LOCATION IN SPACE

A THEORETICAL APPROACH TO ECONOMIC GEOGRAPHY
SECOND EDITION

LOCATION IN SPACE

A THEORETICAL APPROACH TO ECONOMIC GEOGRAPHY
SECOND EDITION

PETER E. LLOYD & PETER DICKEN

Harper & Row, Publishers

London   New York   Hagerstown   San Francisco

Library of Congress Cataloging in Publication Data

Lloyd, Peter E
   Location in space.

   Bibliography: p.
   Includes index.
   1. Geography, Economic.   2.   Space in economics.
3. Industries, Location of.   I.   Dicken, Peter,
joint author. II. Title.
HF1025.L584 1977   330.9   77-23256
ISBN 0-06-044048-1

Printed in Great Britain by A. Wheaton & Company, Exeter.

Contents

Acknowledgements

It is, unfortunately, never possible to acknowledge fully all the individuals who contribute towards a book of this kind. Every effort has been made to obtain permission to use copyright material; we apologize should there be any inadvertent omission. Where we have drawn upon other people's work we have, of course, made due acknowledgement in the text. But the contributions of others—colleagues and students—though often less tangible have been just as valuable. It would be invidious to single out any named individual so perhaps they will all accept a blanket "thank you." Having said this, we must offer special thanks to Jean Mellor who, as they say, performed miracles in typing drafts of the manuscript from almost incomprehensible handwriting in record-breaking time. We also thank Richard Thomas for writing the technical notes on pp. 73–74, 79–80 and 86–87. Finally, we again pay tribute to our respective wives, Ros and Valerie, and to our children, Jennifer and Murray Lloyd and Michael and Christopher Dicken, for tolerating the disruptions we continually force upon them.

Peter E. Lloyd   Peter Dicken

Preface

Location in Space: A Theoretical Approach to Economic Geography is an attempt
to introduce theories and concepts regarding the location and spatial arrangement of economic activities in a logical and coherent framework. The book
has its origins in various courses in economic geography, locational analysis,
and regional economic development taught both jointly and separately by the
authors in North American and British universities. It brings together a wide
range of work by geographers, economists, regional scientists, business theorists
and others in a way which emphasizes their interrelationships rather than their
individual contributions. The emphasis throughout is on *principles* of location
rather than on case studies of specific economic activities. However, this does
not mean that we completely ignore the "real world." On the contrary, a large
number of empirical examples are discussed, but in a particular way: they are
used either to provide some corroboration of a theoretical concept or to illustrate a point in a more concrete manner. We deliberately restrict our attention
to the capitalist economies of Western industrial society and our empirical
examples are drawn mainly, though not exclusively, from the United States,
Britain and Canada.

The substantive material between these covers is by no means entirely new.
It is drawn from a wide variety of sources as the size of the bibliography
testifies. Inevitably, the bias of the authors' own interests tends to show through
in places so that some topics are covered more fully than others. What we
have attempted, however, is the presentation of this material within an ordered

and logical structure rather than simply as a series of separate topics. We are well aware that at times the links are not always smoothly engineered, but we have operated on the principle that it is better to have a structure with some weaknesses than to have no structure at all.

Second edition revisions

Although this revised version was written in the spring and summer of 1976, the process began, in a sense, even before the first edition was actually published. In the period which has elapsed since then we have used the first edition as a course text in a wide variety of contexts. In North America, students at Queen's University, Kingston, and the University of Windsor, both in Ontario, and at the University of British Columbia have been subjected to the book's contents by one or other of the authors. In Britain, apart from continued undergraduate teaching at the University of Manchester, we have extended our joint teaching activities into other levels of education, particularly through our refresher courses for high school and teachers' college teachers. The feedback from these students together with comments and criticisms from many colleagues has provided much of the basis for the second edition.

What we have learned from this experience of teaching with our own text is that *Location in Space*, though well received, was a book that relied heavily on the instructor. In particular, the terseness of the style and the deliberate policy employed in the first edition of not spelling out the detail, particularly of economic concepts, made it perhaps more an instructor's than a student's book. We have, therefore, set improved readability as a primary aim of this second edition. Secondly we have attempted to meet the demands of the student audience for more explanation of concepts and more examples. Inevitably there is a price to be paid for this. The book needed to be longer, but to keep the length within reasonable bounds something had to go. In the event the price was one we were willing to pay. Much of the material on regional development in part three of the first edition has been dropped. In many ways this was the weakest part and certainly one that demanded a more broad ranging treatment than we were originally able to give.

Another of the potential disadvantages of spreading ourselves more in the treatment of the original concepts was that this tended to take precedence over the potential re-working of the conceptual framework on which the book was based. In the event we decided to retain the original progression and chapter sequence from the first edition almost intact. There is, however, a great deal of new material, in particular a totally new Chapter 9 which adds the organizational variable to our discussion of business decision-making. This is currently a fast growing area of research activity in economic geography and one which we felt should be introduced more fully to the wider undergraduate audience.

There are many ways in which the introductory concepts of economic geography can be presented. On balance we felt that the logical framework of the first edition was one that worked though we are, of course, aware of the constraints which the chosen framework puts upon us. Developing a logical argument by relaxing certain variables one by one in a progressive sequence frequently demands that the reader suspend his curiosity for a while. Questions in his mind must be deferred to their "proper" place. This can be a disadvantage but we regard it as a reasonable price to pay for clarity of exposition.

Similarly the approach we adopted in the first edition meant that the interactions between variables tended to become lost in the "one-by-one" progression. The effects of say transport costs (Chapter 5) on the supply of labor (Chapter 6) and on agglomeration economies (Chapter 7) tend to become clouded unless one constantly looks backwards over the progression of variables, summarizing and re-summarizing what has been learned. This is an area we have sought to improve in the second edition but we cannot claim yet to have covered all of these interacting influences in any comprehensive way. Ways of improving the framework have both occurred to us and have been suggested by colleagues but we felt that in this edition readability and fullness of exposition should take precedence over rebuilding the basic structure.

In attempting to communicate with a wider audience both internationally and over the educational spectrum we consciously accepted a major task. We wanted the book to be both trans-Atlantic in its approach and multi-level in its attack. Sometimes in the process there is a danger of meeting the requirements of one group at the expense of others. For example, in lightening the style of the book we are conscious that from time to time we have left the safe ground of accepted written style for the shifting sands of current linguistic fashion. Pre-publication reviewers have pulled us back from some of the more extreme excesses committed in the cause of lightening our style but some still remain. This is a conscious decision on our part, a sin perhaps perpetrated, as so many are, in the name of better communication.

Similarly, explaining very fully what are, to some readers, familiar and well understood concepts, though to others they are distinctly not, produces other problems. Spelling things out inevitably takes some of the pace from the delivery of the concepts, providing more possible side-tracks from which the main-line becomes less strongly defined. To combat this particular problem we have employed two methods which have been used successfully elsewhere. First we have used the extended footnote as a means of explaining concepts more fully. These are provided on what might be called a "self-service" basis. Readers take what they need from the footnote "shelf" leaving the main text unbroken for those whose background permits them the fast route through the conceptual material. Second, where there are opportunities for higher level readers to skip sections we have advised them to do so at appropriate points in the text.

In summary, then, this second edition of *Location in Space* sets out to retain what was generally regarded as good in its precursor, to introduce some new material, to correct the inevitable errors which have come to light over five years but, most important, to produce a more readable book based firmly on theoretical principles.

Organization of the second edition

The overall structure remains, as we have said, basically the same as that of the first edition though much new material has been woven in. Following an introductory chapter in which we set out a particular perspective on economic geography we begin, in Chapter 2, by building a highly simplified model of the spatial organization of economic activities based upon a single variable: distance. Chapter 3 reviews a wide range of empirical studies to see just how far our simplified model "fits" the real world. Chapters 4 through 9 follow a strictly logical sequence in which each of the variables which were regarded as constants in Chapter 2 is relaxed. Thus in Chapter 4 we discuss the impact of spatial variations in the nature of the land surface while in Chapter 5 we look specifically at transportation routes and networks and at transportation costs. Chapter 6 is concerned with spatial variations in production costs—labor, capital, and technical knowledge—while Chapter 7 explores the nature of demand in space together with a consideration of economies of scale and agglomeration. Chapters 8 and 9 focus upon the actual process of decision-making and the structure of complex business enterprises: Chapter 8 deals with the behavior of decision-makers in uncertainty while Chapter 9 explores the nature and behavior of multiplant business corporations.

Throughout the sequence followed in Chapters 4 through 9 the same basic thread is maintained. Each variable is examined individually and then its spatial ramifications are explored. In each case, we attempt to tie the discussion into what has come before thus strengthening the thematic nature of the book. As far as the end of Chapter 9, then, our approach is more or less static, time being introduced to only a very limited extent. In Chapter 10, however, we explicitly consider the time dimension. Instead of simply introducing yet another factor we try to consider *all* the factors we have introduced but in a dynamic framework. The emphasis in Chapter 10, therefore, is upon economic development in space and on the way economic growth evolves at particular points and spreads throughout space. Finally, Chapter 11 presents some concluding thoughts in the form of an Epilogue.

CHAPTER I

A PERSPECTIVE ON ECONOMIC GEOGRAPHY

The geographer is identified not so much by *what* he studies as by *how* he studies it. In examining the economic systems of society the geographer shares a common interest with other academic disciplines—particularly economics—but he has a distinct viewpoint. In other words, economists and economic geographers tend to ask rather different questions about the same phenomena. The essence of the *geographical* approach is that it is *spatial*: it is fundamentally concerned with the ways in which economic activities are arranged on the surface of the earth and with the *processes* which lead to such *spatial patterns*. We shall have more to say about this viewpoint later in this chapter but, before doing so, it is helpful to make some basic points about economic systems themselves.

What is an economic system?

An economic system might loosely be described as a way of organizing human activity to solve what Heilbroner (1972) calls *the economic problem*. In short, this is *the process of providing for the material needs of society against a background of scarcity*. At base it is what the nineteenth-century economists called the "parsimony of nature" that sets the stage for the economic problem. There are inherent scarcities in what nature provides and few human needs can be satisfied by resources which are literally as "free as air." At the level of subsistence, nature's provision is crucial to survival and it is to this that man's ingenuity is applied in devising economic systems finely tuned to making good use of scarce resources. Above the level of subsistence, however, scarcity becomes more a relative than an absolute concept. The economic systems of modern advanced societies seem to be concerned more with the satisfaction of wants than of needs. Under these conditions the economic problem becomes vastly more complex as do the systems designed to solve it. Scarcities appear under these circumstances in relation to *human nature*—to men's aspirations and the wants by which they are expressed. As such the economic problem takes on a complex range of psychological, social and cultural connotations.

In essence, then, whether the society in question is primarily concerned with day-to-day survival or with more trivial matters like "keeping up with the Joneses" or "being fashionable," the bald statement of the economic problem remains the same. Society expresses its material needs and wants as *demand* and some system of social organization must be devised to produce the goods and services that satisfy it. Alfred Kuhn (1966) suggests that several major decisions are involved of which four are most relevant to us:

1. *What kinds* of goods and services should be produced, in *what quantity* and *quality*?
2. *How* are such goods to be produced given the availability of resources and factors of production? In other words, how much of each resource or factor should be applied to the production of particular goods?
3. At what *relative values* should goods *exchange*? In money-based economies, the exchange-ratio is expressed in terms of the relative *prices* of goods, hence the question becomes—at what prices shall various goods be sold?

4. How should the total product be *shared* (*distributed*) among the population? In other words, who gets what?

In addition, we must add a fifth decision:

5. How should the *geographical* (*spatial*) pattern of production be organized?

At first sight it might seem that the "economic problem" could be solved in a myriad of different ways. In fact the solutions which have been adopted during man's history can be boiled down to three major strategies (though these have been used in varying combinations). Each strategy has the necessary ingredients for solving the economic problem: first, a means of *mobilizing effort*; second, techniques for *allocating effort*; third, a means of *distributing output* in such a way as to permit further production to take place. The three solutions can be summarized briefly as follows in terms of their controlling or co-ordinating mechanism:

1. Tradition. The classical solution to the economic problem grew out of the slow evolution of methods of coping with nature's scarcity and man's increasing aspirations. Tried and tested practices from the past were retained and built into the fabric of society by becoming intertwined with laws, customs and beliefs. Deviations from accepted practice were suppressed by heavy sanctions and taboos.

The production problem—that is the allocation of resources to various uses—was solved by recourse to tradition, to what had been done before. In the case of manpower allocations the traditional solution simply assigns sons to the jobs of their fathers, thus ensuring a continuation of the necessary social fabric over time. Similarly, kinship and family links are applied to the solution of the distribution problem with the fruits of production allocated by rank and status in the social hierarchy. This is no less an economic system than the ones with which the modern westerner is familiar. The tools needed for analysis of the traditional system are, however, more appropriately those of the social anthropologist than the economist, and for this reason we shall not be considering them here.

2. Command. This strategy for solving the economic problem is widely applied in the present day, particularly in many of the developing nations and in the Communist countries of the Soviet Union, Eastern Europe and China. It is a quasi-military solution under which allocations and assignments are made by an economic "commander-in-chief" or by some designated group in society. Decisions are made in accordance with some more or less conscious objectives set out by those in authority. Those in positions to command may be either elected or self-appointed. Their programs for solving the economic problem may be based on social justice or self-interest or some particular combination of both.

Regardless of the moral or philosophical basis of the command system, it provides yet another way of organizing human activity to produce a society's material needs. The production problem is solved by direct allocation of men and resources to particular tasks and the distribution problem by some conscious assignment of the fruits of labor by some precepts determined by the group in authority. Once again, although the basic problem is no less economic, the tools of analysis most appropriate to the study of command systems demand a familiarity with topics which range far beyond our present interest in economics and economic geography *per se*.

3. The Market. This will be, for most readers, the most familiar strategy for the solution of the economic problem. Its very familiarity will, however, tempt us into making glib assumptions about its functioning. In fact, short descriptions such as those applied to the tradition and command systems above are very hard to find in the literature when it comes to explaining how the market system solves the production and distribution problem. Whole books are dedicated to it and this one, though based on a strictly geographical viewpoint, will be no exception. Perhaps Heilbroner's splendid parable of the "economic consultant" gives us the best hint of the obscurity which might result from any formal attempt to describe how the marketing strategy works in solving the economic problem. Let us tell it in his terms.

> Suppose, for instance, that we were called on to act as consultants to one of the new nations emerging on the continent of Africa.
>
> We could imagine the leaders of such a nation saying, "We have always experienced a highly tradition-bound way of life. Our men hunt and cultivate the fields and perform their tasks as they are brought up to do by the force of example and the instruction of their elders. We know, too, something of what can be done by economic command. We are prepared, if necessary, to sign an edict making it compulsory for many of our men to work on community projects for our national development. Tell us, is there any other way we can organize our society so that it will function successfully—or better yet, more successfully?"
>
> Suppose we answered, "Yes, there is another way. Organize your society along the lines of a market economy."
>
> "Very well," say the leaders. "What do we then tell people to do? How do we assign them to their various tasks?"
>
> "That's the very point," we would answer. "In a market economy, no one is assigned to any task. In fact, the main idea of a market society is that each person is allowed to decide for himself what to do."
>
> There is consternation among the leaders. "You mean there is no assignment of some men to mining and others to cattle raising? No manner of designating some for transportation and others for weaving? You leave this to people to decide for themselves? But what happens if they do not decide correctly? What happens if no one volunteers to go into the mines, or if no one offers himself as a railway engineer?"
>
> "You may rest assured," we tell the leaders, "none of that will happen. In a market society, all the jobs will be filled because it will be to people's advantage to fill them."

Our respondents accept this with uncertain expressions. "Now look," one of them finally says, "let us suppose that we take your advice and allow our people to do as they please. Let's talk about something specific, like cloth production. Just how do we fix the right level of cloth output in this 'market society' of yours?"

"But you don't," we reply.

"We don't! Then how do we know there will be enough cloth produced?"

"There will be," we tell him. "The market will see to that."

"Then how do we know there won't be *too much* cloth produced?" he asks triumphantly.

"Ah, but the market will see to that too!"

"But what is this market that will do these wonderful things? Who runs it?"

"Oh, nobody runs the market," we answer. "It runs itself. In fact there really isn't any such *thing* as 'the market'. It's just a word we use to describe the way people behave."

"But I thought people behaved the way they wanted to!"

"And so they do," we say. "But never fear. They will want to behave the way you want them to behave."

"I am afraid," says the chief of the delegation, "that we are wasting our time. We thought you had in mind a serious proposal. What you suggest is inconceivable. Good day, sir."

Robert L. Heilbroner, The Economic Problem, *3rd edn*, © *1972, pp. 25–27, Reprinted by permission of Prentice-Hall, Inc., Englewood Cliffs, New Jersey, U.S.A.*

The fact that Heilbroner's parable is set in the context of an underdeveloped economy whereas our central concern is with developed industrial economies is, in itself, unimportant. The key feature is that it points to the major characteristics of a market system.

Difficult as the market process is to describe and grasp in any summary description, it is the one upon which most of the advanced industrial nations based their rise to economic power. It is also the one upon which these nations still largely depend to ensure their livelihood. It is a source of bounty and a source of difficulties. It is effective, as we shall suggest later, in solving many of the production problems of society but far from effective in ensuring the most equitable allocation of the rewards of production.

With time, however, the "invisible hand" by which the market system works has come under increasing pressure from the growing economic "muscle" exerted by government and the large business organization (Galbraith 1966, 1974). Advertising has arrived as a powerful medium for the manipulation of consumer choice. Pricing policies have been evolved which discriminate for some customers and against others. More significantly still, problems of distribution and social justice have promoted a movement toward collective, rather than individual, ownership of such key resources as land. Mixed, command-market economies have begun to evolve even in those countries for which the market solution to the economic problem approximated a national creed only fifty years ago. In short, outside the realms of pure theory the market system as a strategy for solving the economic problem has, with time, lost the essential unbiased simplicity on which it was supposed to function. Yet for analytical purposes there are advantages in assuming initially that the market system operates in a more or less pure form. Not the least of these, from our viewpoint, is that the major body of *location theory*—which forms a central core in this book—was devised in the context of a market economic system. Nevertheless in later chapters we shall be examining some of the effects of the operation of an "impure" system, particularly in terms of the behavior of big business organizations and the involvement of government.

The viewpoint of economic geography

It would be misleading to suggest that all economic geographers possess a single, unitary viewpoint. Not only has the nature of economic geography (as of geography as a whole) changed over time, but also at any one point in time there are differences between economic geographers in their philosophical and methodological approach to economic systems. But throughout the development of economic geography, from the mid-nineteenth century to the second half of the twentieth century, it has been possible to identify a central concern, a particular set of questions which distinguish economic geography from economics. That central concern relates to *space*, though this specific term has become widely used only in the last two decades. Earlier generations of economic geographers would more likely have used such terms as area, region, place, landscape, which, though not exactly synonymous with space *per se*, are particular facets of it.

For the economic geographer, as opposed to the economist, the crucial point is that supply and demand, the regulators of the market system, have a spatial component. For any given good there will generally be a *spatial disparity* between the places at which it is demanded and the points of supply. The interaction or exchange that must take place for it to be consumed is therefore affected by *distance*.

The point is most clearly illustrated in the case of products based on highly localized natural resources that are far from the main industrial centers that use them, but the same is true to a varying degree for most goods and services. All economic activities are space-users, whether they are grain producers occupying thousands of acres in the Midwest or garment manufacturers renting a loft in downtown Manhattan. Similarly, the final consumer—the individual family or household—needs space in which to live. The exchange of goods or services between any of these space-users demands some form of *movement* over the earth's surface, and in this process resources will be used up as money, time, or physical energy are applied to the task of providing the consumer with his good and the producer with his return.

An economic system, therefore, has a spatial dimension and it is this that is the primary concern of the economic geographer. As Berry (1964, p. 3) observed, "the geographical point of view is spatial ... the integrating concepts and processes of the geographer relate to spatial arrangements and distributions, to spatial integration, to spatial interactions and organization, and to spatial processes." It is the spatial viewpoint that distinguishes economic geography as a field of study from economics, although both are concerned with studying economic systems. Mainstream economics remains, as a whole, relatively unconcerned with space as a variable but, as in all disciplines, there is a considerable blurring of boundaries. Indeed, as this book testifies, many of the early and more significant contributions to an understanding of the spatial dimension of the economic system were produced by economists rather than geographers.

An economic system is only one of several human social systems—others include political systems, religious systems, and cultural systems—and as such it is "anchored in the attitudes, perceptions, beliefs, motivations, habits and expectations of human beings" (Katz and Kahn, 1966, p. 33). The spatial pattern of economic activity within an economic system is ultimately the end product of a multitude of human decisions. Quite clearly, then, economic geography is essentially a *behavioral* science concerned with the spatial dimension of economic systems.

Having said all this, however, we should be clear that the current explicit spatial viewpoint differs considerably from its predecessors, even though the concept of space was *implicit* throughout. Economic geography in its infancy was concerned with compiling mountains of factual information about economic activities in different parts of the world, just as geography as a whole accumulated facts about the earth's surface in general. The "capes and bays" of economic geography were the lists of commodities and products, exports and imports. Where attempts were made to seek explanations of geographical variations in economic behavior the deterministic role of the physical environment was almost invariably invoked. Subsequent disenchantment with the naivety of such explanations led many to adopt the view that all geographic phenomena were unique and that generalization and the building of theory were of little value (or even impossible). Hence for a considerable period between roughly the 1930s and the 1950s the primary focus of geographical concern was what Richard Hartshorne (1939) called *areal differentiation*: differences, rather than similarities, between places.

Dissatisfaction with such an approach gathered momentum in the middle and late 1950s. Typical of the feeling was such criticism as that of Ballabon who argued that economic geography needed

> greater rigor in defining concepts, precision in measurement, applicability of conclusions ... unlike economics, where the premium has been placed

on generalizations and principles, economic geography has been short on
theory and long on facts.
Ballabon (1957), p. 217

Today there are few, if any, economic geographers about whom Ballabon's
comments would still be valid. The overall position is very different. There
has been a major shift of emphasis away from the particular question of *how*
economic phenomena are located to the more general question of *why* such
phenomena are located and arranged as they are. Economic geographers are
not simply interested in *spatial patterns*, they are even more concerned with
identifying the *processes* which produce such patterns. The problem is that
whereas pattern is unequivocally spatial, process is not. Thus we cannot expect
to find answers to spatial problems solely in spatial or geographical terms.
We must seek answers in whatever sphere seems most relevant; hence the need
for economic geographers to interact not only with economists but also with
other social scientists: sociologists, and political scientists, to name only two.

Theories and models in economic geography

Perhaps the most important way in which modern economic geography differs
from its immediate predecessors is in its pervasive concern with theory. It is
rather unfortunate that for a long period geography as a whole eschewed theory
very largely because of the transparent naivety of its own early attempts. In
emphasizing the need for theory, therefore, modern economic geography is in
step with the aims of science in general. Science without theory is, as Kurt
Lewin observed, essentially blind. Expressed rather differently,

> a structure (or theory) is essential if we are to effectively interrelate and
> integrate our observations in any field of knowledge. Without an integrat-
> ing structure, information remains a hodge-podge of fragments. Without
> an organizing structure, knowledge is a mere collection of observations,
> practices, and conflicting incidents.
> *Forrester (1968), pp. 1–2*

In accordance with this viewpoint a great deal of the current work of geographers is devoted to the construction of *theories* and *models* in an attempt to
understand the complexity of the real world more readily and to be able to
predict future spatial patterns. This is not the place to explore the complex
definitional issue of what is or is not a theory or a model. The interested
reader should consult David Harvey's authoritative book *Explanation in Geography* (1969)—particularly chapters 7 to 12. However, some very general comments
on what we mean by the term model are necessary at this stage since this
book is built around locational models. It is unfortunate that the relatively
recent upsurge in the use of models in geography has led many to interpret
them as some kind of mystical game that can be played only by those who
know the right kind of jargon. In fact, model-building—the simplified representation of a more complex situation—is part and parcel of all our everyday
lives. Models help us to "cut the world down to our size" and thus assist
us to deal with complex situations. We simplify and concentrate on what we

perceive as the most important element of a situation and behave in accordance with this "model."

Thus, model-building is a fundamental part of the learning process. Children learn by playing with models of trains or cars; they also learn by using "mental models" of the "let us suppose..." type. Similarly, a scientist might use a physical model of a river channel, for example, to investigate how water of varying volume and velocity behaves in flowing through the channel. Another might build a wind tunnel to study the effect of wind velocity on physical structures such as high-rise apartment blocks or supersonic aircraft. Alternatively, a scientist might construct a mental model of the behavior of a gas under pressure using mathematical symbols. Whatever type of model is designed, however, the ultimate purpose is the same: *to further our understanding* of complex objects and processes.

In model-building we try to reproduce the most important attributes of a situation under controlled conditions. For the scientist working in a laboratory the task is relatively simple, because he can hold a range of conditions constant while concentrating on one or a few variables. For the social scientist the task is infinitely more complex, because he cannot control human actions except in very rare and limited circumstances. Instead he has to try to imagine what *would* happen *if* certain conditions were fulfilled. In other words, he makes certain simplifying assumptions. For example, an economist attempting to understand variations in demand might assume to begin with that everybody had the same income and tastes and was prepared to spend an identical proportion of his income on a particular good. Given such constraints, the amount demanded would depend upon the price of the good. If the price were high only small amounts would be demanded; if the price were reduced more would be demanded. Having understood this aspect of the problem the economist could then allow other variables such as consumer tastes or income to operate. This is, of course, only one type of model design, but it is one that has been used extensively. Clearly, therefore, models can be constructed in different ways. Models which begin from a set of assumptions and develop predictions about behavior are known as *deductive* models. Many of the locational models discussed in the early chapters of this book—Von Thünen's model of agricultural location, Weber's model of industrial location and Lösch's economic landscape, for example—are deductive models. Models which are built up from the observation of real events and from simplifying generalizations about them—such as the gravity model discussed in Chapter Two—on the other hand, are known as *inductive* models. In many cases, of course, as models develop they actually contain elements of both deductive and inductive approaches.

A major advantage of model-building is that, although no model can exactly represent reality (except reality itself), it can help not only in our immediate understanding of a problem, but it can also help us to ask the right kinds of questions to increase our understanding. By comparing a model with that portion of reality that it is supposed to represent we often gain clues that help to direct further investigations. But this can be achieved only if the model is tested rigorously. Thus an integral part of the scientific process is the carrying out of factual investigations, although such empirical studies should be clearly defined within an appropriate conceptual framework and not carried out as mere ends in themselves. Testing in this sense does not imply that there is any expectation that models will ultimately be developed that "fit" the real world exactly. It provides a device by which we can review the differential success of the model. In some ways it will have a good fit but in others its assumptions will prove false—encouraging the development and further elaborations of the model. Testing then is a process of model evaluation and does not imply that there is some ultimate model which will tell us the *truth* about the real world. As we have already pointed out the only model which can replicate reality is *reality* itself.

The building and testing of theories and models often demands precision. Such precision is achieved most readily through the language of mathematics, and it is for this reason that geography, like other social sciences, has become involved with "quantification," the use of mathematical and statistical techniques. Inevitably there have been excesses and abuses in the use of such techniques, particularly in the early stages, as the often violent methodological debates of the 1950s reveal. Today, however, a knowledge of quantitative methods is generally accepted as being as necessary a part of the geographer's basic equipment as the topographic map and field notebook. All are basic tools for increasing our understanding of spatial patterns and processes.

The concept of "system"

So far we have used the term "system" without bothering to define it. In fact it is one of the many words that are used loosely by most of us in everyday speech. (For example, talk of rebelling or reacting against the "system" has become commonplace.) But *system* has not only a specific meaning which we shall come to in a moment, it has also become the focus of an entire "interdisciplinary discipline" known as *general systems theory*. There is some disagreement about the validity of such a discipline, but there is little doubt that the concept of system is extremely powerful and adds a great deal to our understanding of the complex world in which we live. Indeed, the geographer Edward Ackerman has gone so far as to claim that

> as the centuries have gone on, men have steadily increased their capacity for problem-solving but the truly important changes in methods of problem-solving have been remarkably few. They might read somewhat as follows: writing, Arabic numerals, analytical geometry and calculus; and the combination of techniques that comprise systems analysis.
> *Ackerman (1963), p. 429*

The use of systems analysis in geographical literature is growing in importance. This is not only because of its purely academic attractions, such as the facility to communicate more easily with scientists in other disciplines, but also because of its operational applications, its importance in problem-solving. In particular, systems analysis provides a framework within which *processes* can be evaluated.

The systems concept permits us to look at the dynamic aspects of ongoing events. It stresses the *functioning* aspects of processes which perform "work," whether this "work" be in the form of erosion and deposition by streams or production and distribution of goods by society. At the academic level, many of the behavioral sciences have come to recognize the particular value of systems concepts in analyzing human behavior, while at the practical level systems analysis has been in use for some time. Systems analysts, cyberneticians, and operations researchers are today employed in almost all branches of industry and commerce, in government, and in other spheres of activity. Large industrial organizations have for some time employed systems specialists to analyze and improve their operational efficiency. Increasingly, too, the planning of large urban agglomerations—in particular transportation planning—is being formulated in systems terms.

Systems in economic geography

Let us look more closely at systems. What is a system, particularly in the context of economic geography? One of the most widely quoted general definitions of a system is that it is "a set of objects together with the relationships between the objects and their attributes" (Hall and Fagan, 1956, p. 18). The "objects" of the economic system are all those activities and institutions that perform a role in the operation of the economy: for example, farms and mines in the primary sector, factories in the manufacturing sector, shops and offices in the tertiary sector. At a higher level of aggregation the objects of the economic system are the towns and cities of varying sizes around which most economic activity ultimately focuses. The "relationships" between the objects are the *connections* that tie the system together. This, in fact, is the crucial component of all systems. Objects that are unconnected do not constitute a system. In the economic system farms, mines, factories, shops, and offices are connected by the *flows* of materials, semi-finished and finished products, people, messages, information, and other types of flow. Economic activities and the connections between them therefore constitute the economic system.

Figure 1.1 is one way of looking at the concept of the economic system. Along the line of our particular interest here, that is the production or work aspect, four basic sectors can be identified. First comes the *primary* sector which combines within it those activities chiefly engaged in the exploitation of naturally occurring resources. Agriculture, forestry, fishing and mining fall into this category. Manufacturing is generally known as the *secondary* sector. The "work" performed here is the transformation of primary resources into useable goods. Several stages are involved as basic materials are converted into more finely processed goods and more value is added by each successive process. The *tertiary* sector includes all those activities associated with commerce and trade. In essence, it covers wholesale and retail trade and the provision of business, personal and entertainment services. Particularly in the more advanced nations it has become common to distinguish a fourth—*quaternary*—sector. Activities under this heading specialize in the assembly, transmission and processing of

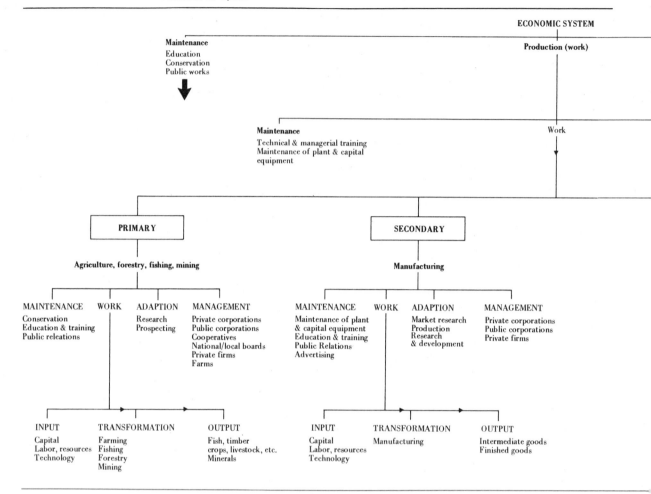

information and in the control of other business enterprises. This includes banks, insurance companies, finance houses, the media, the publishing industry, and so on.

The entire structure is, as Figure 1.1 attempts to show, fully interconnected. The parts of each sector are connected and the sectors themselves are interrelated. Simply to examine the elements of the system would tell us little about how it functions or how changes in one element "ripple" through the system to influence others. It is this *connectedness* which the systems approach enables us to study more closely.

From a geographical viewpoint the elements of the system clearly have a physical expression in space. Buildings, highways, dock installations, telephone lines and so forth form what we shall for shorthand frequently refer to as the *economic furniture* of the landscape. In themselves, however, these are not the system. It is the complex of human activities from which they derive that constitutes the real system and that gives them their meaning. Consider as a simple example the abandoned mining town. Often the physical structures of the "ghost town"

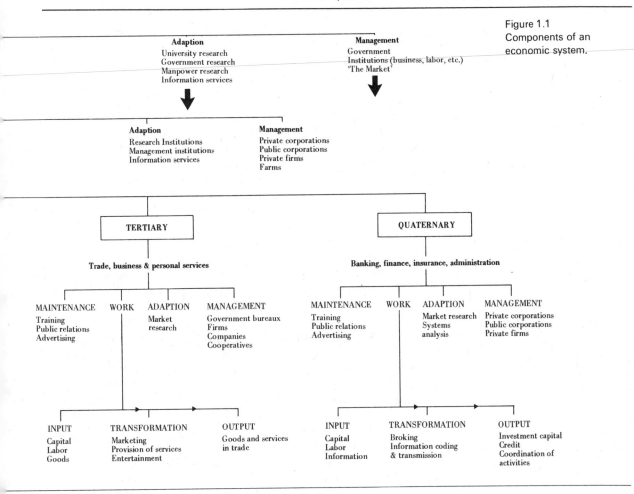

Figure 1.1
Components of an economic system.

remain—the hotel, houses, saloon, telegraph office, blacksmith's yard, the offices of the mining company. The fact that we can describe them as such derives from the way they *used to function* when the town was "alive." They are no longer, however, part of the economic system. The saloon no longer functions as one and except in the historical sense it can no longer be so described. It is the "life" which is brought by human behavior that gives these physical structures meaning as parts of the economic system. Without it they are mere shells, inert bricks and mortar.

It should be clear from the preceding discussion that one of the advantages of viewing the world in systems terms is that it emphasizes *wholeness* and *interdependence* among the components of a system. It is sometimes argued by those who deny the usefulness of a systems approach in geography that geographers have always taken such a view, particularly in their regional interests, and that to introduce the terminology of systems analysis is unnecessary. It is true that some geographers have been concerned with functional interdependence and have attempted to identify functional regions (for example, the urban-centered region). But most regions identified by geographers have not been of this kind. Insofar as the system concept explicitly focuses attention on functional interdependence as expressed through flows, therefore, it does have value for the geographer. This is particularly true when we consider change, because it is obvious that change occurring in one part of a system will have repercussions on other parts of the system, particularly those most closely linked to the part where change occurs.

A second advantage of the system concept is that it applies at all levels of analysis from the microscale to the macroscale and to all kinds of phenomena "from atomic particles, through atoms, molecules, crystals, viruses, cells, organs, individuals, small groups, societies, planets, solar systems, and galaxies" (Miller, 1955). In other words, we can speak of different *levels of resolution*. A primary level of resolution considered in this book is the business firm in the private sector of the economy. Thus, we shall be dealing with the business firm as a system. But a firm is, itself, a sub-system of an industry which, in turn, is a sub-system of the economy and so on. Similarly, the central business district of a city is a system at one level of resolution; at another, that of the level of the city as a whole, it is a sub-system. We could go on and on describing the *nested* relationships between systems. Perhaps the closest everyday analogy is the set of hollow building blocks used by young children whereby each block sits within the block of next largest size. Each block exists in its own right but it also has a place within the context of the larger structure.

This view of different resolution levels of systems raises a further important concept: the *environment* of a system. All open systems exist within, and interact with, an external environment. Expressed in formal terms, "for a given system, the environment is the set of all objects, a change in whose attributes affects the system and also those objects whose attributes are changed by the behavior of the system" (Hall and Fagan, 1966, p. 18). Thus for the economic system as a whole the environment consists of the total society of which it is a part. The demands created by society influence the behavior of the economic system and vice versa. For a business firm the environment consists of all the external elements that influence its behavior, including other business firms, consumer demands, government activities and regulations, and so on.

The idea of the interaction of a system with its environment is crucial to an understanding of the behavior, growth, and survival of any open system. To illustrate this let us take the example of a manufacturer of garments as a particular kind of system. To produce garments the manufacturer must assemble a variety of *inputs*: textile materials of various kinds, thread, capital equipment in the form of sewing and pressing machines among others, lighting and power, a supply of labor of the appropriate skills. Perhaps most importantly there must be a sufficient level of demand for his garments.

These *inputs* have to be acquired from various external sources—the environment—and when assembled they are *transformed* (manufactured) into finished garments. These *outputs* are then exported into the environment, that is, sold to wholesalers or retailers and, ultimately to the general public. (The wholesalers and retailers are, in turn, systems in their own right. Their *inputs* are the *outputs* of another system, in this case a garment manufacturing system.) The sale of these outputs in effect makes possible the continued existence of the manufacturer, because they provide him with the means whereby further inputs can be purchased and so the process continues in a *cyclical* manner. This cyclical feature of all the sub-elements of the production system is shown in Figure 1.2. The interconnections of each can be categorized within the input-transformation-output framework.

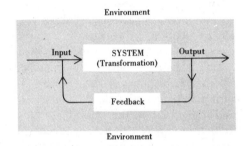

Figure 1.2
A simple open system.

In general terms, then, there is a cyclical exchange of what, again in shorthand, we can call *energy* between a system and its environment. For a system to survive it must import sufficient energy to meet both its current and expected needs. Again, taking the case of our garment manufacturer, he must accumulate extra energy in the form of capital (both in money, and in physical terms such as equipment and inventories) to ensure survival and growth.

Inevitably, of course, the relationship between a system and its environment is in a continuous state of flux. A system must, therefore, be able to identify such changes and *adapt* its behavior accordingly. Thus, a vitally important part of the energy flow process is the *feedback of information* from the environment (Figure 1.2). Information regarding the system's performance forms the basis upon which the system adapts to change. Without such ability to adapt it is unlikely that a system could survive for long except by accident. Adaptation occurs, of course, in relation to the defined *goals* of the system. All human social systems are goal-seeking. A business firm may seek the goal of maximizing profits or of capturing the largest share of a market. In terms of area development, a government may seek the goal of eradicating spatial imbalances in employment or per capita income. Feedback, therefore, may be either negative or positive. Negative feedback, for example, indicates the need for corrective action to keep the system "on target", while positive feedback tends to reinforce and amplify previous behavior.

Systems that survive within a changing environment and are able to keep a dynamic balance between energy inputs and outputs are said to be in a *steady state*. As a system adapts over the long term to a constantly changing environment it tends to change its structure. Indeed, survival may only be possible if such changes occur. For example, if major technological advances revolutionize a manufacturing process, any firm that does not change its process accordingly may be forced out of business by increased competition from lower-cost producers. One aspect of change—the growth of a system itself—undoubtedly leads to structural changes. As a system increases in size its form invariably becomes more complex, and specialized functions may be developed to enable the larger system to operate. The systems concept, therefore, emphasizes wholeness, interdependence, and dynamic relationships both within a system and between a system and its environment.

Turning our attention again to Figure 1.1, we can now look at the economic system in terms of the various specialized supportive structures which it has to keep it running. We have looked at the production or work aspect of the system. In support of this are what we have called management, maintenance, and adaptive structures. *Management structures* provide the necessary organization and control for all the system's functions. *Maintenance structures* seek to preserve the stability of the system by ensuring as far as possible the constancy of input flows such as resources, capital, and trained labor, the smooth running of the plant and the "tuning" of the production sub-system to the needs of the market. *Adaptive structures* carry the maintenance function into the future, seeking out new problem areas and providing solutions, developing new, more efficient plant, and anticipating demand changes and preparing for them. At every level within the complex master system the same basic features are replicated, a fact that emphasizes the applicability of the systems concept at each scale of analysis.

In this book our emphasis will be on the *production sector* of the economic systems of the *developed* urban-industrial economies of the *western* world. But we do not attempt to look at the production sector in its entirety. Our primary focus is the *spatial behavior* of the *business firm* operated by the *producer-capitalist* (we do not consider state-owned economic enterprises, partly because their behavior is often subject to a rather different set of goals and constraints). Returning to our earlier discussion of economic systems in general, we can follow Heilbroner (1972) in defining the basic economic objectives which a society must set itself as a twofold problem:

1. To devise a system to assure the *production* of enough goods and services for its own survival.
2. To devise an arrangement for the *distribution* of the fruits of production so that more production can take place.

Specifically, we shall concentrate upon the *spatial* expression of the first of these. In effect, our purpose is to provide an introduction to economic location theory. Though based in neo-classical economics, however, our approach extends a good deal beyond such a framework into the realms of behavior in uncertainty and the behavior of multi-locational business organizations. Nevertheless, our approach is private producer-oriented and, to that extent, represents an attempt to review and consolidate our knowledge in this area in a logical and consistent framework.

Further reading

Ackerman, E. A. (1963), Where is a Research Frontier?, *Annals of the Association of American Geographers* **53**, 429–440.

Berry, B. J. L. (1964), Approaches to Regional Analysis: A Synthesis, *Annals of the Association of American Geographers* **54**, 2–12.

Bertalanffy, L. Von (1951), An Outline of General System Theory, *British Journal of the Philosophy of Science* **1**, 134–165.

Boulding, K. E. (1956), General Systems Theory—The Skeleton of Science, *Management Science* **2**, 197–208.

Bunge, W. (1966), Theoretical Geography, *Lund Studies in Geography*, Series C, No. 1, 2nd ed., Chapter 1.

Burton, I. (1963), The Quantitative Revolution and Theoretical Geography, *Canadian Geographer* **7**, 151–162.

Chisholm, M. (1967), General Systems Theory and Geography, *Transactions of the Institute of British Geographers* **42**, 45–52.

Chorley, R. J. (1962), Geomorphology and General Systems Theory, *U.S. Geological Survey, Professional Paper*, 500B.

Chorley, R. J., and P. Haggett (1967), *Models in Geography*, London: Methuen, New York: Barnes & Noble, Chapter 1.

Heilbroner, R. L. (1972), *The Economic Problem*, 3rd edn, Englewood Cliffs, N.J.: Prentice Hall.

Katz, D., and R. L. Kahn (1966), *The Social Psychology of Organizations*, New York: Wiley, Chapter 2.

McNee, R. B. (1959), The Changing Relationships of Economics and Economic Geography, *Economic Geography* **35**, 189–198.

Taaffe, E. J. (ed.) (1970), *Geography*, Englewood Cliffs, N.J.: Prentice-Hall, Chapter 1.

CHAPTER 2

SPATIAL ORGANIZATION OF ECONOMIC ACTIVITIES:
A SIMPLIFIED MODEL

Prologue

All of us would probably agree that we live in a very complex world, a world which is particularly difficult for geographers to analyze because of our interest in such a wide diversity of phenomena. This is true even in this book where we deliberately restrict ourselves to *economic* phenomena. A major problem facing any economic geographer attempting to unravel the complexity of his subject matter is just where to begin. There is no unique point of entry—no best starting point—simply because so many of the variable factors which inter-act to produce the economic landscape contribute towards both causes and effects. In everyday language, we face the classic "chicken and egg" dilemma. But as Kenneth Boulding has so aptly pointed out, the egg theory of chickens is every bit as good as the chicken theory of eggs! Thus, wherever we break into the circle of complexity we do so in the knowledge that other points of entry are possible.

This does not mean, however, that our starting point is purely arbitrary because one clue to an appropriate starting point can be found in the nature of geogra-phy itself. As we emphasized in the opening chapter, geography is, first and foremost, a *spatial* discipline. Intrinsically, therefore, one of its central concerns is *distance*; indeed one very much used expression is the *friction of distance*. This simply means the impediment to movement which occurs because places, objects, or people are spatially separate. Movement involves a cost, whether this is actual payment of money to travel by bus, train, or jet, or to transport materials or goods; wear and tear on the soles of the feet; or perhaps the time involved in moving between places. Distance—and especially the cost in-volved in overcoming it—is clearly a logical starting point for geographical analysis and is thus the one we use here.

Suppose we begin by asking ourselves the question: what kind of spatial pattern of economic activities would we expect to find if the only factor affecting the pattern were the friction of distance? To answer this question, we would have to try to isolate distance, separate it out from all the many other variables— economic, social, cultural, even psychological—which together produce the geo-graphical pattern of economic activities which we see around us. Obviously, we can't just go out and "stop the world." But we can use our imagination and assume that, for the time being, all these other variables are not variable at all but constants (that is, they are the same everywhere). If we do this, then we can deduce the kind of spatial organization of economic activities which would occur if the friction of distance were the only influence. In other words, our initial view is *normative*.

In setting about such an exercise, we need to be aware of precisely what is involved; we must specify the nature of our *simplifying assumptions*. These are, in effect, the rules of the game and, as with rules for all games, we have to adhere to them for the duration of the game. We can divide our rules or assump-tions into two categories: those which relate to the land surface and its charac-teristics, and those which refer to the people living on that land surface. Let us look at each of these in turn.

Assumptions about the land surface

Our basic assumption about the land surface is that it is completely flat and homogeneous in every respect. It is, in technical terms, an *isotropic* plain. The word "isotropic" is derived from the Greek and means simply something which has equal physical properties in all directions. Thus, on our isotropic plain there are none of the features so dear to the hearts of physical geographers: there are no mountains or U-shaped valleys, no hills or rivers. Soil fertility is the same everywhere as is climate. All the raw materials needed by economic activities are also available everywhere and at the same cost.

On such a plain there are clearly no barriers to movement. In fact, we can assume at first that movement can, and will, occur in all directions with equal ease, and that there is only one type of transport. Transportation costs—the costs of overcoming the friction of distance—are exactly proportional to distance. This means, as Figure 2.1 shows, that it costs exactly twice as much to travel (or to move materials and goods) 100 miles as it does to move 50 miles. We also assume that the plain is limitless or unbounded, so that we do not have to deal with the many complexities which tend to occur at boundaries.

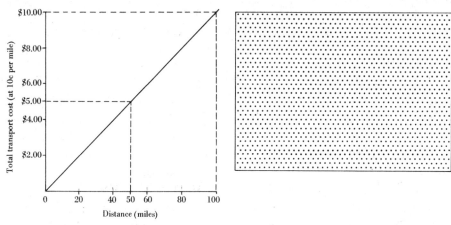

Figure 2.1

Figure 2.2

Figure 2.1
Transport costs which increase in direct proportion to distance.

Figure 2.2
An even spatial distribution of population.

Assumptions about the population living on the isotropic plain

The most important initial assumption about the population is that it is perfectly evenly spread over the plain, that is, the density of population is everywhere the same (see Figure 2.2). We also assume that every one of these people is identical in the sense that each possesses the same financial resources and each spends his or her money in the same way. In other words, their demands and tastes are the same. These people are also given quite remarkable mental qualities. We assume that each one is fully aware of all possible behavioral alternatives (that is, they have perfect knowledge) and that they act in a totally rational way. Because we are dealing with economic matters we mean by such rationality that every producer of goods and services aims to make the largest possible profit and that every consumer aims to satisfy his economic needs as cheaply as possible. All the actions of producers and consumers are therefore guided by the desire to *optimize*. Our plain is populated by Economic Men. These operate in a *perfectly competitive* market in which there are large numbers of producers none of whom can influence the price at which goods are sold (this point is developed further in the note on page 23).

In summary, then, the assumptions on which we will begin to build our simplified model are as follows:

1. The land surface is an unbounded plain which is homogeneous in all respects:
a. The surface is perfectly flat with no barriers to movement. Movement is therefore possible in all directions.
b. Transport costs are proportional to distance and there is a single uniform transport system.
c. Physical resources are evenly distributed, that is, soils are of equal fertility throughout, raw materials are ubiquitous and of equal cost.

2. The population living on the plain has the following characteristics:
a. An even spatial distribution.
b. Identical incomes, demands and tastes.
c. Both producers and consumers have perfect knowledge and act perfectly rationally with respect to this knowledge. They are able, therefore, to behave in an *optimum* fashion. As producers, for example, they are assumed to seek a single goal—the maximization of profits. As consumers they seek to minimize their outlays in meeting their consumption needs.

It is vital that these assumptions are borne in mind throughout this chapter. In emphasizing again why we are using this approach, we cannot do better than use the words of J. H. von Thünen, one of the founders of location theory. Writing more than one hundred years ago, he prefaced his analysis of the location of agricultural production in this way:

> I hope that the reader who is willing to spend some time and attention on my work will not take exception to the imaginary assumptions I make at the beginning because they do not correspond to conditions in reality, and that he will not reject these assumptions as arbitrary and pointless. They are a necessary part of my argument, allowing me to establish the operation of a certain factor, a factor whose operation we see but dimly in reality, where it is in incessant conflict with others of its kind.

> This method of analysis has illuminated—and solved—so many problems in my life, and appears to me to be capable of such widespread application, that I regard it as the most important matter contained in all my work. *J. H. von Thünen (1842)*

The "certain factor whose operation we see but dimly in reality" is the *friction of distance*. By stripping away all the other complicating factors (that is, by using the "other things being equal" formula) we can focus explicitly on the role of distance in the spatial organization of economic activities.

Spatial organization of the production of one good

(i) *One producer*

Suppose that one of the inhabitants on the isotropic plain decides to produce a good—say, sausages—in quantities greater than he must for his own needs. Because all the materials he requires are available everywhere at the same cost he can set up production in his own home. Consequently he does not, at this stage, have to make a location decision. However, he is a small-scale producer and, like most small-scale producers, the price he charges for his sausages if people come to buy them from him will be the "going rate" or the market price* for sausages. In the spaceless world on which many economists have

---

*Demand, supply, and price   Note

The price of a good can be established in a variety of ways, depending upon the kind of economic system being considered. Here we assume that we are dealing with a market system in which no individual can influence the prices of goods. Instead price reflects the balance between demand and supply. Demand and supply are terms which refer to the *willingness* of people in general to purchase or sell goods at different prices. Suppose that the demand and supply schedules for our hypothetical sausages are as follows:

Demand schedule for sausages		Supply schedule for sausages	
Price per pound	Pounds of sausages demanded per week	Price per pound	Pounds of sausages supplied per week
$3.00	0	$3.00	132
2.50	18	2.50	106
2.00	36	2.00	80
1.50	52	1.50	52
1.00	70	1.00	26
0.50	88	0.50	0
0	106		

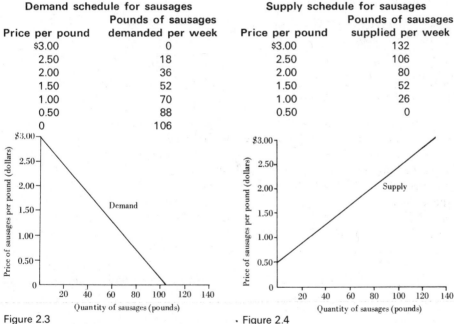

Figure 2.3
Quantity of sausages (pounds)

· Figure 2.4
Quantity of sausages (pounds)

Figure 2.3
A hypothetical demand curve for sausages.

Figure 2.4
A hypothetical supply curve for sausages.

Clearly the higher the price of sausages the less quantity demanded, the lower the price the greater the demand. On the other hand, producers are more willing to supply greater quantities of sausages if prices are high, their enthusiasm fades as prices are lower. Theoretically, however, there is a point in common between the two schedules. In Figure 2.5 this is where the demand curve and the supply curve cross. The crossover point—the point where demand and supply are in equilibrium—is at a price of $1.50 per pound. At that price, suppliers are prepared to sell 52 pounds of sausages per week and this is exactly the amount consumers are willing to buy at that price. In this case, therefore, the market price is $1.50 per pound.

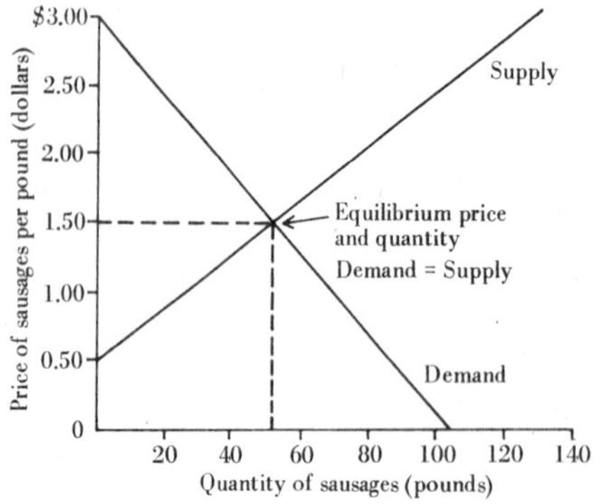

Figure 2.5
Market price of sausages
depends upon the
relationship between
supply and demand.

tended to base their analyses, the market for a good is a point. In fact, of course, we should be concerned with a *market area* and this has very important implications for the spatial organization of production of sausages (and all other goods and services as well, of course). The importance lies in the fact that the amount of sausages any individual is prepared to buy depends on the *real price* he has to pay and this is made up of two distinct elements:

1. The market price, that is, the price at the point of sale.
2. The cost of traveling to and from that point.

In our case it is the second of these elements which both helps to determine whether our sausage producer can sell enough sausages to stay in business and also how extensive his market area will be.

Suppose that the market price for sausages is $1.50 per pound. Any customer living immediately next to the sausage producer pays that price for his sausages. If he sets aside $6 per week for sausages then he will buy four pounds at $1.50 per pound. The assumptions of our model tell us that every individual has the same demands; therefore every inhabitant of our plain is *willing* to spend $6 per week on sausages. But how many sausages each one *actually gets* depends on the two elements identified above: the market price *plus* the cost of travel. Clearly, the further away a person is from the point of sale, the fewer sausages he can buy for his $6 simply because a larger proportion of that $6 has to be spent just on overcoming the friction of distance. Figure 2.6 illustrates this relationship between distance and quantity demanded on the assumption that transport costs are 10 cents per mile for a return trip (i.e. 5 cents per mile each way). A person living 15 miles from the point of sale has to spend $1.50 on traveling. This leaves $4.50 of "sausage money" with which he can buy three pounds of sausages. In other words, for this person the *real price* per pound is $2.00 compared with $1.50 for the person living next door to the producer. As distance increases so, too, does this real price. At 30 miles, the cost of travel ($3.00) leaves only enough to buy two pounds of sausages, at the equivalent of $3 per pound. At 45 miles, transportation costs leave exactly $1.50, just enough to buy one pound of sausages. But to the person living at a 45 mile distance these are really expensive sausages,

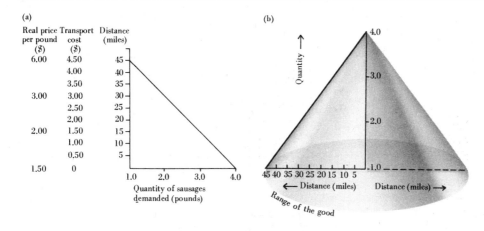

(a)

Real price per pound ($)	Transport cost ($)	Distance (miles)
6.00	4.50	45
	4.00	40
	3.50	35
3.00	3.00	30
	2.50	25
	2.00	20
2.00	1.50	15
	1.00	10
	0.50	5
1.50	0	

Quantity of sausages demanded (pounds)

(b)

Quantity

Range of the good

← Distance (miles)   Distance (miles) →

Figure 2.6
Distance and the "real price" of sausages.
(a) Hypothetical demand curve incorporating distance costs;
(b) Hypothetical demand cone showing the range of the good.

working out at the equivalent of $6 per pound! If the producer is not prepared to sell quantities of less than one pound then it is clear that anybody living beyond 45 miles from the point of sale remains sausage-less.

If we tilt Figure 2.6 over to the left through 90° we get a clearer view of the "ideal" market area for sausages. With an evenly distributed population, the area served is a circle with a radius of 45 miles. This distance, in fact, represents in this example the so-called *range of the good*; beyond 45 miles the real price of sausages is greater than people are prepared to pay. Since we know that the population is evenly distributed over our plain and we also know how many pounds of sausages each person is prepared to buy, depending on their distance from the point of sale, then we can calculate the total demand per week for sausages for the market area. (We assume for simplicity that sausages can only be bought in multiples of one pound; the seller does not sell fractions of a pound.) Figure 2.7 shows three circles, each of which represents both a specific distance and the per capita demand for sausages at that distance. By adding the demand per head for each customer, we find that the total demand is 96 pounds of sausages within the 45 mile range.

Before we leave our first producer of sausages and consider the locations of other sausage producers we need to answer another basic question. If the producer is to set up in business to produce and sell sausages and if he is to remain in business he has to be sure of selling enough sausages to cover his basic costs and to give him some profit. This fundamental requirement also has a spatial form. Suppose that our producer needs a weekly return of $105 to cover his costs. This represents the equivalent of 70 customers buying one pound of sausages per head. But as we have seen, those living near the point of sale can afford to buy more than one pound per head. In Figure 2.7 the minimum demand needed is contained within a radius of 30 miles. Such a minimum level of demand needed to ensure the survival of a producer is generally known as the *threshold* value. These two important concepts, *threshold* and *range* are very closely related to each other. One represents the minimum

Figure 2.7
Variations in total demand
for sausages with distance
from the point of
production.

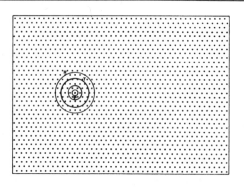

Variations in demand with distance from P

Distance from P	Number of customers and per capita demand	Aggregate demand	Value of sales
0	1 – 4 lbs	4 lbs	$ 6.00
Up to 15 mls	6 – 3 lbs	18 lbs	27.00
16 – 30 mls	24 – 2 lbs	48 lbs	72.00
31 – 45 mls	26 – 1 lb	26 lbs	39.00

R = Range of the good
T = Threshold

demand necessary to support a business, the other represents the maximum distance over which the business can sell its goods. Clearly, the threshold must lie *within* the range or at least equal it; otherwise, as Figure 2.8 shows, the business must fail.

Figure 2.8
Relationship between
threshold and range.

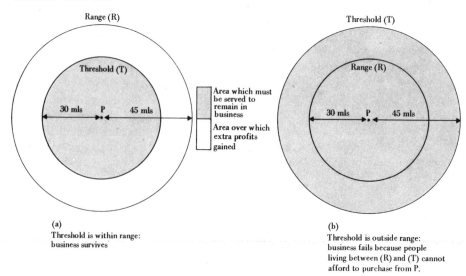

(a)
Threshold is within range:
business survives

(b)
Threshold is outside range:
business fails because people
living between (R) and (T) cannot
afford to purchase from P.

(ii) *More than one producer of the same good*

A glance back to Figure 2.7 shows that there are large numbers of people who cannot buy sausages simply because they live outside the range of sales from point P. Clearly, there is room for other producers. Assuming that conditions facing them are the same as for our first producer (that is, a market price of $1.50 per pound, transportation costs at 10 cents per mile, and a maximum expenditure of $6.00 per consumer), then the threshold and range will be identical for each sausage producer. But there is one very important complicating factor which arises as soon as we consider second, third, or nth producers of the same good. The complicating factor is that each has to take into account the existing location and market area of already established producers. As an example, consider our first producer who, as we have seen, has a market area with a radius of 45 miles. It would be irrational for a second producer of sausages to locate less than 90 miles from the first one, simply because if he did, the two producers would be competing for some of the same customers (Figure 2.9).

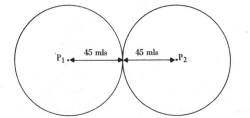

Figure 2.9
The location of a second producer is constrained by the location of the first producer.

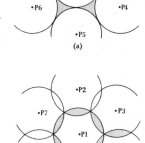

(a)

(b)

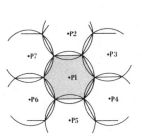

(c)

Figure 2.10
Theoretical spatial arrangement of the market areas of competing producers of the same good. (a) Population of interstitial areas is unserved; (b) Overlap of circular market areas results in competition between producers; (c) One suitable solution: hexagonal market areas.

The same principles apply to all producers of the same good each of whom will sell sausages to a circular market area of equal size. However, as the number of producers increases and covers more and more of the plain, other kinds of problems arise. Figure 2.10a shows that if producers are located so that the edges of their market areas just touch there is no competition between producers but, at the same time, there are potential consumers who live outside the range of any producer. These are left unserved. On the other hand, if the circles overlap, although they give complete coverage from the consumer viewpoint, this is unsatisfactory for the producer because it generates competition which may lower profits (Figure 2.10b). One suitable solution, for both producers and consumers, is that shown in Figure 2.10c where the circles are transformed into *hexagons* (in effect by bisecting the zones of overlap so that overlap is removed). This is a perfectly logical solution to the problem because we have already assumed that consumers will purchase their goods from the *cheapest*—that is *nearest*—producer. Thus a network of equal-sized hexagonal market areas is the most likely spatial structure for producers of the same good, under the simplified conditions of our discussion.

We can, however, take the argument just one stage further before we introduce the complication of different types of goods. Recall that the threshold for the sausage producer is located within the range (Figure 2.8a). This means, in effect, that the area between the two generates sales over and above the level necessary to cover the producer's basic costs plus some profit. In other words, the producer gains "excess profits," though these are unlikely to persist for very long. The existence of excess profits is likely to attract more producers because we assume that there is *free entry* into the industry. (This simply means that there are no barriers preventing a firm from being established; for example, the capital cost of setting up is not prohibitive and there are no institutional limitations on the establishment of new firms.) The result of such free entry is that individual

Figure 2.11
Theoretical development
of market areas from
initial circular form to final
hexagon of threshold size.
[*Source:* A. Lösch
(1954), *The Economics of
Location* (Die räumliche
Ordnung der Wirtschaft),
Stuttgart: Gustav Fischer,
1962, Figure 23.]

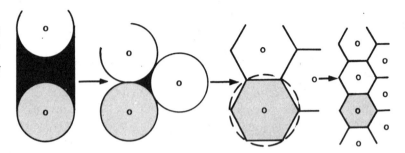

market areas become progressively smaller in size until they approach the
threshold size (Figure 2.11). Any further shrinkage would, of course, drive producers out of business. We assume that the *best* solution for both producers
and consumers as a whole is one in which all producers make the same profit
and all consumers are served at the lowest cost consistent with this level of
profit. The result is a compact, uniform lattice of production centers each serving
hexagonal market areas of identical size equivalent to the threshold size for
that good.

Spatial organization of production of other goods

Even the most avid hot dog enthusiast would probably agree that man cannot
live by sausages alone (if nothing else, he needs the buns to go with the sausages).
Other goods and services will be demanded by the inhabitants of our isotropic
plain. How would the production of these other goods and services be arranged
in space and what would their market areas be like? Fundamentally, the same
basic principles would apply whatever the good or service in question. Each
will have a specific *threshold* and a specific *range* which will apply to every
producer of the same good. But thresholds and ranges differ from one good
to another according to such variables as their basic price (including their relative transport costs) and the frequency with which they are demanded. Some
goods such as bread or milk are required very frequently and are relatively
cheap. Thus a producer of such goods need not serve a very wide geographical
area. On the other hand, most people that we know do not buy a new Rolls
Royce or a Cadillac every week; a dealer selling such luxury cars must therefore
be able to reach a very large number of customers. If, as we have assumed,
the population for both bread and Cadillacs is evenly distributed then the spatial
threshold and range will be very small for goods such as bread and very large
for such rarely purchased and expensive goods as Cadillacs. Thus we can envisage a *continuum* of goods and services from those of *low order* (small threshold,
small range) to those of *high order* (large threshold, large range). All goods,
whatever their order, will be offered in hexagonal market areas but the size
of these areas varies directly according to the order of the good. The network
of market areas of low-order goods is made up of small hexagons, the network
of market areas of high-order goods is made up of large hexagons.

Spatial organization of production of "bundles" of goods: the arrangement of central places*

It should be obvious from our discussion so far that threshold restrictions will govern both the number and the relative location of different goods and services. Low-order goods will be available at a large number of locations but as the order of a good increases, its locational frequency will become less so that high-order goods will be available at only a very few (possibly only one) locations. Even on our unbounded plain it is likely that the production of different order goods will tend to cluster together in certain locations. Walter Christaller suggested that such production clusters would be arranged in a very precise way both on the surface of the earth (that is, in terms of their relative location) and in terms of the comparative importance of different clusters. The clusters he named *central places*, which can be defined as places whose primary function is to provide the surrounding population with goods and services.

The relative importance of each central place depends upon both the number and order of goods and services it provides. Christaller suggested that the central place system takes the form of a regular *hierarchy* of central places. The precise form of the hierarchy is based upon the principle that *a place on a particular level in the hierarchy provides not only goods and services which are specific to its level but also all other goods and services of lower order.* To explain this more clearly we need to rank all the goods and services which are demanded by our evenly dispersed population in order of their threshold values. For simplicity, assume that ten goods of different order are demanded by the population of our plain. Table 2.1 shows how the organization of these ten goods, and of the centers providing them, can be fitted together to form a regular hierarchy of centers. Good 1 is the highest order good which, by definition, must be located so that it can serve the largest possible market. Good 1, therefore, will be produced only in the highest order central place, here called an A center. How many A centers there will be depends upon the total demand for the highest order good and the size of its threshold value. Suppose that the total population of our plain is 1 million and that Good 1 has a threshold value equivalent to the demand of 200,000 people: then no more than five A centers can exist. These will be spaced at an equal distance from each other in exactly the same way as our sausage producers were and for the same basic reasons.

Note

*Walter Christaller

Central place theory originated with the pioneering work of the German geographer, Walter Christaller. In his major published work, *Central Places in Southern Germany*, Christaller posed the basic question: "How can we find a general explanation for the sizes, number, and distribution of towns? How can we discover the laws?" He proceeded to seek an answer by deductive reasoning subsequently tested by a detailed empirical study of settlement patterns in Southern Germany.

Central place theory was one of the earliest location theories devised by a geographer (most other location theory originated with economists) and has had an enormous influence on geographical work.

Table 2.1
Relationship between the order of a good and the central place hierarchy.

| Threshold | Goods/services ranked in descending threshold value | Level in the hierarchy High ———————→ Low | | |
		A centers	B centers	C centers
High	1	✓		
	2	✓		
	3	✓	✓	
	4	✓	✓	
	5	✓	✓	
	6	✓	✓	
	7	✓	✓	✓
	8	✓	✓	✓
	9	✓	✓	✓
Low	10	✓	✓	✓

✓ denotes that the good is provided in the central place

The good of next lowest threshold, Good 2, will also be located in an A center, though, of course, it will serve a slightly smaller area than Good 1. Similarly, Good 3 will also be located in the A centers. However, the extent of Good 3's market area, based on each of the A centers in which it is located, is sufficiently small as to leave a considerable number of people out of reach of Good 3. If, and only if, the unserved demand is equal to Good 3's threshold value, then a new producer of the good can come into existence. As Table 2.1 shows, it will be located in the central place of the next lowest order (which we can call a B center). Figure 2.12 shows us *where* the B centers will be located: they will be located at the midpoint between three A centers. Reference back to Figure 2.10 should make it clear why this is so. The market area for a good from a production point should not overlap with market areas for the same good from other production points. Also, under our assumptions, a good can only be produced if the appropriate threshold demand exists. By locating at the midpoint between three A centers in Figure 2.12, therefore, the B center can just serve a market area which is large enough to meet the threshold requirement of the good (Good 3 in Table 2.1 in this case) without overlapping with the market areas for the same good from centers of next highest order. In Figure 2.12 the market areas for the B centers are shown by the solid lines. Good 3 can be termed a *hierarchical marginal good* because it is a good which "defines" a new level in the central place hierarchy; it is the highest order good provided by central place B.

We can continue this process to produce as many levels in the hierarchy as there are hierarchical marginal goods (that is, goods whose market areas based on particular central places leave sufficient unfulfilled demand for a new center to be established). Table 2.1 and Figure 2.12 show just one more level in the

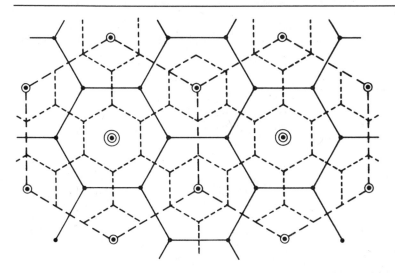

Figure 2.12
A hierarchical spatial arrangement of central places according to Christaller's *k = 3* principle.

◉ *A*-level centers
– – *A*-level market areas
◎ *B*-level centers
—— *B*-level market areas
• *C*-level centers
- - - *C*-level market areas

central place hierarchy—C-level centers. These are defined by Good 7 in Table 2.1 and are located in exactly the same way as B centers: at the midpoint between three centers of the next highest order. Clearly, then, each C center nests within three B centers and each B center nests within three A centers. Thus Table 2.1 shows that each level of the hierarchy is characterized by a specific mixture of goods. A centers, the highest order centers, provide all goods with highest to lowest threshold values. B centers provide Goods 3 to 10 but not the higher order Goods 1 and 2. Similarly, C centers provide Goods 7 to 10 but not Goods 1 to 6 which are of a higher order. Each level in the hierarchy is also characterized by equal distances between centers on that hierarchical level. Thus all A centers are the same distance from each other, each B center is an equal distance from another B center and B-level distances are less than A-level distances, and so on down the central place hierarchy.

Christaller's model, then, implies a fixed relationship between each level in the hierarchy. This relationship is known as a *k* value and indicates that each center dominates a discrete number of lower order centers and market areas in addition to its own. Figure 2.12 shows a *k = 3* system in which the hierarchical arrangement is according to the "rule of threes." The diagram is interpreted in the following way. Recall from the discussion of hierarchical marginal goods that each new center was located midway between three centers of the next highest order. In effect, therefore, each new center (and its market area) is "shared" between the three higher order centers. Within the hinterland of every A center there is *the equivalent of* two B centers (one-third of each of the six B centers surrounding an A center) and six C centers. Christaller used the term *marketing principle* to describe the organization of a *k = 3* system because it was based on the principle of supplying the maximum number of evenly distributed consumers from the minimum number of central places.

Christaller proposed that the *k* value, once established in a region, remained constant throughout the hierarchy so that the number of centers and market areas on each hierarchical level increased according to this regular progression.

Table 2.2 shows the pattern for a five-level hierarchy in which a metropolis would supply highest order goods for the equivalent of two cities (plus itself), six towns, eighteen villages, and so on.

Table 2.2
A central place system organized according to Christaller's marketing principle (*k = 3*).

Level of hierarchy	Equivalent number of central places dominated by highest order center	Equivalent number of market areas dominated by highest order center
1. Metropolis	1	1
2. City	2	3
3. Town	6	9
4. Village	18	27
5. Hamlet	54	81

The central place system

Having begun by considering the logic underlying the decision of an individual to offer a good for sale to his neighbor, we have been able to extend that same logic to make some far-reaching discoveries about the spatial organization of central places in our simplified landscape. On the basis of the distance variable alone it has been possible to generate on the isotropic plain a complex network of hierarchically ordered centers with predictable functional and locational characteristics.

This network takes the form of a spatially organized system. The objects of the system, the central places and the households of the evenly distributed consumers, are linked together by the flows of goods and cash returns as supplies and demands are matched by exchange. The dynamic force which gives the system its structure is the cyclical energy-exchange process in which *inputs* of money (demand) from a dispersed population are transformed into *outputs* of goods and services by the individual production sub-systems (butchers, bakers, printers, etc.) making up the central places. This energy-exchange process, on which both the individual production sub-systems and the central places (as aggregates of these sub-systems) depend for survival, has a spatial form because of the differences in location between points of demand and points of supply. In moving to a central place to exchange some of his income for goods and services, a consumer must use up scarce resources (money, time, physical energy) to overcome the friction of distance. At a certain distance from the supply point this expenditure is so great that when it is added to the price he must pay for the goods and services it reduces his demand for them to zero. At this distance the energy-exchange process stops as the demand input is absent (this is the range of the good).

The spatial extent of the energy-exchange process varies from one good to another, being most extensive for high-order goods (generally those of high value which are purchased relatively infrequently) and least extensive for low-order goods. The entire form and structure of the central place system, therefore, is dependent upon these systematic variations in the spatial amplitude of the energy-exchange process. The perfect hierarchical structure developed above in fact represents the *steady-state* of the central place system—a condition of dynamic equilibrium in which the nature of the functional organization achieves a balance between inputs and outputs of energy. In other words, the demands generated by the population are supplied most efficiently. Thus individual central functions, the central places themselves, and the network of central places in the hierarchy are all in perfect dynamic equilibrium with their respective environments.

Spatial organization of agricultural production

Before taking a deeper look into the nature of the central place hierarchy let us transfer our attention to the areas surrounding the central places and consider the location of agricultural production. So far we have narrowly assumed that the role of the dispersed population was to support the economic activities in the urban centers through their demands for goods and services: that is to provide *inputs* to the central place system. But some of the members of the dispersed population—those operating farms—also provide *outputs* of those agricultural products which are demanded by the residents of the central places. Indeed, the continued existence of such urban centers depends, at least in part, on the supply of agricultural goods. It is clear, therefore, that we have a further energy-exchange process to consider: one involving the production and exchange of agricultural goods. How will such agricultural production be organized on our homogeneous plain, a plain on which most of the "usual" agricultural variables (soil quality, climate, terrain) are held constant and on which the friction of distance is the sole factor?

One basic characteristic of agricultural production compared with the production of manufactured goods or the provision of services is that it uses relatively large amounts of land. Therefore, the focus of attention when we consider agricultural production is how different units of land are used. The farmers on our plain have a choice of what crops to grow or what kind of livestock to raise, though overall their choices are governed by the kinds of agricultural goods which are demanded by the inhabitants of the central places. But given this set of demands, how will the production of such agricultural goods be organized spatially? In general terms, we can say that *different units of land will be occupied by those types of use which can achieve the highest return per unit of land*. The mechanism by which the scarce land resource is allocated in this way is *economic rent*. It is important to note that "rent" in this context has a specific meaning which differs from that implied by the everyday use of the term. Economic rent is the surplus income which can be obtained from one unit of land above that which can be obtained from an inferior unit of land; for the most part it is measured against land at the margin or limit of cultivation. This "marginal land" is land which is just capable of producing a return large enough to cover the cost of bringing it into production. The term "rent" in popular usage refers to *contract rent* which is the *actual* payment which tenants make to others for the use of their land or property. The two concepts are related but not necessarily synonymous (see Chisholm, 1962).

For our present purposes we can define *economic rent* as a measure of the level of return which the market at large (all the potential bidders for land) would expect a particular piece of land to produce. It is basically a measure of the *advantage*, as the bidders see it, of one piece of land over another.* This implies, of course, that land is differentiated in some respect and that such differentiation is reflected in higher or lower returns per unit of land. In our simplified model, the only basis for such differentiation is the friction of distance. More specifically, the only advantage which one piece of land can have over another piece of land is its *location* in relation to the market for agricultural products. For this reason, we will use the term *location rent* to signify this particular interpretation of economic rent.

Each of the central places located in an orderly hierarchical manner in our simplified landscape may be regarded as a potential market for agricultural goods. Obviously the centers vary in importance as markets according to their size and hierarchical status. The highest order A centers in Figure 2.12 are likely to be far larger centers of demand for agricultural products than are the C-level centers. However, different sized market centers pose problems which obscure the essential features of our discussion so, at this stage, we will concentrate on just *one* highest order central place and show how agricultural production is likely to be located in the area around it.†

Spatial organization of one agricultural product

The price of any product at the market is, as we have seen, set by the prevailing relationship between demand and supply. Thus we could construct demand and supply schedules for each of the agricultural products demanded by the central place population in exactly the same way as we did for urban products such as sausages on p. 23. The market price is the price received by the farmer when he sells his product at the market. His net return is this price *less* his costs of production and the cost of transporting his product from his farm to the market. As production costs are assumed to be the same everywhere, then the only factor which can influence the farmer's net return is the cost of transportation.

Note | *There is, in fact, far more to the concept of economic rent than this definition implies, but fuller discussion at this stage would deflect us from our central purpose. The question of economic rent in a more general context is taken up again in Chapter Six.

Note | †*J. H. von Thünen.* This kind of approach originated with J. H. von Thünen who, as we observed earlier in this chapter, can be regarded as one of the founders, if not *the* founder, of economic location theory. Von Thünen was a German estate owner who, in the early nineteenth century, began to investigate with great scientific precision the best way of organizing agricultural land use. His findings were published as a book, *Der Isolierte Staat (The Isolated State)* in 1826, which has had an enormous impact both on economic thinking (we quoted from his preface on p. 22) in general and on geographical analysis of agriculture in particular. A translation of *Der Isolierte Staat* edited by Peter Hall was published in 1966. It contains not only the translation of von Thünen's text but also a commentary and interpretation.

If all farmers could be located at the market, they would all get the same net return. But this is obviously impossible. Farms cannot be piled on top of each other in skyscraper fashion. As we have said, farming uses a lot of land and *where* this land is located with reference to the urban market is the critical factor determining the net advantage which one piece of land has over another piece of land. Clearly, the greatest advantage belongs to land immediately adjacent to the market center and the advantage declines as distance from the market increases. Precisely how this occurs in the case of a single crop can be calculated by using this simple formula:

$$LR = Y(m\text{-}c) - Ytd$$

Each element of this formula can be interpreted as follows:

LR = location rent per unit of land
Y = yield (quantity produced) per unit of land
m = market price per unit of product
c = production cost per unit of product
t = transport rate per unit of distance
d = distance of the unit of land from the market

Let us apply this formula to the production of an imaginary milk producer by substituting numerical values for the letters. Suppose that:

Y (yield)   = 100 gallons per acre
m (market price)   = $5 per gallon
c (production cost)   = $3 per gallon
t (transport rate)   = 5 cents per mile

At the market itself, the value of location rent for milk would be:

$$LR = 100\ (\$5\text{--}\$3) - 100\ (5c \times 0)$$
$$= \underline{\$200}$$

As no transportation costs are involved, the net return to the farmer is at its maximum. However, for the farmer producing milk on a piece of land 10 miles from the market, the situation is rather different. His yield, market price, and production costs are the same as those of the farmer located at the market. But he has to pay to ship his milk to market. Location rent at his location, therefore, is:

$$LR = 100\ (\$5\text{--}\$3) - 100\ (5c \times 10)$$
$$= \underline{\$150}$$

If we follow this pattern outwards from the market the relationship between location rent for milk and transportation costs takes the form shown in Figure 2.13. This shows that the margin of production of milk given these yield, price, and cost figures will be at a distance of 40 miles from the market. At that distance the farmer's net return is completely obliterated by the costs of transporting his milk to market. He cannot, therefore, remain in business without making a loss, something our economic man could not tolerate.

Figure 2.13
Relationship between
location rent for an
agricultural product and
transportation costs to the
market.

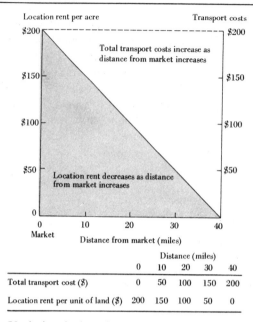

	Distance (miles)				
	0	10	20	30	40
Total transport cost ($)	0	50	100	150	200
Location rent per unit of land ($)	200	150	100	50	0

Variation in location rent with distance is usually shown by the kind of downward-sloping curve of Figure 2.14. It indicates that the closer the unit of land to the market, the more desirable it is. This will stimulate competition to exploit its use. The situation can be understood more easily if we distinguish between the dairy farmer who seeks to use a particular piece of land and the owner of that land. Land will be allocated among dairy farmers on the basis of competitive bidding between them. This location-rent curve, therefore, can also be regarded as a *bid-rent curve* (Alonso, 1960) because it gives an indication of how much dairy farmers would be prepared to pay for a unit of land at varying distances from the market. In the present example, the cash advantage which a farmer located 10 miles from the market has over a farmer located 20 miles away is $50. It would, therefore, benefit the more distant farmer to bid up to $50 to acquire the land close to the market. But it would be useless for him to bid more because any figure above this amount would be higher than the "ceiling rent" at that location, resulting in a loss.

Spatial organization of several agricultural products

Just as in our discussion of goods and services produced in urban centers we progressed from the consideration of one good (sausages) to other goods, so, too, we can examine the spatial organization of agricultural production of other crops and products on our isotropic plain. The basic principles remain the same though the specific values of price and cost will vary for each product. For each agricultural product demanded by the population there will be:

(i) a specific market price depending on the supply/demand relationship for that good;
(ii) a specific transport rate which will vary according to the nature of the product—its bulkiness, perishability and general transportability;

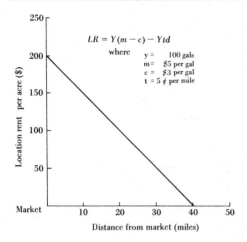

Figure 2.14
Hypothetical location-rent curve for milk.

(iii) a basic cost of production which is assumed to be constant in space for any one good;

(iv) a specific yield per unit of land.

Thus every product will have a different location-rent curve. Its *height* (the value of location rent at the market) depends on the difference between the product's market price and its production costs; its *slope* (the rate at which the value of location rent declines with distance) depends on the transportation characteristics of the product.

Suppose we introduce two more products (in addition to milk): potatoes and wheat. What will their location-rent curves look like and, more importantly, how will this affect the relative location of production of all three products? Figure 2.15 shows how the location-rent curves for the products overlap. The relative heights of the three curves at any given distance from the market determine which of the three land uses will be adopted at that distance. For example, a farmer located 20 miles from the market could achieve the following location-rent values:

Milk $100 per acre
Potatoes $70 per acre
Wheat $55 per acre

Clearly he will devote his land to milk production because this is the land use yielding the highest location rent at that location.* In fact, all farmers located between the market and a distance of some 26 miles from the market

---

Opportunity cost. Note that the farmer could still make a profit if he grew either potatoes or wheat instead of milk. To grow either potatoes or wheat would incur an *opportunity cost* which is the difference between the return *actually* achieved and the maximum which *could* be achieved. Thus the farmer's opportunity cost for growing potatoes instead of raising dairy cattle is $30 ($100–$70) and for growing wheat it is $45. An opportunity cost, therefore, is a measure of the cost of one alternative in terms of the alternative not taken up. But as all our producers aim to achieve optimal solutions, each will adopt the land-use type generating the highest location rent.

Note

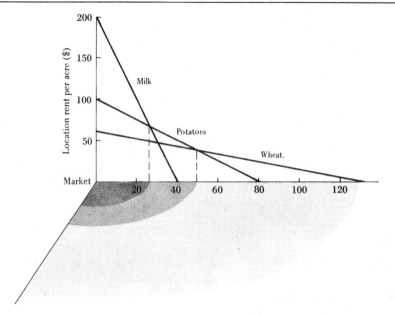

Figure 2.15
Location-rent curves and
production zones for milk,
potatoes, wheat.

would be milk producers because the location rent for milk is higher than that of its nearest rival, potatoes, over the entire distance. But at a distance of 26 miles, milk production would be displaced by potato production; this land use would then dominate over all distances from 26 miles to 40 miles beyond which wheat would be the crop grown until the margin of cultivation is reached at approximately 126 miles from the market. Beyond that distance agricultural production would cease under the prevailing conditions of demand and supply.

Figure 2.15 also shows that if we envisage the land-use zones on the horizontal axis being rotated around the market point, the result is an agricultural land-use pattern of *concentric rings* or *zones*. Each zone accommodates that type of land use yielding the highest location rent. Thus the spatial organization of production of those agricultural goods demanded by the population of our highest order central place takes the form of a series of concentric zones around the central place. The order or sequence of products is determined by the height and slope of their location-rent curves. The transition from one land use to another occurs where their respective location-rent curves intersect.

Although we have considered the possibility of producing only one type of crop at a particular location exactly the same principles apply to *combinations of crops*. In such cases, the location-rent curve applies to the total combination and not simply to the individual elements. Figure 2.16 shows a hypothetical example. A combination of milk, potatoes, and wheat has the location-rent curve AX; that for a combination of potatoes, wheat, and barley is shown by BY, and a combination of potatoes, barley, and beef by CZ. That combination yielding the highest location rent at any given location will be the prevailing type of land use. Figure 2.16 also shows that the same product may occur

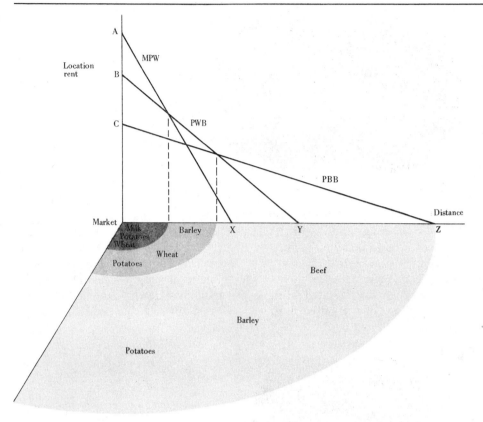

Figure 2.16
Location-rent curves for
combinations of
agricultural products.

in several zones though in different combinations (potatoes are present through-out the area in the diagram). Thus the introduction of crop combinations rather than single crops does not alter the basic concentric pattern of agricultural production; it simply means that the *number* of possible concentric rings is increased to the number of possible combinations of products demanded by consumers.

The effect of more than one market center on the spatial organization of agricultural production

We deliberately isolated one central place from the hierarchical system in order to see more clearly how agricultural production would be spatially organized around that center. We did this to avoid obscuring the basic allocating mechanism—location rent—and its operation. But what happens when we put our single-market center back into its rightful place as only one center in the hierarchy? It certainly makes life more complicated for the location theorist because every central place is, potentially, a market for agricultural goods. Suppose, as in Figure 2.17, we introduce the complication of just one additional market. Both centers have the inner land-use zones organized concentrically around them, as in the single-market example. However, the outer zones are displaced and take on an elliptical shape because of their orientation toward

Figure 2.17
The effect of two market centers on agricultural land-use zones. [*Source:* E. S. Dunn (1954), *The Location of Agricultural Production,* Figure 16. Reproduced by permission of the University of Florida Press, Gainesville.]

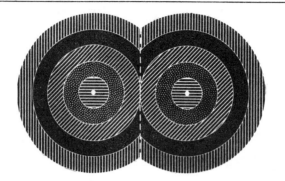

two markets rather than one. The dotted line marks the boundary between the two competing supply areas. The existence of more than two market centers produces a more complex picture as Figure 2.18 illustrates diagrammatically. Here part of the central place system depicted in Figure 2.12 is used to give an impressionistic representation of the agricultural supply areas. Products of the inner rings are oriented towards the individual towns as in the simpler case but those of the outer rings are oriented towards the entire cluster of centers.

Figure 2.18
Diagrammatic representation of the effect of multiple market centers on agricultural land-use zones.

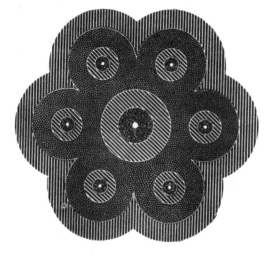

These examples are very general; Figure 2.19 takes a closer look at the effect of several market centers on agricultural location. Five market centers are shown together with three types of agricultural land use: milk, beans, and wheat. The difference in the pattern of land uses is caused by the effect of transportation costs and the movement characteristics of each product on their location rents. Rent curves for milk are very steep because milk is perishable and generally has to be transported quickly. Thus each center, even the smallest, has its own "milkshed." The other two products have gentler rent gradients and are thus produced over a wider area. Thus the existence of several market centers un-

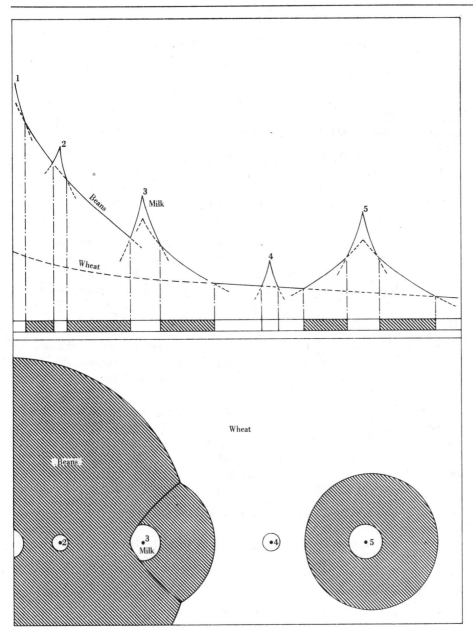

Figure 2.19
Rent gradients and zones of land use tributary to five market centers. [*Source:* from *The Location of Economic Activity* by E. M. Hoover. Copyright 1948 E. M. Hoover. Used with permission of McGraw-Hill Book Company.]

doubtedly produces a more complex picture but it does not alter the basis on which the spatial pattern of agricultural production is founded. The land use at any particular location is the one which yields the highest location rent at that location. This allocative mechanism still operates even though the existence of several markets makes its operation more difficult to visualize.

The agricultural production system

For the agricultural production system, the objects are the dispersed farm units and the nucleated central places. *Inputs* to the agricultural system take the form of money income to the farmer derived from the sale of his products, production factors (farm machinery, fertilizers, etc.), and manufactured goods which are obtained from the central places.

Outputs from the agricultural system are the crop and livestock products. The *transformation* stage in this case involves the use of capital, labor and technical skills in manipulating biotic processes to satisfy consumption needs. The functional structure of the system derives from the continuous interaction process as the demand for crop and livestock products is met by supply. Should it stop the system ceases to exist.

Under the constraints of our model, the spatial organization of the system depends first, on the specific products demanded, and second, on the extent to which this demand is eroded by distance. For some products spatial interaction—the exchange of town-based inputs for crop or livestock outputs—is restricted by the loss of resources incurred in transport costs. For these the spatial amplitude of the interaction cycles is small and in the model the only feasible locations are close to their markets. For others, the friction of distance bears less heavily and their range of feasible locations in relation to markets is wider. The precise spatial allocation of land uses is in the long-run achieved through a competitive bidding process among prospective land users.

Given all the assumptions of our model and the absence of any volatile or disruptive forces the steady-state of the system would be achieved with a regular pattern of zonal land uses. These would be simple and concentric in the single-market case but for a hierarchical network such as that generated earlier for the central place system the pattern would, even under the constraints of the model, be extremely complex.

Thus far, we have treated the central place and agricultural production systems of the model as though they were separate entities. This is convenient for the purposes of exposition. More realistically, however, it is clear that they are inextricably bound up with one another. The two combine in a symbiotic relationship. Together they comprise a higher order, two-sector, economic system, the one interacting with the other to satisfy the consumption needs of society in the model landscape. The inputs of one *sub-system* can now be identified as the outputs of the other. For instance, agricultural produce shipped to the central places (or the money income derived from it) is exchanged for "town-based" production factors or central goods and *vice versa*. The economic system developed up to this point in the simplified model depends therefore on "two region-two sector" trade and interaction to meet consumer demands.

Spatial organization of land uses within urban centers

When we derived the hierarchical structure of central places with its concentrations of functions we ignored the question of *how* such functions would be organized *within* each central place. However, having now explained the way in which location rent "allocates" agricultural land uses in the areas surrounding the central places we can apply the same basic principle to the internal structure of central places. As Isard (1956) has observed, "in many respects, urban land-use theory is a logical extension of agricultural location theory." The two situations are by no means identical but they have sufficient in common to justify brief consideration here.*

We assume that each urban center has one focal point—the center—which, on our isotropic plain is the most accessible location in the urban center. Urban land uses will be arranged around that point in exactly the same way as agricultural land uses were arranged around the central place itself, that is, in concentric rings. The basic reason is the same in both cases: land uses compete for the most accessible location and are "sorted out" on the basis of their location rents which reflect their ability to pay for a particular site. Robert M. Haig expressed this concept in the following way:

> the center is the point at which transportation costs can be reduced to a minimum. Since there is insufficient space at the center to accommodate all the activities which would derive advantages from location there, the most central sites are assigned, for a rental, to those activities which can best utilize the advantages and the others take the less accessible locations. Site rents and transportation costs are vitally connected through their relationship to the friction of space. Transportation is the means of reducing that friction, at the cost of time and money.
> *R. M. Haig (1926), p. 421*

Richard Hurd expressed the same idea though rather more concisely:

> Since value depends on economic rent and rent on location, and location on convenience, and convenience on nearness, we may eliminate the intermediate steps and say that value depends on nearness.
> *R. M. Hurd (1924), p. 13*

In the most simple terms, therefore, the spatial organization of land uses within the central places on our isotropic plain would look like the general pattern of Figure 2.20. Those functions which gain the greatest advantage from locating

---

*The issue of urban land-use allocation and its relationship with land values is highly complex and beyond the scope of this book. Early classic studies are those by Hurd (1924) and Haig (1926), both of whom follow closely the concept of economic or location rent. A more recent interpretation which introduces additional variables is provided by Alonso (1964) in his *Location and Land Use,* while Carter (1975), *The Study of Urban Geography* (Chapter 9) contains a very useful summary of a wide range of studies.

Note

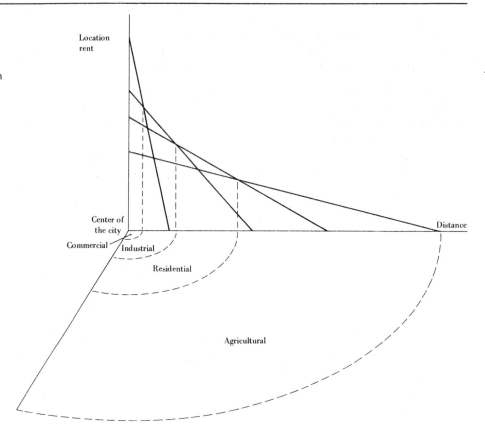

Figure 2.20
Relationship between
location rent and the
spatial organization of
land uses within an urban
center.

at the point of maximum accessibility form the innermost zone with the other
uses arranged in sequence according to their location rents.

Thus the concentric zonation of land uses, from the center of the city and
through urban uses and the various agricultural products to the margin of
cultivation can all be attributed to the operation of the following relationships
(Alonso, 1960):

(i) land uses determine land values, through competitive bidding among users.
(ii) land values distribute land uses according to their ability to pay. This ability
depends upon the level of location rent accruing to a particular product at
a particular location with respect to the market.
(iii) the steeper rent curves capture the central locations: in other words, those
products which have most to gain by locating near the market and most to
lose by being further away.

A reconsideration of the central place hierarchy

Having kept matters as simple as possible while we examined the relationship
between urban centers and their agricultural supply areas, we are now ready
to add a little more complexity to our model. Let us take a more penetrating

look at the spatial organization of the central place system. We ended our previous discussion of this topic by suggesting that its most probable form would be the hierarchical arrangement of centers according to Christaller's *marketing principle* ($k = 3$). Under these conditions a system of central places was evolved in accordance with two basic principles. The first was that all parts of the plain would be supplied with all conceivable goods from a given number of centers; the second, that a central place of given rank provided the goods and services appropriate to its own rank and all goods and services of lower order. Modification of one or both of these principles would present us with alternative hierarchical arrangements.

Christaller, in fact, recognized that a $k = 3$ system of central places was not the only conceivable form for the hierarchy to take. He suggested two other organizing principles in which the size and orientation of the hexagonal market areas is changed, thus altering the functional relationships between centers on different levels of the hierarchy (Figure 2.21).

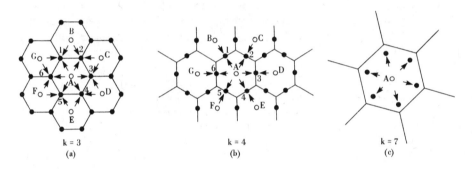

k = 3   k = 4   k = 7
(a)   (b)   (c)

Figure 2.21
Christaller's three alternative spatial arrangements of central places.
(a) Marketing principle ($k = 3$)
(b) Traffic principle ($k = 4$)
(c) Administrative principle ($k = 7$)

Christaller's "traffic" principle: $k = 4$

Even on our isotropic plain where movement is *possible* in all directions, some movement paths are more likely to be followed than others. Christaller pointed out that the marketing principle ($k = 3$) is an awkward arrangement in terms of connecting different levels of the hierarchy:

> In a system of central places developed according to the marketing principle, the great long-distance lines necessarily by-pass places of considerable importance, and the secondary lines built for short-distance traffic can reach the great places of long-distance traffic only in a roundabout way— often even in remarkably zig-zag routes.
> *Christaller (1966), p. 74*

As an alternative arrangement, Christaller suggested that central places could be organized according to what he called the *traffic* principle:

> the traffic principle states that the distribution of central places is most favorable when as many important places as possible lie on one traffic route between two important towns, the route being established as straightly and as cheaply as possible. The more unimportant places may

be left aside. According to the traffic principle, the central places would thus be lined up on straight traffic routes which fan out from the central point.
Christaller (1966), p. 74

Where central places are arranged according to the traffic principle, therefore, lower order centers are located at the midpoint of each side of the hexagon rather than at the corners as in a $k = 3$ system. Thus the traffic principle produces a hierarchy organized in a $k = 4$ arrangement in which central places are nested according to the "rule of 4s." Figure 2.21 shows how this can be interpreted. Take the central places numbered 1 to 6 around the higher order center, A. In a $k = 4$ system, central place number 1 is "shared" equally between the two higher order centers A and B. Place 2 is shared equally between A and C and so on for each of the six lower order centers. Center A, therefore, dominates or serves the equivalent of *four* market areas of next lowest order (six times one half of each of the market areas 1 to 6 together with its own market area). In a $k = 3$ system the market area relationship is one to three. Table 2.3 shows the hierarchical relationship for a five-level system and should be compared with Table 2.2 to clarify the difference between a $k = 3$ and $k = 4$ system.

Table 2.3
A central place system organized according to Christaller's traffic principle ($k = 4$).

Level of hierarchy	Equivalent number of central places dominated by highest order center	Equivalent number of market areas dominated by highest order center
1. Metropolis	1	1
2. City	3	4
3. Town	12	16
4. Village	48	64
5. Hamlet	192	256

Christaller's "administrative" principle: $k = 7$

Christaller's other suggested organizing principle was based upon the realization that from a political or administrative viewpoint centers which are "shared" pose problems. Any pattern of control which cuts through functional units is potentially problematical (an extreme example would be the divided city of Berlin). Consequently Christaller suggested that an arrangement whereby lower order centers were entirely within the hexagon of the higher order center would obviate such problems. Such a pattern is shown in Figure 2.21c: all six lower order centers are fully subordinate to center A which, therefore, dominates the equivalent of seven market areas at the next lowest level (market areas 1 to 6 plus its own).

Whichever of these three hierarchical arrangements ($k = 3, 4, 7$) is adopted, they each share one basic characteristic. Once one of the k values is established in an area then, according to Christaller, this value remains constant so that the hierarchical ordering of central places and of market area sizes follows this strict progression throughout. The result is a very regular, rigid and discrete-level hierarchy of centers in which the relationship between each level is identical throughout.

Lösch's approach to the hierarchical arrangement of centers*

August Lösch, writing just a few years after Christaller published his study of central places, took a far less rigid view of the hierarchical arrangement of centers. Using an argument which is often difficult to follow, he shows how this more flexible hierarchy can be derived. He pointed out that the $k = 3$, 4 and 7 arrangements were but the three smallest of a very large number of possible market area structures. Figure 2.22 shows the ten smallest areas though Lösch in fact identified 150 such areas altogether. Recall that each good in our simple landscape possesses a hexagonal mesh of market areas, the fineness or coarseness of the mesh being determined by the good's threshold value. In Lösch's view, there is no reason why these market areas and their associated production centers should, or could, be arranged in the rigid manner proposed by Christaller.

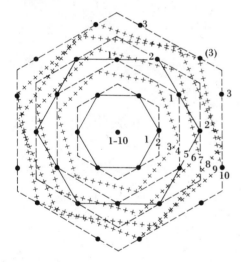

Figure 2.22
Lösch's ten smallest market areas focused on the "metropolis."
[*Source:* A. Lösch (1954), *The Economics of Location* (Die räumliche Ordnung der Wirtschaft), Stuttgart: Gustav Fischer, 1962, Figure 27.]

*August Lösch. Lösch was, without doubt, one of the most original, stimulating and, at the same time, one of the most obscure of the modern location theorists. His major work, *The Economics of Location,* was originally published in German in 1939 but was not available as an English translation until 1954, some nine years after his death at the age of only 39. Lösch's view of the world was extremely idealistic: "the real duty of the economist," he wrote, "is not to explain our sorry reality, but to improve it. The question of the best location is far more dignified than determination of the actual one" (p. 4). Lösch's work shows a breadth and depth of thought unequalled by most other location theorists. We have already employed some of his ideas as building blocks in this chapter. For example, it was Lösch who first demonstrated how hexagonal market areas for different goods could be derived using spatial adaptations of the demand curve (see above, p. 25).

The question he posed was how might this confusion of hexagonal nets of various sizes be combined to form a spatial structure which would be efficient for both producers and consumers? Begin, says Lösch, by arbitrarily choosing just *one* production center from the entire set of production points established on the plain. (Each production point itself is established on the basis of the principles discussed on pages 23 to 28. Then arrange the nets so that this one center is common for all of them. Figure 2.22 shows this for ten goods and their hexagonal nets. This center, at which *every* good would be available, could be regarded as the metropolis, the highest order center of all. The nets are then arranged so that there is an alternation of 30° sectors radiating out from the metropolis.* There will be twelve such sectors (see Figure 2.23)

Figure 2.23
Theoretical spatial arrangement of market areas and production centers according to Lösch. [*Source:* after Isard (1956). Original source: A. Lösch (1954), *The Economics of Location* (Die räumliche Ordnung der Wirtschaft), Stuttgart: Gustav Fischer, 1962, Figure 28.]

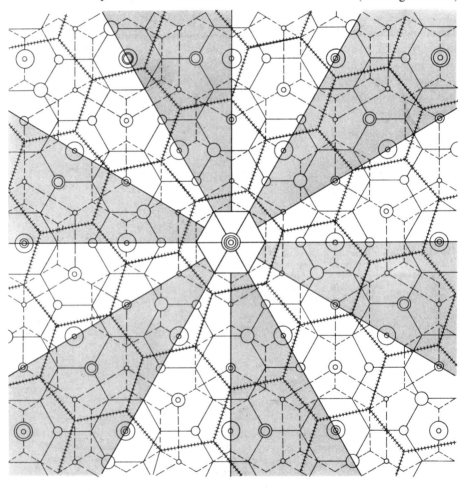

Note

*This particular section of Lösch's work has been the subject of much controversy and misinterpretation. Lösch seems to suggest that, having focused all the nets on one center, the nets are then rotated around that central point until we get "six sectors with many and six with only a few production sites" (p. 124) with a consequent maximum coincidence of production sites. This conjures up a picture of Lösch sitting at his desk with 150 sheets of transparent

Note continued

paper with a pin through the middle spinning each of them round until he reached the sectoral pattern he wanted. This *may* have been so, though recent work by Tarrant (1973) and Beavon and Mabin (1975) suggests a rather different interpretation. The mathematical detail of their argument need not concern us here but their conclusions are particularly illuminating. According to both studies, the production of "city-rich" and "city-poor" sectors is not the *result* of rotation, as many have believed, but a *constraint* upon it. In other words, *if* a sectoral pattern is to be achieved there is a very limited number of ways in which the hexagonal nets can be arranged. Once certain ones are oriented in a particular way the positions of the others are fixed. It is perhaps worth re-emphasizing the idealistic basis of Lösch's view. He was concerned with finding the "best" spatial solution to the arrangement of producers and he regarded a sectoral pattern as part of this best arrangement.

arranged alternately so that six sectors have very many economic activities and six have relatively few. Lösch called these "city-rich" and "city-poor" sectors but these terms are misleading. *Each sector has the same number of production points (central places) but the number of activities at each center varies between the two types of sector.* In other words, there are more higher order centers (in Lösch's scheme these are centers with a larger number of economic activities) in the activity-rich sector than in the activity-poor sector. Figure 2.24 shows this more clearly for just part of the total system. The left-hand sector of the diagram has the same number of centers as the right-hand sector (168) but it has far more centers with a larger number of activities at each. For example, the "activity-rich" sector has 34 centers with more than five economic activities at each and 39 centers with either three or four activities. The "activity-poor" sector by comparison has only 23 centers with more than five activities and 24 with three to four. Conversely, the activity-poor sector has far more production centers with only one activity (52 percent of the total) than has the activity-rich sector (39 percent of the total).

Despite the cloudiness of some of Lösch's statements there is no doubt that he produces a spatial organization of production centers whose form is very appealing. Lösch himself saw this spatial pattern of economic activities as offering several advantages. In particular he claimed that the total distances between production points are minimized and, therefore, both the volume of shipment and the length of transport routes needed to satisfy the demands of the systems are reduced. At the same time, because the largest number of production locations coincide, the maximum amount of purchases can be made locally. Thus Lösch suggested that this spatial arrangement of urban centers was consistent with what he saw to be a basic element in human organization: the *principle of least effort*.

Using similar assumptions but dissimilar approaches, Christaller and Lösch generate rather different urban hierarchies. In Christaller's scheme, the hierarchy is composed of a series of discrete levels in which a center produces *exactly* the same mix of goods as every other center on the same hierarchical level. Lösch's hierarchy, on the other hand, is far less rigid. The less regular coincidence of centers producing different orders of goods means that centers of the same size (in terms of the number of economic activities) may produce *quite different* combinations of goods. In Lösch's scheme functional mixture and hierarchical position are not synonymous. Figure 2.25 illustrates some of the flexibi-

Figure 2.24
Transport lines and
clusters of economic
activities in Lösch's
"activity-rich" and
"activity-poor" sectors.
[Source: A. Lösch
(1954), The Economics of
Location (Die räumliche
Ordnung der Wirtschaft),
Stuttgart: Gustav Fischer,
1962, Figure 32.]

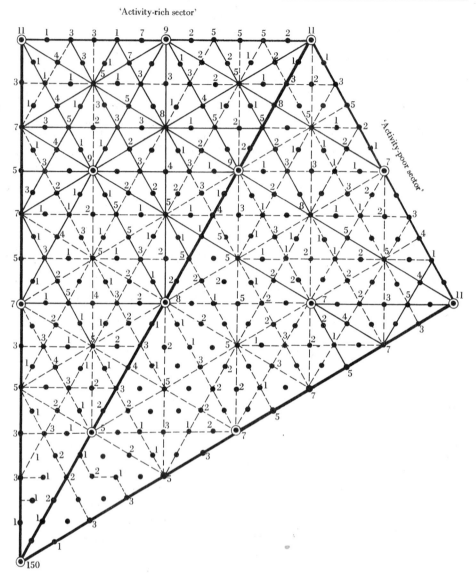

lity of Lösch's structure (the lines represent delivered prices so that the production point of each good is where the appropriately numbered line is at its lowest point or points). Place A may be regarded as the metropolis in which all goods (1 to 7) are produced, but there is no fixed relationship between the type of goods supplied and the other centers as postulated by Christaller. In the first place, it is possible in Lösch's scheme to have different combinations of functions in centers of the same size or rank. For example, centers E, I, and K each provide two functions. E and I both produce goods 2 and 4, but K produces goods 2 and 5. Secondly, functions of the same order may be produced in centers of different size. Thus, good 7 is produced not only in the metropolis but also in what is clearly a lower order center, H. Christaller's

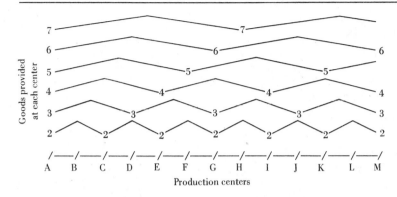

Figure 2.25
Hypothetical distribution
of goods produced by
centers of different order.
[*Source:* W. Stolper
(1955), Spatial Order and
the Economic Growth of
Cities, *Economic
Development and Cultural
Change,* 3, p. 140.
Reproduced by
permission of The
University of Chicago
Press, © 1955 by the
University of Chicago.]

condition that a center on a given hierarchical level will provide the goods of all lower order centers is not fulfilled with the single exception of the metropolis. Thus Lösch's scheme allows the existence of *specialized* production centers while Christaller's does not, except insofar as each level in his hierarchy is distinguished by a specific hierarchical marginal good.

Despite the obscurity of certain parts of the Löschian model, it is more flexible and more comprehensive than Christaller's. Indeed Lösch claims that it is unnecessary to envisage three separate and conflicting principles as Christaller does, on the grounds that his complete regional system of centers and hexagonal market areas subsumes all of these principles at the same time. Two important consequences follow from the kind of economic landscape envisaged by Lösch (neither of which he identified himself). One relates to the implications of the sectoral arrangement on movement and the other to population distribution. Let us take each of these in turn.

A major advantage of Lösch's sectoral patterning of production centers, as he saw it, was that movement was more efficient when channeled along discrete routeways (Christaller's $k = 4$ principle was based upon a similar view). As Figure 2.24 shows, the transport network is denser in the activity-rich sectors though, for some reason, Lösch positioned his major transport routes, of which there were twelve radiating outwards from the metropolis, along the edges of each sector whereas they should logically run *through* the activity-rich sector. However derived, the fact remains that the introduction of linear transportation routes greatly modifies the spatial arrangement of economic activities by modifying the frictional effects of distance. Movement will likely be both easier, quicker, and possibly cheaper, along established routeways than "across country" (indeed movement may well be possible only along such routeways). The result will be the distortion of what would otherwise be regularly shaped hexagonal market areas and circular land-use areas. Figure 2.26 shows how a hexagonal market area might become elongated along the line of a routeway; clearly the impact of routeways on a full network of hexagonal areas would greatly alter the overall spatial pattern of market areas. Similarly for land-use zones, whether within urban centers or surrounding them, differential movement patterns result in a stretching out of zones along the transportation routes. Von Thünen, in fact, recognized that such a distortion would take place (he introduced a river

Figure 2.26
Distortion of a hexagonal
market area by a
transportation route.

Figure 2.27
Distortion of land-use
zones by transportation
routes.

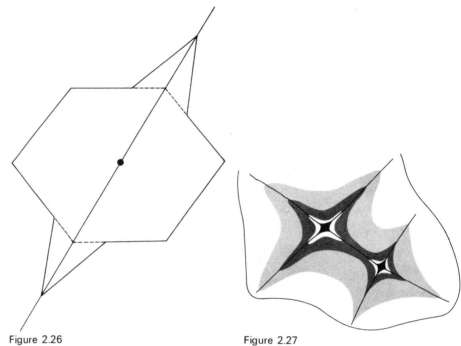

Figure 2.26   Figure 2.27

routeway into his Isolated State) by, in effect, raising the level of location rent along a zone parallel to the route.

The second implication of Lösch's kind of economic landscape is that it inevitably destroys our initial assumption of an evenly distributed population. Not only will population densities (the number of people per square mile or square kilometer) be greater in the individual urban centers but also differential population densities occur on a larger scale because of the sectoral clustering of activities envisaged by Lösch. Inevitably, such differences in density will cause variations in the size of market areas. Figure 2.28 shows this effect diagrammatically. Recall that in a fully developed system of market areas for a particular good the size of each hexagon will be equivalent to that good's threshold value. Suppose that a producer needs the equivalent of one hundred customers to keep his business going. The geographical extent of his threshold market area will be determined by the population density. If the density is 100 people per

Figure 2.28
Market area size varies in
accordance with
variations in population
density.

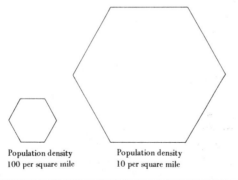

Population density
100 per square mile

Population density
10 per square mile

square mile then his market area will have that geographical dimension. If, on the other hand, people are far less densely settled—say at 10 per square mile—then his market area will be ten times larger, though serving exactly the same number of people. Thus, in areas of high population density, especially nearer the metropolis, a high level of sales can be achieved by a small market area. At a greater distance from the metropolis, however, where population densities are lower, this same level of sales would require a much larger market area. Isard (1956) has attempted to modify Lösch's system diagrammatically by allowing hexagon size to vary, although, as Figure 2.29 shows, such variation makes it very difficult to preserve a true hexagonal structure.

However, introduction of such modifications as linear transportation routes and varying population densities does not destroy the underlying logic of the argument. The spatial organization of economic activities on our simplified landscape is still ordered fundamentally by the frictional effect of distance. Movement and its costs are still the basic influence. So let us finally turn to a more general consideration of movement itself as a geographical phenomenon.

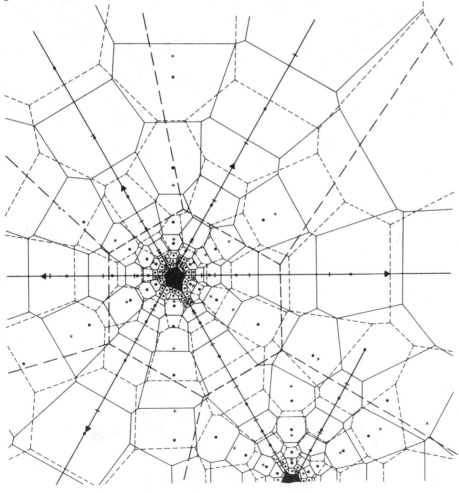

Figure 2.29
Effect of uneven population densities on the size of market areas in a Löschian landscape. [*Source:* reproduced from W. Isard (1956), *Location and Space Economy*, Figure 52, by permission of the M.I.T. Press, Cambridge, Mass. Copyright © 1956 by the Massachusetts Institute of Technology.]

Movement and interaction in the economic landscape: people, objects, and information

Bases for interaction

Interaction—movement between places of people, goods, or information—does not occur in isolation but is stimulated or generated by particular forces. Edward Ullman (1956) suggested that there are three fundamental bases underlying all spatial interaction. First, for interaction to take place between two places, they must be *complementary* to each other. In other words, there must be a demand-supply relationship between them—one place must want what another place has got and the latter must be prepared to supply it. We can illustrate complementarity by referring back to Figure 2.25 and examining two of the production centers, for example, G and K. The mix of products at G consists of goods 2, 3, and 6, while at K only products 2 and 5 are produced. A clear complementary relationship exists between these two centers: G can provide K with goods 3 and 6 while K can provide G with good 5.

The concept of complementarity throws additional light on the two types of hierarchy discussed earlier. Figure 2.30 compares the Christaller and Lösch hierarchies in terms of their differing degrees of complementarity. In the rigid Christaller-type hierarchy (Figure 2.30a), centers on the same hierarchical level are, by definition, *not* complementary. They provide exactly the same mix of functions and are, therefore, identical. In a Christaller hierarchy, then, interaction can only occur between one level of the hierarchy and another. Lateral interaction—that is between centers of the same hierarchical status—is precluded. Thus Christaller's central places are complementary to only a very limited extent (defined by the hierarchical marginal good). In a Löschian hierarchy, on the other hand, as Figure 2.30b shows, interaction can occur in more than one direction within the hierarchy because of its less rigid organization. (As we pointed out earlier, centers of similar order may have different mixtures of economic activities, while low-order places may offer specific goods which higher order centers—other than the metropolis—do not possess). Allan Pred (1971) has suggested that a more suitable solution is one which contains elements of both kinds of hierarchy. In Figure 2.31, for example, in addition to

Figure 2.30
Interaction relationships in (a) a Christaller-type hierarchy and (b) a Löschian hierarchy.
[*Source:* A. Pred (1971), Large-city interdependence and the pre-electronic diffusion of innovations in the U.S., *Geographical Analysis,* 3, 2, Figures 1 and 3.]

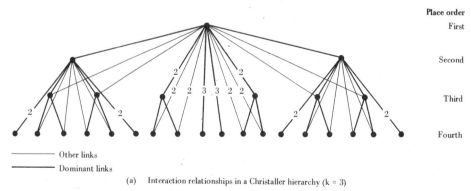

Place order
First
Second
Third
Fourth

——— Other links
———— Dominant links

(a)   Interaction relationships in a Christaller hierarchy (k = 3)

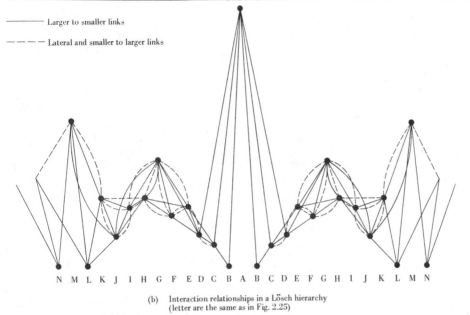

Figure 2.30(b)

Larger to smaller links

Lateral and smaller to larger links

N M L K J I H G F E D C B A B C D E F G H I J K L M N

(b)   Interaction relationships in a Lösch hierarchy
(letter are the same as in Fig. 2.25)

the inter-center links shown in Figure 2.30, there are substantial *lateral* links between higher order centers in particular. In each case the basis underlying such interaction is the *complementarity* of places modified, of course, by other factors dealt with below.

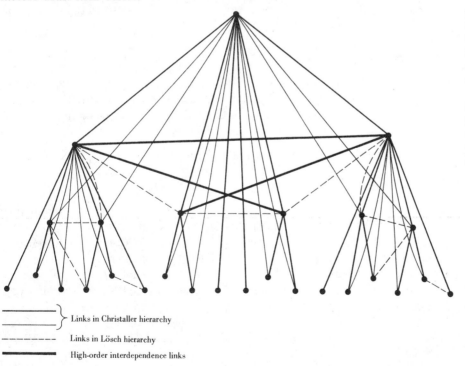

Figure 2.31
One combination of Christaller and Lösch hierarchies with links *between* high-order centers. [*Source:* A. Pred (1971), Large-city interdependence and the pre-electronic diffusion of innovations in the U.S., *Geographical Analysis,* 3, 2, Figure 4.]

Links in Christaller hierarchy

Links in Lösch hierarchy

High-order interdependence links

Figure 2.32
The modifying effect of
intervening opportunity
on interaction between
complementary places.

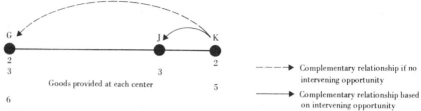

Goods provided at each center

- - - - ▶ Complementary relationship if no
intervening opportunity

———————▶ Complementary relationship based
on intervening opportunity

Ullman's second interaction principle relates to the existence of *intervening opportunities* which can be defined, for our purposes, as an alternative source of supply. For example, one respect in which center K and center G are complementary in Figure 2.25 is that G provides good 3 while K does not. Thus there is a demand at K for center G to provide it with good 3. But this complementary relationship may be negated if, as shown in Figure 2.32, there is an alternative source of supply of good 3 which is nearer to center K. If we imagine the three centers G, J, and K, as towns aligned along a highway in the sequence shown, then center K will obtain good 3 from the closer town J rather than from G.

Thirdly, according to Ullman, even if there is perfect complementarity and an absence of intervening opportunities interaction will be reduced, or even be absent altogether, if the cost of such movement—*transferability*—is excessive. This implies more than just distance. Transferability refers to the transport cost characteristics of different goods and is clearly related to the varying movement characteristics of different *orders* of goods and services and of agricultural products. Some products, as we saw in our discussion of agricultural zonation, are more sensitive to distance than others. This is a point we shall return to again in Chapter Five.

The gravity model

If we "collapse" Ullman's three principles to two on the grounds that complementarity represents a force which encourages interaction while both transferability and intervening opportunity represent different aspects of the frictional effects of distance, then we can focus on:

1. the *generators* of movement and interaction—the push-pull forces of supply and demand; and
2. the *restraints* on movement and interaction—the frictional effects of distance.

It is useful to do this because it allows us to view movement and interaction in our simplified landscape as a variant on the general physical law of *gravity*. A few perceptive observers of human behavior, such as Carey and Ravenstein in the nineteenth century, identified a parallel between the migration of people and the basic Newtonian law of gravity. But it was not until the present century and, especially following the work of John Q. Stewart and his "school of social physics," that the *gravity model* was systematically applied to social and economic interaction. (The gravity model differs from the other models considered so far in this chapter because it is *inductively* based. That is, it is based on empirical observation of regularities in movement. So far, our approach has been *deductive*; we have proceeded by a series of logical steps from a set of initial assumptions.)

Suppose, for instance, we have two urban centers i and j separated by a certain distance d. The gravity concept suggests that the amount of movement or interaction between i and j would, in the first place, be related to the product of the "masses" of these centers (measured, for example, by their population size, P). Other things being equal, for example, we would expect a greater amount of interaction to take place between two very large cities than between two small villages. But other things are rarely equal: in particular the amount of interaction between two centers is likely to be modified to a considerable degree by the magnitude of the *distance* which separates them. This then is the basic gravity model. Expressed as a simple formula it becomes

$$I_{ij} = k \frac{P_i P_j}{d_{ij}^b}$$

where:

I_{ij} refers to the amount of interaction between place i and j.

$P_i P_j$ refers to the product of the population sizes of the two places i and j.

d_{ij} represents the distance separating place i and place j.

b measures the frictional effect of distance. For example, if the value of b is 2, this means that the amount of interaction is inversely related to the square of the distance (d_{ij}^2).

k is an empirical constant.

We can interpret the gravity model formula as indicating that the amount of interaction between any two places will be directly proportional to the products of their populations (or some other measure of "mass") and inversely proportional to some power of the distance separating them.*

Gravity model variables. Each of the symbols *P, d,* and *b* can be expressed in a variety   Note
of different ways. In fact, the whole question of the interpretation of "mass" and "distance" is complex. Various suggestions have been made regarding the most suitable measure of mass. Population size is most common, probably because of the relative ease of obtaining data, but other suggestions include number of employment opportunities, industrial structure, retail sales, per capita income, vehicle registrations. It is also possible to "weight" mass in accordance with supposed differences between places in their "propensity to interact." As Dodd (1950) pointed out, "the average Chinese peasant does not make the same contribution to 'sociological' intensity as the United States urban dweller." Distance likewise can be measured in a number of ways: straight line, road distance, time, cost, and so on. The exponent applied to distance—*b* in the gravity formula—is particularly interesting because this represents, in effect, the *frictional* effect of distance. The higher the value of *b* the greater the friction and, therefore, the more rapidly interaction falls off with distance. Stewart himself argued that to use other than 1 or 2 was out of step with the model's physical derivation. We shall have more to say about *b* in Chapter Five.

A detailed review of the gravity model and its development can be found in Carrothers (1956) and Olsson (1965b).

Figure 2.33
Predicted interaction
between three
hypothetical towns based
on the gravity model.

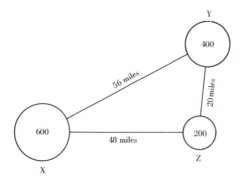

A simple hypothetical example might be the situation shown in Figure 2.33 where there are three urban centers separated from each other by varying distances. If we assume that $b = 1$ and that $k = \frac{1}{3}$ (this is simply a "scaling" factor to ensure similarity in the order of magnitude between predicted and observed values), then the amount of interaction between these centers would be:

$$I_{xy} = \tfrac{1}{3} \frac{(600 \times 400)}{(\quad 56 \quad)} = 1{,}429$$

$$I_{xz} = \tfrac{1}{3} \frac{(600 \times 200)}{(\quad 48 \quad)} = 833$$

$$I_{yz} = \tfrac{1}{3} \frac{(400 \times 200)}{(\quad 20 \quad)} = 1{,}333$$

Thus although x and y are much larger than z and would be expected to exert a major attractive force, the actual flow of people is considerably reduced by the 56 miles separating them. For example, if x and y had been only 20 miles apart then the interaction between them would have been 4,000 instead of 1,429.

Diffusion of information

The gravity model is one very useful way of viewing movement and interaction between two places or areas. But although the gravity model applies to movement of all kinds, the particular case of information flows through space can be looked at rather differently though, again, Ullman's three basic principles are just as relevant. The pioneering studies of the geographical diffusion of information (especially information related to innovations) were carried out by the Swedish geographer Torsten Hägerstrand. His basic model of the spatial diffusion process fits well into our own model of a simplified economic landscape because he uses the same basic assumptions we outlined at the beginning of this chapter, although his approach is *probabilistic* rather than *deterministic*. In other words, he recognizes the fact that there are uncertainties in the pattern of communication. For a moment, then, let us revert to our assumption of an evenly distributed population (even though we have seen fit to modify this in the light of Lösch's ideas).

Suppose we are interested in how an item of information spreads through the population living on our isotropic plain. The information might concern a new agricultural technique or a news item concerning events in one of our urban centers. How does such information diffuse through space, assuming that the information can only be passed on *directly*, that is by face-to-face contact between the person possessing the information and another? All other things being equal, the chance of one person getting to know the information from somebody already possessing it depends entirely on the distance separating them. The closer they are together the greater the *probability* (though not the certainty) that they will come into contact. Here, then, we have another example of the *friction of distance*. Expressed graphically (Figure 2.34) the probability of interpersonal communication taking place declines with increasing distance between individuals. Hägerstrand called this the *neighborhood effect*, whereby

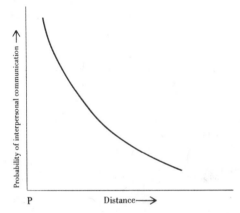

Figure 2.34
The probability of interpersonal communication declines with distance.

information spreads outwards from the originating source in such a way that the adoption of the item of information is more likely to occur in the immediate vicinity of others having the same information.

Hägerstrand devised a *simulation model* (which attempts to recreate an evolving pattern) to demonstrate how information would probably be diffused given the kinds of assumptions about our simplified landscape. Suppose we take a square portion of our plain and divide it up into equal-sized cells as shown in Figure 2.35. Each cell is identified by a letter and a number and each has ten people living within it (we can identify these by the ten digits 0 to 9). At the beginning of the process we assume that one person has the item of information—say one of the people in cell D5. Suppose that it is the individual numbered 6 within that square; we could then give him the James Bond-type label $D5_6$. We can imagine Mr. $D5_6$, in common with every other person on our plain, as being "located" in the center of a *contact field* which simply represents the spatial distribution of all those people with whom he comes into regular contact. Because he would be in contact more frequently with people close to him we could envisage his contact field looking like a smoothly-sloping cone being highest at his own location and falling away regularly with distance, very much like our demand cone or our location-rent surface. (Imagine Figure 2.34 being rotated around point P.) To make life easier (for our purposes), suppose that

Figure 2.35
Hypothetical area over which information can diffuse.

Figure 2.36
Steps in the simulation of spatial diffusion of information. (a) A contact probability field; (b) Accumulated probabilities.

	1	2	3	4	5	6	7	8	9
A	10	10	10	10	10	10	10	10	10
B	10	10	10	10	10	10	10	10	10
C	10	10	10	10	10	10	10	10	10
D	10	10	10	10		10	10	10	10
E	10	10	10	10	10	10	10	10	10
F	10	10	10	10	10	10	10	10	10
G	10	10	10	10	10	10	10	10	10
H	10	10	10	10	10	10	10	10	10
I	10	10	10	10	10	10	10	10	10

Figure 2.35

0.010	0.010	0.020	0.010	0.010
0.010	0.030	0.060	0.030	0.010
0.020	0.060	0.440	0.060	0.020
0.010	0.030	0.060	0.030	0.010
0.010	0.010	0.020	0.010	0.010

Figure 2.36(a)

0-9	10-19	20-39	40-49	50-59
60-69	70-99	100-159	160-189	190-199
200-219	220-279	280-719	720-779	780-799
800-809	810-839	840-899	900-929	930-939
940-949	950-959	960-979	980-989	990-999

Figure 2.36(b)

this contact field is converted to a 5 × 5 square (Figure 2.36a) in which the probability or chance of communicating with others is shown by the values in each cell. The chances are highest (44 in 100) that he will be in contact with another person in the same cell as himself (the central cell) and lowest (only 1 in 100) that he will be in contact with people in the most distant squares. Note that there *is* the *chance* of his communicating with one of these distant people just as there is the *chance* that he will *not* communicate with people closest to him. We do not guarantee contact, we only make it more likely at closer distances than farther away.

Before we can use this contact field to calculate how the information will be spread we have to change the nature of the values in the cells. We do this by beginning with the top left-hand cell of Figure 2.36a. The probability value of 0.010 tells us that there are 10 chances in 1,000 of contact taking place, so we assign ten digits (0 to 9) to that cell. Reading to the right we do the same calculation for each cell and accumulate the values as we go along, so that we give the first cell the range 0 to 9, the second cell the range 10 to 19, the third 20 to 39, and so on to the bottom right-hand cell which has the range 990 to 999. The total range of numbers, therefore, is 1,000. This represents the total probability of contact occurring. As a result we have a second square grid, Figure 2.36b. This gives us a range of numbers from which to select a cell to which information passes. But how do we choose? We could throw a dice (but dice can be loaded); it is better to use a table of random numbers.

We can now begin to simulate the diffusion process using the grid of even population distribution of Figure 2.35 and the contact field of 2.36b. We have already identified the initial possessor of the information being diffused as $D5_6$, so we start by "placing" the contact field over the basic grid so that the center cell is located on D5. We then draw a random number within the range 0 to 999. Suppose the number is 231. This identifies cell D4 because this is the cell immediately to the left of D5 and our contact field shows that all numbers between 220 and 279 are in that equivalent cell. To find which of the ten people living in cell D4 will receive the information we draw another random number from the range 0 to 9. In this case, the number chosen is 1, so the item spreads from individual $D5_6$ to individual $D4_1$. As each teller of information can transmit the item only once in each time period, the first phase ends and at the end of time period t_1, there are two people possessing the information.

Each of these is now a teller. In time period t_2, therefore, we repeat the process for each one by centering the contact field over each in turn and choosing a random number to identify the cell and another to identify the individual within the cell. In our simulation during t_2, $D5_6$ transmits the item to $B7_7$ and $D4_1$ tells it to $C4_2$. So at the end of period t_2 there are four people with the information; the process being summarized in Figure 2.37. A new time

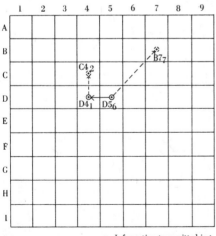

Figure 2.37
Diffusion of information over two "generations".

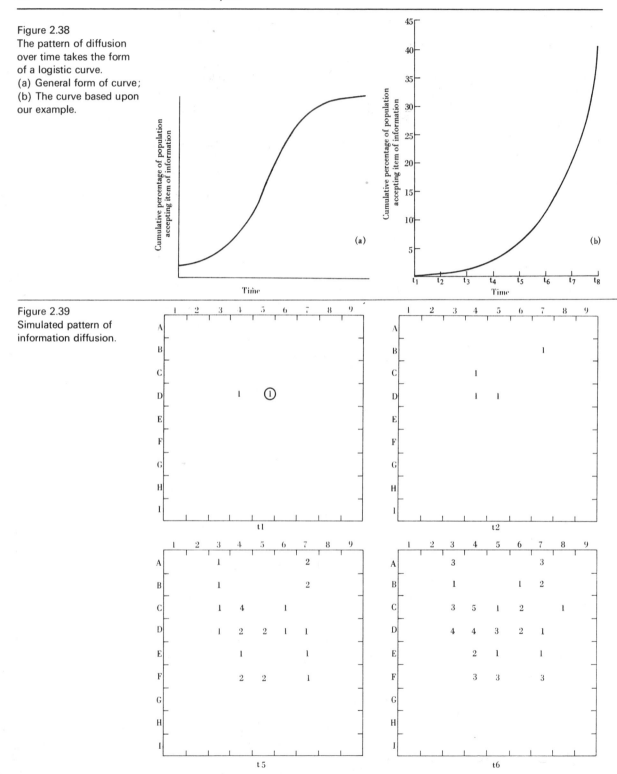

Figure 2.38
The pattern of diffusion
over time takes the form
of a logistic curve.
(a) General form of curve;
(b) The curve based upon
our example.

Figure 2.39
Simulated pattern of
information diffusion.

period begins, the process is repeated, and so on for as many time periods as desired (or until everybody has the information). Because each person who becomes a receiver then becomes a teller in the next time period, the rate of increase should theoretically double each time: 2, 4, 8, 16, 32, 64, 128, 256, and so on. In fact this will not happen because as the process proceeds individuals not already having the information (and nobody can get it twice) become more difficult to "find." Thus the pattern of diffusion over time tends to look like the curve in Figure 2.38a. This S-shaped *logistic curve* depicts the diffusion process as being slow at first because only a small number of people possess the item of information. It then picks up momentum as a larger number of people act as transmitters and then ultimately levels off as the population becomes "saturated."

In our hypothetical example, the simulation ran for eight time periods, the sequence of adopters at the end of each time period being 2, 4, 7, 13, 26, 49, 90, 148. By the end of this time, 41.8 percent of the total population had received the information; to this point, therefore, the diffusion curve appeared

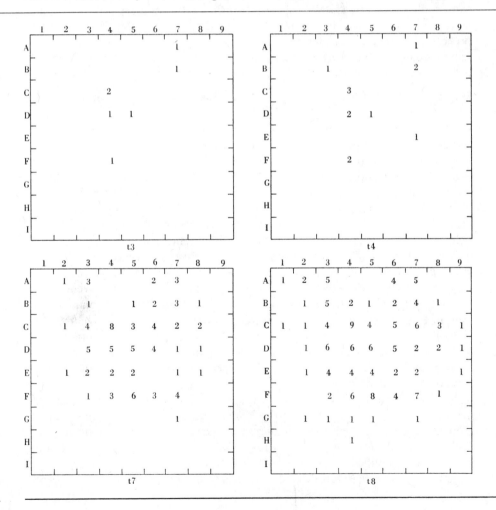

as in Figure 2.38b. Spatially, the information spread is shown in the series of maps in Figure 2.39. Inspection of the maps shows a clear distance-related spread but, as should be the case with such a probabilistic model, there are some interesting departures from a strict distance relationship. For example, cell A3 contains more adopters than cell E6 even though the latter is closer to the originating cell D5. In fact, although the probability of contact was by definition highest in D5, there were fewer adopters in that cell than in C4, F5, and F7. Of course, if we were to run the simulation again we would not get identical results though the same *general* features should be evident.

Although we used an even population distribution in order to clarify the process more easily, the existence of the kind of population variations which arose out of our consideration of the Löschian economic landscape can quite easily be incorporated into the simulation model. This is done by varying the weighting of each cell in proportion to the population of that cell. Thus the probability of contact becomes proportional to both distance *and* population density. Similarly linear transportation routes which alter relative accessibility on the plain can be allowed for by raising the contact probabilities in those cells with higher accessibility and lowering them in cells which are less accessible. The underlying process of diffusion by *expansion* outwards from the origin of the information remains based upon interpersonal contact. In its ideal form, therefore, the pattern of expansion diffusion would look like the situation in Figure 2.40.

Hägerstrand and others have identified another way in which information is diffused. Not all information spreads by face-to-face contact (even if we discount the mass media). Certain types of information also seem to be transmitted through the system of urban centers. Thus we would expect some information to spread over our plain by *hierarchical* diffusion as well as expansion diffusion. Hierarchical diffusion rests upon the notion that connections between urban centers may be closer than connections between an individual center and the rural area surrounding it. Such connections would be based upon the complementarity relationship discussed earlier in this section. Thus the "information richness" of a center will tend to reflect its hierarchical status. The metropolis not only contains all economic functions, it is also the center at which the intensity of information is greatest. Because urban centers interact in the manner suggested earlier—directly proportional to their mutual attractiveness and inversely proportional to the distance separating them—then information may well, in Hägerstrand's words, "short-circuit" the neighborhood mechanism and "jump" from one urban center to another. Precisely how this occurs depends on the kind of hierarchy we envisage. Following our line of argument in relation to Figures 2.30 and 2.31 we would not expect hierarchical diffusion to follow a rigid uni-directional pattern from higher to lower order centers. Rather we would expect information flows to mirror other kinds of flows between complementary centers at whatever level. Insofar as these will tend to emphasize the importance of large, high-order centers, then large-center influence on information flows would also be expected. In summary, therefore, the flow of information in our simplified economic landscape consists of two components shown diagrammatically in Figure 2.41. Information spreads from center A to center

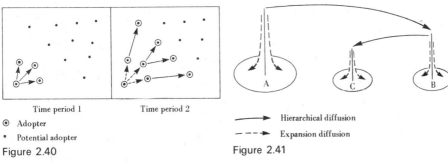

Time period 1   Time period 2

⊙ Adopter

• Potential adopter

Figure 2.40

⟶ Hierarchical diffusion

⇢ Expansion diffusion

Figure 2.41

Figure 2.40
Expansion-type diffusion.
Source: based on Brown
(1968).

Figure 2.41
Relationship between
expansion and
hierarchical diffusion.

B by hierarchical diffusion while at the same time spreading outwards from center A to the area surrounding it. Similarly, when the information reaches center B it too transmits the information in both a hierarchical and expansionary manner. The two diffusion processes operate side by side.

A summary view of the simplified economic landscape

The most important conclusion of our discussion in this chapter is that even if a perfectly uniform land surface were to exist, economic activities would still tend to be organized spatially in a clearly differentiated manner due to the effect of distance. Such organization is both complex and orderly. Its particular form and structure is derived from the patterned nature of economic behavior as goods and services are produced, exchanged, and consumed within the specific assumptions on which our model is based.

Over space this patterned behavior takes the form of interaction: the movement of consumers to central places, of goods to consumers and of agricultural products to central markets. It is the sensitivity of these movements to the attenuating effects of distance, expressed in transport cost, which provides the key to the particular spatial order displayed. The spatial economic system is then a complex of interacting elements, producers and consumers, farms and central places connected together by continuous flows of goods, services, people, and information. It functions as an integrated whole and although its various parts play an individual role in the operation of the system, no part is wholly independent of the others. A change in the functional role of one part will, in such a complex, have an important effect on the operation of all the other parts and on the functioning of the total complex. The *space economy* generated under such idealized conditions therefore represents a system by which men seek to satisfy their wants from the means of production at their disposal in the face of the spatial disparity between those wants and the resources necessary for their satisfaction.

Further reading

Alonso, W. (1960), A Theory of the Urban Land Market, *Papers and Proceedings, Regional Science Association* **6**, 149–157.

Berry, B. J. L. (1964), *Geography of Market Centers and Retail Distribution*, Englewood Cliffs, N.J.: Prentice Hall, Chapters 3 and 4.

Berry, B. J. L., and W. L. Garrison, (1958c), Recent Developments of Central Place Theory, *Papers and Proceedings, Regional Science Association* **4**, 107–120.

Christaller, W. (1966), *Central Places in Southern Germany* (C. W. Baskin, trans.), Englewood Cliffs, N.J.: Prentice-Hall.

Dunn, E. S. (1954), *The Location of Agricultural Production*, Gainesville: University of Florida Press, Chapter Two.

Gould, P. R. (1969), *Spatial Diffusion*, Association of American Geographers, Commission on College Geography, Resource Paper No. 4, Washington D.C.

Hägerstrand, T. (1967a), *Innovation Diffusion as a Spatial Process*, (trans. and postscript by A. R. Pred), Chicago: University of Chicago Press.

Hall, P. (1966b), *Von Thünen's Isolated State*, London: Pergamon.

Lösch, A. (1954), *The Economics of Location*, New Haven, Conn.: Yale University Press, Chapters 9–12.

Olsson, G. (1965b), *Distance and Human Interaction: A Review and Bibliography*, Philadelphia: Regional Science Research Institute.

Ullman, E. L. (1956), The Role of Transportation and the Bases for Interaction, in W. L. Thomas (ed.), *Man's Role in Changing the Face of the Earth*, Chicago: University of Chicago Press, pp. 862–880.

Valavanis, S. (1955), Lösch on Location: A Review Article, *American Economic Review* **45**, 637–644.

CHAPTER 3

EMPIRICAL EVIDENCE OF SPATIAL ORDER

In Chapter Two we built an economic landscape which was characterized by a very orderly and regular spatial arrangement of production centers and agricultural zones. The orderliness of the system was the result of constraining all but one of the many variables which operate in reality and observing what would happen *if* the friction of distance were the only force which could influence spatial patterns. Before we try to introduce more complexity by relaxing each of our simplifying assumptions, we should now pause to consider how far our simplified model corresponds with the reality of the world we live in. The question we pose in this chapter, therefore, is "how far does the *actual* spatial organization of economic activities correspond to the *theoretical* patterns described in Chapter Two?"

An immediate reaction might be "not at all." In gazing down at the landscape from an airliner we do not usually see an orderly hexagonal arrangement of towns and cities. Similarly in looking at an agricultural land-use map we can rarely observe neat, concentric zones of agricultural production focused around urban centers. But such observations are superficial. We need to look far more closely at the world before either rejecting or accepting any model of spatial organization. For one thing, many of the elements—such as hierarchical structure, the movement of people, goods, and information and so on—are not readily apparent without careful measurement and observation. The object of this chapter is thus to "test" (in a loose sense) our model space economy against reality. Naturally, we would not expect to find complete correspondence between the two; after all, we allowed only one out of many variable factors to shape the theoretical spatial pattern. However, if, after allowing for the influence of other variables, distance *is* an important factor in helping to mold the spatial organization of an economic system, then we should be able to see some evidence of this.

The approach we adopt is to review a selection of empirical studies carried out by geographers and other spatial analysts into various aspects of our simplified model. The selection we use is but the tip of a very large iceberg though we believe that this tip gives a clue as to the shape of the entire iceberg; in other words, we have tried to choose a representative set of studies. We have tried, also, to reflect as accurately as possible the views or findings of the original authors but our summaries are no substitute for reading the original studies themselves—hence the rather lengthy list of further reading at the end of this chapter.

Before looking at the variety of evidence it is useful to remind ourselves of the major characteristics of our simplified model. They can be summarized under three headings:

1. Urban centers are organized into a hierarchy. Each level of the hierarchy is characterized by:
a. a specific number of economic functions.
b. specific distance relationships, with uniformity of spacing between centers on the same hierarchical level.

Both of these attributes are a reflection of the differing *threshold* requirements of different functions and the spatial *range* over which they are demanded.

2. The spatial arrangement of agricultural production consists of a concentric zonation of land uses focused around urban market centers. The basis of this structure is the systematic variation of location rent with distance, a factor which also underlies the spatial arrangement of land uses *within* urban centers.

3. Movement and interaction are, in general, positively related to the degree of complementarity between places and inversely related to the distance (including intervening opportunities) separating them.

In discussing the empirical evidence relating to each of these in turn we refer, from time to time, to certain statistical techniques. So as not to interrupt the flow of the argument we provide a brief explanation of such techniques as a note to the text. Readers already familiar with the techniques can obviously proceed without reference to them. (It is perhaps worth pointing out that these notes are not intended as a substitute for a more detailed and comprehensive study of quantitative techniques. A good general introduction is provided by Yeates (1974) while King (1969) presents more advanced discussion).

The urban hierarchy

Hierarchies of central places

Most investigations of urban hierarchies concentrate upon only one facet of urban activities: the *central place* function. In fact, of course, most urban centers perform many functions other than those of providing its own and its surrounding population with central goods and services. In many cases, non-central place functions are far more important to the economy of urban centers. We return to this point again on p. 75 but, for the moment, let us look at some of the investigations of the *central place hierarchy*. Even here, however, we find a strong tendency for most workers to follow the framework laid down by Christaller rather than the more flexible hierarchy devised by Lösch. Much of the pioneering work was carried out in the late 1950s by the geographers Garrison and Berry, work which stimulated an enormous number of studies of central place systems in many parts of the world during the 1960s.

The consensus of most central place studies is that a definable hierarchy of central places does exist and can be identified at a variety of scales and in quite varied geographical conditions. Table 3.1 summarizes the results of seven such studies carried out in a diversity of areas, from the northwest coast of the United States through the almost homogeneous landscape of southwestern Iowa to the Niagara peninsula and southern Ontario; from the heavily industrialized South Wales coalfield to the undulating agricultural region of Baden-Württemberg. In each of the seven areas a distinct grouping of centers according to their functional significance is apparent, though the boundaries between each hierarchical level vary from one area to another. The number of levels also differs, ranging from three in Snohomish County, Washington, to six in southwestern Iowa.

Level of Hierarchy	Snohomish County, Washington (1)			Southwestern Iowa (2)			Southwestern Ontario (3)			Niagara peninsula		
	No. of centers	No. of central functions	Population	No. of centers	No. of central functions	Population	No. of centers	No. of central functions	Population	No. of centers	No. of central functions	Population
Low												
1	20	1–16	15–2586[a]	29	<10	<150	10	1–12	25–1702	20	1–22	49–2064
2	9	22–42	600–2996[a]	32	10–25	150–400	2	19–22	408–486	9	27–43	1900–5400
3	4	56–64	1684–3494[a]	15	28–50	500–1500	2	28–32	673–676	4	55–59	6900–9800
4				9	>55	2000–7000	1	78	3507	2	69–73	18,000–44,000
5							1	99	22,224	2	89–98	57,000–101,000
6							1	150	77,190			

Level of Hierarchy	Owen Sound area, Ontario (4)			South Wales (5)			Baden-Württemberg, Germany (6)		
	No. of centers	No. of central functions	Population	No. of centers	No. of central functions	Population	No. of centers	No. of central functions	Population
Low									
1	10	7.42–15.76[a]	65–213	25	2.33–11.74[a]	?	162	2–24	57–780
2	12	34.52–179.67[a]	73–1501	18	11.69–58.67[a]	?	134	25–50	781–2150
3	6	257.55–655.09[a]	1090–3450	4	83.99–176.05[a]	?	44	51–97	2200–5501
4	1	3013.88[a]	17,421	3	249.27–450.60[a]	?	19	108–207	6200–24,000
5				1	2077.96[a]	?	2	248–292	73,500–90,000
6									

[a]Functional index (see Davies, 1967). Briefly, this weights each function in a central place by its frequency of occurrence in the general study area, summing them to derive the index.

Based on material in:

(1) B. J. L. Berry and W. L. Garrison (1958a), Functional Bases of the Central Place Hierarchy, *Economic Geography* **34**, 145–154.

(2) B. J. L. Berry, H. G. Barnum, and R. J. Tennant (1962), Retail Location and Consumer Behavior, *Papers and Proceedings, Regional Science Association* **9**, 65–106.

(3) R. A. Murdie (1965), Cultural Differences in Consumer Travel, *Economic Geography* **41**, 211–233.

(4) J. U. Marshall (1969), The Location of Service Towns, *University of Toronto, Department of Geography Research Paper* 3.

(5) W. K. D. Davies (1967), Centrality and the Central Place Hierarchy, *Urban Studies* **4**, 61–79.

(6) H. G. Barnum (1966), Market Centers and Hinterlands in Baden-Württemberg, *University of Chicago, Department of Geography Research Paper* 103.

Table 3.1   Selected examples of central place hierarchies.

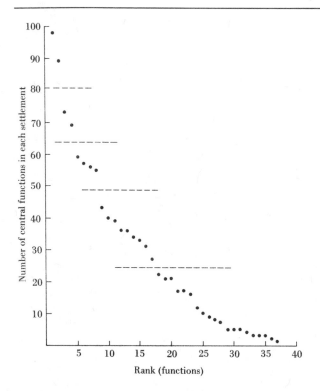

Figure 3.1
A functional hierarchy of
central places in the
Niagara peninsula.

The data in Table 3.1 are arranged into groups on the basis of distinct breaks in the overall distribution of central places. Figure 3.1 illustrates this point for the Niagara peninsula, one of the seven examples summarized in Table 3.1. In Figure 3.1 the thirty-seven central places are arranged in rank order in terms of the number of central functions in each place (central functions are goods and services such as retail shops, professional services, leisure facilities, etc., but excluding manufacturing activities). This rank distribution seems to fall into five broad categories, shown by the dotted lines in the diagram. These lines represent the divisions between hierarchical levels. Quite clearly, there is considerable variation *within* each hierarchical level in the number of functions per central place. Certainly the pattern is some way removed from the very rigid Christaller pattern and closer to the more continuous distribution proposed by Lösch.

Although most central place hierarchies seem to be of this kind, a few studies indicate that some central place hierarchies *do* correspond to the particular k values proposed by Christaller. Tables 3.2 and 3.3 present two such examples. Lösch himself carried out empirical studies in Iowa and concluded that the system of centers displayed a close correspondence with a *k = 4* system. Thus, Table 3.2 shows that if we begin with the largest number of centers (615) and calculate the expected values for a *k = 4* system the values predicted correspond very closely to the actual distribution of centers. Later work in the southwest of the same state by Berry, Barnum and Tennant (1962) also suggests the existence of a *k = 4* structure. They argue that such a system (which, we should recall, was Christaller's traffic principle) was a result of both the rectangular land subdivision and the role of transportation routes.

Table 3.2
Regional systems in Iowa: theory and reality, correspondence with theoretical system $k = 4$.

Size-class of regions	Centers			
	Number		Distance apart (miles)	
	Theory[a]	Reality	Theory[a]	Reality
1	615		5.6	
2	154	153	11.2	10.3
3	39	39	22.4	23.6
4	10	9	44.8	49.6
5	2–3	3	89.6	94.0
6	0–1		179.2	

[a]The values obtained for class 1 were the starting point for the calculation of all theoretical values.
Source: A. Lösch (1954), *The Economics of Location* (*Die räumliche Ordnung der Wirtschaft*), Stuttgart: Gustav Fischer, 1962, Table 34.

Table 3.3
Observed nested areas of South Australian central places compared with Christaller's ideal hierarchies.

Order	South Australia	$k = 7$	$k = 4$	$k = 3$
5	435	435	435	435
4	72	62	109	145
3	11	9	27	48
2	—	1	7	16
1	1	—	2	5
	519	507	580	649

Source: P. Smailes (1969), Some Aspects of the South Australian Urban System, *Australian Geographer XI*, Table 5. Reproduced by permission of the author and editor.

In similar vein, Smailes (1969) concluded that a nested hierarchy of central places exists in South Australia which fits closely a $k = 7$ arrangement. Table 3.3 compares the actual organization of central places in South Australia with what would be expected for each of Christaller's three principles. Again, the starting point for interpretation is the total number of lowest order centers (435). The table clearly shows that $k = 7$ is the closest theoretical approximation to the pattern of central places in the area.

Reference back to Table 3.1 shows that each level in the hierarchies of the seven areas is also associated with a particular population size or range of population sizes. Much of the work into central place systems has in fact been concerned with establishing the existence of a functional relationship between such variables as the number of central functions or the number of establishments of each functional type, on the one hand, and the population sizes of central places on the other. The underlying logic is that settlements with large populations will be able to support more central functions and more units of each function than settlements with small populations. For example, Figure 3.2 is a graph showing the number of functional units in each of the Niagara peninsula settlements on the vertical axis and the population of each settlement on the horizontal axis.

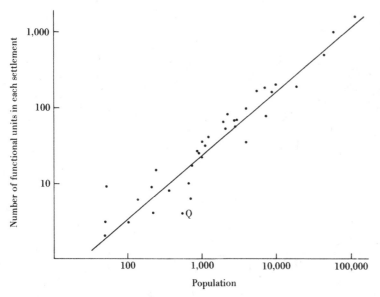

Figure 3.2
Relationship between the number of functional units and population of central places in the Niagara peninsula.

A glance at the graph gives the impression that there is roughly a straight-line (linear) relationship between the population of settlements and the number of functional units they possess. Obviously, however, the relationship is not perfect; if it were we would be able to predict the number of functional units in a town by calculating its population. To help us decide how good the relationship is, and how far we can really be justified in assuming that it is linear, we can employ the technique known as *regression analysis.** The result of such analysis supports the view that, in the case of the Niagara peninsula, an increase in the population of a settlement is positively associated with (we may go even further and say "causes", though many other factors are likely involved) an increase in the number of functional units in the settlement.

Although it is clear that the rigid hierarchical organization proposed by Christaller is not found in more than a few instances it is equally clear that there

---

Simple linear regression. If we think that two variables are linearly related we can measure both the *strength* and *direction* of this relationship using simple linear regression. In regression analysis we assume that one variable (x) is responsible for, or "causes," changes in the

Note

Note continued

second variable (y), and *not vice versa*. Thus x is termed the *independent* variable and y the *dependent* variable. In our Niagara peninsula example we are assuming that the population of a settlement (x) is responsible for the number of functional units (y) in that settlement. Linear regression is simply the statistical procedure for finding the equation of the straight line which best fits such data (represented by the scatter of points in Figure 3.2).

The primary objective of linear regression is to estimate the values of a, b and e in the following linear equation.

$$y_c = a + bx + e$$

where:

a = the value of the intercept of the line on the y axis (see Figure 3.3)
b = the slope of the line = $\Delta y / \Delta x$
y_c = the predicted value of y for a given value of x
e = a random error term whose magnitude depends on how closely the observations fit the line.

Finding the values of "a" and "b" which give the best fit linear equation is usually undertaken by an estimation procedure known as the *"method of least squares."* To understand this procedure we need to define what is meant by a *residual,* which is denoted by d in Figure 3.3. It can be seen that a residual is the difference between the observed value of y and the value of y predicted by the linear equation

$$d_i = y_i - y_c$$

**Figure 3.3
Residuals from a
regression line.**

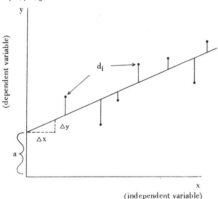

The least squares procedure involves estimating the values of a and b in such a way that the sum of the squared residuals is at a minimum. The required values of a and b may be obtained from the following:

$$b = \sum x_i y_i / \sum x_i$$

$$a = \bar{y} - b\bar{x}$$

Because the residuals are equivalent to errors it can be seen that the least squares procedure involves the minimization of error solely in the dependent variable (y). This is in accordance with the logic of the technique (remember that our initial assumption was x was responsible for variation in y). Clearly for the estimated regression equation to be an acceptable representation of the relationship the error associated with the residuals must be relatively small. A crude assessment of the adequacy of the fit may be obtained by evaluating the *coefficient of determination* (R^2) which gives the percentage of the variation in the values of the dependent variable which is accounted for by variation in the values of the independent variable. For the relationship between population and functional units, $R^2 = 80.5$, which means that 80.5% of the variation in functional units has been explained (or paralleled) by variation in settlement population. The unexplained variation of 19.5% is attributed to the residuals as error variation.

are distinct groupings of central places according to systematic variations in their functional 'significance. The hierarchy is at its clearest in those circumstances in which conditions are closest to the assumptions of the original model, that is towns acting predominantly as centers serving a surrounding area with central place goods and services in fairly homogeneous physical conditions. (Iowa is as close as we are likely to get to a flat plain). The pattern also holds good where a center's manufacturing functions use local or ubiquitous (universally available) materials and serve a local market. These, in fact, were the kinds of manufacturing function envisaged by Lösch in devising his more flexible hierarchical structure. In other words, those manufacturing activities which are most similar to central place activities do nothing to distort the hierarchical organization of centers. But, as we observed earlier, most urban centers, especially the larger ones, are multi-functional. Although all have a central place component (providing the local residents with their daily needs) this is frequently not the center's most important role. This is not the place to become embroiled in the intricacies of urban functional classification*, but it is important to note that "deviations" from the hierarchical arrangement of centers may well be the result of influences which are specific to manufacturing or other specialized activities—for example, the localized nature of material inputs—which we will examine in some detail in subsequent chapters.

Rank-size relationships

Quite apart from studies based upon central place hierarchies, other kinds of empirical regularities have been recognized in the system of urban centers. By far the best known of these is what has become known as the *rank-size rule*, a phenomenon which has a very long history but which was brought to general attention by G. K. Zipf in 1949. If we take all the urban centers in a particular country and arrange them in rank order, beginning with the center having the largest population and ending the list with the smallest sized center then, in many cases, the size relationship between the towns of each rank is extremely regular. If the rank-size rule applies exactly, then the population of, say, the third-ranking center would be one-third of the population of the first-ranking center, the population of the twentieth-ranking center would be one-twentieth of the first-ranking center and so on. Expressed in a formal way, the rank-size rule is:

$$P_r = P_1/r^q$$

where: r = the rank of a city
P_r = the population of a city of rank *r*
P_1 = the population of the largest city
q = an exponent which generally has a value close to 1.0

---

*Geographers have shown a great fondness for devising town classifications on the basis of their economic functions. Unfortunately, there is little, if any, consistency between the many schemes. Some of the best known classifications are those by Harris (1943) and Nelson (1955) for the United States, Maxwell (1965) for Canada, and Moser and Scott (1961) for England and Wales. Smith (1965) presents a critical evaluation of town classification in which he explores some of the methodological problems involved.

Note

If we plot population size against rank for every urban center in a country then the relationship (on a logarithmic scale) appears as a downward-sloping line with a slope defined by q. This simply means that the size of a center is inversely proportional to its population rank.

Figure 3.4
Rank-size distribution of
urban centers in the
United States, 1950.
[*Source:* R. Vining
(1955), A Description of
Certain Spatial Aspects of
an Economic System,
*Economic Development
and Cultural Change,* 3,
Figure 1, p. 152.
Reproduced by
permission of the
University of Chicago
Press, © 1955 by the
University of Chicago.]

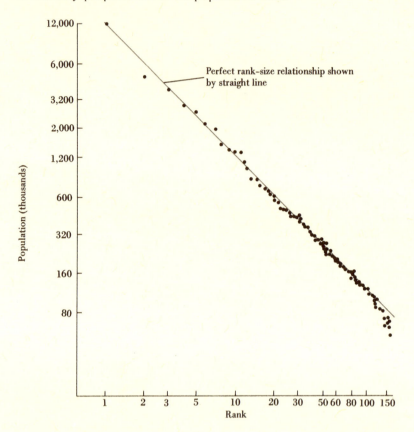

Figure 3.4 shows that for the United States the size distribution of cities in 1950 corresponded extremely closely to the rank-size relationship. The major deviations were, first, the second ranking city (Chicago) which in 1950 had a population of 4.9 million instead of roughly 6.0 million as predicted by the rank-size rule and, second, the lower end of the scale. In general, however, the pattern conforms remarkably well. Thus, the third-ranking center (Los Angeles) would be expected to have a population of a little over 4.0 million; in fact, its population was 3.97 million. The twelfth-ranking center (Baltimore) should have had roughly 1.0 million people (one-twelfth that of New York); in reality it had 1.15 million. Not only does the rank-size relationship appear to hold in the United States for a single point in time but also the relationship has been remarkably stable for more than a century and a half. Figure 3.5 shows that the slope of the rank-size relationship has remained more or less the same since 1790, even though the urban system has grown enormously since that time.

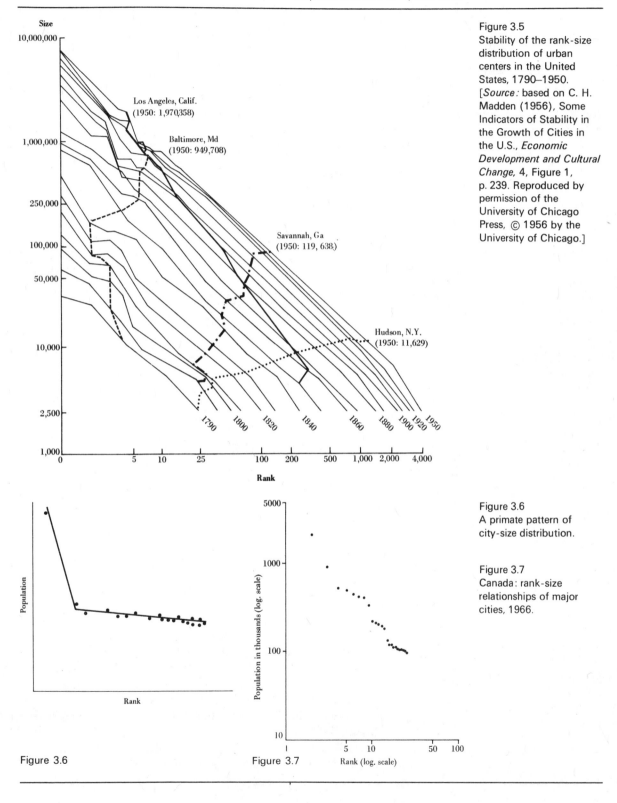

Size

Los Angeles, Calif.
(1950: 1,970,358)

Baltimore, Md
(1950: 949,708)

Savannah, Ga
(1950: 119, 638)

Hudson, N.Y.
(1950: 11,629)

1790 1800 1820 1840 1860 1880 1900 1920 1950

Rank

Population

Rank

Figure 3.6

Population in thousands (log. scale)

Figure 3.7   Rank (log. scale)

Figure 3.5
Stability of the rank-size
distribution of urban
centers in the United
States, 1790–1950.
[*Source:* based on C. H.
Madden (1956), Some
Indicators of Stability in
the Growth of Cities in
the U.S., *Economic
Development and Cultural
Change,* 4, Figure 1,
p. 239. Reproduced by
permission of the
University of Chicago
Press, © 1956 by the
University of Chicago.]

Figure 3.6
A primate pattern of
city-size distribution.

Figure 3.7
Canada: rank-size
relationships of major
cities, 1966.

But how far does this relationship hold true outside the United States? A large-scale comparative study by Berry (1961) of thirty-eight countries at varying levels of economic development showed that thirteen countries had rank-size city distributions. However, a further fifteen had a so-called *primate* distribution in which one or two very large cities dominate and there is an absence of medium-sized cities (Figure 3.6). The remaining countries revealed patterns intermediate between rank-size and primate. As one would expect, the "intermediate" category covers a whole range of city-size distributions from those close to primate at one end to those close to rank-size at the other. Figures 3.7 and 3.8 illustrate one each of these extreme cases. Figure 3.7 is the city-size distribution for major cities in Canada in 1966. The dominance of the twin largest cities, Montreal and Toronto, is clear. Figure 3.8 shows the size distribution of Standard Metropolitan Labor Areas (SMLAs) in England and Wales for 1966. Although one city—London—is again dominant, the overall pattern is rather closer to rank-size than is Canada's, especially if we take just the first 25 cities in England and Wales and compare their distribution with that of the leading 25 Canadian cities.

Figure 3.8
England and Wales:
rank-size relationships of
Standard Metropolitan
Labor Areas, 1966.

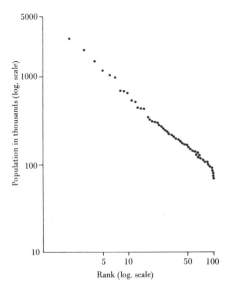

Table 3.4 suggests that there is no obvious explanation for these differences. For example, although some underdeveloped nations do have primate patterns, others do not. Numerous factors probably account for these differences: level of economic development, changes in political status, length of time urbanized, and others. Berry suggests that as the economic, political, and social life of a country becomes more complex its urban size distribution will tend to develop toward a rank-size pattern which represents the *steady-state* of an urban system. Looked at in this way, the rank-size distribution can be regarded as a special case of the *law of allometric growth.** In essence, this implies that the ranks of all cities in the urban system remain constant over time.

Countries with rank-size pattern	Countries with primate pattern	Countries with intermediate patterns
Belgium	Austria	Australia
Brazil	Ceylon	Canada
China	Denmark	Ecuador
El Salvador	Dominican Republic	Malaya
Finland	Greece	New Zealand
India	Guatemala	Nicaragua
Italy	Japan	Norway
Korea	Mexico	Pakistan
Poland	Netherlands	England and Wales
South Africa	Peru	
Switzerland	Portugal	
United States	Spain	
West Germany	Sweden	
	Thailand	
	Uruguay	

Source: based on data in B. J. L. Berry (1961), City Size Distributions and Economic Development, *Economic Development and Cultural Change* **9**, 573–588.

Table 3.4
City size distributions in selected countries.

Yet in the case of the United States, despite the high degree of *general* stability over time shown in Figure 3.5 the relative position of individual cities has varied considerably. Between 1870 and 1950, for example, Los Angeles gained 314 rank places while New Haven, Connecticut lost 32 places. Of cities with more than 100,000 population in 1950, 14 had a relatively stable pattern (i.e. they changed less than 10 places) while 10 experienced extreme variation of

Allometric growth models. It has been suggested, for example by Beckmann (1958) and Nordbeck (1971) that the rank-size distribution is an outcome of the process of *allometric* growth similar to that operating in the growth of biological organisms. The term *allometry* embraces a variety of simple growth models although the original biological formulation (see Huxley, 1932) simply states that, "the relative growth of an organ is a constant fraction of the growth of the whole organism." Symbolically we write this statement as:

$$y = ax^b$$

where y is a measure of the size of the organ at one point in time, and x is the size of the organism at the same point in time. The simplest form of this model is the linear case where constant proportions are assumed to govern the growth of organisms. Consequently "a" is a coefficient denoting the size of y when x equals one, and "b" is a second coefficient whose value is obtained by dividing the dimensions of the y variable by the dimension of the x variable. For example, if both x and y were measures of volumes then b = 3/3 = 1, whereas if y measures the area of the organ and x the volume of the organism then b = 2/3 = .67.

It is not essential for allometric growth to be tested by looking at the growth of a *single* individual or object; it is possible to study the growth of a sample of similar objects (for example, cities) even though there are size differences between them. In this case, the urban system as a whole represents the organism while each city in the system is analogous to an individual organ. Hence we can regard the rank-size rule for cities as a special case of the linear allometric model. Let us briefly explain this for a city system following the

Note

Note continued

work of Nordbeck (1971). First, the population of each city is denoted by the variable P. If we then rank the city populations from highest to lowest such that the largest city has a rank of 1, we can use these ranks as a second measure of city size, r. An allometric model relating r to P would be of the form:

$P = ar^b$

Because P and r are both measures of population size they must be scaled in units of the same dimension so that b in this case is equal to 1. However, because r, the rank, increases in numerical value as P, the population, decreases, b must have a negative value of -1 to indicate the negative slope of the relationship. For allometric models. a is the value of P when $r = 1$ which, by definition, implies that $a = P_1$, where P_1 is the population of the largest city. Our allometric model now takes the form:

$P = P_1 r^{-1}$

which is the same as the rank size rule where $q = 1$. Expressed in terms of the common version of the allometric relationship:

$P = ar^b$

where a is the population of the highest ranking city, r is the rank of the city and $b = -1$.

Many other features of urban systems have been found to behave in rough accordance with allometric principles. The interested reader should consult Nordbeck (1971), Ray, Villeneuve, Roberge (1974), Thomas (1975).

more than 100 places (Madden, 1956). However, this need not be incompatible with the allometric growth law which can be modified to allow for variations in the growth rate of individual elements.*

Reconciliation of hierarchical and continuous city distributions

We have evidence, therefore, of both *hierarchical* distributions of centers, based on functional complexity, and of *continuous* (rank-size) distributions of centers,

Note

*The rank-size rule with random errors. We begin by incorporating an element which will allow for some random variation in the allometric growth law and then proceed to show how this applies to the rank-size rule. The element of randomness can be added by making use of Gibrat's (1927) law of proportionate effect. This states that "a variable undergoing a process of change will obey the principle of proportionate effect if the change in the size of the variable at any step in the process is a random proportion of its previous value." We can build this principle into the allometric growth law by re-writing the allometric equation as:

$y = eax^b$

where e is the random error term. Basically, we have relaxed the allometric growth law to allow for random deviations in the value of y for any value of x. Because of the relationship between the rank-size rule and the allometric growth law we can write a revised rank-size rule in the form:

$$P_r = \frac{eP_1}{r}$$

This revised model implies that, in a given time period, the growth of the rth city will be proportional to the growth of the largest city (P_1) plus or minus a random error term. Notice that e is a multiplicative error which causes the errors associated with large towns of low rank to be larger than those associated with small towns of high rank. The magnitude of e for an observed city system may be estimated using *regression* techniques (see note on p. 73). Rederiving the rank-size rule in this manner allows for chance changes in the ranks of cities as a national urban system evolves.

based on population size. Not surprisingly, there has been a good deal of contro-versy as to whether these two distributions are compatible or totally conflicting. The problem is most acute in the context of Christaller's central place hierarchy. Stewart (1958) and Vining (1955), for example, argue that the central place hierarchy based on function and the rank-size distribution based on population are quite incompatible. On the other hand, Beckmann (1958) claims that the two may well be compatible on the grounds that centers of similar functional status will not have exactly the same population size but a *range* of such sizes. As a result, the steps of a strict hierarchy tend to be smoothed out resulting in a more continuous distribution of population sizes. The problem is less acute if we take Lösch's form of the hierarchy which, as we have seen, produces a more continuous functional hierarchy. A further suggestion has been made by Berry, Barnum and Tennant (1962) who argue that because most studies of the central place hierarchy have been in small areas, aggregating the results will likely blur any clear steps between hierarchical levels defined at the sub-national scale and the continuous distributions observed at the national scale.

The hierarchy and the movement of consumers to central places

In looking at empirical evidence of an urban hierarchy so far we have concen-trated on the "objects" of the system—the urban centers themselves in terms of their functional structure. But how far does the actual movement of con-sumers to these centers to satisfy their demands for goods and services—the "flows" which bind the system together—correspond with the predictions of central place theory? This is rather more difficult to ascertain because informa-tion regarding the spatial behavior of consumers is less readily available than that concerning the number and type of functions in urban centers.

Our theory tells us that consumers will travel to the *nearest* center providing the desired good so that movement for low-order goods, which are available at a large number of centers, should tend to be short-distance, while movement for high-order goods should be characterized by longer distances. In other words, distance traveled to acquire central place goods should be directly related to the order of the good. Let us take just two or three examples of low and high-order goods and see how far the spatial pattern of consumer purchases corresponds with our expectations based on central place theory.

This aspect of central place theory is generally tested by questioning a large number of people about their shopping habits for different goods. For each good, a map can be drawn connecting the location of each consumer with that of the center in which the good is purchased with a straight line known as a *desire line*. Patterns of consumer behavior for low-order goods would there-fore show many very short desire lines focusing upon a large number of small places. Patterns for high-order goods would show much longer desire lines focused on a smaller number of larger centers. Let us take the example of food purchases as a typical low-order good. Figure 3.9 shows the spatial pattern of food purchases in a part of eastern Ontario, the area between Ottawa and Cornwall on the St. Lawrence. It is clear that most of the dispersed population

Figure 3.9
Spatial pattern of food
purchases in a part of
eastern Ontario. [*Source:*
D. M. Ray (1967),
Cultural Differences in
Consumer Travel Behavior
in Eastern Ontario,
Canadian Geographer, XI,
Figure 3. Reproduced by
permission of the author
and editor.]

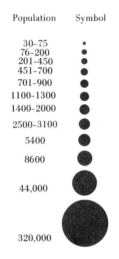

Population	Symbol
30–75	•
76–200	•
201–450	•
451–700	•
701–900	•
1100–1300	•
1400–2000	•
2500–3100	•
5400	•
8600	•
44,000	●
320,000	●

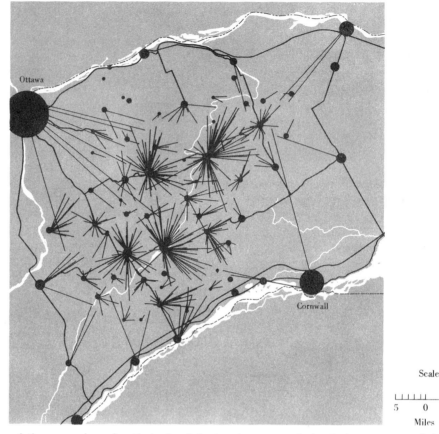

of the area shop for their food in local centers; indeed the pattern of desire
lines not only indicates predominantly short-distance movement but also gives
some idea of the extent of each center's general market area for food. Figure
3.10 is a similar example based on investigations in South Devon, England.
Again the prevalence of short-distance moves is clear.

At the other end of the scale, Figures 3.11 and 3.12 show the spatial pattern
of the purchase of two higher order goods. Figure 3.11 shows that the movement
for optical services in eastern Ontario consists of longer distance travel, predominantly to the two major urban centers, Ottawa and Cornwall. Desire lines
are much longer than in the case of food, reflecting the lack of provision of
optical services in most of the lower order centers. Figure 3.12 illustrates the
shopping pattern for another relatively high-order good, clothing, in South
Devon, and shows that, compared with food purchases in the same area, trips
to purchase clothes are far longer and emphasize the importance of Plymouth
and Exeter as major high-order centers.

These examples, which could be replicated many times over from the very large
number of central place studies in different areas, clearly suggest some correspondence with theory. On the whole the length of a shopping trip *is* directly
related to the order of the good or service and it does seem that, to a certain

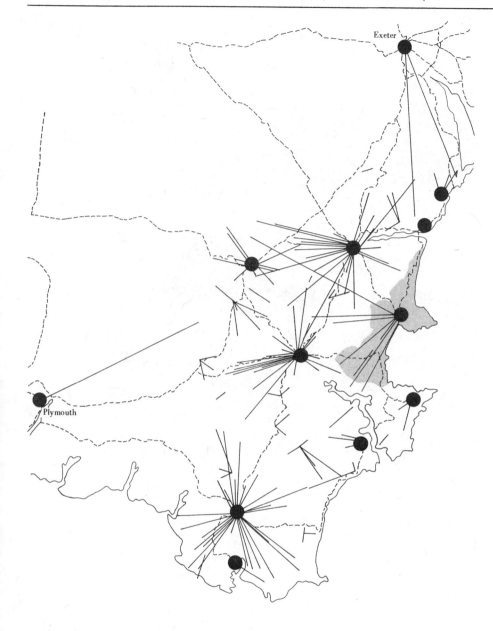

Figure 3.10
Spatial pattern of grocery
purchases in a part of
South Devon.

extent, consumers attempt to minimize their movement costs by visiting nearby
urban centers. However, a study of consumer behavior in Iowa (Golledge, Rushton, Clark, 1966) reveals that this relationship holds to a greater extent for
low-order "convenience" goods than for high-order "shopping" goods. Table
3.5 shows the distances traveled by a sample of the Iowa farm population for
various types of good. Column 1 shows the mean distance traveled to the "maximum purchase town" (calculated on the basis of dollars spent on a good at

Figure 3.11
Spatial pattern of movement for optical services in a part of eastern Ontario. [*Source:* D. M. Ray (1967), Cultural Differences in Consumer Travel Behavior in Eastern Ontario, *Canadian Geographer,* XI, Figure 8. Reproduced by permission of the author and editor.]

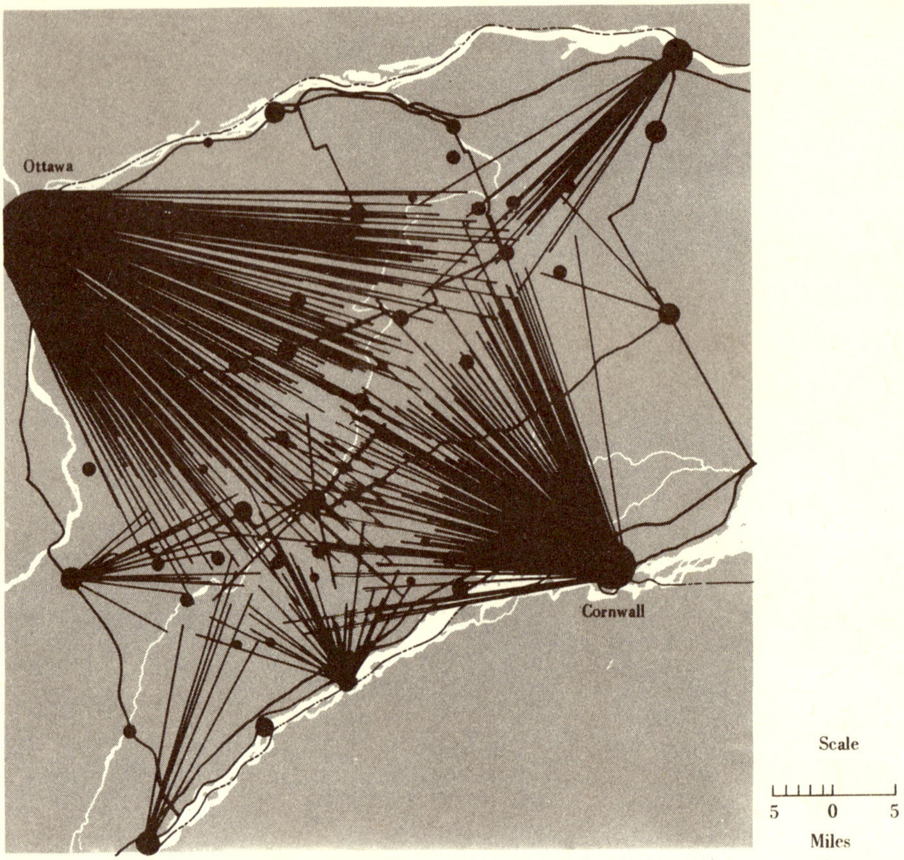
Ottawa
Cornwall
Scale
5 0 5
Miles
Population Symbol
30-75
76-200
201-450
451-700
701-900
1100-1300
1400-2000
2500-3100
5400
8600
44,000
320,000

different places in a single year), while Column 2 indicates the mean distance traveled to the "nearest purchase town" (the nearest town in which an actual purchase was made).

Table 3.5
Consumer travel in Iowa.

Good/service	Mean distance to maximum purchase town (miles)	Mean distance to nearest purchase town (miles)
Beauty/barber	7.4	6.1
Food/groceries	7.8	5.2
Dry cleaning	10.5	10.3
Major appliances	14.5	13.8
Male clothing	15.6	8.2
Boys' clothing	15.6	11.4
Furniture	18.7	17.6
Car purchases	19.7	18.8
Girls' clothing	29.3	13.4
Female clothing	30.3	14.1

Source: based on R. G. Golledge, G. Rushton, and W. A. V. Clark (1966), Some Spatial Characteristics of Iowa's Dispersed Farm Population, *Economic Geography* **42.** Table 1. Reproduced with permission of the author and editor.

Figure 3.12
Spatial pattern of clothing
purchases in a part of
South Devon.

The distances in Table 3.5 reveal two interesting features. First, they confirm that on the whole distance traveled does vary with the order of the good as already suggested (for example, compare distances traveled for food with those traveled for female clothing). Second, there is considerable variation between "maximum purchase" distances and "nearest purchase" distances, implying that consumers do not invariably purchase goods at the nearest center. This, too, is related to the order of the good. Differences tend to be least for low-order goods; in the case of high-order "shopping goods" consumers appear to travel a great deal further than the nearest center providing the good. For example, there is a difference of only 2.6 miles between the mean maximum purchase town and nearest purchase town for food and groceries. In comparison, there is a 16.2 mile difference for female clothing. Such differences may be related to a desire on the part of the consumer to "shop around" for higher order goods, to compare competing products at different outlets and so on. The relation with order is not unequivocal, however; for example there is very little difference between the two distances for furniture or car purchases.

One final point should be made before leaving this very brief discussion of shopping distances. Reference back to the desire-line maps of low-order purchases (Figures 3.9 and 3.10) reveals that although most trips are short, there are a few very long desire lines to the higher order centers. This is probably because in making a trip to such centers for high-order goods consumers may at the same time purchase low-order goods. In effect this reduces the total travel expenditure: a single trip to a higher order center replaces the need to make separate trips to different centers. Where only low-order "convenience" goods are being purchased, of course, the nearest center is likely to be chosen. One implication of such multi-purpose trips is that the spatial range of low-order goods provided by high-order centers is likely to be greater than the spatial range of the same goods provided from low-order centers.

Spacing of urban centers

In our discussion of the urban hierarchy we found that if urban centers are considered in terms of their central place functions a hierarchy is evident, though its structure is less rigid than central place theory would suggest. On the other hand, if urban centers of *all* types are considered in terms of their population size, the result is a more or less continuous (rank-size) distribution although, as we have suggested, the two may well be compatible. When we turn to consider the *spatial* distribution of urban centers we are faced with a similar problem. We would expect to find some spatial regularity between central places but if urban centers of all types are considered we would now hardly expect to find complete spatial uniformity (such as a hexagonal distribution). We would however expect evidence of *some* regularity.

One means of objectively measuring the spatial pattern of urban centers is the technique of *nearest neighbor analysis**. This is a method for determining

Note

**The nearest neighbor statistic.* This test was developed by the ecologists Clark and Evans (1954) as a method for comparing observed point patterns with theoretical random patterns. An observed pattern will consist of r points distributed over a predefined study region. We first measure the distance between each point and its nearest neighboring point (d_i in Figure 3.13c) and then calculate the average nearest neighbor distance from the formula:

$$\bar{d}_o = \sum_{i=1}^{r} d_i / r$$

The fundamental idea of nearest neighbor analysis is that we compare the *observed* mean nearest neighbor distance ($\bar{d}_o$) with the *expected* one ($\bar{d}_e$) for an infinite number of points in a *randomly* distributed pattern. It can easily be proved that, if an infinite number of points are placed in an infinite plane such that the average number of points per unit area (i.e. the density) is λ, then the expected mean nearest neighbor distance is given by:

$$\bar{d}_e = 1/2 \sqrt{\lambda}$$

Note continued

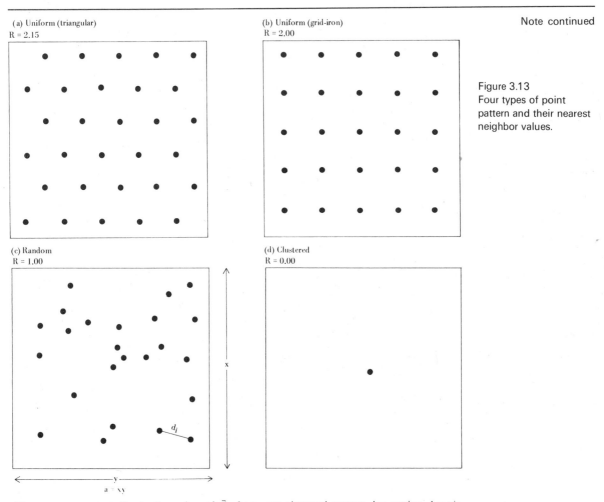

(a) Uniform (triangular)
R = 2.15

(b) Uniform (grid-iron)
R = 2.00

(c) Random
R = 1.00

(d) Clustered
R = 0.00

Figure 3.13
Four types of point pattern and their nearest neighbor values.

Moreover, we can estimate the value of $\bar{d}_e$ from our observed pattern by setting $\lambda = r/a$, where a is the area of our study region. The *nearest neighbor statistic* is defined as

$$R = \bar{d}_o/\bar{d}_e$$

It can be seen that R takes on a value of 1 when the observed mean distance ($\bar{d}_o$) is identical to the random expectation ($\bar{d}_e$). Departures from a value of 1 are indicative of an orderly pattern. Values between 1.0 and 0.0 suggest an increasingly clustered pattern of points (see Figure 3.13d), while values between 1.0 and 2.15 are indicative of increasing uniformity of spacing (Figure 3.13ab). Indeed, 2.15 is the maximum value for R; it denotes a pattern in which the points are located at the corners of a grid of equilateral triangles.

how far a distribution of points (and at an appropriate scale we can regard urban centers as points) differs from a random distribution. The method consists simply of measuring the straight-line distance between every urban center and its nearest neighbor in the area in question. The resulting mean nearest neighbor distance value can then be compared with the values expected if the pattern were either completely clustered (a nearest neighbor value of zero), random (a value of 1.0), or completely uniform (a value of 2.15). A perfectly hexagonal arrangement of centers would have a value of 2.15.

King (1962) used this technique to investigate the spatial pattern of urban places in twenty sample areas in the United States and his results are summarized in Table 3.6. There is clearly considerable variability in the spacing of settlements due, presumably, to the differential influence of physical, economic, cultural and other forces. In fact 12 of the 20 areas (including, of course, Iowa) had patterns which could be described as "approaching uniform" though in no case was the approach especially close to the predicted value of 2.15. The remainder had predominantly random patterns or, in the cases of Utah and Washington, patterns tending toward the clustered.

Table 3.6
Spatial pattern of
settlements in twenty
selected areas of the
United States.

Clustered		Random		Approaching uniform	
Area	Nearest neighbor value	Area	Nearest neighbor value	Area	Nearest neighbor value
Utah	0.70	California	1.08	Georgia	1.32
Washington	0.71	Florida	0.94	Iowa	1.35
		Louisiana	1.08	Kansas	1.33
(Ideal value =	0.00)	New Mexico	1.10	Minnesota	1.38
		N. Dakota	1.11	Mississippi	1.28
		Oregon	1.02	Missouri	1.38
				Ohio	1.27
		(Ideal value =	1.00)	Pennsylvania	1.22
				Texas (NW)	1.23
				Texas (SE)	1.16
				Virginia	1.22
				Wisconsin	1.24
				(Ideal value =	2.15)

Source: based on L. J. King (1962), A quantitative expression of the pattern of urban settlements in selected areas of the U.S., *Tijdschrift voor Economische en Sociale Geografie*, 53, Table 1.

But if we concentrate on urban centers which are predominantly central places in a *functional* sense then, presumably, the correspondence with theory should be closer. Central place theory tells us that there should be a characteristic distance separating centers on a given hierarchical level and that high-order centers should be widely spaced with the distance separating centers on each level decreasing as we move down the hierarchy.

Numerous writers have claimed to identify "typical" distances separating central places on different hierarchical levels. Reference back to Table 3.2 shows that Lösch claimed to find a close correspondence in Iowa between theoretical distances and actual distances among central places in what appeared to be a $k = 4$ hierarchy. Brush's (1953) study of central places in southwestern Wisconsin also identified mean distances between central places which appeared to vary in accordance with theory. Brush recognized a three-tier hierarchy in the area of hamlets, villages, and towns; their relative distances are shown in Table 3.7 and they appear to correspond closely with theoretical expectations.

Between-center distances	142 hamlets	73 villages	19 towns
Theoretical distance	5.6 miles	10.0 miles	19.8 miles
Mean measured distance	5.5 miles	9.9 miles	21.2 miles
Range of variation	1.0–12.0 miles	3.5–18.5 miles	7.0–38.0 miles

Source: J. E. Brush (1953), The Hierarchy of Central Places in Southwestern Wisconsin, Table 2. Reprinted by permission from the *Geographical Review*, **43**, copyrighted by the American Geographical Society of New York.

Table 3.7
Spacing of central places in southwestern Wisconsin.

However, Dacey (1962) rejected this conclusion after carrying out a nearest neighbor analysis of the same centers. He found, in fact, that the central place system in southwestern Wisconsin more closely approximated a random pattern rather than a uniform pattern. As Dacey pointed out, this does not necessarily deny the existence of a central place hierarchy in southwestern Wisconsin but rather suggests that the hierarchy *as identified by Brush* does not conform to the uniform spatial pattern he had claimed. Thus there appear to be two possible explanations in this case. Either the levels of the hierarchy were wrongly identified, or the central places are not uniformly spaced because of the operation of other factors.

A third possibility, however, is that the measure of distance itself is inappropriate. Indeed it is extremely doubtful whether straight line physical distance is a truly valid measure of the functional spacing of central places.

Population density and urban spacing

A more realistic measure might well be one that takes into account variations in population density because, as we saw in Chapter Two, population density has a marked effect on the size of market areas. Where population densities are high, threshold market areas tend to be smaller and, presumably, centers will be located closer together and vice versa. Olsson and Persson (1964) investigated the spacing of central places in Sweden in precisely this context. First, using the nearest neighbor technique, they measured the straight line distances between central places. They then used correlation and simple linear regression (see note on p. 73) to compare the relationship between the centrality of places and their nearest neighbor distances. The resulting correlation coefficient was +0.31, not a very high level of association. (A perfect relationship would have a value of +1.0.) Investigation of the residuals revealed that those places which were closer to their nearest neighbor than they should have been were mainly clustered in the densely populated parts of the country while those which were further apart than predicted were in the more sparsely populated areas. By allowing for such variations in population density—in effect by measuring the distance between centers in numbers of people rather than straight-line distance—they were able to explain far more of the variation in the actual spacing of central places (46 percent compared with less than 10 percent).*

*Experiments in which attempts are made to transform distance in other ways to allow for more realistic testing of spatial theories are discussed by Bunge (1966) and Tobler (1963). Getis (1963) used a transformation of distance based on disposable income with some success in a study of the spatial distribution of grocery stores in Tacoma, Washington.

Note

Figure 3.14
Relationship between size
of market area and
population density.
[*Source:* B. J. L. Berry
and H. G. Barnum
(1962), Aggregate
Relations and Elemental
Components of Central
Place Systems, *Journal of
Regional Science,* 4,
Figure 2. Reproduced by
permission of the author
and editor.]

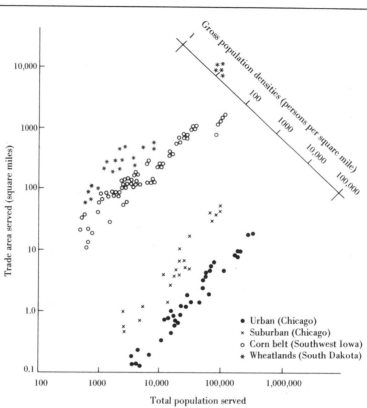

Figure 3.14 illustrates the same general relationship between population density and the size of market area for samples of central places in four quite disparate geographical areas in the United States. The graph relates three variables: the area served (in square miles), the total population served, and the population density. Note how the symbols for the four areas are, on the whole, clearly distinguishable from each other and that the relationship is remarkably regular. Market areas in the wheatlands of South Dakota are extensive and serve a relatively small population at low densities. At the other extreme, the pattern of solid black dots representing centers in the highly urbanized Chicago region indicate very small trade areas serving large numbers of people at very high densities. Thus evidence in both Sweden and the United States appears to bear out the importance of taking into account variations in population densities in explaining the spacing of central places.

Empirical regularities in the distribution and density of population

Quite apart from the effect of varying population density on market area sizes, certain regular and systematic spatial variations in population density itself have been identified. Following the pioneering work of Colin Clark (1951), a number of studies have verified that, in general, the density of population declines systematically with increasing distance from the center of the city. Clark claimed that the actual form of this variation corresponded to a *negative exponential* relationship between population density and distance:

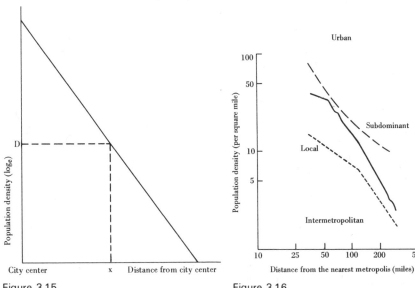

Figure 3.15

Figure 3.16

Figure 3.15
Decline of population density with increasing distance from the city center.

Figure 3.16
Decline of population density by sector.
[*Source:* D. J. Bogue (1949), The Structure of the Metropolitan Community, Ann Arbor: University of Michigan Press. Reproduced by permission of the author.]

$$D_x = D_o e^{-bx}$$

where

D_x = population density at distance x from the city center
D_o = population density at the city center
b = rate of decline in density, i.e. the slope of the density curve
e = the base of natural logarithms.

Expressed graphically, and using the natural logarithm of the population density values, the spatial variation in population density from the city centers slopes away regularly as in Figure 3.15. Although the *rate* at which density declines with distance varies from place to place and over time (that is the *b* value changes) a lot of evidence has been accumulated to confirm this density-distance relationship. Clark himself claimed that

> the falling off in density is an exponential function . . . (which) . . . appears
> to be true for all times and for all places studied, from 1801 to the present
> day, and from Los Angeles to Budapest.
> *Clark (1951), p. 490*

In fact, Clark's assertion was based on only 36 cases but by 1963, when more than 100 cases had been examined in many different countries, Berry, Simmons, and Tennant were able to observe that no evidence had been found to refute Clark's claim.

The above studies of population density variations were concerned with patterns *within* urban centers. On a much broader scale—that of the metropolis plus its surrounding hinterland—Bogue (1949) was able to shed further light both on density-distance relationships in general and on *directional* variations in the relationship. Recall that Lösch suggested that the optimal arrangement of production centers was a *sectoral* pattern; alternating wedges of activity-rich and activity-poor patterns. Though Bogue was not testing Lösch's ideas, his findings do confirm the existence of sectoral variations in population density. He identified three types of sector radiating outwards from the metropolis:

(i) *Intermetropolitan (or route) sectors*—containing a major routeway connecting metropolitan centers.
(ii) *Subdominant sectors*—lacking the major routeways of the route sector but having a major center of more than 25,000 population.
(iii) *Local sectors*—lacking both major routeways and major centers.

Figure 3.16 shows that the first two sectors contain much higher densities than the third. It seems not unreasonable to equate the intermetropolitan and subdominant sectors with Lösch's activity-rich sector and Bogue's local sector with Lösch's activity-poor sector.

Periodic markets in a central place framework

In looking at the central place system in terms of both its vertical or hierarchical organization and its horizontal or spatial structure we have been concerned with the kind of urban place familiar to most of us—the village, town, or city of the western world. But an interesting finding of recent research work is that some of the basic logic of central place theory may also apply to the quite different marketing conditions of the less developed economies of Asia, Africa, and possibly elsewhere. Although our central concern in this book is with the spatial organization of economic systems in the urban-industrial economies of the western world it is worthwhile at this stage, when we are looking at the validity of the theoretical models of Chapter Two, to briefly consider this aspect.*

Despite the rapid rates of urbanization which have been experienced in recent decades, many parts of Africa and Asia are still essentially rural. In such areas, per capita income levels are generally low and personal mobility very restricted. Away from the major urban centers, such income and mobility conditions may well be such as to preclude the establishment of permanent central places. Stine (1962) was one of the first to point out that this did not necessarily imply that central place theory was inapplicable in such circumstances. He argued that although for a trader in a fixed location the *threshold* may well lie outside the *range* (see Figure 2.8) this problem could be overcome if the trader moved from place to place to sell his goods. In effect he accumulates sufficient demand to meet his threshold requirements. But such movement is not random or haphazard: it is synchronized in both time and space. If both time *and* space are considered, instead of space alone, then it is suggested that the pattern

---

Note

*After the intense activity of the 1960s, interest in examining central places in developed economies has dwindled. The focus of interest has shifted very markedly to marketing systems in non-industrial societies. There is a considerable and rapidly growing body of literature which, among other qualities, examines the complex spatio-temporal structure of periodic markets. Bromley (1971) provides a useful general survey while specific research investigations are presented in Hay (1971), Hill and Smith (1972), Eighmy (1972), McKim (1972), and Scott (1972).

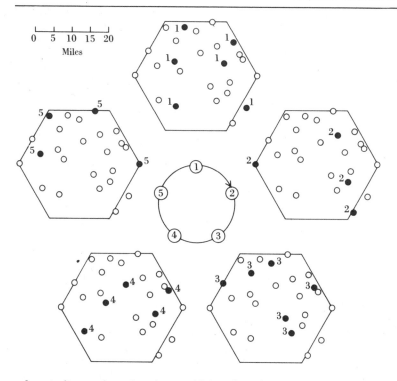

Figure 3.17
Periodic central places in
Korea. [*Source:* J. H.
Stine (1962), Temporal
Aspects of Tertiary
Production Elements in
Korea, in F. R. Pitts (ed.),
*Urban Systems and
Economic Development,*
Eugene: University of
Oregon Press, Figure 1.
Used by permission of the
editor.]

of *periodic markets* (markets which take place at a particular location on one or more fixed days every week, month, or other time period) can be explained, at least partially, in terms of a modified central place framework.

For example, Figure 3.17 shows the structure of a system of periodic markets in a small section of Korea. In this area of roughly 650 square miles there are 25 periodic central places and their functioning is based upon a five-day cycle. The sequence is shown by the numbers in Figure 3.17. During the five-day period, each periodic market functions once and then the cycle is renewed.

The central place system in Korea is mixed, there being both permanent and periodic elements. This is true also in China where, as Skinner (1964) shows, a hierarchical structure can be identified which, he suggests, corresponds closely in some places to a $k = 3$ system, in others to $k = 4$. Skinner identified three hierarchical levels in pre-revolutionary China. "Central" markets were the highest order central places: these were located in key positions and performed both retailing functions for its own market area and wholesaling functions for lower order centers. "Intermediate" and "standard" markets—the latter being the lowest level in the hierarchy—made up the rest of the hierarchy. Skinner suggested that the area covered by Figure 3.18a revealed a $k = 3$ hierarchical arrangement between the intermediate and standard markets. By regularizing the actual market areas of Figure 3.18a, Skinner produced a Christaller-type $k = 3$ arrangement as in Figure 3.18b.

Two levels of periodic cycle can be discerned for the system focused on Chung-Ho-Chen. Both are based on a ten-day period with markets operating on nine

Figure 3.18
Periodic central places in
a part of China. (a)
Distribution of markets;
(b) Distribution of
markets interpreted as a
k = 3 system. [*Source:* G.
W. Skinner (1964),
Marketing and Spatial
Structure in Rural China,
Journal of Asian Studies,
24, Figures 3.2 and 3.3.
Reproduced by
permission of the editor,
(c) Association for Asian
Studies, Inc.]

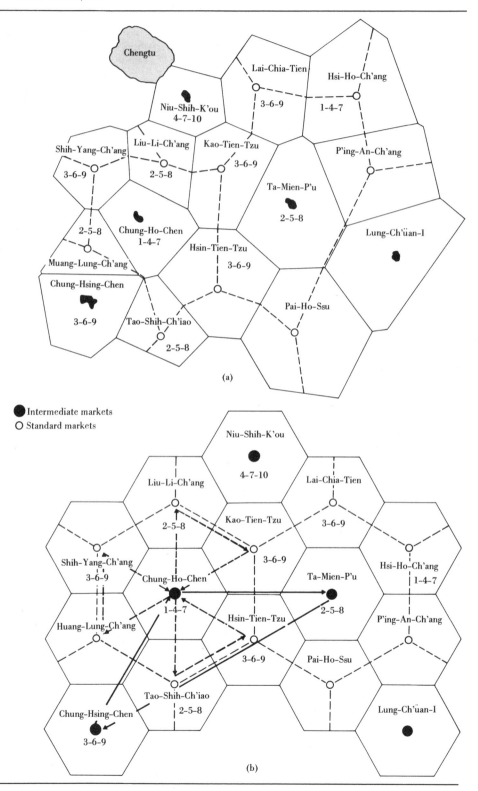

● Intermediate markets
○ Standard markets

days, the tenth being one on which the markets did not operate. In the $k = 3$ arrangement, this cycle was divided into three–day segments. The lower level of the cycle involved interaction between Chung-Ho-Chen and the six standard markets located at the corners of the large hexagon surrounding it. The arrows in Figure 3.18b show the sequence of markets. For example, on the first day of the cycle the market was located in the intermediate center itself. On day two, markets were held in Liu-Li-Ch'ang, Tao-Shih-Ch'iao, and Huang-Lung-Ch'ang. On day three, the standard markets operating were in Kao-Tien-Tzu, Hsin-Tien-Tzu, and Shi-Yang-Ch'ang. On day four, the intermediate market functioned again, after which the same sequence was repeated, returning to the intermediate market on the seventh day. Thus each market functioned on three separate days within one period of the cycle. Superimposed upon this was the cycle involving the intermediate centers: Chung-Ho-Chen, Ta-Mien-P'u, and Chung-Hsing-Chen.

Not all students of periodic market systems accept such a clear central place interpretation of their organization. Clearly, many other variables are involved as in the case of central places of a permanent kind. Nevertheless, there do appear to be significant time-space regularities in periodic market systems in many parts of the world. Hill and Smith (1972), for example, found that in part of northern Nigeria periodic markets are synchronized in such a way that markets which are close together in geographical space tend to be separated in time. Conversely, markets held on the same day tend to be geographically dispersed. They show some evidence to suggest that such spacing (measured by the nearest neighbor technique) tends towards uniformity, the markets being more or less equally spaced.

Spatial regularity of agricultural production

The model of the spatial pattern of agricultural production constructed in Chapter Two predicted that the growing of crops and the raising of livestock would be located in a regular series of concentric zones focused on urban markets. Such zonation was produced by the influence of transport costs on the *location rent* yielded by units of land at increasing distances from the market together with the sensitivity of different products to the cost of transport. Now let us see how far this helps us to understand the spatial pattern of agricultural production in the real world.

Zonation of agricultural production around individual urban centers

Von Thünen based his theory upon careful observation and measurement of agricultural practices in the northern Germany of the early nineteenth century. Thus his suggested spatial organization of agricultural production—Table 3.8 gives a detailed picture of the contents of his land-use zones—had a strong empirical content. It is clear from the variety of evidence assembled by Chisholm (1962) in particular that a pattern very like this was a dominant characteristic of agricultural production in the past. Chisholm quotes a contemporary source in describing the location of agriculture around London in 1811 and shows that despite the wide variety of soil types, agriculture around London was arranged in a series of concentric zones. Harvey's (1963) study of the historical development of the Kentish hop industry also revealed that regularity in the land-use pattern may override physical differences. In the case of this single crop, there was clear evidence of a decline in the density of hop acreage with increasing distance from the central core area of production, although Harvey's interpretation of this pattern was based on more than simply the location-rent principle.

Table 3.8
Von Thünen's agricultural land use system.

Zone	Area percent of state area	Relative distance from central city	Land-use type	Major marketed product	Production system
0	Less than 0.1	−0.1	Urban-industrial	Manufactured goods	Urban trade center of state; near iron and coal mines
1	1	0.1–0.6	Intensive agriculture	Milk; vegetables	Intensive dairying and trucking; heavy manuring; no fallow
2	3	0.6–3.5	Forest	Firewood; timber	Sustained-yield forestry
3a	3	3.6–4.6	Extensive agriculture	Rye; potatoes	Six-year rotation: rye (2), potatoes (1), clover (1), barley (1), vetch (1); no fallow; cattle stall-fed in winter
3b	30	4.7–34		Rye	Seven-year rotation system; pasture (3), rye (1), barley (1), oats (1), fallow (1)
3c	25	34–44		Rye: animal products	Three-field system: rye, etc. (1), pasture (1), fallow (1)
4	38	45–100	Ranching	Animal products	Mainly stock-raising; some rye for on-farm consumption
5	—	Beyond 100	Waste	None	None

Source: P. Haggett (1965), *Locational Analysis in Human Geography*, Table 6.4, London: Edward Arnold.

Such regularities in the agricultural land-use pattern are a good deal less evident in today's more complex world, particularly in the highly industrialized economies, but it does appear that some "remnants" of the pre-existing zonal pattern can still be identified. The most widely occurring remnant is that of the survival of parts of the innermost zone of agricultural production—intensive market gardening and liquid milk production—around urban centers. Despite increased concentration of these activities in areas of greatest comparative advantage, most major cities retain considerable horticulture and dairying on their urban-rural periphery. Jean Gottmann's classic study of Megalopolis—the highly urbanized seaboard of the northeastern United States—amply confirms this. Agriculture in Megalopolis is highly specialized, with particular emphasis on market gardening, dairying, and poultry husbandry. These goods are produced at a very high degree of intensity, giving one of the highest productivity per acre levels for these goods in the whole of the United States. Theoretical discussion of bid-rent curves in Chapter Two would suggest that farm property values in such a situation should be high and this is indeed the case. Not only this, but these high values are directly related to *location* with respect to the market.

> A farm with good soil usually commands a better price than one of the same size with poor soil, *but only if their locations are equal.* The rockiest pasture ten miles from Boston is more valuable than the finest black loam in central Illinois.
> *Gottmann (1961), p. 263*

Despite the development of specialized areas of milk production based upon factors other than market proximity (see Chapter Five), urban-oriented liquid milk production is still evident. Durand's detailed study of the major milksheds of the northeastern United States clearly illustrates this. Within the broad zone of specialized dairy production stretching from Maine to Minnesota which capitalizes on favorable natural conditions to serve a national market, Durand identified pockets of liquid milk production which are related solely to local urban markets. As one would expect in a region of strong urbanization, the milksheds of the major cities generally overlap and also intermingle with the milksheds of smaller cities, but the basic direct orientation of liquid milk production to urban markets is indisputable. Similar conclusions regarding the persistence of urban-oriented agriculture can be drawn in other developed countries. Most cities have pockets of intensive agriculture on their urban periphery.

Sinclair's "reversal" of Von Thünen's analysis

A rather different view is taken by Sinclair (1967). He suggests that although in developed economies the basic allocating force governing land use is, in fact, *economic* or *location rent*, the major force influencing spatial variation in such rent is no longer simply transport cost to the market, but rather the massive urban expansion which has occurred on a scale not envisaged in Von Thünen's day. Urban land invariably commands a higher value than rural land and, where the two types of use are in direct competition, urban uses generally win. But land which is *expected* to become urbanized also has a higher value—an "anticipated" value—and this has a considerable effect on the type of land use practiced in rural areas. Recall that in the Von Thünen model land adjacent to the urban market tended to be farmed at the highest intensity. However, Sinclair argues that such land is most likely to become urbanized and thus has the highest anticipated value. Under these circumstances a landowner or farmer is unlikely to invest large amounts of capital and labor in agricultural production when, by waiting a little while, he may make a very large financial gain by selling his land to property developers.

Figure 3.19
Relationship between the
value of land for
agriculture and distance
from urban center.
[*Source:* R. Sinclair
(1967), Von Thünen and
Urban Sprawl, Figures 5
and 7. Reproduced by
permission from the
Annals of the Association
of American Geographers,
57.]

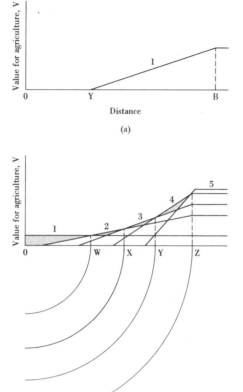

The value of land for agricultural purposes therefore, according to Sinclair, is *lower* very close to an expanding urban center and increases with distance as the likelihood of urban encroachment declines. This relationship is shown in Figure 3.19a for one type of agricultural land use. The value of land for this type of agriculture is lowest near the urban area but gradually increases outwards until at B urban expansion is no longer anticipated and thus has no influence on agricultural land values. In Figure 3.19b a competitive situation between five agricultural types is shown, their competitive position being governed by the steepness of their slopes. These, in turn, depend upon the intensity of agricultural investment.

Using these principles, Sinclair proposes a hypothetical progression of land uses around an expanding urban center in an area such as the specialized feed-grain livestock economy of the Midwest (Table 3.9). Although this is a hypothetical scheme it does appear to reflect many of the characteristics of agricultural land use around expanding cities in developed economies such as the United States. In fact, Sinclair summarizes a variety of empirical evidence which adds support to his scheme.

Zone	Type of land use
1 (adjacent to urban area)	Land changing to urban use. Subdivision. May be held vacant by speculators. Some "industrialized farming": poultry, greenhouses, etc.
2	Vacant land. Subdivision not begun. Zone of uncertainty, owners awaiting most profitable time to sell. Land may be leased temporarily for grazing or recreation.
3	Field crop and grazing zone. Low level of intensity. Zone of transitory agriculture.
4	Dairying and field crop zone. Outside "area of anticipation" except at inner margin. But oriented to urban market. Major milkshed.
5	Beyond specific urban influence. Part of nationally oriented agricultural system, e.g., specialized corn belt agriculture.

Source: Based on R. Sinclair (1967), Von Thünen and Urban Sprawl, *Annals of the Association of American Geographers* **57**.

Table 3.9
Sinclair's suggested land-use zones around an expanding urban area in a developed economy.

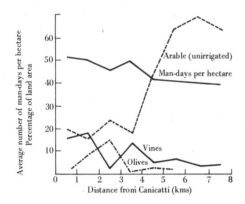

Figure 3.20
Percentage of land area in different crops around Canicatti, Sicily. [*Source:* M. Chisholm (1962), *Rural Settlement and Land Use*, London: Hutchinson, Table 6. Reproduced by permission of the publisher.]

More recently, a study by Mattingly (1972) of rural land use around Rockford near the Illinois–Wisconsin border produced results which corroborate Sinclair's hypothesis.

Agricultural zonation in developing economies

In contrast to the situation in developed economies, agricultural land use in less developed countries *does* seem to be spatially organized in terms of the influence of transportation costs on economic rent. Again, Chisholm (1962) provides a lot of the relevant evidence though there are a number of other studies which show support for this view. Figure 3.20 shows how the percentage of land devoted to each of three crops—olives, unirrigated arable, and vines—varies with increasing distance from the village of Canicatti in Sicily. The crops grown closest to the village tend to absorb more labor inputs (man-days per hectare). Evidence of similar agricultural zonation has been collected for many of the less developed parts of Europe, for India (Blaikie, 1971), Brazil (Katzman, 1974) and elsewhere, but distance is rarely the sole influence on land-use patterns.

Figure 3.21
Agricultural production
around Addis Ababa.
[*Source:* R. J. Horvath
(1969), Von Thünen's
isolated state and the area
around Addis Ababa,
Ethiopia, Figure 4.
Reproduced by
permission from the
Annals of the Association
of American Geographers
59.]

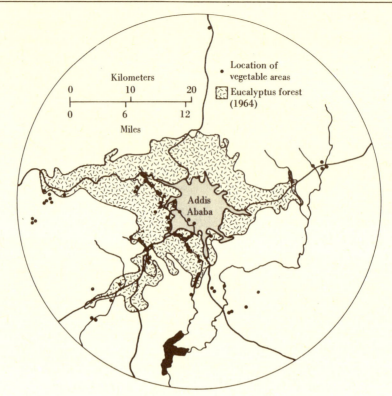

Horvath's study of agricultural patterns around the city of Addis Ababa in Ethiopia is especially interesting because of his suggestion of a direct parallel with Von Thünen's forestry zone. Literal interpreters of Von Thünen have made much of his apparently anomalous positioning of forestry in the second zone from the city. As Grotewold (1959) has emphasized, however, Von Thünen was writing in the context of conditions prevailing in the early nineteenth century when forest products were among the most fundamental and widely used materials by city dwellers. Though this no longer applies in developed economies, it may well still apply elsewhere as Horvath's work suggests. In Addis Ababa, the importance of timber as the major source of building materials and fuel has preserved its position close to the city. This is shown in Figure 3.21 as the zone of eucalyptus forest surrounding the city. Vegetable production, which requires irrigation and a good deal of labor, is located as close to the city as access to water permits. Beyond the forest zone, Horvath identified a zone of mixed, semi-subsistence farming with some possible "incipient zonation" within the mixed farming area.

Thus, although the pattern of present-day land use around cities in developed economies differs considerably from our Von Thünen-based model, this does not necessarily imply that economic rent is no longer the basic allocating mechanism. It probably is, even though the forces influencing it are no longer dominated by transportation costs from farm to market. On the other hand, agricultural land use in less developed countries, where the friction of distance is generally still very high, shows a pattern much closer, though not identical to, that predicted by our location-rent model.

Agricultural zonation and a change of scale

Yet such findings do not inevitably mean that the zonation of agricultural production no longer applies to the developed industrial economies. It may not be much in evidence around individual cities within individual countries; but if we alter our lens to the much larger geographical scale of entire continents or even the world as a whole, then we may still be able to discern some spatial order in the pattern of agricultural production. This, at least, is the view of a number of writers, though it should be pointed out that it is extremely difficult to obtain sufficiently detailed data to fully confirm such a hypothesis. The basis of agricultural zonation on a continental or global scale is that such a pattern is oriented towards very large clusters of urban markets rather than to individual cities. Figure 3.22 shows that if we regard the whole of northwestern Europe

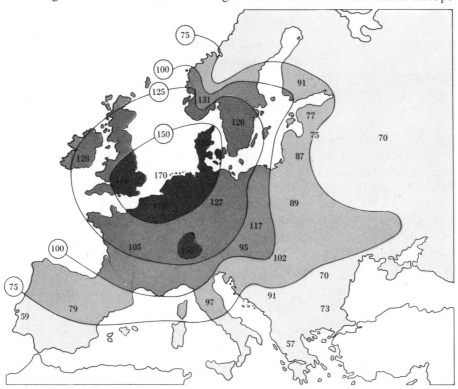

Figure 3.22
Intensity of agriculture in Europe. The index of 100 is the average European yield per acre of eight main crops: wheat, rye, barley, oats, corn, potatoes, sugar beet and hay. [*Source:* S. Van Valkenburg and C. C. Held (1952), *Europe,* Map A 105, New York: John Wiley.]

as a single vast market for agricultural products then the spatial pattern of variation in intensity in eight major crops shows a very clear zonal pattern. Intensity is highest at the core of the urban-industrial region centered on southeastern England, northeastern France, the Low Countries, northern Germany and Denmark and declines fairly regularly with increasing distance from that core.

Figure 3.23
Net income per acre for
the United States, quartic
trend surface (contour
interval = $10). [*Source:*
P. O. Muller (1973),
Trend Surfaces of
American Agricultural
Patterns, *Economic
Geography*, 49, Figure 8.]

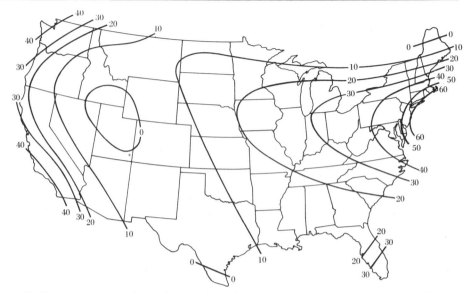

A similar broad zonation of agricultural production also seems to exist in the United States oriented predominantly to the massive urban-industrial complex of the northeast. Recent work by Muller (1973) certainly lends support to this idea. Muller's approach was to collect data on net farm income per acre for 1964 on a county basis and to fit a trend surface to the spatial distribution of income values. (The trend surface is a mapping technique designed to produce *generalized* spatial patterns rather than individual detail.) His hypothesis was that if distance to market is still a factor in agricultural activity as reflected in farm productivity then the contours of the trend surface should be broadly concentric around the Megalopolis national market. Figure 3.23 shows this to be broadly so. There is a marked concentricity around Megalopolis with a persistent decline in net income per acre as distance increases. However, there is clearly an indication of a secondary national market on the west coast toward which the income contours begin to rise again.

Thus we should not rush too quickly to deny the existence of some distance-based agricultural zonation in advanced industrial economies. It could even be argued, as Schlebecker (1960) does, that on a global scale the northeastern United States and northwestern Europe form a *world metropolis* (of which New York and London form the axis) around which agricultural production is arranged as a series of gigantic zones. Certainly if we put Figures 3.22 and 3.23 together we can envisage such a pattern, albeit in very general terms.

Spatial regularities within urban areas

Land uses within urban areas

In our simplified model we extended the basic location-rent mechanism from its original agricultural context to the organization of land uses within cities. Our expectation based on such theory would be that urban land uses should display a strong concentric regularity around the central point, modified by the extension of zones in a sectoral fashion along major routeways. When we try to see how far this pattern actually occurs, however, we are faced with a number of problems. First, we are interested primarily in the arrangement of *economic* activities, yet, in terms of their share of urban land, these are not the dominant uses. Niedercorn and Hearle's (1964) study of 48 large American cities showed that industrial uses occupied only 10.9 percent of total urban land while commercial uses occupied only 4.8 percent. By far the largest user was the residential sector which occupied 39 percent of the total with a further 25.7 percent in roads and highways and 19.7 percent in other public uses. Second, cities are exceedingly complex structures which have not only a horizontal dimension but a vertical dimension as well, so that urban land uses tend to intermingle in both dimensions. A third point is that few if any large cities today have their single most accessible point at their geographical center.

Just as in the case of agricultural location patterns around individual cities in developed economies, we do not find a neat concentric pattern *within* cities. Such a pattern may well have been present in the past; certainly Burgess's classic descriptive model of concentric land-use patterns in Chicago was a better description of cities at the turn of the century than it is today.* Sectoral patterns along major transportation routes are certainly a common feature of modern cities as are clusters of activities at key locations within the city. Smith's (1962) study of Calgary is interesting for our present purposes because the pattern he identifies (Figure 3.24) shows some evidence of concentric elements especially around the center and to the northwest together with a strong sectoral component to the east and southeast. There is also an indication of pockets of manufacturing activity on the periphery of the city.

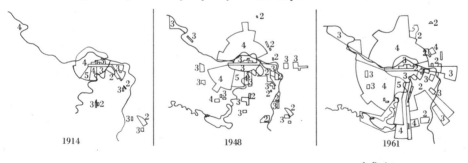

1914   1948   1961

1 Business
2 Industry
3 Low value residences
4 Medium value residences
5 High value residences
□ Park

Figure 3.24
Land-use zones in Calgary, 1914, 1948, 1961. [*Source:* P. J. Smith (1962), Calgary, A Study in Urban Pattern, *Economic Geography*, 38, Figures 6, 7 and 8.]

Three features of the arrangement of economic activities within cities are abundantly clear. First, all cities contain a central business district which our rent theory would predict, though especially in North America its importance as

*For a discussion of urban land-use models, including the "classic" examples of Burgess, Hoyt, Harris and Ullman, see Yeates and Garner (1976), Chapter 9, and Carter (1975), Chapter 9.

Note

a retail center has been declining as peripheral shopping centers have developed. Second, most cities have an industrial zone (not necessarily a continuous one) surrounding the CBD with manufacturing industry extending along particular transportation lines (see Chapter Five) and, more recently, industrial clusters in more peripheral suburban locations. Third, most cities contain a transitional zone close to the center, a zone of incipient speculation similar to Sinclair's urban fringe. In both cases, land tends to be in short-term usage pending possible future development.

Land values within urban areas

Another way of looking at spatial regularities within cities is to examine the pattern of *land values*. As we pointed out in Chapter Two, land uses tend to be arranged according to their ability to bid for specific locations. The value of land within cities, therefore, should display some spatial order. The study of land values is not easy because of both data limitations and variations in the way land value itself is defined. But there are a number of studies which demonstrate some of the regularity we would expect from our theory. The consensus of most studies is that distance from the location of maximum accessibility is an important, though not the sole, factor producing spatial variation in land values.

According to Seyfried's study of Seattle, for example,

> market forces result in a structure of site values with the highest value occurring at the location with maximum market accessibility or lowest transportation costs. Thus accessibility tends to centralize site values in a directional sense so that value declines with decreased accessibility at a measurable rate.
> *Seyfried (1963), p. 283*

Both Knos (1962) in his analysis of land values in Topeka, Kansas, and Yeates (1965) in Chicago, identified a similar situation. Figure 3.25 illustrates the variations in land values in Topeka. There is clearly an extremely precipitous fall in land values within a very short distance of the peak value location. Yeates also found that over the entire 1910 to 1960 period, land values in Chicago were highest in or close to the central business district (the peak land value being at the intersection of State Street and Madison Street). Land values declined markedly with increasing distance from the CBD. But Yeates also points out that distance from the center became progressively less important over the 50-year period.

The general configuration of the land value surface is thus far less regular than would be the case if all cities had a single center and equal movement possibilities in all directions. More likely, the actual land value surface resembles that shown in Figure 3.26 where there are a number of peaks and ridges of high values separated by areas of lower values. Nevertheless, it does appear that at least some aspects of the spatial organization of land values (and, therefore, of land uses) can be explained by the operation of location rent though the relationships are much more complex than our initial formulation suggested.

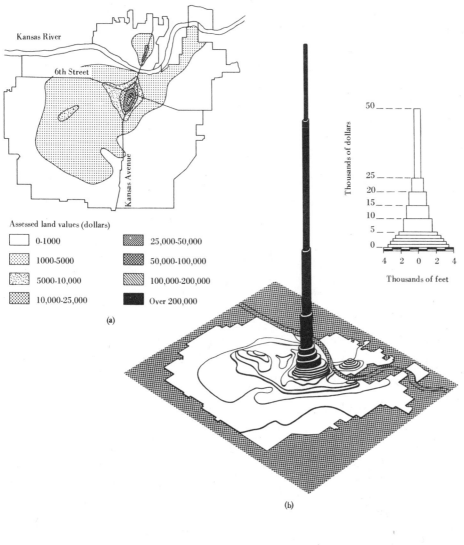

(a)

(b)

Figure 3.25
The pattern of land values
in Topeka, Kansas. (a)
Assessed land values,
1954–1959; (b) Isometric
land values. [*Source:*
D. S. Knos (1962), *The
Distribution of Land
Values in Topeka, Kansas,*
The University of Kansas
Institute for Social and
Environmental Studies,
Figures 1 and 2.]

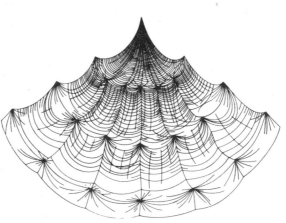

Figure 3.26
A generalized urban land
value surface. [*Source:*
B. J. L. Berry (1963),
*Commercial Structure and
Commercial Blight,*
University of Chicago,
Department of
Geography, Research
Paper No. 85, Figure 3.]

Distance and interaction

Finally, in this somewhat brief survey of empirical evidence of distance-based regularity in the spatial organization of economic activities, we turn to movement and interaction. To what extent do actual movements of goods, people, and information reflect the theoretical principles outlined in Chapter Two?

The gravity model

Movement and interaction of any kind within an economic system is a highly complex phenomenon that is influenced by a whole variety of interrelated variables. Nevertheless, there is general agreement that the intensity of movement and interaction falls off as distance increases. Three examples are used here as being fairly typical of the large number of studies which have used the gravity model. It is worth reiterating the point made in Chapter Two that the gravity model is *inductively*-based. We would, therefore, expect to find a higher degree of correspondence between such models and empirical data than in the case of the deductively-based models.

Zipf (1946, 1949) was one of the first to assemble a large body of empirical evidence on this basis even though studies using a gravity-type formula date back to the end of the last century. Zipf gathered together data on highway,

Figure 3.27
The flow of bus passengers between pairs of United States cities.
[*Source:* G. K. Zipf (1949), *Human Behavior and the Principle of Least Effort,* Reading, Mass,: Addison-Wesley, Figure 9.15.]

Figure 3.28
Relationship between truck trips and distance in the Chicago area.
[*Source:* M. Helvig (1964), Chicago's External Truck Movements, University of Chicago, Department of Geography Research Paper 90, Figure 18. Reproduced by permission of the author.]

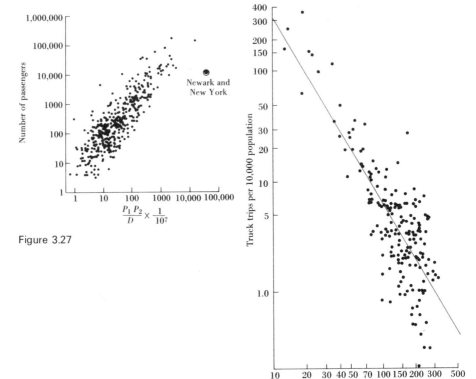

Figure 3.27

Figure 3.28

rail, air traffic and telephone traffic between pairs of cities in the United States and compared them with what would be expected if such flows were directly related to the product of the populations and inversely related to the distance separating them. Figure 3.27 shows his findings for the movement of bus passengers. The actual number of passengers traveling by bus between pairs of U.S. cities is plotted on the vertical axis of the graph, while the predicted value (P_1P_2/D) is plotted on the horizontal axis. Although there is a scatter of points there is a clear relationship between the two. High predicted values are matched by high actual values and vice versa. The second example relates to truck trips in the Chicago area (Figure 3.28). Here the distance-decay element is more immediately obvious because the intensity of truck trips (measured per 10,000 population) is plotted directly against distance. Again the relationship is not perfect but the general decline of movement intensity with distance is undoubtedly present.

Studies by Taaffe (1962; Taaffe and Gauthier, 1973) of air passenger traffic in the United States have shown how the gravity model ties in with the concept of the urban hierarchy. Taaffe calculated the expected interaction between 100 large United States metropolitan areas using the formula:

$$I_{ij} = \frac{P_iP_j}{d_{ij^2}}$$

Each center was categorized as being "dominated" (in air passenger terms) by the center with which it had the highest I_{ij} (that is, expected) value. Exceptions were made if that center was located within 120 miles of the city. Figure 3.29 is the map of *expected* air passenger dominance while Figure 3.30 is the map of *actual* air passenger dominance based upon observed air passenger flows between the 100 metropolitan areas. Without doubt, there is some correspondence between the observed and the expected patterns of air passenger dominance. Equally, however, there are important differences. New York is far more important to the cities of the United States manufacturing belt than the gravity model predicts; its air passenger hinterland extends a good deal further west to incorporate Detroit, Cleveland, and Cincinnati in particular. In this respect, therefore, Taaffe points out that the gravity model has overestimated the frictional effect of distance. On the other hand, some of the interaction linkages between New York City and some southern cities are weaker than predicted. Taaffe concludes, therefore, that

> the historical ties that have created strong linkages between New York and the other large cities of the manufacturing belt, but weak linkages between New York and many southern cities, are too complex to be completely described by the model. It is clear, however, that the overall pattern of air passenger flows between major metropolitan areas is set within a general context of population and proximity.
> *Taaffe and Gauthier (1973), pp. 87, 90*

Although there is a good deal of agreement that the intensity of interaction declines with distance there is far less unanimity regarding the *rate* at which

Figure 3.29
Expected air passenger
dominance, United States.
The city circles on the
map are shaded according
to the city that *should* be
dominant using a
modified gravity model in
which a distance
exponent 2 was used and
all cities within 120 miles
of each other were
excluded from the
calculations. [*Source:*
E. J. Taaffe and H. J.
Gauthier (1973),
*Geography of
Transportation,* © 1973,
Figure 3.8. Reprinted by
permission of
Prentice-Hall, Inc.,
Englewood Cliffs, New
Jersey, U.S.A.]

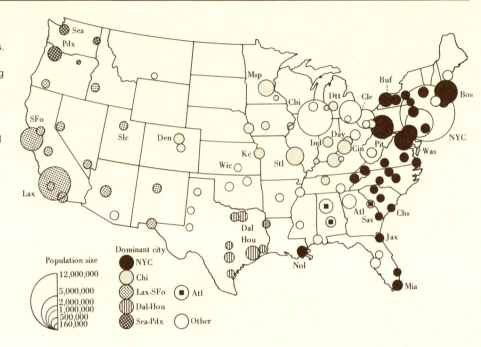

Figure 3.30
Air passenger dominance
1962. [*Source:* E. J.
Taaffe and H. J. Gauthier
(1973), *Geography of
Transportation,* © 1973,
Figure 3.9. Reprinted by
permission of
Prentice-Hall, Inc.,
Englewood Cliffs, New
Jersey, U.S.A.]

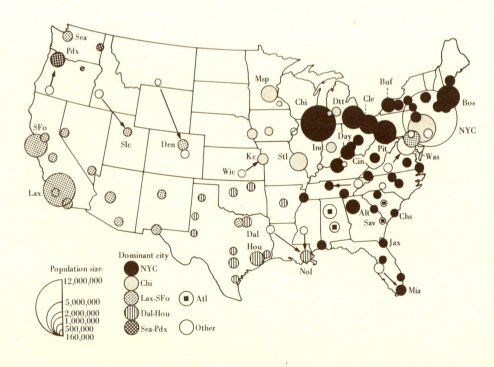

such fall-off occurs. In other words, what is the "frictional value" of distance? As we saw in Chapter Two, this frictional effect is incorporated in the gravity model by fitting an exponent (*b*) to the distance measure. For example, Zipf's study referred to above used an exponent of 1.0 whereas other studies have used exponent values varying from a little less than 1.0 to around 3.0. Almost certainly there is no uniquely correct exponent of distance. It is likely to vary from one type of movement to another, from place to place depending on such factors as the efficiency of the transportation network and degree of congestion, and from time to time because as transportation improves the frictional effect of distance is likely to decline (see Chapter Five). Clearly, the frictional effect on a journey between, say, New York City and San Francisco was a great deal higher in the days of the '49ers than it is today.

Evidence of complementarity

Compared with the number of studies which have made use of the gravity model, attention to one of the basic generators of movement—*complementarity*—has been rather sparse. Figures 3.31 and 3.32 show two of Ullman's own maps. Figure 3.31 maps the flow of forest products from the state of Washington to other states. Ullman attributes the low volume going to the southern states to a low level of complementarity. Both regions at the time had economic structures in which forest products were dominant. Figure 3.32 shows flows of animals and animal products from the state of Iowa. The pattern is dominated by heavy flows of these products to the northeastern states and to southern California (despite the considerable distances involved). Other livestock states, though geographically close, are also livestock specialists and, therefore, there is no complementarity between them.

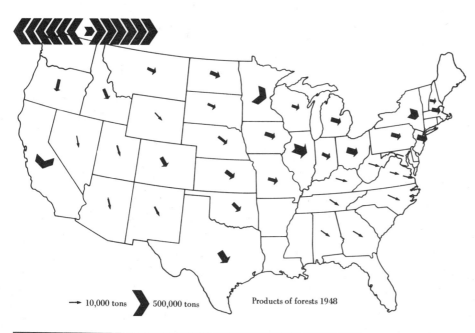

Figure 3.31
Destination, by states, of forest products shipped by rail from Washington, 1948. Width of arrows is proportionate to volume. Arrows within Washington represent intrastate movements. (Tons are short tons of 2,000 pounds). [*Source:* E. Ullman (1956), in W. L. Thomas (ed.) *Man's Role in Changing the Face of the Earth,* Figure 162. Reproduced by permission of the University of Chicago Press, © 1956 by the University of Chicago.]

Figure 3.32
Destination, by states, of
animals and products
shipped by rail from Iowa,
1948. [*Source:* E. Ullman
(1956), in W. L. Thomas
(ed.) *Man's Role in
Changing the Face of the
Earth,* Figure 165.
Reproduced by
permission of the
University of Chicago
Press, © 1956 by the
University of Chicago.]

Destination of Iowa animals and products 1948

Smith (1964) tried to look more closely at the nature of the complementarity existing between states. In particular he was concerned to establish *degrees* of complementarity: the extent to which the complementarity between state A and state C was higher or lower than that between state B and state C. Figure 3.33 shows the pattern of agricultural commodity shipments by rail to New England in absolute terms. It clearly reflects the well-established regional pattern of agricultural production. But although it shows that complementarity

Figure 3.33
Agricultural commodity
shipments by rail to New
England, 1959. The
proportional circles are
shaded according to
the commodity group
accounting for 50 percent
or more of shipments. The
composition of
commodity shipments
from Delaware was
assumed to be grain
products. [*Source:*
R. H. T. Smith (1964),
Toward a measure
of complementarity,
Economic Geography, 40,
Figure 1.]

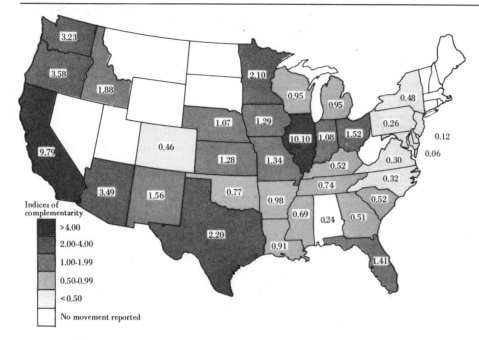

Figure 3.34
Complementarity indices
for shipments of
agricultural commodities
to New England from 34
states, 1959. [*Source:*
R. H. T. Smith (1964),
Toward a measure
of complementarity,
Economic Geography, 40,
Figure 3.]

Indices of
complementarity

>4.00
2.00-4.00
1.00-1.99
0.50-0.99
<0.50
No movement reported

exists between, say, California and New England and between New York and
New England, it does not tell us whether one level of complementarity is greater
than the other. Smith's attempt to solve this problem was based on a modification of the *numerator* of the gravity model which involved multiplying the population of the New England states by the agricultural rail surplus of each state
(this was calculated for four agricultural commodities from the total rail shipments out of each state weighted by the share which New England imported
of that surplus). Distance was calculated as straight-line distance with a *b* value
of 1.0.

Figure 3.34 is a map of the *complementarity indices* calculated by Smith for
the shipment of agricultural commodities to New England. These indices are
simply ratios of actual flow to expected flow. The map makes an interesting
contrast with that of absolute shipments (Figure 3.33). New York, for example,
is seen to have low complementarity with New England in the sense that its
actual shipments were lower than predicted. Illinois shipped ten times more
than predicted on the basis of distance. New Mexico, which shipped only a
small volume of agricultural goods to New England, has a complementarity
index of 1.56, indicating that its supply-demand relationship with New England
offsets, at least partially, the considerable distance between them.

Spatial diffusion of innovations

Although the basic concepts of complementarity and distance are common to
movement of all kinds, we saw in Chapter Two that studies of information
flows have focused more specifically on the manner in which information
spreads through a population either by interpersonal communication (expansion

diffusion) or within the framework of the urban hierarchy (hierarchical diffusion). Again we can only hint at the kind of empirical studies carried out by geographers and others.*

One of the many examples of expansion diffusion studies by Hägerstrand was the spread of adoption of subsidies to improve pasture in a part of Sweden. The objective of this government program was to encourage farmers to abandon their practice of open grazing during summer time. His hypothesis was similar to that which formed the basis of our simulation model in Chapter Two: that the spread of the innovation would be by face-to-face contact between farmers

Figure 3.35
Diffusion of pasture subsidies among Swedish farmers. [*Source:*
T. Hägerstrand (1967), On Monte Carlo Simulation of Diffusion, in W. L. Garrison and D. F. Marble (eds.), *Quantitative Geography Part 1, Economic and Cultural Topics,* Northwestern University Studies in Geography, 13, Figure 6.]

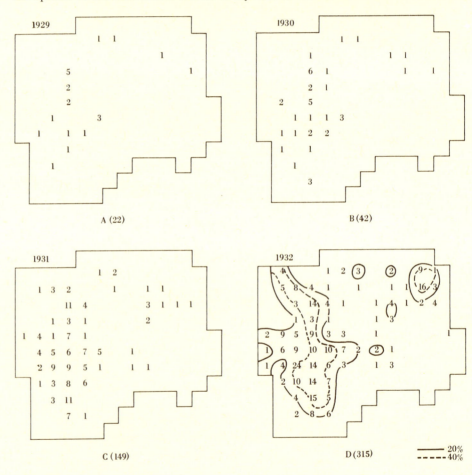

Note

*The literature on spatial diffusion has been growing steadily since Hägerstrand's pioneering work of the early 1950s. His basic work, *Innovation Diffusion as a Spatial Process,* was published in English translation in 1967 (Hägerstrand, 1967a) while other key articles are Hägerstrand (1952, 1966, 1967b). Gould (1969) has gathered together a great deal of diffusion material, both conceptual and empirical, and provides a good general introduction to the topic. Specific studies of hierarchical diffusion can be found in Berry (1972), Pedersen (1970). Discussion of both expansion and hierarchical diffusion is provided by Brown (1968a,b), Brown and Cox (1971), while Pred (1971) presents a critique of hierarchical diffusion.

and that this pattern would be strongly related to distance between tellers and potential receivers. Figure 3.35 shows the actual spread of adoption of the subsidy for four years 1929 to 1932. The numbers in each cell represent the cumulative number of farmers who had adopted in each year. In 1929 there were small, though distinct clusters of adopters in the west of the region with isolated adopters in the north and east. As the diffusion spread these two initial elements became reinforced so that by 1932 there was a broad belt of adopters in the west with adoption rates of 20 percent enclosing a narrow belt with a 40 percent adoption rate. In the east a smaller cluster was also evident.

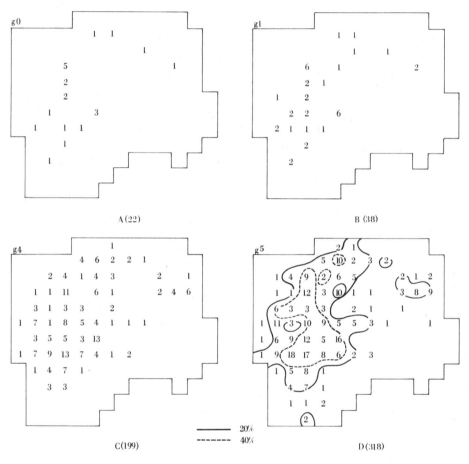

Figure 3.36
Simulated diffusion of pasture subsidies among Swedish farmers. [*Source:* T. Hägerstrand (1967), On Monte Carlo Simulation of Diffusion, in W. L. Garrison and D. F. Marble (eds.), *Quantitative Geography Part 1, Economic and Cultural Topics,* Northwestern University Studies in Geography, 13, Figure 9.]

Comparison of this observed pattern with one of the simulation runs (Figure 3.36) based upon the assumptions of Chapter Two (see p. 58) shows a remarkable degree of correspondence. Essentially the same general features appear in each case with only a few differences. Both the western belt of high adoption and the isolated eastern cluster are evident. The major difference is that the simulated pattern (g_5) extends the major adoption belt to the north and east, whereas the actual pattern was to the north and west. Nevertheless, the basic simulation model replicates the real diffusion pattern very closely indeed, suggesting that an expansion diffusion process with a strong distance-decay element was indeed present. This example is similar to many carried out by Hägerstrand and by subsequent workers. In circumstances where face-to-face contact is an important component of the communication process the distance-based diffusion model shows a close correspondence with actual diffusion patterns.

The other type of diffusion mechanism observed in Chapter Two we termed *hierarchical* diffusion. We noted there that precisely how information flows within an urban system depends very much on the hierarchy envisaged: a Christaller-type hierarchy producing uni-directional flows, a Lösch-type hierarchy allowing for flow in more than one direction. Berry (1972) certainly argues that "entrepreneurial innovations"—television transmitting stations for example—diffuse through the urban hierarchy in a regular manner:

> The innovation potential of a center is a product of its position in the urban hierarchy, and the force exerted upon it by centers that have already adopted the innovation ... Therefore, looking back at an entire diffusion sequence, adoption time should be a function of the product of hierarchical position and population potential.
>
> *Berry (1972), p. 114*

Figure 3.37 demonstrates this relationship. Population of United States cities are plotted on the vertical axis and the date each city opened a television station is plotted on the horizontal axis. Apart from the break imposed by the Korean War in the early 1950s there is a *general* inverse relationship between size (i.e. hierarchical position) and date of acquiring a TV station. But visual inspection of the graph shows that the sequence was by no means strictly hierarchical in a Christaller sense—especially at later dates. Insofar as Berry's urban hierarchy was based on the rank-size distribution of United States cities his view of the diffusion process would seem to be most compatible with a more flexible Löschian hierarchy. Thus it was possible for a small city of less than 10,000 population to acquire a TV station some six years before a city of some 200,000 population even though, as Berry justifiably claims, the diffusion of television stations was "largely hierarchical."

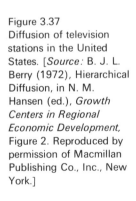

Figure 3.37
Diffusion of television stations in the United States. [*Source:* B. J. L. Berry (1972), Hierarchical Diffusion, in N. M. Hansen (ed.), *Growth Centers in Regional Economic Development,* Figure 2. Reproduced by permission of Macmillan Publishing Co., Inc., New York.]

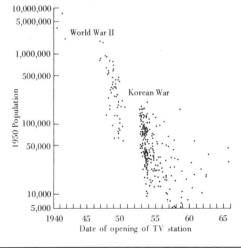

Summary

The variety of empirical evidence presented in this chapter does reveal that there is a considerable degree of order and regularity in the spatial organization of economic systems, although such regularity is a good deal less than the models of Chapter Two suggested. Central places in particular and urban centers in general are hierarchically organized and this is reflected in both their functional structure and population size, as well as in the flows of consumers to centers of different hierarchical levels, and, to a lesser extent, in the regularity of their spatial patterns. The basic elements of a central place system were also shown to be present in both developed and underdeveloped economies. Similarly there is a degree of spatial regularity in the pattern of agricultural production and of urban land uses though, again, this does not correspond exactly with the pattern predicted. Finally, interaction between places does appear to show a fairly strong relationship with both distance and complementarity.

Despite the evidence of regularity, however, the simplified constructs of Chapter Two are clearly not a complete replication of reality. One reason for the observed gap between observation and expectation is the difficulty of testing the models under the kind of homogeneous conditions on which they are based. For example, most of the empirical work described in this chapter has used straight-line physical distance as a measure. But this concept of distance, as we have seen, is not necessarily the most valid. A more realistic approach is probably to use such measures as "economic" distance (cost, incomes etc.), "time" distance, "social" distance or "perceived" distance rather than physical distance. Attempts to "transform" distance to more readily test the kinds of models discussed in Chapter Two are still at an experimental stage but they undoubtedly offer the prospect of introducing greater rigor into the testing of locational hypotheses.

A further reason, of course, for the gap between model and reality is the nature of the simplifying assumptions on which the model was based. We deliberately held most variables, which in reality mold the spatial form of the economic system, constant in order to concentrate on the single variable of distance. We must now begin to progressively relax these constraints, in other words to introduce causal factors other than distance into our discussion.

Further reading

Beckmann, M. J. (1958), City Hierarchies and the Distribution of City Size, *Economic Development and Cultural Change* **6.** 243–248.

Berry, B. J. L. (1961), City Size Distributions and Economic Development, *Economic Development and Cultural Change* **9.** 573–588.

Berry, B. J. L. (1964), Cities as Systems Within Systems of Cities, *Papers and Proceedings, Regional Science Association* **13.** 147–163.

Berry, B. J. L. (1972), Hierarchical diffusion: the basis of developmental filtering and spread in a system of growth centers, in N. M. Hansen (ed.), *Growth Centers in Regional Economic Development*, New York: Free Press, pp. 108–138.

Berry, B. J. L., H. G. Barnum, and R. J. Tennant (1962), Retail Location and Consumer Behavior, *Papers and Proceedings, Regional Science Association* **9**. 65–106.

Berry, B. J. L., and W. L. Garrison (1958a), Functional Bases of the Central Place Hierarchy, *Economic Geography* **34**. 145–154.

Berry, B. J. L., and W. L. Garrison (1958b), A Note on Central Place Theory and the Range of a Good, *Economic Geography* **34**. 304–311.

Bogue, D. J. (1949), *The Structure of the Metropolitan Community*, Ann Arbor: University of Michigan Press, Chapter Three.

Bromley, R. J. (1971), Markets in the Developing Countries: A Review, *Geography*, **56**. 124–132.

Brush, J. E. (1953), The Hierarchy of Central Places in Southwestern Wisconsin, *Geographical Review* **43**. 380–402.

Chisholm, M. (1962), *Rural Settlement and Land Use*, Chicago: Aldine, London: Hutchinson.

Dacey, M. F. (1962), Analysis of Central Place Patterns by Nearest Neighbor Analysis, *Lund Studies in Geography Series B*, **24**.

Golledge, R. G., G. Rushton, and W. A. V. Clark (1966), Some Spatial Characteristics of Iowa's Dispersed Farm Population and Their Implications for the Grouping of Central Place Functions, *Economic Geography* **42**. 261–272.

Gould, P. R. (1969), *Spatial Diffusion*, Association of American Geographers, Commission on College Geography, Resource Paper No. 4, Washington D.C.

Hägerstrand, T. (1967b), On Monte Carlo simulation of diffusion, in W. L. Garrison and D. F. Marble (eds.), *Quantitative Geography, Part 1, Economic and Cultural Topics*, Northwestern University Studies in Geography **13**. 1–32.

Horvath, R. J. (1969), Von Thünen's Isolated State and the Area Around Addis Ababa, Ethiopia, *Annals of the Association of American Geographers* **59**. 308–323.

Isard, W. (1956), *Location and Space Economy*, Cambridge, Mass.: M.I.T. Press, Chapter 3.

King, L. J. (1962), A Quantitative Expression of the Pattern of Urban Settlements in Selected Areas of the U.S., *Tijdschrift voor Economische en Sociale Geografie* **53**. 1–7.

Madden, C. H. (1956), Some Indicators of Stability in the Growth of Cities in the United States, *Economic Development and Cultural Change* **4**. 236–252.

Olsson, G. (1965b), *Distance and Human Interaction: A Review and Bibliography*, Philadelphia: Regional Science Research Institute.

Ray, D. M. (1967), Cultural Differences in Consumer Travel Behavior in Eastern Ontario, *Canadian Geographer* **11**. 143–156.

Sinclair, R. (1967), Von Thünen and Urban Sprawl, *Annals of the Association of American Geographers* **57**. 72–87.

Skinner, G. W. (1964), Marketing and Social Structure in Rural China, *Journal of Asian Studies* **24**. 3–43.

Smith, R. H. T. (1964), Toward a Measure of Complementarity, *Economic Geography* **40**. 1–8.

Stine, J. H. (1962), Temporal Aspects of Tertiary Production Elements in Korea, in F. R. Pitts (ed.), *Urban Systems and Economic Development*, Eugene: University of Oregon Press.

Vining, R. (1955), A Description of Certain Spatial Aspects of an Economic System, *Economic Development and Cultural Change* **3**. 147–195.

Yeates, M. H., and B. J. Garner (1976), *The North American City*, 2nd ed., New York: Harper and Row, Chapter 9.

Zipf, G. K. (1949), *Human Behavior and the Principle of Least Effort*, Reading, Mass.: Addison-Wesley, Chapter Nine.

CHAPTER 4

A HETEROGENEOUS LAND SURFACE

Relaxing the simplifying assumptions

The empirical evidence presented in Chapter Three revealed that the operation of a single variable—distance—even in its most simplified form is responsible for some of the spatial variability in the pattern of economic activities. Clearly, however, the gap between the model situation and the real-world situation is still considerable. To reduce this gap we need to relax some of the rigid simplifying assumptions on which the model of Chapter Two was based. For ease of explanation and to help us understand the spatial impact of each factor, the constraints will be relaxed one at a time. However, because all of these factors are interrelated, there is no unique sequence in which this operation should be performed. The order adopted here is believed to have some logic, but it will be apparent that other arrangements are possible.

The fundamental concern of Chapter Two was the relative location of economic activities in space. Given a homogeneous plain with resources of uniform quantity and quality available everywhere, the problem was to determine the distances that separated economic activities. The resulting pattern was one of *spatial order and regularity in relative location*. In the central place system producers of the same good were uniformly spaced, while in the agricultural system production patterns followed an ordered spatial zoning.

In both cases the only variable costs to each producer were those derived from the movement of *evenly distributed* input factors and of final products to an *evenly distributed* market. Implicitly, of course, there were also cost differentials derived from the lower unit costs of large-scale enterprise; without them there would be no incentive to shift from a subsistence economy in the first place. Apart from this, however, no allowance was made for other variable costs of production.

In a real world things are very different. Many other factors enter the determination of production costs in space. Transport costs both for input factors and final products are highly variable over space and vary widely with the type of medium used, the nature of the terrain and the type of good carried. Factors of production like labor, capital and technical knowledge are not available everywhere nor are they all infinitely and equally mobile. Perhaps the first thing to strike the geographer about the unreality implicit in the model is the fact that material resources are in no sense of equal quality and ubiquitous in location. We shall begin "dismantling" the constraints of the model with this question of variable material resources taking each of the other "unrealistic" constraints in their turn in subsequent chapters.

Spatial variations in resource quality and availability

For the present then, we retain all those constraints of the model which we set up in Chapter Two with the exception of that dealing with spatial variations in resource quality. We now want to look at the way natural resources of all kinds influence the location of economic activity and this takes us on to look at the "traditional" variables of economic geography.

Let us pause for a moment, however, to remind ourselves of what we mean by the word "resource." In its most general usage it implies anything that is useful to man, a definition so wide as to render it generally unhelpful. What we have in mind here are *natural resources*—those elements from the *stock* of material components in the environment that man finds useful. These might be mineral and energy sources, climate, soils, natural vegetation, animal life and so forth. What makes them resources, however, is not their intrinsically valuable properties such as the energy they contain or their food value, but the fact that a given culture *expresses a use for them* and is willing to pay for their extraction. Resources, as Haggett (1975) points out, are a "cultural concept." They are drawn from the stock of the earth's material properties when man has a use for them and returned to it when that use disappears. A stock becomes a *resource*, then, when some effective demand like the need for food, shelter, warmth, or clothing brings it into use.

We begin our analysis with that sub-set of the natural resource complex providing industrial raw materials and sources of energy. This exerts its most powerful locational influence on mining and manufacturing industries in particular, an aspect of economic activity which the model constraints have given us little opportunity to explore so far. Indeed, one of the main conclusions of Chapter Three, in which the simplified model was tested against conditions in a real world, was that there was a relatively poor correspondence in the case of manufacturing industry. The most obvious, though by no means the only, reason for this was the model's assumption of a uniform availability of materials of homogeneous quality. In reality most industrial raw materials and energy sources are restricted in their spatial availability or *localized* rather than *ubiquitous* (available everywhere) as the model assumed them to be. Thus the Lösch-Christaller principles around which the simplified model is constructed are more applicable to the location of tertiary activities and those manufacturing industries that use such ubiquitous materials as do exist, like air (oxygen manufacture) or small amounts of soft water (soft drinks). For them transportation costs are most important from the point of view of the distribution of the good or service, but most manufacturing industries must use some localized materials and thus the cost of *assembling* material inputs from a variety of sources is a significant component of this total cost structure. What effect, then, will the procurement of *spatially localized materials* have on location patterns? We can begin to answer this question by drawing upon some of the ideas of Alfred Weber.*

*Alfred Weber, a German economist, first published his classic work *Über den Standort der Industrien* in 1909. This followed a long tradition of German interest in the economics of location. It was begun by Von Thünen in 1826, whose work formed the basis for our discussion of agricultural location in Chapter Two. Another German, Wilhelm Launhardt (1882, 1885) preceded Weber in paying specific attention to the location of industry, but the translation of Weber's book into English in 1929 as *The Theory of the Location of Industries* assured him of wider recognition as the acknowledged pioneer of this aspect of location theory. In any case, however, Weber's work was far more comprehensive and rigorous than any of his predecessors'.

Note

The particular format of our treatment in this book denies us the opportunity to treat Weber's theory as a whole, and the reader is encouraged to consult, for example, the work of Daggett (1968) and D. M. Smith (1971, pp. 113–119) for a more rounded view. In brief, however, what Weber set out to do was find the answer to the question "What causes an industry to move from one place to another?". In seeking his answer he made use of the "model" approach of the classical location theorists, setting up, as we did in Chapter Two, a series of constraints which assumed a flat plain, conditions of perfect competition, and so forth. What he was looking for were those *general factors* that influenced the location of manufacturing industries.

In essence, Weber saw the location of industry as a response to two interconnected sets of forces: *primary causes* for the regional distribution of industry (regional factors) and *secondary causes* of the redistribution of industry (his agglomerating and deglomerating factors). At the regional level his general regional factors were the *costs of transportation* (our particular concern in this chapter and in Chapter Five) and *labor costs* (which are taken up in Chapter Six). The secondary factors by which Weber saw industry to be redistributed within the regional context are taken up under the heading of scale economies in Chapter Seven.

Weber closes the introduction to his work with the statement "This book is expected to be a beginning not an end." So it has been. His work has, for the past six or seven decades, been constantly reviewed, attracting both commendation and criticism. It has been updated, embellished and even computerized. In the process, however, almost all have gained something from Alfred Weber and his approach to the problems of industrial location theory.

Weber's analysis of the minimum transport point

In the absence of spatial differences in basic production costs, Weber observed that manufacturing plants will locate at the point where total transport costs are minimized. He suggested that transport costs are, in effect, determined by two factors:

1. The *weight* of the materials to be assembled together with the weight of the final product to be shipped to market.
2. The *distances* over which the materials and the product have to be moved.

The combination of these two elements permits him to come up with a simple index of cost, the *ton-mile*. The locational problem is then simply to find the point where the total ton-mileage is minimized for the particular production-distribution process.

The key which determines the suitability of a particular location for a manufacturing activity is the total number of ton-miles accumulated at that site. If every possible site is examined in this way, then the site which accumulates the lowest total of ton-miles for assembling materials and getting the product to market is the best location (i.e. it is the minimum transport-cost location). In looking at the ton-mileage calculations for a variety of situations, however, it becomes obvious that certain key principles of location can be extracted which make copious calculation unnecessary. These give some general indications as to the best sites for potential classes of industry depending upon certain characteristics of the materials they use.

1. Ubiquitous materials, those available everywhere, exert no separate locational force on manufacturing. For industries subject only to assembling them it is the *principles of marketing alone* which condition locational choice and the best location will be at the market site. (The simplified model case).*

2. Localized materials exert a specific influence on location. They are of two types depending upon the ratio between the weight of material and the weight of the product which is produced from it. First, there are *pure localized materials* for which the entire weight enters into the product. For example, yarn for the manufacture of cloth can be regarded as a pure material because no loss of weight occurs in the manufacturing process. Second, there are *gross localized materials*, which do suffer a loss of weight in the process of manufacture. Perhaps the most widely quoted example for this is the manufacture of sugar from sugar beet. The weight of raw sugar extracted by this process is only one eighth of the weight of the raw material that goes into the process of extraction.

3. The material index (MI) calculated as follows:

$$MI = \frac{\text{weight of localized materials used in the industry}}{\text{weight of the product}}$$

shows the extent to which a particular industry will be material-oriented or market-oriented. *Where the material index is greater than one, this indicates a tendency toward a material site location.* In this case the sum of the weights of the localized materials used in the industry is greater than the weight of the product. In those industries where ubiquitous materials are involved, however, it is possible that the product may have a weight greater than that of the localized materials. Take the case of brewing. The heaviest material used by far is, to all intents and purposes, ubiquitous; that is *water*. Compared to the weight of the beer itself then (mostly water), the weight of the *localized* materials such as hops, sugar, chemical additives and so forth is small and the resultant material index will be less than one. In cases such as this *where the material index is less than one this indicates a tendency to favor market location.*

For those industries using only pure localized materials or where the balance of gross materials and ubiquities gives a *material index exactly equal to one, then, in theory, location can be at the materials site, the market or any point in between.* For reasons connected with transport rates, a subject taken up in the next chapter, intermediate locations are in fact less likely to result in this case than locations fixed at either the market or the materials site.

---

*Weber's market assumption   Note

It is perhaps worth emphasizing here that Weber assumes the market for manufacturing to be *punctiform* rather than areally dispersed. That is, the market is concentrated at one or a number of discrete points in space. Isard (1956, p. 143 fn) suggests that this is not conceptually different from the areal market assumed in the central place model. It merely represents a special case derived from a change in the scale at which the market is treated. For the central place model the household is the smallest point of reference; for Weber's analysis of manufacturing the scale of the smallest unit is higher at the level of, say, the village or town.

Having established some of the basic principles of Weber's approach to the location of manufacturing let us consolidate our understanding with the help of a simple example. Take the simple case of a manufacturer who requires only one raw material and sells his entire output at a single market (Figure 4.1). Location depends simply on the nature of the material used in production. If it is gross (weight-losing) then the production site will tend toward the material source. For example, suppose the manufacturing process is the refining of

Figure 4.1
Simple location problem: a firm using one material and selling to a single market.

Figure 4.2
Location of a firm using two inputs and selling to a single market.

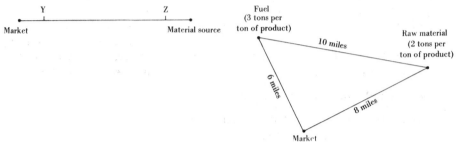

Figure 4.1   Figure 4.2

sugar beet, a material that, as we saw earlier, contributes only about one-eighth of its weight to the final product. A location at any point other than the raw material source would involve paying unnecessary transport costs for the shipment of the seven-eighths of each beet that are not required in the manufacturing process. The same argument would apply in the case of any other gross material. Why pay transport costs to ship unwanted material? Only pure materials, whose entire weight enters the final product, could be processed at a location other than the source. Thus in the single-market, single-material situation, all production processes with material indices greater than one will be located at the sources of their materials, while those using pure materials will, in theory, be free to locate at any point along the lines connecting their markets and material sources.

Clearly, the two-point case is too simplistic; very few, if any, manufacturing processes use only a single material input. However, even where the production process is more complex the same basic principles apply. Figure 4.2 illustrates the situation in which a manufacturer requires one raw material and an input of fuel, both derived from separate localized resources, and ships his product to a single market. By looking separately at each of the three extreme points of the triangle and calculating the ton-mile total at each of them we can establish which of them is the "best" location.

The total ton-mileage that would be incurred in manufacturing one ton of the product at each of the locations is as follows:

Location at the market:
Fuel cost: 18 ton-miles (3 tons over 6 miles)
Raw material cost: 16 ton-miles (2 tons over 8 miles)
As the product would be manufactured at the market there is no transport cost incurred in marketing the product.
Total transport cost at market: *34 ton-miles*

Location at the fuel source:

Raw material cost: 20 ton-miles (2 tons over 10 miles)

Marketing product: 6 ton-miles (1 ton over 6 miles)

There would be no transport cost on fuel as manufacture would be at the fuel source.

Total transport cost at the fuel source: *26 ton-miles*

Location at the raw material source:

Fuel cost: 30 ton-miles (3 tons over 10 miles)

Marketing product: 8 ton-miles (1 ton over 8 miles)

There would be no transport cost on the raw material as manufacture would be at the raw material source.

Total transport cost at raw material sources: *38 ton-miles*

In this case the fuel source is the minimum transport-cost point. Only by locating the plant there could the manufacturer avoid the heavy costs involved in moving around those three tons of fuel that he needs for every ton of his product. The material index for this industry is 5, that is every ton of product requires five tons of localized materials (three of fuel and two of raw material). We should have known, then, without the ton-mile calculation that the industry would have a strong tendency to be materials-oriented. It is also a general rule that where a single gross localized material input exceeds the sum of all the others then the least-cost location will be the source of that input. A quick glance could therefore have told us that the fuel source was the best decision and that any deviation from it would incur costs which no "economic man" such as our manufacturer would be willing to bear. There was in this case no possibility of an intermediate location between the three extreme points.

An intermediate location is possible however where the ton-mile cost of any single input (or output) does not exceed all others. It is in such circumstances that the locational polygon is useful; in the previous example the solution could be achieved without such a device. In terms of a locational polygon, Weber

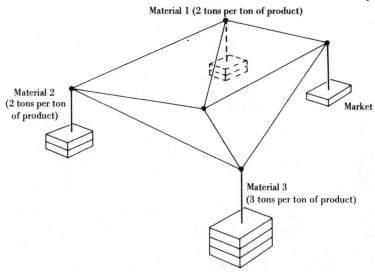

Material 1 (2 tons per ton of product)

Material 2
(2 tons per ton
of product)

Market

Material 3
(3 tons per ton of product)

Figure 4.3
A mechanical solution to the multi-point location problem.

described the locational problem in terms of a "struggle" between the corners of the polygon (each corner representing an input source or a consumption point). The outcome of the struggle, however, still depends on the material index. One method of determining the minimum transport-cost point is to use a mechanical model such as the *Varignon frame*, in which distances and weights in the locational polygon are simulated by appropriately scaled weights and pulleys connected by wires. The point where the connected wires come to rest at a point of balance is the optimum location. Figure 4.3 illustrates this diagrammatically. The respective weights represent the strength of the attractive force of each corner of the polygon.

Table 4.1
The influence of Weber's material types on the location of a manufacturing plant

Types of materials used	Material index	Location at		
		Material source[a]	Intermediate location	Market
Ubiquitous material only				+
1 pure material	1	=	=	=
1 pure material + 1 ubiquitous material	< 1			+
> 1 pure material	1			+
> 1 pure material + > 1 ubiquitous material	< 1			+
1 gross material	> 1	+		
1 gross material + ubiquitous materials	< 1			+
> 1 gross material	> 1	→		
Gross materials + pure materials	> 1	→		
Gross materials + pure materials + ubiquitous materials				→

[a]Symbols used:
+ indicates definite location
= indicates equally possible locations
→ indicates a tendency for production to be *attracted toward* a particular type of location.

Source: Based on A. Weber (1909), *Theory of the Location of Industries*, Chicago: University of Chicago Press, and F. E. I. Hamilton (1967), Models of Industrial Location, in R. J. Chorley and P. Haggett (eds.), *Models in Geography*, London: Methuen, p. 371.

Table 4.1 shows for various combinations of pure and gross localized and ubiquitous materials the particular locational tendencies that would arise. Again this provides a short-cut to judging the location which a given industry might choose without going through the arithmetic of the ton-mile calculation. The *definitive* locational types marked by + signs are interestingly biased toward the *market location*. Only two definite *material locations* occur: those where there is either a single gross material or where there is one gross material and a ubiquitous material. The reason for this is, of course, that a number of gross materials may neutralize the pulls of each other at the corners of a locational polygon leaving an intermediate location as the resolution of these forces. This will *tend toward* a material location but may not be sited directly at one. Weber has often been criticized for over-emphasizing the attractive force of raw materials in his model but the number of "pluses" in the market column shows how frequently a market location is a final solution for many combinations of raw materials.

There is little doubt that Weber's distinction between ubiquitous and localized materials and between pure localized materials and gross (weight-losing) localized materials has had a profound influence on the economic geographer's approach to industrial location problems. But how efficient in reality is the material index in predicting the orientation of manufacturing industry? The most comprehensive test of the index was undertaken by Smith (1955). Basing his analysis on 65 British industries using 1948 census data, Smith investigated the extent to which weight-losing materials are tied locationally to their raw materials.

In the case of primary industries, the initial processing stage of manufacture, the relationship between high weight-loss materials and location of production was strong. Thus, for example, sugar beet (MI = 8), manufactured dairy products (MI = 6) and pig iron manufacture (MI = 3 to 4) were all strongly materials-oriented. Table 4.2 summarizes Smith's findings for industries located entirely at the materials source, partly at the materials source, and at other locations. The real-life significance of Weber's claim that industries with a material index of greater than one tend to locate at material sources is validated. Out of all 22 industries sited at materials locations, not one had an index of less than one. Of those "partly at materials" nine out of twelve had a material index above one. For industries defined as "not located at materials" Smith's findings are, however, less clear but so also is the basis for the classification. The group of eight industries with a material index between 2 and 5 classed as "not located at materials" invites caution in applying Weber's simple principles to real-life situations.

Location	Material index				
	>5	2–5	1–2	<1	Total
At materials	2	4	16	—	22
Partly at materials	—	4	5	3	12
Not located at materials	—	8	12	11	31
Total	2	16	33	14	65

Source: Based on W. Smith (1955), The Location of Industry, *Transactions of the Institute of British Geographers* **21**, Table 1, p. 7.

Table 4.2
Observed relationship between Weber's material index and locations of manufacturing: 65 British industries, 1948.

As Wilfred Smith pointed out "the material index provides us with a tool of analysis but it is a blunt tool and is effective only at the very extremities of the classification" (Smith, 1955, p. 109).

One of the problems with the material index is that by standardizing inputs and outputs as a ratio it loses the power to distinguish the sheer size of the quantities of materials which some industries have to move. For those already heavily committed to materials in the sense that they have a high material index this is no problem. There are, however, many "middle range" industries whose relatively low material indices fail to indicate strongly enough how far they are committed to a materials location because of the scale of the raw material movements they need to undertake. Smith (1955) suggested combining an index of the *weight of materials per operative* with Weber's material index to make this clearer.

> Loss of weight has significant locational effects only when it is combined with large weight per operative, for variations in transport costs are substantial enough to affect location only if weights handled are large.
> *Smith (1955), p. 111*

He goes on to make the point that for some industries like engineering trades which produce large amounts of waste in processing, the material index itself is misleading and this in part explains the tendency shown in Table 4.2 for some industries with high material indices not to be located at material sites. Though some engineering trades have a high propensity to generate scrap in their operations the weight of material per operative in these industries is small. Using the two indices in combination it is easier to see why engineering industries in general are not tied to materials, despite the fact that some of them have high material indices.

Further evidence of the relevance of Weber's formulation to the location of certain industries is provided, for example, by Kennelly (1954), Craig (1957), and Lindberg (1953). One conclusion of Kennelly's classic study of the location of the Mexican steel industry was that the industry is located in accordance with Weber's transport-orientation principle and that, in this case, weight and distance are the principal factors of transport cost. Also, the Weberian distinction between ubiquitous and localized material was found to be valid. On the other hand, Kennelly found the material index to be inadequate because it *emphasized the relative weight of materials and product at the expense of their relative locations.* Similarly, Craig's investigation of location factors influencing the development of steel centers in the United States revealed that its basic transport orientation could be formulated in Weberian terms. Lindberg (1953) made a detailed study of the Swedish paper industry. He found that, although the industry is not, as commonly believed, oriented toward materials it is undoubtedly located so as to minimize the cost of transporting materials and product. (We shall look at two of these studies in detail later in this chapter.)

Thus Weber's work shows how the existence of localized materials will affect the location of manufacturing industry. In particular, he points out how the need by some industries for gross localized materials will draw them to resource sites. This distorts the logic of a central place location under the predictions of the simplified model for some, but by no means all, types of manufacturing industry. Weber also provides a simple, but still remarkably useful, predictive model for industrial location studies in general, although its lack of flexibility has been a major inhibiting factor in its application to more complex locational situations.

Isard's substitution framework

Walter Isard (1956) took Weber's basic theoretical logic and greatly enhanced its scope and flexibility by placing it in a new methodological context, that of *substitution* analysis. While this added little to the theoretical implications of the model it did make it a more powerful predictive tool, and a review of Isard's technique at this stage will greatly simplify later discussion.* The fundamental basis of Isard's approach can be illustrated by looking again at the simple two-point location problem shown in Figure 4.1. Let us assume that location can occur at any point along the straight line connecting the material source and the market, as would be the case if the material were pure (see Table 4.1). There are thus two variables in this locational situation: distance from the market and distance from the material source. This relationship can be plotted graphically, as in Figure 4.4, to yield a *transformation line*, which expresses all possible substitution relations for the two variables. The market and the material source are seven miles apart. Thus, the two axes have a length of seven units. At the extreme points a location at the market is seven miles from the raw material source and, of course, zero miles from the market. Conversely, a location at the material source is seven miles from the market and zero miles from the material source. On the transformation line which connects these two extreme points all the possible combinations of distance adding up to seven miles are shown. At point Y location is six miles from the material source and one from the market. At Z it is six miles from the

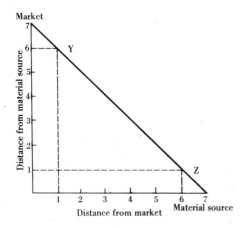

Figure 4.4
A transformation line for the two-point location problem. [*Source:* Reprinted from W. Isard (1956), *Location and Space Economy*, Figure 16, by permission of the M.I.T. Press, Cambridge, Massachusetts. Copyright © 1956 by the Massachusetts Institute of Technology.]

*We shall be making further use of substitution analysis in subsequent discussion of (i) the impact of transport rate structures on industrial location, p 180 (ii) the distortional effects of cheap labor sources on the minimum transport location, p 242 (iii) the substitution of factor inputs in production, pp 203–205 and (iv) the effects of scale on the choice of factor inputs and on plant location, pp 284–285.

Note

market and one from the material source. Each mile over which shipment must be made represents a necessary transport-cost input which the producer will have to bear. Location at Y, then, involves "six miles' worth" of transport input on materials and "one miles' worth" of transport input on the finished product. Of course the two-point problem, especially for a pure material, is a trivial one since we already know that location at any point along the straight line is equally costly and that the "seven-mile" transformation line for distance inputs covers all the possibilities. It does, however, help us to get the transformation principle established in simple terms before we go on to make it more complicated.

Suppose now that we add a second raw material to the producer's input requirements. There are now not just two but three sets of substitution relations to be taken into account. Take the case set out in Figure 4.5. Transformation lines for distance inputs can now take the following form:

Figure 4.5
Solution of the
three-point case using a
transformation line.
[*Source:* (a), (b),
Reprinted from W. Isard
(1956), *Location and
Space Economy*, Figures
17 and 18, by permission
of the M.I.T. Press,
Cambridge,
Massachusetts. Copyright
© 1956 by the
Massachusetts Institute of
Technology.]

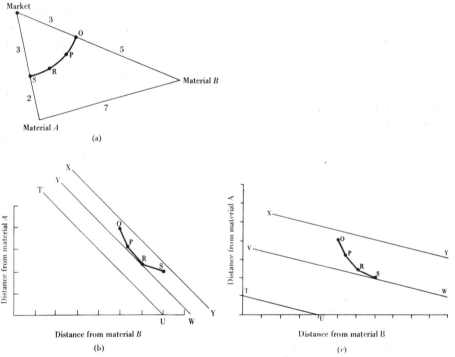

1. For any *fixed distance* from the market there will be a transformation line showing possible substitutions between the distance from material A and the distance from material B.
2. For any *fixed distance* from material A there will be a transformation line that shows substitutions of distance from material B against the distance from the market.
3. For any *fixed distance* from material B there will be a transformation line that shows substitutions of distance from material A against distance from the market.

These cover all the substitution possibilities. The reason for fixing one of the distance variables each time is simply because the graphical approaches used in generating transformation lines demand that the problem is stated in two-dimensional form. In effect we "creep up" on the solution to the problem by looking at *pairs of distance inputs* from two of the corners of the triangle while we give the third corner a controlled series of fixed-distance values. In a sense, then, we *search* the inside of the triangle by giving the fixed corner a series of arbitrary distance values at a radius of, say, one mile, two miles, and so forth, stopping at each stage to look at the transformation relationship between the two corners whose distances are free to vary.

The overall minimum cost point is found by identifying the point at which total mileages are at their lowest for each of the three individual sets of transformations. In effect, the minimum mileage point for each pair of transformations forms a *partial solution* and the partial solutions are used as "stepping stones" in finding the optimum (or minimum transport-cost) location. Figure 4.5a shows a transformation example for the first of the possible cases of substitution. Here distance from the market is fixed at an arbitrary three miles. If we assume, to make things simple, that three miles is known to be the "best" distance from the market we can follow the process through. Figure 4.5b shows the transformation line for the variables labeled distance from material A and distance from material B (with distance from the market fixed to the distance represented by the arc OS). In this example it is assumed for the sake of simplicity that location can take place at only one of four discrete points O, P, R, S along the arc (perhaps because these are the only points located on direct transportation routes between materials and market). The optimum location will be that which involves the minimum total cost of both material A and material B to some point three miles from the market. If we assume that material A and material B are either both pure materials or have equal weight-losing properties then there is no problem. The best location is simply that with the *least accumulated mileage*. On the graph it will be the point on the transformation line nearest the origin—R in the case shown in Figure 4.5b. The lines TU, VW and XY are known as *iso-outlay* lines* and they would help us find the point nearest the origin if it were not immediately obvious. In this particular case the iso-outlay lines simply connect the vertical and horizontal scales of the graph in a one-to-one ratio. One unit on the vertical axis joins one unit

---

*Iso-outlay Lines   Note

Iso-outlay lines show the possible alternative combinations of goods, resources (or, in our specific case, transport services) that can be obtained for a *given value of total expenditure*. The concept appears under a variety of alternative titles in economics. Price-ratio lines, budget lines and consumption-possibility lines all derive from the same idea; the difference between them depending on context, viewpoint or terminological choice.

To make things clearer, let us take a simple example. Suppose in spending the surplus money we have left at the end of the month we are presented with a straightforward binary (or two-way) choice. For the same amount, say, $60.00, of spending money our preferences are for either textbooks, which sell at a fixed $20.00 each, or long-playing records selling at $10.00 each. Our consumption possibilities within this budget are not difficult to determine.

We could buy three books, six L.P. records, or any finite combination of the two items (no half books or half records). For the "sixty-dollar" level of outlay (iso-outlay) we could draw up the following schedule of choices:

Consumption possibilities for a budget of $60.00

Books @ $20.00 each		L.P. Records @ $10.00 each		Total
Amount	Cost $	Amount	Cost $	outlay $
0	0	6	60	60
1	20	4	40	60
2	40	2	20	60
3	60	0	0	60

If we were to draw a simple graph of the available choices with the number of books on one axis and the number of records on the other, we would derive the *iso-outlay line* for $60.00. The slope of the line would reflect the *price-ratio* between the two types of good. In this case 2:1 the ratio of the price of books to the price of records. The reader is encouraged to draw the "books-records" iso-outlay line for himself and to experiment with other sets of binary (two-variable) choices.

on the horizontal axis, two joins two, and so on. This is consistent with the particular situation where the material coming from site A has *equivalent weight per ton of product* to that coming from site B.* Their *price-ratio* in terms of the costs of moving them is one-to-one. The lines drawn on the diagram are just a selection from an infinite number of lines rising upwards and rightwards in a one-to-one ratio. It is easy to visualize the process in terms of a parallel ruler being moved upwards and rightwards from the origin of the graph until it just touches the point marked by R.

In the specific case under consideration here let us remind ourselves that what we are trying to do in Weberian terms is to *minimize the number of ton-miles moved by a particular production unit*. So far in the case of substitution analysis we have said a good deal about miles but very little about tons. Only in the case where there are pure materials or where there is no weight-loss differential between materials can we get away with this. To avoid getting involved in dollars and cents, and in accordance with Weber's basic ideas, we have so far assumed that the *costs* which a producer bears are measured solely in ton-miles. Thus his *outlays on production* are ton-mileage amounts. Bearing this in mind let us return to the example of Figure 4.5 under slightly changed circumstances. Suppose the material that comes from A contributes four times as much weight to each unit of the product as that from B. For a given total outlay (measured in ton-miles) by the producer the material located at A would have a price-ratio four times that of the material located at B.

Let us begin by setting a budget on the amount our producer could afford to spend in ton-mile terms. Suppose he can afford the money equivalent of only four ton-miles. Figure 4.5c shows that he could have four full units of the material from B and no materials from A (the point U). Alternatively at

*Since ton for ton the materials are identical, the producer's costs (or outlays) vary only with the mileage he accumulates in moving materials and product. To all intents and purposes his outlays are measured in *units of miles* and the iso-outlay lines represent selected numbers of miles for this special case.

the other extreme he could have just one unit of material from A and none from B (the point T). He could also choose any combination which lies between these limits (the line TU). The iso-outlay lines for this situation are shown in Figure 4.5c. Their slopes now reflect the additional weight which must be given to material from A in the transport calculation. Our producer can afford to carry material A over fewer miles than material B if he is to stay inside his budget. The whole range of iso-outlay lines above and below four ton-miles now slopes parallel with the new iso-outlay line, TU. Going back to Figure 4.5a it can now be shown that the "best" location has shifted from R to S; that is, closer to the more expensive (in ton-mile terms) material source and slightly further away from the cheaper material source.

Smith's space-cost curve

Smith (1966) provides another technique that is used in subsequent chapters. Like Isard's substitution method, it can be used in relatively complex situations but it can also be introduced here in its most elementary form to demonstrate the impact of raw-material and finished-goods shipment costs on the location of industry.

The basis of Smith's method is the *isodapane* technique developed by Weber himself, primarily to examine the impact of a second factor, the cost of labor, on the locational pattern that he had derived purely by minimizing transport costs. We shall be taking up the case of labor costs in Chapter Six.

Weber's *isodapane* is a line drawn through all those points in space that have equal total transport costs from the point of view of a given production unit. It is best visualized as a *contour map*, except that in this case the contours join places with equal total transport costs instead of heights above sea-level. It can be interpreted in exactly the same way as a contour map with its troughs and basins of low transport costs, peaks or ridges of high ones, and plateaux or plains where there is little spatial variation. There are two stages involved in the construction of an isodapane surface:

1. Plot isotims (isovectures) around each separate supply or market point. An *isotim* is a line connecting points of equal transport costs on each material and on the finished product. It shows how the cost of transporting each individual component increases as distance from *its* minimum cost point increases. Thus isotims are drawn around each point in the locational situation (materials and market). Where the costs of transport are the same in all directions and cost increases away from each point are strictly proportional to distance, the isotims are an equal distance apart and take the form of concentric circles running out like ripples from each supply and market point. They form the construction lines used in the second stage of the operation. In Figure 4.6a only two-point sources are used, a materials site and a market, but depending on strength of eyesight and patience, a large number can be incorporated.

2. Sum the total transport costs for assembling the materials and shipping the product to market for a series of convenient points over the "search" area. These

Figure 4.6
Trànsport-cost surface (a)
and space-cost curve (b).

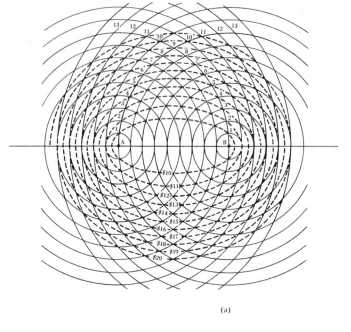

(a)

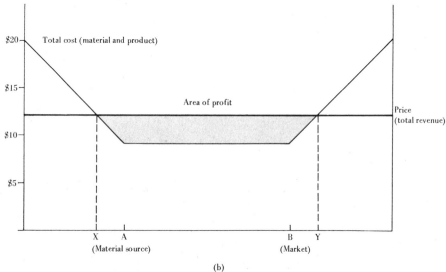

(b)

are likely to be the intersection points of a series of isotims. If the isotims
are set at one mile intervals and we are shipping only one ton of material
or product then the total ton-mile cost at each intersection becomes very simple.
The number of isotims or rings are counted from the material source. This
is the ton-mileage incurred in getting enough of the materials together to make
one unit (ton) of the product. The number of rings from the intersection to
the market then gives the ton-mileage which must be added to get one unit
(ton) of the product to market. For example in Figure 4.6a the intersection

of the $7 isotim around the material source and the $8 isotim around the market gives a total transport cost at that point of $15. The same total cost is clearly obtained at the intersection of the $9 and $6 isotims and so on, thus defining the position of the $15 isodapane. The process is continued for all isotim intersections until a total transport-cost surface is obtained.

In effect the sample points are like transport-cost "spot heights" and they are simply used as "markers" from which the contour surface of transport cost is built up.

If there were a unique point at the bottom of the cost surface "basin" this would obviously represent the minimum transport-cost point under the assumptions made. The case we have chosen for ease of explanation does not provide us with one, but under other assumptions of the weights to be moved, with non-uniform transport or with more sources, a point solution could result.

For Smith the isodapanes are interpreted more generally as "cost isopleths" or "cost contours"—lines of *equal total cost*, including costs other than transport. Only in the model as we have it at this stage are they synonymous with isodapanes, since we have constrained all cost factors other than those allowed by the Weberian example. From such cost isopleths Smith derives two important concepts.

The first is the *space-cost curve* (Figure 4.6b), which is simply a section drawn through the cost-contour map discussed above (Figure 4.6a). The lowest point of the curve, where one exists, is the least-cost location. In some cases, of course, like the one in our example, several locations on a "cost-plain" are equally likely. The steepness of the slopes on the surface give some notion of the sensitivity of the industry to locational or space-derived costs. Those with a high sensitivity to weight and distance would have steep slopes, those with a low one would be shallow in form.

Smith's second concept, derived from the *space-cost curve*, is that of *spatial margins to profitability*. The manufactured product will be sold at a price that, for simplicity, here, is assumed to be constant in space. At some point on the total-cost surface there will be a contour that coincides with this value. Everywhere above this level will have costs which exceed this delivered price. This contour represents the spatial margin to profitability under the conditions of the model (X, Y in Figure 4.6b). Inside the margin, profits will be made, outside it, losses. Weber's least-cost point now becomes, more realistically, only one point within a varying zone where profits could be made at a given price. Entrepreneurs could miss the least-cost point slightly but still survive. Other factors could also pull them to new sites within the margin. Something of the imprecision of real-world locational choice is introduced into the model by this notion. Although Smith does not add anything fundamentally new to basic Weberian theory, his method, like Isard's substitution framework, adds analytical power to the theory, as subsequent sections will demonstrate.

Several writers expanded and developed various aspects of Weber's work, in particular Palander (1935) and Hoover (1937). More recently, Kennelly (1954) and Lindberg (1953) applied the basic concepts discussed above to examine real-world locational problems and it is to their work that we now turn to give some empirical substance to what has, up to now, been a purely theoretical concept.

Weber's theory and reality: two case studies

The Mexican steel industry

Kennelly (1954) presented one of the most comprehensive studies in the literature of economic geography in which the simplified models of location theory are put to the test of practicality. The brief synopsis which follows cannot do him justice, and we shall concern ourselves here only with that part of his work which bears in particular on Weberian theory.

Kennelly set himself two main tasks of relevance to us here. First, he set out to examine actual transport costs on raw materials and finished products for two existing steel plants in Mexico—the Fundidora plant at Monterrey and the Altos Hornos plant at Monclova. Second, by using data from the existing plants as a guide, he applied a variety of location theories including that of Weber to the determination of the minimum transport location for steel manufacture in Mexico.

We are less concerned here with the comparative cost analysis for the two plants than with the determination of the minimum transport point. We do, however, need to know something about the technical and spatial requirements of the Mexican steel industry in the early fifties as represented by the two plants. Table 4.3 summarizes the details. For the shipment of basic input materials each plant, as the table shows, gains in some respects and loses in others. Both have heavy inputs of iron ore, most of which is derived from a single source at Durango. In the case of fuel, however, there are differences. Fundidora

Table 4.3
Sources of materials, amount from each source and transportation cost on materials and finished product for Fundidora and Altos Hornos, 1950.

Raw Material Inputs	% total weight of inputs	Fundidora Monterrey weight (kgs)	Pesos	% total weight of inputs	Altos Hornos Monclova weight (kgs)	Pesos
Iron Ore	51.0	1940	24.15	42.2	1691	24.38
Coke	36.8	1400	31.57	26.4	1059	8.63
Oil	6.9	263	9.42	23.3	931	36.17
Scrap	5.3	200	5.65	8.1	323	10.09
			70.79			79.27
Shipment to Markets	% total weight shipped					
Mexico City	50.0	500	39.14	80.0	800	64.92
Monterrey	50.0	500	0.0	20.0	200	4.64
			39.14			69.56
Total Shipment Costs			109.93			148.83

Source: based on Kennelly (1954), Table XII.

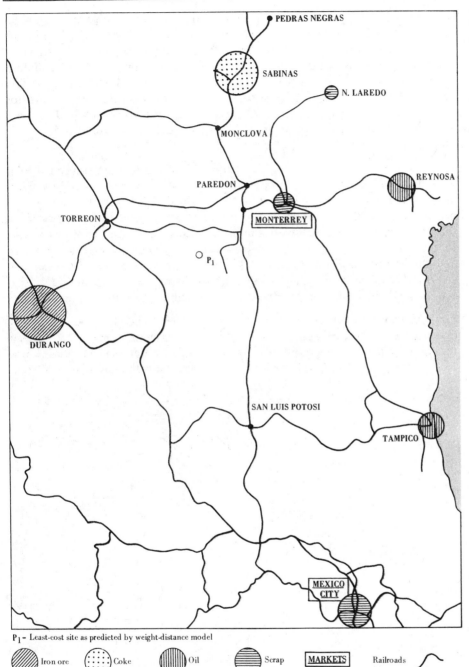

Figure 4.7
Material supply-points and markets for the Mexican steel industry, c. 1954. [*Source:* R. A. Kennelly (1954), Location of the Mexican Steel Industry, *Revista Geografica,* Tomo XV, No. 41, Map 4.]

P_1 - Least-cost site as predicted by weight-distance model

Iron ore   Coke   Oil   Scrap   MARKETS   Railroads

is connected to an industrial gas pipe-line and thus saves substantially on oil inputs. On the other hand, Altos Hornos is close to a coke supply and the relative savings almost even out. The only real difference in shipment costs between them lies in the cost of moving the product to market. For Fundidora shipments are divided equally between Mexico City and Monterrey. Thus fifty percent of the product *goes at virtually no cost to a local market*. At Altos Hornos the split is 80 percent to Mexico City and 20 percent to Monterrey. The savings for finished product shipment are thus much smaller for Altos Hornos.

In attempting to apply theory to the estimation of a minimum transport point a number of assumptions need to be made. Figure 4.7 shows the spatial configuration of the resources and market complex. Since gas is only really available near the U.S. border its influence is dropped from the model, and oil, assumed to be equally available at Reynosa and Tampico, is made the only *fuel source*. In the case of *iron ore* there is assumed to be a single source at Durango and this is not far from the truth. The real supply conditions for *coke* and *scrap* are retained as are the locations and relative sizes of *markets*. Kennelly now has the basic parameters needed for a simple locational-weight model.

Looking simply at weight and distance as in the Weberian model Kennelly first applies the vector-weights method of the Varignon frame. This gives a resultant location at the point P_1 roughly half-way between Monterrey and Durango (Figure 4.8a). Using the isodapane technique with assumptions of equal

Figure 4.8
(a) An adaptation of Varignon's Frame and its application to Mexican steel manufacture. (b) Isodapanes based on weight and distance (in ton-kilometers): Mexican steel industry c. 1954. [*Source:* R. A. Kennelly (1954), Location of the Mexican Steel Industry, *Revista Geografica,* Tomo XV, No. 41, Figures 7 and 10.]

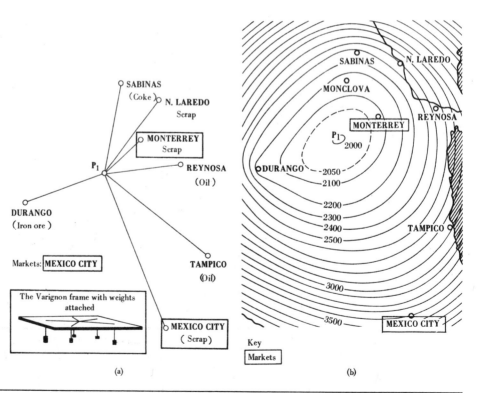

transport cost, he also constructs a space-cost surface (Figure 4.8b). The lowest point on the cost surface is also, of course, at P_1. Monterrey, the site of the Fundidora plant, is only 100 ton-kilometers above the least-cost location selected on the basis of the extensive simplifying assumptions in the isodapane method. With further modifications such as measuring distance by network routes instead of straight lines or by using realistic freight-rates the least-cost location moves still nearer to Monterrey. The remarkable feature of the analysis is not, however, that modifications will produce the "right" result. It lies much more in the fact that for a complex industry as it existed some two decades ago the use of a crude weight-distance model predicted a location with relative costs only five percent different from those at the existing "best" site.

The Swedish paper industry

Lindberg (1953) provides us with another valuable case study illustrating in particular the use of isoline techniques for space-cost surfaces. Again he has much more to say than can be reported here, and the reader is strongly encouraged to consult the original work. Lindberg examines the historical evolution of the paper industry over the period since 1830. During that time the nature and therefore the locational attributes of both raw materials and markets for paper changed considerably.

Figure 4.9
Isodapanes and the analysis of locational changes in the Swedish paper industry 1839–1939. (a) Handmill period. (b) Ground-wood period. (c) Chemical pulp period. [*Source:* O. Lindberg (1954), An Economic-Geographical Study of the Localization of the Swedish Paper Industry, *Geografiska Annaler,* **35** 1, Figures 5, 6 and 7.]

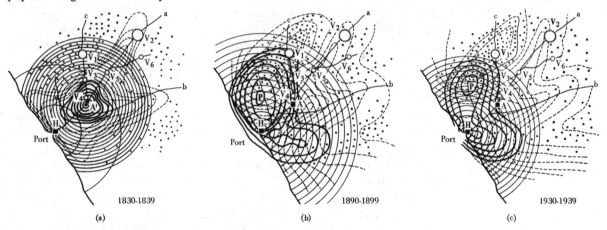

1830-1839   1890-1899   1930-1939

(a)   (b)   (c)

Figure 4.9a shows the isodapane-based space-cost surface during the *handmill period*. The isotims or, as Lindberg calls them, *isovectures* connect points with equal total transport costs for a certain commodity to a certain place. They are based on more realistic cost estimates than the simple, concentric, equidistant rings of our earlier example. Their closeness, for instance, represents the steepness with which shipment costs rise with distance. This is more for some commodities and over certain types of route than for others. Take the tight network of concentric circles around the point A in Figure 4.9a. These represent movement costs on the *finished product*. Their close spacing implies that movement of finished paper over any distance acquires a heavy space-cost penalty. The second, more elongated set of isovectures, which spreads out at the extremities to follow the rivers like normal topographic contours, is that for raw materials. At this time raw material inputs for paper-making consisted chiefly of *straw* and *rags*. Their primary source was the centers of dense population, places like A and H on Figure 4.9a. Once again the smallest movement in distance away from these centers carried a heavy cost penalty. Only where river transport made movement easier was it possible to ship such materials over any reasonable distance. This explains why the materials set of isovectures begins to follow the rivers as distance from the center A increases.

The summation of the two sets of isovectures for raw material assembly and the shipment of the final product produces the *isodapane* surface (the heavy lines on Figure 4.9a). On balance in the period 1830–1839, marketing considerations were dominant over raw material assembly in the transport-cost structure of the Swedish paper industry. As a result around the market center at A the isodapanes approximate the concentric circles that might have been derived from the marketing principle of the central place model as we described it in Chapter Two. The relative ubiquity of straw and rags close to the market makes the isodapane surface there insensitive to their differential pull. Further away from A, however, where materials are potentially scarce and must be moved, at high cost, to production sites, the shape of the isodapane surface begins to reflect the relative benefits of riverside locations for cheap movement of materials.

Even small handmills for making paper, however, need *power* and, in the early years of the nineteenth century, power meant a waterfall site. Despite the fact that the best site in relation to transport costs is at A (the lowest point on the isodapane surface) the absence of a waterfall at that point is critical. In effect the best *practical location* at which to site the paper mill is at the *nearest waterfall* to A. This is shown in Figure 4.9a as the point V4.

Turning to the *ground-wood period* from 1890–1899, Lindberg shows how conditions have changed. Figure 4.9b shows the new situation. Now the raw material is wood and as a "harvesting" activity the pattern of isovectures includes considerations of the density of forest cover. Where there is dense unbroken forest, wood is in effect ubiquitous. Near the settled areas, however, and where the forest is sparse, the isovectures close up to register the situation. The port at H has now replaced A both as the effective market site for the export trade and as a source of coal for power. Water power, a "free" gift of nature, still has crucial importance as a power source and at this stage its energy still cannot be transmitted.

At this time the isodapane surface shows P, at the center of rich forest resources but near the port at H, as the "best" location. But once again, the demands of the least mobile input veto this choice and production takes place at the nearest waterfall big enough to support the scale of production: V1.

Finally, in the modern era represented by what Lindberg calls the *chemical pulp period* (Figure 4.9c) there has been another key change. This owes its origin to a technological innovation. Now, while the locational conditions regarding markets and wood materials have hardly changed, water power can be *transmitted as electricity*. Although earlier developments have produced mills at the larger waterfalls, new plants are *free to move*, the least-cost sites being determined by other inputs.

Although the configuration of isovectures is much the same as in Figure 4.9b the large waterfalls at V1 and V2 have now become sites for power stations. For the first time the best transport location P is now also the best practical site.

From this conceptual model based on the known series of technological developments in the industry Lindberg goes on to look at actual spatial changes in the industry over time. In summary, he found a good correspondence between model and reality. The early handmill period saw an industry dispersed more in accordance with demand than with weight-distance considerations. The chemical pulp-wood period showed a marked concentration of activity at water sites favorably located to timber resources. The modern period shows the impact of "transport-economy" more fully, since electric power has removed the locational constraints of water power sites.

Taking his theory into practicality, Lindberg constructed an aggregate isodapane map for transport costs on paper-making. This is shown in Figure 4.10. He concludes his analysis as follows:

> Thus for Sweden, the generally accepted idea that the paper industry is mainly dependent on its raw material does not apply ... since the paper industry is a "harvesting" industry Weber's ideas are not entirely applicable to it. The raw material—wood—is ubiquitous to such a great extent that its localizing effect is small despite its ... material index (3 tons of wood to one ton of paper).
> *Lindberg (1954), p. 125*

What Lindberg's study provides in particular is an example of the power of the isoline or contour technique for space-cost surfaces. It is far more flexible in application and interpretation than teaching examples tend to suggest. His use of the model to explore a real situation and raise questions for the investigator in the process indicates that models do not have to "fit" to be useful. The exercise of investigating their goodness or lack of fit itself justifies the modeling process even where the model itself may prove weak.

Localized industrial raw materials and the space economy: summary and historical perspective

Let us now recapitulate and turn our attention to the probable impact of industry's need for localized resources on the form of the space economy as we have developed it thus far. Allowing that the primary resource base of the economic system will be composed of various industrial raw materials unevenly distributed over its geographical environment, we can now see how, for some elements of manufacturing, there will be a strong pull to locations away from existing central places. The effectiveness of these pulls in determining the final location will depend upon their total weight in the cost structure of the industry

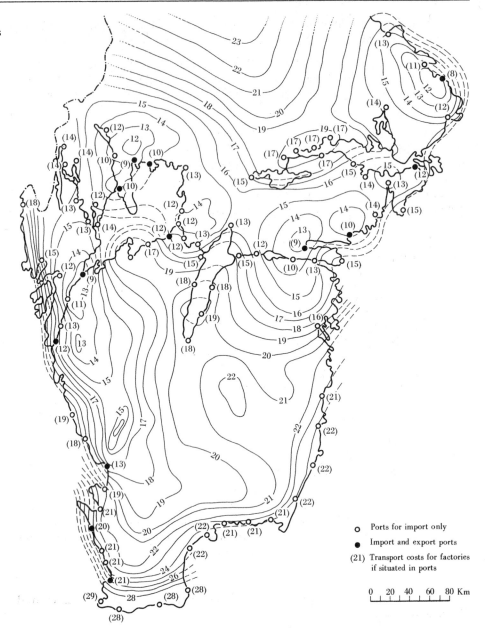

Figure 4.10
Transport cost isodapanes for assumed paper manufacturing centers in Sweden. [*Source:* O. Lindberg (1954), An Economic-Geographical Study of the Localization of the Swedish Paper Industry, *Geografiska Annaler,* **35**, 1, Figure 20.]

o Ports for import only

● Import and export ports

(21) Transport costs for factories if situated in ports

0 20 40 60 80 Km

in question. Industries with a large proportion of their total costs incurred in acquiring and processing gross, localized raw materials will be powerfully drawn to resource sites. On the other hand, those processing semi-finished goods or with a relatively low proportion of gross materials in their total cost structure will behave more like the central service functions of the Lösch-Christaller model. They will attempt to maximize their access to a market while minimizing distribution costs. Both the materials-oriented and market-oriented industries comply with the basic requirement of all economic activities to locate where the maximum possible number of customers can be served at the lowest possible cost. The spatial heterogeneity of the resource base now means that in pursuing this end (of maximizing profits) the solution to the locational problem varies from industry to industry depending upon the particular input and market requirements.

There are, therefore, important locational differences between producers of manufactured goods and suppliers of services. Manufacturers assemble a variety of predominantly localized inputs, process them, and distribute them to primarily punctiform markets (i.e., wholesalers and retailers in central places). They must therefore "look both ways" to procurement costs and distribution costs. A whole spectrum of industry types spans the range from those in which resources dominate location to those dominated by considerations of access to markets. Services, on the other hand, where they do require non-labor inputs, employ essentially pure materials (e.g., the goods handled by wholesalers and retailers). For them the localization of the source has little impact. They perform their specific service function and market the result. This goes to sources of demand that range widely from highly localized seats of government through the entire hierarchy of central places to the dispersed domestic consumer. Here the primary locational concern is access to the market. The spectrum of service industry types covers the range from those relatively loosely tied to a specific market to those totally so. In general, however, the choice of location begins and ends in some central place within the overall hierarchy.

The locational outlook of manufacturing and services is thus different (although the difference is primarily one of emphasis). This is important when it comes to reviewing the nature of the space economy with localized manufacturing added to it. As we have seen, many manufacturing industries with a high degree of market orientation would offer little disruption to the central place-dominated space economy. They would seek to minimize the distance to at least one punctiform market by locating there. Those industries processing inputs with high material indices would be different. They would find locations at raw material sites and to perform their operations would attract labor, and so population. This would distort the regular central place lattice (Figure 4.11). A manufacturing town of this kind would itself provide a market for central goods and services, drawing to it those tertiary services, primarily of low order, that could gain a profit by supplying its needs.

For example, the very high volume of coal needed for most heavy industrial processes in the nineteenth and early twentieth centuries ensured that many such industries located on the coalfields. The result was the generation of new urban centers based on resource utilization. Such urban areas invariably acquired lower order services to provide for their local populations, but their service status was often a good deal lower than their population size would suggest.

Figure 4.11 is a diagrammatic representation of the distortion of the uniform pattern of urban centers by this kind of resource localization. Towns A_1 and B_1 are examples of towns based on direct utilization of a high weight-losing

Figure 4.11
Distortion of the spatial
pattern of urban centers
due to resource
localization.

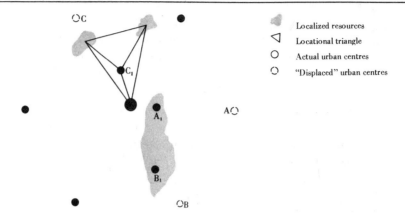

material. The location of the resource precludes the development of urban centers A and B at their "expected" locations in the corners of the hexagon. C_1 is an example of a town based on an industry whose minimum transport-cost point is intermediate between materials and market. The consequence of resource localization, therefore, is to produce specialized industrial centers in the settlement pattern. These tend to be "out of step" with the spatial uniformity of central places in the Lösch-Christaller model.

In a real world, however, the nature of demand and the technology of production is constantly changing. The nature of the resource base and its distortional impact on settlement and population distribution also changes. Resources are exploited for a period and then are either worked out physically or become too costly to win. Alternatively, a shift of demand may lead to the abandonment of a previously exploited raw material. A new technique may significantly change its material index, weakening the localizing pull of the resource on the other factors needed for production. The resource complex available to any economic system changes constantly in tune with the evolution of the system itself (Firey, 1960). As a result the space economy at any given point in time carries within it structures derived from a previous stage in its functional evolution. Sometimes these structures carry sufficient momentum from their early growth to exert a long-standing impact on the future development of the space economy. Take, for example, the coalfield areas of Pennsylvania or the Black Country of Great Britain. Long after the basic resources on which they were founded have passed the peak of production, their growth and development continues. Their impact on the space economy remains. Other raw material sites fail to achieve the necessary momentum and are short-lived. They distort the regularity of the space economy only in an ephemeral way, as in the case of the abandoned mining towns of Arizona and New Mexico.

Some of the most powerful resource-oriented "distortions" of the space economy have been generated by the evolution of the iron and steel and the fuel industries, both of which have experienced volatile changes in locational orientation since the beginning of the nineteenth century. In the case of iron and steel the impact of shifts to new ore resources and in particular of changing technology has been widely studied.

Warren (1973) in his study of the *American Steel Industry 1850–1970* provides what is for our purposes a valuable model framework set against the background of actual events in the United States. This is hardly the place, however, to attempt a comprehensive review of the growth and spatial development of this key industry. Our present needs are satisfied if we simply take that part of his work which illustrates the impact which localized raw materials exert on a central place-type economy. To do so we follow developments in the iron industry up to 1859, to the "break point" represented by the arrival of the railways and the new technology of steel.

Happily, in view of what we are trying to achieve here, Warren begins by pointing out that

> a time honored simplification in locational analysis is to start with a uniform plain on which patterns of economic activity gradually evolve. For the American iron industry this is perhaps as good a starting point as any.
> *Warren (1973), p. 2*

Iron manufacture develops initially out of the needs of the farms and central places. But, since there are both minimum scales at which efficient manufacture can take place (a point which we take up later in Chapter Seven), and also localized raw materials, *iron manufacture will tend to be less widely distributed* than basic central goods manufacture like baking or brewing. New specialist locations will grow up closely related to mineral working or manufacture will gravitate to the intermediate or larger-sized centers in the hierarchy.

In real terms this period is shown in Figure 4.12 which shows the spatial extent of U.S. iron-making as it existed before 1859. The market concentration is shown by the production points in the hinterland of Philadelphia. The emphasis on high-grade ore sites is represented by the blast furnaces of southwestern New England. But, in general, *the picture is a scattered one* reflecting the pattern of demand and the relative ubiquity of input needs under prevailing technology. Since fuel at this stage was chiefly provided by wood charcoal, the extent of the abandonment of blast furnaces shown should hardly be surprising. As a "harvesting" activity (recall Lindberg's Swedish paper example) growing settlement and rising demand "pushes" the effective resource sites further away from the market. In this process transport costs on raw material inputs increase and spatial thresholds are reached. Beyond these, transport costs on materials discourage production imposing strict technical limits on the scale and permanency of the blast furnace.

Warren sees the next stage as follows:

> Rising wood fuel costs and the opportunity of increased production to serve bigger market areas may cause a transfer to mineral fuel but at this point the vagaries of mineral distribution ... become even more significant. Depth, water conditions, richness and accessibility of coal and iron

Figure 4.12
The United States
charcoal iron industry
before 1859. [*Source:* K.
Warren (1973), *The
American Steel Industry,*
Figure 1. Reprinted by
permission of The
Clarendon Press, Oxford.]

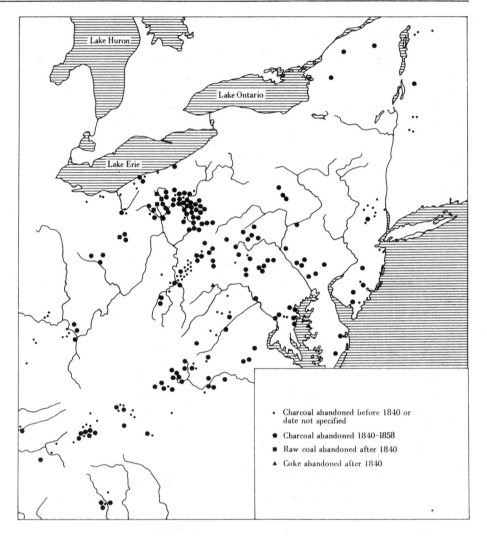

ore become factors which will *favor one old established center and penalize
another.* [*present authors' italics*]
Warren (1973), p. 2

Figure 4.13 shows how this *selection* process had come into operation by 1859.
The dispersed pattern has now "crystallized". The canals and rivers in particular
drew iron-making to their banks. Where this asset combined with the availability of key fuels like anthracite and local sources of iron ore as it did in
the Lehigh, Schuylkill and Susquahanna rivers, there was a particularly powerful
basis for industrial growth. Similarly in the west of Pennsylvania along the
Ohio river system it was the availability of iron ore, charcoal, coal and, critically,
coke that formed the basis for the emergent industrial complex. Despite their
inaccessibility, the ore sources close to the New York-Massachusetts border
also formed the basis for a significant cluster.

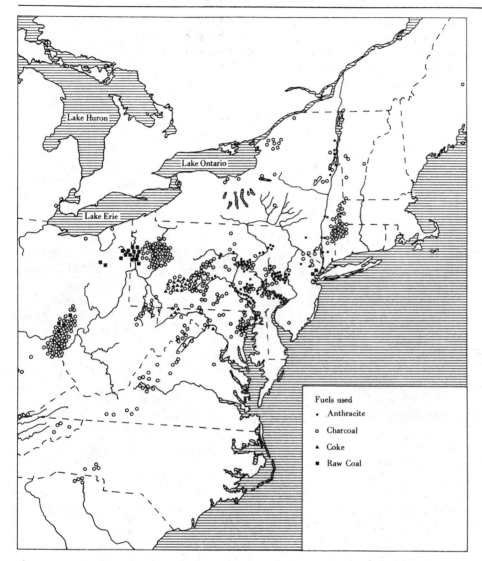

Figure 4.13
The United States iron industry in 1859: blast furnaces and the clustering of production sites. [*Source:* K. Warren (1973), *The American Steel Industry*, Figure 2. Reprinted by permission of The Clarendon Press, Oxford.]

The "distortional" influences of localized raw materials at this stage are thus set out as *selecting certain existing sites for growth*. Part of this selection process also revolves around the characteristics of local markets. Favored sites on the sea coast, accessible to cheap raw material and fuel supplies, become specialized in providing iron and steel for shipbuilding. Later they perhaps diversify into other activities. River-crossing points and victualling places for settlers, especially those with easy water access to coal, coke and iron ore, also grow up as iron-manufacturing centers. These specialize perhaps initially in the production of nails, roofing or fencing. Water access is again the broad key to locational choice since only by this means of transport is the assembly of dispersed raw materials possible in any reasonable quantity.

In this way then a limited phase in the evolving economic geography of the United States provides of itself a model for the impact which localized resources produces on a space economy. A largely dispersed central place-type economy drawing its resources from ubiquitous materials existed at the outset. Once the scale of demand and the demands of technology called localized resources into use, there came a process of crystallization. Selected places became the sites of specialized clusters. For the iron industry in particular it was the transport connotations of the particular resources-markets complex which favored some locations over others. After 1859 the arrival of the railways and the new technology of steel manufacture shifted the configuration of resource and market needs. It also changed the effective friction of space. The theoretical implications of this process take us beyond the impact of localized resources *per se* and we will leave discussion of them to later chapters.

In the particular case of the power industries the trend over time has been for a more progressive substitution of more efficient and more mobile energy sources. In the pre-steam phase factory production was highly localized at water and wind power sites. In effect, with no opportunity for effective transmission of generated power, those industries with substantial energy needs were tied immovably to rivers, waterfalls, the edges of escarpments and so forth. Lindberg's Swedish paper example showed how restrictive such locations were in the days before the arrival of the steam engine.

Steam power released energy-using activities from the *total restriction* of the previous era but itself imposed new localizing constraints. As a gross localized material in an era of pack horse, coastal and navigable river transport, the movement threshold of coal was highly limited. Power-hungry industries moved to coalfield sites. At this stage then a largely dispersed pattern of industrial activity based on wood fuels and charcoal began to cluster on the coalfields. In the birthplace of the new industrial technology the historian C. R. Fay described it as follows: "Depicted geographically the industrialization of Britain is a laying of population and enterprise upon the areas which had coal underneath" (Fay, 1950, p. 260). With the coming of canals another shedding of spatial restrictions occurred. Coal could be moved along avenues not determined by the whim of nature but by the conscious objectives of man. Again Fay's summary comment puts the situation in a nutshell: "The advent of canals endowed pit coal with the ubiquity of the forest waste—at a price. The heavy price of transport from the pit head to the place of use" (Fay, 1950, p. 260).

In Weberian terms, however, ubiquity *at a price* is no ubiquity at all. There was certainly more freedom in location. But, in general, since iron ore moved to coal and the metal-using industries found materials, energy sources and demand in the same places, the coalfield clusters simply grew. The resolution of the materials-markets problem at this stage required no lengthy computation. As every elementary textbook points out (making it needless to spell out the details here) early industrialization grew in localized clusters on the coalfields. Once again there was both a *selection* process and the *crystallization* of growth around locations which to the present day have lost little of their geographical importance.

With further passage of time came the railways to offer more freedom to move coal but resulting in still greater concentration on coalfields. Gas, oil and electric power subsequently almost obliterated the locational "pull" of coal resources for all but a few activities. That this failed significantly to "shift" the spatial basis of industrial power was a product of more complex causes which it is the purpose of later chapters to review.

On the basis of the previous summary discussion we can demonstrate the effectiveness of Smith's *space-cost curve* as an illustrative device. What we shall show is the locational impact of the substitution of a ubiquitous energy source (electric power) for a highly localized one (coal). Figure 4.14 shows the evolutionary situation.

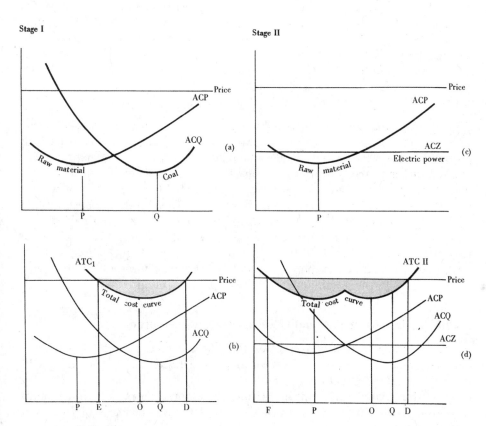

Figure 4.14
Locational impact of supplementing a highly localized fuel with a ubiquitous one. [*Source:* based on D. M. Smith (1966), A Theoretical Framework for Geographical Studies of Industrial Location, *Economic Geography,* **42,** Figure 12. Reproduced by permission of the author and editor.]

In the first technological era which we have called Stage I the industry in question uses a single raw material with coal as an energy input (Figure 4.14a). The source of the material is at the location shown by P and the space-cost curve derived from a section through its space-cost surface is the curve ACP. The source of coal is at Q and the space-cost curve rises steeply away from this point. Coal has the stronger localizing pull.

When total costs for both inputs are added together (Figure 4.14b) the overall cost curve ATC_1 "favors" coal but generates an intermediate low point at the place O. For the total situation the spatial margins to profitability (where costs just equal price) are at E and D. There is thus a relatively limited portion of space over which profitable operation is possible.

Moving to the new era of fuel technology (Stage II) electric power becomes available. It is as near to any (reasonable scale) producer as the nearest plug socket and has a flat space-cost curve (ACZ) (Figure 4.14c). The space-cost surface for the material is retained as before (ACP). The new space-cost curve for fuel, then, offers two possibilities (Figure 4.14d). Coal can still be used (ACQ) or electricity can be adopted (ACZ). For any producer in the system the overall space-cost curve now looks different (ATC_{II}). The new spatial margin to profitability expands to cover the area between F and D. Coal retains its pull in the area around Q but electricity has opened up a new area over which profits are possible. Of course this has its most cost-effective impact around the source of the material at P. It is not now necessary to move fuel and since production savings are made by not having to move the material, a new dip in the total cost surface appears around P. On balance the new combination of electric power at the resource site is marginally cheaper and P becomes the overall least-cost location replacing O which had this status in Stage I.

Times change and so does fuel technology. What we have shown is how this may alter the resource complex available to industry and how this in its turn produces a basis for spatial change (though it does not make it happen). We referred earlier to the "distortional" impact of localized materials on the central place-type space economy. Some locations probably from the old farming-central place network are favored over others and a clustering of industry-based settlement takes place. This pattern in its turn becomes the "normal" one of an industrial society and other forces which we shall examine later then come into play to add further distortions. The previous phase is not entirely obliterated, however, and at any point in time the economic furniture of the space economy reflects the accumulated results of previous events.

Spatial variations in the quality of agricultural resources

In the preceding section we suggested that the localized pattern of particular material resources "distorts" the central place-derived pattern of settlement. Now we turn our attention to another "distortion". This time it is the way in which the spatial variation of agricultural resources alters a farming space economy developed (as ours was in Chapter Two) on the basis of *locational* rent alone.*

By definition, agriculture is concerned with the utilization and where possible the improvement of "the natural genetic and growth processes of plant and animal life, to the end that these processes will yield the vegetable and animal

Note   *Seeing the real-world variety in the pattern of world resources as a distortion is, of course, a function of nothing more substantial than the particular way we have chosen to structure our analysis, i.e. beginning with a study of the impact of the distance variable.

products needed and wanted by man." (Zimmerman, 1951, p. 148). Quite clearly, therefore, the quality of land (here "land" is taken to include all its physical attributes, including climate) is of fundamental importance. In particular, the complex interaction of three basic elements—climate, soil, and topography— plays a large part in influencing the spatial pattern of agricultural production.

Crops and livestock have particular fundamental physical requirements, especially certain levels of temperature, moisture, and nutrient supply. Not only is the provision of these uneven in space but also the actual requirements differ from one crop or livestock type to another. Each has its optimum requirements. There is, too, a considerable range around the optimum within which growth is possible, for most crops have a degree of tolerance of sub-optimal conditions. Nevertheless this tolerance has its maximum and minimum limits and it is this that helps, first, to delimit the absolute limits of crop and livestock production and, second, to influence the proportions in which the various crops are grown.

We can set this situation graphically within the framework suggested by McCarty and Lindberg (1966). Two sets of effective limits on agriculture are defined. The first of these are *physical* limits. They are set at the points where for a given crop or husbandry activity production becomes physically impossible. The second set of limits are limits to *profitability*. These are set by economic considerations but physical conditions exert a powerful impact in their determination. We know something of the nature of economic limitations already since we have already met them in the simplified model. We will return to them in due course but first let us look at physical limits and their impact on the spatial pattern of agriculture.

Figure 4.15 illustrates the physical "optima and limits schema" set out by McCarty and Lindberg. Two key variables are employed: temperature and moisture. Over a particular area (in the center of the graph) there is an optimum combination of both inputs for a particular crop. Outwards from this, however, the restrictions which physical limits of the two variables impose make conditions less and less favorable. Ultimately under extreme conditions physical limits are reached which make production impossible. Of course, it is always possible, even within the context of physical limits, to provide artificial growing conditions. Technically it would be possible to grow strawberries at the South Pole

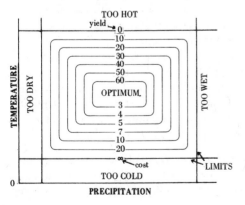

Figure 4.15
An optima and limits schema for the impact of physical factors on agricultural production. [*Source:* H. H. McCarty and J. Lindberg, *A Preface to Economic Geography*, © 1966, Figure 3.3. Reprinted by permission of Prentice-Hall, Inc., Englewood Cliffs, New Jersey, U.S.A.]

given sufficient market incentive. Costs, however, rise with a degree of steepness that depends upon the particular product as the optima is left behind. At the margins of the square figure in Figure 4.15 they rise to infinity, meaning a real technological barrier exists. In effect, the optima provide the farmer free of charge with the maximum benefits which nature can provide in terms of temperature and moisture. To move away from the optimum imposes costs and the use of other scarce resources.

For all practical purposes the economic production of agricultural commodities is spatially restricted. Large areas of the earth's surface are useless agriculturally. Under *prevailing technological conditions* they do not provide the critical physical requirements of crops and livestock. However, these outer limits are by no means fixed. Changes in agricultural technology—the development of special- and general-purpose fertilizers, the innovation of more suitable crop varieties such as hybrid corn, and the introduction of types of livestock suited to particular environmental conditions such as drought-resistant breeds of cattle—may have the effect of extending the margin of agricultural production.

Outer limits to agricultural production are controlled very largely by climatic conditions. There appears to be general acceptance that, on average, plant growth ceases below a daily mean temperature of 41–43°F. This is the base, or threshold temperature, at which growth begins to take place. This threshold value varies somewhat from one crop type to another. For satisfactory growth to occur there must also be a sufficiently lengthy period during which temperatures exceed the threshold and the longer this period the greater the growth, other things being equal. This fundamental temperature requirement is either completely or partially unfulfilled over very large areas in the high latitudes and in areas of great elevation. Apart from the polar regions themselves, more than half the area of Canada and Siberia are temperature deficient and thus unsuitable for agricultural production on any significant scale.

Similarly, extensive areas are deficient in moisture and agriculture is precluded except in a most rudimentary form. Moisture deficiency is a product not only of shortage of precipitation but also of the relationship between evaporation and precipitation. The lack of sufficient moisture to ensure growth has been estimated to preclude or severely restrict crop production in no less than one-third of the United States and Asia, one-half of Africa, and two-thirds of Australia. It is important to realize that both extremes of temperature limit the amount of available moisture. On the one hand, consistently high temperatures encourage rapid evaporation; on the other, sub-zero conditions convert water into an inaccessible form. At the other end of the precipitation scale excessive moisture also imposes limits on agricultural production. Very high and prolonged rainfall leads to the waterlogging of soil and the virtual asphyxiation of plants. Under certain topographic conditions, the vital plant nutrients are leached or washed out of the soil, rendering it impoverished and infertile.

The extreme effect of the climatic forces, then, is to preclude, or very greatly restrict, agricultural production from large areas of the world. Within the feasible limits, of course, physical conditions help to modify land-use patterns. This is partly because, as we have pointed out, certain combinations of physical conditions are more suitable for some crops than others. In this respect soil quality is a particularly important differentiating factor. The varying demands of crops for soil-based nutrients means that some soils favor certain types of crop and produce higher yields. Thus, in the southern United States, the higher cotton yields are generally associated with high-nutrient black soils, while the soils of the Blue Grass Basin of Kentucky have produced yields of tobacco 75 percent greater than those obtained from adjacent but less suitable soils. Local topographic conditions can also modify land-use patterns. Apart from the altitudinal influence on temperature, precipitation, and so on, the slope of the land surface may be significant, especially in the case of modern, large-scale, highly mechanized farming operations. Hidore (1963) tested the hypothesis that an association exists between the spatial distribution of cash-grain farms in the Midwest and the distribution of flat land. (Hidore defines "flat land" as that having a slope of 3° or less.) Figure 4.16 shows this relationship cartographically, and it is apparent that the two variables are related. Hidore found that at the county level almost half the total variation in cash-grain farming could be statistically "explained" in terms of the variation in flat land, although the level of explanation varied considerably from one midwestern state to another, being particularly high in North Dakota and particularly low in Missouri.

Our discussion of the influence of the more important environmental factors on agricultural production has been deliberately superficial because it is a well-documented topic in the literature of economic geography.* Let us turn at this point to consideration of the *profitability* aspects of the "optima and limits" approach to agriculture. As far as the individual producer is concerned, his major aim is still to maximize his profits and he will, therefore, choose to produce that combination of crops and livestock most likely to achieve this end. Particularly favorable or unfavorable physical conditions will influence the broad range of choice, affect productivity or yield, and thus modify unit production costs, for it is primarily through spatial variations in costs and revenues that environmental factors operate. In other words, favorable natural conditions, such as a more fertile soil, will increase the *economic rent* accruing to that unit of land.

We have already met the concept of economic rent in the case of the simplified model. We described it then as "basically a measure of the *advantage*, as the bidders see it, of one piece of land over another." At that stage in the development of our model, land could achieve this advantage only in one way. It could be *better located* in relation to the market for its products than were other parcels of land.

It was for this reason that we termed the particular form of rent in the model *locational rent*. Now we have introduced another way one piece of land can have an advantage over another. This is by virtue of those *physical-environmental*

---

*The reader is referred to such texts as Alexander (1963), Kolars and Nystuen (1974, Chapter 1) and Thoman and Corbin (1974) for a more detailed treatment.

Note

Figure 4.16
The relationship between
cash-grain farming and
flat land in the Midwest.
(a) Percentage of total
farms classified as
cash-grain. (b)
Percentage of flat land per
county. [*Source:* J. J.
Hidore (1963), The
Relationship Between
Cash-Grain Farming and
Land Forms, *Economic
Geography,* 39, Figures 1
and 4. Reprinted by
permission of the author
and editor.]

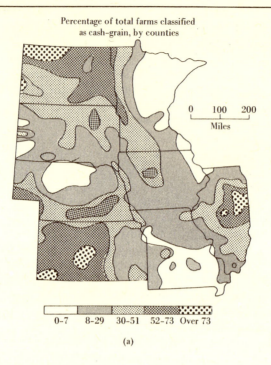

Percentage of total farms classified
as cash-grain, by counties

0   100   200
Miles

0-7   8-29   30-51   52-73 Over 73

(a)

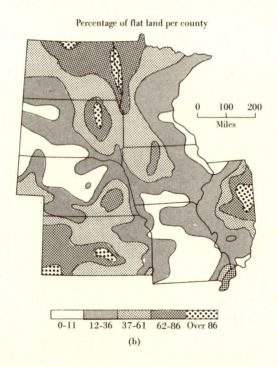

Percentage of flat land per county

0   100   200
Miles

0-11 12-36 37-61 62-86 Over 86

(b)

properties we have just discussed. These, as we pointed out, are offered as free benefits to certain crops or pastoral activities. They are "gifts of nature." *In combination with location*, these special attributes of land give it a *value* to those bidders who want to make use of it in production. They would compete with each other to *hire the services* of a piece of "good" agricultural land (of course its "goodness" would depend on what they had in mind). What they would, in general, be prepared to bid for, say, a fertile acre of flat land on Long Island would depend on how many bidders were in the market for it and what return they would expect to get from hiring it. The bidder who finally succeeded in hiring it (in a perfect world run according to the laws of economics) would be the one who would expect to get the highest return from doing so. The *economic rent* of the piece of land would be measured in terms of what he, the highest bidder in the market, would expect to get in return for its use.

Extending the argument from a single piece of land to land in general with all its attributes, locational and physical, we can see yet again how *economic rent* is a device for allocating parcels of land to various uses. Good land near the market will fetch high returns. Poor land in the backwoods will fetch low ones. Some land which is "useless" will fetch no returns at all and it will have no bidders and therefore no economic rent. Economic rent measures the *relative advantage* of land as a factor for producing the goods which a market wants. It is also an *allocative device*, ensuring in a perfect world that the best land goes to uses with the highest returns and so on down the line. At this stage in our discussion, then, we have given a more realistic basis for the valuation of land. In the simplified model it was location alone. Now it is location *plus* fertility, climatic attributes, flatness, and so forth.

Having extended and revised our understanding of the economic rent concept let us turn to look further at the *profitability* limits as they apply to the use of land which is inside the boundary of physical limits. Figure 4.17, again from McCarty and Lindberg (1966) illustrates the way rents contribute to the determination of economic limits. (Interestingly, the exact reverse is also true; economic limits set the base value for rents.) The productivity characteristics assigned to land by the two variables, temperature and moisture, in Figure 4.15 are now translated into unit costs of production. The "free-rider" effects which nature provides in the zone of optima are now converted into cost savings (compare Figure 4.17 with Figure 4.15). Movement away from the physical optimum promotes a rise in unit costs of production. This is shown by what readers will recognize as a graph which looks like that by which we previously showed the space-cost curve in Figure 4.6. If a price is set for a particular product, this will determine the *level of return* possible for that product. Suppose, as McCarty and Lindberg do, that this price is set at 7. No part of the producer region with unit costs above seven will offer a *net return* (profits less costs). The isoline marking the *margin to profitability* (but this time not a directly spatial one) will be that at which nature's bounty gives *not less than seven units of cost saving* to a prospective hirer of land. Land outside this production cost margin will have *no economic rent* as the diagram shows. This is because

Figure 4.17
Productivity translated
into unit costs and rent
for land under agricultural
production. [*Source:* H.
H. McCarty and J.
Lindberg, *A Preface to
Economic Geography,* ©
1966, Figure 3.4.
Reprinted by permission
of Prentice-Hall, Inc.,
Englewood Cliffs, New
Jersey, U.S.A.]

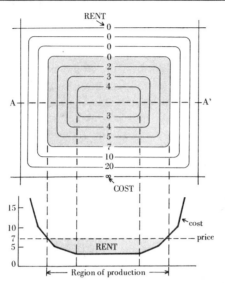

it offers *no return* to those who hire it. From the isoline for seven inwards, however, rent is acquired by land for the particular use and it rises to a peak where four units of rent are returned in the center of the optimum zone.

Logically, the diagram in Figure 4.17 offers a direct analogy to the *bid-rent lines* which allocated land use with reference to *locational* advantage in the Von Thünen model. We must be careful to note, however, that the "regions" of Figure 4.17 are not regions in the *spatial* sense. They are regions of *temperature and moisture conditions* as determined by the axes of Figure 4.15. Similarly, the margins to profitability are not *spatial* ones but the temperature and moisture margins. But, bearing this in mind, it can be seen that in the competitive struggle by bidders to hire land with good temperature and moisture advantages those uses which give the highest returns to moisture and temperature optima will capture the "inner" segments of the diagram. Uses with lower returns to temperature and moisture will be outbid and will occupy "locations" of lower quality.

What we now have to do is to put the attributes of physical resource quality and location together. We want to see how the addition of differential resource quality influences the regular order which location rent alone gave to the pattern of land use in the simplified model. At first sight it would seem that little spatial order could possibly remain because the quality of the natural environment varies spatially in a largely non-systematic manner. This is in direct contrast to the effect of distance that, by its relatively predictable influence on transport costs, tends to create a more regular spatial pattern around the major spatial reference points, urban markets.

As Dunn (1954) has pointed out, however, all is not lost:

the lack of regularity in the distribution of these (environmental) attributes would seriously distort the regularity of the land-use patterns. However, the phenomenon of the systematic progression of crops would not be altered. All crops could earn more on the more productive land, but, for any given degree of productivity, the crop that would earn the most would be the crop which had the highest marginal rent-line established by the economic influence of distance. The systematic nature of crop progression would be preserved because the more productive land would be more productive for all uses. The principal location influence would be a distortion of the regularity of the pattern by extending the crop boundaries in the areas of high productivity and restricting them in areas of low productivity.

Dunn (1954), p. 67

An example of such *distortional* effects is shown in Figure 4.18. Shaded area A to the east of the market town presents an area that is unsuitable for agricultural use. Shaded area B is an "inlier" of crop 3, which is otherwise produced at a greater distance from the market. However, area B is particularly suited to the production of crop 3 and gives much higher yields at lower cost. This increases the economic rent of crop 3 above that of crops 1 and 2 in this restricted area and allows crop 3 to be substituted for crops 1 and 2.

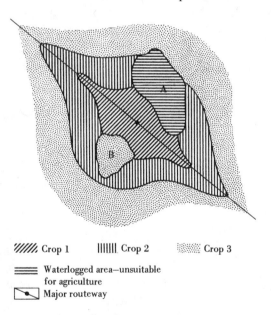

Figure 4.18
Distortion of agricultural land-use patterns by variation in the physical quality of the land.

////// Crop 1 ||||||| Crop 2   ········ Crop 3

≡≡≡ Waterlogged area—unsuitable
     for agriculture
◥◣ Major routeway

Variations in land quality, therefore, are important primarily for their influence on the spatial pattern of economic rent in the course of agricultural production. Such variations may also be significant for other forms of economic activity. Those manufacturing industries requiring very extensive sites for efficient plant layout will be influenced, to some extent, by the availability of sufficiently large areas of flat land. The extent to which this factor is significant depends, of course, on the importance of site costs in the industry's cost structure (in most cases this is not very great). Similarly, climatic influences may, in certain cases, be a consideration for the manufacturing process. The often-quoted example of the advantages of the California climate for aircraft manufacture may be cited. But, as in the case of the relationship between the physical environment and agriculture, the impact is generated through economic costs primarily. On a larger scale, variations in the physical environment may have an impact on population distributions and therefore on settlement patterns. In the days when settlements *had* to be supplied with food from their local area there was some relationship between land quality (hence crop-yield) and population density. Over time, of course, this relationship has ceased to exist, but the inertial element has meant the perpetuation of such patterns. For, as with industrial raw materials, the forms generated by the functioning of earlier agricultural systems under different conditions of demand and technology exert a strong impact on agricultural patterns in the space economy at any subsequent point in time.

Thus the impact of the physical environment on the location of agricultural production is seen as one controlling cost factor among many. Its effect on a space economy such as that of the simplified model will be to contribute its influence to the distortion and complication of conditions on the isotropic plain, making it more realistically heterogeneous.

Further reading

Dunn, E. S. (1954), *The Location of Agricultural Production*, Gainesville: University of Florida Press, Chapter Five.

Hidore, J. J. (1963), The Relations Between Cash-Grain Farming and Land Forms, *Economic Geography* **39**, 84–89.

Isard, W. (1956), *Location and Space Economy*, Cambridge, Mass.: M.I.T. Press, Chapters 4 and 5.

Kennelly, R. A. (1954), The Location of the Mexican Steel Industry, in R. H. T. Smith, E. J. Taaffe, and L. J. King (eds.), *Readings in Economic Geography*, Chicago: Rand McNally, 126–157.

Lindberg, O. (1953), An Economic-Geographic Study of the Swedish Paper Industry, *Geografiska Annaler* **35**, 28–40.

McCarty, H. H. and J. B. Lindberg (1966), *A Preface to Economic Geography*, Englewood Cliffs, N.J.: Prentice Hall.

Peet, J. R. (1969), The Spatial Expansion of Commercial Agriculture in the Nineteenth Century, *Economic Geography* **45**, 283–301.

Smith, D. M. (1966), A Theoretical Framework for Geographical Studies of Industrial Location, *Economic Geography* **42**, 95–113.

Smith, W. (1955), The Location of Industry, *Transactions of the Institute of British Geographers* **21**, 1–18.

Warren, K. (1973), *The American Steel Industry, 1850–1970: A Geographical Interpretation*, Oxford: Clarendon Press.

Weber, A. (1909), *Theory of the Location of Industries*, Chicago: University of Chicago Press, Chapter III.

CHAPTER 5

TRANSPORTATION AND THE SPATIAL ORGANIZATION OF ECONOMIC ACTIVITIES: ROUTES, NETWORKS, TRANSPORTATION COSTS

Throughout our discussion so far we have been concerned with *movement* and its fundamental role in influencing how economic activities are arranged on the earth's surface. We have gradually relaxed some of our initial assumptions, in particular the notion that movement was both equally possible and equally likely in any direction on our plain. But we have still retained some restrictive assumptions concerning both the form of transportation *routes* and the structure of transportation *costs*. In this chapter, we examine the effect on the spatial organization of economic activities of removing both of these constraints.

The location of transportation routes and networks

We saw in Chapter Two that even on our homogeneous plain movement would tend to become channeled into specific lines or routes. But transportation routes do not exist in isolation; they are organized into *networks* with varying degrees of interconnection. Such networks are the physical expression—the trace left on the earth's surface—of the *flows* of materials, people, and information which bind together the economic system. The question we pose in this section, therefore, concerns the nature of the forces which influence the spatial form of the transportation routes and networks which play such a fundamental part in our daily lives.

It is perfectly obvious that variations in the form of the land surface will have an impact on the location of transportation routes and networks. Mountain ranges and extensive plains, river valleys and expanses of swampland clearly provide differential resistances to movement. Such variations in physical geography led many geographers in the past to explain the location of particular routes almost entirely in terms of the influence of such physical conditions. It seems obvious, perhaps, when looking at a map showing, say, a mountainous region dissected by river valleys, that the highways or railroads "choose" the "natural routeways." It is tempting to suggest that the river valleys represent the *raison d'être* of the railroads and highways that pass through them. But as Appleton (1963, p. 21) so aptly pointed out, "a so-called 'natural routeway' is a means and not an end. It affords the opportunity for communication; it does not create the demand."

In fact, Appleton goes on to observe that in the development of transportation routes in the Great Australian Divide for example the most obvious physical routeway was, in several cases, *not* used. Other studies of route development have reached a similar conclusion. Meinig's comparative study of railroad development in the Columbia basin of the western United States and in southern Australia showed that many alternative routes other than the obvious ones were surveyed and considered by the developers. In the case of underdeveloped countries too it seems that variations in the physical landscape can be relatively unimportant in determining the development of transportation facilities (Taafe, Morrill and Gould, 1963).

To find the fundamental reason for the location of a transportation route we have to return again to demand and, especially, to the principle of *complementarity*. As we saw in Chapter Two, interaction occurs between places if they have some kind of demand-supply relationship. If two urban centers are complementary but not connected by a transportation route then it is likely that such a route will be constructed to meet the need. It is in the context of construction costs, therefore, that variations in the land surface are influential. The *costs* of traversing difficult terrain have to be set against the *benefits* which such construction would bring. The cost of a transportation route consists of two basic elements:

1. *Fixed or capital costs.* These are the costs involved in actually building the route. Land may have to be purchased (in heavily urbanized areas this may well be the largest single element in the cost of building a route), uneven ground may have to be leveled or waterlogged ground drained and filled. Cuttings may have to be blasted through solid rock. Fixed costs are closely related to the length of the routeways.

2. *Variable or operating costs.* The cost of a transportation route does not end when it is built and opened to traffic. There are recurrent costs which vary according to both the length of the route and the volume of traffic flowing along it. Routes have to be maintained and kept in good repair. They may have to be ploughed or salted in winter to keep them clear and maintenance staff have to be employed to carry out these and other tasks.

These two cost elements may well vary from place to place in terms of their relative importance. In some cases, fixed costs may be extremely high and operating costs relatively low and vice versa. Thus the relationship between fixed and variable costs goes some way toward explaining the precise form of transportation routes and networks. To some extent, we can view the route problem as one involving two extreme sets of goals. One goal is to build the route or network as cheaply as possible—what Bunge (1966) called the "least-cost-to-build" motive. The other extreme is to build the route or network with the aim of keeping the costs to the user as low as possible—the "least-cost-to-user" goal. The former objective would result in a network as small as possible, while the latter would result in a highly-connected route network in which every place is directly connected to every other place.

As an example, let us suppose we wish to build a transportation network in an area which has within it five towns (Figure 5.1a). What form should the network take? The answer clearly depends upon our basic objectives; in particular, do we wish to keep construction costs as low as possible or do we wish

Figure 5.1
Alternative ways of connecting five settlements by a transportation network. (a) Relative locations of the settlements. (b) "Least-cost-to-use" solution. (c) "Least-cost-to-build" solution. [*Source:* W. Bunge (1966), Theoretical Geography, *Lund Studies in Geography,* Series C, 1, Figures 7.10 and 7.14.]

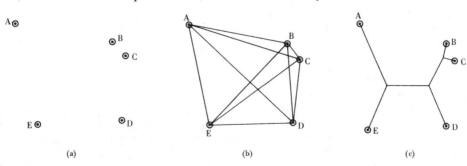

(a) (b) (c)

to build a network offering greatest convenience to the people who are going to use the network and perhaps thereby increase total revenue? There are many different ways in which the five towns could be connected into a network. Figure 5.1b and 5.1c show the two extreme alternatives which correspond to the least-cost-to-user and least-cost-to-build principles. In Figure 5.1b we see the network which gives maximum benefit to the user insofar as each of the five towns is *directly* connected to every other town. There is no problem, therefore, of having to change trains to pick up an airline connection to the next town. Figure 5.1c shows the solution which meets the criterion of least-cost-to-build because it minimizes the total route length. But, clearly, this is far less convenient for the user.*

Bunge suggested that the railroad pattern of North America in the 1950s could be at least partly understood in terms of these two basic patterns (Figure 5.2).

Note

*The networks in Figure 5.1 can be regarded as *topological graphs*. Topology is the most general and abstract of geometries which is concerned with the *connections* between points (that is, their *relative* location) and not with their absolute location. All networks, whether they are rivers, transportation networks, or blood vessels, can be analyzed using *graph theory* and a considerable body of geographical literature now exists. The pioneering application of graph theory to geographical problems was Garrison's study of the interstate highway network (Garrison, 1960), although Kansky (1963) did much to develop its application. More recent summaries can be found in Haggett and Chorley (1969), Hay (1973), and Taaffe and Gauthier (1973).

Topologically, a network consists of two elements:
1. A set of *vertices* or *nodes* (v)
2. A set of *edges* or *links* (e)

Using these two elements a number of different descriptive indices have been devised to describe the properties of networks. Some measures refer to the network in its entirety, others to parts of the network, such as the nodes. Just one example will be given here—the *beta index* (β). Other measures are described fully in the studies listed above. The *beta index* measures the degree of *connectivity* which a network possesses and does this by simply relating the number of edges or links (e) to the number of nodes or vertices (v). Thus

$$\beta = \frac{e}{v}$$

Where there are a large number of edges to vertices, the *beta* value will be large, signifying a well-connected network. On the other hand, more vertices than edges signifies a poorly-connected network. Thus we can measure the difference in connectivity between the two networks in Figure 5.1:

Network	Number of edges	Number of vertices	$\frac{e}{v}$	β
"least-cost-to-user"	10	5	$\frac{10}{5}$	2.0
"least-cost-to-build"	7	8	$\frac{7}{8}$	0.87

There can be no doubt that the least-cost-to-build network has much the lowest degree of connectivity. More generally, the *beta* index is a useful measure for comparing networks, either several different networks at the same time or one network as it changes through time.

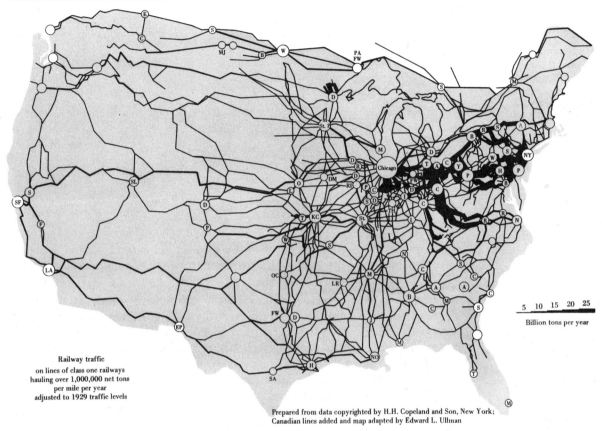

Railway traffic
on lines of class one railways
hauling over 1,000,000 net tons
per mile per year
adjusted to 1929 traffic levels

5 10 15 20 25

Billion tons per year

Prepared from data copyrighted by H.H. Copeland and Son, New York;
Canadian lines added and map adapted by Edward L. Ullman

Figure 5.2
Density of rail traffic in the United States. [*Source:* E. L. Ullman (1957), *American Commodity Flow,* Seattle: University of Washington Press.]

The "least-cost-to-user" network was characteristic of the Northeast and Midwest where the large metropolitan centers are spatially clustered and transportation demands greater. Elsewhere in North America, urban centers are relatively scattered involving greater distances and smaller traffic volume. In such conditions, the dominant consideration would tend to be construction costs and a "least-cost-to-build" network would be expected.

In locating a transportation route, therefore, a balance has to be struck between making the route short enough to keep construction costs down and making it long enough to connect places generating a large amount of traffic and revenue. We can thus identify two forces which help to deviate transportation routes from a straight-line connection between origin and destination. Positive deviations are those which result in making a route longer in order to increase revenue. Figure 5.3 shows a hypothetical example in which the problem is to locate a transportation route in an area where there are eight towns. The two major towns, X and Y, both generate revenues of 10 units while the others vary in their revenue-generating capacity. The problem is that increasing the length of the route to take in other centers raises construction costs. Which is the best route? In Figure 5.3a the net benefits of the straight-line route connecting only X and Y are 10 units. Lengthening the route to connect two additional places raises costs but greatly increases revenues (Figure 5.3b). However,

Figure 5.3
Alternative ways of
locating a transport route
to maximize net benefits.
[*Source:* R. Abler, J.
Adams, P. Gould (1971),
*Spatial Organization: The
Geographer's View of the
World,* Figure 8.42.
Reprinted by permission
of Prentice-Hall Inc.,
Englewood Cliffs, New
Jersey, U.S.A.]

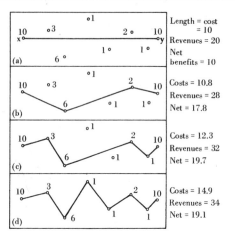

connecting every town does not give the greatest net benefit; this is achieved by connecting six of the centers and by-passing two of the smallest ones (Figure 5.3c).

Negative deviations of transportation routes are produced mainly by the effects of a heterogeneous land surface in differentially raising or lowering construction costs. This effect is not simply restricted to the more obvious physical phenomena such as mountain ranges, river valleys, glacial spillways and marshland areas. Political boundaries, differences in the cost of acquiring land, and other socio-economic phenomena all contribute towards the "distortion" of transportation routes and networks. Even airline routes are not simply straight-line paths between airports: they, too, become distorted by variations in atmospheric pressure and wind strength and direction.

As transportation routes pass through space, therefore, they encounter varying degrees of "resistance." Lösch saw this as being analogous to the way in which light rays become *refracted* or bent as they pass from one medium to another, just as a stick partly immersed in water appears bent rather than straight. As an example, consider Figure 5.4 which depicts a transportation situation in which goods have to be moved over two different media, land and sea. Each of these has a different "resistance" to movement in the sense that transport costs per mile are higher over land than over sea ($1.50 per mile compared with 75 cents per mile). The problem is what will be the optimal route for moving the goods from A, which is a port, to B, which is an inland location in a different country? The diagram shows three alternative routes using different combinations of land/sea distances.

1. Route ANB is the straight-line route crossing equal distances over land and sea. At the prevailing transport rates the total transport cost will be:

$$(20 \times 75c) + (20 \times \$1.50) = \$37.50$$

2. Route AMB is the route which maximizes the distance traveled over water (the lower cost medium) and minimizes the distance traveled over land. Total transport costs will be:

$$(30 \times 75c) + (10 \times \$1.50) = \$45.00$$

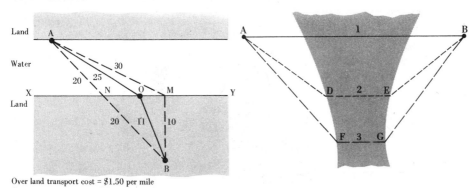

Figure 5.4
Application of the principle of refraction to transportation routes: movement over land and water.

Figure 5.5
Refractive effect of a mountain barrier. [*Source:* Based on A. Lösch (1954), Figure 51.]

Over land transport cost = \$1.50 per mile
Over sea transport cost = 75 cents per mile

Figure 5.4   Figure 5.5

3. Route AOB is the "compromise" route with total costs of:

(25 × 75c) + (11 × \$1.50) = \$35.25

The least-cost route, therefore, is the one which crosses the coast at 0.

Lösch also suggested that "refraction by lenses" occurs in both natural and human conditions. In Figure 5.5 the problem is to transport a consignment of goods as cheaply as possible from A to B, two cities which are separated by a high mountain barrier. The excessive cost of crossing the barrier rules out the possibility of the straight-line connection. Lösch saw the shaded area in Figure 5.5 as being exactly like a "biconcave lens." "The greater the refractive index of the lens—that is the more it resists the passage of a beam of light—the more will the beam be deflected." He referred to the changing pattern of trade between the eastern and western coasts of the United States in the nineteenth century as an example. Initially overland transport costs were so exceptionally high that much of the trade was via the long sea route round Cape Horn. Subsequently, the degree of refraction was lessened by the construction of the Panama Canal while, today, east–west movement is barely refracted at all by overland barriers.

We can quite easily extend this basic idea by considering a case where an origin and destination point are separated by several areas of varying resistance to movement. In Figure 5.6 there are four such areas which affect the level of construction costs. The darkest shaded areas represent the highest construction costs per mile. These areas could be seen as different types of physical terrain—a mountainous region with intervening valleys across the desired line of movement—or as a land value surface in which the cost of acquiring land for the route is much higher in some places than in others. Whatever their exact nature, the presence of such areas of differential resistance is to deflect the optimal route from the straight-line path between P_1 and P_2. It is interesting to note that in Figure 5.6 the route with the lowest total cost is, in fact, the longest (Route 3).

Transportation routes are not only distorted by variations in the land surface

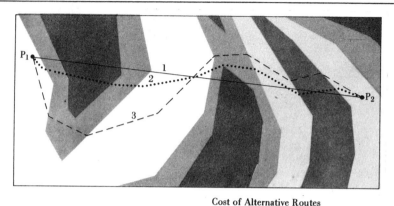

Figure 5.6
Effect of areas of different
construction costs on the
location of a
transportation route.
[*Source:* C. Werner
(1968), The Law of
Refraction in
Transportation
Geography, *Canadian
Geographer,* 12, Figure 6
and Table 1. Reproduced
by permission of the
author and editor.]

High ▮▮▯▯ Low

Total cost per mile

Cost of Alternative Routes		
Route	Length (miles)	Total transport costs
1	22.7	$743,995
2	23.7	$622,972
3	28.6	$512,135

itself. Boundaries, especially political boundaries, also have a very considerable influence. In some cases the effect on the network structure is quite spectacular. One of the best known cases is that either side of the United States–Canadian border. In the approximately 700-mile stretch of country shown in Figure 5.7 only eight railroad lines cross the border though more than twenty approach it and are terminated before reaching the border. Two major east–west routes run parallel to each other on either side of the border. As Wolfe pointed out,

> If the boundary between Canada and the United States were removed from the rail network map, one would have little difficulty in putting it back again in about the same place.
> *Wolfe (1962), p. 184*

Figure 5.8 shows an even more striking example of the effect of political boundaries on transportation networks. The line XY on the map marks the boundary between the provinces of Quebec and Ontario. To the east of the line, there is a dense network of roads; to the west there are virtually none until the railroad is reached.

One likely result of such disruption and distortion of transportation networks at political borders is a reduction in the intensity of movement and interaction between one side of the border and the other. In the extreme case, the barrier may be almost total, allowing no transportation routes to cross from one side to the other. More usually, the barrier is permeable, that is, it acts as a kind of filter through which some, though not all, movement passes. The two cases shown in Figures 5.7 and 5.8 are of this type. In the particular case of the Quebec border an interesting study of interaction was carried out by Mackay (1958). Mackay used the gravity model to analyze the flow of telephone traffic between, on the one hand, three Quebec cities—Montreal, Quebec City, and Sherbrooke—and on the other, fifty Canadian and twenty United States' cities. By predicting the intensity of telephone traffic from the gravity model and test-

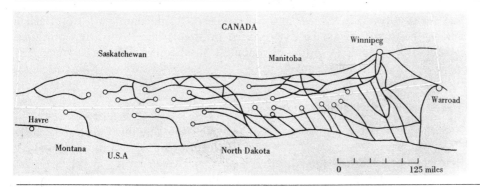

Figure 5.7
Effect of the
U.S.-Canadian border on
railroad networks.
[*Source:* A. Lösch
(1954), *The Economics of
Location* (Die Räumliche
Ordnung der Wirtschaft),
Stuttgart: Gustav Fischer,
1962, Figure 85.]

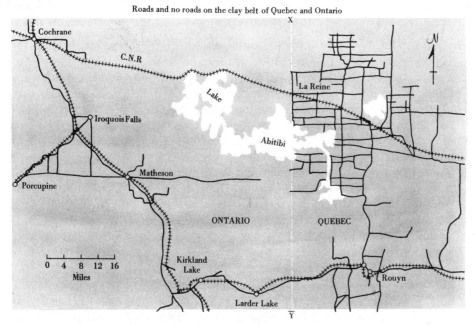

Figure 5.8
Road patterns astride a
section of the
Ontario-Quebec border.
[*Source:* R. I. Wolfe
(1962), Transportation
and Politics, Figure 4.
Reproduced by
permission from the
*Annals of the Association
of American Geographers,*
52.]

ing the values against actual telephone traffic he was able to measure the effect of the border on such interaction. He found that telephone traffic across the border was consistently lower than expected on the basis of the actual distance between cities. In the case of interaction between Quebec cities and Ontario cities, the Ontario cities received between one-fifth and one-tenth of their predicted telephone calls while United States cities received only one-fiftieth of the predicted calls. As Mackay points out, the border in effect *increased* the distance between places, by between five and ten times for interaction within Canada, and by fifty times for interaction between Quebec and the United States.

For a number of reasons, therefore, both physical and human, transportation routes and networks have a complex spatial form. Insofar as all economic activities are locationally related to transportation facilities, then the intricacies of the network result in location patterns which are considerably removed from the regularity presented in Chapter Two. The relative positions of urban centers and the distortions in the size and shape of market and supply areas and urban and agricultural land-use zones produced by simple linearity of transportation facilities (see Chapter Two) become infinitely more complex though the underlying locational principles remain.

The structure of transportation costs*

A particularly important assumption on which the simplified economic landscape of Chapter Two was based was the form of transportation costs. These were characterized as being strictly proportional to distance; in other words, each additional unit of distance added an equal increment of cost to total transportation costs (Figure 2.1). Movement of a good over a distance of 100 miles therefore costs twice as much as movement of the same good over 50 miles.

In reality, transportation costs are rarely exactly proportional to distance for several reasons. First, all transportation media, whether railroad, truck, airline, waterway, or pipeline, incur a certain level of *fixed costs* which do not vary with the length of journey. We have mentioned some of these costs in connection with the construction of transportation routes, but there are also "handling" costs which are part of fixed costs—costs of picking up and loading freight and of billing customers. Such handling costs are also unrelated to the length of journey and have to be incurred whether the goods are moved one mile or one thousand miles. These unvarying-with-distance costs are collectively termed *terminal costs*. Although terminal costs are not dependent on the length of journey, they greatly influence transportation costs because, as length of haul increases, terminal costs are spread to a greater extent than on a short journey. *The result is that the cost per mile tends to decline with increasing distance.* Figure 5.9 shows this for a situation in which *terminal costs* are $1.00 and *line haul* (*movement*) *costs* are 5 cents per mile. The total cost per mile (terminal plus line-haul costs divided by the distance traveled) falls very rapidly and then flattens out. Thus, the cost per mile if the journey is only one mile is $1.05, whereas it is 25 cents per mile for a journey of five miles and only 6 cents per mile for 100 miles. In terms of *total* transportation costs the effect is as shown in Figure 5.10: the cost curve "tapers off" with increasing distance.

For the most part, tapering transportation costs are the result of spreading a fixed terminal cost over a greater distance but there are other influences too. One is that line-haul costs themselves are not always exactly proportional to distance; another is that rates for longer distances are kept lower than they might otherwise be in order to encourage longer distance movement. Figure 5.10 also shows how tapering cost curves compare with those where transportation costs are strictly proportional to distance. In effect, short-distance movements are more expensive and longer-distance movements are less expensive when tapering transportation costs are in operation.

Note   *Transportation cost structures are extremely complex; in this section we do no more than review some of the more spatially significant features. For more detailed and expert treatment, the following sources are recommended: Sampson and Farris (1966), Locklin (1960).

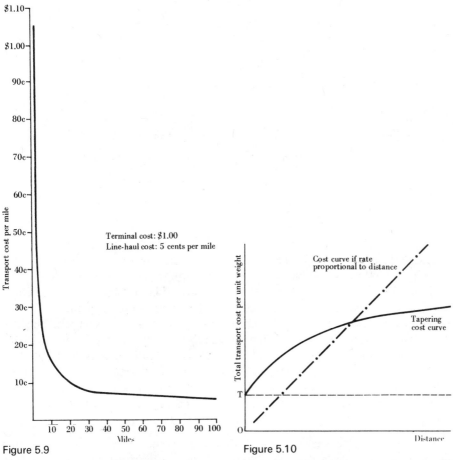

Terminal cost: $1.00
Line-haul cost: 5 cents per mile

Cost curve if rate
proportional to distance

Tapering
cost curve

Figure 5.9

Figure 5.10

Figure 5.9
Relationship between
transport cost per mile
and length of journey.

Figure 5.10
Comparison between
transport costs
proportional and
less-than-proportional to
distance.

The general form of transportation costs, therefore, is for them to "taper off"
as distance increases. However, the degree of tapering varies greatly from one
type of transportation to another, depending upon their respective terminal
and line-haul costs. Figure 5.11 is an idealized representation of transportation
cost curves for three types of transportation: highway, railroad and waterway.
Highway or truck transportation costs are seen to be only slightly less than
proportional to distance. This is because fixed costs are low, possibly only about
ten percent of total costs. One reason for this, of course, is that truck operators
do not maintain their own highways unlike railroad operators who incur track
maintenance costs. Such contributions as are made towards highway costs (e.g.
through gasoline taxes) vary largely according to the use made of them. Conversely, line-haul costs are high for truck operators so that trucking costs increase more or less directly with distance.

Railroad and waterway costs, on the other hand, are characterized by far higher
terminal costs but lower line-haul costs. Both railroad and waterway networks
are coarser than highway networks, providing fewer terminal facilities which
generally involve costly trans-shipment of goods from truck to freightcar (or
barge) and finally to truck again. For example, in 1962 the route mileage of

Figure 5.11
Idealized transportation
cost curves for three
transportation media:
truck, railroad, waterway.

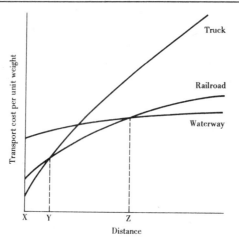

Figure 5.11
Idealized transportation
cost curves for three
transportation media:
truck, railroad, waterway.

highways in the United States was ten times greater than railroads and 100 times greater than navigable waterways (Barloon, 1963). Rationalization of the railroad network in particular, with the closure of large stretches of "uneconomic" routes in North America, Britain, and western Europe in the 1960s and 1970s has increased this already considerable difference between the fineness of highway networks on the one hand and rail networks on the other. Although the development of standardized containers has greatly facilitated trans-shipment from one type of transportation medium to another, terminal costs on rail and waterway remain high. However, line-haul costs are relatively low, particularly in the case of waterways, producing cost curves which are convex upwards.

As a result of these varying cost characteristics, each transportation medium offers advantages over different lengths of haul. For short distances such as XY in Figure 5.11 truck transportation is cheapest. For medium-length hauls (YZ) the railroad is least costly, whereas over very long distances (beyond Z) water transport, if available, is cheapest. The extent to which these media can compete for traffic therefore is somewhat limited. If, for example, railroads wish to compete in the "short-haul" market they must offer rates over such distances which are comparable with trucking rates and vice versa. However, such competition is probably restricted to certain types of freight since there is a considerable degree of specialization in the type of freight moved by road and by rail. Table 5.1 summarizes some of the basic characteristics of the major transportation media.

Although most transportation rates take the general form described in this section, there are a number of other influences which have a significant geographical impact on transportation costs. We shall look briefly at just three of these:

1. Grouping of freight rates into zones.

2. Variations in freight rates according to the nature of the freight being moved.

3. Variations in freight rates according to traffic characteristics.

Mode	Costs	Unit cost (mile) (Rail = 1.0)	Distance	Characteristic goods	Distinction	Drawbacks
Railroad	Capital intensive: large initial investment (incl. right-of-way). Profit-ability rests on intensity of use: 350,000 to 500,000 tons/mile/year is operational margin. Terminal costs high.	1.0	Increasing effectiveness with length of haul. Large shipments. Large shipments cheaper by long or short haul.	Minerals; unprocessed agricultural products; building mats., chemicals. Passengers minor.*	Large volumes of bulk goods in comparatively short time at low costs.	Cost and time of assembling units.
Waterways	Investment low, especially where natural waterways utilized. Terminal and handling costs several times line-haul costs.	0.29	Increasing effectiveness with length of haul.	Marine: semi finished and finished products. Inland: bulk raw goods—coke, coal, oil, grain, sand, gravel, cement. Passengers negligible.	Low freight rates; slow speed; spec. of goods carriage.	Slow speed.
Motor transport	Fixed costs negligible. Operates on small margins—operating costs high; vehicle turnover high.	4.5	Short haul, less costly than rail. Wide area coverage.	Perishable goods; lumber. Passengers important.	Light loads, short distances, short time. Flexible and convenient. Minimizes distribution costs. Improved service.	Inadequate capacity for moving heavy volumes, bulk materials. High costs of long hauls. High vehicle operating costs.
Air transport	Fixed costs low. Investment in stock very high. Terminal, take-off costs, high.	16.3	Long hauls, economy with distance.	Passengers dominant. Perishable, lightweight, high value goods.	Speed.	Very high costs.
Pipelines	Fixed costs high. Large economies through diameter of pipe. Costs increase almost directly with distance. Viscosity adds costs.	0.21	Long haul in bulk.	Crude oil and petroleum products in large volume.	Bulk movement.	Restricted commodity use. Regular flow and demand needed. Large market.

*In Europe, passenger revenues usually exceed freight revenues.
Source: From *A Geography of Economic Behavior: An Introduction* by Michael E. Eliot Hurst. © 1972 by Wadsworth Publishing Company, Inc., Belmont, California 94002. Reprinted by permission of the publisher, Duxbury Press.

Table 5.1 Characteristics of major transportation media.

Grouping of freight rates into zones

Two aspects deserve our attention. The first relates to the practice, prevalent until the 1950s in the United States, of allowing different rate *levels* to exist in different parts of the country. For the first half of this century, in fact, railroad freight rates were grouped into five major regions. Figure 5.12 shows how the *average* rate varied from region to region compared with the eastern or official region. The disparities are quite remarkable; for example, railroad freight rates in the southwestern region were, on average, 61 percent higher than those in the eastern region. In part these differences reflect the principles discussed earlier—areas of high demand will likely generate a dense transportation network and such high demand may also be reflected in lower freight rates. The operation of this regional differential between 1887 and 1952 gave the Northeast a pronounced rate advantage, with an average cost of shipping goods significantly lower than in the rest of the nation. Though no longer operative these regional differences in freight rates will continue to exert a spatial impact on economic activities for some time because of the stimulus they gave to economic activity.

Figure 5.12
Relative freight rate levels by major freight rate region, United States.

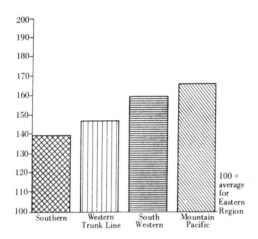

More significant today, however, is the almost universal practice of charging freight rates in *zones*. In theory, every separate journey would be charged a specific rate which varied precisely according to its length. But this is time-consuming and costly to administer. Consequently, most transportation companies operate a zonal rate structure. In the case of railroads, for example, a common practice is to group stations into areas and to charge a single rate within that area. Most commonly rates are set in relation to a "control point" in each area; frequently this is the largest center. Figure 5.13 illustrates this zoning principle for rail freight rates in Wisconsin. In Figure 5.13a, the zones are those for *interstate* traffic (traffic moving between Wisconsin and another state) while Figure 5.13b shows the *intrastate* zones (traffic moving *within* Wisconsin). Interstate zones are approximately 40 miles wide while intrastate zones are a good deal smaller, reflecting the shorter distance moves involved.

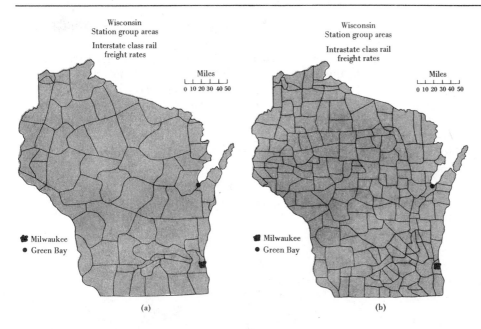

Figure 5.13
Rail freight rates in Wisconsin. (a) Interstate movements. (b) Intrastate movements. [*Source:* J. W. Alexander, S. E. Brown, and R. E. Dahlberg (1958), Freight Rates: Selected Aspects of Uniform and Nodal Regions, *Economic Geography,* 34, Figures 12 and 13. Reproduced by permission of the author and editor.]

Closely associated with the zoning of origin and destination points is the common practice of quoting freight rates in *steps* of varying width. Figure 5.14 shows the stepped freight rate pattern for the same interstate and intrastate movements in Wisconsin. In Figure 5.14a, it can be seen that *interstate* rates are not quoted on distances of less than 40 miles (the average size of interstate zones). Between 40 and 100 miles the zones increase in steps of 5 miles; between 190 and 240 miles the steps are 10 miles wide and beyond 240 miles each step represents 20 miles. In the case of *intrastate* traffic the steps are 5 miles wide for movements of less than 100 miles and 10 miles wide beyond that distance. The stepped-rate pattern, with steps becoming wider with distance, retains the tapering principle and favors longer-haul movements.

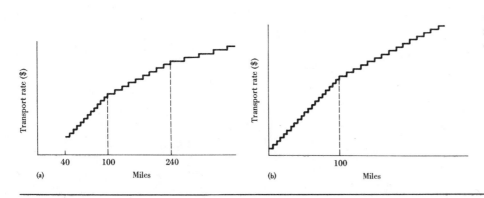

Figure 5.14
Stepped freight rate curves in Wisconsin. (a) Interstate movements. (b) Intrastate movements.

Figure 5.15 illustrates freight rate zoning on a larger, trans-continental scale. The rate pattern shown in **Figure 5.15a** shows the blanket or zonal rate for shipping lumber from western Oregon and Washington to various parts of the United States, while the profile in **Figure 5.15b** is for shipment of the same commodity to the Gulf Coast via the southern route. This graph is especially interesting because it shows a combination of blanket or zonal rates and mileage rates. Over the first few miles the rate per 100 lbs increases very rapidly but then takes on a blanket level of 40 cents per 100 lbs for several hundred miles. This is again interrupted by a lengthy stretch of short-stepped progressions before the level of about 140 cents per 100 lbs is reached at roughly 2,100 miles. From that point the rate remains exactly the same. Again, therefore, we have a freight rate structure which tapers off with distance but in a more complex way.

Figure 5.15
Blanket-rate freight profiles on the shipment of lumber from Portland, Oregon. [*Source:* R. J. Sampson and M. T. Farris (1966), *Domestic Transportation: Practise, Theory and Policy,* Boston: Houghton Mifflin, Figures 19 and 20.]

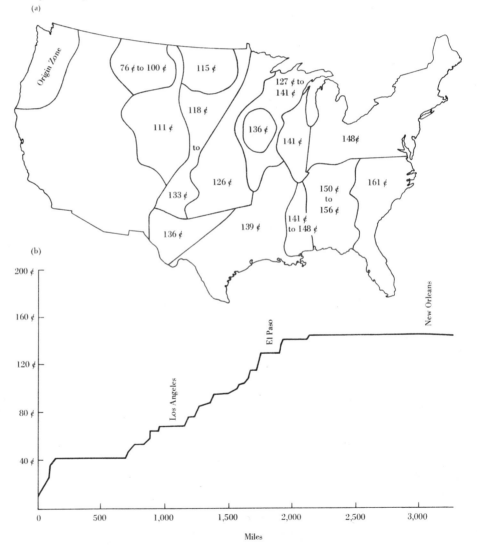

Variations in freight rates according to commodity characteristics

The characteristic shape of transportation rates over distance is, as we have seen, a stepped, convex-upwards curve. However, the *level* of transportation costs varies markedly according to the general characteristics of the commodities involved. Just as the tapering of freight rates has its origin in the existence of fixed costs, so these same costs encourage transport operators to vary their rates in order to cover these costs. The result is a considerable degree of discrimination between commodities in the level of freight rates and the existence of rates which are above or below those justified by the actual costs of transportation. This is shown in Table 5.2 in which the revenue received from carload shipments is expressed as a percentage of the "fully distributed cost" of transporting these commodities. Thus, commodities with a figure of less than 100, such as lettuce, bituminous coal and iron ore, were transported at rates which, overall, did not cover the fully distributed cost. Conversely, those with values greater than 100 covered the fully distributed cost often with a considerable margin. Clearly, therefore, a degree of cross-subsidization may be practiced whereby "losses" on transporting some commodities can be offset by "gains" on others. But why should such rate discrimination between commodities exist? Two reasons seem to be especially important. One is the fact there are differences in the cost of providing a transportation service for various kinds of freight. The other relates to the ability of various types of traffic to pay high transportation charges.

Commodity	Percent of fully distributed cost	Commodity	Percent of fully distributed cost
Corn	121	Paint, putty and varnish	157
Cotton, in bales	135	Drugs and toilet preparations	141
Oranges and grapefruit	78	Agricultural implements	158
Lettuce	62	Machinery and machines	207
Butter	112	Automobiles, passenger	171
Anthracite coal	101	Refrigerators	142
Bituminous coal	80	Liquors, alcoholic	208
Iron ore	63	Cigarettes	192

Table 5.2
Revenue from railroad freight (selected commodities) as a percentage of fully distributed cost, 1956.*

*Includes variable costs together with an allocation of constant costs, including an allowance for a return on investment.
Source: Reproduced with permission from D. P. Locklin (1960), *The Economics of Transportation*, 5th ed., Homewood, Ill: Richard D. Irwin, p. 136.

A. Differences in the cost of providing a transportation service. A number of factors contribute to differences in the cost of providing a transportation service:

1. *Loading characteristics.* Of particular importance is the weight-density of the commodity (weight per cubic foot). Consequently, light though bulky articles are likely to incur higher freight charges than heavy, compact articles. This explains the common practice of charging more favorable rates on "knocked-

down" than on "set-up" articles. The decentralization of the automobile industry from Detroit owes a good deal to the fact that there was a significant freight saving in shipping packaged components over the shipping of finished automobiles. Similarly, articles which load compactly are preferable, from a rate viewpoint, than articles of odd shapes and large dimensions.

2. *Size of shipment.* Up to a point there is a direct relationship between the size of shipment and the level of transportation costs. Large, single consignments of goods permit economies in administrative, terminal, and in some cases, line-haul costs, per unit weight. A significant distinction is between shipments in carload (CL) and less-than-carload (LCL) lots. Table 5.3 shows quite clearly that average costs were very much lower the larger the quantity shipped. Thus in the case of rail shipments over a 60-mile journey, a carload shipment cost only 1.8 percent of the cost for a shipment of less than 100 lb. The differential was rather less for truck transport. The table also reveals that truck transport is a good deal cheaper than rail transport even on longer hauls where LCL loads are involved, thus partially reversing their relative competitive positions discussed earlier.

3. *Susceptibility to loss or damage and risk liability.* There is considerable variation between commodities in their susceptibility to loss or damage. As a result freight rates must often be calculated to cover such contingencies. The more fragile and perishable a good—such as delicate instruments and components, on the one hand, and vegetables and fresh fruits on the other—the higher is the rate likely to be. Often the type of packaging influences the rate level, glass containers being more susceptible to breakage than cans. Closely related to this is the need for certain commodities to be transported in special equipment, such as refrigerated or insulated cars, or by special services; for example, rapid transportation is necessary for perishable goods. Finally, the amount of the transporter's liability must also be taken into account.

B. Elasticity of demand for transportation*. It is generally accepted that goods of high unit value are better able to "bear" relatively higher transportation charges than goods of lower unit value. This, as Hoover has pointed out, is related to the good's elasticity of demand for transportation which is less for

Note

**Elasticity of demand* measures how much demand for a good or service *changes* in response to change in the price of that good or service (both usually being measured in percentage terms). At the most basic level we can recognize three major types of elasticity:

1. *Unitary elasticity of demand.* Where the percentage change (increase or decrease) in demand is exactly the same as the percentage change in price we speak of elasticity of demand being *unitary.* (For example, where the price of a good decreases by 5 percent and demand for the good increases by 5 percent).

2. *Elastic demand.* Where the percentage change in price produces an even greater percentage change in demand, such demand is said to be *elastic.*

3. *Inelastic demand.* Where the percentage change in price produces an imperceptible change. in demand, we speak of *inelastic* demand, that is it changes very little in response to a change in price.

In reality, of course, elasticity of demand generally falls somewhere along what is a continuum.

goods of high unit value. Such variations allow the transportation agency considerable flexibility in rate-making. High value goods are generally charged at least the full cost of the service, including overhead charges, while goods of low unit value may be charged rates which do not meet the actual costs involved.

Size of shipment	60-mile haul			500-mile haul		
	Rail	Truck	Barge	Rail	Truck	Barge
Under 100 lb	301	138	—*	366	173	—*
501–2000 lb	54	30	—*	120	65	55
Carload (30 tons), truckload (10 tons), or equivalent quantity of package freight by barge	5.5	6.2	11	18	33	16

Table 5.3
Average cost of rail, truck, and barge transport (including return on investment) in the Lower Mississippi Valley, 1939–1940 (cents per 100 lb.).

*Data not available.
Source: From E. M. Hoover (1948), *The Location of Economic Activity*, Table 2.2. Copyright 1948. McGraw-Hill, New York. Used with permission of McGraw-Hill Book Company.

Variations in freight rates according to "traffic" characteristics

A. Competition between transportation media. Where only one effective form of transportation exists, the operator can set rate levels to cover costs and, in the absence of government intervention, there is considerable scope for establishing high rate levels. But, as we have seen, the major transportation media each have the advantage over certain distances. If, for example, railroads wish to compete with trucks for traffic on short hauls they must keep their rates down to a comparable level. A similar effect occurs because of competition between different routes of the same transportation medium, particularly railroads. The general effect of competition, then, is to lessen the rate differences between direct competitors. There are numerous examples of this in the literature of economic geography; for example, the presence of the New York State Barge Canal had a pronounced effect on railroad rates between Buffalo and New York. Thus freight rates have been observed to be lower from Chicago to New York than from Chicago to Philadelphia. The opening of the St. Lawrence Seaway in 1959 resulted in a decline in rail freight rates on those commodities most likely to be affected by low water transport rates. But the improvement of a transport route will not in itself reduce freight rates to the *users* of the route if there is no competition between *suppliers* of the transport service. The effect will be simply to lower the costs to the suppliers of the service and increase their profits. This has occurred in British Columbia, for example.

B. Traffic density. Where demand for transportation is areally concentrated with the consequent heavy volume of traffic over certain routes there is a justification for setting lower rates. This is because the greater the traffic density, the lower is the unit cost of transportation as the fixed costs can be spread more extensively. Obversely, areas or routes of light traffic may charge higher rates. The variations between freight rate territories discussed earlier reflected such differences in traffic density as did the network patterns.

C. Direction of haul over a particular route. A common practice is for freight rates to be lower along a route in the direction of light traffic flow. Such a difference is based on the fact that the railroad cars, trucks, or other vehicles must in any case be returned to the point from which the major traffic originates. Where a return journey has to be made it costs little more to carry a freight load than to return empty. Thus more favorable "back-haul" rates can be offered and these have been significant in a number of cases, a notable example being the development of iron and steel plants in the upper Great Lakes region. Here coal was shipped by water transport at low back-haul rates and used with local ores.

Transportation costs and the location of economic activity

The introduction of more realistic transportation costs and, especially, of the tapering characteristic of many freight rate structures inevitably modifies our view of the spatial organization of economic activities. The existence of tapering freight rates compared with rates which are proportional to distance encourages longer-distance movements, as Figure 5.10 showed. Clearly, this greatly alters distance relationships in our economic landscape; long-distance movements become relatively cheaper, short-distance movements are less advantageous. We can examine the locational implications of this revised view of transportation costs under three broad headings: first, the effect on supply and market areas and, second, the effect on the actual location of production units. Third, we will examine some of the ways in which producers may themselves operate different spatial pricing policies by manipulating their transportation rates.

Effect on supply and market areas

Long-haul economies make possible sales and purchases at greater distances than would be feasible if transportation costs were proportional to distance. The result is that market and supply areas for all kinds of products—agricultural, manufacturing, and central place goods—become spatially extended. In the case of agricultural production, for example, tapering transportation costs modify the shape of the location-rent curve. Instead of being linear the rent curve becomes *curvilinear* implying that location rent declines more rapidly close to the market than at greater distances. The result is to spread production zones, especially the outer ones, thus extending the boundary of agricultural production as shown in Figure 5.16. Clearly non-linear transportation costs in general do nothing to destroy the overall pattern of zonation; they simply modify the size of the zones.

However, if different products have different levels of transportation costs, as well they might depending upon such characteristics as perishability, fragility, or bulkiness, the zonal pattern may be quite drastically altered and some production zones may disappear altogether. In Figure 5.17, for example, the relatively high transportation costs incurred by product 2 give a steeper location-

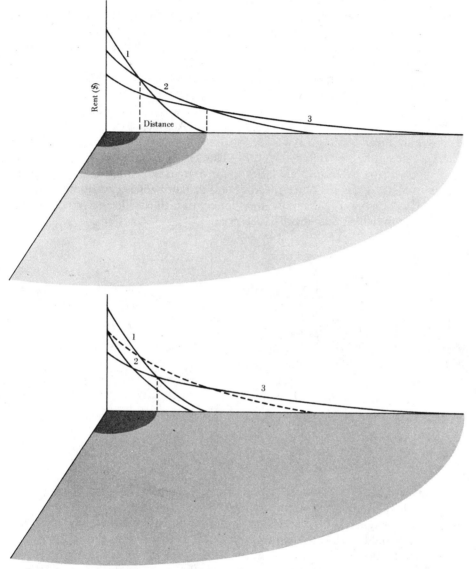

Figure 5.16
Effect of tapering freight
rates on agricultural rent
curves.

Figure 5.17
Effect of different levels of
transportation rates on
agricultural land-use
zones.

rent curve which is never higher than that for product 1. Product 2, therefore, will not be produced. As a result the transition point between one crop and another also changes so that product 1's zone of production is extended outwards while product 3 can be produced rather closer to the market.

Long-haul economies will also tend to extend the *market areas* of producers. In the absence of competition this would simply result in an extension of the outer boundary, a shift outwards of the *range* of the good. In the more usual situation in which producers are competing for sales the effect of tapering transportation costs will depend, as in the agricultural supply area example of Figure 5.17, on the *relative* transportation costs of each competitor. Suppose that, as in Figure 5.18, there are two producers of the same good. If transportation costs were linear (that is, proportional to distance) the market area boundary would be exactly halfway between the two producers, at M. But suppose that not only are transportation costs not linear but also that the producer at A pays a lower transport rate than B. This could occur, for example, if A can ship his products in larger consignments. The result could be that A may push the market area boundary to M′ and even isolate B's market area (M′—M″) by being able to charge a lower delivered price beyond M″ even though consumers in that area are closer to B than to A. Such extensions to market and supply areas are not, of course, spatially uniform but vary according to the cost advantage of different routes. The result is not only larger market and supply areas but also boundaries to such areas which are highly irregular. In addition, the grouping of freight rates into distance zones contributes towards the overlap of market and supply area boundaries, thus reducing the clear spatial monopoly which would otherwise exist.

Figure 5.18
Effect of tapering freight rates on the market areas of two competitors.

Figure 5.19
Tapering freight rates encourage location at terminal points.

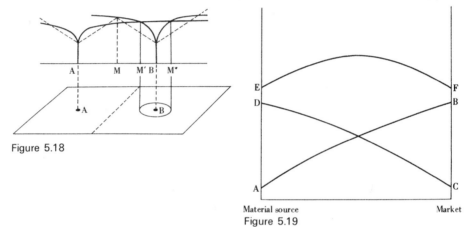

Figure 5.18

Material source   Market
Figure 5.19

Effect on the location of production

In Chapter Four we examined the locational problem facing a producer of manufactured goods who had to assemble materials which were available only at certain locations and to distribute his product to a market. We saw that production could be located either at the end points of the locational figure or at an intermediate location depending upon the size of the material index in Weber's approach to the problem or upon the specific substitution relationships in Isard's analysis. With tapering transportation costs, however, an intermediate location becomes distinctly less likely simply because the cost of two separate short hauls is likely to exceed the cost of one long haul from either a material source or a market location (two sets of terminal costs would be incurred rather than one). We can illustrate this in a number of ways to correspond with our discussion in Chapter Four. Figure 5.19 shows the simple two-point locational problem in which both material and product have a tapered freight rate structure. The curve AB represents the cost of transporting the material, the curve CD represents the cost of transporting the finished product. Adding the transportation cost on each at every point between market and materials source (curve EF) shows that an intermediate location is out of the

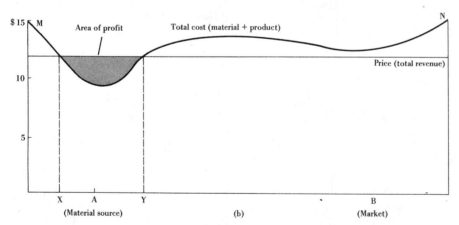

Figure 5.20
Effect of tapering freight
rates on isodapanes.

question because, in every case, it would be more costly in transportation terms than location at either market or material source.

Tapering transportation costs can be accommodated quite easily into the *isodapane* technique. The effect is basically to progressively increase the spacing between each set of isotims as in Figure 5.20. This is the same situation as shown in Figure 4.6 except that now transportation costs are higher on the material than on the product (shown by the closeness of the isotims around the material source). The least-cost production point under these conditions is at A (the material source) while the cost surface itself is also modified with repercussions on the extent of the spatial margins to profitability (X-Y).

The existence of stepped and tapering freight rates certainly makes Isard's substitution analysis rather more complex at first sight as Figure 5.21 suggests. This graph shows the substitution relationships between two materials, M_1 and M_2. Two tons of M_2 and one ton of M_1 are needed to produce one ton of the final product. The graph contains three iso-outlay lines (lines of equal total expenditure on transportation) of $24.00, $26.40, and $30.00. In the comparable Figure 4.5, such iso-outlay lines were straight because they reflected linear transportation costs. In Figure 5.21 they are both curved and stepped, each step representing a distance zone. The derivation of the optimal location is the same as in all such analysis—it is the point where the transformation line just touches the lowest iso-outlay line. At first sight this would seem to be location D on the $30.00 line in Figure 5.21. In fact it is location B. This is because a tapering cost structure produces "tails" on the iso-outlay lines which converge with the axes of the graph. For example, the stretch LM represents the tail of the $30.00 iso-outlay line. BG, however, represents the tail of the $26.40 iso-outlay line; hence B—the location of material M_1—is on a lower iso-outlay line than D and is, therefore, the minimum transport cost point.

Tapering transportation costs, then, tend to encourage location at terminal or end points—material sources or market locations—rather than somewhere between. However, there are many examples of manufacturing activity which have been established at neither material sources nor their main market centers. As subsequent chapters will show there are several "non-transport" reasons for this but as far as transportation costs are concerned, there are two major ways in which such intermediate locations may arise.

Figure 5.21
Isard's analysis and realistic freight rate structures. [*Source:* reprinted from W. Isard (1956), *Location and Space Economy,* Figure 22, by permission of the M.I.T. Press, Cambridge, Massachusetts. Copyright © 1956 by the Massachusetts Institute of Technology.]

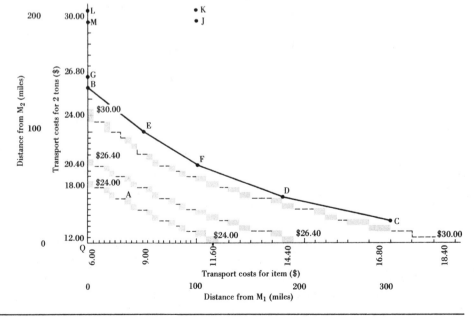

First, and most important, is the case where different transportation systems converge. Where goods must be trans-shipped from one type of transport to another, additional terminal and handling costs are incurred which destroy any long-haul advantage. These extra costs can be avoided by locating production at the *break-of-bulk point.* If we examine the two-point case again but introduce the additional complexity of different transport media the effect of their convergence can be seen (Figure 5.22). Between A (material source) and B (trans-shipment point) movement is by water transport; between B and C (the market) rail transport is used. The differing cost characteristics of the two media is shown by the differences in cost gradient. The cost of transferring the good from water to rail at B produces the marked upward jump in both procurement and distribution costs. Consequently it is cheaper to establish production at B. This simple example demonstrates why ports and rail terminals in particular tend to have considerable importance as manufacturing centers, especially in the processing of bulk materials. A similar phenomenon may occur at political boundaries where crossing from one country to another may result in the journey being regarded as starting afresh at the border even though no actual break occurs. The result, however, is an increase in transportation costs which can be avoided only by establishing production at the artificial trans-shipment point.

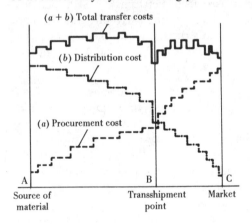

Figure 5.22
Effect of the convergence of two transportation media on total transportation costs. [*Source:* from E. M. Hoover (1948), *The Location of Economic Activity,* Figure 3.8. Copyright © 1948 McGraw-Hill, New York. Used with permission of the McGraw-Hill Book Company.]

A second, and far less important cause of intermediate location in the transport context has been the granting of "in-transit" privileges by transportation agencies, particularly in the past when railroad companies were anxious to attract traffic to their routes. The objective of the in-transit privilege is to remove the disadvantage of intermediate locations which, as we have seen, would generally involve the combined greater costs of two short hauls. Under this arrangement, the material can be shipped from its source to an intermediate point, processed, and shipped onwards to its market destination at the through rate. In the United States flour milling has been perhaps the most notable example of this practice, but it has also been present in the iron and steel industry. For example, in 1909, the Wheeling and Lake Erie Railroad permitted the stopping of steel in transit at Canton and Toledo for fabrication. This facilitated the introduction of new fabricating plants there to compete with those in the Pittsburgh area (Fulton and Hoch, 1959).

LIS—G

The nature of transportation facilities and the use made of them by different types of economic activity helps to explain *some* of the locational arrangement of manufacturing functions *within*, as well as between, urban areas. In particular, differences in the medium of transportation—whether road, rail, or waterway—seem to be especially important because the media themselves differ in the extent to which they exert a locational constraint.* For example, industries using entirely truck transportation to serve local or regional markets will not be particularly constrained in their locational choice by transportation considerations simply because of the fineness of the road network and the flexibility of truck transportation. Those serving a more geographically extensive market, of course, may well be attracted to strategic locations such as interchanges on the interstate highway or national motorway system.

The concentration of manufacturing activities which developed along Route 128, a ring highway around Boston and connected into the interstate highway system, well illustrates this tendency. As Ball and Teitz (1958) were able to demonstrate, the potential value of such a routeway for industrial use was recognized long before construction began. Tracts of land were purchased as soon as the right-of-way was announced in the late 1940s. It was estimated that land values alongside the highway increased from between $50–$100 per acre to between $2,000 and $5,000 per acre. Certainly in the early stages of development the heaviest investment was at the southern end, close to south and west rail connections, although the emphasis tended to shift as the Massachusetts Turnpike was completed and connected into Route 128.

Industries using ubiquitous or light material inputs or producing a very high-value product will tend to be less concerned with transportation considerations as a specific location factor at the intra-urban scale. But there are some industries which are both "transport sensitive" and which also rely upon those media which are more spatially restrictive. In his study of the San Francisco Bay area, Groves (1971) identified a number of manufacturing activities—for example, glass container and metal can manufacture, paints and varnish, fabricated structural steel, brewing—all of which showed a marked tendency to be located with reference to railroad facilities, generally for the acquisition of non-local raw material inputs.

Spatial pricing policies

In our discussions so far we have assumed that the price which a consumer pays for a good is related directly to his location in relation to the good's point of origin. This form of pricing is known as F.O.B. (free-on-board) or ex-works pricing whereby a price is quoted at the point of production. The cost of transport is then added to this ex-works price. Obviously the existence of transportation costs imposes limits on the spatial extent of a firm's market

Note   *The medium of transportation is one of the six variables on which Groves (1971) built his typology of intra-metropolitan manufacturing location. The same variable played an important part in the earlier typological scheme devised by Pred (1964). We shall have more to say about intra-urban manufacturing patterns in Chapters Seven and Ten.

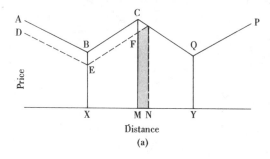

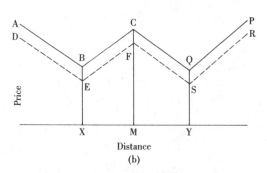

Figure 5.23
Competition for markets: the result of change in delivered price. [*Source:* reprinted from M. L. Greenhut (1956), *Plant Location in Theory and Practice,* Figure 23, by permission of the University of North Carolina Press, Chapel Hill.]

while, at the same time, it gives a degree of spatial monopoly to a producer over the area in which his delivered price is lower than that of competing producers.

F.O.B. pricing is *nondiscriminating* in the sense that each consumer pays a price in exact accordance with his location relative to the point of supply (factory price plus transportation cost). In Figure 5.23, for example, two firms, X and Y, both charge F.O.B. prices for an identical product. Where both factory price and transportation costs are the same they share the market between them equally (the market area boundary in Figure 5.23a being shown by the line MC). If firm X reduces his delivered price uniformly, from ABC to DEF—he may do this by lowering his profit margin in order to increase his sales volume— then he can invade producer Y's market area as far as N. Such an advantage is likely to be short-lived, of course, because Y will probably retaliate by reducing his delivered price by at least the same amount and the market area boundary will revert to M (Figure 5.23b).

However, a producer need not adhere to F.O.B. pricing, especially if he wishes to increase his sales at greater distances. He can practice *discriminatory pricing* by manipulating his transportation costs in a number of ways. In each case the price paid by a consumer is *not* directly related to his distance from the point of sale as it would be if F.O.B. pricing were followed; in other words, there is a degree of spatial discrimination.

The aim of discriminatory pricing is to increase total revenue by achieving sales in markets at distances beyond those that could be served using the F.O.B. pricing system. The basis of such discrimination is the spatial monopoly imposed by distance and the extent to which elasticity of demand for the good varies

Figure 5.24
Potential for price
increases is related to the
degree of spatial
monopoly. [*Source:*
based on M. Chisholm
(1966), Figure 4.]

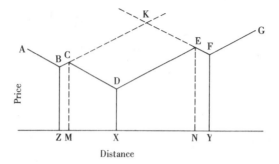

as a result of the location of competitors. In Figure 5.24 the boundaries of X's market area under F.O.B. pricing are M, N. Beyond these points, consumers are supplied at a lower delivered price by Z and Y. The price to consumers within X's market area is a point along CDE, depending upon their distance from X. But X *could* charge prices as high as CK and EK without losing sales to Z or Y. Clearly, X's scope for raising prices is greatest close to his location and least at the outer margins of the market area, where potential competition from other suppliers is greatest. In other words, the elasticity of demand for good X is greater farther from the seller's location.

In order to extend sales spatially, therefore, a seller must be able to charge a delivered price to distant consumers that is lower than that of his competitors. This can be achieved by "absorbing" some or all of the freight cost to the distant consumer. Instead of operating an F.O.B. pricing policy a firm may operate an *equalized* delivered price system in which a uniform price is charged over a wide area. As Figure 5.25 shows, this, in effect, discriminates *against* consumers near to the point of production or sale and discriminates *in favor* of more distant buyers. In other words, local customers pay rather more and distant customers rather less than they would if delivered price varied directly with distance. A uniform delivered price system, which may extend over the entire national market in certain cases, is justified if it encourages sales to distant areas that would not exist otherwise, provided that the cost of producing additional units of output to such distant consumers is less than the revenue received in selling these units, allowing for the extra cost of freight absorption.

A good deal of controversy exists regarding the extent to which uniform delivered prices operate in practice. On the whole the system has been most prevalent on consumer goods, especially those advertised and sold on a state-wide or nation-wide basis, rather than on producer goods. In the latter case, much depends upon the relative importance of transport costs in the industry's cost structure and upon the distances involved. The small spatial extent of the British market, for example, means that uniform delivered prices are characteristic of a very wide range of economic activities and not merely of those with low transport costs. However, Chisholm (1966) presents evidence to suggest that even in the United States uniform delivered prices are characteristic not only of consumer goods but also of a range of commodities including rubber products, printing and publishing, aluminum, rayon yarns, and electric turbine generators.

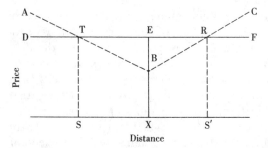

Figure 5.25
The relationship between
F.O.B. pricing and
uniform delivered pricing.

Probably the most widely known discriminatory pricing policy is *basing-point* pricing (single or multiple), although today it is relatively unimportant and probably restricted to one or two economic activities. But in the past, basing-point pricing was a characteristic of a large number of industries. In the United States, Machlup (1949) suggests that no fewer than 18 major industries used this system at some time until it was finally declared illegal by the federal authorities in 1948.*

Basing-point pricing is, in effect, a rigid pattern of delivered prices systematically followed by all firms in an industry. The system operates in the following way. A base price is fixed at a certain location and the price quoted to all consumers is this base price plus the freight charge from the base point to the consumer, whether or not he buys the good from the base point or from some other location. In an industry operating on basing-point pricing, all sellers will quote an identical delivered price to any one consumer.

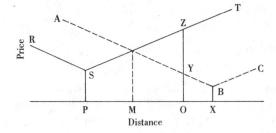

Figure 5.26
The distortional impact of
single basing-point
pricing. [*Source:* based
on M. Chisholm (1966),
Figure 5.]

Figure 5.26 shows two production centers. Center P can quote an F.O.B. price of PS while RST shows its delivered price at all locations. Center X is also a producing center, which has much lower production costs (XB) than P and which could quote a delivered price ABC. Under a nondiscriminatory pricing system, X would supply to all consumers to the right of M and P would serve the market to the left of M. Suppose, however, that P is the basing-point for the industry. In this case all consumers must pay the appropriate delivered price along RST. For example, O represents a consumer who purchases from X, the nearest producer. Under the basing-point system O must pay OZ instead of OY even though the good is transported only from X. In other words, he

*The U.S. steel industry was perhaps the best-known example of basing-point pricing (Rodgers, 1952). A comprehensive analysis of the pricing system is given by Stocking (1954). See also Chisholm (1966).   Note

must pay a non-existent or "phantom" freight. Quite clearly, the existence of a basing-point pricing system is likely to stimulate the location of users of the good close to the basing point. Only in this way can they reduce the delivered price of the good to them. In the case of the United States steel industry, where a single basing point focused on Pittsburgh operated until 1924, and a multiple basing-point system prevailed until 1948, it has been claimed that it greatly helped to keep steel fabricating activity in the long-established areas of steel production. In particular, Stocking (1954) argued that the development of steel production and fabrication in the southern states was inhibited for some considerable time despite the low-cost advantage of the Birmingham, Alabama site. In fact in Figure 5.26 point P could be regarded as representing Pittsburgh and point X as representing Birmingham.

Thus variations in pricing policies together with the zonal characteristics of freight rates tend to reduce the occurrence of distinct market area boundaries. As Greenhut (1956) has observed, the ultimate goal of the various pricing practices, both nondiscriminatory and discriminatory, is to maximize revenues by increasing sales. Where a nondiscriminatory F.O.B. policy is adopted, with consumers bearing the cost of transport, there is a stimulus for the seller to be as close as possible to the largest number of buyers. If the market is spatially extensive, firms are likely to be dispersed, other things being equal. Under such circumstances the location of competitors is of vital importance. On the other hand, where equalized delivered prices are quoted such locational interdependence is less marked. Location patterns are more likely to differ according to spatial variations in procurement costs (see Chapter Four), costs of production (see Chapter Six) and agglomeration economies (Chapter Seven).

Transportation improvements and their spatial impact

An efficient transportation system is, in many ways, the life-blood of an economic system because it is the means whereby the friction of space is overcome. The need to move goods and people from place to place as rapidly and as cheaply as possible has resulted in major changes in transportation technology. These have, in effect, progressively altered the spatial dimension of the economic system. As a result we live in a "shrinking" world, but the amount of shrinkage is not everywhere the same. We might imagine that the earth's surface is like a sheet of highly flexible material which, over time, becomes changed and distorted: relatively stretched in some areas and contracted in others.

Let us look more closely at this process using Janelle's concept of *time-space convergence* as a framework for our discussion. Janelle set out to demonstrate the cumulative, though spatially uneven, impact of transportation improvements on the spatial organization of activities, an issue we shall return to again in Chapter Ten. His starting point is the same as the one we chose at the beginning of this chapter: the *demand* for improved accessibility generated by an economic system as a whole or by one or other of its component parts (individual businesses, urban centers, etc.). In Figure 5.27, therefore, *demand for accessibility* (1) is the driving force. If potential demand is sufficiently large it is likely that

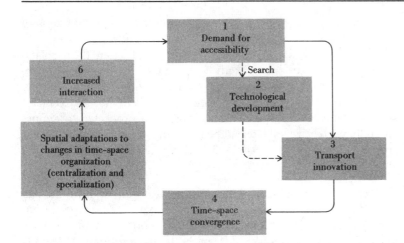

Figure 5.27
A process of spatial reorganization in response to transportation improvements. [*Source:* based on D. G. Janelle (1969), Figure 3.]

search for the means of satisfying this demand will occur (2). Those searches that prove to be successful result in a *transport innovation* (3) which may be of one of two kinds. The innovation may be an entirely new form of transportation, as when the railroad superseded the stagecoach, or it may be an improvement in existing types, for example, paved highways instead of dust tracks, steamboats instead of sail. In either case, the result may be to increase the speed of movement, thus reducing the time-distance separating places or to reduce the cost of moving from place to place. Or the innovation may permit the movement of a much larger volume of traffic.

This is not the place to indulge ourselves in a detailed discussion of transport innovations but we need to take a brief look at such changes to provide a perspective from which to examine their spatial impact. As many economic historians have observed, the nineteenth-century industrial revolution cannot be considered in isolation from developments in transportation. Indeed, it has been suggested that the industrial revolution, at least in its early stages, might more realistically be called the transportation revolution. Because of the high cost and low level of efficiency of overland transport prior to the development of the steam engine, most industrial and commercial freight was carried by water: hence the early dominance of coastal centers and those on navigable waterways. Development of the steam engine in the eighteenth century and its application in the early nineteenth century, first to water, and later to land transportation in the form of the locomotive, was nothing short of revolutionary. This heralded the beginning of a series of transportation improvements which have continued to the present day.

The transportation revolution of the nineteenth century was based on the rapid spread of the railroads which, in the United States, was most marked in the 1850s. In 1830, only 23 miles of railroad track existed in the United States; by 1848, the figure had risen to 6,000 miles, followed by a sharp increase to 30,600 miles in 1860, a stage which marked the completion of the basic railroad network east of the Mississippi River. By 1890, the United States railroad network consisted of 166,703 miles of track (Chandler, 1965). The transportation revolution of the twentieth century is associated with quite different, but equally revolutionary transportation innovations. First in importance is the automobile, the current symbol of western urban–industrial society and, later, the airplane and a more specialized form of transportation, the pipeline. The automobile, in particular, has become the most pervasive transportation medium, with a phenomenal growth rate since the turn of the century. In 1910, 468,500 vehicles were registered in the United States; by 1915 this figure had rocketed to almost two and a half million; ten years later almost twenty million vehicles were registered. At present there are approximately eighty-nine million automobiles on United States highways.

Introduction and development of each successive transportation medium has led to changes in the competitive position of existing types of transportation. This is mainly because each new development generally represented an improvement either in speed or efficiency of service, or both. In addition, as demonstrated on page 168, each type offers particular advantages, either over certain distance ranges or for particular types of freight. In general, the share of freight carried by truck has increased very markedly since the Second World War while railroads have experienced a considerable decline except in the movement of certain kinds of freight. Airlines remain more significant as people-movers than as freight-movers, although some kinds of low-weight/high-value goods do move by air.

Thus, the two major trends in transportation innovations have been, first, the development of improved means of transportation and, second, technical developments within the transportation media themselves. The beneficial effects of such developments have been further enhanced during the last few years by improvements in coordination and linkage between the different transportation media. The development of "piggy-back" and "fishy-back" techniques—standardized containers which are interchangeable between truck, railroad car and ship—is making an enormous difference to both freight-handling times and costs.

These successive developments have resulted not only in greatly improved transportation facilities but also in a drastic general decline in the average costs of transportation. For example, the opening of the Erie Canal in 1825 reduced the cost of transportation between Buffalo and Albany from $100 to $10 and ultimately to $3 per ton (Locklin, 1960).

As far as the railroads were concerned:

> Late nineteenth-century innovations in motive power, carrying capacity, and operating procedure reduced average railroad freight charges to a revolutionary degree. On a representative line, the New York Central and Hudson River Railroad, average freight tariffs per ton–mile fell from 3.31 cents in 1865 to 0.70 cents in 1892. Over a somewhat shorter time span, 1865–1884, the average ton–mile rates levied by a smaller railroad, the Boston and Albany, were diminished from 3.90 cents to 1.09 cents. For

U.S. railroads as a whole, rates dropped 41 percent between 1882 and 1900, from 1.236 cents per ton–mile to 0.729 cents per ton–mile.
Pred (1966), p. 49

Chisholm (1962) suggests that between the 1870s and the 1950s the *real* cost of ocean transport fell by almost 60 percent.

Such a universal decline in transportation costs combined with the changes discussed in Chapter Four towards a more efficient use of raw materials in production processes and the substitution of one material for another (for example, electricity for coal) means that transportation has become a relatively less important factor in the overall cost structure of many industries. For some heavy industries, of course, transport costs remain a very substantial cost element. However, the tendency in recent decades has been for most products to undergo a greater degree of processing. In other words, the *value added* by production to that of the original materials has tended to increase. The greater this degree of value added the less important proportionally are transport costs, which, as we have shown in this section, have in any case been falling relatively.

Not only has the *cost* of overcoming the friction of space declined spectacularly over the last century and a half, but also the *time* involved has greatly decreased. For example, the construction of the railroad shortened the journey time between New York and Chicago from more than three weeks to less than three days. Figure 5.28 shows the progressive reduction in travel time between Detroit and Lansing in the United States and between London and Edinburgh in Britain because of transport innovations. As a result of such changes these places (and many others) are effectively closer together than before. In Janelle's terminology they are characterized by *time-space convergence*—step 4 in Figure 5.27. He calculates, for example, that the average rate of such convergence between London and Edinburgh was roughly 29 minutes per year over the period 1776–1966. It is clear from Figure 5.28, of course, that such convergence

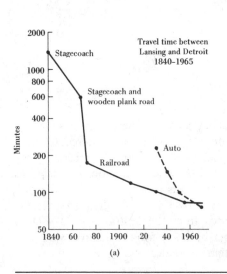

(a)

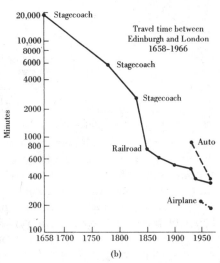

(b)

Figure 5.28
Reduction in journey times as a result of progressive transportation improvements. [*Source:* (a) D. G. Janelle (1969), Spatial Reorganization: A Model and a Concept, Figure 4. Reproduced by permission from the *Annals of the Association of American Geographers,* 59. (b) D. G. Janelle (1968), Central Place Development in a Time-Space Framework, Figure 1. Reproduced by permission from the *Professional Geographer,* 20.]

does not occur evenly (nor is it likely to occur at the same rate indefinitely)—long periods of comparatively little change in time–space relationships between two places are punctuated by abrupt changes corresponding to major transport innovations.

The general result of such developments is an overall reduction in the friction of distance. In terms of the gravity model (see Chapter Two) the distance exponent, b, has been progressively reduced as transportation improvements have occurred. Insofar as b describes the *rate* at which interaction or movement declines with distance (it defines the slope of the distance-decay curve) the changing situation resembles that of Figure 5.29. As we move from t_1, a period in which movement was costly and the friction of distance very high, through successive time periods, t_2 to t_4, the diminished frictional effect is reflected in gentler and gentler slopes as defined by b and interaction takes place over greater and greater distances.

More specifically, the result of the kinds of transportation developments we have described briefly in this chapter is to greatly alter the spatial relationships between economic activities. Their *relative* locations have been altered (step 5 in Figure 5.27). This spatial reorganization has three major characteristics:

1. The spatial pattern of production has been transformed from a dispersed to a concentrated pattern.

2. There has been increased differentiation between locations on the basis of their intrinsic qualities.

3. The degree of geographic specialization and the spatial extent of production have both increased.

Figure 5.29
Changes in the frictional effect of distance.

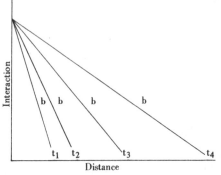

The production and distribution units (farms, factories, central places) which, under primitive or high-cost transport conditions, had to be scattered to serve distant markets, have tended to become spatially concentrated in areas of greatest advantage. Market areas, therefore, have become even more extensive as transportation has improved. Similarly, supply areas have expanded. In the case of agriculture, production becomes profitable over a wider area so that the zones of production tend to move outwards from the central market. Figure 5.30 presents a striking illustration of this by comparing estimated values of wheat at increasing distances from the market under two different transport

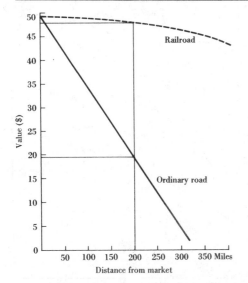

Figure 5.30
The impact of improved
transportation (railroad)
on wheat values per ton
at various distances from
the market, United States
1852. [*Source:* calculated
from data in D. P. Locklin
(1960), *The Economics of
Transportation,* 5th ed.,
Homewood, Ill.: Richard
D. Irwin, p. 3.]

technologies, the railroad and the "ordinary" road in 1852. The value of wheat declined very rapidly if road transport was used whereas its value was retained over far greater distances as a result of the railroad. At a 200-mile distance wheat was worth $19.50 per ton under road transport but $46.50 under rail. Clearly, the margin of cultivation for wheat (and, of course, for other crops) was very greatly extended.

Such expansion of agricultural production zones based on transportation improvements partly explains the continental-scale zonation noted in Chapter Three. Peet (1969) has demonstrated how the large-scale spatial expansion of commercial agriculture in the nineteenth century can be interpreted in a Von Thünen framework. He shows how the growth in demand for food and raw materials generated by the industrializing and urbanizing "world metropolis" focused on northwestern Europe and northeastern U.S.A. was met by tapping increasingly distant agricultural areas in a way made possible by the transportation improvements of the nineteenth century. Figure 5.31 shows how the average distance from London to regions from which imports were derived increased over the period 1831 to 1913. In the 1831–1835 period, no significant imports of fruit and vegetables or live animals occurred (products originating in Ireland were not classed as imports). By the 1856–1860 period, however, fruit and vegetables were being imported from an average distance of 324 miles from London and live animals from 630 miles on average. As the century progressed, these eight products were derived from increasing distances from London. In 1831–1835 the maximum distance involved was 2,430 miles (for wheat and flour); by 1891–1895 this maximum distance had increased to 11,010 miles (for wool and hides). Thus although the outward expansion of agricultural zones was not regular in every case the general trend shown in Figure 5.31 is for an overall progressive increase in the distances involved.

Decline in the relative importance of transportation costs, therefore, implies that other factors increase in significance. In particular, specialization of produc-

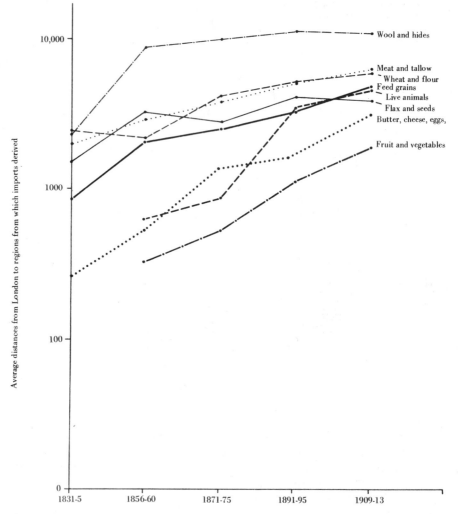

Figure 5.31
Expansion of agricultural
import zones, Great
Britain 1830–1913.
[*Source:* compiled from J.
R. Peet (1969), Table 1.]

tion on the basis of comparative advantage other than market accessibility emerges with an accompanying increase in geographical specialization. In agriculture, for example, remote locations with particularly advantageous physical conditions can be exploited whereas their location relative to the market precludes their optimal use under less favorable transport conditions. An obvious example is the change which has occurred in the location of intensively cultivated horticultural crops. They were formerly tied to the area immediately adjacent to the market; today they tend to be concentrated in areas offering the greatest natural advantages with only small pockets remaining at the urban periphery (see Chapter Three). In Denmark a general agricultural economy with mixed farming has become transformed during the present century to a highly specialized dairy and livestock economy taking advantage of a favorable natural environment for such products. As O. E. Baker (1921) observed, the general effect of improved transportation in the location of agricultural production is to increase the relative importance of natural environmental factors.

Such spatial changes at what might be termed the interregional scale have been paralleled by changes at the intraregional level. In particular, the spread of automobile transport has induced profound changes within metropolitan areas primarily by allowing the infilling of interstitial areas between major transportation arteries. Developments in intra-metropolitan accessibility have permitted a rearrangement of urban-economic functions resulting in greater growth at the periphery than in the central area (see Chapter Ten).

As Figure 5.27 shows, the result of such spatial reorganization is a higher level of interaction (6). Whereas under more primitive transport conditions most needs could be satisfied locally, the greater spatial concentration and specialization of production means that this is no longer the case and interaction must inevitably increase as places engage in trade with each other. This, in itself, generates new demands for further improvements in transportation as the routes and networks become congested and obsolescent after a period of time and so a renewed cycle is initiated (step 1 in Figure 5.27).

But although in general terms the friction of space has greatly diminished over time and continues to do so, the process has not been spatially even: some areas have benefitted far more than others. This is a point we shall return to in more detail in Chapter Ten. Suffice it at this stage to observe that transportation improvements tend to enhance the strategic position of some areas and to diminish that of others. In effect, they change the entire spatial form of the economic system by altering the functional distances between places. Invariably, transportation improvements tend to be greatest in those areas and between those places which already possess considerable economic status, generate a high level of demand for transportation, and which are likely to benefit most from such improvements. These are the places, therefore, which tend to "converge" most significantly in time-space. Figure 5.32 illustrates the extent of this differential process on urban centers in Britain. Transport innovations, such as the introduction of rapid transit passenger services on the railroads and inter-city airline services, have produced time-space convergence between London and the major provincial cities such as Birmingham, Manchester and Liverpool. On the other hand, less important places are becoming increasingly remote (in relative terms) because of the differential impact of transport innovations. Such places may be said to be characterized by *time-space divergence*. For example, as Figure 5.32 shows, Burnley, a town only 25 miles north of Manchester, is twice the time-distance from London. Pwllheli in North Wales is almost as far from London as New York or Montreal in time-distance, even though it is less than one-tenth the distance in terms of physical mileage!

Developments in transportation thus have a pronounced effect on the spatial dimension of economic systems. As well as increasing the general level of interaction within and between systems such developments profoundly alter space relationships. The implications of this process for regional economic development are profound because in many cases areas which are peripheral to the main concentrations of economic growth become increasingly remote and their degree of real integration within the system diminishes. Finally, at a more specific

Figure 5.32
Travel times from London
to selected cities.
[*Source:* Richard Natkiel
for *New Society,*
London.]

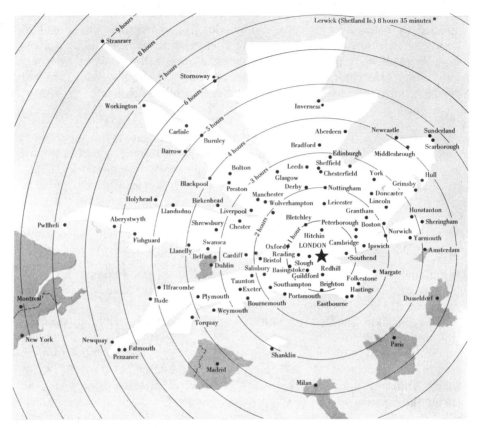

level, we should mention the impact of transportation improvements on the overall cost structure of business firms. As transportation costs decline they become relatively less significant in a firm's cost structure and other costs—for example, costs of production—become relatively more important. It is to the spatial form of such costs and their locational impact that we turn in the next chapter.

Further Reading

Alexander, J. W., S. E. Brown, and R. E. Dahlberg (1958), Freight Rates: Selected Aspects of Uniform and Nodal Regions, *Economic Geography* **34,** 1–18.

Chisholm, M. (1966), *Geography and Economics,* London: Bell, Chapter 7.

Greenhut, M. L. (1956), *Plant Location in Theory and Practise,* Chapel Hill: University of North Carolina Press, Chapter 6.

Haggett, P. (1965), *Locational Analysis in Human Geography,* London: Edward Arnold, Chapter 3.

Isard, W. (1956), *Location and Space Economy,* Cambridge, Mass.: M.I.T. Press, Chapter 5.

Janelle, D. G. (1969), Spatial Reorganization: A Model and a Concept, *Annals of the Association of American Geographers* **59**, 348–364.

Sampson, R. J., and M. T. Farris (1966), *Domestic Transportation: Practise, Theory and Policy*, Boston: Houghton Mifflin, Chapters 2–5; 9–12.

Smith, D. M. (1971), *Industrial Location: An Economic-Geographical Analysis*, New York: John Wiley, Chapter 5.

Taaffe, E. J., and H. Gauthier (1973), *Geography of Transportation*, Englewood Cliffs, N.J.: Prentice Hall, Chapters 4–5.

CHAPTER 6

SPATIAL VARIATIONS IN PRODUCTION COSTS

The production of any good or service requires that the producer assemble together a number of basic inputs. He will, as we have seen, require land on which to place his factory, farm or office. He will also need to assemble together various raw materials, and we have seen in the Weberian model of Chapter Four some of the particularly geographical considerations which he must take into account in attempting to find the best location at which to assemble them. But he will need other basic things as well. He will probably need *labor* over and above that which he can provide himself. He will certainly need *capital*, both as money to set himself up in business and buy his first inputs of materials from suppliers, and as machinery, office furniture, or perhaps, if he is a farmer, just seed from which to grow next season's crop. He will also need *technology* in one form or another. This may be provided simply as the stock of basic notions about how best to go about producing things handed down in culture and applied practically in methods of forging iron, rotating crops or curing customer's ailments. In its more advanced forms technology may be provided by setting up a research and development department, hiring graduates as employees, or sending managers to business school. In simple terms, and divorced from the people or machines that carry it, technology is simply "know-how" and, elusive though it is to categorize and measure, it is critical to the productive process in society, be it ancient or modern.*

It is worth reminding ourselves of the reasons why individuals or groups set out to assemble these combinations of inputs. They do so because there is some identified demand for the goods or services that come out of the production process. An economist would call this a *derived demand*. From the wishes of a consumer population demands are derived for a variety of things from automobiles to asparagus and from garbage collection to psychoanalysis. These in turn increase the demand for the land, labor, capital and technology required to produce them as would-be producers enter the market for these fundamental *factors of production*. Clearly, as time passes tastes will change as will the prescribed methods for producing the goods and services which satisfy those tastes. As a result, factors of production will be in more or less demand by particular groups of producers who are more or less able to pay for them at the going price. Thus, there is a *market* for factors of production like land, labor and capital, just as there is a market for potatoes or gasoline. In this market the twin forces of supply and demand determine the price for a given factor in much the same way as they did for various commodities as we demonstrated in Chapter Two.

Note

*Although land, labor and capital are relatively easily distinguishable from one another and are, in theory at least, discrete measurable factors, technology is both difficult to define and even more difficult to separate out and measure. Much technology is "built in" to the tools available to a society. Tools, however, would be more readily identifiable as capital. Even more "know-how" is built into the particular "social technology" which represents the institutions which different societies provide for "getting things done". For the sake of simplicity we shall concentrate here on the factors of land, labor and capital, implying that technology is built into them, although at a later stage we shall look briefly at technology as a separate entity.

Looked at from the viewpoint of the individual businessman who sees his chance to make a profit by selling some product on the market, his first investment decision will be how many factors to hire and in what proportions to combine them (Figure 6.1). The word "hire" here needs some emphasis since what a man "buys" in the factor market is not a whole human being but the *labor services of a person.* When he acquires a plot of land it is the *productive properties of the land* he seeks, not a set of geographical coordinates defining a two-dimensional space. True, if he wants the land to build a newsstand and those geographical coordinates would set him down in the middle of Grand Central Station, they have some critical importance by having a positive impact on his likely sales. Thus, as we have already demonstrated, location has its special utility, and newsagents, farmers, or any others sensitive to place in their productive operations, will bid against each other to acquire it. Similarly, producers bidding to acquire capital are not seeking gold bars or banknotes in their own right, but they are seeking to hire the *productive services of that currency* by turning it into paying assets like machinery, hospitals or office blocks. Hence, as with land and labor they will value money or other more fixed forms of capital in terms of its particular *utility* in relation to the productive tasks they have set themselves. The factors of production then are traded in the market for factors on the basis of *the value of the productive services* which it is anticipated they will provide at some point in the future and this adds a speculative element into the trading. (See Heilbroner, 1972, p. 488.)

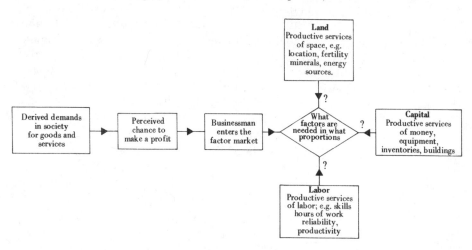

Figure 6.1
Choices in the hire of production factors.

All along we have been looking at the particular requirements of aspiring producers in society and attempting to assess the particularly spatial features which have both entered into their decision-making and have resulted from their decisions. In essence, we have been examining the spatial constraints which have been involved in determining what factors a producer has hired. Under the constraints of the simplified model these have been explicitly reduced to a single factor—*land.* In effect, when we looked at the concept of *locational rent* in such models as that of Von Thünen, we were examining the role of a constrained factor market for land (that is land of uniform quality at different locations) in generating particular patterns of agricultural land use on the isotropic plain. With the notion of heterogeneity in the landscape introduced in Chapter Four, we have relaxed some of these constraints—those of differential topography and fertility in particular—but have still retained the assumption of free access to other factors of production such as labor, capital and technology. At this point we must go on to consider in a more realistic way the spatial connotations of those key questions which every aspiring businessman must ask himself. "Which factors of production do I need and in what amounts? How shall I combine them together to create the most effective unit for the production of the output I am going to supply to my customers?"

Clearly, knowing what it is he is going to "output" and in what amounts (a question which for the sake of simplicity we shall treat only superficially here, deferring it for fuller consideration until a later stage—see Chapter Seven), the first logical step he will take will be to consider the set of *production possibilities* open to him. Does he have a choice, or is there a single unique combination of factor inputs to make the product he has in mind? In the modern world the second is rarely the case. For the most part he will have choices and frequently the success or failure of the venture will depend upon making the right one.

Suppose, for instance, our businessman is an aspiring shirt manufacturer. Even for the same output of shirt "units" per week he will have choices to make. Given perhaps that the smallest factory site worth acquiring is fixed at, say, 500 square feet, he would still have to choose between quantities of capital and labor employed on it. Should he, for instance, invest in a set of computer-controlled cutting machines to cut his cloth, or is it better to take on skilled workers? Should buttonholing be done by machine or man? Should the shirts be handstitched or sewn on a machine? Should he allow for floorspace and shelving to carry a reserve stock of shirt-cloth or should he buy as he goes? Should he have a boy and handcart to get his shirts to the wholesaler or should he invest in a truck? Obviously, many of these choices will be more critical in relation to the likely scale of the operation, but even at the same scale of output choices of *factor mix* would have to be made. It is also clear that in some activities *technical substitution* of, say, capital for labor, or land for capital, is not possible. For any production unit, therefore, there is some notional range of production possibilities which implies an ability to substitute one factor of production for another. An economist would express this as a *production function*. In its fullest aggregate form we could set out the production function for our aspiring businessman in the form of a simple logical statement like the following:

O	= f	(K, L, Q, T)
The output he will produce	*Will be some function of*	*The amounts and combinations of the Land (K), Labor (L), Capital (Q) and Technology (T) which he assembles together*

If we were to attempt to graph the possible combinations made available for substitution from this full set we would, of course, need four dimensions—one for each of the factors. Even if we assigned technology to the capital category we would still need a three-dimensional diagram—difficult to draw and interpret. So let us go one step further and subsume both capital and technology for the moment into the land factor. Under these constrained conditions the logical expression for the production function would be reduced as follows:

$$O = f(K, L)$$

–and we could draw a two-dimensional graph of the production function for the enterprise (Figure 6.2). The axes represent increasing amounts of the land and labor factors from the origin, O. The curves OU_1 and OU_2 show for given levels of output the possible combinations of amounts of land and labor. We have encountered similar curves before in the section (Chapter Four, p. 128) on substitution analysis. In that case we were using the curves or *transformation lines* to show possible substitutions of distance from pairs of locations in attempting to solve the manufacturer's distance-minimization problem. In this case we are looking at the substitution possibilities between land and labor inputs for a new business. To produce 1000 units of output on the basis of the production function shown in Figure 6.2 our businessman could choose, for example, to hire 50 units of land combined with 10 units of labor. Alternatively, he could go to the other extreme and hire only 20 units of land but 35 units of labor. These would represent the extremes of land intensity or labor intensity open to him. There is, however, a wide selection of intermediate choices. Every combination of land and labor inputs at any point on the curve between its two extremes offers an opportunity for substitution of one against the other.* Clearly some combinations represent more rational choices than

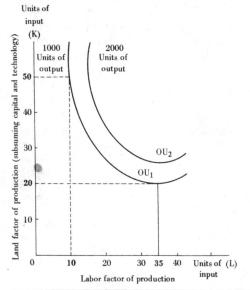

Figure 6.2
Production function for two factors of production: land and labor.

*A point worth noting here, but one which we will pursue in more detail in the next chapter, is that for the production function illustrated in Figure 6.2 the production of 2000 units of output does not demand twice as much land/labor input as the production of 1000 units. We could clearly draw up a production function for each possible scale of output—3000

Note

Note continued

units, 4000 units and so on. This would enable the businessman to see how much more of each factor he would need to hire for each successive increase in output and perhaps to determine the best scale of operations for his new enterprise.

others. Where the production possibility lines "re-curve" towards their extremities more of *both* factors would be required for the same output. No rational businessman would choose such a combination.

We have looked at the *possibilities* available to the businessman in deciding on his particular factor mix. So far, however, we have said nothing about cost. Clearly, while several combinations of factors may be *technically* feasible, many of them may be out of the question when costs are taken into account. Factors of production are priced on the market on the basis of their *economic* (or *quasi*) *rent*.* We met this before in the context of land allocation in the simplified model of Chapter Two. It is essentially a "premium" paid to the holders of a production factor because of its relative scarcity. The more bidders for a factor the higher its value to the owner in terms of economic rent. In common with most average houseowners over the last two decades, the landowner needs to do nothing to see the value of the resource he owns appreciate in value. It does so by virtue of the rising demand from the population at large for a land factor in short supply. Valuation by economic rent is a principle applied to all factors of production, not just land. They are valued by their relative scarcity.

To hire a production factor, a would-be user makes a *transfer payment*. In the case of land we call this *rent*. This is not the same as economic rent which is a measure of value and not something which is paid at all. It is unfortunate that the terminology encourages confusion. Clearly, there is a relationship between the two. The rent which a landlord demands as compensation for letting you, rather than someone else, have the use of his property will be based upon what bidders in general see as the "going rate"—something approximate to economic rent—as well as his own costs in providing furniture, services, and so on.

Note

Economic Rent: Figure 6.3 shows the supply and demand situation for prime office space in a major city. At time $t = 1$ there is office space of this type for all on demand and no scarcity exists. The *real rent* OY_1 represents the basic costs of bringing the factor into production and this is paid to landlords to compensate them for doing so. Once demand for prime office space shifts to the right of X_1, however, the price rises. Office space is now becoming relatively scarce and the cost of supplying new prime office space rises as more expenditure is required, perhaps to bring second grade offices up to the standard needed. The new higher price of prime office space is no longer, however, simply a payment to bring more of the factor onto the market. It is paid not only to those who supply more office space, but also to those already holding offices. It has now become a "surplus" payable to holders of the factor because of its scarcity. This additional value placed on office space by virtue of its short supply is *economic rent*. It is added to real rent to give rent levels Y_2 and Y_3 on *all* office space at the relevant times. Under these conditions of relative scarcity only those who can afford to "bid" up to the economic rent of prime office space can acquire it. Those who cannot must look to secondary office space or to that on which their bids relate to the economic rent of the factor in demand. Economic rent serves as an *allocative* indicator, the market making sure that the "best" of a factor is hired only to bidders who can make the best returns from using it.

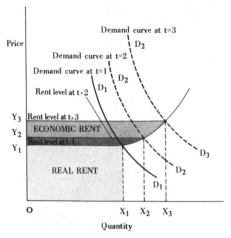

Figure 6.3
Economic rent and real
rent for prime office
space.

To acquire capital a person makes a transfer payment which is called *interest*. It should surprise no one to learn that interest rates rise and fall in accordance with the demand for capital and that holders of capital "earn" a variable premium on the factor which they hold as general levels of demand rise and fall. Similarly in order to hire the productive services of labor a transfer payment of *wages* is made. This compensates the resource-holder for the labor time he puts in to the producer's tasks. What makes labor different, however, as a factor of production is that it is a factor provided by some men to other men on terms of contract or agreement. It has moral, social and political connotations which would divert us if we were to enquire too closely into them at this stage.

Let us go back to our aspiring businessman. He is now confronted not simply with the technical possibilities of substituting one factor of production against another but with the *relative costs of the various factors.* As a notional profit maximizer he will be concerned to make that decision in the context of his production function which minimizes his costs. (We are still retaining for the moment the assumption of uniform demand.) He will, therefore, go for those factors which, other things being equal, involve him in the lowest technically feasible outlays for a given volume of output.

Figure 6.4 provides a graphic illustration of what might be involved. Taking the production function for 1000 units of output from Figure 6.2 we can show the impact which differential factor costs might have. Costs are added to the graph by means of *iso-outlay lines* drawn diagonally from axis to axis. Suppose the relative prices of land and labor per unit of output are in the ratio 2:1. In other words, land for the businessman's particular application is twice as expensive as labor for each unit he produces. There will then be an infinite number of iso-outlay lines running upwards to the right of the graph's origin. We have only drawn a selection of them and for the sake of clarity (though not realism) we have expressed them in real dollar values.

Take first the iso-outlay line for $6000. If the businessman decides that his total budget would be $6000 dollars then he would have choices in the way

Figure 6.4
The production function
and factor outlays for a
given scale of output.

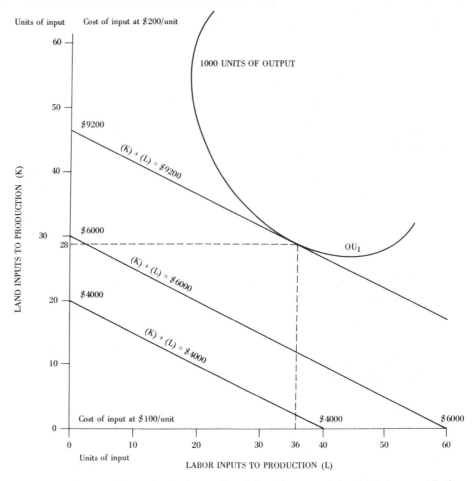

he spends it. Applying the logic outlined in Chapter 4 (p. 129) he could, for
instance, spend it all on land and, at $200 per unit, he could obtain 30 of
our notional units of land. Alternatively, he could spend it all on labor and
get 60 units of this at $100 per unit. He could also combine inputs of land
and labor so long as their total cost did not exceed $6000. The iso-outlay
line for $6000 shows all the possible combinations at this cost.

However, if he had set himself to produce a minimum of 1000 units as shown
by the production function OU_1 it is obvious that a $6000 expenditure would
not be enough. The outlay line does not nearly begin to reach the level at
which his chosen scale of production is technically possible. Unless he reduced
the number of units production would be impossible. For the 1000 units he
set himself the actual level of outlay on production factors could only be represented by iso-outlay lines which *intersected the curve of the production function*.
Since he wishes to minimize his costs of production he would be sensible to
choose the one which gave him the lowest total outlay on the two production
factors in combination. In finding the point at which the production possibility
curve intersects the lowest iso-outlay line he would discover that the least-cost

combination of factors would be that demanding 28 units of land at $200 per unit and 36 units of labor at $100 per unit—a total of $9200. With the production function shown in the curve OU_1 this is the lowest feasible cost at which he could produce 1000 units of output. Notice that the slope of the iso-outlay lines, which reflects the relative costs of the two factors, tends to encourage the *use of more labor*—the cheaper factor—and less land. Were the relative cost positions of the two reversed, the slope would be steeper and would favor land over labor. In the real world such simple solutions would be made more difficult by the problems of quantifying the variables and by the fact that the relative costs of factors is not static but ever-changing. For example, if labor was a cheap factor input for all businessmen and they exercised their choices to hire more of it, the relative scarcity of labor would increase. Its value (economic rent) would rise and the price of the factor would rise with it. Soon the price advantage of taking on labor as a substitute for other factors would be significantly reduced and other factors would become relatively more attractive.

So we have seen, in outline, the sort of considerations which an aspiring businessman would have to take into account in setting up his enterprise. He would have to consider what factors he needed to produce his good; what combinations were technically feasible at the chosen scale; and what would be the least-cost combination. Each choice, as we have seen in Chapters Two and Four, has its *spatial ramifications*. In the case of the *land factor*, we have already shown how the geographical heterogeneity of the landscape has influenced the location of economic activity in space. The need for appropriate soil or climatic conditions at an economically feasible distance from the market absorbed our attention in the case of agriculture, while for manufacturing we have concentrated thus far on the "space costs" associated with assembling those resources needed for a given productive activity. But these considerations only tell part of the story. However good the "space-cost" models have proved themselves to be in providing a working basis for the understanding of location, they are necessarily limited in their application. Where the influence of space has great importance, say, for economic activities needing large amounts of specific localized raw materials, or land of a special type, the models (as we saw both in Chapter Three and in Chapter Four) give a good "fit." Equally, activities serving spatially localized markets in a situation where shipment costs contribute a major proportion of total costs are also appropriate subjects for analysis with models founded on space costs.

For some activities, however, space or land costs have never had a special importance in comparison with, for example, labor or capital costs. For the small handicraft manufacturer space inputs are traditionally small; a loft or workshop is often sufficient. Transport costs on inputs or the final product tend equally to be small. For this kind of businessman the availability of labor with the right skills at the right price or the presence of a friendly financier to help him set up in business is the crucial element in the decision process. He will be drawn to locations where such attributes exist. In this sense, labor and capital, though not by nature intrinsically "spatial" like land or distance, are no less critical to location. Thus they are equally deserving of intensive treatment in a textbook devoted to the theory underlying the location of economic activity in space. Further, as we pointed out in Chapter Five, the distance element in "space costs" has been *drastically reduced* with the transport revolutions of the last 150 years. This being so, *in relative terms* non-space factors of production have increased their importance in the cost structure of businesses of all kinds. Indeed, with the exception of certain craft-based industries (see Chapter Seven), it is arguable that while the "space-cost" models developed during and around the turn of the last century provided a good *general* approximation for understanding locational choice in the nineteenth and the first half of the twentieth century, models for the late twentieth century demand that more attention be given to the locational impact of capital, labor and technical knowledge.

We now turn our attention to those other ingredients of the production function, to *labor*, *capital* and the particular forms of *technology* on which human productive effort is so dependent. The simplified model assumed them to be available everywhere. Let us now remove this constraint.

Labor

As we have pointed out, some input of labor is fundamental to the operation of all production systems. The relative importance of the labor factor varies widely, however, from one business enterprise to another. For the manufacturer of high quality watches, for example, the availability of labor with the right skill is critical to the success of the business. On the other hand, for the manufacturer of gasoline or fertilizer there will be a greater concern with the costs of raw materials and with the need to raise capital to buy expensive plant. For him the supply problems associated with labor will rank small in the calculus of total costs.

Up to this point we have assumed for the sake of simplicity that, despite such differences in labor requirements among economic activities, labor has had no significant impact on locational choice. The simplified model assumed that labor was evenly distributed over space and that workers were equally endowed with an infinite variety of labor skills which they could perform with uniform productivity. Nothing is, of course, further from the real-world truth. Labor, defined as the productive services offered by human beings, is highly variable in its spatial distribution. Even if we were to equate labor availability simply with the distribution of population, a glance at any population density map would immediately indicate the extreme spatial variety in the supply of this factor. If we were to take into account differences in skill, productivity, reliability, versatility and so on, labor supply would take on the most complex patchwork of pattern and variety over space. Such spatial variety by itself, however, would not necessarily make labor supply a key variable in business location. If, as it has frequently been convenient for geographers and economists to assume, labor were *infinitely mobile*, its long-term locational significance would still be negligible. If this were the case, a manufacturer with a need for skilled watchmakers would be able to choose a location on other grounds (close to the market perhaps), and if this gave him the chance of good profits he could offer more than the going rate and wait for his watchmakers to arrive to snap up the high wages. That the infinite mobility attributed to labor is no more than an assumption similar to those we made earlier about flat plains and equal fertility should be fairly clear. How, for example, do our watchmakers get to hear about the higher wages? What happens when a competitor in the next state raises his wages to watchmakers? Do they pack up and move again? What do their wives and children think about all this mobility? What about the low-paid watchmaker who likes it in Peoria, Illinois, because he grew up there? What if the costs of moving exceed the net benefits of his wages? The mobility of the factor, labor—simple as it is in the abstract—involves the movement of those complex, often illogical creatures who provide it and for them high wages is merely one criterion among many when it comes to uprooting home and family.

Having established that labor is neither evenly distributed over space nor infinitely mobile, we can go on to assume that it does have a significant impact on the locational choices made by businessmen. The next question we must ask is—how significant and for what kinds of economic activity?

The importance of labor as a location factor

For U.S. manufacturing as a whole, even in these days of mechanization and automation, labor costs are still, as almost any businessman will be willing to assert, a significant proportion of business costs in general. Wages and salaries of production workers still account on average for more than 30 percent of the value added in manufacture for all industries. If non-production workers— managers, technical and office staff and so on—are added, the figure is nearer 45 percent. Though, in a society becoming more dominated by computers and machines, wage and salary payments to production workers are steadily falling, the drift of the labor force from "blue collar" to "white collar" jobs is maintaining the *overall* cost significance of labor as a production factor. Segal in 1960 calculated that labor costs (to production workers) were 15 times greater than "space" costs and 21 times greater than costs levied through state and local taxes. While the total contribution of "blue collar" wages to costs has fallen by 5 percent since then, there seems little reason to dispute the relative contributions of each cost element as Segal saw them. *Labor costs are still critical to most industries.*

For the United Kingdom, the relative importance of labor in the calculus of cost is even more important than in the United States. Taking the wages and salaries of all workers (production and non-production) as a proportion of value added in manufacturing, the equivalent figure is 54 percent. No one exposed to the British economic scene over the past decade can be in any doubt as to the importance attributed by business and government to labor costs as a factor in profitability. A recent sample survey conducted by the U.K. government on the key criteria taken into account by firms moving to new locations in Britain found more than 70 percent of the firms interviewed concerned with aspects of labor cost (H.M.S.O. 1973). In Britain, as in the United States, however, there has been a growing shift from "blue collar" to "white collar" occupations and a greater emphasis on the substitution of capital for labor in the production process. The traditional pools of skill in "shop-floor" occupations which did so much to mold the industrial geography of nineteenth century Britain are becoming increasingly less important (see above p. 289).

Figure 6.5
Wages of production
workers as percent of
value added by
manufacture, United
States, 1974. [*Source:*
Statistical Abstract of
United States (1975),
Table 1266.]

Looked at more specifically in terms of those industries for which labor has greater than average cost significance, Figure 6.5 shows the main classes of U.S. manufacturing activity ranked by decreasing contribution of the payroll for production workers to value added. Those industries retaining a substantial handicraft element head the list. Leather goods, textiles and the manufacture of clothing remain those most likely to give primary consideration to the cost and availability of labor skills in their locational choices. At the other end of the scale, petroleum products and the manufacture of chemicals represent the most obvious cases where considerations other than labor are likely to be most important. Since the aggregation of industries into the major classes tends to obscure some of the more extreme cases where labor is (or is not) likely to influence location, Table 6.1 selects from the detailed industries of the standard classification those with the greatest (or least) contribution of production workers' wages to value added.*

Note   *Since the selection is made with reference to standard deviations (>1.5 and <1.5) from the mean percentage value and the distribution is negatively skewed, there are more classes with a low labor cost element.

	%
Ship and boat building and repairing	52.8
Weaving mills, cotton	52.1
Iron and steel foundries	49.0
Yarn and thread mills	45.9
Weaving mills, synthetics	45.0
Men's and boys' suits and coats	44.9
Wood containers	44.8
Cut stone and stone products	44.5
Reclaimed rubber	43.8
Nonferrous foundries	43.3
Boot, shoe cut stock, findings	43.0
Office and computing machines	18.4
Dairy products	18.0
Grain mill products	18.0
Greeting card publishing	17.8
Petroleum refining	17.8
Misc. foods and kindred products	17.5
Misc. publishing	17.4
Paints and allied products	16.5
Books	15.7
Industrial organic chemicals	15.4
Chewing and smoking tobacco	14.6
Agricultural chemicals	14.5
Beverages	14.3
Cigarettes	13.1
Misc. petroleum and coal products	12.5
Drugs	9.5
Soap, cleaners, toilet goods	9.0
Periodicals	4.0

Source: Statistical Abstract of U.S. (1975), Table 1266.

Table 6.1
United States: wages and salaries of production workers as a proportion of value added in manufacture: the highest and the lowest.

At this scale it becomes clearer that for those industries in which the adoption of mechanization and production line methods has been less effective, such as shipbuilding, weaving, tailoring and so on, access to the right labor at the right cost is still a primary production (and therefore locational) criterion. At the lower end of the relative labor cost scale there is a combination of those industries with a high degree of capital substituted for labor, like petroleum refining or those such as books and periodicals where production workers *per se* are less important in the work force than "office" workers. There are also those industries for which duties and taxes levied on production inflate the value added in processing.

For the United Kingdom, Figure 6.6 and Table 6.2 provide the best available comparable data with that for the United States. In this case, however, the figures shown are for all operatives. These give less variation about the mean value of 53 percent than would be the case with production workers only. At the top of Figure 6.6, with more than 74 percent of value added accounted for by labor cost, is shipbuilding and marine engineering. This also ranked high in the U.S. case. Clothing and footwear similarly ranked high in both cases and the different status of the leather goods category in the case of the

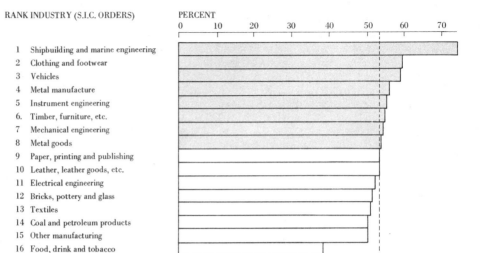

Figure 6.6
Wages and salaries as percent of net output (value added), United Kingdom, 1968. [*Source:* Report on the Census of Production (1968), Summary Tables, 156, Table 1.]

U.K. simply reflects differences in the methods of classification for this order. At the more detailed level of Table 6.2, the high ranks associated with railway products manufacture reflect the fact that they form the basis of a nationalized industry where value added figures include no profits (not that there were any). In this sense they cannot be regarded as comparable either with other U.K. industries or their U.S. counterparts. Watch and clock manufacture and pottery fall into the expected class of craft-based industries for which mechanized production is difficult. At the reverse end of the labor-intensity scale in the U.K. the predictable industrial groups are to be found. Foremost among them are the various elements of the chemicals industry for which most value added is derived from the application of plant and technology rather than the direct efforts of production workers. As Lewis (1969) points out and as Table 6.3 indicates, one of the keys to measuring the relative importance of the labor input is the *stage of production*. The earlier stages of the production process chiefly involve the reduction of raw materials to their more refined elements. These are "heavy" on raw materials, energy and plant inputs and relatively "light" on labor. Toward the *final stages of production* labor exerts a more powerful effect on value added and becomes more critical as a cost factor.*

In the case both of the United States and the United Kingdom it is clear that there are some industries whose *key factor input is labor*. Equally there are those which are all but insensitive to cost variations in this particular factor. When Alfred Weber set out his model of industrial location in 1909 he was aware of this fact. Labor costs ranked at the highest level as a "locational factor." They were given the status of a *general regional* factor of location along

Note

*In the example shown in Table 6.3 there is almost a perfect negative rank correlation ($r = -0.9946$) between the importance of materials and fuel costs and the importance of labor costs in relation to total product value.

with "the relative price range of deposits of materials and the costs of transportation." He saw all industries as being affected in their location to some degree by labor costs but he also acknowledged that some have a more specific degree of labor orientation due to the greater importance of the labor input in relation to that of other factors.

	%
Locomotives and railway track equipment	94.1
Railway carriages, wagons and trams	86.8
Ship building and marine engineering	74.3
Motor cycle, tricycle and pedal cycle mfr.	72.4
Watches and clocks	66.5
Pottery	65.3
Iron castings, etc.	65.1
General chemicals, inorganic	34.7
General chemicals, organic	33.9
General chemicals, other than organic or inorganic	33.8
British wines, cider and perry	33.7
Surgical bandages	32.9
Polishes	32.7
Production of man-made fibers	31.5
Starch and misc. foods	30.9
Brewing and malting	30.3
Soaps and detergents	30.2
Pharmaceutical chemicals	30.1
Toilet preparations	29.8
Lubricating oils and greases	28.1
Grain milling	27.4
Tobacco	25.4
Mineral oil refining	22.0
Spirit, distilling and compounding	17.9

Source: Census of Production (1968), Summary Tables, 156, Table 1.

Table 6.2
United Kingdom: wages and salaries of all workers as a proportion of net output (value added): the highest and the lowest.

Within the terms of his analysis Weber sought to provide some measure of the degree of labor orientation applicable to various industries. His *index of labor cost* measures the average cost of labor required to produce a given unit weight of product. Thus those industries with a high index will be more generally sensitive to spatial variations in labor costs than those with a low index. However, the real significance of the labor factor in location depends upon its relative weight as compared with those other elements in the production function of the industry which have an identifiable locational impact. In Weber's analysis the prime component among these was the total weight of materials to be moved for the production of a unit weight of product, that is the *locational weight*. Thus in Weberian terms the sensitivity of an industry to spatial variations in the cost of labor as an input factor is simply given by the *labor coefficient*, that is the ratio of the labor index to the locational weight.

Apart from the logical simplicity of Weber's theoretical constructs, the determination of the relative importance of labor as a locational factor is far more complex. As Segal (1960) points out, it is often the need for particular scarce

Table 6.3
Ratio of cost of raw
material, fuel and wages
to total value for major
British industries.

Industry	Ratio of raw material and fuel costs to total value		Ratio of wages to total value	
	%	Rank	%	Rank
Blast furnaces	77.6	1	10.3	22
Non-ferrous	76.1	2	10.8	20
Leather	74.5	3	13.3	16
Steel sheets	72.0	4	12.0	19
Textiles	71.6	5	12.7	17.5
Chemicals	67.6	6	12.7	17.5
Iron and steel	64.2	7	16.9	13
Paper and board	63.5	8	10.5	20
Clothing	61.8	9	22.4	12
Stationery	61.0	10	15.4	15
Cardboard boxes	58.8	11	16.2	14
Wood and cork	58.6	12	25.0	9
Precision	58.1	13	23.0	10
Vehicles	56.7	14	26.8	8
Electrical engineering	54.7	15	28.9	7
Other metal	54.6	16	22.6	11
Food and drink	50.3	17	7.3	23
Iron foundries	42.9	18	33.3	2
Shipbuilding	42.4	19	33.6	1
Treatment of non-metalliferous	41.9	20	29.4	6
Engineering	41.3	21	30.4	4
Printing	31.9	22	31.7	3
Newsprint	29.3	23	29.8	5

Source: P. W. Lewis (1969), A Numerical Approach to the Location of Industry, *Occasional Paper Series*, No. 13, Table 1, p. 17, Hull University Publications. The rank correlation rho is, $p = -0.9946$

and spatially localized types of labor possessing certain skills which makes some industries especially labor-sensitive in the modern world. The total contribution of such workers to value added may not always be quantitatively large nor may their total impact on costs, but the existence of the enterprise in any form may depend heavily upon their sheer availability.

In the past the existence of such skills exerted a far more powerful locational pull on the craft-based industries in particular. The precision instrument, fashion, gun, jewellery, pottery, textile and clothing industries were all, as a wide range of empirical studies have shown, and as we shall demonstrate in Chapter Seven, strongly attracted to particular sites and maintained there by, among other things, the availability of specialized skills.* However, modern trends toward increasing division of labor and more mechanized forms of production are making jobs not necessarily less skilled but more similar in nature.

The craftsman makes less and less contribution to production in "modern times" as machines are substituted for manual skill. Under these circumstances the

Note   *See, for example, Wise (1949), Rodgers (1958), Hall (1960).

contemporary businessman tends to be more powerfully drawn in his locational choice toward pools of *reliable* labor with the capacity for *high productivity* while working with a machine. So crucial have these attributes become in recent times that U.S. and European businesses have gone "global" in their search for the right type of labor (at the right price, of course), abandoning the homeland for Taiwanese or Korean labor services (more of this later—see Chapter Nine). Within a national context attributes such as reliability, versatility and productivity per labor hour tend to be industrial "virtues" present in the population at large. They tend to be more readily available in those areas already long industrialized and among those people fully "integrated" to the needs of modern society. They are more likely to be *regionally* distributed characteristics of the population unlike the skills and crafts which were highly localized in particular "quarters" of cities or in smaller scale industrial districts. Thus while the *general* pull of labor on location has gradually but not dramatically decreased over time the *specific* attractions of pockets of labor for particular industries has certainly declined. In strictly geographical terms many more industries have been released from the need to choose sites closely associated with clusters of skilled labor. In this respect they have become relatively more "footloose"— released from the localizing influence of a key factor input.

Spatial variations in the cost of labor

We have spent a good deal of time thus far talking about labor costs. But what transfer payments actually constitute the costs of labor to the businessman? In short, what does he have to pay to acquire it? The first and most obvious answer would be wages and salaries. These, as we have seen earlier, are determined like all factor costs on the economic-rent principle, taking into account the relative scarcity of the factor in relation to total demand for it.* There are also many *fringe benefits* which are generally paid to or on behalf of workers both as cash payments like social security or superannuation contributions and as facilities such as safety equipment, mess rooms and so on. In paying out wages, salaries and fringe benefits to hire labor, a key criterion is what the businessman gets for his money—the amount of output achieved per labor hour.

Marginal Productivity and Factor Costs: In attempting to maximize profits a firm will apply the factors of production to increasing output just up to that point at which the last unit of a factor adds as much to revenue as it does to costs. An economist would call this the stage at which *marginal cost* equals *marginal revenue* (with the word "marginal" implying the concept of the last unit to be added). If certain other conditions were met about the economic system in question and in particular if it were in what an economist would call equilibrium, we can show how factor prices can be determined. Simply, the price of a factor will be equal to the addition to revenue which results from the sale of the output produced by the marginal unit of the factor in question. In the case of labor, for instance, the cost of taking an extra man onto the payroll if he were to be the "marginal man" would be equal to the revenue which his efforts produced and all wage rates would be derived from this base—*the marginal productivity of labor.* Clearly, different types of labor and different "pools" of labor within a nation will have varying marginal productivities, but the general wage rate for labor will be determined by the level of wages paid to the marginal individual—in other words, the "last man in" at the lowest rate. When this rises, so will all other rates in relation to it. The same is true for interest rates in relation to the marginal unit of capital and for rents in relation to the marginal unit of land.

Note

The costs of labor vary from place to place, from time to time and from industry to industry in accordance generally with prevailing supply and demand conditions for the factor and with its *marginal productivity*. Estimating the impact of spatial variations in the cost of labor is not, then, simply a question of looking at the geographical distribution of wage rates any more than it is solely concerned with patterns of labor productivity over space. The two are closely related and both are fundamental to any realistic evaluation of labor cost.

We have established from the outset that the *demand* for labor exerted by production systems is unevenly distributed over space. Even under the constrained conditions of the simple model the need for labor varied widely from the central places to the extensive farming regions. For a variety of reasons, social and demographic as well as economic, the *supply* of labor also varies widely over space. In particular there is wide variation in the supply of different types of labor: skilled, unskilled, male and female, productive and unproductive. Thus there are powerful forces at work within the space economy promoting wage differentials from place to place through inherent imbalances in supply and demand for the factor at various points. With perfect competition and no social or economic barriers to mobility, such imbalances would, as we have already pointed out, tend to be only short-term features. They would be adjusted over time by the operation of the labor market as supplies and demands sought to equalize themselves (Borts and Stein, 1961).

But labor is not infinitely mobile and the labor market does not operate freely under conditions of perfect competition, at least not outside the realms of pure theory. In the real world, while it is certainly true that a good deal of migration during the present century has been from low-wage, mainly rural areas, to higher wage urban areas, the classical notion that,

> labor reacts to wage differentials by moving to the jobs offering the most favorable terms and conditions. Workers compare alternative jobs and choose the ones that are superior.
> *Gitlow (1954), p. 62*

as we pointed out earlier (p. 207), requires substantial qualification. Even where such movements have taken place they have conspicuously *failed to remove spatial wage differentials*.

Long-distance labor movements have to be examined in the context of migration as a whole, a complex behavioral process the parameters of which are far from simply economic in nature.* In general labor tends to be *relatively immobile*, particularly where long-distance movement is involved. Estall and Buchanan (1973) put it more strongly and conclude that, in the short run at least, labor is an immobile factor of production. Given that this is so and that in addition many other factors (such as differential capital to labor ratios, differential income elasticities of demand for the products of industrial and agricultural regions, differential labor productivities, differential costs of living and so on) all serve

Note   *See Chapter Eight for a general discussion of location decision-making; also Olsson (1965a,b), Newson (1959), Kariel (1963), Okun and Richardson (1961).

to influence the geographical pattern of wage rates, then significant disparities in wages do exist within a space economy.

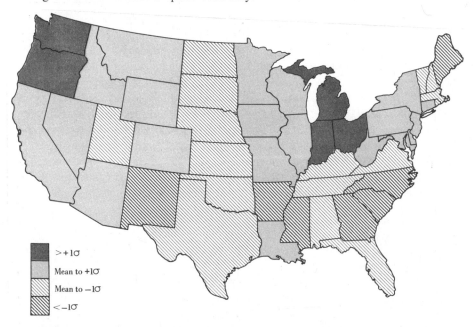

For the United States Figure 6.7 indicates the interstate difference in average hourly earnings for production workers in manufacturing for 1974. Earnings are, as expected, lowest in the South as a whole. They are also low in Maine and New Mexico. Wage rates are highest in the eastern part of the North Central division with Michigan, Ohio and Indiana; and in the west with Washington and Oregon in the top bracket.

Not only do wages differ from state to state but also between rural and urban areas and according to city size. Table 6.4 demonstrates this quite clearly. In

		Urban Places		**(Dollars per hour)**	S.M.S.A.'s		
	Rural	**Under 10,000**	**10,000– 99,999**	**Under 250,000**	**250,000– 499,999**	**500,000– 999,999**	**Over 1,000,000**
Total	$2.00	$2.12	$2.23	$2.39	$2.43	$2.56	$2.84
South	1.71	1.82	1.94	2.15	2.31	2.34	2.62
Non-South	2.22	2.30	2.39	2.54	2.50	2.67	2.87
Northeast	2.33	2.37	2.41	2.41	2.36	2.51	2.79
North Central	2.11	2.22	2.33	2.61	2.61	2.79	2.90
West	2.36	2.43	2.50	2.65	2.62	2.71	2.98
White males	2.24	2.43	2.61	2.78	2.77	2.96	3.29
Non-white males	1.28	1.26	1.33	1.53	1.89	2.00	2.08

Table 6.4
Average hourly earnings,
non-agricultural employed
persons, by city size,
1959.

Source: V. R. Fuchs (1967), *Differentials in Hourly Earnings by Region and City Size*, New York: Columbia University Press, Table 3, p. 25. Reproduced with permission of the National Bureau of Economic Research.

each of the five major regions average hourly earnings are highest in the larger cities. The intraregional variations are greatest in the South and least in the Northeast.

These data on earnings are, of course, subject to qualification. Apart from the artificial nature of the areal units on which the data are based, it must be stressed that the figures are averages for all manufacturing industries. Much, therefore, depends on the "*industry mix*" of the various states and cities. Some may have an excessive proportion of low-paying industries and this will clearly depress the average wage level. Wonnacott (1964) attempted to correct for such interstate variations in industrial structure. His ranking of states according to the highest comparable wages in fact produced a picture broadly similar to that discussed above. Even within the same industry, however, major wage differentials occur from place to place and Figure 6.8, derived from Smith (1971) shows for a sample of three occupational classes how wage rates vary over the United States.

Similar variations in wage levels exist even in such a small country as the United Kingdom. Table 6.5 shows the regional variation in average hourly earnings for workers employed in engineering industries. In these particular industries, hourly earnings for skilled workers were highest in the West Midlands, an area of heavy concentration in certain types of engineering, and lowest in Yorkshire and Humberside. It is interesting to note that hourly earnings in Wales, Scotland and the Northern Region were relatively high, despite the general economic characteristics of these regions.

Table 6.5
Great Britain: average hourly earnings in engineering industries by skill, June 1969 (pence per hour).

Region	Skilled	Semi-skilled	Unskilled
Southeast	143.5	132.5	104.3
East Anglia	138.2	125.8	99.2
South Western	138.0	112.8	94.5
West Midlands	156.3	126.6	105.0
East Midlands	136.3	110.1	92.3
Yorkshire & Humberside	126.0	104.0	91.4
North Western	137.3	125.8	94.3
Northern	140.3	116.2	98.7
Scotland	142.7	124.7	104.9
Wales	142.0	122.0	105.5

Source: Dept. of Employment and Productivity Gazette (October 1969), p. 916.

Labor costs are not, as we pointed out earlier, merely a function of wage levels. The crucial factor is not so much what a businessman has to pay for labor but rather the return he gets for a given payment. In other words, we must now turn to a consideration of *productivity* or output per worker. For example, suppose wages in city A were 5 percent lower than in city B but the productivity of the labor force at B was 10 percent higher than in A. It would clearly benefit the businessman to locate in the higher-wage location because of the greater volume of output he would receive for his money.

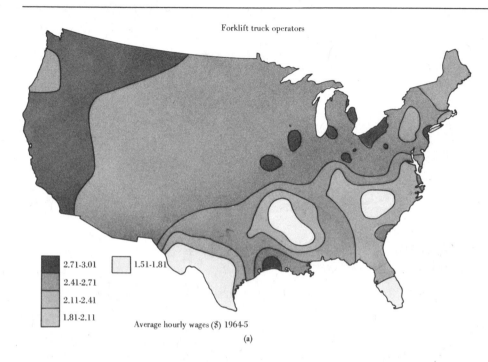

Forklift truck operators

2.71-3.01   1.51-1.81

2.41-2.71

2.11-2.41

1.81-2.11

Average hourly wages ($) 1964-5

(a)

Figure 6.8
Industry specific wage
rates for a sample of
occupations, United
States. [*Source:* D. M.
Smith (1971), *Industrial
Location,* Figures
15.5–15.7. Reproduced
by permission of John
Wiley & Sons, New York.]

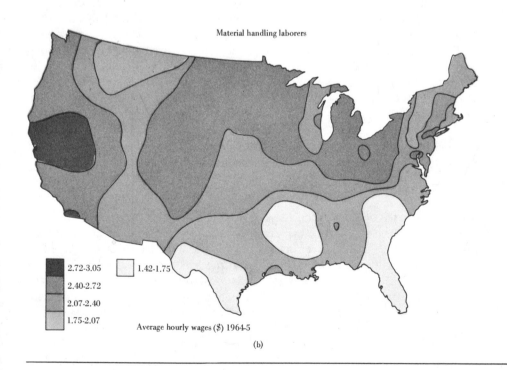

Material handling laborers

2.72-3.05   1.42-1.75

2.40-2.72

2.07-2.40

1.75-2.07

Average hourly wages ($) 1964-5

(b)

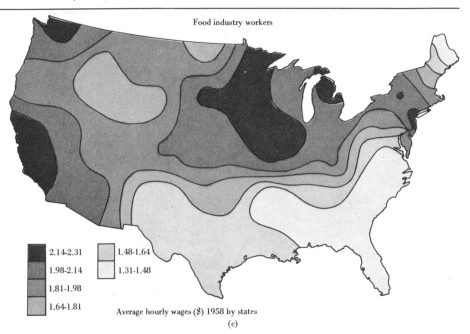

Food industry workers

2.14-2.31
1.98-2.14
1.81-1.98
1.64-1.81

1.48-1.64
1.31-1.48

Average hourly wages ($) 1958 by states

(c)

Low wage areas, therefore, are not such an obvious attraction to business enterprises as a first, uncritical glance would suggest. Frequently it costs a business a substantial amount to initiate training programs to meet even the most modest productivity targets. High levels of labor "turnover" while the local populace "try out" the new jobs often means that many more workers are trained than ever produce output. Similarly, high levels of initial absenteeism mean disruption of training programs and manning schedules with a consequent loss of output. It is for this reason that many governments, in attempting to attract industry to the more depressed areas where wages are likely to be low, are still bound to offer further inducements. In the United Kingdom this takes the form of a "regional employment premium"—a fixed subsidy payable to a company for each manufacturing worker employed. In addition, both in the U.K. and elsewhere, businesses opening up in areas of high unemployment and low wages are granted "tax holidays" (exemption from taxation for a limited period), training and investment subsidies and so on. These help tide them over an initial period of heavy outlay, part of which is concerned with the need to raise productivity levels in the labor force to a point where any wage savings constitute a *real* gain in cost efficiency.

The productivity of labor, then, depends upon many things. If we ignore, for the moment, considerations such as the equipment a man is given or the management skills which direct his activities (both of which are critical to effective productivity) then we might see *labor attitudes* as the critical variable. When talking of the quality of their labor force most businessmen would speak in terms of rates of labor turnover, rates of absenteeism, the frequency of industrial disputes, willingness to adapt to new production methods and so on. Indeed for a very large percentage of industrial enterprises moving to new locations it is the labor attitudes and labor relations aspect which tends to come to the fore in discussions of the role of labor as a factor in locational choice. Not that wage rates are not important as a consideration; they are. But to the everyday operation of a business enterprise, differentials in "strike prone-ness" or absenteeism tend to weigh more heavily these days on a decision-maker's mind than a few cents an hour differential in cash labor outlays.

The key to both wage levels and labor attitudes in modern society lies in the extent to which labor is organized and in the bargaining power of the labor organizations. Arguments about the cost of labor as a factor of production which make assumptions about its pricing as if trades unions did not exist must be seen in the same light as those other approximations to reality with which we began this book. They aid in the understanding of the problem but must be evaluated critically in the light of the assumptions on which they are based. The organization of labor into politically powerful groups like the AFL-CIO in the United States and the TUC in the United Kingdom takes much of the pricing for this factor out of the realms of neo-classical economics and into those of national politics. At lower levels of labor organization, in the individual trades unions themselves, bargaining for wages, fringe benefits and conditions of work has become a matter of confrontation or negotiation and compromise between employers and unions, the balance of which differs from time to time, from place to place, and from industry to industry. The price of labor is no longer determined in a *free* market by the marginal productivity of the factor, but the harsh economic realities are, at bottom, still present. Where bargaining drives labor as a factor to a point where marginal revenue is less than marginal cost, *substitution of capital and land for labor* (where this is technically possible) will become an attractive proposition to the businessman with profit as his basic motivation. Making such a substitution technically possible has been one of the driving forces behind the technological evolution of modern society. Where it has not been possible, the search for non-unionized, high-productivity labor has been pursued globally.*

Unionization, even within a single country, varies considerably from industry to industry and from region to region. Our analysis here, primarily for reasons connected with the availability of data, concentrates on the United States. Taking the sectoral distribution first, it is broadly true to say that union membership is lowest among office workers and highest among production workers in manufacturing, mining and public utilities. Table 6.6 shows some of the salient features in more detail. Perhaps the most interesting figures are those in column 5. These show a quotient value based on the assumption that every class of industry has just that proportion of union membership which would be expected if this were allocated across all industries strictly in proportion to their share of total employment. In short, a quotient of 1.0 shows a "par" value with just as many union members as expected, while a quotient of 2.0 means twice as many and a quotient of 0.5 means half as many.

---

*To explore more realistically the background to modern labor costs would demand another book and another approach. We shall content ourselves here with a brief look at the geographical distribution of union membership as a political key to the problem of labor attitudes and wage rates.

Table 6.6 Unionization in major classes of non-agricultural industry, United States 1970.	Union membership		Number of employees		Quotient	
	1 No. of Union Members '000	2 %	3 No. of Employees '000	4 %	5 Percent total Union Members Percent total Employees	6 Percent of Workers in Unions
Manufacturing						
Ordnance and accessories	157	0.92	242	0.50	1.84	64.9
Food and kindred products	906	5.32	1,783	3.67	1.45	50.8
Tobacco manufactures	36	0.22	83	0.17	1.29	45.8
Textile mill products	191	1.12	976	2.01	0.56	19.6
Apparel and related products	852	5.01	1,365	2.81	1.78	62.4
Lumber and wood products	215	1.26	573	1.18	1.07	37.5
Furniture and fixtures	214	1.26	460	0.95	1.33	46.5
Paper and allied products	453	2.66	706	1.45	1.84	64.2
Printing, publishing and allied industries	370	2.18	1,102	2.27	0.96	33.6
Chemicals and allied products	361	2.12	1,049	2.16	0.98	34.4
Petroleum refining	80	0.47	191	0.39	1.21	41.9
Rubber and miscellaneous plastics products	272	1.60	580	1.19	1.34	46.9
Leather and leather products	140	0.82	320	0.66	1.24	43.8
Stone, clay, glass and concrete	284	1.67	640	1.31	1.27	44.4
Primary metals industries	788	4.63	1,316	2.71	1.71	59.9
Fabricated metal products	918	5.40	1,380	2.84	1.90	66.5
Machinery, except electrical	550	3.23	1,982	4.08	0.79	27.7
Electrical machinery equipment	1,034	6.08	1,917	3.95	1.54	53.9
Transportation equipment	1,109	6.58	1,799	3.70	1.76	61.6
Professional, scientific and control instruments	49	0.29	460	0.95	0.31	10.7
Miscellaneous manufacturing	194	1.14	426	0.88	1.30	45.6
Non-manufacturing						
Mining and quarrying	369	2.17	623	1.28	1.70	59.2
Contract construction	2,576	15.14	3,536	7.28	2.08	72.9
Transportation	2,441	14.35	4,504	7.28	1.55	54.2
Telephone and telegraph	533	3.13	1,125	2.32	1.35	47.4
Electric, gas and services	312	1.83	691	1.42	1.29	45.2
Wholesale and retail trade	1,549	9.11	15,040	30.97	0.29	10.3
Finance, insurance and real estate	55	0.39	3,687	7.59	0.42	14.9
Total	17,010		48,556			

Source: Statistical Abstract of United States (1975), Table 608.

From this we can see that at the low end of the unionization spectrum are wholesale and retail trade (with only one-third as many union members as it should have); professional, scientific and control instrument manufacture; the finance, insurance and real estate category, and textile mill products. Only the latter concerns a significantly large number of production workers in manufacturing. At the high end of the unionization scale the contract construction class is outstanding with more than twice its expected share of union members. Following this comes the ordnance accessories class, the primary metals industry and, perhaps least surprising of all, mining and quarrying.

Column 6 of Table 6.6 shows the proportion of the workers in each industry class registered as union members. Contract construction has nearly 73 percent of its employees registered, while at the opposite end of the scale only just over 10 percent of workers in the wholesale and retail trade category belong to unions. At the highest level almost 80 percent of all union members in United States industry are in affiliates of the AFL-CIO.

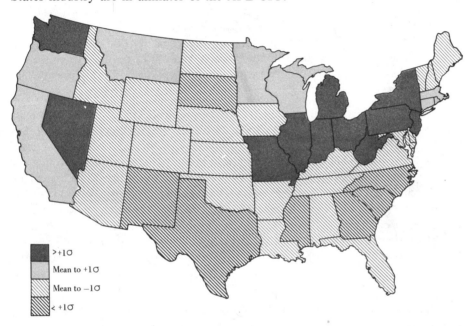

Figure 6.9
Labor union membership—percent of non-agricultural employment by states, United States, 1972. [*Source:* Statistical Abstract of United States (1975), Table 608.]

If we turn to spatial variations in union membership, Figure 6.9 shows the state by state distribution. It is perhaps, not surprisingly, a very similar picture to that presented in Figure 6.7 of variations in wage rates by states. The industrial northeast and east-north-central regions show high proportions of union members in the work force along with the far western states. The south has uniformly low levels of union membership. In North Carolina, for example, only 17.5 percent of non-agricultural workers belong to labor unions and this kind of figure is repeated in South Carolina (9.0), Mississippi (12.6), Georgia (13.9) and Florida (14.7). Away from the deep south there is also low unionization in Texas (13.5 percent) and South Dakota (11.8 percent) but in predominantly non-industrial states there is little tradition of unionization.

There is, of course, a significant cross-correlation between those sectors with low rates of unionization and those states with the same characteristic. The textile products category, still predominantly localized in the south, had low levels of union membership while the least unionized elements of the lumber and wood products industry and clothing and apparel manufacture are those still to be found in the southern states.

From the employer's viewpoint, as we have shown, there are a number of features associated with unionization which significantly affect costs. First, wage rates are likely to be higher because of the improved bargaining position achieved by workers acting collectively.* Second, the employer's freedom of manipulation of the labor force is likely to be restricted with respect to work assignments and work loads and the introduction of labor-saving machinery may be inhibited. Again the north-south differential is significant, particularly regarding employment conditions for certain types of labor. Vyver (1951) noted that whereas no southern state restricted night work by females at least five northern states had such regulations. This has been especially important for the textile industries which not only employ a large proportion of female operatives but also need to operate a three-shift system. A third result of unionization is that freedom to lay off, transfer, or discharge workers without consultation is likely to be curtailed.

Interstate variations in the strength of labor organization are reflected, at least partly, in differences in the costs associated with workmen's compensation, unemployment payments and other benefits. There is little doubt that, at least in the 1950s, workmen's compensation laws were less costly in the south, mainly because maximum cash benefits and the maximum duration of such benefits were a good deal lower there. For example, maximum weekly payments ranged from an average of $29 in the north to $23 in the south. Differences in the total cost of compensation can be seen in the relative insurance rates per $100 payroll in 1950. The average for the northern states was $1.02 per $100 payroll with values as high as $1.61 in New York. On the other hand, the southern average was only $.67 with a range from $.96 in Louisiana to $.41 in Alabama (Vyver, 1951).

This discussion has emphasized the major factors producing spatial variations in labor costs. But even if such differences did not exist, some locations would be more attractive in terms of labor *supply* than others. Two such attractions may be cited. First, development of a localized concentration of a particular economic activity leads to the existence of a specialized labor pool with a range of skills particularly suited to that activity. Second, the sheer size of the labor force associated with major metropolitan areas offers a number of real advantages such as a greater range of skills and a large reserve labor force for those activities whose labor requirements are seasonal or periodic. Also a greater concentration of managerial, technical and professional talent is likely in metropolitan centers.

For all these reasons, then, and despite migrational adjustments and other factors, *labor supplies and labor costs vary significantly from place to place and exert differential locational attractions.* However, in modern society a man's output is often less a function of his own attitudes and abilities than of the capital equipment and facilities with which he is provided. It is to the role of the capital factor that we turn next.

Note   *It has been suggested that the existence of collective bargaining has been a force likely to lead to a general reduction in the spatial variation of wages, but as Figure 6.8 and Table 6.4 show this is not the case in practice. Wage rates in the same trade under the same bargaining agreements still differ from city to city and from place to place in general.

Capital

Capital is defined as:

> all those man-made aids to further production such as tools, machinery,
> plant and equipment, including everything man-made which is not con-
> sumed for its own sake but which is used up in the process of making
> other goods.
> *Lipsey (1963), p. 38*

Capital is by definition a key element in the production function of any business.
In a more basic sense it was man's unique ability to create and use capital
as "man—the toolmaker" which first distinguished him from the animals. In
applying his higher powers of reason to the problem of survival and of improving his lot *homo sapiens* came up with a unique solution. This was to commit
less of his labor-time today to direct consumption and to use it to manufacture
tools to give him better prospects of consumption tomorrow. Thus the emergence of modern man and the first formation of capital were simultaneous
events.

This simple truth applicable to the first identifiable man is still the basis of
advanced industrial society. Capital to produce the output of the future is derived from the deferment of direct consumption in the present. The act of con-
verting such *savings* into productive tools is termed *investment*.

Let us briefly take a more formal look at the origins of capital and the characteristics of investment. Figure 6.10 shows in a very simple form the flows of income

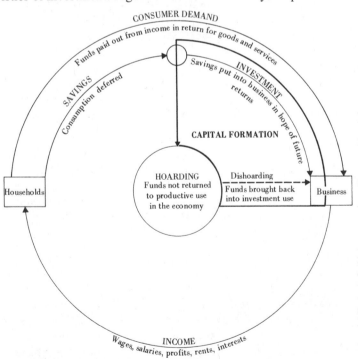

Figure 6.10
The circular flow of
income.

and expenditure in society. The flow is, essentially, circular. Businesses provide incomes (the lower half of the circle) to individuals or, as we have termed them, households. These incomes are derived from the wages, interest, rents and profits paid out to compensate those whose factor services and entrepreneurial skills are hired to make the business work. Incomes are "spent" (the top half of the circle) by households in two main ways. First, there is direct consumption of the goods and services produced by the business sector, and this we have called *consumer demand*. This tends to be a relatively steady flow of funds from households to businesses and is not normally subject to violent ups and downs. People's consumption habits once formed are generally fairly stable. Second, and more important to our present concern, is that part of household expenditure which is not directly consumed. Consumption is deferred and this creates *savings* out of income. Where the saver is relatively confident that he will get a good future return for the consumption he denied himself he might put his income to use as *investment*. He is now a holder of a more or less scarce factor of production—investment capital—and is entitled to *interest* from those willing to hire it from him. The "price" of capital to the hirer will depend upon the marginal productivity of the factor and capital, like labor and land as we saw earlier, will be assigned a value in terms of its economic rent. Holders of capital derived in this way from savings out of income will be more or less willing to hire it to others depending upon the level of return and their expectations. Where uncertainty exists about likely future returns or where interest rates are low in relation to expectations, savings may not be put back into use as investment but may be *hoarded* or taken out of circulation altogether. This will lower the overall level of demand in the economy since funds have been taken out of the system. Rates of deflation and unemployment or of inflation are dependent on the magnitude of investment flows and the willingness of savers to invest rather than hoard. This aspect of the expenditure side of the circle tends to be, unlike consumer demand, highly volatile, giving rise to booms and slumps in the economy over time. It is not our purpose here to develop the notion of national income flows further but simply to point to the underlying mechanisms behind the supply of capital as a factor.

Let us now look at capital from the viewpoint of our businessman. To set up his business, be it a farm, factory or store, he needs some capital. He needs to persuade holders of this capital to hire it to him (invest in his enterprise) where he cannot finance it directly himself. He, himself, needs to invest in buildings, equipment, inventories of production materials and so on. Where does this capital come from in a realistic modern world?

Unless the enterprise is small or the potential businessman is unusually rich it is not likely that capital will come from his own savings. He is much more likely to go to the bank or finance corporation for a loan, to the government for a grant, or to the stock market to raise money from a share issue. In fact, when looked at more realistically the "saver households" of Figure 6.10 are likely to be far removed from the businessman seeking investment funds. Between the two will be a complex interface of financial institutions—banks, finance corporations, insurance companies, government agencies and so on—which serve to accumulate savings and disburse investment capital to would-be hirers of the factor. Most domestic savings in the modern world come in an institutionalized form. The government "saves" and reinvests household income through taxation. Pension funds and insurance premiums channel savings to assurance companies and their associated banks who form the largest private sector sources of finance in the modern era. These represent the effective sources of supply to the developer seeking funds. They have a particular spatial distribution. Similarly, the aggregate demand for capital has a spatial pattern. We can, therefore, as in our discussion of labor, look at the locational impact of capital in terms of the spatial disparity between supply and demand for the factor and its mobility in matching the two at different locations. First, however, let us examine the importance of capital as an input to different classes of economic activity.

The importance of capital as an input factor

As we have emphasized, all economic activities make some use of capital. In general terms, however, it is possible to distinguish broadly between the relatively *labor intensive* service sector and the more *capital intensive* manufacturing and mining sectors of an economy. Wholesale and retail trade, finance, insurance and personal and business services are heavy on men and light on machines. Though the advent of the computer has revolutionized many aspects of the work in these industries in recent years, it has not significantly altered their degree of labor bias. By contrast, the mining and manufacturing sectors depend very heavily in general on expensive inputs of capital equipment and there has been a consistent tendency over the years to substitute capital equipment for the hire of labor services. Within each of the sectors themselves there is, of course, a wide variation in capital intensity. Figure 6.11 shows for the major classes of U.S. manufacturing the amount of capital invested per production worker in 1971. It is hardly surprising that the petroleum industry appears as far and away the most capital-intensive of the major classes with more than three times as much capital invested per shop-floor worker as tobacco which comes second in the rank order. Chemicals, the transportation industries and primary metals are also highly capital-intensive by this measure. Predictably the rank order in this case is almost the polar opposite of that shown for labor intensity in Figure 6.5. Apparel, furniture, leather and textiles, as the set of most labor-intensive industries, rank lowest in capital invested per worker.

The story is the same as that for labor. All economic activities require capital inputs but some, particularly mining and those elements of manufacturing concerned with the primary processing of raw materials, demand large programs of capital investment. We now turn to the question of variations in the availability and price of capital over space and to the role of mobility for the factor in adjusting differences in the pattern of supply and demand.

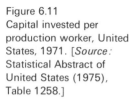

Figure 6.11
Capital invested per
production worker, United
States, 1971. [*Source:*
Statistical Abstract of
United States (1975),
Table 1258.]

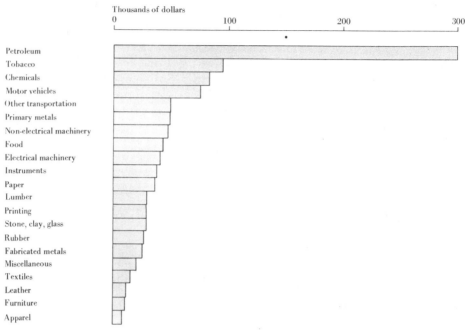

Spatial variations in the availability of capital

The accumulation of capital within an economic system depends, as we have seen, on the level of savings, the willingness of savers to invest, and the level of net capital inflows from outside. This represents broadly the supply side of the situation. On the demand side we must take into account the level of actual or expected profits in the system and their relationship to profit levels in other systems to which capital might flow (Siebert, 1969).

In some regions, for instance, old, established, successful industrial regions, capital may have been accumulating over a long period to give a large basic stock of physical capital in the sense of plant, equipment and infra-structural facilities as well as an abundant supply of monetary investment capital from savings out of profits and wages. These regions may also be large sources of demand for capital, the high levels of profits within them absorbing internally generated investment funds and drawing in additions from outside.

Other regions, perhaps old and established but less successful, may still exhibit a large accumulation of physical capital and may, from the fruits of a more successful past, still accumulate large supplies of investment capital. They may, however, be unable to absorb all of this investment capital within themselves and stand out as regions of capital surplus. At the other end of the scale, developing areas, perhaps new frontiers for settlement, may be sources of a limited supply of capital but may at the same time exert a powerful demand for capital inputs through the potential returns to be had from mining and agricultural ventures.

Thus over space as well as over time, and from one industry to another there exist variations in levels of supply and demand for capital as a factor of production. The allocative mechanism by which scarce supplies are distributed among competing uses (regional, sectoral) is a market system regulated by economic rent in which capital has its "price"—the *interest rate*. As in the case of labor, given perfect mobility and a free competitive market for capital, geographical differences in interest rates, and, therefore, the cost of capital as an input, would virtually disappear. Capital would flow from surplus areas to deficit areas until a balance, with equilibrium rates of interest, was achieved. In fact, capital like labor is far from infinitely mobile as a factor of production, and free competition is, like the isotropic plain, an idealized concept employed as a datum from which the wide variations in real conditions are measured.

The mobility of capital

The mobility of capital differs according to the specific form of the capital involved. *Physical capital* in the form of plant or equipment is largely immobile as a factor once it is put in place. In this respect it is useful to distinguish between the existing stock of capital and newly produced capital goods (Siebert, 1969). The new capital units are more mobile than the established capital stock but once they are themselves put in place they become functionally immobile. This is one of the sources of the phenomenon often referred to as *geographical* or *industrial inertia*.* Once put to work at a particular place, the value of physical capital lies in its being used as much as possible and every moment of lost production costs money. The cost of taking it out of production to move it to another location is one which any businessman would seek to avoid and is therefore a significant barrier to mobility. Thus physical capital once set in place becomes a powerful locational force guiding the development of the space economy through its inertial impact.

Monetary capital on the other hand is considerably more mobile. Its movement is restricted more by institutional barriers than by distance or the "frictional drag" of space in general. The boundaries between nations, economic communities, trading blocs or currency areas represent steep "steps" in the path of its flow, tending to keep finance capital within homogeneous financial systems. Within the same currency area, trading bloc or nation, monetary capital has traditionally been assumed to be highly or even perfectly mobile—free to move at no perceptible cost from place to place. But as Estall (1972) has pointed out, there may be a number of impediments to the free flow of investment funds which are not necessarily directly reflected in aggregate figures for the cost of capital at different places. Especially for the small business or for businesses wanting to invest in unusual or "non-standard" activities, the physical presence at a given place of some institution willing to finance them may provide a point-source of investment funds which would simply not be available at other places. Estall quotes the willingness of the financial community in Boston

---

**Industrial Inertia* is the tendency for an industry to remain in operation at a location when the reasons which brought it there in the first place have either lost their significance or completely disappeared.   Note

to invest in research and development projects with potentially nebulous pay-offs. He also suggests that Philadelphia bankers are apparently less willing to fund science-based projects of this type.

Small industry is often dependent upon *local finance* from banks or loan finance institutions where there are close, often personal, contacts between businessman and financier. A move away from the effective range of such personal contacts may make finance for development purposes difficult or even impossible to obtain. There may, therefore, be a strong distance-decay effect in the mobility of capital for the small business with financiers willing to put up funds just so long as they can "keep a close eye on them." The presence of "specialist" lending institutions particularly in the inner city with a long tradition of sup-porting the small clothing, jewellery or furniture trade may well provide a source of capital to these industries which is to all intents and purposes *fixed* in its effective location. Indeed there may be particular ethnic or religious traditions in the lending process which effectively restrict certain investment projects to particular quarters associated with such groups.

Estall (1972) points to a further neglected consideration influencing the effective spatial and sectoral mobility of capital. Most new investment funds go into the support and expansion of *existing* capital investments which are, as we have seen, themselves constrained by the immobility of physical capital once in place. It has been estimated that up to 80 percent of all new manufacturing investment in the advanced nations goes to support the expansion of existing plants. Clearly, if this is the case, whatever the potential returns to be obtained at new greenfield locations, there is only a limited proportion of total capital stock available to finance development. In this sense capital as a production factor is far less mobile than we have hitherto tended to assume.

The modern activities of national and state governments seeking to promote investment in the less developed regions provide an effective testimony to the immobility of capital as a production factor. Almost all of the advanced indus-trial nations find it necessary to provide investment capital in the form of grants and subsidies paid for out of taxes in regions where they hope to promote new development. This form of capital (derived from income the state "saves" on behalf of households as taxation) is becoming an increasingly important source of investment funds for *new development*. Indeed the assistance schemes are designed for just this purpose—to pull new investment to depressed regions against an inertial trend which would reinforce those regions previously capita-lized. Capital of this order is clearly mobile in an imperfect sense. It is available in some regions and not in others and among those regions where it can be obtained there may be "tariffs" which restrict its availability to specific locations.

In summary, then, social, political and economic "discontinuities" tend to dis-courage the free flow of monetary capital between different economic systems. The most significant of all these discontinuities is that between the advanced and underdeveloped nations. Even within homogeneous systems, however, the free flow of monetary capital cannot be said to be "perfectly" mobile either sectorally or spatially. In some senses it is—for the large, well-known corporation, funds may be as close as the nearest telephone. But for the small firm or for the "non-standard" capital application there may be no effective mobility, spatially or otherwise, in the factor. Finally, governments these days exert a powerful impact on the flow of capital for development, regulating its overall levels by policy instrument and making it more readily available in some areas than in others.

In general, then, like labor, capital is localized (or perhaps more accurately—regionalized) in its supply and is not in any broad sense mobile. This means that the price of capital—the interest rate—does vary spatially and it is to this variation that we now turn our attention.

Spatial variations in the "cost" of capital

A number of writers have pointed to the existence of spatial variations in the cost and availability of capital and its impact on the evolving economic geography of the United States. Davis (1966) showed how in the mid-nineteenth century the financial network of the United States was dominated to such a large extent by the established centers of New England and the middle Atlantic states that capital movement was unable to keep pace with demand generated by the westward expansion of economic activities. Davis suggests, for example, that acute shortage of capital in the south prevented the major redevelopment of the region's textile industry until after the Civil War. Even then local capital was insufficient and northern capital had to be acquired at high interest rates. This situation was a result of the prevailing condition of the financial market which consisted not of an integrated national network but of a series of small separate markets. The result was a wide divergence in interest rates: in 1870, for example, there was a 10 percent interest differential between New York City and the smaller centers of the west coast.

At a more localized level the work of Burgy (quoted in Estall, 1972) points to the impact of differential availability of capital and interest rates on the evolution of the New England textile industry in the nineteenth century. The effective source of investment funds was the shipping and commercial enterprises of Boston and the region around Narragansett Bay with a marked rise in interest rates culminating in a total reluctance to venture funds increasing with distance from the source. It was this which contributed substantially to the early localization of the textile plants in Boston and the Providence-Pawtucket area in the early years of the century. Gradually, with improvements in communication promoting a more realistic appreciation of the risks involved in investing money further away, Boston capital began to fund new developments in New Hampshire and Maine. Later funds were available to the whole of New England and with time Boston capital was to become one of the key sources of finance for developments over the entire United States.

It seems reasonable to assume that with time and the spread of the communications network, with effective national integration and with universally applicable legislation and security services protecting the interests of capital, investment funds would become freely available over the United States. Lösch (1954), however, showed that in the 1920s and 1930s there were still significant spatial variations in general interest rates. Figure 6.12a is based on data for twenty financial centers at varying distances from New York, the key source of U.S. capital. It shows average interest rates on six major types of bank loan for the period 1919–1925. The graph shows that, although interest rates in each of the twenty centers were above that for New York and that there was a general increase with distance, the increase was not uniform. Highest rates were in the southern states (average 6.84 percent) and in the mountain region at El Paso (7.68 percent) and Helena (7.73 percent); beyond this region rates fell again towards the west coast. The implication is that all the major banking centers were subordinate to New York. But, in turn, each major center dominated a surrounding region within which interest rates increased with distance from the dominant center. Figure 6.12b demonstrates this phenomenon for the area round Houston, Texas.

Figure 6.12
Spatial variations in interest rates within the United States. (a) Increase in the rate of interest with distance from New York City, 1919–1925. (b) Increase in the rate of interest with distance from Houston, Texas, 1936. [*Source:* A. Lösch (1954), *The Economics of Location* (Die raümliche Ordnung der Wirtschaft), Stuttgart: Gustav Fischer, 1962, Figures 94 and 95.]

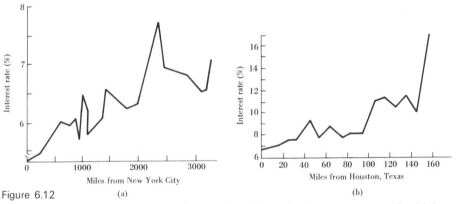

Figure 6.12   (a)   (b)

Lösch attempted to explain the observed tendency for interest rates to be higher in the west than in the east in two ways. First, he suggested that *demand* for capital at the same rate of interest was greater in the west because of the larger range of undeveloped possibilities there together with the need for more credit to bridge over agricultural losses. Second, the total *supply* of capital, at the same rate of interest, was held to be smaller in the west. This was produced by a number of factors. One was the fact that the supply of *local* capital was smaller because of a predominance of agriculture, whose profits were lower than those of the major eastern industries. Another factor was the need for western banks to keep larger cash reserves in hand, and a third factor was the higher costs of banking in the west (partly because of the great distance from New York).

Not only was the local supply of capital smaller but also the supply of *eastern* capital was smaller. Again a number of factors inhibited capital movement despite the high interest rates. Lösch mentions the inaccessibility of the New York market in terms both of distance and knowledge and the need to employ middlemen. He suggested, too, that the risk increases with distance because creditors cannot have full knowledge of conditions at a distance. More recently Moroney and Walker (1966) attempted an explanation of development differentials in the north and south by reference in part to the comparative capital abundance of the former as compared to the latter. The high cost of capital in the south and the relatively low cost of labor are hypothesized as the basic factors underlying the region's strong attraction on the labor-intensive industries rather than more capital-intensive ones during the 1950s.

Smith (1971) puts forward the view that today's rates of interest appear not to differ very much from place to place in advanced industrial nations. He quotes in support of this contention the findings of a company specializing in plant location studies for clients. These indicated that for a selection of U.S. and Canadian cities there was no significant difference in average annual financing costs regardless of the size or location of the city concerned. Of 34 cities examined, only eight had figures outside the range 8.30 to 8.60 percent per year and Chicago, the largest city in the sample, at 8.30 percent had exactly the same figure as Bentonville, Arkansas, the smallest. Smith (1971, p. 38) concludes that on this evidence, "The cost of financial capital is thus not very influential in locational choice in the modern industrial state."

Estall (1972, p. 195), whose work we quoted earlier, does not go along with this. He suggests that even where such conditions as Smith describes are general, "The *costs* of capital remain an imperfect index of the actual, or potential mobility of investment funds." He then adds that "the growth or expansion of enterprise in different locations is affected by marked differences in the availability of capital."

Perhaps an approach to the question by way of general average interest rates is too crude as Estall suggests. While these may not, in the modern era, vary widely from place to place, the willingness of finance capital institutions to lend money for development is certain to vary. Any reader who has ever sought an overdraft or a bank loan will know that while base interest rates do not tend to vary from bank to bank nationally, the willingness of the manager to lend money certainly does. For some industry, then, the evaluation of capital as an input factor with an impact on location will depend solely on its availability or the reverse. The "first-time" businessman wishing to open a liquor store in the ghetto might not find capital available to him at any price, while General Motors could presumably raise capital almost anywhere at any time.

Technical knowledge

No study of the impact of variations in production costs would be complete without a consideration of the role of technology. As we pointed out earlier (fn. p. 198), this is a somewhat slippery subject to handle and frequently economists have avoided trying to tackle it because of the uncertainties involved in its measurement. Galbraith in particular is highly critical of the way in which modern economics has handled the question of technology:

> Changing technology, it is conceded, alters progressively and radically what can be obtained from a given supply of factors. But there is no way by which this intelligence can be developed at length in a textbook.

> So economic instruction concedes the important, and then discusses the unimportant.
> *Galbraith (1966), p. 46 fn.*

In its broadest possible definition as "society's pool of knowledge regarding the industrial arts" (Mansfield, 1968, p. 10), technology is clearly fundamental to the production process and a new method, technique or machine can alter literally overnight the production possibilities open to a businessman. It may fundamentally alter the choices of factor mix which he makes and may therefore substantially alter the cost effectiveness of a given locational choice. Technology cannot therefore be either assumed to be given and effectively ignored, as is done by much of modern micro-economics (Johnson, 1975), nor can it be, in a realistic view of the modern world, assumed to be a constant over time (Keynes, 1936).

Technology is worthy of treatment as the third of the non-land factors of production and it is expressed as such in the production function shown earlier on page 200. But because of its resistance to quantification or precise, unambiguous definition, it is often treated as a *"residual factor,"* accounting for the residual output that is left after the contributions of land, labor and capital are accounted for. Table 6.7 derived from Denison (1967) shows for the U.S. and northwestern Europe how important is this "residual factor" once the contributions of labor and capital are abstracted. In the case of the U.S. approximately 23 percent of the growth in national income, 1950–1962, is attributed to the broad category of improvements in technical knowledge. This compares

Table 6.7
Percentage distribution of growth rates of adjusted National Income[a] among the sources of growth, 1950–62, for the US and NW Europe.

Source of growth	US	Belgium	Denmark	France	Germany	Netherlands	Norway	UK	Total NW Europe
	%	%	%	%	%	%	%	%	%
Adjusted National Income[a]	100	100	100	100	100	100	100	100	100
Total factor input	58	39	46	26	38	42	30	47	36
of which: Labor	*33*	*25*	*18*	*10*	*19*	*19*	*4*	*25*	*18*
Capital	*25*	*14*	*29*	*17*	*19*	*23*	*26*	*21*	*18*
Output per unit of input	42	61	54	74	62	58	70	53	64
of which: Improved allocation of resources and economies of scale	*20*	*34*	*39*	*41*	*40*[b]	*31*	*43*	*20*	*36*[c]
The "residual" (ie advances of knowledge and changes in the lag in application of knowledge general efficiency, and errors and omissions)[d]	*23*	*28*	*15*	*32*	*22*	*27*	*27*	*33*	*28*

[a]The adjusted figures are arrived at by deducting from the actual growth rates the estimated effect of (i) irregular fluctuations in farm output and (ii) incomparabilities between terminal years with respect to the intensity of resource utilization. These deductions are made by Denison to improve comparability of growth rates between countries.
[b]Includes 4 percentage points for balancing of capital stock.
[c]Includes 2 percentage points for balancing of capital stock.
[d]As mentioned in the text, Denison assumes that the residual in the US countries consists solely of advances in knowledge.
Source: E. F. Denison, assisted by Jean Pierre Poullier *Why Growth Rates Differ, Postwar Experience in Nine Western Countries*, Washington, Brookings Institution (1967) Chapter 21. Detailed figures may not add to subtotals because of rounding.

with 33 percent attributed to labor and 25 percent to capital. Scale economies and improved use of resources takes up the balance. For the same period in the U.K. the respective factor contributions were 25 percent labor, 21 percent capital and 33 percent technology. Slippery to measure or not, factors connected with the improvement of technical knowledge are critical ingredients in the economic growth process of advanced industrial nations.

The most comprehensive early treatment of technical knowledge as an input factor was made by Joseph Schumpeter (1939). He saw the accumulation of knowledge as a function of two discrete but co-related processes, *invention* and *innovation*. Invention was envisaged as the introduction of new production processes and techniques to the existing stock of knowledge. Innovation, which we have encountered already in Chapter Two, is the adoption of those processes and their translation into actual production processes. He further distinguished *autonomous invention* from *induced invention*. The former represents the long-term, spontaneous and apparently random contribution of those occasional geniuses who invent things. They extend the existing stock of technical knowledge by the application of intuitive thought to the existing body of technology. Induced invention by contrast is the fruit of a deliberate expenditure of time, effort and resources for the purposes of generating new knowledge. Today we would see this element of invention as being generated by research and development activity, or R and D for short.

Critics of Schumpeter's classification see one of the main problems as that of trying to divide the indivisible. If invention is the first *practical* application of some abstract idea, how does one distinguish whether "making it work" was defined as part of the invention or innovation process? Is innovation different only in *scale* of application from invention? The first automated spindle cotton picker was made to work in the United States in 1889. Was this its invention? Full commercial use had to wait until 1948 for the development of the invention by the inventor using the capital of the firm that took it up. Invention and innovation together? Clearly, semantic hair-splitting is unhelpful to our present purpose, but it should encourage the reader, while accepting the Schumpeter typology for the moment, to give careful thought to the "gray areas" of its application. For Schumpeter, innovation is seen in terms of *commercial* exploitation at a significant scale and this is important to the present discussion because it implies the widespread application of capital and labor inputs whose spatial availability is, as we have seen, a constraining influence on location. Similarly, induced invention, or the application of R and D, demands significant inputs of other production factors. Both innovations and the sources of R and D activities may therefore have a different probability of occurring over a region or nation than the more esoteric autonomous invention. If this is the case, then the availability of technology as a factor of production to its potential users may also vary significantly over space in the same way as those factors which we have examined previously. Before taking this up in more detail, let us once again attempt to identify those particular economic activities which will demand heavy technology inputs and which might well be locationally sensitive to the availability of the factor.

The importance of technical knowledge as an input factor

It is impossible to put a realistic quantitative measure on technical knowledge as an input factor to various kinds of economic activity. All industries require some technology just as they require some labor, some capital and some resources, but the problem of differentiating between possible *technology-intensive* industries and those in which technological inputs are not so great, is difficult. As an attempt to find some surrogate measure of such inputs, Table 6.8 shows for a selection of U.S. industries the relative importance of research and development expenditures as a proportion of the sales dollar. This measures the degree to which industries themselves expended funds on promoting technological inputs for their own use.

Table 6.8
Importance of research and development in the sales dollar 1960.

Industry	Amount (in cents)
Aircraft, missiles	22.5
Communication equipment, electronic components	12.9
Scientific and mechanical measuring instruments	11.8
Other electrical equipment	9.4
Optical, surgical, photographic, and other instruments	6.5
Industrial chemicals	5.3
Drugs, medicines	4.4
Machinery	4.3
All manufacturing (average)	4.3
Motor vehicles, other transportation equipment	3.1
Non-industrial chemicals	2.2
Rubber products	2.1
Fabricated metal products	1.5
Other manufacturing industries	1.4
Primary metals	0.8
Paper and allied products	0.7
Textiles, apparel	0.6
Lumber, wood products, furniture	0.6
Food and kindred products	0.3

Source: U.S. National Science Foundation, *Research and Development in Industry*, 1960 (Washington, U.S.G.P.O. 1963), p. 82.

Looking at the same problem by means of a different measure for the U.K., Table 6.9 shows the percentage of QSEs (qualified scientists and engineers) per 1,000 workers over a range of British industrial classes. It is clear from this that as in the United States' case, aircraft manufacture, electronics and particular elements of the chemicals industry rank high as "technology-based" activities. At the other end of the scale in both cases come the food, textiles and clothing industries which are low on technology inputs. Table 6.9, designed for the purposes of an enquiry into small firms, points up another feature of technology-intensive industry. While aircraft and electronics use large numbers of QSEs at whatever scale they operate, this is not so across the board. For most industries it is the larger business which mounts the heaviest expenditures on R and D and which would therefore seek out the highly qualified elements in the available labor force—another potential constraint affecting the location of this kind of industry over space.

Table 6.9
QSEs in small firms in R
and D compared with all
firms in survey.

| | Number per 1000 employees | |
	Small firms	All survey firms
All manufacturing	1.4	5.0
Food, drink, tobacco	0.4	1.9
Chemical and allied industries	7.9	22.1
Metal manufacturing	0.4	3.0
Mechanical engineering	1.4	2.8
Electrical engineering	1.8	5.5
Electronics	14.0	21.6
Aircraft	13.4	18.2
Motor vehicles	2.4	2.0
Other vehicles	1.7	4.6
Textile, clothing, etc	0.2	1.4
Other manufacturing	0.6	2.0

Source: J. G. Cox, *Scientific and Engineering Manpower and Research in Small Firms* (Committee of Inquiry on Small Firms, Research Report No. 2) London, HMSO (1971) Table 7.

The question of size of firm rather than type of industry which is particularly technology-intensive is further emphasized when it comes to innovation—commercial application—of the products of R and D. The case of Terylene quoted by Johnson (1975) is instructive here. When Terylene was invented the research laboratory was running on a budget of £200,000 per year (in 1940). Pilot developments cost £4 million and the final plant for making it initially available on the commercial market cost £15 million. Only the very largest businesses could mount the "innovation expenditure" in this case, even though the R and D stage was relatively small in scale. We shall return to the further implications of this in Chapter Nine. For the moment it is sufficient to point out that the "technology-producing" and the "technologically innovative" businesses are more likely not only to be in aircraft, electronics and chemicals, but at the top of the size scale in those and other industries.

Variations in the spatial origin of technical knowledge

Technical knowledge is simply a sub-set of total knowledge and, while this is no place to delve into such a deep philosophical problem as the factors promoting the growth and development of knowledge, it can be said with some conviction that the processes of communication and interaction are fundamental determinants. Following from this it might be argued that those locations in space with the highest probability for the generation of new technical knowledge of a spontaneous (autonomous) nature will be the points of greatest human interaction.

From what we know thus far of the space economy these points would be identified as the foci of the communications and interaction network, in particular as the higher order central places, a phenomenon which we discussed at length in Chapter Two and which is verified by Pred (1966). Table 6.10 shows the dominance of existing and emerging high-order centers in the late nineteenth-century United States in terms of their share of the number of patents granted.

Table 6.10
Percentage of patents granted in U.S. for selected cities 1860, 1880, 1900.

	1860	1880	1900
U.S. Total	100.00	100.00	100.00
New York	14.75	13.19	10.27
Chicago	0.90	3.87	6.92
Philadelphia	4.88	4.28	3.98
St. Louis	0.81	1.37	1.62
Boston	2.91	3.32	2.02
Baltimore	0.95	1.54	1.11
Pittsburgh	1.13	1.61	2.05
Cleveland	0.95	1.05	1.58
San Francisco	0.60	1.32	1.08
Detroit	0.21	0.76	0.87
Los Angeles	0.00	0.02	0.49

Source: Based on figures in Pred (1966), Table 3.1, Table 3.2, Table 3.3.

Ulman (1958) points to the dominance of the industrial belt, the focal point of U.S. interaction in general, for such indicators of innovation potential as number of patents issued, membership of learned societies, etc. (Figure 6.13). Discussing the obverse situation he quotes the poet Sidney Lanier, who found that in the south, away from the main crossroads of interaction, there was "not enough attrition of mind on mind... to... bring out any sparks from a man."

The sources of much of the *autonomous invention* which contributes to the stock of technical knowledge may thus be identified as localized in their distribution. Central places in general, but in particular those of higher order with greater levels of functional interaction and wider hinterlands, dominate and polarize the availability of invention.

In spatial terms as we have seen, the processes of induced invention—the conscious promotion of new technical knowledge and innovation—the conversion of ideas into practice and process—have much in common. Both depend upon the application of substantial investment inputs and upon the willingness of entrepreneurs to utilize their capital resources in this way. They therefore tend to exhibit a space preference for those "capital-rich" locations with ready availability of investment funds and with, on Schumpeter's definition, a favorable "entrepreneurial climate."

In effect, therefore, all forms of invention and innovation have a tendency toward spatially localized patterns of evolution (Seibert, 1969). Autonomous invention tends to take place with greatest probability at the points of greatest interaction and information exchange in space. Induced invention and innovation have a stronger association with those foci of interaction towards the apex of the urban hierarchy which are economically the most successful—*the centers of control* (Ullman, 1958).

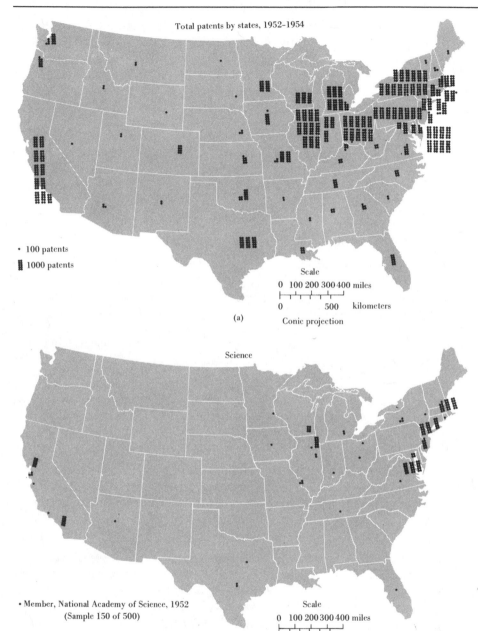

Total patents by states, 1952–1954

• 100 patents

▓ 1000 patents

Scale

0 100 200 300 400 miles

0   500   kilometers

(a)   Conic projection

Science

• Member, National Academy of Science, 1952
(Sample 150 of 500)

Scale

0 100 200 300 400 miles

0   500   kilometers

(b)   Conic projection

Figure 6.13
Surrogate measures to
show some aspects of the
distribution of technical
knowledge in the United
States. (a) Distribution of
patents 1952–1954. (b)
Membership of the
Academy of Sciences in
the United States.
[*Source:* E. L. Ullman
(1958), Regional
Development and the
Geography of
Concentration, *Papers and
Proceedings, Regional
Science Association,* **4,**
Maps 4 and 6.
Reproduced by
permission of the
Regional Science
Association.]

The mobility of technical knowledge

Given that new technical knowledge does not originate in all regions at the
same rate, its availability at different locations depends, like other factors, on
its mobility. As before, with complete and free mobility spatial disparities in
its initial origin would have no significance, since the factor would move to
attract high returns at favorable locations.

Technical knowledge (as our discussion of Hägerstrand's diffusion model showed in Chapter Two) is not perfectly mobile any more than is capital, though once again some writers have assumed it to be so.* Like all information its movement is attenuated by the effects of distance and its precise flow patterns are determined by a variety of complex factors. Suffice it to say at this stage that the exchange of technical knowledge over space tends to be sharply affected by the particular communications network in existence and by the relative spatial locations of senders and receivers. There is a strong conservative element in information flow. Existing structures tend to maintain and reinforce themselves because, to a considerable degree, the existing spatial distribution of economic activities determines the potential application of new knowledge and information.

The availability of technical knowledge over space

Technical knowledge therefore may be considered a spatially localized factor input for most economic activities. Its localization as we have seen tends to be oriented towards the larger and more successful existing concentrations of production and the foci of the geographical network of communications. In terms of mobility it behaves like the other non-land production factors: it is sensitive to movement over space, it tends to be attenuated by distance, diffusing only slowly from its origin, and it is channeled along existing lines of movement and interaction.

In view of this it tends in locational terms to be a strong polarizing agent in the evolution of economic activity. In particular its polarizing function, that is its capacity to draw development to *its location*, is especially powerful when other factor inputs such as labor and capital tend to be relatively mobile:

> Process, product and organizational innovations have a strong polarizing incidence. The more mobile capital and labor, the stronger are the polarizing effects which technical knowledge induces with respect to these determinants.
> *Siebert (1969), p. 40*

For those industries which may be described as "technology-intensive" the costs involved in relation to the technical knowledge factor are essentially the *opportunity costs* which a business would incur by being, in popular jargon, "in the wrong place at the wrong time." They would be notional costs that would add up to the total savings that might have been made if they were better placed—the costs of "foregone opportunities." The quantification of such costs in such a way as to compare them with money costs of labor or capital is a matter of fine judgment. For industries like electronics the relative importance of "new ideas" as an input is likely to be so great as to encourage a location close to the main foci of technical knowledge in this field, even if the cost of other factor inputs at that point is high.

Note   *See, for example, Borts and Stein (1964), p. 81.

One of the problems associated with the evaluation of technology as a *factor of location* as well as a factor of production is, as we pointed out earlier, one of measurement. It is not difficult to gain some idea of the way in which *technology-producing* activities are located in space. Figure 6.14 gives a broad indication of this for the United States. Clearly, the western division ranks highest (26 percent) if technology-producing activities are measured by the amount of federal and private expenditure attracted to research and development activities. It is worth noting, however, that its dominance rests primarily on the provision of federal rather than private funds. The manufacturing belt (if its three constituent divisions are added together) accounts for more than 50 percent of the remainder. Here the balance of private to federal funding is reversed. When it comes to measuring *technology-consuming* activities, say, those in aircraft and missile manufacture and the making of electronic and scientific equipment and chemicals, it is equally clear that they are to be found, together with most other industries, in precisely the same regions. Indeed, the technology-producing activities and those which consume technology as a major input are very largely one and the same. But who is to say that the one attracted the other? Both grew up more or less in parallel. As the aircraft and missile industry grew up in the west, so too did the research and development expenditure which keeps it ahead of the world. Similarly as the vehicles industry evolved in the midwest, so too did vehicle technology and the research activity that goes with it. If there is a direct, perceptible link between them it is their twin *association with success.* Successful industries these days remain successful by investing in invention and innovation. Embedded within a regional structure of industries with heavy research and development expenditure there are identifiable geographical clusters of research-producing activities. The Palo Alto complex in California, the cluster of electronics industries along Route 128 near Boston, the Cape Kennedy complex, the science-based industrial complex along the

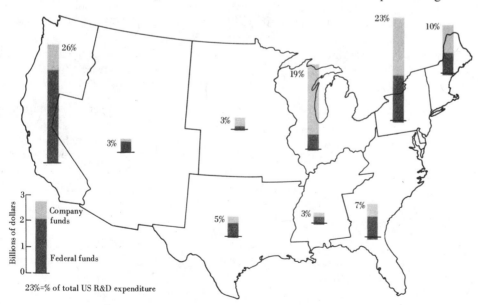

Figure 6.14
Expenditure on industrial research and development by division and source of funds, United States, 1968. [*Source:* R. C. Estall (1972), *A Modern Geography of the United States,* Figure 45, London: Penguin Books. Reproduced by permission of the author.]

Queen Elizabeth expressway near Toronto, and the cluster along the M4 west of London, are well known. The complexity of the issues surrounding the production and "consumption" of technical knowledge in modern society and the sheer difficulty of measuring any aspect of the whole phenomenon makes generalization unprofitable in this particular case.

At best, we can argue that technology is *critical to economic growth* in the advanced industrial nations. It draws a high proportion of the venture capital generated by both industry and government. As a factor we have suggested that technology is *not as perfectly mobile* as many economic models would ask us to accept. There are places where it is more available than others and deliberate expenditure to create it has a localized pattern of allocation. Even the transmission of technical knowledge through the channels of communication tends to be between such centers of specialization and thus reinforces its relative spatial concentration. As to its role as a location factor we can do no more than suggest that there is a *geographical association between research and development expenditure and successful industries*. For a new enterprise, whether it simply searches out success or the technological innovation which tends to accompany it, the opportunity costs of being "in the wrong place at the wrong time" could be critical in locational terms.

The locational impact of spatial variations in factor costs

Now that we have seen something of the "real-world" variety of the structural and spatial conditions affecting the input of production factors to economic activities, let us make some summary generalizations on the impact of this variety on the location of economic activity in space.

The tradition of analysis in location theory has been to take a single factor of production (generally labor) and to show how it would "distort" locational patterns made with reference to other criteria. We shall begin this section with a brief review of this kind of analytical approach, concluding with a discussion of the general locational issues that arise where, under more realistic conditions, production factors are combined together in a given production function.

Under the greatly simplified conditions of his model Weber devised a technique for the evaluation of the locational impact of localized sources of relatively cheap labor, on the location of an industry, the initial site for which had been determined by reference to transport costs alone. He begins with the proposition,

> when labor costs are varied an industry deviates from its transport locations in proportion to the size of its labor coefficient.
> *Weber (1909), p. XXV*

In other words it was established that the locational pull of an additional factor on a location previously set by other factors would depend upon the relative importance (labor coefficient) of that factor in relation to all other factor inputs for the industry.

Weber went on to determine the precise spatial extent of the locational shift under the conditions of his model by the use of *isodapanes* (see Chapter Four). He introduced the notion of the *critical isodapane* which has particular relevance to us here. This is the isodapane whose value represents the additional transport costs (above those of the minimum transport-cost point) which are equivalent to the *savings* which might be made through reductions in other production costs at alternative locations. The method is illustrated in Figure 6.15. Total production costs which for the moment we assume to be simply transport plus labor, are $5 per unit of output higher at A, the minimum transport point, than at B, C, or D. This means that some differential in non-transport production costs exists between them. For instance, labor may be $5 per unit of output higher at A, the minimum transport point, than at B, C or D; alternatively it might be capital, perhaps a function of development cost subsidies or taxes.

The critical isodapane, therefore, has a value of $5. It can be seen that, of the three alternative locations, C lies exactly on the critical isodapane so that in the absence of other factors a producer would be indifferent as to a location at either A or C. Location D incurs excessive transport costs, while B appears as the location at which *total costs* of production including transportation are minimized. As a general rule, therefore, if the location with lower production costs lies *inside* the critical isodapane it is worthwhile for the producer to transfer to that point from the minimum transport-cost location. Strictly speaking, a separate critical isodapane exists for each alternative location, though in Figure 6.15, the production cost savings are the same at each location other than A, so that only a single one need be used.

Weber thus established that the evaluation of least-cost location for an economic activity using diverse factor inputs is essentially one of spatial substitution. In his special case the producer substitutes transport outlays for labor outlays. His isodapane technique provided a simple method for solving this two-factor substitution problem in spatial terms within the constraints of his own model.

Figure 6.15
Deviation of location from the minimum transport-cost point to the point of lowest production costs.

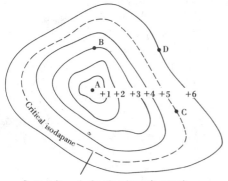

Costs at alternative locations (per unit output)

	A	B	C	D
Transport costs:	$10	$13	$15	$16
Production costs:	$20	$15	$15	$15
Total costs:	$30	$28	$30	$31

Figure 6.16
Substitution relationships
between labor outlays and
transport outlays.
[*Source:* Reprinted from
W. Isard (1956), *Location
and Space Economy*,
Figure 25, by permission
of the M.I.T. Press,
Cambridge,
Massachusetts. Copyright
ⓒ 1956 by the
Massachusetts Institute of
Technology.]

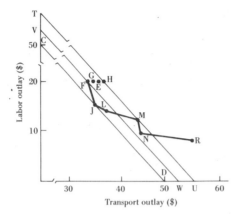

Applying Isard's substitution technique to the same problem it can be shown that while the theoretical implications are the same the method is perhaps a little simpler. Figure 6.16 depicts a similar situation by means of an outlay substitution line (F J L M N R). The substitution in this case is again between transport and labor, though it is possible to apply the method to all other input costs. Under the conditions assumed in Figure 6.16, labor costs are equal at locations F, G, E, and H ($20 per unit of output) but lower at J, L, M, N, R. Point F is the minimum transport-cost point but J, with only slightly higher transport costs, has labor costs which are $5 cheaper. J, therefore, lies on a lower iso-outlay line ($50) and thus represents the optimum solution. It is worth noting that the solution might be affected by a shift in the slope of the iso-outlay lines, in other words, in the relative cost importance of labor and transport in the total situation. This is logically the parallel of Weber's solution by labor coefficient.

Not only is the substitution method simpler to apply, it is also considerably more flexible in its application. Substitutions over a wide range of input factors can be examined (providing that they are expressed in two-dimensional form). It is also possible, as was pointed out in Chapter Five, to take into account the curved and stepped nature of realistic transportation rates. Thus by use of such a technique and in particular some of its multi-dimensional mathematical extensions solutions can be attempted in accordance with the theoretical principles expounded earlier, although these could not be in any sense considered final solutions.

In general terms, although we began with the land factor of production and the role of transport costs, each factor with its specific localization pattern and mobility characteristics exerts a more or less powerful influence on location in space. The particular factor or combination of factors that has the dominant role varies from sector to sector and from industry to industry. For some, like agriculture, a fundamental tie to a totally fixed factor is the dominant force (though, of course, land is "mobile" in the sense that the use to which it is put can change); for others it is a pull to sites of bulky raw materials, pockets of specialized labor or "seed-beds" of new technical knowledge.

For most economic activities, however, an identifiable "pull" to one or other production factor is difficult to isolate. In effect, as we pointed out at the beginning of this chapter, the production function *offers a businessman choices.* Where labor is a demanded factor in short supply he may be able to substitute capital for it. Alternatively, he may adopt or develop some new form of technology which raises the same productivity from a similar labor force. Similarly, where capital is in short supply, perhaps in remote regions or in those far-from-remote inner city locations where finance capital sees investment as "risky," labor can be applied as a substitute. Since in the modern world the kaleidoscope of possible factor substitutions is changed almost from day to day by new developments in technology, generalization about production factors as location factors is made extremely difficult.

The simplicity of the analytical approach where one factor is isolated and its locational "pull" is estimated by making the classical "other things being equal" assumption ignores a salient feature of modern economic life. At the extremes where activities are tied to particular factor needs, there are *imperatives* but, over the entire range between, there are factor mix *choices.* Perhaps in the last century and in the first half of the present one, the imperatives tended to hold sway. But, certainly in more recent years there appear to be more choices and fewer imperatives in the locational decision. One imperative which we have observed as being drastically reduced during the past 150 years has been that imposed by the "tyranny of distance." Both through the transport revolution and the accompanying revolution in the communications media, flows of people, goods, credit and new ideas have all been made easier. As we have suggested there is still not as perfect a mobility in these phenomena as the economists' models frequently assume for ease of exposition. Production factors are still to some degree localized and exert localizing forces on those economic activities which demand them. But in the second half of the twentieth century the nature of these localizing forces is subtle and complex. Perhaps the nineteenth century was the heyday of the influence of key factor inputs (generalized in the literature as location factors) as a positive determinate force underlying economic geography.

In this chapter we have introduced some of the complexity associated with the choices open to a businessman in selecting a mix of production factors. One of his choices has, however, been constrained still—that of choosing the *scale* at which he will set his operations. To evaluate this he needs to know something of the *demand* which his production is to satisfy. It is to these questions of demand, scale, and the associated spatial form of agglomeration that we turn our attention in the next chapter.

Further reading

Estall, R. C. (1972), *A Modern Geography of the United States*, London: Pelican, Chapters 10, 11, 12.

Estall, R. C., and R. O. Buchanan (1973), *Industrial Activity and Economic Geography* 3rd ed., London: Hutchinson, Chapter 4.

Fuchs, V. R. (1967), *Differentials in Hourly Earnings by Region and City Size, 1959*, New York: Columbia University Press.

Isard, W. (1956), *Location and Space Economy*, Cambridge, Mass.: M.I.T. Press, Chapter 6.

Johnson, P. S. (1975), *The Economics of Invention and Innovation*, London: Martyn Robertson, Chapter 1.

Pred, A. (1966), *The Spatial Dynamics of U.S. Urban-Industrial Growth, 1800–1914*, Cambridge, Mass.: M.I.T. Press, Chapter 3.

Segal, M. (1960), *Wages in the Metropolis*, Cambridge, Mass.: Harvard University Press.

Siebert, H. (1969), *Regional Economic Growth: Theory and Policy*, Scranton, Pa.: International Textbook Co., Chapter 4.

Vyver, F. T. de (1951), Labor Factors in the Industrial Development of the South, *Southern Economic Journal* **18**, 189–205.

Weber, A. (1909), *Theory of the Location of Industries*, Chicago: University of Chicago Press, Chapter IV.

CHAPTER 7

DEMAND, SCALE AND AGGLOMERATION

In the previous chapter we looked at the various ways in which businessmen responded to spatial differences in production costs. In effect we showed how each would-be producer decided on the amounts and proportions of the factor inputs he will need and how variations over space in the availability of production factors will influence his attitude to location. Notionally, the businessman is faced with a *space-cost surface* for each factor and with a composite cost surface for all his inputs added together depending upon which combinations he chooses in his factor mix. The idea is not new to us. We encountered it first in the *space-cost curve* concept at the end of Chapter Four. Let us use it again here to introduce the subject of demand variation and its impact on the simplified model.

For a given industry there exists at a point in time a space-cost surface like that shown in Figure 7.1 for the manufacture of electronic equipment.* Each point on the surface represents the aggregate costs of production at that location and there is assumed to be a regular progression in costs between the points.

Figure 7.1
Cost surface for all spatially variable costs—electronic equipment manufacture. [*Source:* D. M. Smith (1971), *Industrial Location,* Figure 18.17. Reproduced by permission of John Wiley & Sons, New York.]

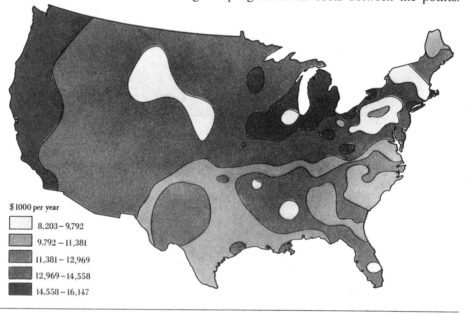

$1000 per year

	8,203 – 9,792
	9,792 – 11,381
	11,381 – 12,969
	12,969 – 14,558
	14,558 – 16,147

Note

The space-cost surface for electronic equipment manufacture. Although our concern here is simply to use the space-cost surface to make a general, conceptual point, Smith's (1971, pp. 376–387) example of electronic equipment manufacture presents a rare opportunity to show the form of the surface for a real-world case. As such, it deserves further comment. The total cost surface shown in Figure 7.1 is derived by summing together five input cost surfaces—labor costs, freight costs, occupancy costs, utilities costs and tax costs. Added together they produce a total surface for what Smith calls "spatially variable operating costs." The *least-cost* location on this basis is found to be in rural eastern South Carolina while highest costs prevail in Detroit, Michigan. Since labor costs constitute a substantial element in total costs the total cost surface follows closely the form of the labor cost surface with the south showing up as the most likely source of a low-cost location for the industry. Comparing the actual location of the electronics industry with that suggested by the variable-cost analysis Smith was forced to conclude, however, that there was very little correspondence between the two.

Cost isopleths show the detail of spatial variations and the form of the surface. As we saw in Chapter Four, highly localized activities will tend to respond to steep cost variations while "footloose" ones will respond to "plateau-like" conditions. So far we have proceeded on the assumption that the locational problem is the same in every case. Find the *lowest point on the production cost surface* and there is the point of maximum profit and the best location. This is of course the case only *where the pattern of demand does not vary over space*. Notice that the assumptions of Figure 4.6 about spatial margins to profitability—reproduced here as Figure 7.2a—depended entirely upon the total revenue or price line being horizontal, that is pro-rated as being constant over space. Where this is not the case as in Figure 7.2b and we permit revenue and price to vary more realistically over space the situation is drastically altered. First, the area of profit is not now a single contiguous zone. It would appear over space as two separate regions. Second, the material source, while it provides the least-cost location, no longer provides the maximum-profit one. Third, there are clearly some as yet unexplained subtleties to be explored with respect to the interrelations of costs, prices and likely levels of demand for a product.

Figure 7.2
The impact of variations in revenue on the spatial pattern of profitability. (a) Spatial margin to profitability with total revenue constant over space. (b) Spatial margins to profitability with total revenue variable over space.

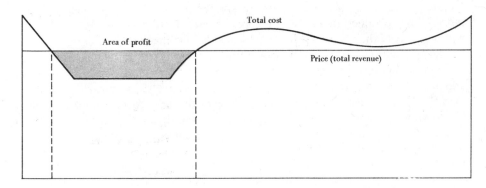

(a)

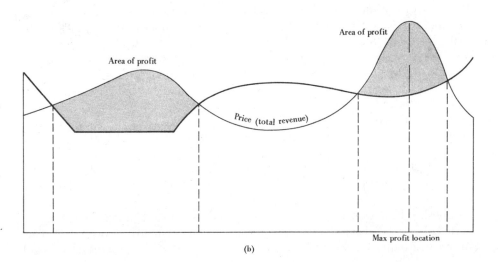

(b)

Although up to this point we have proceeded tacitly on the assumption that the only real consideration in locational choice was the minimization of costs in serving a given market, the importance of spatial variations in demand was recognized (i.e. through variations in population distribution) as early as the end of Chapter Two. We are in good company in adopting this approach. In common with many location theorists we have chosen to ignore the subject of demand variations and their impact until we could get the notion of the least-cost location across to the reader in simple terms. Now we must try to set the record straight.

Spatial variations in demand

At the outset it is worth reminding ourselves that we are seeing demand here as the *initiating* force which prompts the businessman to go into production. Where he sees a level of actual or potential demand for a good or service he can supply or perhaps in a more familiar modern context where he can "create" demand by advertising or by skillful marketing techniques, he puts together his production factors at a particular location in the belief that he will profit from the venture. Once established he has made certain commitments. He has committed mobile, monetary capital into fixed buildings, plant and equipment. He has put his own savings or the "savings" of others into stocks and inventories in the hope that beyond this initial "stocking up," cash flow into the business from his customers will pay the bills to his suppliers. From our particular viewpoint a most important commitment is that *he chooses a particular place* to do all this and that having made his choice many forces are brought into play which will make him reluctant to leave it. For an established firm as opposed to a new one it is the "tuning" of the enterprise—responding to factor and market price changes, adopting new techniques, making the most of the advantages of his chosen location which become critical. He must *use a location rather than choose one.* But we should not forget that in choosing his initial location and operating from it he has already molded the spatial pattern of demand as those who supply him would see it. *He is both supplier and customer* as is every other element in the economy (even the household is both a supplier of labor and a consumer of goods and services). As his customers increase their demands on his output so he exerts a demand on his suppliers and they on theirs. The whole system "cascades" along as demands are supplied and newly derived demands are created. Over time relatively small shifts in these short-term transactions between customers and suppliers accumulate to generate aggregate long-run changes in the structure and pattern of demand. Just as the horse and buggy era gives way to the automobile or the dance hall gives way to the discotheque, so new technology or new tastes generate new demand conditions and a new "game board" for the upcoming or established businessman. Once demand is introduced to the model in an unconstrained form so also is the full dynamic complexity of evolving society. (Perhaps on these grounds readers will forgive us for apparently doing things backwards.)

Sources of demand in the economic system

As we showed in Chapter Six (p. 224) the demand available to an economic system can be expressed in two ways: by the amounts of income returned to the system as *consumption* or as *investment*. In the first of these, this demand brings into production such *consumer goods* as food or clothing, washing machines or automobiles. In the second, it stimulates the production of *producer* or *capital goods* like power stations, oil tankers or steel mills. For consumer goods the chief source of demand is consumption in the household sector of the economy. The investment funds which bring about the production of capital goods largely emanate from business, the financial institutions, and government.

We have already seen how the savings-investment cycle operates and how the factor market for capital operates (see Figure 6.10). We should not forget, however, that when a businessman starts or expands his enterprise the plant, equipment and inventories he assembles are all produced by someone. For the building and construction trades, the shipbuilders, machine tool manufacturers, the steel industry and so on, most of their effective demand comes from *other producers assembling capital goods* as part of an investment program. When investment flows these industries are busy; when it does not they are slack. It is, of course, true that at the bottom of the demand "cascade" there is still the household itself exercising a demand for the *consumer goods* that, say, the textile manufacturer is looking to supply when he orders a new machine from a weaving-frame producer. The usefulness of the distinction comes, however, in realizing that investment flows are much more volatile than flows of consumer demand, giving booms and slumps in the steel industry rarely felt by the food manufacturer. Investment flows respond to different stimuli. These days they are increasingly a response to government policies and public sector spending but they also clearly reflect such complex determinants as the rate of inflation and the economic "mood" of a nation. More importantly from our specific viewpoint the spatial pattern of demand for producer or capital goods will be a function of the geographical distribution of *other producers* rather than of consumers in general. In other words, in assessing the likely location of *his* "consumer demand" a capital goods manufacturer manufacturing, for example, tire-making machinery, would want to consult a map measuring the intensity of automobile production in a country rather than one showing the distribution of automobile owners.

Turning our attention to the consumer side of demand, we can remind ourselves that consumption is paid for by that part of income which is not saved or hoarded. It goes into payments for the direct consumption of goods and services, some of which, like food and clothing, have a relatively short life. Others, known as *consumer durables*, have a long life, as do washing machines or automobiles. With rising average incomes it is the latter rather than the former which become the primary focus (in relative terms) of consumer demand. No one living in a modern western society can be in any doubt as to the key role which the demand for such goods as television sets, washing machines and especially automobiles plays in sustaining levels of production in the economy.

Many of the key principles underlying the way households in a market society make their consumer choices were discussed in Chapter Two. We do not propose to repeat them here but the reader is prompted to review, in this more general context, topics like the demand schedule, demand and price, and elasticity which were originally introduced in the specific case of the central place model.

One key source of demand in the modern economy which can neither be ignored nor given the treatment it deserves in the present text is that derived from the activities of government.* While the household sector accounts for by far the largest share of total demand available to the economic system, government is becoming an increasingly large consumer of the national output in most western capitalist nations. The income which government receives and which is then disbursed on the citizens' behalf is derived from taxation. About nine-tenths of this comes from direct taxation in the form of income taxes and social security contributions. Although the overall figure varies substantially between nations, government spending in the western capitalist countries accounts for something beween ten and twenty-five percent of the value of gross national product. Public spending is therefore becoming an increasingly important source of demand in modern economic systems.

When we look at the sections of the modern economy where government spending has its greatest impact, perhaps the first areas that spring to mind are such obvious ones as defense and space exploration. Against the prominence of these sectors, however, is the less obvious truth about the pervasiveness of public activities and the expenditure they generate on everyday life. Teitz provides a concise and effective summary for modern America:

> Modern urban man is born in a publicly financed hospital, receives his education in a publicly supported school and university, spends a good part of his life traveling on publicly built transportation facilities, communicates through the post office or the quasi-public telephone system, drinks his public water, disposes of his garbage through the public removal system, reads his public library books, picnics in his public parks, is protected by his public police, fire, and health systems; eventually he dies, again in a hospital, and may even be buried in a public cemetery. Ideological conservatives notwithstanding, his everyday life is inextricably bound up with governmental decisions on these and numerous other local public services.
> *Teitz (1968), p. 36*

Note

*Investigation of the basis for public spending in general and for its allocation across production sectors in particular takes us far from the precepts of neo-classical economics which have absorbed most of our attention so far. Questions of social and distributive justice, of the proper role of government in democratic society, of the right of government to intervene and exercise command in the economic system and so forth, all burning issues of our day, demand exploration if we are properly to understand the basis for government involvement in modern mixed command-market economies. For this reason we have deferred such discussion to a companion volume and our treatment here can be no more than superficial.

The demand which governments exert for everything from nuclear warheads through hospitals to printed tax forms, is one which businesses, both privately and publicly owned, move in to satisfy. Indeed, government contracts are highly prized targets for business enterprises of all kinds since at the very least the state is a reliable, if often demanding, customer. As a source of demand public expenditure rarely fits the pattern which would be expected under the operation of the free enterprise system under market control. In fact, much government spending and therefore, the productive activity generated by it tends to "fill in" areas of the economy where the operation of market forces alone fails to achieve a satisfactory distribution of wealth. Government welfare and reconstruction schemes and attempts by the state to bring investment to depressed areas easily spring to mind. In addition there are many facilities demanded by modern society such as, for example, education, police and fire services, defense, transportation systems, which are better consumed and paid for collectively (that is by government) than individually. These are potentially massive sources of demand for both private and public enterprise and they produce a powerful impact on levels of economic activity throughout the economy as a whole.

The spatial distribution of demand

In looking for some approximation to the spatial distribution of *household consumer demand* it is clear that it will, to some degree, vary with the pattern of incomes. In general terms the higher the level of household income the higher the anticipated level of demand. However, bearing in mind our preliminary discussion of demand in Chapter Two and what we know from our own daily experiences about consumer choice, there are at least three other important determinants of the level of demand for a good or service:

1. The market price of the good or service.
2. The relative prices of all other goods and services in the consumer's bundle of demands.
3. The weightings given by the consumer to each element in his bundle of tastes and preferences.

We know, even for the constrained conditions of the simplified model in Chapter Two, that the price of a single good and the relative prices of a bundle of goods will vary over space. We can further assume, given the nature of the species, that the way men *weight* their tastes and preferences varies with age, sex, income level, culture and most of the other variables attributable to humanity. Under these circumstances we are certainly never going to get very close to an accurate overall measure of aggregate consumer demand. Even for a single product with a clearly defined consumer group the measurement of spatial patterns of demand is a slippery task outside the controlled world of the simplified model. Various attempts have been made, however, to measure the intensity of aggregate demand over space and we can make use of them here, tempering our criticism of the methods by the sheer difficulty of the task.

One possible way of describing spatial variations in the intensity of demand is to use the concept of *potential*, an idea closely related to the gravity model that we looked at in Chapter Two.* Recall that the gravity model tells us that interaction between two areas will be related to the product of their "masses" divided by the distance separating them. We can extend this idea to encompass the level of interaction between one area (i) and all other areas (n) by simply adding together the interaction between i and every other area. For example, interaction between area i and area 1 is calculated as for the gravity model:

$$I_{i1} = \frac{P_i P_1}{d_{i1}^b}$$

Similarly, interaction between i and area 2 is calculated as

$$I_{i2} = \frac{P_i P_2}{d_{i2}^b}$$

This process is repeated for all other areas to give the *population potential* at area i (we can use the symbol PP_i to denote this). Because the process involves merely adding together a whole series of pairs of interactions, we can express the *population potential* in general terms as

$$PP_i = \sum_{j=1}^{n} \frac{P_j}{d_{ij}^b}$$

For place i, therefore, its *population potential* gives some indication of the "intensity of the possibility of interaction" of place i with all other places in the system. In a sense it is a measure of the "nearness" of place i to the population of the entire system. If we carry out the same calculation for every place in the system then the resulting values can be mapped using isopleths to give a *surface of population potential*.

If, as we assumed initially in Chapter Two, every individual in the population did have an identical income, spent the same proportion of that income on purchasing goods, and had similar tastes, then a *population potential* surface would represent a reasonable approximation to a household sector demand surface. But since these assumptions can no longer be retained, one possible solution would be to "weight" population by some measure of income as in Figure 7.3.

An alternative measure used by Harris (1954) was the value of retail sales per county, from which he derived a *market potential*,

$$MP_i = \sum_{j=1}^{n} \frac{M_j}{d_{ij}}$$

Note   *Detailed discussion of the potential concept can be found in Carrothers (1956) and Isard (1960).

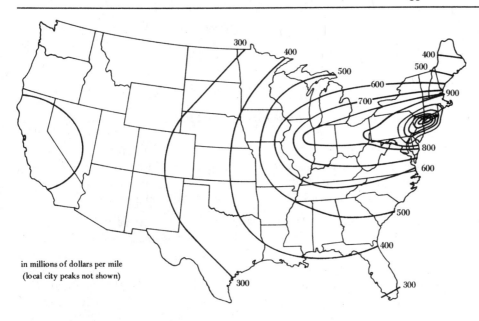

in millions of dollars per mile
(local city peaks not shown)

Figure 7.3
United States—income
potential 1956. [*Source:*
W. Warntz (1956),
*Macrogeography and
Income Fronts,*
Philadelphia: Regional
Science Research
Institute, Figure 1.]

where

MP_i = market potential at i
M_j = size of market at j measured in terms of retail sales per county
d_{ij} = distance between i and j based on an estimate of the transportation cost, allowing for long-haul economies

Market potential at point i, therefore, is obtained by dividing the retail sales of each jth point (group of counties) by the distance between i and j and summing the result. The process is carried out for all points to yield values on which an isopleth map of the *market potential* surface can be based.

Figure 7.4a indicates that market potential in the United States is consistently high in a belt between Illinois and the east coast (an area roughly coterminous with the traditional manufacturing belt), reaching a peak at New York City. Away from this ridge of maximum potential there is a consistent decline to the north, south, and west, with a subsidiary peak in southern California. Assuming that market potential is a valid measure of the spatial pattern of demand then it follows that location at points of high potential should offer closer proximity to the market, a better assessment of current and changing demands, faster delivery, and other locational advantages (Isard, 1960).

Market potential provides an indication of the *general* proximity of a location in relation to total demand, the peak giving an approximation of the maximum sales location. It gives no indication, however, of the cost involved in transporting goods to that market. According to Harris, the minimum transport-cost point in relation to the national market may be derived as follows:

$$TC_i = \sum_{j=1}^{n} M_j d_{ij}$$

where

TC_i = total transportation costs at i

$$\left.\begin{array}{l} M_j \\ d_{ij} \end{array}\right\} \text{as defined in formula for } \textit{market potential}$$

The calculation of transportation costs at i involves multiplying the retail sales of each jth area by its distance from i. The transportation-cost surface is then obtained by repeating the calculation for each point and constructing cost isopleths. Figure 7.4b, the transportation-cost surface, reveals a rather different pattern from the market-potential surface. The location at which total transportation costs to the entire U.S. market are minimized is at Fort Wayne, Indiana.

So far we have been concerned with spatial variations in the pattern of aggregate demand as this is reflected by such indicators of *household consumption* as income or retail sales potential. As we have already pointed out, however, not all sectors of economic activity are concerned directly with this market. Manufacturing is to a great extent its own market. Roughly 80 percent of all U.S. industries make use of materials previously processed by other industries. To estimate the spatial pattern of this market for intermediate and capital goods, Harris substituted employment in manufacturing in the potential and transport-cost formulas. Figure 7.5 shows the surfaces of *manufacturing potential* and *transportation cost* to the U.S. "manufacturing market." In the former case the optimum location is New York City, in the latter, Cleveland.

A problem therefore exists: which of these locations, New York or Fort Wayne in the case of the total market, New York or Cleveland in the case of the manufacturing market, offers the most advantageous market location? The differences between the two surfaces arise because in the market-potential case the contribution of a given-sized market declines with increasing distance whereas in the transportation-cost case the contribution of the same market increases with distance. Harris gives the example of the impact of the Pacific coast market on the values for Chicago. Pacific coast retail sales represented roughly 11 percent of total U.S. sales yet they contribute less than 5 percent to Chicago's market potential because of the magnitude of the distance between the coast and Chicago. Because of this distance, however, they account for 22 percent of the transportation cost of serving a nationwide market from Chicago.

The problem of the optimal location with respect to the market remains unsolved. Dunn (1956) attempted to combine the two measures of market potential and transport cost in a single index, but without much success. Dunn's study was based only on Florida and, in this respect, emphasized one of the basic problems of potential models: the extent to which the area for which potentials are measured is self-sufficient. In the case of Florida this is clearly far from being so, for the state is but a fragment of the total U.S. market. But even the U.S. market as used by Harris is not a closed system. In particular, Canada should be included, although given the spatial pattern of Canada's population distribution, it seems likely that the surfaces calculated for the United States

Market potential

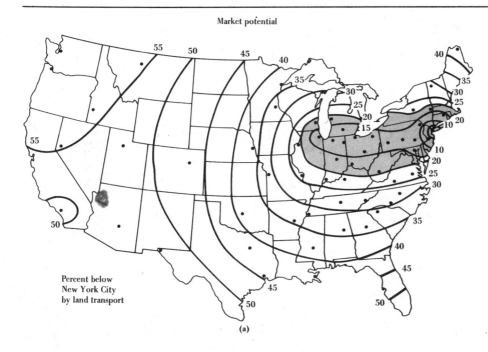

(a)

Figure 7.4
(a) Market potential and
(b) transport-cost
surfaces, United States.
[*Source:* C. D. Harris
(1954), The Market as a
Factor in the Localization
of Industry in the U.S.,
Figures 4 and 7.
Reproduced by
permission from the
*Annals of the Association
of American Geographers,*
44.]

Transport cost to the national market

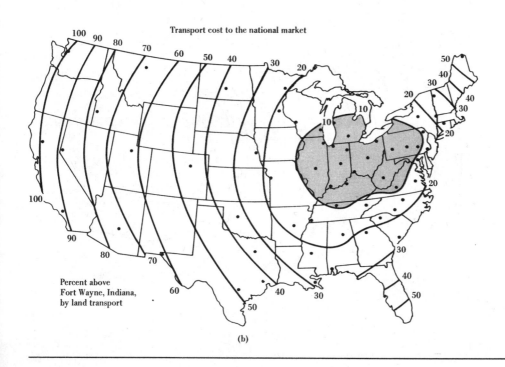

(b)

Figure 7.5
(a) Manufacturing
potential and (b)
transport costs to the
national manufacturing
market, United States.
[*Source:* C. D. Harris
(1954), The Market as a
Factor in the Localization
of Industry in the U.S.,
Figures 28 and 29.
Reproduced by
permission from the
*Annals of the Association
of American Geographers,*
44.]

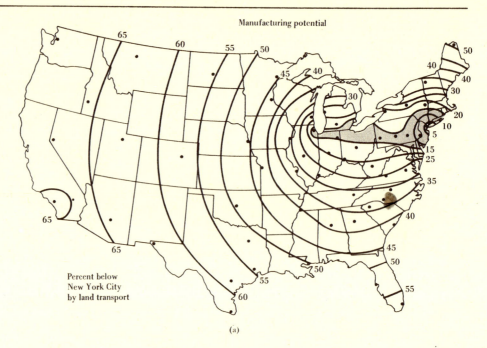

(a)

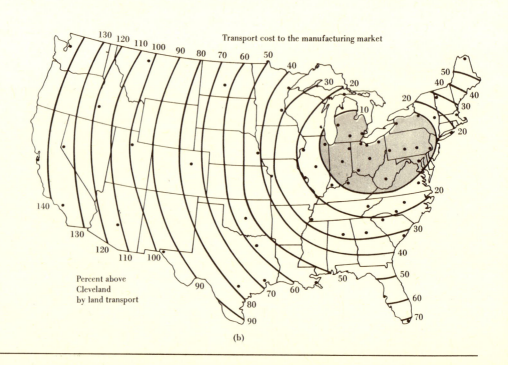

(b)

alone would be altered only marginally. Despite the difficulties inherent in the potential model, however, it does provide a useful means of estimating the overall magnitude of spatial variations in demand. Spatial variations in such aggregate indicators as incomes, retail sales figures, or manufacturing employees give some notion of the *potential* demand available throughout a space economy. The *actual* level of demand for a given good or service will, however, depend upon all those additional factors that influence consumers' demand schedules for the item in question. The market price of the good, the prices of other goods, and the particular tastes and preferences of the consumer will all have an impact.

The determination of market price for a particular good will depend on supply and demand. We know that demand varies spatially and our accumulated knowledge of the structure of the space economy testifies strongly to the spatial variability of supply. Warntz (1959) made an ingenious attempt to examine the geography of price for various agricultural commodities in the United States. He showed how prices for wheat, potatoes, onions and strawberries varied between 1940–1949 and went on to try to explain these variations in terms of a spatial interpretation of the law of supply and demand. Prices, he suggested, would vary geographically over an economic system *directly* with the pattern of demand and *inversely* with the pattern of supply. In simple terms—for those areas with high supply and low demand prices would tend to be low, and vice versa—the problem was to devise some continuous valid measure of spatial variations in the supply and demand conditions for each crop. He wanted, in effect, to superimpose a spatial surface of supply onto a spatial surface of demand and derive a third spatial surface of price from the interaction of the two. Given also that in the specific case of agricultural commodities, supply is seasonally variable, he wanted to take *time* into account. From a price point of view this is critical, as any strawberry lover will know. The propensity to consume strawberries is costly to satisfy if it is not carefully regulated to fit with seasonal peaks in supply.

Warntz, like Harris, used the potential concept to develop spatial *surfaces* from discrete data for individual states. His *gross economic population potential* is in effect a population potential surface where each state's population is weighted by its annual per capita personal income for the relevant period. It looks very similar to the situation shown in Figure 7.3 and Warntz suggests that it can be looked on as a map of *spatial variations in the intensity of effective consumer demand*. He agrees that the demand for each individual commodity will be a sub-set of this general picture and that demand, like supply, will vary over time. The measurement problems inherent in trying to produce these "lower order" demand surfaces, however, lead him to assume that the *gross* surface will be reasonably representative of demand for various commodities at all times.

On the supply side he produces a series of potential surfaces for each of the commodities in his analysis. The method of calculation is basically the same. For wheat, whose pattern of *supply space potential* is shown in Figure 7.6a, the basic data are the wheat "population" attributable to each state at a given

Figure 7.6
(a) Supply space
potential for wheat and
(b) demand space
potential. [*Source:* W.
Warntz (1959), *Toward a
Geography of Price*,
Philadelphia: University of
Pennsylvania Press,
pp. 67–68.]

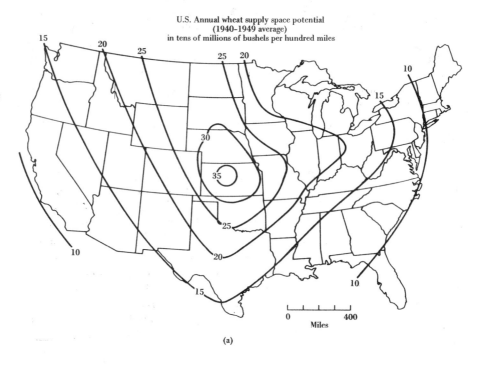

U.S. Annual wheat supply space potential
(1940–1949 average)
in tens of millions of bushels per hundred miles

(a)

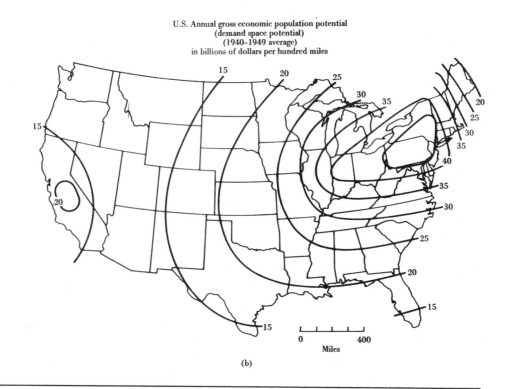

U.S. Annual gross economic population potential
(demand space potential)
(1940–1949 average)
in billions of dollars per hundred miles

(b)

time. Where the supply space potential is highest, that is in Kansas and Nebraska, the influence of supply on price is at its maximum. Away from the midwestern wheat-growing states supply falls away spatially. Looking at *demand space potential* in Figure 7.6b, the peak of the aggregate demand surface is in the northeast and here the influence of demand on price will be at its maximum. Clearly then, given the admittedly restrictive assumptions of the model and the potential technique itself, one would expect the geographical distribution of wheat prices to vary from *low* where supply is greatest in relation to demand to *high* where the reverse is true. It is but a short step from this to the integration of time into the framework. The wheat, potato, onion and strawberry "populations" varied seasonally in the ways shown in Figure 7.7, and as different producer areas brought crops onto the market the pattern of supply space potential would reflect both the overall trend and the regional variations at different times. Hence the price of commodities can be shown to be constantly varying both over time and over space as supply and demand conditions change. Warntz's analysis is highly aggregative but it does serve to emphasize the fact that supply, demand, and, as a result, price all have a spatial component. For our purposes it provides some hint of the complex logic underlying spatial variations in commodity prices and therefore points to other factors that must be taken into account in determining the spatial pattern of actual demand at a point in time. Among these other demand determinants there remains the elusive factor of consumer tastes and preferences. That these are spatially variable is indisputable, although their precise measurement and impact is difficult to assess. Indeed an entire industry of market research and consumer analysis is supported by the need of industry to predict such tastes.

We have shown, therefore, that demand like all the other factors we have considered which influence the location of economic activities is extremely variable

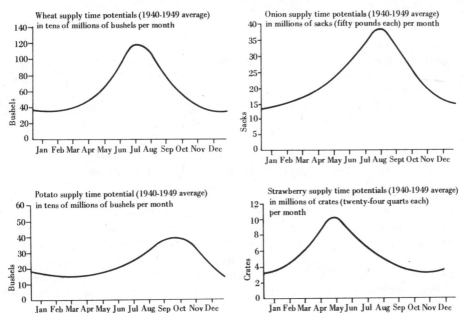

Figure 7.7
United States: supply time potentials for a selection of agricultural products. [*Source:* W. Warntz (1959), *Toward a Geography of Price*, Philadelphia: University of Pennsylvania Press, Figures 7, 8, 9 and 10.]

over space. As such it becomes another complex input to the substitution problem that faces every potential producer. The point of lowest production cost is only in rare circumstances likely to coincide exactly with the point of maximum profit. He must look "forward" to demand as well as "backward" to cost in making his judgment of the best location. There is, however, another important component in the producer's substitution problem which, in a sense, "closes the circle" by connecting the size of a producer's market with the costs of production he is likely to face. This is a factor which though not obviously "spatial" in itself has the most far-reaching locational implications. In choosing his *scale of production* a businessman makes a key decision which both influences and is influenced by his costs and the level of demand he can serve.

Economies of scale

Let us for the moment go back to the businessman we encountered at the beginning of Chapter Six. He was at that stage concerned primarily with problems of getting the right factor mix for the product he was going to produce. We made the convenient assumption then that he knew *what amount* he was going to produce. That was a burden lifted from him at that stage which real world businessmen are not allowed. Indeed one of their first decisions and in some ways a difficult one to get right is "*how many units of output to produce?*" Hinged on this, of course, is the question of the amount of each production factor that will need to be hired to meet the chosen level of output, and we demonstrated in Figure 6.4 how these amounts could be determined *for a given level of output*. Perhaps the simple answer to the question "how many units?" is "as many as can be sold at a profit." This clearly links scale with levels of *demand* and, since lower prices will generally produce greater sales, also with *price*. Some effort in market research will need to precede the scale decision.

But there are also important implications for *costs* in the choice of scale of operation. Up to this point we have followed the example of most of the early location theorists and assumed, once again for the sake of simplicity in exposition, that the average cost of producing each additional unit of output remains the same no matter how many units are produced. We have, in fact, assumed the cost implications of scale away. This situation is shown graphically in Figure 7.8a with average costs as a horizontal straight line. We have further assumed that there is no lower limit to the scale of production. Not only can a businessman (if he has a buyer) produce one unit or 10,000 but in production terms alone there will be no difference in the cost per unit.

In reality there is a minimum scale of production necessary for competition. For the most part this is determined by prevailing technology. (Few single-handed manufacturers of computers, television sets or even pencils would be likely to survive in a production-line world of high technology; more of this later, p. 273.) As far as the progression of costs with scale is concerned this is more likely in a realistic world to describe a U-shape or L-shape like those shown in Figure 7.8b, c, d.

Above the initial starting threshold, average costs tend at first to fall as the number of units of production begins to rise. They may then begin to rise beyond a certain size of production or to level out. For some activities this "straight-and-level" situation appears to be maintained while for others costs rise at the higher levels of output to give an extended U-form. We shall return to the implications of these cost considerations in more detail later, but for the moment let us briefly explore the question of *returns to scale* in production to see how they come about.

The basis of scale economies

To begin with let us assume that our businessman has not, in fact, decided on a fixed scale of operations. The market for his product seems unlimited, and he sets out to keep on increasing the size of his operation. As before, let us assume for the sake of exposition that he uses only two factors, labor and land (with capital and technology subsumed in the latter). Suppose also that he holds the *land input constant* so that he can see the short-run effect on his production of varying amounts of labor. He might well find that under these circumstances the progression of his output with variable inputs of the labor factor follows the trend shown in Table 7.1.

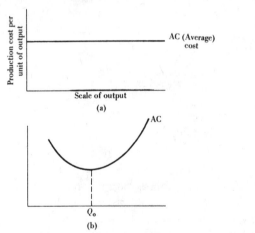

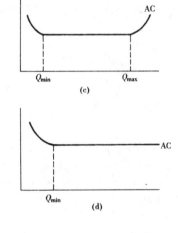

Figure 7.8
Various possible
cost-scale curves.
[*Source:* J. S. Bain
(1968), *Industrial
Organization*, 2nd ed.,
Figures 2–5. Reproduced
by permission of John
Wiley & Sons, New York.]

Table 7.1
Returns to scale.

Labor units added No. of men	Total output	Marginal productivity (change in output)	Average productivity total output per man (rounded)
1	500	500	500
2	1,500	1,000	750
3	2,750	1,250	917
4	3.900	1,150	975
5	4,900	1,000	980
6	5,800	900	967
7	6,550	750	936
8	7,150	600	894

At first he will notice that the effect of hiring an additional man will increase dramatically the level of output he gets. It is not difficult to see why. If our production unit is a farm of fixed size and capital equipment, then a second pair of hands on the farm will be enormously valuable. The new man in the hypothetical example *triples* the total output. He adds 1,000 output units to the total. This, in the terms which we used in Chapter Six, is the *marginal productivity* (the amount added to production) by two as opposed to one unit of labor. Average productivity (the total output now divided by two) is lower than marginal productivity at 750. Hiring a third man pushes up marginal productivity by another 1,250 units and average productivity rises to 917. At this stage we can talk of *increasing returns to scale*. As the variable factor is added both marginal and average returns in output also increase.

On hiring the fourth man the increase in marginal returns is for the first time lower than before, but average returns are still rising. By the time the fifth man is hired marginal returns have slipped back to the level which the *second* man's inclusion brought about but average returns have increased to their peak at 980 production units. From here on, as extra units of labor are added, both marginal and average returns decrease with the scale of the input.

Figure 7.9
Returns to scale with one
variable factor input.

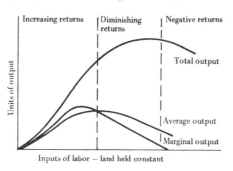

The graph in Figure 7.9 shows the basic trends. It is worth noting that marginal output falls while average output is still rising. This is because the fifth man added, although producing less than the fourth, is still producing more than the average output of all his predecessors. Output clearly varies with scale as our businessman would have discovered. In this case the scale we are discussing is the scale of input of a single factor with all others held constant. Had our businessman chosen to vary his capital inputs with land and labor constant or land inputs, with labor and capital constant, a similar progression would have resulted. First there is a stage of *increasing* (average) *returns*. This is followed by *diminishing returns* where average output falls as more units of the variable factor are added. Finally comes *negative returns* where the marginal return of the next unit of the factor is less than that of the first unit to be added.*

Note

*Known as the *law of variable proportions* this sequence of events will occur in the output of a production system wherever a single variable factor is increased in the scale of its input while the others are kept constant. Nature or the demands of technology frequently apply these constraints to man's productive activities by restricting the availability of land, labor or capital and the law of diminishing returns is one frequently encountered not only by would-be businessmen but by humanity in general.

In judging the scale at which he should "pitch" his enterprise, our businessman should be aware, then, that in hiring his variable factors of production there may well be physical or technical constraints that will make certain factor combinations become at first more and then increasingly less productive. Just as there will be some minimum threshold size he must be above, so also will there be a point higher up the scale of production where diminishing returns are likely to set in as the supply of certain factors tends to become fixed relative to others.

Let us look at the situation from the cost viewpoint. Hiring factors costs money and what our man should be looking for is the point at which he gets most units of output for his money (always assuming that he can sell that many units once he identifies it). Turning to Table 7.2 we could attempt to calculate the businessman's total *variable* costs per unit of output. (These must be distinguished from fixed costs which we will come to in a moment.) Let us suppose that the going wage rate is $10,000 per year per man to keep the arithmetic simple. The unit cost calculations for variable factor inputs would then come out as follows:

Table 7.2
Variable costs and scale of output.

Labor units added no. of men at $10,000 p.a.	Total output units/p.a.	Total labor cost/p.a.	Average labor cost/unit of output
1	500	10,000	$20.00
2	1,500	20,000	$13.33
3	2,750	30,000	$10.91
4	3,900	40,000	$10.26
5	4,900	50,000	$10.20
6	5,800	60,000	$10.34
7	6,550	70,000	$10.69
8	7,150	80,000	$11.19

It is all too obvious that beyond the fifth man hired, labor costs per unit will start to rise although there have been substantial *scale economies* in the cost of labor up to this point. If we graph the situation as in Figure 7.10 we can begin to see where the U-shaped cost-scale curves encountered at the beginning of the chapter have come from. Taking our simplified model using only two factors as representative of the more general situation where factors are used in combination, we can see how *variable* costs of production change with increasing output. If there were only variable costs to be considered and demand conditions were met it would clearly be best for our businessman to produce at the scale of 4,900 units a year at a cost of $10.20 per unit in factor outlays.

We are almost there but not quite. There is the additional question of *fixed costs*. Our simple case study assumed that labor was a variable cost and we have looked at its progression as production levels rise. But we assumed land, capital and technology *to be fixed* as labor varied. Fixed or not, they must

Figure 7.10
Variable costs per unit of
output, labor variable,
land constant.

Figure 7.11
Fixed costs per unit of
output for land (including
labor and technology).

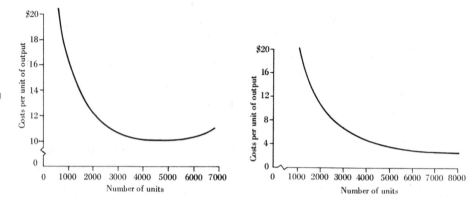

still be paid for and though they will not vary as production rises they must still be added to the total cost per unit of output. In effect, under the chosen strategy they will be "once-and-for-all" payments made when the business is set up. (If it is decided to change them, of course, they will take on the characteristics of variable costs).

How will fixed costs vary over units of production? Suppose there is a single initial outlay on these fixed "overheads" of $20,000. For one unit of output the effective cost will be all of this at $20,000 per unit. But for two units the cost per unit will be $10,000; for three, $666.66 and so on. The curve produced will be of the type shown in Figure 7.11. Starting at 1,000 units of output fixed costs stand at $20.00 per unit, but by the time 8,000 units have been produced they are down to $2.50. Beyond this point they will fall still further until in the long-run they become infinitesimal—(supposing they can remain fixed for long enough).

All that remains is to add the fixed-cost curve and the variable-cost curve together to obtain the *total-cost curve* for our businessman's enterprise. (Figure 7.12).

Table 7.3
Total costs per unit of
output.

No. of men	Total output units/p.a.	Total cost $20,000 fixed costs plus $10,000 per man	Average cost per unit of output
1	500	30,000	$60.00
2	1,500	40,000	$26.66
3	2,750	50,000	$18.18
4	3,900	60,000	$15.38
5	4,900	70,000	$14.29
6	5,800	80,000	$13.79
7	6,550	90,000	$13.74
8	7,150	100,000	$13.98

The effect of the sharp improvement in returns to scale due to the spreading of fixed costs over more units has been to "push" the minimum unit cost point from the level associated with the five-man firm to the level of the seven-man firm (Table 7.3).

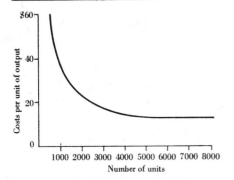

Figure 7.12
Total costs per unit of
output, fixed and variable.

Our businessman, then, in attempting to decide the scale at which he should "pitch" his enterprise will now be aware that over a certain range of scale in production he can expect to encounter what we can now call *economies of scale* and the unit cost will tend to fall as each new unit of output is added. At first this fall in unit costs will be sharp as fixed costs are paid off over more units of output. But as the size of the output increases, restrictions on the physical or technical availability of factors begins to activate the law of diminishing returns and *diseconomies of scale* begin to appear. But, as we shall show later, for long-run conditions in a real-world context this is by no means invariably the case. If he is "lucky" there may be a definable scale point determining exactly at what scale his unit costs are lowest—the bottom of the U-shaped cost-scale curve. This is known as the *minimum optimal scale* (MOS) and we shall be making use of the concept in later sections.

We have talked in analytical terms about the basis of scale economies: let us now explore in a more general way where these economies come from in a more realistic world.

Specialization of manpower and equipment

In looking more generally at the factors underlying scale economies in production the logical place to begin is with Adam Smith's classic principle: *division of labor*. We saw in the simplified example the economics underlying the old saying that "two heads are better than one." Two men working a farm in combination produce more than the sum of their individual outputs working singly as we showed.

Adam Smith in the first chapter of *Wealth of Nations* described at great length the advantages in production brought about by the division of labor. Perhaps his description of the pin-maker which follows has never been bettered as a way of making the principle clear:

> ...a workman not educated to his business nor acquainted with the use of the machinery employed in it could scarce, perhaps, with his utmost industry, make one pin in a day, and certainly could not make twenty. But in the way in which this business is now carried on, not only the whole work is a peculiar trade, but it is divided into a number of branches, of which the greater part are peculiar trades. One man draws out the

wire, another straights it, a third cuts it, a fourth points it, a fifth grinds it at the top for receiving the head; to make the head requires two or three distinct operations, to put it on is a peculiar business, to whiten the pins is another; it is even a trade by itself to put them into the paper; and the important business of making a pin is in this manner, divided into about eighteen distinct operations, which, in some manufactories are all performed by distinct hands, though in others the same man will perform two or three of them.

I have seen a small manufactory of this kind where ten men only were employed and where some of them consequently performed two or three distinct operations... Each person... making a tenth part of forty-eight thousand pins might be considered as making four thousand eight hundred pins in a day. But if they had all wrought separately and independently and without any of them being educated to this particular business, they could certainly not each of them have made twenty, perhaps not one pin in a day, that is, certainly, not the two hundred and fortieth, not the four thousand eight-hundredth part of what they are at present capable of performing, *in consequence of a proper division and combination of their different operations.* (authors' italics)
Adam Smith, Wealth of Nations, *edited by Edwin Cannan, London: Methuen, pp. 6–7.*

It is in itself instructive, as well as perhaps sad, to consider that all of these operations are now performed more than likely by a single machine in the control of a single man and that their combined output would render Smith's then staggering output figures quite trivial.

In analyzing the key features of cost saving through producing so many units of output per worker Smith identified three basic elements:

1. **Increase of dexterity:** A man who works at the same task for some time will acquire a degree of basic skill and rhythm, giving an economy of motion and enabling him to produce a higher rate of output for a longer period. Those with natural gifts can apply them to tasks for which they are best suited.

2. **Saving of the time which is commonly lost in passing from one type of work to another:** Where one or a small number of workers produce complex articles like automobiles in a "one-off" mode, or where a single farmer handles a variety of different jobs around his farm, a great deal of labor time is used up in moving from task to task. To add labor and assign specialized continuous production tasks to each individual in a complementary system immediately produces a rise in output for the same factor cost.

3. **Capability of equipping specialist workers with equally specialized machines:** By simplifying work tasks there is the enhanced possibility of inventing machinery to facilitate production. In this way one man can do the work of many. Humanity would have had to wait a long time for a machine to be invented which would make a whole automobile the way a small group of men would. But by breaking the exercise down into enough simple tasks, the

automated production-line assembly plant became a possibility shortly after the turn of the century.

While the pin-maker might have been the classic example of division of labor in the late eighteenth century, there is no doubt that the automobile manufacturer leads the field in the late twentieth. It was Henry Ford who learned the most from Adam Smith's three principles of division of labor. In particular by bringing the product to the worker—the assembly line principle—the most complex tasks on even large items of equipment could be performed simply, efficiently, and with minimum loss of labor time.

Division of labor up to the level permitted by the size of the market is one of the means by which an increase in the input of labor as a production factor produces lower unit costs in output. As we have shown, however, there is a limit to its application. Over-manning—too many men for the capital equipment and space available—pushes the scale-cost curve upwards as the law of diminishing returns takes its toll.

Just as specialization in the application of one factor—labor—brings about scale economies, so also will *specialization in the use of capital or land*.

Let us turn to the case of capital equipment. We have seen how the specialization of tasks facilitates the more efficient use of labor and how this permits greater opportunities for the invention of machines. Once available, machines can further enhance the productivity of the system, this time through the *combined* application of capital and labor. In accordance with the principles we established for the human worker, a machine performing a simple repetitious task has certain important cost advantages. It is likely to be simple in design, using fewer complex parts and performing operations each of which contributes directly to generating the product. A highly complex machine, besides having more parts to go wrong, may have some parts waiting unproductive while other parts do their tasks. Specialization in the use of machines contributes to production efficiency. True there are complex machines which cannot meet the requirement that every part contributes output at all times, but part of the drive behind technological improvements in design will be to achieve more output per hour of machine time.

In strictly cost terms a machine is bought with *a single outlay* to perform a productive task. It is not, like a worker, paid by the hour and is not subject to human constraints like getting tired, bored, or hungry. Humanitarian organizations do not spring up to protect machines from exploitation and machines do not re-negotiate the terms on which they produce if the cost of living changes. Thus the simple economic principle for getting the best return from the use of a machine is this: *having bought it and installed it, make use of it to produce output every feasible second of its working life*. As a fixed outlay (per machine) capital equipment has those cost characteristics we discussed earlier. The more units of output it produces the more units of output bear the initial cost and the cheaper the unit cost of each marginal unit. The use of machines, then, contributes heavily to the economies of scale achieved by a business as its output rises. Remember, though, that other factors are needed to make the machine function. By adding more machines—each one paying off its cost as it produces more units—and therefore making the input of capital a variable, albeit "lumpy," cost factor, the other factors also need to be expanded. Too many machines in too small a space (land fixed-capital variable) will give ultimate diseconomies from diminishing returns. So also will too many machines and too few men to man and maintain them (labor fixed-capital variable).

We need to look more closely at this "lumpiness" in capital inputs since it has profound effects on scale. For the most part this constraint depends upon the state of technology at a given time. An economist would call this the problem of *indivisibility*. Put in its simplest sense this means that machines tend to come in single, whole units with a given capacity for output. Take the case of the sewing machine. For the handicraft worker using a needle and thread to make shirts which he sells at a rate of seven a week, the sewing machine has significant indivisibility problems. First the purchase of the machine costs him money, a substantial sum by comparison with his needle which has a much lower indivisibility threshold. To justify the outlay on a sewing machine he must earn enough from using the machine to repay the fixed cost of buying it. Remember the first shirt he makes will effectively bear the whole cost of the machine plus his materials and labor. It will be a long way along the production run before he is able to produce a shirt at the same unit cost as by needle and thread methods. Let us say he needs to produce thirty shirts a week to achieve this. He must then be able to make twenty-three more shirts a week to justify the purchase of one sewing machine. What if he cannot sell more than fifteen? He would be sensible to stick with his needle and thread. There is, therefore, an *indivisibility threshold* of 23 shirts to be overcome before he can begin to mechanize his operations. Perhaps the reader would like to consider what the ramifications of buying a second sewing machine would be supposing he could meet the indivisibility threshold of the first one? Like sewing machines, metal presses, drop forges, blast furnaces, power stations, and so on, all tend to present indivisibility problems. To proceed from zero to one or from one to two requires that certain demand conditions be met as well as a "step" in the availability of the other factors. Manning the second blast furnace or finding space for it, for instance, demands an equivalent "jump" in the provision of labor and land.

When we talked earlier of the lower threshold limit to production imposed by technical factors it was this sort of consideration that prompted it. The scale-cost curve for a given form of business does not begin at zero and follow a smooth progression. Where significant inputs of capital are involved there is an indivisibility threshold, like that for our shirt manufacturer, below which production is impossible unless the method of operation is different.

The economy of the large machine

A further point on the subject of the scale economies associated with the use of capital equipment is worth making. The cost of producing many types of capital equipment increases less rapidly than the capacity of such equipment. For this group it is more the laws of mathematics than those of economics that determine the nature of the relationship. Consider the cost of raising the capacity of an oil storage tank in relation to its capacity to store oil. The first (cost) increases regularly in proportion to the surface area of the tank. That is the *square* of its dimensions. The second (capacity) increases with the inside volume and therefore with the *cube* of its dimensions.

Take another example from the field of transport. A ship is essentially a container and so it has the technical advantages in capacity of the oil storage tank above. In addition to this, however, it must move over a viscous medium—water—and energy is used up in overcoming the resistance both of this and (to a lesser extent) the air through which it moves. The "interface" between ship and water is the area over which the surface of the ship is in contact with the water. In increasing the size of a ship this water-ship interface is increased by the square of the ship's dimensions below the water line. Its capacity is increased by the cube of its overall dimensions. Up to a technically determined point, therefore, a large ship will require *less horse-power per unit of carrying capacity than a small one.*

The advent of the wide-bodied jet airliner which had to await technical developments in the thrust capacity of jet engines exploits the same technical principle. Doubling all the dimensions of an aircraft gives an eight-fold increase in cubic capacity for a four-fold increase in air resistance. The passenger-carrying capacity of the "jumbo" series of jets has therefore increased dramatically for a less than proportionate increase in engine thrust and wing lift. Once again, of course, such increases have indivisibility connotations as the international airlines have found to their cost. The large machine must generate sufficient output to reap its scale benefits and, as we must constantly emphasize, *the market must be available for this to take place.* Further restrictions on the economies of the large machine come from the problems of making the technically correct amounts of other factors available. The need to add the land factor in extending airport runways to parallel "jumbo" jet developments is one example. In the same context restrictions in the amounts of the labor factor to meet the huge capacity expansions following the introduction of the wide-bodied jet have brought diminishing returns. Many readers will doubtless have first-hand experience of the time diseconomies of the big jet brought about by a less than proportional increase in the supply of baggage handlers, immigration officers and customs officials as passenger capacity has expanded.

Economies of massed reserves

Another of the clear advantages of size in the scale of a business's operations is where contingency plans have to be made against the effects of machine failures or breakdowns. For any business, regardless of its size, the breakdown of a machine is a costly event. As we said earlier, machines pay their way most efficiently by round-the-clock usage on activities that produce returns. Should a machine fail, its "down-time" costs money. This is a contingency against which all businesses need to take out some insurance. For the small operation with a single machine, how does it proceed? The quick answer might be to have a second machine always ready in reserve. This would be cost-foolish, however, because every unit of output produced by the one machine would have the cost of two machines in its overhead. More sensibly it might be best to carry reserve stocks of the moving or most vulnerable parts, but this too goes directly into the overhead costs chargeable against every item of output. Here is another of the businessman's basic trade-off problems. Should he risk it and not carry spares, bearing the cost of breakdowns as they come? On the other hand, should he go for more security by carrying basic spares even though holding them unused adds cost to each unit of output? Either way there are expenses to be covered which raise the unit costs of output.

The bigger operation, however, has a significant cost advantage over the smaller one in one key respect. Where there are a large number of machines in operation the loss of one makes for a smaller proportion of production loss than where there is only a single machine. Equally, though in this case there are more machines to fail, there is a low probability that more than one will fail *at the same time* by virtue of the breakdown of the same part. Thus, where supplies of a part are held in the bigger plant they *service the potential needs of more machines and the costs of holding them in stock (unused) is spread over more units of output.*

Crisis demands of any kind can more easily be met by the larger plant than by the smaller one. Sudden increases in demand at one point may take up slack capacity at another, making overall factor usage more efficient.

For the smaller operation sudden shifts in the demand for resources or the allocation of capacity in emergency can only be met by carrying reserve stocks. These use resources without producing returns. The electricity grid network provides a good example of the massed reserves principle. Separate power generators not connected together would each need to carry contingency reserves against emergency or breakdown. Connecting them all together in a grid system means that a far smaller allocation of total resources needs to go into reserve stocks. Failures at one point can be compensated by allocation of slack capacity from another and the entire system needs only a minimal back-up in terms of spare parts. The same part is most unlikely to fail everywhere at the same time.

Economies of large scale purchasing

Everything said so far in this section contributes to the notion that larger production units are (up to a point) more cost-efficient per unit of output. To achieve these economies on his own part each producer must seek to find a market of sufficient size to absorb the extra units of output that take him nearer the scale optimum.

Take, for example, the owner of a small plant producing high quality paper for the publishing industry. At the current scale of output unit costs are relatively high. The plant is somewhere on the low side of the output needed to achieve the minimum optimal scale. Costs are high but given sufficient demand to permit the purchase of the latest high-capacity polishing and cutting machine unit costs could sharply be brought down. At this stage the publisher of a new glossy magazine presents himself to discuss a possible long term order for large quantities of high quality paper. From the paper producer's viewpoint capturing the order would take him over the indivisibility threshold for the new machine. He could then produce all his output at lower unit cost, including that to his existing customers and any new customers who might be attracted by the lower prices he could then offer. What should he do? Any sensible businessman would obviously try to gain new business by offering at least a major discount to the publisher. He would, in effect, offer to "share" some of the gains from the return he would make on becoming more scale-efficient. With the new business his unit costs would in any case be lower and being more price-competitive he might well attract even more trade and become even more scale-efficient.

What does the publisher gain from all this? He gains high quality paper at a discount price. Why? Because his demand has made the paper maker more efficient by enabling him to profit from scale economies. Take the situation one step further back. The paper maker, once the deal has been made, can go to his suppliers and offer them in turn an increase in demand for the long term. If they were not already into diminishing returns and had either slack capacity or, like himself, were near an indivisibility threshold, he would be sensible to demand a hefty discount too. So it goes on. *Large-scale purchasing may well make suppliers more efficient and attract discount rates to the buyer.*

Recalling our discussion of the economics of transport in Chapter Five, there is another area in which economies are achieved for large-scale purchases. We saw then that freight rates on large consignments such as full carloads are a good deal more favorable than those on less-than-carload quantities. We can set this situation clearly within the context of scale economies. A railway company invests capital in a freight car. That car is only at maximum efficiency where *all of it* is used all of the time to produce returns on the initial capital investment. That way the unit costs of the items carried in it can be reduced to a minimum. With a half-carload fifty percent of the capital equipment paid for out of scarce resources returns no income to the operator. To compensate he charges higher rates where the market will bear it.

Utilities such as gas, electricity and water are areas in which the "lumpiness" of capital investment is particularly pronounced. Modern town gas plants or gas pipelines, power stations and dams or generating stations come as large, very expensive indivisibles. They are most efficient at very high levels of output and the "step" in output between, say, one power station and two is very large indeed. Frequently utilities are, for the best of social reasons, built ahead of demand for their output. They carry excess capacity. Should a large-scale purchaser like a steel-works or railway come along as a potential customer discount rates are to be anticipated as the utility shares its increased scale-efficiency with a customer. Where there is a transfer of the savings from scale economies to a producer to one of his customers and where these turn up as cost savings in the latter's production, gained as it were "second-hand," an economist would term them *external economies of scale*. We shall be taking this concept much further in a subsequent section and will content ourselves here with a mention in passing.

We have then made a strong case for the observation that while big may not necessarily be beautiful, it certainly tends to be cost-efficient—other things, of course, being equal. We have, however, tempered this with the view that the cost-efficiency of size tends to disappear beyond a certain scale of operations. We should also emphasize that "bigness" and "efficiency" are very different for different industries. A big, efficient manufacturer of diamond rings may employ less than 20 people in a second-floor workshop while the smallest of the major American automobile producers may employ upwards of 30,000 over acres of land and still be below the notional optimal scale. There are some advantages of scale and size which we have chosen not to discuss here. These are concerned with the sizes of firms and organizations rather than plants—a story taken up in more detail in Chapter Nine. In general terms then it can be asserted that over certain ranges of scale there are *significant cost advantages to be obtained from concentrating production into larger scale processing units.*

In fact, despite our attempts to assume away scale economies in the discussion so far it was the prospect of such scale economies from increased production that led the first subsistence farmer to set up a central bakery or brewery in the simplified model. It was the same prospect that led the subsistence farmer of the Von Thünen system to specialize in the most favorable crop type. Both were able to set up and maintain commercial production systems because of the increasing returns to scale as they expanded their output. By adding additional factor inputs to those required for their own subsistence and by achieving economies of scale such that the returns from the new output exceeded the cost of the extra factor inputs, they were able to make a profit from centralized production. So long as this increase in returns existed they could continue to expand their scale of operations.

Ultimately, however, other things being equal, we would now expect their expansion to have slowed down as the production units approached their minimum optimal plant size, the point at which under existing conditions of technique they achieved the lowest average cost of production per unit. Under these conditions we could have divined something of the logic that underlies the determination of plant size in the space economy. Given the average share of the total market which a plant at the optimal size could supply we could have *determined the number of plants or farms likely to exist at a given point in time.*

Under conditions of free entry and perfect competition plants, firms, farms, even towns and cities, in fact all identifiable production systems, would strive toward an equilibrium condition—their numbers, sizes and, in part, their location depending upon their minimum optimal scales of production and the share of the total market that they could expect to achieve at such scales. From such a concept as the MOS, once again given conditions of free entry and perfect competition, *much of the structure of the space economy could theoretically be determined*: the equilibrium number of plants, firms, multi-plant firms, and so on in a given industry at a given point in time.

However, under more realistic conditions such simple solutions to complex questions tend to disappear although, like the hexagon and the Von Thünen ring, the minimum optimal scale may be considered a latent force molding the form of economic structures. The precise nature of its influence, although relatively simple under the conditions of the constrained model, is however extremely complex once such constraints are removed. Perhaps the most potent force for variability in a realistic situation is the fact that the MOS itself is constantly changing and that there is no uniquely identifiable scale to which any economic enterprise can strive in an open, constantly developing system.

Economies of scale in reality

While it is relatively simple to put forward logical reasons for the existence of scale economies in theory, it is quite another matter to prove their existence in practice. Empirical work by Blair (1972), Bain (1954, 1968) and Moroney (1972) for the United States and Pratten and Dean (1965) and Pratten (1971) for the United Kingdom, shows how difficult it is in practice to measure scale economies under realistic conditions. There is great variation in the minimal optimal scale conditions to be found both between industries and, perhaps less obviously, within industries. In reality those constraints which make the conceptualization of the problem so simple are absent. "Free entry," as Bain (1968) shows, is largely a myth. Businesses can survive in an environment with less than "perfect competition" whether their operations are at the technically efficient scale or not. In addition the river of technological change flows continuously, changing the technical "optimum" of one plant or another every day. The conditions under which an economy operates will not stand still while we measure "optimal" scales of technical production.

It is hardly surprising then that there has been much debate over the existence of *real* scale economies in recent years over a wide range of industry types. Few seem willing to deny that scale economies were a powerful economic force for industrial "bigness" up to the end of the 1920s. But for the post-war period there has been less certainty in some quarters.

Before proceeding we must make something clear. Our subject here is the impact of scale economies on the operating costs and therefore the locational characteristics of *the plant*. We shall have much more to say in Chapter Nine about the economies which can be achieved by the *multi-plant firm* whose recent growth is indisputable. As yet we restrict our analysis to the level of the technical unit for producing output—the plant or, in more general terms, the establishment.

It was when the steam engine replaced water power and steel replaced wood that the first effective scale economies at the plant level were realized. Water power provided a slow, cumbersome means of generating energy and its transmission by belts and pulleys so quickly dissipated its power that plants were necessarily small and geographically localized. Similarly wood as the basic structural material was singularly inappropriate for the mass production of standardized articles. Its tensile strength characteristics, ability to be shaped and molded and general variability as a material, made wood a material for the craftsman rather than the factory.

Steam power and steel together revolutionized unit production costs for the majority of articles demanded in trade and brought to light new ones whose cheapness and mass availability was undreamed of in the craft era. Steam power, with greater effective energy, made the transmission of power throughout a mill or factory so efficient that division of labor by men equipped with *powerful* machines became available for the first time. It raised the sheer speed of output of the individual as compared with the cumbersome slowness of water power. At the same time a medium which could be melted, poured, molded, forged and milled while retaining strength and durability revolutionized the production possibilities open to the businessman. Given that both developments took place, as we have seen in Chapter Five, against a background of a revolution in transport and the accessibility of producers to markets, all the key ingredients were present for a dramatic upward shift in the scale of plant operations. Since technological change made upward shifts in output subject to increasing returns to scale, there in a nutshell is one key to the economic change which swept the advanced nations in the century and a half after 1750.*

The era of massive scale economies, however, seems not to have lasted "across the board" in industry far into the twentieth century. Blair (1972) shows how Ford, the epitome of scale economies and the production-line technique, ran into diseconomies as early as the middle 1920s with its River Rouge factory. The automatic assumption that "bigness means greater efficiency," the American business creed of the late nineteenth and early twentieth centuries, took a long time to become qualified by the phrase "up to a point." Many industries like Ford pushed ahead on the first assumption only to realize that in Boulding's words while "growth creates form, form limits growth"! Plants became too big, too vulnerable to breakdown, too dependent on division of labor to cater for human dignity, too big to manage, and so on. The drive for scale increases had pushed on ahead of the technical limit to efficiency and into rising unit costs. There was a need to wait for technology to raise the MOS with operating practices *following* to make use of the cost advantages.

At this stage, as Blair (1972) points out, the decentralization of plant capacity began. Branch plants were set up to tap regional markets, each operation gaining what it could in scale advantage. Even this, however, was a drive made possible by another revolution in technical operations. The advent of electric power and the solution to problems of effective transmission freed industry from the *concentrated* power and energy of the steam engine as we have already seen in the case of the Swedish paper industry in Chapter Four. While the latter had been a major breakthrough from the previous stage of industrial power technology, it too enforced scale limits which were broken by the new

Note   *These generalizations do scant justice to the vast literature on technology and scale during the Industrial Revolution though they suit our present purpose. The reader is encouraged to consult, in particular, Mumford (1934), Jerome (1934) and Florence (1933) for essential background.

electric era. Industry was now *free to spread spatially*, to tap new resources and new markets. The parallel widespread availability of the motor truck, another "decentralizing technology" complemented electric power in the 1920s and 1930s. Instead of the "super giant" River Rouge type of plant there was a spawning of more plants of more modest scale. Looked at nationally then, this "spawning" process and the drive toward the multi-plant firm shows itself as a *leveling off in the drive for fewer, bigger and bigger plants*. More plants of similar sizes, perhaps under the control of a single, ever-growing organization, replaced the drive for "giant" firms "across the board." This generalization, like every one made in the area of scale economies, is subject to wide qualification. For some industries a small number of large plants has become the norm. For others the small, largely handicraft operation is as viable today as it ever was (see Chapter Nine). Economies of scale, as we said at the outset, is a slippery area for generalization. The section which follows attempts to provide some empirical substance to what is frequently a simply conceptual discussion of the impact of scale economies. It is not vital, however, to a general understanding of the topic. Some readers may, therefore, wish to skip to p. 280 for a continuation of general discussion.

Let us turn to Pratten's (1971) work on modern, technical scale economies in the United Kingdom. Since this provides the best available, up-to-date source of *technically based* information on what he calls minimal efficient size (our MOS), we shall depend heavily upon it. In this case the scale economies relate to *long run* conditions in industry under more general circumstances where all inputs of production factors are variables but where some are *relatively* less readily available than others.

Table 7.4
Estimates[a] of the minimum efficient scale (M.E.S.) for new plants.

	Capacity/ output	Percent of U.K. capacity/ output	Percent increase in costs at 50% of M.E.S.	
			Total costs per unit (inc. materials)	Value added per unit
Steel: Integrated with strip mill	4 m tons p.a.	80	8	13
Motor Cars: Range of models	1 m cars p.a.	50	6	13
Steel: Blast and L.D. furnace	9 m tons p.a.	33	5–10	12–17
Synthetic fibers: Polymer plant	80,000 tons p.a.	33	5	23
Soaps and detergents	70,000 tons p.a.	20	2.5	20
Domestic appliances: Range of ten	0.5 m appliances p.a.	20	8	12
Chemicals: Sulphuric acid plant	1 m tons p.a.	30	1	19
Chemicals: Ethylene plant	300,000 tons p.a.	25	9	30
Motor Cars: One model and variants	0.5 m cars p.a.	25	6	10
Cement: Portland works	2 m tons p.a.	10	9	17
General purpose oil refinery	10 m tons p.a.	10	5	27
Beer: Brewery	1 m barrels p.a.	3	9	55
Bread: Baking plant	30 sacks flour/hr.	1	15	30

[a]There are many qualifications to each estimate and the reader should consult the original source to appreciate them.
Source: C. F. Pratten (1971), Economies of Scale in Manufacturing Industry, *Department of Applied Economics Occasional Papers*, No. 28, University of Cambridge, Table 30.1.

Table 7.4 shows for a variety of plant specifications the minimum efficient scale calculated according to technical estimates. As Pratten points out, these are no more than engineering estimates and have to be interpreted cautiously. Taking the case of steel first, this gives direct emphasis to the point that for some industries the "giant" plant is the most technically efficient. For an integrated steel plant strip mill the estimated efficient size is one which would take up 80 percent of the total U.K. demand. Small wonder at the throes of the nationalized British steel industry in attempting to become more efficient by rationalization. There are currently five such plants in operation and economic decisions to close, say, four of them in the interests of scale efficiency are by no means

Table 7.5
The economies of scale for the production of crude steel.

Output of plant—000 tons per annum					
Output of iron	250	1,000	2,000	5,000	10,000
Number of blast furnaces	1	1	2	4	7
(Index number of costs per ton for sinter and blast furnace plant)					
Materials[1]	100	70	68	67	67
Net fuel[2]	100	100	100	100	100
Operating charges	100	63	62	60	58
Capital charges[3]	100	57	55	50	48
Total (average cost)	100	83	82	80	79
Output of steel	250	1,000	2,000	5,000	10,000
Number of steel furnaces:					
Installed	2	2	2	3	6
Operating at one time	1	1	1	2	4
(Index numbers of costs)					
Materials[4]	100	84	81	80	79
Operating cost	100	67	61	60	60
Capital charges[3]	100	68	52	41	40
Total (average cost)	100	80	75	73	72
(marginal cost)			74	74	73

(1) The blast furnace material costs decline with increasing size of plant because it is assumed that a small works would receive a number of small ships, rather than a few large ships—this assumption may not apply. For example a small works may be near a quay which can take large bulk carriers, and which is used to supply other works not necessarily steel works. For the purpose of these calculations it is also assumed that special ore selection is practiced at small works. No allowance was made for a reduction of port charges for small-scale operations. (If a quay would have to be built this could cost as much as £20 m., and would be a source of economies of scale. If capital charges were 10%, spreading the capital charges for such a quay over an output of 5 m. tons instead of 2 m. tons, would reduce costs per ton of steel by about 2%.)

(2) There is no evidence that the N.C.B. supplies coal to large works at lower prices than to small works. The costs of making coke and by-products would be slightly reduced as scale increased, and there would be small economies for fuel costs for large furnaces, but no allowance is made for these economies.

For some overseas plants there are substantial economies for transporting and buying fuel in large quantities.

(3) Capital charges, depreciation and interest on capital, are included at 15% of the initial capital employed. (Working capital would form a small proportion of the capital for a new plant—less than 20 percent.)

(4) Materials for steel include iron, scrap, oxygen and other materials. The iron/scrap ratio is assumed to be 70:30. The iron required for a steel plant with an output of, say, one million tons would be approximately 780,000 tons. Materials costs for steel do not move in step with the costs of iron from blast furnaces because there are assumed to be no economies for purchases of scrap—this damps down the economies—and because of discontinuities attributable to the optimum size of capacity of blast furnaces—about 1.5 million tons when these estimates were prepared.

Source: C. F. Pratten (1971), Economics of Scale in Manufacturing Industry, *Department of Applied Economics Occasional Papers*, No. 28, University of Cambridge, Table 12.2

Table 7.5 continued

politically or socially cost-free. Nor would this be *geographically* insignificant. Which four locations would be chosen for closure? Where should the one efficient plant be located?

Table 7.5 shows Pratten's estimates of the technical scale economies which apply in the manufacture of crude steel as output is increased. What is demonstrated most effectively here is the tendency of scale-cost curves in steel to be L-shaped. Notice how at the first "scale jump" from 250,000 to 1 million tons per year there are dramatic scale economies on the input of all the main factor inputs. After this, however, the marginal decrease in factor costs shows up sharply.

If we turn our attention to automobiles—the motor cars entry in Table 7.4—it is clear that both the structural and spatial rationalization of this industry over recent years has been closely associated with the availability of technical scale economies. We talk of the "big three" in automobile terms, perhaps if the situation in the United States paralleled that in the United Kingdom, the "big two" would be the long-run efficient situation. It is interesting in the context of recent events in the British vehicles industry to consider that Pratten's estimates of the minimum efficient scale would allow for only two major producers sharing the market between them. Ford, Leyland (now government controlled) and the Vauxhall division of General Motors dominate the market. Chrysler, the smallest of the domestic producers, recently mooted a desire to pull out but were encouraged to remain by a massive subsidy from the British government. Technical efficiency might suggest rationalization, but once industries become very large the social disruption of their closure *at particular places* generates an extra cost which governments are frequently unwilling to bear. Table 7.6 shows Pratten's estimates of the technical scale economies available in a multi-model automobile plant. Here the cost economies with scale do not level off as quickly as was the case with steel. There are relatively large marginal cost savings to be made still as automobile plants increase in size. In addition, the enormous capital outlays necessary on re-tooling to bring out new models and stay in the competitive race for customers favors the big operation.

Table 7.6
Estimates of costs and scale for a range of models (consisting of three basic bodies with variants, and five basic engines)[a].

Output (thousands a year)	100	250	500	1,000	2,000
Initial costs for model £m	40	50	60	80	110
			Costs per vehicle £		
Initial costs	100	50	30	20	14
Materials and components bought out	290	270	255	247	240
Labor (direct and indirect)	120	100	92	87	84
Capital charges for fixed and working capital	75	65	58	53	48
Total ex-works costs	585	485	435	407	386
Index of average costs	100	83	74	70	66
Index of marginal costs		72	65	66	62

(a) Costs have been "standardized". If the range of models included large and sophisticated models this would, of course, raise average costs per unit, but we have ignored this factor.

Source: C. F. Pratten (1971), Economies of Scale in Manufacturing Industry, *Department of Applied Economics Occasional Papers*, No. 28, University of Cambridge, Table 14.4.

Space prevents us here from looking at the breadth and depth of detail available in Pratten's work, but let us finally go to the other end of the size scale as it appears in Table 7.4. The baking plant and brewery in the U.K. are of interest because, while plants in each industry need to take up only 1–3 percent of the total demand, the "scale penalty" for having a less than efficient plant is high. For bread total costs for operations at half the efficient scale would be 15 percent higher and for beer 9 percent. Taking out the effects of raw material inputs and looking at the "finer" scale as measured by factor inputs in value added the respective figures are 30 percent and 55 percent. Not surprisingly, both industries have undergone spectacular rationalization over the past 20 years as the small *local* bakery and brewery has succumbed to competition from the technically more efficient *regional* operation.

For the United States comparable detail in technical estimates is harder to come by. The interested reader is encouraged to consult the work of Bain (1954, 1956, 1968) for the most comprehensive statement of the impact of scale on U.S. industry. Commenting on technical considerations of scale for a sample of 20 industries in his 1968 work, *Industrial Organization*, Bain made the following observations. He found:

1. That *two industries* had "very important" scale economies. In each the minimum optimal (efficient) plant scale exceeded 10 percent of total market capacity. Unit cost penalties at half the efficient scale would be of the order of five percent. These were:
automobiles
typewriters

2. That *five* industries had "moderately important" plant scale economies with efficient plants operating at between four and six percent of total market capa-

city. Again unit cost penalties at half the efficient scale were of the order of five percent. These were:

cement
farm machinery
tractors
rayon
steel

3. That *nine* industries had unimportant scale economies with either small efficient plant sizes in general or "flat" scale curves. These were:

cigarettes	*liquor*
petroleum products	*soap*
rubber tires	*shoes*
flour	*meat*
canned goods	

Bain emphasizes, as we should, that this is only a *sample* of 20 industries and a disproportionately weighted one at that. But there are at least tentative grounds here for the empirical verification of the role of scale economies in the contemporary U.S. economy. Moroney (1972, p. 32), however, looking at the scale problem somewhat differently and not on the basis of technical estimates, is able to make the following statement: "there seems to be a substantial amount of supplementary economic evidence consistent with the hypothesis of constant returns in American manufacturing."

Whether or not there are significant scale returns in an economy in the last quarter of the twentieth century seems in fact to depend more on the way the problem is examined than upon the underlying reality. Looked at as Pratten does by assessing costs in terms of the technical capacity of plant it appears that there are. Looked at by aggregate analysis of national concentration of industry into plant size classes there are not. The reader is therefore, exhorted to caution in his interpretation of the *real* as opposed to theoretically expected existence of scale economies.

Scale factors, certainly in the past and less certainly in the present, have exerted a significant impact on business production costs. This makes life for the businessman choosing a location even more difficult. First, he has to choose the right factor mix. Second, he has to find the place at which distance–related costs are lowest in collecting factors and materials together. Now, on top of all this, *he has to choose an appropriate scale of production.* These things, of course, "trade-off" against each other. Opening a technically efficient scale of plant in a prime position to dominate a large market may be a good solution even though more factors and materials may have to be moved over greater distances. The requirements of a large, possibly more technically efficient plant will differ from a small one not only in quantity but in quality. Indeed, the entire locational problem may look significantly different with each successive estimate of the scale of the production unit. In making ready-to-wear clothing, for instance, there may well be scope for plants to operate successfully over a wide range of plant-sizes. For a small operation the businessman might look for cheap premises, accessibility to down-town fashion stores, nearness to cloth wholesalers and so on. For a large one the criteria change. Now maybe it will be a new, custom-built factory on a green field site with good access to freeways, near to a pool of reliable and adaptable female labor.

Looked at this way, *scale has an important influence on location* even though, of itself, it is a non-spatial, technical consideration. A trap into which we may sometimes fall is to believe that only geography may affect geography. In this case, without a knowledge of the technical and economic importance of scale, we cannot comprehend fully the importance of one of the critical factors taken into account in locating a factory. Not that this makes the problem simpler. Quite the reverse. As we have suggested, the minimum optimum (or efficient) scale is essentially a theoretical abstraction. It varies over space, time, from industry to industry, and even within the same industry. Moreover, in some industries technological changes come so fast that plants are obsolescent before they are completed and production process is always at least one innovation behind. Small wonder, then, that the question of scale is one which generates much dispute and one which proves difficult to handle in any model whether designed by geographers or economists. We cannot, however, choose to ignore it, and in the next section we shall look more closely at the locational impact of scale, knowing in advance that it will be incomplete.

Scale, demand and location

At this stage in our analysis the substitution problem facing a producer as he chooses a location has three main dimensions:

1. The costs incurred in assembling input factors over space.

2. Technical considerations of the minimum efficient scale for production.

3. Estimation of demand conditions and gaining access to the market.

All three are, of course, inextricably tied together. Factor costs and scale affect price; price affects the level of demand; the level of demand affects scale and, to complete the circle, scale affects factor costs. There are several ways of going round this particular circle, but the important consideration for us at this stage is to realize that the process is a *circular* one. It begins nowhere and ends nowhere. We choose to cut into it where we like, but the act of "cutting in" by itself destroys something of the reality of the situation.

One of the acknowledged weaknesses of location theory to date has been its tendency to neglect scale. Where scale has been taken into account it has been treated as a secondary factor helpful in determining the size of the market area for a *given* location. The prior assumption is made that the plant has *already been located* on the basis of other criteria. These are usually traditional ones based on minimization of input factor costs. By treating the problem this way the vital interaction between costs, scale and demand *in choosing the location in the first place* is lost.

Hoover (1937), for instance, shows the way reductions in unit costs with increasing scale reduce the delivered price of goods for an established plant. This extends the market area over a wider range than would be the case with the assumption of constant returns to scale. To show this, Hoover uses the *margin line*. This shows how delivered prices at the edge of a producer's market vary as the spatial extent of the market itself varies. The underlying idea is relatively simple. Suppose an already-located producer serving a spatially dispersed market finds a way of expanding his territory. Two things at least will happen. His total transport costs will rise as he ships his product to more customers who are further away. But, compensating for this, if he is operating below his minimum efficient scale, a rise in the volume of his output will lower the unit costs of his product. There will be a circular effect. If the fall in costs due to the additional sales volume *exceeds the additional shipment charges*, he can offer lower delivered prices at the margin of his market and carry on expanding. Where the "trade-off" between scale economies and extra shipment charges equalizes itself then further expansion would mean higher delivered prices beyond this margin.

Isard (1956) shows how this works for two competing producers and the situation he describes is shown in Figure 7.13. Assume that potential consumers of the good produced at A are located geographically along the line AB. If only those consumers located at A want to buy the good, the producer's marginal cost (and in this special case, delivered price also) will be equivalent to the amount AK. But if other consumers perhaps from as far away as L are willing to buy the good then marginal production costs could fall. This is because (assuming previous output levels to be somewhere below the MOS) scale economies in producing the greater volume of output reduces unit costs of production. However, in tapping the new market to achieve these scale economies there will be *additional transport charges to be paid*. The slope of the line JG shows a linear uniform freight rate and adding the appropriate shipment cost to the basic production cost the new delivered price to the customer at L becomes LG. Further expansion of the geographical extent of the market, say to the site of M, permits still further production economies (down to AE) but adding the additional costs of transport incurred (the slope EF) gives a delivered price of MF.

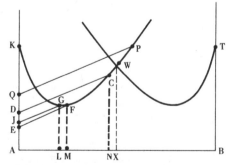

Figure 7.13
Relationship between scale of output and spatial extent of market. [*Source:* Reprinted from W. Isard (1956), *Location and Space Economy*, Figure 27, by permission of the M.I.T. Press, Cambridge, Massachusetts. Copyright © 1956 by the Massachusetts Institute of Technology.]

This, however, represents the optimal combination for this case of market area served and scale of production. Any further increase in demand will incur *higher unit production costs* as well as the extra shipment charges for covering more distance. Delivered prices to customers rise to, say, NC or XW. The curve connecting points KGFCP is called a *margin line*. Any point along this line, as we have seen, expresses the delivered price at the edge of the market area. Before going on to look at the second producer, consider for a moment what would happen if transport rates rose steeply with distance (that is if the slope of lines like JG or DC were steeper). The benefits of production scale economies would be "bought" at a very high price in extra shipment costs as markets further afield were tapped and would quickly disappear. Whatever the *technical* feasibility of scale economies at the plant, steeply rising space-costs would preclude the achievement of scale economies. Thus, economies of scale are not only limited by the size of the market in a non-spatial sense but they may also be limited by the *spatial* extent of the market and the character of transport rates.

Figure 7.13 also shows a second producer of the same good, located at B with identical initial costs BT. His margin line has the same form as that of the producer at A so that the market is shared equally at X, the point where the two margin lines intersect. If, however, scale economies are more readily available to one firm than to the other it is possible, as in Figure 7.14, for the former to charge a lower delivered price over a wider area. Reference back to our discussion of spatial pricing policies in Chapter Five is useful at this point. In Figure 5.23, for example, one reason why firm X could lower his delivered price might well be that he was able to produce at a larger scale than producer Y. In Figure 7.14, then, A's market area is increased from X to Y at the expense of B because A can achieve greater scale economies in production. Figure 7.14b shows the extreme case in which A's delivered price is below that of B at all points within the market area, thus excluding B completely.

Figure 7.14
Achievement of economies of scale permits extension of a firm's market area by reducing the delivered price. [*Source:* Reprinted from W. Isard (1956), *Location and Space Economy,* Figure 30, by permission of the M.I.T. Press, Cambridge, Massachusetts. Copyright © 1956 by the Massachusetts Institute of Technology.]

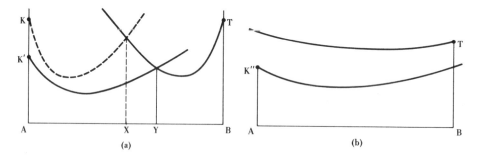

In this way both Hoover and Isard have shown that scale of production is inextricably linked with the level of demand available to a producer. As we have pointed out, however, this kind of analysis neglects the fact that the optimum location itself varies according to scale of output. Not that Isard himself is not aware of this:

> In any location decision, the scale of output is one of several basic, interdependent variables. As scale varies, so may the substitution points between any part of transport outlays, between any two sets of outlays, between outlays and revenues and so forth.
> *Isard (1956), p. 175*

Let us look at another piece of the jigsaw which has been filled in, this time by Leon Moses (1958). His analysis involved that identified by Isard above as scale affecting any two sets of outlays. To follow Moses' methodology it is necessary to recall the techniques for the analysis of substitution previously outlined in Chapters Four and Six. Essentially what Moses set out to demonstrate was that the optimum combination of inputs and the *optimum location of the plant may change* as the scale of output changes.

Consider two locations where the production of a good can possibly take place. One is at the materials site, the other at the market. All that is needed in production here is a raw material and some labor.

Take first the production possibilities for a given total outlay at the material site. Suppose to start with that the producer estimates total expenditure at X dollars per year. For location at the materials site, materials are relatively cheap while labor is dearer in the ratio of 3:2. To add a touch of reality one might consider the site to be a booming mining town where labor, still relatively scarce, is at a premium. As Figure 7.15a shows, our producer could draw up his budget or iso-outlay line against these constraints. At the limits he could obtain either 60 units of materials or 40 units of labor for the expenditure of his total X dollars. The line drawn between these two extremes gives the possible combinations of both labor and materials for the same total expenditure. It is steeply sloping and reflects the fact that three units of materials "trade-off" against two units of labor—the latter being the more expensive.

Let us shift our attention now to the market site where the iso-outlay situation is shown in Figure 7.15b. This time three units of labor get you two units of materials—the relative trading positions are reversed. Here labor is cheaper while materials are dearer since they now have a transport item in their cost. The iso-outlay line slopes the other way. For the same total expenditure of X dollars the producer can buy either 60 units of labor or 40 units of materials.

If we superimpose the two iso-outlay lines as on Figure 7.15c, the choices in outlays between the two locations are clearly laid out. Suppose the producer decides that the best production system functions with 30 units of labor. If he were to choose location at *the materials site* he would need to consult the lower half of the line ST. This would show him that with this choice of location at 30 units of labor input he could afford 14 units of materials with the balance of his X dollars expenditure limit.

Before committing himself it is to be hoped that he bothers to have a look at the same sum for the alternative location at the market. This time he would look for his 30 units of labor on the lower half of the line OP. Following it across to see how many units of materials he would have for the balance of his expenditure, this time he would find the answer as 20. He would be able to have more material units from the balance of his funds with a constant input of labor if *he chose the right location*. For the amount of inputs at the intersection of the solid curves it would not matter where he located his factory. But for every other combination of inputs there are advantages in location

Figure 7.15
Scale and location for a
firm using two production
factors.

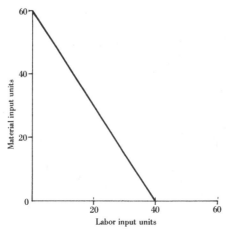

(a) Iso-outlays at the materials site

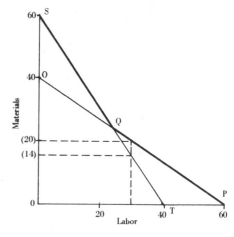

(c) Iso-outlay choices between locations

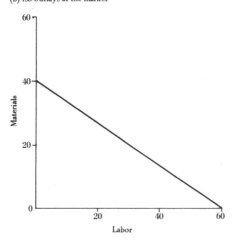

(b) Iso-outlays at the market

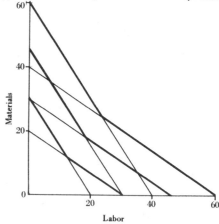

(d) A selection of iso-outlays for different levels of expenditure

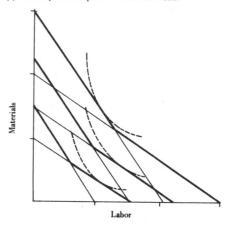

(e) Iso-outlays and iso-quants – the effect of scale

either at the market or at the source of materials, depending on the amounts of each he proposes to use in production.

As Figure 7.15d shows, the iso-outlay line for X dollars which we used in the previous example is only one of many (in fact an infinite number) of possibilities. For every budget figure the producer could name there would be a particular substitution possibility or iso-outlay line for materials and labor.

Now what about scale? One thing we have learned about scale is that at different levels there are different factor mixes. A small operation may need far more labor in relation to materials, while a bigger one may demand more materials and less labor. These depend on the particular *production function* of the establishment and the technical possibilities available for producing the good. Remember in Chapter Six we showed the production function as a curved line showing the possible factor combinations *for a given level of output.* Clearly, the technical possibilities in production will vary with the scale of the output to be produced. We have, then, superimposed these production possibility curves for different levels of output or *isoquants* on the set of iso-outlay lines used in the previous example. These show that for a small plant in this hypothetical case the best location will be the market. For a large one the point at which the isoquant *just touches* the lowest possible iso-outlay line is above Q and therefore the material source is the best location. Thus as the *scale of output changes so also does the optimum location.*

Most location theory has adopted a rather one-sided approach to the problem of defining the optimum location. Whereas the "least-cost" school concentrates on spatial variations in costs with little attention to demand as a primary locational force, the "market area" approach over-emphasizes demand at the expense of cost variations. Both tend to neglect the influence of scale of output. But the major conclusion arising out of the preceding discussion is that the locational problem is tripartite. Variations in costs, revenues, and scale must be considered simultaneously. Change in any one of these will alter the optimum location which is the point of maximum profits.

Perhaps one of the reasons for the failure of location theorists to treat scale of production adequately has been the problem of *isolating its specific locational effect.* Scale interacts with all the elements of the locational problem. By influencing the nature of the factor inputs in the production function it affects the whole character of an industry. As a result the particular importance assigned to factor inputs as *location factors* changes with scale. Similarly, there is an interaction with demand and the market. As we have seen, economies of scale can be achieved up to an extent permitted by the size of the effective market. But by affecting the basic costs of producers and, consequently, the delivered prices they can offer, it is also the case that scale economies contribute to the increases in the size and spatial extent of markets. In all this the impact of space itself is pervasive. The ability of a plant to achieve scale economies may, as we have seen, depend upon the relationship between the production economies derived from serving a wider market and the space costs which must be overcome to obtain access to such a market. Scale is a difficult subject to treat analytically. It is equally difficult to treat empirically. Problems are encountered particularly in attempting to translate the assumed theoretical benefits of scale economies into measurable quantities amenable to empirical testing. This is especially the case with those scale economies which are assumed to be derived from the geographical clustering of economic activities, and it is to these that we now turn our attention.

Agglomeration-localized external economies of scale

One of the characteristic features of economic activities is their marked tendency to occur in spatial clusters. Regular spatial groupings of specialized activities were shown to exist even on the homogeneous landscape of Chapter Two. The chapters that followed demonstrated still more the propensity for economic units to cluster at material sites, terminals and trans-shipment points, cheap labor locations and at the focal points of major markets as businesses moved in to exploit the comparative advantage offered by these points in space. But the process of clustering itself offers further economies of a particular kind to those who take part in it. These are called *economies of agglomeration* and they are a particular kind of *external economy of scale*.

The scale economies that we considered earlier may be classified into two types. These are *internal economies of scale* and *external economies of scale*. The distinction between them depends on their source as seen from the viewpoint of a particular system. Those economies which derive from a production unit as a result of *its own efforts* would be identified as *internal* economies. Take, for instance, the development of the transistor which has revolutionized the field of electronics since the last war.

Bell Telephone Laboratories started a project in 1946 to undertake extensive research on semiconductors. The enormous demand for electronic gadgetry, boosted during the war, encouraged the company to pull together a team of physicists, chemists and metallurgists to apply atomic theory to electronic applications. In 1948 they came up with the first transistor. This replaced the large cumbersome, short-life thermionic valve with a compact economical, "long-life" replacement that performed most of the valve's basic functions. From the viewpoint of Bell Telephone these developments, which dramatically reduced unit production costs of electronic components, could be seen as an internal economy sponsored by the firm's own efforts to overcome a technical restriction against a background of rising demand.

Looked at from the viewpoint of the electronics industry *as a whole* the unit cost savings derived from production with transistors is also an *internal* economy. It was the demand for the products of the industry as a whole which encouraged it (since Bell Telephone is a part of the electronics industry) to invest research funds in making the breakthrough to new, more efficient, levels of output.

But what of firms in the industry other than Bell Telephone, and what of other firms in other industries now able to use, say, transistorized computers to control their operations? For them the economy is derived at second-hand. For other firms in the electronics industry the transistor, made available through Bell Telephone Laboratories' research, comes as an *external economy of scale*. It is available to them because demand for electronic products as a whole has enabled the electronics industry (in the form of Bell Telephone) to exceed the "threshold" needed to develop and make use of the transistor. They gain scale economies through no direct effort on their own part. For other industries reaping the benefit of the transistor's cost-saving properties, they gain *external* economies passed on to them from the electronics industry. When it comes down to it, however, all of these production systems, Bell Telephone included, might see the transistor as an *external* economy passed on to them by courtesy of the wartime research program to develop the atomic bomb.

The distinction we have been making between internal and external economies of scale, as Chisholm (1966) points out, is simply one based on whatever viewpoint the observer chooses. It is another of those "slippery" concepts associated with economies of scale which often serve more to confuse than to enlighten. It does, however, have a wide currency in the literature and it is as well to be clear about its meaning.

In the specific case of agglomeration economies the external economies experienced by a production unit derive from its particular *locational* association with a larger scale spatial cluster of economic activities. Scale economies internal to the major cluster, for example the economies achieved by a city during the early phases of its growth, are passed on as *external* economies to the individual production units that make it up. Without necessarily raising their own scale of production, their spatial association and functional linkage with the larger agglomeration permits them to derive cost economies at second-hand from scale factors operating outside themselves. Under these conditions agglomeration economies become yet another element contributing to the businessman's decision to locate and therefore have a significant impact on the location of economic activity in space. It was Alfred Weber (1909) who focused attention on this particular phenomenon. Weber visualized agglomeration economies as exerting a deviational force on the minimum transport-cost location in a similar way to that exerted by cheap labor locations (see Chapter Six). In both cases the existence of a locational deviation was seen to depend upon the location of the attracting force in relation to the *critical isodapane*. For agglomeration to occur, the *critical isodapanes* of the firms in question must intersect as in Figure 7.16b; where intersection does not occur, as in Figure 7.16a, agglomeration will not take place.

Although Weber's analysis is consistent with the rest of his location theory, it is perhaps one of its weaker aspects; first, because he failed to probe sufficiently deeply into the nature of agglomeration economies and second, because of his highly simplistic view of the mechanism of relocation in this context. It must be stressed that agglomeration economies differ from other locational economies, such as cheap labor or materials, in that they depend upon the coincident decisions of a number of firms:

Figure 7.16
Weber's concept of agglomeration. (a) The critical isodapanes *do not* intersect: There is no agglomeration. (b) The critical isodapanes *do* intersect: Agglomeration may occur.

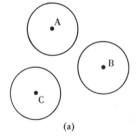

(a)

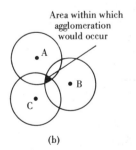

Area within which agglomeration would occur

(b)

An agglomeration point is merely a place to which a number of persons engaged in industry decide to resort. Without the decision it does not exist; after the decision it is there. Looked at from another point of view, a point for agglomeration is not one to which it is to the advantage of any single producer to transfer his plant. While it may be to the advantage of two producers to come together, neither will gain unless the other also acts.
Daggett (1955), p. 450

The question of location decision-making will be pursued in detail in Chapters Eight and Nine. At this point we focus our attention on the specific nature of the external economies that may accrue given that firms cluster together in space for whatever initial reason.

Figure 7.17
Major functional linkages of a hypothetical manufacturing firm.

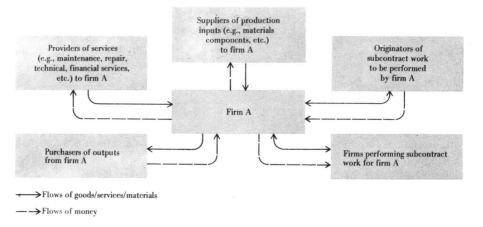

The study of agglomeration economies emphasizes the *connections* or *linkages* between economic activities within a relatively restricted geographic area. In the final analysis, of course, any firm is but one part of a complex chain of production held together by direct or indirect linkages between a series of firms. It is through such linkages that external economies are transmitted to the individual production unit through its network of interconnections with other elements in a system. Figure 7.17 shows, in a highly simplified form, the major linkages possessed by a hypothetical manufacturing firm. These linkages are of three main types.

1. *Production linkages.* In this case there is a physical movement of goods from one firm to another as part of the production process. A tailor's cutter, for instance, obtains cloth from a wholesale business and his product goes on to a "maker-up." In this way he is linked *backwards* to his suppliers and *forwards* to those next along the chain of production. In general, the smaller the business the more dependent it is upon sub-contract linkages in production and the more specialized are the linked elements in the process chain. For the larger firm there are, of course, such linkages—to raw material suppliers and to metal-users in, say, the case of the steel industry—but many more processes are internalized within the production unit itself.

2. *Service linkages.* These are defined as those which connect a business to a different sub-set of sub-contractors whose functions are to supply services ancillary to the production process itself. Under this heading come suppliers of machinery, equipment, tools and dies. Suppliers of services like window cleaning, catering, specialist repairs to plants, office stationery, accountancy, and so forth come under this heading. Once again, larger firms can be clearly distinguished as those which tend to internalize these services while smaller firms look to obtain them from outside sources. In some classifications like that of Townroe (1969), those services connected with finance and commercial institutions are given the status of a separate major category in their own right.

3. *Marketing linkages.* These connections are to separate businesses whose task is to sell and distribute the goods of a particular producer. Under this heading would come packaging firms, wholesalers, transport undertakings and sales agencies, all those who deal with the distribution of the good to final demand or to the next link in the process chain.

An agglomeration economy may exist, therefore, where some or all of these linkages are present *within a relatively small geographic area,* thus either lowering a firm's costs or increasing its revenue (or both). In addition there may be other economies derived, as it were, "by association." Complementary or similar industries, by recruiting and training a labor force for instance, provide a localized cluster of particular labor skills. These "skill pools" add to the attractiveness of such areas for particular specialized industries.

Commonly, a distinction is made between two types of agglomeration economy: *localization economies* and *urbanization economies. Localization economies* are those gained by firms in a single industry (or a set of closely related industries) at a single location, economies accruing to the individual production units through the overall enlarged output of the industry as a whole at that location. *Urbanization economies,* on the other hand, apply to all firms in all industries at a single location and represent those external economies passed to enterprises as a result of savings from the large-scale operation of the agglomeration as a whole. The economies of scale to the higher order systems such as the localized industry, or the city as an economic unit, are essentially the same as those discussed for the individual producer on pp. 265–271—specialization, economies of massed reserves, and economies of large-scale purchasing. Indeed, a real distinction between localization and urbanization economies is often difficult to establish, and to avoid what is often a confusing issue, we shall avoid making a formal distinction in what follows.

Although all firms have linkages of the type described above, the literature dealing with economies of agglomeration in general has tended to focus primarily on those at the smaller end of the plant size spectrum. Here, highly specialized trades under separate ownership exploit a complex constellation of linkages to each other, often replicating in this way the characteristics found under single ownership in the multi-plant firm. At this scale it seems easy to identify one of the keys to agglomeration economies as the *minimization of the distance between each linked firm and its trading partners.* Under these circumstances, the economies achieved would not be fundamentally different from those out-lined by Adam Smith in his description of the pin maker, except that in this case each sub-process is under separate ownership. Each small firm can special-ize in its particular trade to a degree which promotes a high level of efficiency in the operations of both men and machines. Where the firms cluster together in the same street, block or quarter, the movement of goods along the "produc-tion line," instead of being by conveyor belt, can be by handcart along the street or by motor truck. In the "handcart" example, there are obvious imme-diate savings to each producer since the "conveyor belt"—the street—is paid for and maintained not by any individual firm but by the community at large.

Apart from the apparently obvious transfer-cost benefits of close spatial juxtapo-sition and the "production line in the street," there are certain other advantages associated with plants which keep their linkages within a closely confined area. Hoover (1948) points to the particular scale economies which come from *special-ization of function.*

> Certain operations and services that a firm in a smaller place would do
> for itself can in the city be farmed out to separate enterprises specializing
> in these operations and operating at a scale large enough to do the job
> more cheaply.
> *Hoover (1948), p. 120*

It is the economies of scale from serving the large city market which is reputed to make the small specialist cost-efficient since his level of output can move closer to the minimum efficient scale. These *internal* economies to each firm are then passed on as *external* economies to the other firms that use their goods or services. The example of the quality paper manufacturer and the pub-lisher quoted earlier was an arrangement of this sort.

In the same way the *economies of massed reserves* that lowered unit costs for the single large firm can also be seen to operate at the level of the urban-indus-trial agglomeration. This may apply to the supply of materials, labor, or perhaps floor space. For instance, an isolated firm may have to tie up its funds by carrying a considerable inventory of materials and components to cover it for possible delays in delivery or temporary shortages. The firm that is part of an agglomeration of activities, however, may well be able to call on supplies at very short notice. This is because the high level of aggregate demand, as we have seen, permits the operation of a wide range of specialist factors or merchants. As a result, far less capital needs to be immobilized in inventories. In the case of the printing industries of New York City, for example, it was found that firms need only 9.7 percent of their total assets in inventories com-pared with 19 percent for printing firms outside New York (M. Hall, 1959). The benefits of access to a large labor pool for the individual firm were discussed in Chapter Six. Large agglomerations offer a wide range of skilled and unskilled labor that can be drawn upon relatively easily to meet sudden shifts in produc-tion activity. Similarly, industrial and commercial floor space of all kinds is widely available in most major agglomerations and can be taken up or discarded to meet short-term shifts in production needs.

Economies of large-scale purchasing are also available as external economies to the firm in an urban-industrial complex. The advantage of the single large firm, obtaining favorable rates on the bulk purchase of supplies and services, may also be available to the cluster of firms of all sizes in agglomerations. In the case of transportation, for example, small firms that individually ship small quantities of their goods can share the services of freight forwarders. Dealing with a large number of spatially concentrated firms, these can combine shipments to make up full carload lots and theoretically pass on some of the resulting economies to the customer.

Another of the acknowledged benefits of agglomeration for certain industries is the *rapidity with which communication can take place between customer and supplier.* This is particularly important for firms producing non-standardized or "one-off" articles or services where direct and frequent contact is essential. Groves (1971) identifies these as a distinctive group. He picks out in particular commercial printing, lithographing, women's apparel and certain small-scale elements of the electronics industry. All of these tend to occupy small premises close to their concentrated downtown local markets since successful businesses in these fields are those able to respond quickly to the shifting demands of the customer.

The concept of localization economies outlined above sets out the particular gains that accrue to localized firms in purely material terms. Some of the critics of this approach, however, and Taylor (1970), and Gibson (1974) in particular, wonder whether the clearly observed tendency for small firms to agglomerate owes much at all to the benefits derived from *material* linkages. Perhaps the benefits are far more subtle and of a "social" rather than economic nature, though as Estall and Buchanan (1966) pointed out, even this might be expressed in terms of economic advantage:

> the social relationships among linked firms in the main center which commonly create a feeling of loyalty to the group, may make it difficult for a newcomer in a location away from the recognized geographical area to obtain regular and reliable orders.
> *Estall and Buchanan (1966), p. 96*

Taylor's (1970) concept of *seedbed growth* follows the same line but sees the contribution of linkage benefits in agglomeration in a rather different light. They are seen to be much more subtle in the way they operate, having more to do with the fact that particular localized concentrations of industry once evolved *become known as centers suitable for particular trades.* For the new small businessman in particular, they provide quick access to the "contacts" he needs to get going. Frequently, since small plants have a high turnover rate, they also provide suitable premises for the trade. For these less material and less tangible reasons, it is suggested that areas of specialized agglomeration provide a suitable *seedbed* for newly established businesses (see Chapter Eight). Even though the strictly economic and material benefits of locating there may be "long gone," they retain an attractiveness for nascent small industry which gives them a pull based on inertia rather than on the contemporary benefits of localized external economies of scale.

Unfortunately, when it has come down to establishing *in fact* the source of the real or perceived benefits drawing industry to particular clusters or maintaining it there, most empirical studies of local linkages have been qualitative rather than quantitative in nature. They have tended to provide verbal descriptions testifying to the presence of functional linkages but little indication of their strength. Gilmour (1974) has been particularly critical of the location theorist's approach to agglomeration economies to date. In reviewing the elements of agglomeration theory which we have just put forward he makes the following comments:

> First, the theory was deductively derived. Second, it has never been shown to be completely valid. Third, it has generally been assumed to be valid and for pedagogical purposes has provided the explanatory basis of agglomeration absorbed by several generations of university students.... The theory has enjoyed a long life. It has never been demonstrated that it is completely invalid but neither has the converse been demonstrated. More than anything else this noteworthy state of affairs reflects the theory's difficulty of verification.
> *Gilmour (1974), pp. 336–7*

Yet again it is worth making the point that economies of scale tend to be a "slippery" area for generalization. It is one where conceptualization comes easy but verification difficult.

Much of the early work on agglomeration economies pointed to the localization of specialized industries in particular "quarters" of cities. Such was the richness and variety of specialized trades in these areas as Wise's (1948) map of Birmingham's jewellery quarter in Figure 7.18 shows, that strong linkages between the elements was easily inferred. Similarly, Hall (1960), commenting on the clothing "quarter" in the East End of London, could make the observation that:

> in Stepney today, despite a trend towards vertically integrated production in large factories, it is still fairly common for a making-up firm to sub-contract buttonholing, pleating, embroidering and button-covering to specialist firms.
> *Hall (1960), p. 174*

Most of these, styling themselves "suppliers to the trade," were in localized clusters serving the high fashion West End clothing firms and the "down-market" garment makers of the East End. Sargant Florence (1948) and Beesley (1955) made detailed studies of the linkage phenomenon from the viewpoint of the West Midland metal trades, finding significant scale economies in the clustering process.

In the particular case of the United Kingdom it was still possible to find some vestige of the inner city industrial quarter in most large cities in the 1950s and 1960s. Small factories in the clothing, printing, woodworking and light

Figure 7.18
The Birmingham jewellery
quarter, 1948. [*Source:*
M. J. Wise (1949),
Evolution of Jewellery
and Gun Quarters in
Birmingham, *Transactions
of the Institute of British
Geographers,* No. 15,
Figure 1.]

Key

■ Goldsmiths and manufacturing jewellers
□ Silversmiths
⊡ Electro-platers
▢ Medallists
⊟ Gilt and imitation jewellery

▼ Factors and merchants
▽ Dealers in bullion and precious stones
▼ Jewellers material suppliers

◆ Gem setting
◇ Stamping and piercing
◇ Engraving polishing and enamelling
⬦ Die sinkers
△ Jewellery repairer
▲ Refiners
◇ General outwork

○ Manufacturers of optical goods
⊕ Manufacturers of fancy leather goods
⊖ Watchmakers
○ Miscellaneous manufacturers

(a)   (b)

● Watchmakers   (74/1018)   ■ Clock makers (15/181) ○ Watch case makers (23/43) ○ Watch glass makers (4/8) G Watch material dealers (2/9)
s Watch spring makers (5/15) ◆ Allied trades (183/257)

The figures in brackets show the number of makers engaged in trades listed   map area are expressed as proportions of the total numbers of makers in
in Post Office London Directory, 1861. The numbers of makers within the   the London area.

Figure 7.19
(a) The Clerkenwell
watch and clockmaking
quarter, 1861. (b) The
Clerkenwell watch and
clockmaking quarter,
1951. [*Source:* P. Hall
(1960), Industrial
London, a General View,
Figures 46 and 47.
Reprinted by permission
of Faber and Faber Ltd
from *Greater London*
edited by J. T. Coppock
and H. C. Prince.]

engineering industries could be found still clinging to premises originally built
in the early years of the Industrial Revolution. More recently, however, these
specialized quarters have increasingly come under threat of extinction. Redevelopment of the central areas of the main cities has all but wiped out many
manufacturing clusters including the traditional ones of London and Birmingham. Even by 1951, as Figure 7.19 shows for Clerkenwell, London, some of
the best-known agglomerations of industry were disappearing. During the redevelopment boom of the 1960s the process accelerated forcing the kind of "flight"
from the inner city shown in the case of Manchester, England in Figure 7.20.
During the period 1966 to 1972 alone, central Manchester lost over 30,000
manufacturing jobs. The majority of these were associated with traditional clusters of small inner city industry. The clothing, printing and publishing, and
small engineering trades bore the brunt of the losses, most of which resulted
directly from the compulsory purchase and demolition of factory premises under
the city's rehousing program. As Figure 7.20 shows, many displaced firms sought
out new premises elsewhere, though only 20 percent of the total jobs lost to
central Manchester could be labeled as being "saved" through the migration
process. Significantly, the favored sites for transfer of small, particularly clothing,
industries displaced from the central city were clusters of cheap mill premises
close to the centers of the traditional cotton textile towns which form a ring

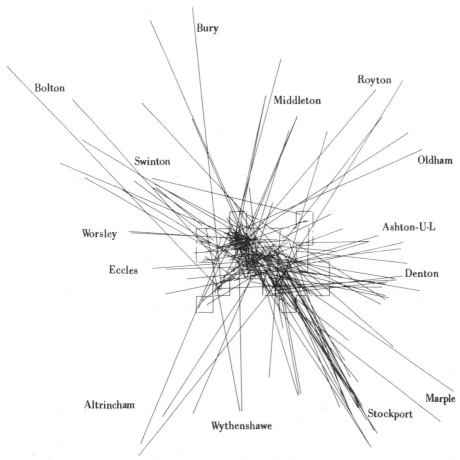

Bury

Bolton

Royton

Middleton

Swinton

Oldham

Worsley

Ashton-U-L

Eccles

Denton

Altrincham

Marple

Wythenshawe

Stockport

Figure 7.20
The migration of
manufacturing
establishments from
central Manchester,
1966–1972.

around Manchester. In general in the United Kingdom, residential and commercial uses have either gained or been granted preference over manufacturing in the central areas of cities, promoting the sort of "death or flight" alternative to small industry observed in the case of Manchester.

For the United States and Canada the situation is much less clear. Although the mid-town Manhattan industrial quarter is well known and has been explored in detail in the work of Seidman (1947) and M. Hall (1959)—particularly in the case of the "needle trades"—other clusters appear to exist only in the very largest metropolitan centers. Lack of empirical work again makes comment on the subject speculative, but *timing* in the industrial growth process seems to be important. Since the origins of the industrial quarter lie in the low-mobility "walkabout city" of the early and middle nineteenth century, many North American cities with later industrial growth missed this particular phase. Later-growing cities developed in the motor-truck era under vastly different mobility conditions for industry.

In both the United Kingdom and North America, however, the advent of the automobile brought about a sorting process which left only certain specialized types of industry in the inner city. The notion of *localization* on which the concept of cluster economies was founded changed dramatically with the arrival of automobile transport. What was "local" before this was quite different from what was perceived as "local" afterwards. Traditional linkages to railway termini, stockyards, docks and other central city break-of-bulk points had kept much manufacturing industry tightly localized. The new medium of transport, however, with its greater flexibility and tendency to favor the *outer* less-congested parts of cities began the shift of industry to the urban periphery. This has continued unabated to the present, partly by means of a physical transfer of plants to the periphery. More important, however, has been the *net shift* produced as *new* industry has chosen to locate in the suburbs rather than in the inner city.

"Local" industrial linkages now span entire metropolitan areas though as Norcliffe (1975) points out there are certain "non-goods linkages" which still have to be provided in close proximity to a plant. These are services which are frequently used; the study of metal industries in Hamilton, Ontario by Bater and Walker (1971) found nine such services. These are (in rank-order) transport services, banks, security, investment dealers, data processing, sub-contract work, waste disposal, repair shops, and advertising printing and photography. In most other respects the closeness with which industries need to be associated in space seems to have diminished significantly as transport developments have redefined the impact of space on economic efficiency. It is perhaps for this reason, as we suggested earlier, that a real distinction between localization economies and the more general urbanization economies is difficult to determine.

Let us now change the level of resolution finally to consider the broader aspects of external economies as they exist in the modern urban environment. One of the general economies of agglomeration afforded to the constituent firms of a major urban-industrial complex is the provision of wide-ranging public utility and welfare services. As the size of such complexes increases the unit costs of "producing" utility services such as power generation, urban transportation, water supply, and sewage disposal should fall. Scale economies should, in theory, continue to increase until a point is reached that is equivalent to the minimum optimal scale of the individual plant. Up to this point lower costs should be passed on to the individual user in the agglomeration as external economies of scale. In theory, therefore, there should be optimal sizes for agglomerations just as there are for individual plants; sizes at which public utilities and services are "produced" at optimum levels of efficiency, maximizing the external economies that they pass on to constituent firms.

Isard (1956) attempted to investigate this aspect of agglomeration economies by means of his net economy curves (economies less diseconomies) for utilities such as power generation, urban transportation, water supply, and sewage disposal. Figure 7.21 depicts a set of hypothetical net economy curves for agglomerations of varying size, with the individual curves summed to give a total economy curve. Unfortunately, as Isard himself points out, such a procedure involves numerous problems, including the question of weighting each curve according to relative importance and the fact that there is a degree of interdependence between, for example, power economies and transportation economies.

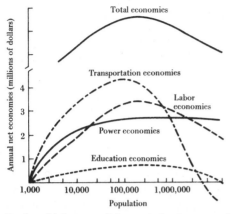

Figure 7.21
Hypothetical net economy
curves. [*Source:*
Reprinted from W. Isard
(1956), *Location and
Space Economy,* Figure
35, by permission of the
M.I.T. Press, Cambridge,
Massachusetts. Copyright
© 1956 by the
Massachusetts Institute of
Technology.]

It should be possible to calculate a minimum optimal scale of agglomeration but just as the quantitative evidence of external economies in the case of individual firms is scanty and often ambiguous, so also is that for urbanization economies.

Most writers seem to assume that beyond a certain size of agglomeration the scale advantages of size begin to disappear and diseconomies of scale begin to appear. One might envisage this as the point at which an expanding urban area becomes incapable of maintaining certain key elements of its complex structure. The arrival of raw material shortages, overspecialization, prohibitive cost and congestion problems in the transport network, inefficiencies in administration and so forth, could, it is presumed, lead to what Weber called deglomerative tendencies. These imply the movement away from overcongested cities. Many of these features are recognizable in modern cities yet there seems, with one or two exceptions perhaps, to be no slackening of the drive to urban growth. One reason for this lies in the difference between *private costs* and *social costs* in the context of urbanization economies. In the city some of the apparent economies to a business derive from its ability to have the use of some facilities at *no cost to itself.* The "conveyor belt in the street" is an obvious example. It is the city as a whole that pays for the construction and maintenance of the street. Other "costs" in production are borne by the community at large: congestion, pollution, noise, longer journeys to work and so on. These are in a sense a powerful source of external economies—the economy comes from the fact that the city offers plants what are known as "free rider" economies. The costs are borne socially by the *community at large*, not privately by the firm itself. For this reason the expected deglomerative forces are slow to appear since their impact is dispersed over a community. Only as the community as a whole begins to feel the strain is the build-up of external diseconomies to its constituent producer units identifiable. Hansen (1968b, p. 14) points to the overall effects of this.

> There is nothing in the nature of things to halt this process (of increasing agglomeration) because the costs of congestion are usually not internalized costs for private producers; or if they are internalized, they are not sufficient to balance the external economies of agglomeration.

Seen in this context, it may well be the community at large which bears most of the costs which arrive as external economies to producers in the modern city. Only when the community acts to limit them by anti-pollution legislation, noise control schemes, planning restrictions for industrial uses and so forth do diseconomies become effective in retarding growth. At this point and for what are perceived to be non-economic reasons economies of agglomeration may begin to disappear.

Summary

Relaxing our initial assumption about the spatial uniformity of demand and giving more explicit attention to the question of scale economies in production has introduced a substantial degree of sophistication into our analysis. It has also, however, promoted a sharp increase in the complexity of the subject matter. By restricting our early investigation to cost considerations alone we were able to deal with a single source of variation in the conditions facing the business-man. By opening up questions of variable demand and scale, however, not only have new sources of complexity been introduced but, more importantly, we have been able to show the existence of key *interaction effects* between costs, scale and demand. Each influences the other in an unbroken circle of cause and effect.

Lösch, reviewing Weber's least-cost approach to location made the following observation:

> The fundamental error consists in seeking the place of least cost. This is as absurd as to consider the point of largest sales as the proper location. Every such one-sided orientation is wrong. Only search for the place of greatest profit is right.
> *Lösch (1954), pp. 28–29*

While Lösch is, of course, correct, the problem which has clearly arisen in this chapter is that what he recommends is far easier said than done. The place of greatest profit will depend not only on choices related to material and factor inputs and their costs of assembly. It will also depend upon the chosen scale of production and the size and geographical disposition of the market. As we have emphasized, all three are closely interrelated and the real choice of the location of greatest profit involves a "multi-way" problem of substitution in which there are many complex trade-offs.

For example, in some industries the substitution choices may span the whole range of plant sizes. The small plant with low overheads located in an area offering agglomeration economies may provide one alternative. At the other extreme a large plant with many of its material and service requirements internalized and available under the same roof may well form a realistic alternative as a production unit. By contrast, in other industries there may be a closely constrained set of plant size possibilities from which to choose. Further, with time and technological change, previously wide ranges of choice may be narrowed or narrow ones widened, leaving some producers in a "favorable" position while others previously in the right place at the right scale become less favorably placed.

There is nothing simple about "multi-way" substitution problems in a continously changing economic system. No doubt the uncertainty associated with it has asserted itself on the reader's mind during the course of the chapter. Equally, however, for the real-world businessman there are few Weberian certainties. He too must make his choices with the best information available to him in a world full of uncertainty. It is to this aspect of locational choice—decisions in the face of uncertainty—that we turn our attention in the next chapter.

Further reading

Bain, J. S. (1968), *Industrial Organization*, New York: Wiley, Chapters 4 and 6.

Chisholm, M. (1966), *Geography and Economics*, New York: Praeger, London: Bell, Chapters 4 and 7.

Greenhut, M. L. (1956), *Plant Location in Theory and Practise*, Chapel Hill: University of North Carolina Press, Chapters II and VI.

Harris, C. D. (1954), The Market as a Factor in the Localization of Industry in the U.S., *Annals of the Association of American Geographers* **44.** 315–348.

Isard, W. (1956), *Location and Space Economy*, Cambridge, Mass.: M.I.T. Press, Chapter 8.

Isard, W. (1960), *Methods of Regional Analysis*, Cambridge, Mass.: M.I.T. Press, Chapter 11.

Keeble, D. E. (1969), Local Industrial Linkage and Manufacturing Growth in Outer London, *Town Planning Review* **40.** 163–188.

Moses, L. N. (1958), Location and the Theory of Production, *Quarterly Journal of Economics* **72.** 259–272.

Richter, C. E. (1969), The Impact of Industrial Linkages on Geographic Association, *Journal of Regional Science* **9.** 19–28.

Robinson, E. A. G. (1958), *The Structure of Competitive Industry*, Cambridge: Cambridge University Press.

Warntz, W. (1959), *Toward a Geography of Price*, Philadelphia: University of Pennsylvania Press.

Weber, A. (1909), *Theory of the Location of Industries*, Chicago: University of Chicago Press, Chapter V.

CHAPTER 8

DECISIONS IN AN UNCERTAIN WORLD

So far in discussing how economic activities are arranged on the earth's surface we have concentrated on a number of important variables. We have examined the bases and locational effects of spatial variation in the cost and availability of such major input factors as land, labor, capital, and technology. We have investigated the effects of network structure and transport costs on the location of economic activities and we have explored something of the complex relationship between scale of production and spatial variations in demand and location. We have introduced the concept of agglomeration as a cost-reducing and demand-increasing function. But we have deliberately retained one of the biggest constraints of all: the nature of the decision-maker. We have assumed that the producers inhabiting our economic landscape—whether they be farmers or industrialists—behave perfectly rationally, in a strictly economic sense, to achieve the single, clearly defined goal of maximizing their profits.

To place this view in clearer perspective and to provide a basis for the kind of discussion presented in this chapter it is useful to refer to the most fundamental elements of all purposive decision-making systems. Figure 8.1 is a very simple *cybernetic** model in which behavior is reduced to three basic components:

1. A *detector* (or sensor) which picks up information signals from the environment and feeds it back to:
2. A *selector* (or governor) which chooses what to do about the information on the basis of some predefined goal or objective and then passes instructions to:
3. An *effector* which carries out the instructions and performs the chosen act of behavior.

Figure 8.1
Fundamental components
of decision-making
systems: a simple
cybernetic model.

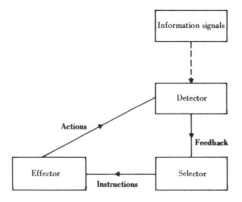

Our producer was able to *detect* all the information signals—we endowed him with powers of omniscience—so that he was fully aware of all possible spatial variations in the costs of acquiring inputs and in the pattern of demand. He could thus *select* the *optimum* location because his choice was based on only one criterion: making the largest possible profit. We also made it possible for him to adjust his location easily if circumstances changed. For example, in Chapter Six we showed how the availability of, say, a cheap labor supply could attract a producer away from the minimum transport-cost point. Adjustment to change, therefore, was regarded as a self-regulating process based on perfect feedback of information.

In effect, we have been looking at the spatial behavior of a very special kind of human being who is generally labeled *Economic Man* for rather obvious reasons. The models we have constructed on the basis of such a "person" are *normative* economic models in that they are concerned with what *should* be done according to, in this case, the economic desires of producers. Without question, such models have proved of enormous value, and we shall see later that some of the simple location models we have discussed based upon optimizing assumptions retain much of their validity even in more complex circumstances and at a much enlarged organizational and geographical scale. But, clearly, decision-makers in the real world are far less perfect than we have assumed, so that if we are to develop a clearer understanding of the spatial organization of economic activities, we should look rather more closely at decision-making. In this chapter, therefore, we adopt what has come to be called a *behavioral* approach to the location problem. Our view will be more general than particular because it would be a pointless and futile exercise to try to probe the basis of every individual decision, even if that were possible. After all, we have enough on our hands without attempting to become amateur psychologists!

Despite the general feeling that the decisions that interest us may not be as unambiguous and efficient as our normative models lead us to believe, there have been remarkably few attempts to investigate the *magnitude* of the difference between theoretical and actual decisions. The most comprehensive and detailed study by a geographer is the one carried out by Julian Wolpert (1964) in which he examined the spatial patterns of farming in middle Sweden and made an explicit attempt to compare the geographical variation in farming practice with the pattern that *would* exist if all farmers were *economic men* with the single goal of optimizing returns and perfect information on how to do it.

The basis of Wolpert's comparison was the level of labor productivity actually achieved, and potentially achievable, *given* the prevailing resources available to the farmer. Obviously, climate, soil quality, evenness of terrain, farm size, type of farming equipment and other elements vary from place to place and contribute to the volume of output which each farm worker can produce. Figure 8.2 shows how the actual labor productivity per farm varies and, quite clearly, only a very few areas achieve relatively high levels. The question posed by Wolpert was whether this pattern was the *best* that could be achieved taking into account the nature of the existing resources possessed by the farmer. Figure 8.3 shows that high levels of productivity were potentially attainable over far larger areas than Figure 8.2 would suggest if all farmers had used their existing resources in the most efficient manner; by concentrating on the most suitable type of production for their particular circumstances, for example. Combining

Figure 8.2
Actual labor productivity
per farm in middle
Sweden. [*Source:*
J. Wolpert (1964), The
Decision Process in
Spatial Context, Figure 2.
Reproduced by
permission from the
*Annals of the Association
of American Geographers,*
54.]

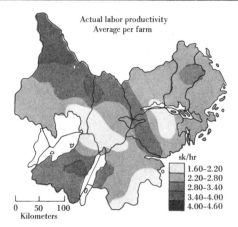

Figure 8.2

Figure 8.3
Potential labor
productivity per farm in
middle Sweden. [*Source:*
J. Wolpert (1964), The
Decision Process in
Spatial Context, Figure 3.
Reproduced by
permission from the
*Annals of the Association
of American Geographers,*
54.]

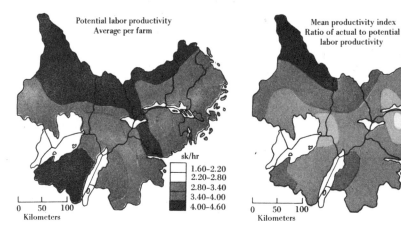

Figure 8.4
Mean productivity index:
ratio of actual to potential
labor productivity in
middle Sweden. [*Source:*
J. Wolpert (1964), The
Decision Process in
Spatial Context, Figure 4.
Reproduced by
permission from the
*Annals of the Association
of American Geographers,*
54.]

Figure 8.3   Figure 8.4

the two surfaces—actual and potential productivity—as in Figure 8.4 shows
that the average farmer achieved only about two-thirds of the potential productivity which his resources permitted. Wolpert's conclusion, therefore, is that
farmers lack "one or both of the prerequisites for economic rationality (perfect
knowledge and optimizing behavior)." These two prerequisites are not independent but closely related, so let us look at them more carefully.

The problem of uncertainty

> Dynamically there is no best location because we cannot know the future.
> *Lösch (1954), p. 16*

Lösch's statement, despite its truistic nature, captures the essence of the problem.
However extensive our knowledge of the present, we cannot accurately predict
the future; consequently a fundamental feature of all decision-making situations
is that they take place in an environment of uncertainty. Such uncertainty may

relate to the future economic or political situation at the *macroscale* (for example, the state of the national or world economy or the stability of the political system) or at the *microscale* (such as the behavior of other producers who are competing for the same resources or striving to capture an increasing share of the same market). Indeed, some would argue that the pace of change is now so rapid that uncertainty is increasing at a faster rate than we are able to cope. Be that as it may, let us look at one way in which social scientists have attempted to incorporate uncertainty into their theoretical models: the use of *game theory*.

Application of game theory to locational situations

Game theory originated in essentially mathematical approaches to *conflict* situations. It aims at providing the best solutions to problems in which the outcome for one "player" depends not only on his own actions but also on the actions of an "opponent." Thus the best strategy or move is not simply the one *most* preferred in an absolute sense, but *the one which promises to give the best return in the light of what future actions the opponent might take.** Hence, the approach in its simplest forms can be used to illustrate the problems of making spatial decisions in the face of uncertainty. The following examples refer to three rather simplified hypothetical situations. Strictly speaking, situations such as the first two examples are not true games in that only one of the players is actively aiming to "win." The other "player" is what we might call "the environment" though this is only a general term to cover a variety of possible future states of affairs over which the individual has no control. Thus, in our first example, the environment consists of possible government actions which will affect the locational behavior of a small manufacturer. The manufacturer has no influence over which action the government will take. In the second example, the environment is the state of the weather over which, again, the individual has no control. Our third example is a genuine conflict situation—a true game-theory situation—represented by a competitive struggle between two producers for a marketing location. In this case, both players are actively striving to win: one's gains are the other's losses. Where one of the players is the environment, the gains and losses apply only to the one player.

The location decision of a manufacturer as a game-theory situation

Imagine the case of a small-scale manufacturer of electrical machinery who is located in rather cramped, though low-rent, premises close to the center of a large city. Demand for his goods is increasing and to meet this he needs to install additional equipment to produce more goods. He perceives that he could do this in one of three ways; in game-theory terms he identifies three strategies. Obviously there are many other possibilities open to him but we assume that these are the only feasible alternatives he identifies.

---

*Derivation of strategies and the structure of games can be very complex. Excellent general introductions to game theory are provided by Shubik (1964), Vajda (1960), and Williams (1966). Some geographical applications of the game-theory approach can be found in Daly (1972), Found (1971), Abler, Adams and Gould (1971), Isard and Reiner (1962).

Note

Strategy 1—remain at the existing location and install new equipment to increase output.

Strategy 2—close down the central city plant and move to a suburban site in the same city.

Strategy 3—close down the central city plant and relocate in a different part of the country where there is surplus labor.

Suppose again for the sake of simplicity that the future state of the environment can take one, *and only one*, of three alternate forms (the environment's strategies). The manufacturer, of course, is uncertain as to which one will actually occur.

State of environment I. The government implements a program of equipment grants for manufacturing firms.

State of environment II. A new suburban expressway (motorway) is built, linking suburban industrial areas with the national interstate highway (motorway) systems.

State of environment III. Government implements a regional development policy with major financial assistance for manufacturing firms locating in designated areas of high unemployment.

We can now put these two sets of strategies together in the form of a matrix or table in which the numbers in each cell represent the *payoffs* or values of each strategy. The values in the cells are, of course, quite hypothetical. They are designed to represent differences in the value to the manufacturer of the various location choices. Hence they could be interpreted in various ways: for example, they could represent annual profit in hundreds or thousands of dollars.

Table 8.1
Payoff matrix for the electrical machinery manufacturer.

		States of the environment		
		Government equipment grants	New suburban motorway	Government regional policy
Manufacturer's alternative strategies		I	II	III
Re-equip at existing location	1	200	155	145
Move to suburbs	2	130	220	130
Move to surplus labor area	3	118	118	225

Each of these alternative strategies has its advantages and disadvantages. Staying put is the "least-effort" solution, but the premises may be rather obsolescent and city congestion increasingly costly. Moving the plant either to the suburbs or to a more distant location may be a costly and inconvenient process but may offer the prospect of better factory premises, perhaps a more amenable environment and, in the more distant case, the prospect of lower labor costs. However, which strategy is actually adopted will depend on more than this kind of consideration; it will depend upon the manufacturer's perception of future events and upon his attitude toward risk and uncertainty. In this sense, different kinds of persons may choose quite differently between identical sets of alternatives. We can apply this line of reasoning to the locational problem of our electrical machinery manufacturer.

(i) **The "cautious" manufacturer.** The cautious individual does not like to take chances; he opts for the strategy which will minimize his possible disadvantages. In game-theory terms, he adopts a *maximin* strategy, that is, he looks at each row of the payoff matrix and identifies the worst possible outcome for each strategy. In Table 8.1 these would be:

145 for Strategy 1
130 for Strategy 2
118 for Strategy 3.

He thus assumes the worst will happen and chooses the "best of the worst"—*Strategy 1*—which is to stay where he is and install new equipment. Whichever state of the environment occurs, therefore, the cautious electrical manufacturer will achieve a payoff of *at least* 145 which is the lowest payoff for Strategy 1 and could achieve a good deal more. If environment State II occurs he would get 155 or 200 if State I of the environment occurs.

(ii) **The "reckless" manufacturer.** At the opposite end of the attitude-to-uncertainty scale is the reckless individual who is prepared to stake all on the chance of gaining the largest possible return. In game-theory terms, we can imagine him scanning the payoff matrix, choosing the largest payoff for each strategy:

200 for Strategy 1
220 for Strategy 2
225 for Strategy 3.

As an "100 percent optimist," therefore, he will choose the strategy associated with the largest possible payoff (*Strategy 3*) and relocate his plant in a surplus labor area. We would label this a *max-max* strategy.

(iii) **The manufacturer who tries to assess the relative probabilities of each environmental state.** Some environmental states may be regarded as being more likely to occur than others; that is, our manufacturer may be able to "weight" the value of each strategy by guessing at the relative likelihood or probability of each state of the environment occurring. Suppose he believes that these probabilities are as follows:

The probability of State I of the environment occurring is 0.2
The probability of State II of the environment occurring is 0.5
The probability of State III of the environment occurring is 0.3

(Note that the values add up to 1.0, as they must, because these three states represent the totality of the future in our simple world.)

Using these probabilities, the manufacturer can calculate the total expected value for each of his three strategies by multiplying each payoff value by the appropriate probability and adding the results together:

Strategy 1. 0.2(200) + 0.5(155) + 0.3(145) = 40 + 77.5 + 43.5 = *161*
Strategy 2. 0.2(130) + 0.5(220) + 0.3(130) = 26 + 110 + 39 = *175*
Strategy 3. 0.2(118) + 0.5(118) + 0.3(225) = 23.6 + 59 + 67.5 = *150.1*

Clearly *Strategy 2*, a move to the suburbs, is most appropriate given the manufacturer's assessment of the relative likelihood of future events.

(iv) **The manufacturer with a less sophisticated view of the future.** Calculation of different probabilities for each environmental state may be difficult. A less sophisticated method would be to assume that there is an equally good chance of each state of the environment occurring; that is, he gives an equal probability weighting to each payoff value. The overall values for each strategy, therefore, will be:

Strategy 1. 0.33(200) + 0.33(155) + 0.33(145) = 66 + 51.15 + 47.85 = *165*
Strategy 2. 0.33(130) + 0.33(220) + 0.33(130) = 42.9 + 72.6 + 42.9 = *158.4*
Strategy 3. 0.33(118) + 0.33(118) + 0.33(225) = 38.9 + 38.9 + 74.25 = *152.05*

Thus *Strategy 1* is the best one to use under this kind of assumption.

(v) **The manufacturer who wishes to minimize his "regret."** Most of us, at some time or other, having made a particular decision and observed its outcome, wish we had made a rather different decision. In other words, we suffer from a degree of regret whose "size" is reflected in the difference in the payoff between the decision we made and the decision we would have made if only we had known better. We can apply this *regret criterion* to the decision-making of the electrical manufacturer* in the following way. Suppose our manufacturer chose Strategy 3 and State I of the environment occurred. His payoff amounts to 118. But if he had known that State I was going to occur he would not have chosen Strategy 3; he would have chosen Strategy 1 which has the highest payoff value for State I of the environment. The difference between what he *actually* achieved—118— and what he *could have* achieved—200—is a measure of his regret (in this case, the regret value is 82). If we apply exactly the same line of reasoning to all the other payoff values—that is, compare each payoff value with the maximum value in its respective *column* of the payoff matrix (Table 8.1)—then we can construct the kind of *regret matrix* presented in Table 8.2.

Table 8.2
Regret matrix for the
electrical machinery
manufacturer.

Manufacturer's strategies	States of the environment		
	I	II	III
1	0	65	80
2	70	0	95
3	82	102	0

Assuming that the manufacturer wishes to minimize his regret, he adopts a *minimax* strategy whereby he identifies the largest regret value for each strategy:
80 for Strategy 1
95 for Strategy 2
82 for Strategy 3
and chooses the lowest of these large values—80. Thus, Strategy 1 is the appropriate strategy.

Despite its high level of simplification, our hypothetical example does highlight some interesting and pertinent aspects of decision-making under uncertainty.

Note   *Such measures of regret are analogous to the economist's concept of *opportunity cost* which is a measure of the cost of one alternative in terms of the alternatives which are not taken up (see note on p. 37).

Not only does it indicate the importance of *attitudes* towards uncertainty but also it shows that, locationally, the safest strategy is often not to relocate at all, but to remain at the existing location. This is an issue we shall return to later in this chapter.

A farmer's crop decision as a game-theory situation

If we retain our basic assumption that all manufacturers are single-plant organizations then, clearly, the electrical machinery manufacturer is faced with an either/or situation: either he remains at his central city site or he transfers production to one of the two alternative locations. A rather different kind of decision faces the farmer operating in an uncertain world. His most usual spatial decision is to decide what kinds of agricultural production should be practiced on his farm. Should he grow one crop or a combination of crops? Which crop or crops are most suitable for his particular circumstances? Again we can look at this problem in game-theory terms. Again we take a simple example, this time that of a farmer choosing between three possible crop types and faced with an environment which, for simplicity, can be wet, dry, or average. Table 8.3 sets out the payoff matrix and Table 8.4 summarizes the outcome of the different strategies based upon the same five attitude types as in the case of the electrical machinery manufacturer. (Table 8.5 is the regret matrix for the farmer.)

Farmer's crop strategies		States of the environment		
		Dry I	Average II	Wet III
Wheat	1	23	18	10
Barley	2	13	16	20
Rice	3	11	20	21

Table 8.3
Payoff matrix for the farmer.

Attitude	Strategy	Payoff anticipated
(i) *"cautious"*	2. Barley	13
(ii) *"reckless"*	1. Wheat	23
(iii) *assign different probabilities* 0.3 Dry 0.4 Average 0.3 Wet	3. Rice	17.6
(iv) *assign equal probabilities* 0.33 Dry 0.33 Average 0.33 Wet	3. Rice	17.2
(v) *minimize regret*	2. Barley	(10 regret)

Table 8.4
Summary of solutions to farmer's problem for different attitudes towards uncertainty.

Table 8.5
Regret matrix for the
farmer.

Farmer's crop	States of the environment		
strategies	I	II	III
1	0	2	11
2	10	4	1
3	12	0	0

Table 8.4 shows which of the three crops should be grown by the farmer depending upon his attitude towards uncertainty; in each case the solution is in terms
of one of the three crops. But it may be better for the farmer to *mix* his strategies,
either over a period of years (sometimes growing one crop, sometimes another)
or by dividing up his farm and *growing a combination of crops each year.* One
very simple way of deciding upon the correct mixture of strategies is to use
a graphical technique. To do this we need to reduce the strategies of one of
the opponents to two. If we do this for the environment and assume that the
weather will either be *dry* or *wet*, then we can arrange the farmer's payoffs
into two vertical columns, as in Figure 8.5, and join the appropriate values
by straight lines. For example, a glance back to Table 8.3 shows that the payoffs
for wheat are 23 in a dry year and 10 in a wet year; in Figure 8.5 the value
of 23 on the "dry scale" is connected to the value of 10 on the "wet scale."
The same procedure is carried out for barley and rice respectively. If we then
focus upon the upper boundary of the graph and, in particular, upon the lowest
point of that upper boundary, we can identify the optimum crop combination,
which happens to be wheat and barley. This, as should be evident from an
earlier discussion, is the *minimax* solution.

Figure 8.5
Graphical solution for the
game-theory crop
combination problem.

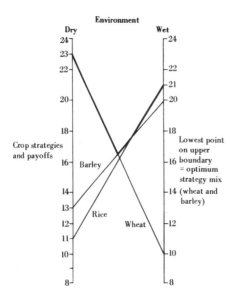

The graph tells us which is the best crop combination; it does not tell us in which proportions the crops should be grown either over a period of time or on a particular farm at one point in time. Table 8.6 shows how this may be resolved (see also Gould, 1963). For each of the two crops, the difference between the high and low payoff value is taken (regardless of sign). This difference is allocated to the other strategy because it is an indication of the size of loss experienced if the wrong choice has been made. Table 8.6 reveals that the ratio between wheat and barley should be 35:65. This means either the farmer should, over a period of years, grow barley roughly two years in every three and wheat one year in three or, more realistically, that he should grow wheat and barley every year, with 35 percent of the available land being put under wheat and 65 percent under barley.

	Dry	Wet		
Wheat	23	10	$\|23 - 10\| = 13$	$\dfrac{7}{13 + 7} = \dfrac{7}{20} = 35\%$
Barley	13	20	$\|13 - 20\| = 7$	$\dfrac{13}{13 + 7} = \dfrac{13}{20} = 65\%$

Table 8.6
Solution to the crop combination problem.

Competition between two sellers of a good: a game-theory view of locational interdependence

As a final illustration of the application of game theory (in the genuine sense) to the question of decision-making in an uncertain world, let us take the problem of two sellers of a good who are competing for the best location from which to serve their market. This is a situation which emphasizes the *interdependence* of location decisions (Greenhut, 1956). Again, our example is deliberately a very simple one, based upon a problem analyzed many years ago by the economist Harold Hotelling. Benjamin Stevens (1961) has shown how this problem of locational interdependence can be analyzed in game-theory terms. The rules of the game are as follows:

1. Imagine a limited stretch of highway along which potential consumers of hot dogs are evenly spread.
2. Each customer is prepared to buy one hot dog no matter what the price may be (in technical language, their demand is infinitely *inelastic*), but he or she will buy from the seller with the lowest total price.
3. Each hot dog costs $1 at the point of sale (these are inflationary times!), to which must be added the cost of the customer traveling to the point of sale. In terms of our discussion of spatial pricing policies in Chapter Five, we are dealing here with an f.o.b. pricing system.
4. The two hot dog sellers are spatially mobile—they can move without cost—but they are confined to the five equally spaced locations, *a* to *e*, shown in Figure 8.6.

Figure 8.6
Possible locations for two
competitors in an evenly
spaced linear market.

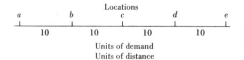

Quite obviously, given these rules, the success of each hot dog seller (measured in terms of one's *net* advantage over the other) depends not only on his own location but also on the location of the other seller. In other words, their locations are *interdependent* and they are competing for the location which will give them the largest volume of sales. Let us see how this competitive struggle may be resolved, using Figure 8.7 as a guide.

Suppose Seller I is rather quicker off the mark than Seller II and enters the market first. In the time period t_1 he can, by locating at *a*, serve the entire market and make sales of 40 hot dogs. When Seller II eventually enters, his

Figure 8.7
Competition and
locational change in the
two-seller situation.

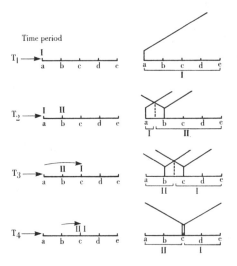

location decision is fundamentally influenced by the fact that Seller I is already in business. Seller II assumes that Seller I's location is fixed so that by locating at *b*, while Seller I is at *a*, Seller II gains a very considerable advantage. As Figure 8.7 shows, he captures the entire market between *b* and *e*, gaining a *net advantage* over Seller I of $30 (made up of the $30 of sales between *b* and *e* plus the $5 for the half of the market between *b* and *a* less the $5 sales which Seller I achieves). This is obviously a severe financial blow to Seller I, so he retaliates spatially by moving to location *c*. In time period t_3, therefore, the market is divided in such a way that Seller I has converted his net disadvantage of $30 to a net *advantage* of $10 ($25 − $15). This, of course, forces Seller II to reconsider his locational strategy. By relocating at *c*, immediately adjacent to Seller I, in fact, neither gains an advantage over the other but each gains exactly the same volume of sales. In the period t_4 Seller II supplies all the hot dog needs of the consumers between *a* and *c*, Seller I supplies all the customers between *c* and *e*.

We can summarize this competitive situation as a payoff matrix as in Table 8.7 in which the values represent the *net advantage* of one seller over the other. Note that although there are nine cells in which a zero appears, only one of these—the one corresponding to the situation where both sellers are located at *c*—represents a stable or equilibrium situation for the sellers.*

			(f.o.b. price per unit = $1) Locational strategies of Seller II				
		a	b	c	d	e	Row minima
	a	0	−30	−20	−10	0	−30
Locational	b	+30	0	−10	0	+10	−10
strategies of	c	+20	+10	0	+10	+20	0
Seller I	d	+10	0	−10	0	+30	−10
	e	0	−10	−20	−30	0	−30
Col. max.		+30	+10	0	+10	+30	

Table 8.7
A payoff matrix for the game-theory solution of the "two-seller" problem.†

†Plus signs represent payoffs to Seller I, whose strategies are listed in the left-hand column. Minus signs represent payoffs to Seller II, whose strategies are listed across the top of the table.
Source: B. H. Stevens (1961), An Application of Game Theory to a Problem in Location Strategy. *Papers and Proceedings, Regional Science Association* 7, Table 1. Reproduced by permission of the publisher.

If they both locate at *c*, neither can gain an advantage from moving elsewhere. The reverse is true of the other eight zero positions where it will always be advantageous for one of the sellers to relocate. Thus, if Seller I is at *b* and Seller II at *d*, neither gains a net advantage; however, if either one of them moved to *c*, he would immediately achieve a net advantage of $10. If both were located together at the extremes of the market (that is, both at *e* or both at *a*) a move by one seller to the next nearest location would produce a large net advantage but also an unstable situation, because the other seller would then retaliate by relocating. Clearly, then, the best position for both sellers, given potential retaliation from each, is for them to locate together at the center of the market.†

Games with saddle points. Although there are nine cells in Table 8.7 with zero values, indicating that neither seller has a net advantage with those locational combinations, there is only one position where the locational solution is stable; that is where both locate at *c*. By this we mean that neither player benefits by moving because the other can retaliate also by moving. This single position in the game is known as a *saddle point*; it is the strategy where the row minimum and column maximum coincide. Not all games have saddle points but in those which do the saddle point is the unique solution to the game which is best for both players.

Note

†This solution, while being optimal for the producers, is not the best solution in a welfare sense. The *total* cost to consumers would be minimized if one seller located at *b* and the other at *d*. This point allows us to emphasize once again that the basic viewpoint in this book is that of the producer.

Note

Game theory certainly helps us understand something of the complexity underlying decision-making, particularly because of its explicit focus upon uncertainty and upon attitudes toward uncertainty as key variables in the decision-making process. Despite its many simplifying assumptions, therefore, it has considerable value in providing insights into complex situations. It forms a kind of bridge between the behaviorally rigid assumptions of normative location theory and the more flexible approach of the behavioral viewpoint. Nevertheless, game theory takes us only so far. Although it incorporates uncertainty and attitudes it still assumes optimizing behavior. As Herbert Simon has pointed out, game theory is still *essentially* normative and presupposes that the decision-maker not only possesses a high level of information but also computational ability of a very high degree in order to set up a payoff matrix. Thus, there are two particularly important questions posed by game theory which merit further attention in our discussion:

1. The nature of the payoff values and the criteria employed for choosing between one payoff and another.
2. The way in which information is acquired to construct such a matrix of payoff values.

Both are very closely related to one another, although greater clarity is achieved by looking at each of them separately.

Payoff values and choice criteria

The kinds of location theory we have discussed are based, as we have seen, on the assumption that producers are motivated by profit. Thus we could conceive of the payoff values in the game-theory situations examined in this chapter as being levels of profit. But an increasing number of economists and business theorists take the view that pursuit of profit is only one of a number of objectives likely to determine business behavior. This is not the place to explore the controversial issue of business goals other than to observe that such objectives as sales volume, share of the market, size of assets, and so on, may be just as important, if not more so, than profit *per se*. Whichever of these constitutes the criterion on which payoffs are evaluated, it is most commonly assumed that such a preference scale is *transitive*. Put at its simplest, this means that if an individual prefers alternative A to alternative B and prefers alternative B to alternative C, then he will prefer A to C and not vice versa. The problem is, of course, that payoffs for a particular decision are likely to be multi-dimensional, so that A may be preferred to C according to one criterion but C may be preferred to A if another criterion is used. In other words, we should perhaps envisage a whole series of payoff matrices, each representing a separate kind of value. To arrive at a single value for such a multi-dimensional problem we must assume that each element can be expressed in the same units. Where the elements are financial, the problem is not very great, but some of the elements may not be readily measurable in monetary returns at all.

For example, many empirical studies of location decisions have found that so-called *personal factors* loom just as large as, if not larger than, the more clearly "economic" elements such as access to materials and labor, or proximity to markets. Table 8.8 gives a representative sample of such findings. At this stage we will simply note the existence of a personal category accounting for a large proportion of the responses; later in this chapter we will return to a more detailed interpretation of what such a category might mean. It is quite conceivable, then, for one course of action to be preferred in terms of one criterion and for a different course of action to be preferred if another criterion is used.

Table 8.8
Reasons given by manufacturers for choosing a location.

(i) *Manufacturers locating in New England*

Principal reason	All firms %	New firms %	Branch plants %	Plant relocations %
Personal reasons	31.4	69.0	3.8	26.1
Market advantages	23.7	16.6	20.7	43.5
Production relationships	16.1	2.4	34.0	—
Material availability	9.3	4.8	11.3	13.0
Management relationships	6.8	2.4	11.3	4.3
Labor considerations	5.1	4.8	3.8	8.7
Other considerations	7.6	—	15.1	4.3
Total	100.0	100.0	100.0	100.0

(ii) *Manufacturers locating at a particular site in Michigan**

Principal reasons	All Michigan %	No. of plants operated by firm 1 %	No. of plants operated by firm 2–4 %	No. of plants operated by firm 5 or more %
Personal reasons; chance	33	55	32	20
Opportunity—found good site, etc.	18	27	16	14
Proximity to customers; central loc'n.	15	16	15	14
Proximity to auto industry	13	7	14	12
Labor advantages	7	4	9	7
Proximity to materials	12	7	6	15
Local concessions and inducements; encouragement	4	2	4	7
Better tax situation	3	4	6	2
Area already established as a center for the industry	2	1	2	4

*Question asked was: "What were the main reasons that operations were set up here in (name of town)?"

Totals differ from 100% because some respondents mentioned more than one reason while for some others the reasons were not ascertained.

Sources: (i) calculated from data in Tiebout (1957), Table I. (ii) from Mueller & Morgan (1962), Table 2.

The crucial role of information

Our game-theory approach assumes that the producer faced with a decision can assemble sufficient information to complete his payoff matrix. However, a moment's reflection will reveal that this may often be an incredibly difficult task, particularly for the kind of simple business organization which is the focus of our attention in this chapter. Such an enterprise patently does not possess the omniscience of economic man. In the first place, all decision-makers, from the single individual to the highly complex large-scale organization, acquire information *selectively*. On the one hand, they neither acquire nor have access to, "complete" information (if such a commodity exists). On the other hand, they *interpret* the information to which they have access in terms of their own "coding" mechanism. As Katz and Kahn have pointed out, organizations (or open systems in general):

> can react only to those information signals to which they are attuned....
> They develop their own mechanisms for blocking out certain types of alien influence and for transforming what is received according to a series of code categories.
> *Katz and Kahn (1966), pp. 22, 60*

In the context of our earlier discussion of information diffusion (Chapter Two) individuals being made aware of an item of information do not necessarily *adopt* that information immediately. Several studies of innovation diffusion, for example, suggest that potential adopters must be subjected to the information a number of times to overcome resistance. Apart from familiarity, many other factors seem likely to influence levels of resistance to information adoption. Among the most important seem to be variables relating to the individual such as his age, social status, financial position, mental ability, "cosmopoliteness" (a person's breadth of values and experience), and the norms or standards of the groups or society to which he belongs.*

Thus all individuals are aware of only a limited part of what we might call the total *objective environment*. The part of which they are aware has been given various names. Some writers use the general psychological term *Behavioral Environment*, a number of geographers working in the field of behavior and cognition prefer the term *Action Space*, while many business organization writers use the label *Task Environment*. All three terms seem to be used more or less synonymously. The behavioral or task environment is the segment of the objective environment about which information signals are received and interpreted. Only a limited proportion of the information transmitted by the "objective" environment is effectively received, it is this that determines the nature of the individual's behavioral environment, and it is this, and only this, that is relevant to *purposive* behavior. Insofar as this is the only environment of which people are aware it is, for them, the *real* environment. Phenomena, places, or events outside the behavioral environment have no relevance to, and no influence on, conscious decision-making. For example, the existence of a potentially valuable

Note   *In terms of simulation models of diffusion, such differences in resistance to information adoption can be built in by weighting. Thus persons with low resistance (a high likelihood of adoption) would be weighted by higher probability values than those with high resistance. For example, the probability of accepting information from a person in the same social group may be greater than the probability of accepting information from somebody in a different social group. In this sense, resistance is simply another of the many *barriers* to the flow of information.

mineral resource or raw material is economically relevant only if it exists within the behavioral environment, that is, if it is *known* to exist and its potential value is appreciated. Within the behavioral environment we can identify an even more limited component—the individual's *activity space*—which refers to all those people, organizations, or places with which the individual is in direct, and regular (possibly day-to-day) contact. Figure 8.8 shows the nested relationships between these various "environments."

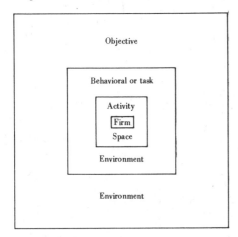

Figure 8.8
Nested relationships between environments.

Whatever terminology is used, it is clear that the precise form of the behavioral or task environment will vary from individual to individual, though there will almost certainly be a commonality of viewpoint for "similar" individuals. This is particularly true because

> the vast bulk of our knowledge of fact is not gained through direct perception but through the second-hand, third-hand, and nth-hand reports of the perceptions of others, transmitted through the channels of social communication. Since these perceptions have already been filtered by one or more communicators, most of whom have frames of reference similar to our own, the reports are generally consonant with the filtered reports of our own perceptions, and serve to reinforce the latter.
> *March and Simon (1958), p. 153*

In Figure 8.9 we indicate very approximately some of the variables which seem likely to account for both differences and similarities in behavioral environments. Individuals having one or more of the variables in common with other individuals will likely possess a similar *image* of the world.

We have seen already in Chapter Two and in our subsequent discussions that, for example, information is not available everywhere in the same quantity and quality but is spatially variable. We noted, particularly, the influence of distance as a frictional force in attenuating information flows and the critical role of the urban hierarchy in channeling information flows. Clearly, then, geographical location is, as Figure 8.9 suggests, an important variable in determining the form and extent of an individual's behavioral environment.

Figure 8.9
Elements in the
perception process: the
behavioral environment
and the "objective"
environment. [*Source:*
based in part on D. L.
Huff (1960), A
Topographical Model of
Consumer Space
Preferences, *Papers and
Proceedings, Regional
Science Association,* **6,**
Figure 3, by permission of
the Regional Science
Association.]

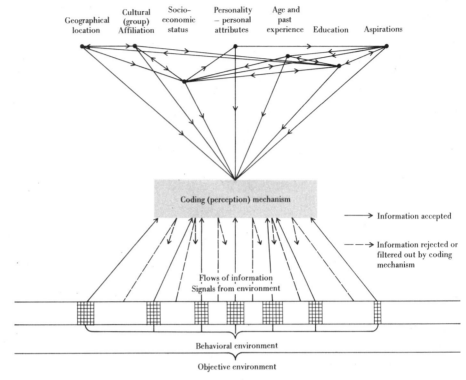

People sharing the same culture or belonging to the same group (both of which may or may not be geographically specific) are also likely to share a similar view of the world. In fact, the existence of groups is of profound importance in the flow of information because, in general, information flow *within* groups is greater than information flow *between* groups. Thus the *functional (or social) distance* separating individuals belonging to different groups may be very much greater than the physical distance separating them. Figure 8.10 shows five hypothetical situations illustrating the relationship between group membership and information flow. Situations A to E represent increasing difficulty of communication. Information flows most readily when both the possessor of an item of information and the seekers of such information belong to the same group (Situation A) and with greatest difficulty when each are members of different and mutually exclusive groups.

An ability to overcome the frictional effects of geographical space and to participate in a diversity of groups and associations will reduce the restrictive influence of both geographical location and of group limitations. Socio-economic status seems to be particularly important in this respect. Hägerstrand has commented on this in the following way:

> from daily experience we know that the links in the network of private communications must differ in spatial range between socio-economic groups .... Some individuals are wholly bound to the local plane, others operate on the regional and local planes, and still others operate more

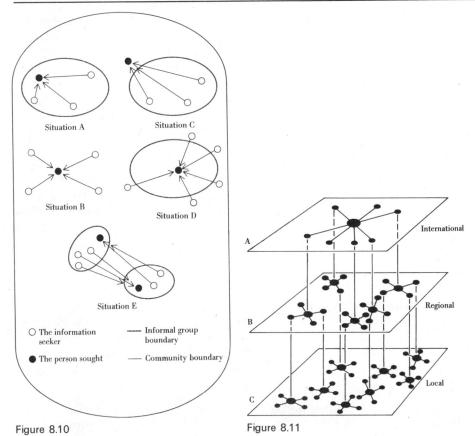

Figure 8.10

Figure 8.11

Figure 8.10
The effect of informal social groups on the flow of interpersonal communication. [*Source:* Reprinted by permission from H. F. Lionberger (1960), *Adoption of New Ideas and Practices,* Figure 5. Copyright © 1960 by The Iowa State University Press, Ames, Iowa.]

Figure 8.11
Diffusion of information between individuals at different geographical levels of interaction. [*Source:* T. Hägerstrand (1967), A Monte Carlo Simulation of Diffusion, Figure 3. Reprinted by permission from W. L. Garrison and D. F. Marble (eds.), *Quantitative Geography, Part I, Economic and Cultural Topics,* Northwestern University Studies in Geography, **13.**]

or less on all three. Those belonging to a wider range and at the same time having links in common with lower ones form the channels through which information disseminates among the planes.
Hägerstrand (1967), p. 8

Figure 8.11 shows three of these spatial ranges.

Simon's concept of bounded rationality

The kinds of problems which we have seen to arise out of our earlier game-theory approach to decision-making—the complexity of payoff values and the limited information on which to calculate such payoffs—are the ones which led Herbert Simon to conclude that the view of the decision-maker as a *globally rational* economic man is untenable. Instead, he suggested, decision-makers should be regarded as *boundedly rational* individuals. Not everybody would accept Simon's views in their entirety but they have been so influential in recent work on decision-making in general and on location decision-making in particular that they merit some attention here.

Simon's argument is based upon two premises. First, information is not a free good but has to be searched for within constraints of time and financial resources in particular. Second, decision-makers have a limited capacity to process such information as they can acquire. For these reasons, therefore, Simon asserts that optimal decisions are probably unattainable. Instead, he suggests that decision-makers are *satisficers**; that is, they make a choice between those payoffs they can identify on the simple criterion of whether they are satisfactory or unsatisfactory compared with some threshold or reference point. Psychologists generally use the term *aspiration level* to describe this but, although it is a valuable concept, it is extremely difficult to measure and such measurement is, in any case, probably outside the geographer's terms of reference. Not only is the aspiration level a composite of multiple variables related to age, personality, socio-economic status, attitude to risk, and so on, but also it is a dynamic phenomenon that, as psychologists have demonstrated, changes over time for a given individual. Aspirations, it is claimed, are expectations that tend to adjust in the long-run to realities—to the result that can be reasonably attained. For example, suppose a person wishes to sell his automobile and decides that he would be happy to get $1,000, and suppose that he does not advertise the price but simply asks for offers. Insofar as $1,000 represents his initial aspiration level, any offer at or above $1,000 would, therefore, be regarded as satisfactory and anything below as unsatisfactory. If, however, the seller is inundated with offers for his car above $1,000 he may try to raise his price (and his aspiration level) to, say, $1,250. On the other hand, if no offers are forthcoming, he may be forced to lower his price to $750. A fundamental influence, therefore, is the experience of the decision-maker: his expectation of success and his confidence in his ability to attain a given goal.

For our purposes, it is not necessary to accept every detail of Simon's theory. The most useful and relevant aspect for us is not the issue of satisficing but the view of decision-making as a *search process*. So let us take this view, first in the context of decision-making in general and, second, as a means of understanding specifically *spatial* decision-making.

A search-based model of decision-making

Decision-making of whatever kind is complex. However, we can simplify it into three basic stages (though an individual making a decision may not be aware of these):

Note

Satisficer concept. The concept of *satisficing* is, as David Harvey (1969) has pointed out, rather ambiguous. He observes that it can be interpreted in at least three different ways. First, it can be regarded as "a form of optimizing behavior in which the criteria used are non-economic"—that is, the decision-maker makes choices on the basis of "personal" considerations. Second, it can be seen as "optimizing behavior (of any kind) with respect to a number of pre-selected alternatives out of a much larger (sometimes infinite) set of alternatives." Third, it could be interpreted to imply that "the decision-maker does not seek *any* optimal solution. In this case, satisficing behavior means non-optimizing behavior." Neither the first nor the third seems to offer much of a basis for development; more promising is the second interpretation, the idea that decision-makers do the best they can on the basis of such information as they can acquire. This would seem to fit most closely Simon's own term: *bounded rationality*.

1. The perceived stimulus to make a decision and definition of the nature of the problem.
2. Search for a satisfactory solution.
3. Evaluation of the consequences of alternative courses of action and choice of solution.

In the case of a business enterprise, whether it is a farm or a manufacturing firm, interaction with its environment consists of both material (production resources and products) and information (Figure 8.12). The information is the basis upon which the enterprise monitors its performance in relation to its predefined goals and objectives, which we can now regard as representing the aspiration level or threshold of satisfactory performance. On the basis of our simple cybernetic model in Figure 8.1 we can envisage the firm as continuously adjusting its behavior to minor fluctuations in both its environment and its own internal structure. Indeed, there will rarely be a perfect balance or equilibrium between firm and environment; there will always be some degree of *stress* which we can define as

> any influence, whether it arises from the internal environment or the external environment, which interferes with the satisfaction of basic needs or which disturbs or threatens to disturb the...equilibrium.
> *Wolpert (1966), p. 93*

In the day-to-day affairs of any business, small stresses are constantly occurring, most of which are corrected by minor operational adjustments or even ignored. In terms of Figure 8.12, what we might call the *stress tolerance threshold* is not exceeded and there is no major change in behavior. But if the threshold is exceeded, if the imbalance between expectations and experience is greater than the firm is prepared to tolerate, then stage 2 of the decision-making process is initiated.

Most students of decision-making now agree that the search process generally displays certain fairly predictable features. Almost invariably when faced with a problem an individual will revert to past precedent, to solutions adopted for similar problems on previous occasions if they proved to be satisfactory. If such a solution can be found, then search may well cease. Where such a solution cannot be identified, either because a similar situation has not occurred before, or because the solution was deemed in retrospect to have been unsatisfactory, there are two commonly followed procedures. One is to adopt a random, trial-and-error, strategy; the other is to imitate the behavior of other decision-makers with similar problems. In this respect, the general characteristics of the information diffusion process are obviously extremely important.

But whatever strategies are employed, their duration and thoroughness are heavily constrained by the pressures to find a solution as quickly as possible—businessmen in particular are very fond of asserting that "time means money." Because of the time constraint, which is present to a greater or lesser extent in all decision-making, *the order in which the search process is carried out is very important.* As Simon and his followers have pointed out, few decision-makers are able to set out a whole string of possible alternative solutions side

Figure 8.12
A simplified model of the
decision-making process.

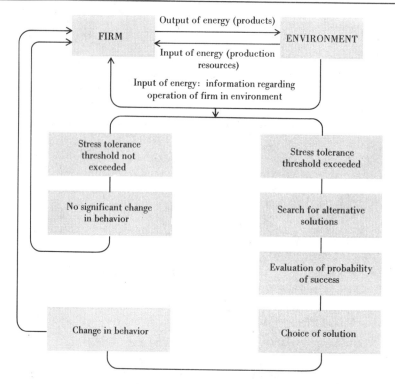

Figure 8.12
A simplified model of the
decision-making process.

by side in order to choose between them. More commonly, possible alternatives are encountered one or two at a time and this sequential form means that a choice may have to be made without knowing whether a better alternative may be found if the search is continued. If we return to the example of the person selling his car, the seller has to decide whether to accept an offer of $1,050 because it is the best he has received so far and meets his notional price, or whether to hold out in the hope of receiving a higher offer. In Simon's terminology, as soon as a *satisfactory* alternative is found it will be chosen and search will terminate. Very often, the ultimate criterion for choosing one alternative rather than another is whether or not it can be implemented easily rather than whether it is the best solution. The principle of least effort is, without doubt, a powerful influence on many forms of human behavior.

The search-based decision model of Figure 8.12, with its inherent circularity is, in fact, a simple *learning* model. A stimulus is identified, search for a response is carried out, an appropriate response is chosen which changes the system's behavior. As experience is accumulated regarding the outcomes of successive decisions then we can imagine the decision-maker improving his capacity to deal with similar problems. If a decision-maker is faced by the same problem on a large number of occasions, he will eventually adopt a routine or standard response which, once learned, will be employed whenever the same problem arises. A distinction can be made, therefore, between *habitual* or *programed* decisions on the one hand and *genuine* or *non-programed* decisions on the other.

The distinguishing characteristic between the two is the amount of previous experience available to the decision-maker; where this is small (i.e. where the problem is novel and unfamiliar), the decision will be genuine or non-programed and involve the kind of search procedure outlined above. Of course, these represent polar extremes; many decisions occupy the "gray area" in which there are both programed and non-programed elements.

Spatial behavior in an uncertain world

Our discussion in the preceding section has been deliberately general and not concerned specifically with "geographical" or "spatial" decisions. All decisions, of course, take place *in* space but not all decisions are regarded as being within the geographer's purview. For our present purposes, we are interested in those decisions made by *producers* of goods which have a significant impact on the economic landscape. In terms of this definition, the main spatial decisions of the farmer are, for example, whether to grow one crop or another; whether to adopt an innovation; whether to sell his output in one market rather than another. For the manufacturer significant spatial decisions are those concerning his selection of location(s) at which to manufacture his products, and those relating to his choice of suppliers and distributors. Most attention tends to be focused on locational choice, but it is worth emphasizing here that such decisions are a good deal more complex than has often been assumed. Geographers and other location analysts have, until recently, concentrated mainly on the actual initial choice of location or on the relocation of an activity, or, more rarely, on the choice of market area. But equally, if not more important, is the decision by a firm with more than one operating unit to expand production at one location and contract operations at another. This, and other decisions relating to such business behavior as mergers and take-overs, will be discussed in the next chapter. For the present, we retain our assumption that the firm (whether agricultural or manufacturing) is a *single location facility*.

Farming decisions as a learning process

As we have said, most human behavior is a *learning* process and spatial behavior is no exception. But the learning process is greatly facilitated in those decision-making situations which occur most frequently, and there is considerable variation in frequency for different types of spatial decision. Thus the farmer may be able to reconsider his product-mix each year, or every few years and can "grope" his way toward a land-use system which yields satisfactory returns (by whatever criteria these are measured). Very likely this will be by a combination of direct experience and experimentation and observation of the behavior of others in similar situations. Because of the kinds of spatial regularities in the diffusion of information which we have seen to exist, much of the local or regional uniformity in agricultural production (crop zones, crop regions, etc.) is almost certainly related to learned patterns of behavior which are found to be satisfactory in the prevailing environmental circumstances.

David Harvey (1967) has suggested that we can view this learning process either as a random, trial-and-error procedure, in which there is a strong imitative element, or as a situation in which certain alternatives are eliminated as they are found to be unsatisfactory on the basis of experience. Figure 8.13 illustrates the first of these situations in which a farmer begins from a position of complete ignorance and strives over a period of time to evolve a production system which is satisfactory to him by a completely random process. The violent swings in the path shown in Figure 8.13 are some indication of his mistakes in attempting to develop a production system which is above his aspiration level (the "minimum satisfaction" line). Figure 8.13 also suggests that the first successful searcher will likely be imitated by others also striving to achieve the same ends; hence the convergence of the three lines once the first searcher finds a satisfactory solution. Figure 8.14 shows the same situation, though in this case it is assumed that the farmer accumulates information about the environment over time; he learns to eliminate certain types of production system. As Harvey points out:

> the choice which any producer makes at any one point in time is thus a function of his knowledge at a preceding point in time.
> *Harvey* (1967), *p. 593*

Figure 8.13
The learning process based on random search. [*Source:* D. Harvey (1967), Models of the Evolution of Spatial Patterns in Human Geography, Figure 14.11A in R. J. Chorley & P. Haggett (eds.), *Models in Geography,* London: Methuen & Co.]

Figure 8.14
The learning process based on accumulated experience. [*Source:* D. Harvey (1967), Models of the Evolution of Spatial Patterns in Human Geography, Figure 14.11B in R. J. Chorley & P. Haggett (eds.), *Models in Geography,* London: Methuen & Co.]

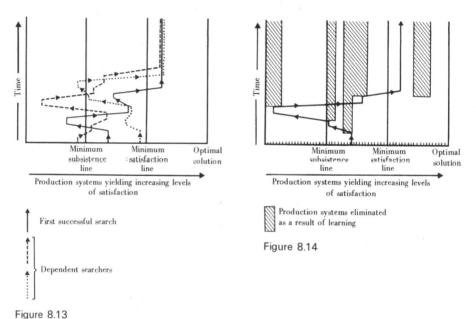

Figure 8.13

Figure 8.14

Of course farmers, or other decision-makers for that matter, rarely operate in isolation, but neither do they have access to complete information. As we have seen, information flows are spatially and socially differentiated. For these reasons, Harvey devised a "synoptic" model to show how the evolution of spatial patterns (e.g. the development of farming systems) can be viewed as both an individual and a group learning process (Figure 8.15).

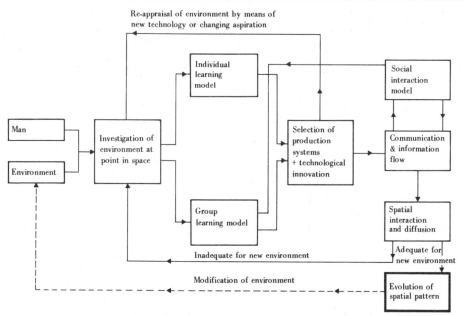

Figure 8.15
A synoptic model of individual and group learning in a spatial context. [*Source:* D. Harvey (1967), Models of the Evolution of Spatial Patterns in Human Geography, Figure 14.12 in R. J. Chorley & P. Haggett (eds.), *Models in Geography*, London: Methuen & Co.]

The location decisions of a simple manufacturing organization

Learning, as we have emphasized several times, is facilitated by frequency of experience. In the case of agricultural decisions, many are made on at least an annual basis. But this is not true of many other spatially significant decisions. For the manufacturer, and especially for the kind of simple manufacturing organization we are considering in this chapter, the *location* decision *per se* is a relatively infrequent occurrence. Only in comparatively rare circumstances is it undertaken sufficiently frequently for it to become a *routine* decision. Locationally, most manufacturers, particularly those operating on a modest scale, are highly conservative.

Leaving aside until the next chapter the location decisions of large multi-plant organizations, we can distinguish quite clearly between two sets of "locational circumstances": the initial location decision, taken when a manufacturer sets up in business for the very first time, and a subsequent occasion when, having already been operating at the initial location, there arises a need to consider a new location. The basic framework for our discussion of the location decision process is Figure 8.16 which, in effect, elaborates in an explicitly spatial context the simple decision-making model we have already examined. But diagrams like this are very formal-looking devices; to make the discussion rather more digestible let us try to construct the possible experiences of an imaginary small manufacturer of garments.* The numbers in the margin correspond to the numbered boxes in Figure 8.16.

---

*We take the garment manufacturer to be a typical example of the small manufacturing organization, and one which is especially well known to one of the authors. Although some aspects of the behavior of garment firms are specific to that particular industry, for the most part

Note

Note continued	the problems faced and solutions adopted are common to many different kinds of small single-plant manufacturing enterprises. For a detailed analysis of research into manufacturing location decisions at the level of individual enterprises the reader should consult such studies as Cameron and Clark (1966), Keeble (1968), Mueller and Morgan (1962), North (1974), Townroe (1969, 1971, 1972).

The initial location decision

**(1)
Initial entry into
the industry**

Most businesses start small and with pedestrian objectives. Their purpose is to do something similar to what is already being done, and their prospects depend on an expanding demand for their product or on their ability to take some of the custom away from existing firms.... Most new businesses are imitators not innovators.... New firms generally begin by doing the same sort of things as old ones because their founders have gained their experience in existing businesses.
Edwards and Townsend (1958), pp. 4, 6

The hero of our story, Morris Needler, fitted this description very well. He had been in the garment industry for most of his working life, mainly as a cutter with several firms in the same large city and had eventually risen to the position of factory manager with a prominent garment company. But he was an ambitious individual who was impatient with the constraints imposed by the organization which employed him, and he felt that he could achieve greater satisfaction (and more money) by setting up in business on his own account. He did not consider anything other than garment manufacture—it was the industry he knew best both technically and in terms of the many contacts he had with both suppliers and customers. Perhaps as important, relatively little capital and labor is needed to set up a garment business: space requirements are modest in both scale and specification, and machinery can be rented or bought second-hand, especially in an established center of the industry.

**(9)
Locational
requirements**

**(10–12, 14)
Locational search**

Not only did Morris stay in the *same type of production* as he had worked in but he also remained in the *same geographical locality*. Again he never even considered looking outside the city in which he was already established.* In terms of Figure 8.16, Morris Needler's search process for his first factory loca-

(14)

Note	*The sentiments of one of Mueller and Morgan's Michigan manufacturers are an apt reflection of this view: "It's my home, I've never gone anywhere, I was trained here, my contacts are here, where else would I go?" *Mueller and Morgan (1962), p. 209* All the evidence points to the fact that genuinely new businesses (i.e. those not associated with existing firms or formed by merger) locate *initially* in the locality where the founder is already established. Commenting on newly established businesses in the British plastics industry, David North (1974) writes: firms created by new entrepreneurs ... invariably located in the areas where their founders previously lived and worked .... A familiar environment and long-standing contacts were considered to be crucial to the initial success of a new firm, so the possibility of opening a factory in another region was rarely considered. New firms were therefore created from and located near established firms, thereby supporting the concept of "seed-bed growth." *North (1974), pp. 239–240*

These are the kinds of consideration which most readily explain the prevalence of the so-called "personal reasons" shown in Table 8.8 and referred to earlier. It is significant that personal reasons are most important for new firms (69% of all responses in the New England example) and for single-plant firms where entrepreneurs were asked why they located in a specific town (55%).

Note continued

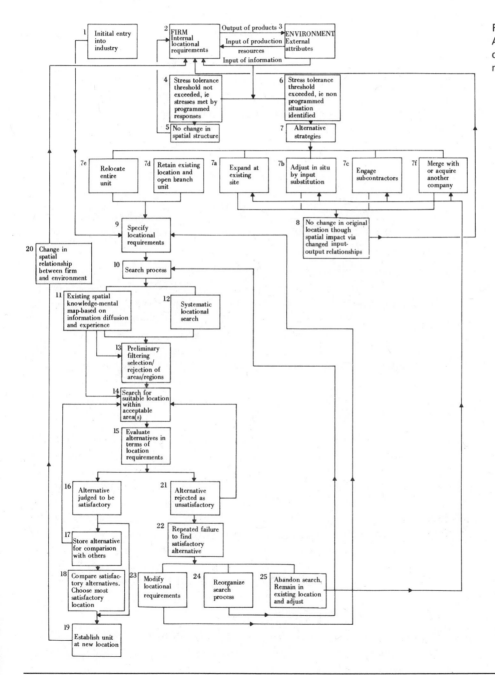

Figure 8.16
A model of the location decision process of a manufacturer.

tion was immediately narrowed down to a search for a suitable site *within* the city with which he was already associated. Here again, the process was basically very simple. His initial production was to work as a subcontractor for several established garment manufacturers. They supplied the design and the material, Needler Ltd. performed the cutting and making up. This kind of work required quick and easy contact with the contracting firms so this was one force which pulled Morris towards that part of the inner city where most garment manufacturers were already concentrated and focused his search there. This area had the added advantage of being not only the part of the city he already knew best, but also the area where there was generally a pool of small, often upper-storey or loft, premises which could be rented relatively cheaply on short-term leases. But how did he seek out particular premises to see if they were suitable? He used the most common methods of all in such circumstances: he walked or drove around the pre-selected area looking for vacancy signs; he scanned the advertisement columns of the city newspaper; he sought out estate agents; he asked his contacts if they knew of any suitable premises. In this context, one of Logan's findings regarding the locational behavior of firms in Sydney, Australia, is relevant. He concluded that:

> personal contacts and local knowledge were more important than advice given by real estate agents or by government departments.
> *Logan (1966), p. 46*

(15–19)
Evaluation
and choice

(17)

For a new entrepreneur like Morris Needler evaluation of alternative sites is likely to be as simplistic as search. In both cases he lacks previous experience and has few criteria on which to base his decision. Given that the general area has been, in a sense, self-selecting, his ultimate location decision boils down to the suitability and relative cost of premises. If he is in no hurry to begin production he may try to "store" several possible premises and then judge between them; more likely he will choose the first premises he can find at the "right price."

Subsequent location decisions

Having started producing garments in the rather small, third-floor premises of a building occupied by a number of other similar small-scale manufacturers, Morris Needler rarely pauses to consider whether he might have found better premises if he had searched for a longer period of time. All his energies are devoted to "keeping his head above water"—meeting production schedules, solving the day-to-day problems of his small workforce, and attempting to develop his business beyond the confines of the original subcontracting operations. As long as no major stresses occur to upset the general balance between his firm and the environment in which he has to operate, the question of an alternative location simply does not occur to Morris Needler.

The stimulus for a location decision

But, of course, neither part of the equation—the firm itself and its environment—remain fixed and unchanging. Stresses may arise in either one which are sufficiently strong as to exceed Needler's stress tolerance threshold. (In other words, problems may occur which cannot be solved by programed or routine responses but which require *genuine* decisions.) Figure 8.17 summarizes the major elements which seem most likely to produce locational stress for the small firm.* Let us take the *internal* forces first of all. If Needler Ltd. is successful and increases the scale of its operations it is likely sooner or later to outgrow its existing premises. Future growth will therefore require some solution to this problem. Alternatively, Needler's location in the inner area of the city in multi-purpose premises, possibly closely juxtaposed with other commercial and perhaps even residential functions, may make it particularly vulnerable to one or more of the *external* stresses shown in Figure 8.17.

**(6)
Stress tolerance
threshold exceeded**

There is every likelihood, for example, that Needler's original lease was a short-term lease and it may be either impossible to renew it or the rent associated with a new lease may be excessive. If Needler's factory is located in an area of city redevelopment then he may be served with a compulsory purchase order preceding demolition. Alternatively, this process of city redevelopment which has so drastically altered the inner areas of most cities in Britain and elsewhere may leave the Needler factory intact but, by rehousing local residents at a considerable distance, drastically reduce Needler's labor supply. As a garment manufacturer, Needler is especially sensitive to labor considerations. Not only is garment manufacturing a labor-intensive industry, but also it uses predominantly female labor which, because of domestic commitments, tends to dislike long-distance commuting. If, on the other hand, he is located in a part of the country where industrial expansion is inhibited by government policy (as in the southeast and other prosperous parts of England where expansions of more than a certain size must obtain a government Industrial Development Certificate), then this may be the dominant stress factor.

Assuming, then, that Needler is faced with one or more of these stresses, what alternative locational strategies might the firm pursue? To some extent, the answer to this question depends upon the nature of the stress itself. Clearly, the termination of a lease or the demolition of premises immediately precludes any strategy which involves remaining at the existing site. Apart from such unequivocal circumstances, however, Needler may be able to choose between the six alternatives shown in Figure 8.16 (the letters roughly indicate the *relative* likelihood of each strategy being adopted on the basis of what we know in general about locational choice).

**(7)
Alternative locational
strategies**

Without much doubt Needler, like most other firms, would prefer to remain where he is and expand *in situ*, either by building an extension or by acquiring

(7a)

---

*Detailed empirical studies of actual location decisions carried out by Cameron and Clark (1966), Keeble (1968), and Townroe (1971) provide us with some indication of the relative importance of the stresses shown in Figure 8.17. In particular, all three studies indicate that expansion of output by the sample firms was the primary internal factor in the majority of cases. Thus 73 percent of Townroe's sample of 59 companies, 88 percent of Cameron and Clark's sample of 68 companies, and 85 percent of Keeble's sample of 266 firms were primarily stimulated to make a location decision by internal expansion. In most cases, of course, other factors were involved. In some instances, for example, as Figure 8.17 suggests, expansion was associated with new products and/or processes.

Note

Figure 8.17
Forces stimulating the
decision to seek a
secondary location.

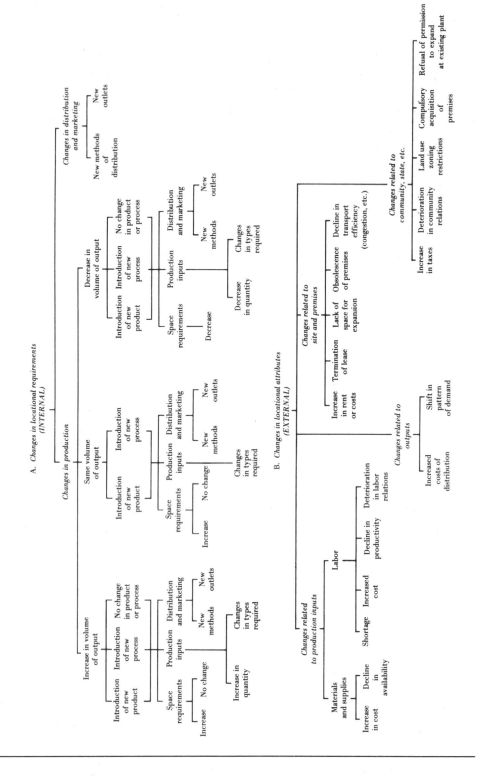

additional space within the same building. If this is impossible, then he may try to adjust by investing in more efficient plant and machinery in order to get more output from his existing space, though because of the particular technical-demand characteristics of garment manufacture this may be quite difficult to achieve. More likely he will employ another producer on a subcontract basis, especially if there are periodic fluctuations in the demand for his goods, thus reversing his own original role when he first set up in business. A more extreme, though related, strategy is to acquire, or merge with, another producer who possibly has spare capacity, but a small manufacturer like Needler is perhaps more likely to offer himself for acquisition to a larger established firm. We shall have a good deal more to say about merger and acquisition in the next chapter; it is sufficient at this stage to note its existence as a possible strategy. **(7b)** **(7c)** **(7f)**

If none of these strategies is possible, or if they are regarded as undesirable, Needler has two other possible ways of solving his problem—these are the ones to which geographers have paid most attention because they represent more obvious *location* decisions. One is to retain the existing location, where this is possible, and to open a *branch* plant elsewhere. In this way it may be possible to gain the extra capacity needed or to tap an alternative source of labor if that happens to be an important stress factor. (Though not usually relevant to garment manufacturers like Needler, it may also be a means of increasing penetration of a spatially dispersed market.) The other strategy is to *relocate* the entire unit*, a measure which Needler will not undertake lightly for a number of reasons. **(7d)** **(7e)**

The basic point about the implementation of these alternative locational strategies is that they clearly reflect a very strong reluctance by manufacturers to abandon their existing production site unless such abandonment is made inevitable by external stresses. There are three major reasons for such locational conservatism. The first is the phenomenon which forms part of the title of this chapter: *uncertainty*. If nothing else, an existing location offers a degree of security in that its attributes are known, whereas those of other locations are not, except indirectly through the reported or observed experiences of others. A second, related, factor is the fact that a firm often builds up strong local identity, allegiances and connections which it is reluctant to surrender unless absolutely necessary. In particular, reliance on local sources of finance—relationships with the friendly neighborhood bank manager—are especially important

---

**Branch locations and relocations.* Most studies seem to indicate that branch location decisions are far more common than relocations. For example, a large-scale study of industrial movement in the United Kingdom between 1945 and 1965 (Board of Trade, 1968) revealed that of the 3,014 recorded moves *between* regions, 1,913 (63.5 percent) were branches and 1,101 (36.5 percent) were relocations (transfers). This study also found that transfers tended to be smaller, in terms of employment, than branches. Both Keeble (1968) and North (1974) provide evidence from their studies which corroborate such a view. They also find that relocations tend to be more characteristic of younger, smaller firms, while branches tend to be established by older, rather larger enterprises. One possible reason for such a distinction is that a newly established firm's first location often allows little space for subsequent growth and that larger premises are required at a stage in the firm's development when it cannot even consider operating at more than one location. After a relatively early relocation, therefore, subsequent expansion is more likely to be achieved by opening a branch factory.

Note

for small firms which do not have access to the wider capital sources (see Chapter Six). In some cases, the desire to preserve a particular local identity reflects a desire to retain the element of prestige that certain locations are perceived to offer. This is particularly true of areas that have established a high reputation for a particular product and of the major metropolitan centers such as New York or London. Third, and perhaps most important, locational inertia is encouraged by the sheer cost and disruption of movement (it is not, after all, as easy and instantaneous as our location theory would suggest, particularly for small firms).* Inherent in each of these considerations is the basic attitude towards risk-taking which we examined in a game-theory context earlier in this chapter. Apart from the essentially personal characteristic of a "gambling instinct," much of the research into attitudes towards risk suggests that an important determinant is the size and strength of the firm. The larger and more economically healthy the economic unit the more likely, other things being equal, is a positive attitude towards location decisions. Other variables associated with a willingness to consider change are the age of the decision-maker, income, amount of working capital, and so on.

The search process

Assuming that Needler Ltd. has decided to either relocate or to open a branch plant, the first stage in the search for a suitable location involves the entrepreneur in specifying what *kind* of location he wants. Ideally, the basis of this assessment should be a thorough knowledge of the relative importance of those factors that are spatially variable and of the prevailing cost structures and marketing methods of the firm. In fact, like many small businessmen, Morris Needler

**(9)
Locational
requirements**

Note

Cost of industrial movement. Two examples can be used to illustrate the costs of movement. Logan (1966) writes of a pharmaceutical products manufacturer considering relocating at the periphery of the Sydney metropolitan area:

> total capital costs for land and air conditioned factory space of 182,000 square feet was almost £1 million. Against this the improved capital value (a fairly reliable indicator of market value) for the existing premises was £540,000. A well-known removalist firm quoted a cost of £37,000 to dismantle and move equipment and stock from the old factory to the proposed new site. The firm estimated, however, that it could achieve savings of £31,800 in its operating expenses through relocating mainly by the installation of automatic equipment and a reduction in labor. But additional selling costs from the periphery would amount to an additional £37,280. The interest on capital borrowed to finance the entire undertaking had to be included as an additional expense. At a rate of six percent per annum this amounted to an additional £25,500. In the light of these additional costs, the management decided to remain at its present site.
> *Logan (1966), p. 463*

In similar vein, though in the specific context of very small firms in northwest London, Keeble comments that

> the area's smallest firms . . . have been far less mobile than larger concerns . . . Indeed, it is not really surprising. Small firms generally lack the capital necessary to tide them over the considerable dislocation of production, and extra cost, caused by a complete move . . . A loss of £60,000 worth of production was reported by one firm which moved only 17.5 km (11 miles) from its former factory.
> *Keeble (1968), p. 21*

has only a vague idea of his *precise* locational requirements. Most of all he is concerned with the problem of labor, in particular with finding a location which is accessible to a sufficiently large supply of female labor. He is also very aware of variations in the cost and availability of premises, though this largely reflects the fact that information on rent, taxes and so on is very easily obtained, whereas information on other locational variables is not. If he were asked to summarize his locational requirements, therefore, he would probably say: "Cheap premises close to a large housing estate with a lot of female labor."

The problem is, of course, that he has very little previous experience on which to draw, having made only one previous location decision, so his search process **(10)** tends to be unstructured and heavily biased. The bias comes about in two ways. First, Morris Needler, like the rest of us, operates within a limited behavioral environment (refer back to p. 316) which, as we have seen, is strongly influenced by his position in both geographical and social space. In beginning his search for a factory site, therefore, he already possesses a store of spatial knowledge; he has a *mental map* which represents not only what he *knows* **(11)** about places but also how he *feels* about the places he knows about. Some of these places he knows from direct experience, particularly those close to where he lives or works or those places he visits either for business or pleasure. His knowledge about other parts of his mental map, however, is based upon more tenuous connections—information and impressions gleaned from friends and acquaintances and from the mass media. Nevertheless, these all contribute toward the "world inside his head" and help to influence the search process.

Unfortunately, almost all the investigations by geographers and others into the form of mental maps of an evaluative kind have been confined to restricted segments of the population (mostly students) and to a particular kind of evaluation (the suitability of areas as places to live).* None so far refers to the mental maps of manufacturers, though Newby (1971) was able to show that manufacturers' attitudes to the business environment of southwest England were greatly influenced by the publicity created by the local authorities aiming to attract new industrial investment. Manufacturers clearly do have preferences for some locations and prejudices against others, opinions which in most cases are based not upon a systematic and "objective" evaluation of the relative merits of places but upon a hotch-potch of impressions. Whether or not such subjective assessments are "true" in any absolute sense is not the point; it is enough that places are *believed* to vary in their locational qualities.

Mental maps. Detailed discussion of such investigations is beyond the scope of this book. The pioneer work was that of Gould (1966) who established a pattern of research which has been widely followed. Gould and White (1974) provide an excellent elementary survey of such work while recent research is reviewed in Downs and Stea (1973). Figure 8.18 shows two examples drawn from Gould's original study: the perceptual maps of Californian and Alabaman students.

Figure 8.18a depicts the mental map of the United States held by students living in California. The strong preference of Californians for their home state in particular and the west coast in general is shown by the ridge of high desirability running north to south. Desirability declines eastward, but at about the 95th meridian the trend of the contours changes noticeably

Note

Note continued

and the California students begin to distinguish very clearly between the Midwest and North-east on the one hand and the South on the other. The South in fact marks the lowest "perceptual trough" on the Californian surface. The Northeast, with its historic connotations of the birth of the nation, is highly regarded by California students.

The Californian surface was found to be very similar to that of students in Minnesota and Pennsylvania, apart from a shift in the local peaks of desirability. A totally different mental map of the United States, however, is held by students living in Alabama, as Figure 8.18b shows. In particular, whereas students of other states perceived the South as a whole as a generally undesirable area, southern students discriminated carefully between individual southern states. In particular, Mississippi is rated as one of the least desirable states.

Figure 8.18
Mental maps of the
United States.
(a) Students living in
California. (b) Students
living in Alabama.
[*Source:* P. R. Gould
(1966), On Mental Maps,
*Michigan Inter-University
Community of
Mathematical
Geographers,* **9,** Figures 2
and 5. Reproduced by
permission of the editor.]

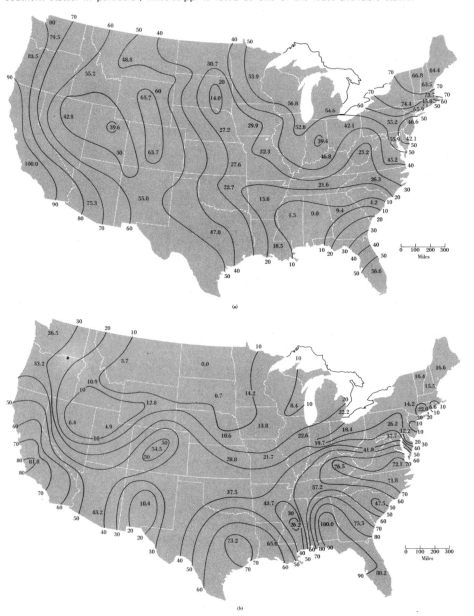

Note continued

Two generalizations can be made from these maps. First, the point of perception is invariably rated very highly regardless of the opinions of others (compare the desirability of Alabama in Figures 8.18a and 8.18b). This creates a local dome of desirability that tends to distort the area immediately around the point of perception. Second, there is a tendency for people to discriminate carefully between states and counties close to their own location even though these may be lumped together by people located elsewhere. The perceptual surface therefore seems to be composed of two elements: a general surface and a highly peaked dome representing a local effect. The importance of the local effect seems to vary considerably from one location to another.

Thus the form of Mr. Needler's mental map is very important in influencing his search for a factory site; it inserts a bias which acts as a *spatial filter*. Certain areas are likely to be excluded immediately from consideration regardless of their *actual* suitability. In many cases a preconceived idea of the suitability of an area or a few areas is formed and search for a specific site concentrated there. Little attempt may be made to increase the level of spatial knowledge through systematic search. In terms of Figure 8.16, Mr. Needler may proceed directly from Stage 11 to Stage 14. Indeed, it seems likely that many manufacturers do just that. **(12)**

(11–14)

Where systematic search does occur it is likely to rely heavily on the kinds of information disseminated by the public agencies and institutions listed in Table 8.9. These, like other information sources, are not equally available everywhere but tend to be most prevalent in major urban centers. **(12)**

The second source of bias in the search process (which is not unrelated to the question of existing spatial knowledge) arises because a distance constraint is often imposed right at the beginning. Indeed, it can often be regarded as one of the basic locational requirements themselves. Because of the basic uncertainty involved in changing locations, firms like Needler often prefer to move only a very short distance. Not only does this simplify the search process because the businessman is aware of far more potentially suitable alternative sites at such short distances; it also increases the likelihood of preserving existing links with suppliers and customers and of preserving the labor supply. For Needler this latter point is especially important because, as we noted earlier, female (especially married female) workers are reluctant to travel very far. If Needler is concerned to establish a branch plant rather than to transfer operations completely, he may be less concerned about distance, though he will have to consider the problems of supervision and communication between the two plants.*

Note

*The studies of branch and transfer decisions referred to on p. 331 corroborate these statements regarding distance and locational choice. In general complete transfers take place over much shorter distances than branch plants. Writing of locational change in the British plastics industry, North noted that

> for all but four of the firms that relocated a factory, the search for a suitable location was confined to the region of their existing factories . . . very small, privately-owned firms, usually concerned with trade conversion, confined their search to a radius of no more than ten miles about their present factory. Normally, the search was unsystematic, discontinuous and made without specified objectives or requirements for the new

Table 8.9
Provision of locational information by public sources.

Source	Type of information							
	General community information[a]	Prevailing economic structure (competition)	Market growth potential	Labor characteristics and costs	Transportation freight rates, schedules	Energy and power supplies and costs	Taxes, local and state	Housing
Federal/national Govt. agencies, departments		1		1		1	1	
State/local development agencies	1							
Municipal officials	1	1	1	1	1	1	1	1
Banks	1		1					1
Chambers of commerce	1		1	1	1	1	1	
Agricultural/industrial/ commercial associations	1	1		1				
Unions				1				
Real estate firms	1							
Local newspapers	1							1
Specialized journals	1	1	1	1	1	1	1	
Transportation agencies					1	1		
Utilities	1					1		

[a]Includes general amenities, educational facilities, community attitudes, political climate.

Source: Compiled from information in M. C. Neuhoff (1953), *Techniques of Plant Location*, Washington, D.C.: U.S. G.P.O.; H. F. Lionberger (1960), *Adoption of New Ideas and Practices*, Ames: Iowa State University Press; J. H. Thompson (1961), *Methods of Plant Site Selection Available to Small Manufacturing Firms*, Morgantown: West Virginia University Press; E. Mueller, A. Wilken, and M. Wood (1961), *Location Decisions and Industry Mobility in Michigan, 1961*, Ann Arbor: Institute for Social Research, University of Michigan.

location. Dominating the search was the constraint of retaining most of the existing
workers since it often took a small firm several years to build up a loyal labour force:
the loss of key workers could be disastrous to the firm's development. The avoidance
of moving executives' homes and familiarity with the local business environment were
added inducements for a short-distance transfer.
North (1974), p. 233

Note continued

Evaluation and choice

(15–19)

Thus for both conscious, and possibly subconscious, reasons, Needler's search
for a suitable factory location is both biased and limited in scope. Search, other
than of a simple and rudimentary nature, is costly in terms of both time and
money. As we observed in our discussion of decision-making in general, alternatives are likely to be discovered sequentially and must be evaluated as and
when they arise or, at best, in groups of two or three. A choice may, in fact,
be made of the very first location which seems to meet Needler's requirements
and no further search undertaken.* On the other hand, the satisfactory alternative may be "stored" and search continued until a number of satisfactory alternatives can be compared and the most satisfactory alternative chosen. Similarly,
if an alternative is rejected as unsatisfactory, search is continued until a satisfactory location is found.

(16–19)
(17)

(14–16)
(18)
(21)

It is quite conceivable, however, that prolonged search may not yield a location
that meets the decision-maker's aspiration level, either because he has set exces-
sively high locational requirements or because his search methods have been
inefficient. Repeated failure to find a satisfactory location, therefore, may stimulate the decision-maker to modify his locational requirements, reorganize his
search process, or alter both of these simultaneously. If a satisfactory alternative
is still not discovered, the entire search may be abandoned and an attempt
made to remain in the existing location and adjust the locational requirements.
This latter course of action cannot be followed, of course, if the existing premises
must be vacated.

(22)

(23)
(24)

(25)

The search process may be prolonged, therefore, either to produce a number
of satisfactory alternatives that may be evaluated simultaneously or because
search has failed to produce a satisfactory alternative. In practical terms, however, search cannot proceed indefinitely. Not only is the search for alternative
locations an expensive process in terms of both cost and time, but also there
is generally a strong motivation to get the new unit into operation as quickly
as possible. The strength of these two forces therefore largely determines the
duration and scope of the search process.

Whatever the locational criteria and however prolonged the search, one thing
is abundantly clear: Morris Needler, like most other small manufacturers, is
anxious to reduce the level of uncertainty inherent in location decisions. This
is shown in his unwillingness to consider locations very far from his existing

---

*Townroe (1971) found that 40 of his sample of 59 companies (68 percent) took the first
satisfactory solution and 17 of this 40 (42 percent) chose that location which was the "first
possible answer for their particular situation."

Note

location because, in this way, he is in effect repeating, as far as circumstances allow, his previous locational behavior or (the next best thing) locating in an area of considerable familiarity. Circumstances may arise, however, where neither of these strategies is possible and a move to a less familiar location is inevitable. How can Needler Ltd. minimize its uncertainty in such a situation? One particularly common way is to follow the lead of others, to imitate the locational behavior of other manufacturers. Such behavior is a common feature of migration in general. Hägerstrand observed some years ago that:

> in emigration it is obviously a very important fact that one emigrant, in selecting a destination, is dependent on earlier emigrants...once they have arisen, irregularities in the shape of migration fields have a tendency to perpetuate themselves because migrations at any one time are dependent on preceding migrations...we have to regard a present-day migration field as a result of a feedback process.
> *Hägerstrand (1957), pp. 127, 130, 131*

Hägerstrand goes on to distinguish between two kinds of migrant. *Active* migrants depend less on the locational experience of others and are more prepared to locate in "new" or more distant places. *Passive* migrants, as the term suggests, are essentially cautious and imitative, reducing locational uncertainty by locating in or around existing clusters. Such clustering may be based either on direct communication between successive "generations" of migrants or merely on observation of their apparent success. In either case it is quite clear that the spatial pattern of information flows and the position of a migrant (whether an individual or a manufacturing firm) within such communications networks is fundamentally important. But even the choice of location by active individuals or locational innovators is not without bias. The spatial biases in information flows and the nature of pre-existing space preferences restricts locational choice. The fact that information flows are greatest in and between major urban centers means that these centers are likely to be most prominent in the individual's mental map. Thus agglomeration is as much a behavioral as a strictly economic phenomenon, heavily dependent upon the nature of information flows in space and the imperfections of the decision-making process.

The fact that businessmen possess neither the ability nor the information to act as perfectly rational economic men adds a great deal more complexity to the analysis of economic activities in space. As yet we know very little about the spatial nature of information flows, the form of mental maps, and even less about the process of locational choice itself. As in many other branches of the subject, the geographer may be on the threshold of exciting and important discoveries. One of the many challenges facing the geographer today, therefore, is to build a healthy body of location theory based on sound behavioral principles because, in the final analysis, the economic landscape is the cumulative expression of decisions made at different points in time and under a variety of conditions. But the decisions which affect the overall spatial pattern of economic activity are not only location decisions *per se* (that is, the choice of a specific production site). Many spatially significant decisions—for example those involved in business decisions in general (selection of growth strategies, product mixes and so on)—are not obviously locational in themselves though they may well have very important locational and spatial repercussions. However, increasingly the most important decisions are being made not by individuals acting as individuals or by small single-plant, single-product firms but by very large, highly complex *organizations*. The final piece in our spatial jigsaw, therefore, involves us in an examination of the spatial behavior of large business organizations.

Further reading

Daly, M. T. (1972), *Techniques and Concepts in Geography*, Melbourne: Nelson, Chapter 4.

Found, W. C. (1971), *A Theoretical Approach to Rural Land Use Patterns*, London: Edward Arnold, Chapter 6.

Gould, P. R., and R. R. White (1974), *Mental Maps*, London: Penguin.

Hägerstrand, T. (1966), Aspects of the Spatial Structure of Social Communication and the Diffusion of Information, *Papers and Proceedings, Regional Science Association*, **16**, 27–42.

Harvey, D. W. (1967), Models of the evolution of spatial patterns in human geography, in R. J. Chorley and P. Haggett (eds.), *Models in Geography*, London: Methuen, New York: Barnes & Noble, pp. 549–608.

Kirk, W. (1963), Problems of Geography, *Geography*, **48**, 357–371.

Mueller, E., and J. N. Morgan (1962), Location Decisions of Manufacturers, *American Economic Review, Papers and Proceedings*, **502**, 204–217.

Pred, A. (1967a), Behavior and Location, Part I, *Lund Studies in Geography, Series B*, **27**.

Simon, H. A. (1952), A Behavioral Model of Rational Choice, *Quarterly Journal of Economics*, **69**, 99–118.

Stevens, B. H. (1961), An Application of Game Theory to a Problem in Location Strategy, *Papers and Proceedings, Regional Science Association*, **7**, 143–157.

Townroe, P. M. (1971), *Industrial Location Decisions*, Centre for Urban and Regional Studies, Birmingham, Occasional Paper 15.

Wolpert, J. (1964), The Decision Process in Spatial Context, *Annals of the Association of American Geographers*, **54**, 537–558.

Wolpert, J. (1965), Behavioral Aspects of the Decision to Migrate, *Papers and Proceedings, Regional Science Association*, **15**, 159–172.

Wolpert, J. (1966), Migration as an Adjustment to Environmental Stress, *Journal of Social Issues*, **22**, 92–102.

CHAPTER 9

SPATIAL BEHAVIOR OF MULTI-PLANT BUSINESS ENTERPRISES

Throughout our discussion so far we have deliberately glossed over the complexities of modern business organizations. Although we have shown that *organization* in itself is a key variable in the way productive resources are combined and used (Chapter Six) and that by increasing the *scale* of production savings in costs can be achieved (Chapter Seven), we have all the time retained the assumption that the firms inhabiting our economic landscape are extremely simple organizations. We have been concerned with "small business" which

> means, typically, an identity of management and ownership, an absence of specialized staff for separate functions and of facilities designed specifically for research and analysis, inability to finance itself by floating securities or to secure its funds through sources such as investment bankers, personal relationship between owners and employees and customers, the affiliation of the firm with a local community, and chief dependence for its market on the local area. These factors, when present in combination, make a small business recognizable as such, even when its volume of business is substantial.
> *Kaplan (1948), p. 37*

More explicitly, we have regarded each firm as being located at a single point in space, producing a single product. But although the small single-plant enterprise is still the most common type of firm in the sense that there are still very many thousands of them operating even in the highly sophisticated North American and western European economies (for example, in the United States more than 80 percent of all manufacturing establishments employ fewer than 100 workers), they are no longer the most important type of enterprise. Measured in terms of employment or financial resources, purchases of materials or sales of products, they are relatively insignificant compared with the comparatively small number of very large, very powerful business corporations.* These are the enterprises making the decisions which have a far greater impact on the spatial organization of economic activities (and hence on the everyday lives of people) than the decisions of the far larger number of very small enterprises. Thus any analysis of how economic activities come to be arranged on the earth's surface must take account of this. In the present chapter we organize our discussion around four main elements. First, we look at the changing balance between large and small firms in order to set the scene. Second, we examine *why* the large firm has increased so much in importance; this allows us to return to the subject of *economies of scale* (discussed in Chapter Seven) but in a broader context. Our third section deals with *how* business organizations develop and grow because it is in such processes that changes in *spatial* organization occur. Location decisions *per se* are neither isolated events nor the only kinds of decision which are spatially significant. Most of the important decisions which

Note   *In making this kind of statement we are not adopting a value judgement on whether large or small organizations are preferable. There is, of course, a considerable debate concerning the economic, social, and political costs and benefits of "bigness" or "smallness." Some would argue that "big is best," others that "small is beautiful"; all would agree, however, that in fact the very large business enterprise has come to dominate modern industrial economies.

concern us as geographers, in fact, arise out of the general strategic decisions of business enterprises of which the actual decision to choose a new location is only a small part. Thus the fourth section looks explicitly at the spatial effects of the behavior of large enterprises.

The increasing scale of business enterprise

The *general* trend during the present century has been for a larger and larger share of economic activity at the industry, national, and international scale to be performed by a relatively small number of extremely large business corporations. Table 9.1 shows how concentration* in United States manufacturing industry increased between 1929 and 1971. In 1929, the leading 100 manufacturing corporations in the United States (a minute fraction of the total number of manufacturing firms) held 40 percent of *total* manufacturing assets; by 1971 this share had increased to almost half. The 100 largest United States industrial corporations in 1972 controlled a larger share of national manufacturing facilities than did the 200 largest in 1950. Similarly, the top 200 had a greater share of total manufacturing assets than did the 1,000 largest corporations thirty years earlier. In 1973, the leading 500 corporations accounted for 65 percent of the sales, 76 percent of the employment, and 79 percent of the profits of all United States industrial corporations.

	1929[a]	1947/8[b]	1970/1[b]
100 largest manufacturing corporations:			
% share of total assets	40	40	49
% share of total value added	n.a.	23	33
200 largest manufacturing corporations:			
% share of total assets	46	48	61
% share of total value added	n.a.	30	43

Source: [a]Blair (1972), p. 64; [b]U.S. Statistical Abstract (1973), p. 483.

Table 9.1
Concentration in United States manufacturing, 1929–1971.

The same kind of picture can be observed in both Britain and Canada. Table 9.2 shows how, for example, the 50 largest firms increased their share of total manufacturing output and employment from around 15 percent in 1935 to almost one-third in 1968. Something like one half of all manufacturing output and employment in Britain was concentrated in only 200 firms. In Canada

---

*Industrial concentration (in a non-geographical sense) is a term which expresses the proportion of an economic activity which is accounted for by a specified number of business enterprises. At the level of manufacturing industry as a whole the leading 50, 100 or 200 firms are generally used (as in Tables 9.1 and 9.2); at the level of an individual industrial sector (e.g. automobiles or bread manufacture) concentration is usually measured by the share of, say, output, sales or employment, which is held by the leading four to eight enterprises in that sector (as in Table 9.3). Because of variations in the fineness of industry classifications used and because changes in definition may occur over a period of years it is sometimes difficult to get a truly unambiguous picture of concentration trends. Hence the fact that, on occasion, the evidence can be interpreted in different ways. For a recent and detailed discussion of concentration the reader is referred to John M. Blair (1972).

Note

in 1963, the 101 firms with assets of more than 100 million dollars accounted for 32 percent of the assets of all firms, even though they represented less than 0.5 percent of the total number of firms in Canada.

Table 9.2
Concentration in British manufacturing, 1935–1968.

	1935 %	1958 %	1963 %	1968 %
Share of largest firms in net output				
Largest 50 firms	14.9	24.7	27.9	32.4
Largest 100 firms	24.0	32.3	37.4	42.0
Largest 200 firms	n.a.	41.0	47.9	52.5
Share of largest firms in employment				
Largest 50 firms	15.0	21.2	24.3	29.4
Largest 100 firms	22.0	27.7	32.6	37.8
Largest 200 firms	28.0	35.5	42.0	47.1

Source: S. Aaronovitch & M. C. Sawyer, The Concentration of British Manufacturing (1974), *Lloyds Bank Review* 114, Table 9. Reprinted by permission of Lloyds Bank.

Similar patterns of increasing concentration of production have been occurring in other sectors of the economy. In agriculture, for example, the trend towards larger production units has been particularly marked. Although the total acreage of land in farms in the United States was virtually the same in both 1940 and 1969 (a little over 1 billion acres) the actual *number* of farms declined very drastically. In 1940, the census recorded a total of 6,350,000 farms; in 1969 the total had fallen to 2,730,000. The decline was greatest among small farms while the number of farms of more than 1,000 acres increased from 100,531 in 1940 to 151,000 in 1969. Table 9.3 provides a slightly different perspective on the same process. In this table, farms are categorized according to the value of farm sales (at 1959 prices). In 1949, 42.3 percent of the farms and 16.3 percent of the total sales were in the $2,500–$4,999 category. By 1969, the figures were 22.8 percent and 3.0 percent respectively. At the other end of the scale, the percentage of farms in the "greater than $10,000 sales" category increased from 23.2 percent in 1949 to 54.7 percent in 1969 and the value of total sales in this category from 57.8 percent in 1949 to 90.7 percent in 1969.

Table 9.3
U.S. farms classified by value of farm sales, 1949–1969 (at 1959 prices).

		$2,500–$4,999	$5,000–$9,999	More than $10,000
1949	Farms	42.3%	34.5%	23.2%
	Sales	16.3%	25.9%	57.8%
1959	Farms	29.9%	31.6%	38.5%
	Sales	7.9%	16.3%	75.8%
1969	Farms	22.8%	22.5%	54.7%
	Sales	3.0%	6.3%	90.7%

Source: based on data in U.S. Statistical Abstract, 1967, p. 750; 1975, p. 612.

Figures which apply to such a highly diverse and aggregated sector like manufacturing conceal very considerable variations *between* different manufacturing industries in the extent to which they are dominated by a small number of firms. Despite the *overall* trend toward increasing concentration it would be quite misleading to suggest that all industries have been, or are, experiencing this to the same degree. Blair calculated that between 1947 and 1967 the following broad changes in concentration occurred. Of 209 industries, concentration increased in 95 (45 percent), decreased in 75 (36 percent) and remained more or less stable in 39 (19 percent). Rather more detail of these changes is given in Table 9.4 for those whose concentration ratios either increased or decreased by more than 3 percent between 1947 and 1967.

| Industrial sector: | Level of concentration (%) | | | | | |
	1947	1954	1958	1963	1967	Net change 1947–1967 (percentage points)
Food and kindred products						
Increasing concentration						
Prepared feeds for animals and fowls	19	21	22	22	23	+4
Bread, cake and related products	16	20	22	23	26	+10
Confectionary products	17	19	18	15	25	+8
Malt liquors	21	27	28	34	40	+19
Bottled and canned soft drinks	10	10	11	12	13	+3
Flavorings, extracts and syrups	50	53	55	62	67	+17
Soybean oil mills	44	41	40	50	55	+11
Decreasing concentration						
Meat-packing plants	41	39	34	31	26	−15
Ice cream and frozen desserts	40	36	38	37	33	−7
Distilled liquor	75	64	60	58	54	−21
Textiles; Apparel						
Increasing concentration						
Weaving mills, cotton	n.a.	18	25	30	30	+12 (1954–1967)
Weaving mills, synthetic	31	30	34	39	46	+15
Knit outerwear mills	8	6	7	11	15	+7
Men's and boys' suits and coats	9	11	11	14	17	+8
Men's dress shirts and nightwear	19	17	16	22	23	+4
Men's and boys' separate trousers	12	12	9	16	20	+8
Women's and misses' suits and coats	n.a.	3	3	8	12	+9 (1954–1967)
Women's and children's underwear	6	8	8	11	15	+9
Decreasing concentration						
Knit fabric mills	27	17	18	18	15	−12
Lumber, Stone, Clay, Glass						
Increasing concentration						
Logging camps and logging contractors	n.a.	8	13	11	14	+6 (1954–1967)
Decreasing concentration						
Glass containers	63	63	58	55	60	−3
Primary metals						
Increasing concentration						
Gray-iron foundries	16	26	24	28	27	+11
Iron and steel forgings	24	27	31	30	30	+6
Decreasing concentration						
Steel foundries	23	21	25	23	20	−3

Table 9.4
Share of output accounted for by the four largest firms in each sector, selected U.S. industries 1947–1967.

Table 9.4 continued

Industrial sector:	Level of concentration (%)					
	1947	1954	1958	1963	1967	Net change 1947–1967 (percentage points)
Transportation equipment						
Increasing concentration						
Motor vehicles and parts	56	75	75	79	78	+22
Decreasing concentration						
Aircraft engines and parts	72	62	56	57	64	−8
Railroad and street cars	56	64	58	53	53	−3
Instruments; Miscellaneous products						
Increasing concentration						
Photographic equipment and supplies	61	n.a.	65	63	69	+8
Games and toys	20	18	13	15	25	+5
Chemicals and allied products						
Increasing concentration						
Toilet preparations	24	25	29	38	38	+14
Decreasing concentration						
Industrial organic chemicals	n.a.	59	55	51	45	−14 (1954–1967)
Plastics materials and resins	44	47	40	35	27	−17
Pharmaceutical preparations	28	25	27	22	24	−4
Tobacco; Petroleum products						
Decreasing concentration						
Cigarettes	90	82	79	80	81	−9
Tobacco stemming and redrying	88	79	83	70	63	−25
Petroleum refining	37	33	32	34	33	−4
Printing and publishing						
Decreasing concentration						
Newspapers	21	18	17	15	16	−5
Periodicals	34	29	31	28	24	−10
Fabricated metals; Non-electrical machinery						
Decreasing concentration						
Metal cans	78	80	80	74	73	−5
Sheet metalwork	21	19	15	11	10	−11
Screw machine products	17	11	9	5	6	−11
Miscellaneous fabricated wire products	20	18	13	13	11	−9
Valves and fittings	24	17	17	13	14	−10
Ball and roller bearings	62	60	57	57	54	−8

n.a. = not available.

Source: J. M. Blair, *Economic Concentration: Structure, Behavior and Public Policy*, pp. 20–22, © 1972 by Harcourt Brace Jovanovich, Inc. and reprinted with their permission.

It is quite clear from the figures in Table 9.4 that some industries are highly concentrated while others remain far more fragmented and have not experienced much increase in concentration (some, in fact, were *less* concentrated in 1967 than they were in 1947).

However, large enterprises have not only come to dominate many individual industrial sectors. They have also become involved in an increasingly wide variety of industries so that, among the very large enterprises, the single-product firm is a good deal less common than the *multi-product diversified* enterprise. Measurement of a firm's product diversity is difficult because very few data exist at a sufficiently fine level of classification. But we do have information for the mid-1960s on the variety of products manufactured by the leading 1,000 industrial corporations in the United States. Figure 9.1 shows that only 50 of the leading 1,000 companies were engaged in a single 5-digit industry.* That is, only 5 percent of the biggest firms were single-product firms. Thirty-two percent of the firms were engaged in between five and ten industries and 27 percent in 11 to 20 industries. Perhaps even more remarkable was the existence of 4 industrial corporations operating in more than 100 industrial categories. Whatever the limitations of these data, the undoubted multi-product nature of the majority of large enterprises is very clear.

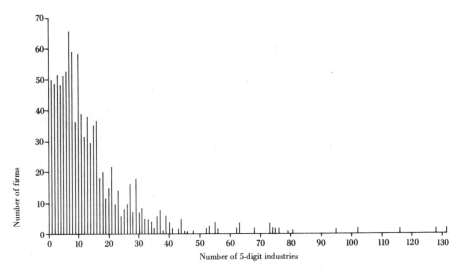

Figure 9.1
Product diversity of the leading 1,000 U.S. industrial corporations, 1965. [*Source:* compiled from data in *Fortune Plant & Product Directory,* © 1966 Time Inc.]

A corollary of the multi-product nature of most large enterprises is that they are also *multi-plant* enterprises, operating in a wide variety of geographical locations and often at a vast geographical scale. Figures 9.2 to 9.5 provide just a hint of the scale and diversity of three of the leading industrial corporations in the United States: General Motors, Textron, and Litton Industries, together with that of ICI in Britain. Again as with Figure 9.1 the data refer to the

---

*The term "5-digit industry" simply refers to a particular level of industrial classification. In the United States, as in Canada, Britain and elsewhere, economic activities are officially grouped into Standard Industrial Classifications. In the case of the United States example discussed here, industries are divided into very broad major groups such as "food and kindred products" or "primary metals industries" which are given a two-figure (digit) identification. These broad categories are then further subdivided. Thus a 5-digit industry within the "food and kindred products" group might be "ground coffee" (SIC 20951); within the "primary metals" group an example would be "steel tubing" (SIC 33176). Though the details vary from one country to another (and over time as individual countries modify and update their schemes), the general principle of classifying industries, first of all very broadly and then subdividing them more finely, appears to be universal.

Note

mid-1960s (the latest available) and depict only those plants located within the firms' domestic territories. Nevertheless, the spread is impressive. At that time, General Motors was the largest industrial corporation in the world, operating some 122 plants in the United States (Figure 9.2). All but a handful of these were located in the eastern half of the country with the expected high level of concentration in the Detroit area in particular and the southern Great Lakes region in general. Figure 9.2 also shows how GM's 95 different products were spread between these 122 plants. Almost half the plants concentrated on a single product but eight plants had more than five products at each and one of GM's two Indianapolis plants produced twelve products.

Figure 9.2
Location of General Motors plants and products in the United States, 1965. [*Source:* compiled from data in *Fortune Plant & Product Directory,* © 1966 Time Inc.]

Figure 9.3
Location of Textron plants and products in the United States, 1965. [*Source:* compiled from data in *Fortune Plant & Product Directory,* © 1966 Time Inc.]

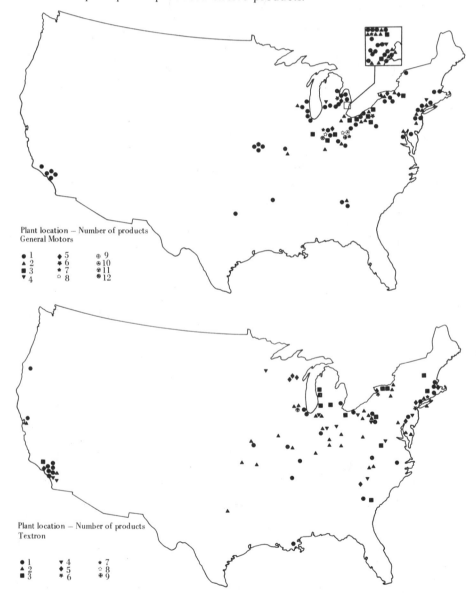

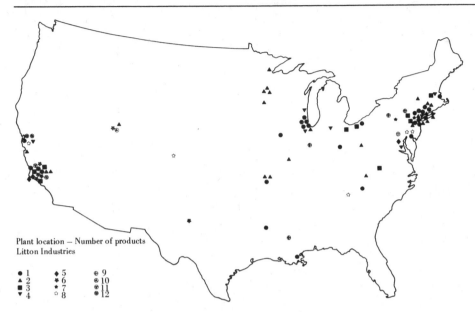

Figure 9.4
Location of Litton
Industries plants and
products in the United
States, 1965. [*Source:*
compiled from data in
*Fortune Plant & Product
Directory,* © 1966 Time
Inc.]

Plant location — Number of products
Litton Industries

● 1	◆ 5	⊕ 9
▲ 2	✦ 6	⊛ 10
■ 3	★ 7	◉ 11
▼ 4	☆ 8	◐ 12

Textron's 116 products and 100 plants were, as Figure 9.3 shows, spread somewhat more widely with more plants in California and in the southeastern states
and less emphasis on the Great Lakes area. The cluster of plants in southern
New England possibly reflects Textron's headquarters' location in Providence,
Rhode Island. Roughly one-quarter of Textron's U.S. plants concentrated on
a single product. Litton Industries was engaged in almost as many product
classes (102) as Textron. As Figure 9.4 indicates, the geographical distribution
of its 97 plants was rather different from that of GM and Textron. Litton's
plants in the mid-1960s showed two distinct clusters plus a fairly wide spread
of the remainder across the country. One cluster of 16 plants was focused upon
Los Angeles, around the corporation's headquarters at Beverly Hills, with a
further six plants in the San Francisco area. The other major cluster was on
the northeast coast around New York City. Litton was the only one of our
three examples to have plants in the mountain states of Colorado and Utah
and in Alaska. The map of ICI locations in Britain (Figure 9.5) reflects the
situation when the corporation had 60 plants in eight product groups in the
United Kingdom (Rees, 1972). Since that time, a good deal of further development has occurred though the importance of the major clusters on Teeside,
in northwest England, and in the southeast remains. We shall have more to
say about such highly diversified firms later in this chapter; for the moment,
we should simply note these as four examples of many multi-product, multi-
plant enterprises.

The large business enterprise is not only increasingly dominant within particular
countries and in many industries within those countries, but it is also increasingly significant at the international or global scale. Indeed, the *multi-national
enterprise* has grown so rapidly in recent years that there is now very widespread
concern over the activities of such enterprises, as the 1976 Senate hearings reveal.

Figure 9.5
Location of ICI plants and
divisions in England and
Wales. [*Source:* J. Rees
(1972), The industrial
corporation and location
decision analysis, *Area,* 4,
3, Figure 1.]

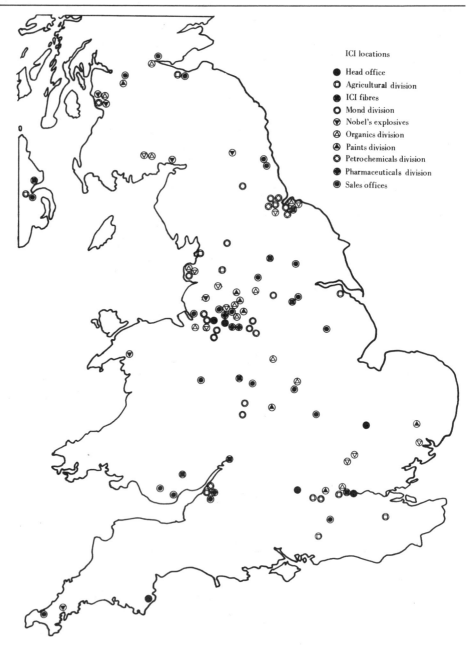

ICI locations

● Head office
◑ Agricultural division
◕ ICI fibres
○ Mond division
▼ Nobel's explosives
△ Organics division
▲ Paints division
◎ Petrochemicals division
◕ Pharmaceuticals division
◉ Sales offices

It has been calculated that direct investment by multi-national enterprises today
accounts for more than one-fifth of total industrial output in the world as
a whole (excluding the centrally-planned economies). They penetrate every
country in the world, in almost every case they have been increasing their
share of the country's national domestic production, and in more than twenty
countries they are responsible for more than one-third of total manufacturing
output.

Dunning (1971) has assembled some of the salient characteristics of multi-national companies which give us some idea of their increasing importance in today's world.

1. In 1968, the value of total assets belonging to multi-nationals outside their country of incorporation amounted to approximately $94 billion.

2. Their total foreign sales (exports plus local output) were probably greater in value than the Gross National Product of any individual country except the United States and the Soviet Union.

3. United States' enterprises owned more than half of all multi-national assets, British firms owned 20 percent of the total, most of the remainder was owned by Japanese and European countries, particularly West Germany.

4. The foreign output of multi-national firms in the late 1960s was growing at 10 percent per year, a rate twice that of the growth of world GNP and 40 percent faster than the level of total world exports.

5. Multi-national companies are far more prominent in some economic sectors than in others. On the whole, they are dominant in the technologically advanced industries, those which have the highest present and future growth potential. Some four-fifths of the overseas investment on plant and equipment by United States multi-nationals is in four main economic sectors: vehicles, chemicals, mechanical engineering, and electrical engineering. Some industries are totally dominated at the world scale by multi-nationals: oil, tobacco, pharmaceuticals, motor vehicles, rubber tires, for example. By 1968, the big three United States automobile manufacturers controlled almost one-third of the total European car market, while 75 percent of all the computers sold in Europe in the mid-1960s were produced by American companies.

The picture emerging in most developed market economies, then, is of a two-part industrial structure of the kind Robert Averitt has called the *Dual Economy*. According to this view there are two types of business enterprise which are fundamentally different from each other. On the one hand there are *center firms*—large, complex in organization and strong in resources—on the other, there are *periphery* firms: the small, simple organizations of the kind we discussed in the previous chapter, although not all periphery firms are quite as small and simple as the type discussed in Chapter Eight.* Although it is far easier to speak generally of center and periphery firms than it is to draw a precise boundary between them it can be argued that certainly the leading two hundred or so industrial corporations at least form the nucleus of the center economy. At the global scale, it has been calculated that the vast bulk of multi-national activity is performed by a relative handful of firms. One estimate puts the size of this "international center economy" at between 500 and

---

*The idea of a dual economic structure forms the basis of Galbraith's analysis (see, for example, his *Economics and the Public Purpose*), although his terminology differs from that of Averitt. Galbraith uses the terms *planning system* and *market system* in a way which suggests that they are the equivalent of center and periphery firms respectively. It is worth pointing out that the term "dual economy" is used rather differently by development economists. They use it to refer to the existence of a modern export-based sector and an indigenous subsistence economy within a single country.

Note

700 firms. Some 70 percent of United States' foreign investment is performed by between 250 and 300 firms, 80 percent of British foreign investment by roughly 165 firms and 70 percent of West German foreign investment by 82 firms. These leading firms, as many studies have shown, are exceptionally large by whatever criteria of measurement one chooses to employ. Tables 9.5 and 9.6 show just the upper echelons of the largest corporations in the United States and in the rest of the world (excluding the communist bloc) in 1974. As it happened, 1974 showed a considerable number of changes over previous years because of the impact of the 1973 oil crisis. Ironically, it was the oil companies which made the greatest improvement in their sales performance. In particular, General Motors lost its first-ranking position for the first time in 40 years. Such changes apart, however, the tables simply give some indication of not only the identity of the largest business corporations but also their sheer size in terms of sales, assets and employees.

Table 9.5
The twenty largest industrial corporations in the United States, 1974.

Rank by sales	Company	Sales ($000)	Assets ($000)	Employees
1	Exxon	42,061,336	31,332,440	133,000
2	General Motors	31,549,546	20,468,100	734,000
3	Ford	23,620,600	14,173,600	464,731
4	Texaco	23,255,497	17,176,121	76,420
5	Mobil Oil	18,929,033	14,074,290	73,100
6	Standard Oil (Calif)	17,191,186	11,639,996	39,540
7	Gulf Oil	16,458,000	12,503,000	52,700
8	General Electric	13,413,100	9,369,100	404,000
9	IBM	12,675,292	14,027,108	292,350
10	ITT	11,154,401	10,696,544	409,000
11	Chrysler	10,971,416	6,732,756	255,929
12	U.S. Steel	9,186,403	7,717,493	187,503
13	Standard Oil (Indiana)	9,085,415	8,915,190	47,217
14	Shell Oil	7,633,455	6,128,884	32,287
15	Western Electric	7,381,728	5,239,551	189,972
16	Continental Oil	7,041,423	4,673,434	41,174
17	Du Pont	6,910,100	5,980,300	136,866
18	Atlantic Richfield	6,739,682	6,151,608	28,771
19	Westinghouse Electric	6,466,112	4,301,804	199,248
20	Occidental Petroleum	5,719,369	3,325,471	34,400

Source: Reprinted from *Fortune Magazine*, May 1975, by special permission © 1975 Time Inc.

The small firms making up the periphery economy are not only small; they are also in many cases functionally subordinate to, and dependent upon, the center firms. Averitt divides periphery firms into three types in terms of their relationship with center firms:

1. *"Satellite" firms.* These are functionally linked to center firms either on the input (backward linkage) or output (forward linkage) side. Often they are specialist subcontractors performing functions which the center firm does not choose to perform itself and are dependent upon the center firm.

Rank by sales	Company	Country	Sales ($000)	Assets ($000)	Employees
1	Royal Dutch/Shell	Neth-Brit.	33,037,116	30,194,285	164,000
2	British Petroleum	Britain	18,269,240	15,088,946	68,000
3	National Iranian Oil	Iran	16,802,000	6,935,000	50,000
4	Unilever	Brit-Neth.	13,666,667	7,116,405	357,000
5	Philips Gloelampenfab	Netherlands	9,422,386	11,304,376	412,000
6	Cie.Française des Pétroles	France	8,908,563	8,266,075	27,400
7	Nippon Steel	Japan	8,843,550	9,456,071	97,814
8	August Thyssen-Hütte	W. Germany	8,664,021	5,212,566	150,888
9	BASF	W. Germany	8,497,038	6,074,799	110,989
10	Hoechst	W. Germany	7,821,054	7,795,485	178,710
11	ENI	Italy	7,172,831	11,379,626	92,241
12	ICI	Britain	6,911,813	7,428,303	201,000
13	Siemens	W. Germany	6,701,681	6,246,892	309,000
14	Volkswagen	W. Germany	6,568,717	5,841,467	203,730
15	Bayer	W. Germany	6,300,940	6,800,582	134,837
16	Daimler-Benz	W. Germany	6,288,668	2,607,505	154,865
17	Montedison	Italy	6,189,753	6,864,807	153,200
18	Hitachi	Japan	6,183,309	7,147,595	144,863
19	Toyota Motor	Japan	5,948,335	3,900,712	58,862
20	ELF Group	France	5,900,381	7,432,271	22,331

Source: Reprinted from *Fortune Magazine*, August 1975, by special permission © 1975 Time Inc.

Table 9.6
The twenty largest industrial corporations outside the United States, 1974.

2. *"Competitive fringe" firms*. These are the non-dominant firms which compete with center firms in their "home industry." They tend to have a relatively short life, often being absorbed by center firms.

3. *"Free Agent" firms* are those which Averitt regards as a residual category, operating

> on the economic fringes of the raw material processing–finished manufacture–retailing continuum, filling in production cracks and crannies... Manufacturing free agents often specialize in producing unique articles or unique batches of articles.
> *Averitt (1968), p. 66*

Such firms may be able to operate, for example, if markets for a particular product are geographically dispersed. In a growing economy there are, as Edith Penrose has pointed out, numerous *interstices* in the economy, productive opportunities which small firms may be able to exploit.

Despite the general trend toward larger business units, therefore, small firms continue to exist. Some members of the small-firm population are destined to die early (the mortality rate of small businesses is very high even in non-recessionary times); other members will be absorbed by center firms or will combine with other small firms. But, allowing for both of these processes, the small firm does continue to survive. Quite apart from the kinds of relationship with center firms other factors help to explain this. One reason is that although most technological advances have favored larger production units, some innovations have been advantageous to the small firm. For example, the replacement of the steam engine by the electric motor allowed small firms to introduce motive power at relatively small cost and for small-scale operations. More recently, the development of small-scale data processing and computing equipment has brought these powerful media within the range of the small company. A further contributing factor is the nature of the scale curve and the level of the minimum optimal scale. Our earlier discussion of the nature of scale economies showed clearly that not only does the minimum optimal scale vary considerably from industry to industry, but also that the shape of the scale curve below the optimum was almost horizontal in some cases, indicating that small-scale operations could exist without incurring excessive unit costs (see Figure 7.8). In industries where the minimum optimal scale is low, then many small optimal-sized firms could compete in the market. Where, on the other hand, the scale curve is relatively flat, a wide range of firms of different sizes can exist.

The fact remains, however, that the general tendency has been for business enterprises to get larger and even though the cult of bigness may not be quite as untarnished as it was only a few years ago, it is still a very powerful force. So let us turn briefly to examine the reasons underlying such growth because, although this is not our central concern, it helps us to understand the *spatial* manifestation of business behavior more clearly.

Why firms grow

Undoubtedly, one of the reasons why business enterprises have become increasingly large is the existence of *economies of scale*. When we discussed these in Chapter Seven, it was in the restricted framework of economies at the level of the *individual plant*. However, many economists have argued that similar, though even greater, economies may be present in firms operating more than one plant. In other words, the very existence of a multi-plant organization may further increase the economies of size in a way shown by the shaded area in Figure 9.6 (which should be compared with Figure 7.8). But why should firms operating several plants be supposedly more efficient (in cost terms) than single-plant firms? Part of the answer lies in the broader relevance of the components identified in Chapter Seven: economies of specialization, mass reserves, and large-scale purchasing.

Figure 9.6
Hypothetical scale-cost curves for single and multi-plant firms.

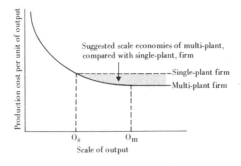

Managerial economies—the better use of managerial skills and the benefits of a more sophisticated organizational structure—are claimed to be especially significant. The creation of specialist departments to carry out research and development, organize marketing and arrange finance and expenditure is the hallmark of the large multi-plant enterprise. Marketing is especially important in consumer goods industries where not only can very large enterprises operate a larger and more comprehensive sales organization, but can also engage in sales promotion and advertising on a scale quite beyond the scope of the small firm. For example, it has been estimated that roughly half of all the costs which make up the final price to the consumer are marketing costs.

In both consumer and producer goods industries it is frequently argued that the necessary scale of expenditure on research and development in fact can be carried out only by the very large firm. J. K. Galbraith thus writes of the *imperative of technology* which he sees as being a major contributor to the existence of very large business corporations. Such technological imperatives are based upon the idea that the increasingly specialized nature of production processes requires a long time-lag between initial invention and innovation (subsequent application of a new technique or product). Such a time-lag is very costly in terms of resources and is also risky. Hence by this argument only the very large enterprise has the resources to carry out major technological advances. We referred to this issue in our more general discussion of technology in Chapter Six. Certainly there is a positive relationship between size of firm and level of research and development expenditure. An OECD survey carried out in 1967 showed that in the United States the four largest firms (measured in terms of size of R and D programs) accounted for 22 percent of all industrial R and D expenditure, the eight largest for 35 percent and the twenty largest firms for 57 percent. (The comparable figures for the United Kingdom were 25.6, 34.0 and 47.2 percent).

The concept of mass reserves also applies to the multi-plant enterprise in the sense that such an organization can transfer financial and other resources between its component units to bolster flagging performance in one or to increase the enterprise's overall performance in ways which the small firm simply cannot do. Likewise, in terms of large-scale or bulk purchasing, very large orders for materials and services generally bring lower prices. In the case of finance, the very large enterprise can generally acquire funds for expansion on cheaper terms than small firms.

However, not everybody would accept these advantages of multi-plant firms without reservation. As with plant economies, it is argued that beyond a "certain" size of firm diseconomies of scale will set in. One reason is what Anthony Downs called the Law of Diminishing Control created by the overload of responsibility and information and the remoteness of top decision-makers from the day-to-day operations of the enterprise. But this does not necessarily imply that there is an absolute limit on firm size imposed by such diseconomies of coordination. Indeed, as we shall see, one of the major activities of large, growing enterprises has been to devise new organizational structures which can cope with problems of coordination and control in very large organizations.

An increasingly common criticism of business size relates to the issue of research and development and to the argument that, under present circumstances, only the very large firms can be technologically innovative. There is no doubt, as we observed earlier, that large firms generate a larger *input* of research and development expenditure. But do they produce an *output*—in the form of inventions and innovations—commensurate with the size of such input? Unfortunately this is a difficult question to answer because evidence is both scanty and conflicting.* In terms of basic inventions (for example, xerography, automatic transmissions for automobiles) the individual or the small firm remains very important as the initiator of new ideas, products, or processes. If we measure inventive activity by patent figures then it has been suggested that for the leading 500 United States corporations, inventive activity increases as firm sales increase but at a decreasing rate implying that very large size is not an advantage in this respect. For such reasons and others, some critics of big business argue that the very large enterprises may, in fact, be "creatively backward" in that they not only get a relatively poor return for their investment but that they also, in effect, inhibit technological advance which may conflict with their own vested interests. In fact, the argument is unresolved, partly because where invention ends and innovation begins is difficult to pinpoint, although this is a critical distinction. What does seem to be likely, as Johnson (1975) suggests, is that large firms are likely to be especially important innovators in industries which are highly capital-intensive (for example, aerospace, motor vehicles, steel) and less important in industries where capital intensity and entry barriers are lower.

Our concern here however is not simply whether large multi-plant firms are "better" in some sense than smaller firms but rather with why business firms in general continue to strive for larger and larger size. There is not much doubt that the very large firms are far larger than can be either explained or justified simply in terms of economies of scale. To answer the question of why large firms continue to seek even larger scales of operation we need to make two basic distinctions. First, we must separate *economies of size* (scale) from *economies of growth*. Edith Penrose emphasizes this point very strongly. She suggests that economies of growth may exist independently of economies of size when there are unused or under-used resources within the firm. In such circumstances, increase in size which makes use of such spare resources may be justifiable in itself. Second, we should distinguish between *actual* and *perceived* scale economies. As Starbuck observes:

> in a sense, the actual relationship between cost per unit and size is irrelevant. The relationship which is relevant is the relationship which executives believe holds true.
> *Starbuck (1965), p. 457*

It could be argued, then, that the tendencies towards increasing scale of business enterprise are based upon the motivating force of *growth* itself either as an

Note

*The pros and cons of the size/invention-innovation controversy are well summarized in Blair (1972), Chapters 9 and 10. Johnson (1975), Mansfield (1968), and Parker (1974) are particularly valuable sources which deal specifically with technology.

end in its own right or as a means to an end. Several writers have suggested, in fact, that the twin criteria of *survival* and *growth** may best explain much business behavior, particularly as growth may be the best means of securing survival. For example, it is probably no coincidence that most business "deaths" are of small rather than large firms.

Regardless of *actual* cost economies, large-scale business organization carries with it a great deal of *power* and *leverage* over parts of what is, without doubt, an increasingly dynamic and changeable external environment. We discussed the general question of uncertainty in the previous chapter. More specifically, Table 9.7 identifies the principal elements of the business environment. The important point is not simply the diversity of the elements but rather the fact that many of the elements are extremely volatile, changing rapidly and, sometimes, unpredictably because of changes generated both by technological and other (social, political, cultural) forces. As illustration, we can refer to the recent furore in the raw materials sphere (particularly oil, but other minerals and commodities as well), the increasing involvement of governments in business affairs whether as a regulator or as a provider of incentives, and the growing "social–ecological" lobby with its concern for the quality of the human environment.

Although, in some cases, very large size may make firms more obvious and vulnerable to external forces (as Edwards and Townsend comment, "in dealing with governments it is well to be large but not too large"), in most cases the large enterprise has a higher degree of *adaptability* to environmental influences through the amount of power and leverage it can exert. Like all open systems it can, by growing, absorb or ingest elements of its environment in order to reduce the level of uncertainty (see next section). More generally, it can, through its possession of power, gain greater access to government (often through personal contact as the Lockheed case revealed) and secure price reductions from suppliers below those justified on cost grounds. Few suppliers are willing to risk losing a large customer. The larger a firm's share of a market the greater is its ability to set prices at the level which *it* wants rather than at the level set by the "market."

---

*Discussion of business goals and motives is bedeviled by a number of problems. One is the question of whether organizations as such can have goals or whether only individuals possess such attributes. Another is the nature of the organization itself, particularly whether it is controlled and operated by its owners or whether ownership and control are separate. Most commonly, the large business enterprise is operated and controlled by a management group which is quite separate from the legal owners of the enterprise (the stockholders). Thus, it is the goals of this management group which are important. Galbraith (1974) suggests that this group (which he calls the technostructure, though the term is not widely accepted) has two sets of goals. First it has *protective* goals—*survival*—and second it has *affirmative* goals of which *growth* of the firm is paramount in importance because it also ensures the increased security, power, and prosperity of the management group. Whether expressed in growth of sales, assets, profits or whatever, how the firm performs "compared with last year" or some other past date is a visible measure of success.

Note

Table 9.7
Principal elements of
organizational
environments.

Cost conditions

(a)   Physical conditions of production.
(b)   Existing technical knowledge and its availability to firm and others.
(c)   Conditions, including availability, prices, terms of sale, in markets in which firm is buyer, borrower or renter of:
    (i)   Labor
    (ii)   Land and natural resources
    (iii)   Materials and supplies
    (iv)   Capital

Government actions:

International, national, provincial or state, local:
(a)   Incentive
(b)   Protective
(c)   Regulatory
(d)   Persuasive

Demand conditions

(a)   Conditions, including extent, elasticity and steadiness of demand, in markets in which firm is a seller.
(b)   Extent of competition and potential competition and behavior of competitors:
    (i)   in same industry
    (ii)   in other industries

Informal social pressures

Deriving from accepted traditions, practices, values and definitions of roles:
(a)   Local community
(b)   Business community
(c)   General social *milieu*

Influences or pressures exerted by other firms:

e.g.   (a)   Bankers
      (b)   Suppliers/customers

or interested groups:

e.g.   (a)   Stockholders
      (b)   Pressure groups

Source: based on Bowen (1955) pp. 31–2; Steed (1971) p. 325.

How firms grow

Both the "why" and the "how" of firm growth are related to the firm's evolving position in such a changing environment. In one sense, therefore, the multi-plant firm is no different from the single-plant firm in that its behavior is stimulated by events generated internally or externally (see Figure 8.12)—either within the firm, or as a result of interaction with the environment, or within the environment itself. The major difference lies in the far greater complexity of the multi-plant firm's operations and the fact that it has more points of contact with its environment. Returning to the terminology of Figure 8.8, it has a far more extensive *task environment* and, therefore, has a far greater information spread than the single-plant firm.

Evolution of the large, complex business enterprise

How an enterprise grows and develops is determined both by the kind of *strategy* the enterprise follows in adapting to its changing environment and by the *structure* it evolves to implement its strategy.* Both of these have very

Note

*This distinction between *strategy* and *structure* is fundamental to the understanding of the large business enterprise. The distinction was made initially by the American business historian Alfred D. Chandler, Jr. (1962) and has been followed by most writers since. Chandler defines these terms in the following manner:

Note continued

Strategy can be defined as the determination of the basic long-term goals and objectives of an enterprise, and the adoption of courses of action and the allocation of resources necessary for carrying out these goals. Decisions to expand the volume of activities, to set up distant plants and offices, to move into new economic functions, or become diversified along many lines of business involve the defining of new basic goals. New courses of action must be devised and resources allocated and reallocated in order to achieve these goals and to maintain and expand the firm's activities in the new areas in response to shifting demands, changing sources of supply, fluctuating economic conditions, new technological developments, and the actions of competitors. As the adoption of a new strategy may add new types of personnel and facilities, and alter the business horizons of the men responsible for the enterprise, it can have a profound effect on the form of its organization. *Structure* can be defined as the design of organization through which the enterprise is administered. This design, whether formally or informally defined, has two aspects. It includes, first, the lines of authority and communication between the different administrative offices and officers and, second, the information and data that flow through these lines of communication and authority. Such lines and such data are essential to assure the effective coordination, appraisal, and planning so necessary in carrying out the basic goals and policies and in knitting together the total resources of the enterprise. These resources include financial capital; physical equipment such as plants, machinery, offices, warehouses and other marketing and purchasing facilities, sources of raw materials, research and engineering laboratories; and, most important of all, the technical, marketing, and administrative skills of its personnel. The theories deduced from these several propositions is then that *structure follows strategy and that the most complex type of structure is the result of the concatenation of several basic strategies* (present authors' italics).

Reprinted from Strategy and Structure: Chapters in the History of the Industrial Enterprise *by A. D. Chandler, Jr by permission of The M.I.T. Press, Cambridge, Massachusetts. Copyright © 1962.*

---

significant geographical relationships for, as we shall see, both strategy and structure have geographical inputs and geographical outputs. Figure 9.7 outlines some of the more important types of growth strategy that we shall be looking at in this chapter. We can see from the diagram that expansion strategies may be on the one hand either *internal* or *external* and, on the other, *vertical, horizontal* or *diversified*. Let us discuss the first of these initially. *Internal* expansion refers to growth—whether of existing products in existing markets, of existing products in new geographical markets, or of new products—created from within the enterprise itself. *External* expansion is achieved by combination with other enterprises by merger or acquisition. In most cases these are not mutually exclusive categories: many firms have grown by a mixture of internal and external expansion. However, there seems to have been a distinct shift of emphasis in recent decades toward a much greater dependence upon external growth strate-

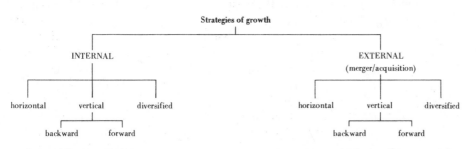

Figure 9.7
Strategies of growth for a business enterprise.

gies. Growth by merger seems to have been particularly important in enabling medium-sized enterprises to develop into the kind of very large enterprises discussed earlier in this chapter.

In the United States since the turn of the century (and probably in Britain, though there is not such detailed information for earlier years) the intensity of merger activity has followed a pattern of increasingly high peaks separated by troughs of relatively less activity. Figure 9.8(a) shows that there have been three major peaks of merger activity in the United States since the 1890s. The merger activity of the turn of the century formed the basis on which the modern industrial structure of the United States was built. A structure which was, in the economist's terminology, "competitive" (i.e. consisting of large numbers of relatively small firms) was transformed primarily by the wave of mergers into an "oligopolistic" structure (one dominated by a relatively small number of large enterprises). Between 1897 and 1905, an average of 352 firms per year disappeared by merger, the peak year being 1899 when 1,208 firms were absorbed. It was during this period that the first really gigantic business enterprises came into existence, firms such as U.S. Steel, American Tobacco, Du Pont, Corn Products, Anaconda Copper, American Smelting and Refining, for example, together with firms such as Imperial Tobacco and Distillers Company in Britain. United States Steel was the first billion dollar business combination in history, the prototype of what was to become commonplace. According to Blair,

> few events in history have contributed more to concentration in U.S. industry than the formation in 1901 of U.S. Steel, referred to at the time as the "giant of giants." All in all, its creation brought together some 170 subsidiary concerns consisting of over 80 mining companies, 40 manufacturing companies, over 30 transportation companies, and several gas and miscellaneous enterprises. When formed, U.S. Steel had steel works with an annual capacity of 9.4 million tons, 1,000 miles of railway, 112 lake ore vessels, iron ore deposits estimated to contain from 500 to 700 million tons of ore, more than 50,000 acres of high-grade coal lands, and numerous related properties. The total number of plants under the control of the corporation exceeded 200.
>
> *Reprinted from J. M. Blair* Economic Concentration: Structure, Behavior, and Public Policy, *p. 260,* © *1972 by Harcourt Brace Jovanovich, Inc. and reprinted with their permission.*

The second major peak of merger activity took place in the latter half of the 1920s. Between the beginning of 1925 and the end of 1929, almost 4,500 United States firms disappeared by merger, an average of 890 per year, with over 1,200 disappearing in 1929 alone. The deep recession heralded by the 1929 Wall Street Crash brought this second wave to a close and, as Figure 9.8 shows, the high levels of these two peaks were not equalled and surpassed until the 1960s even though, of course, mergers and takeovers still continued. Without any doubt, however, the 1960s merger peak was the biggest of the three in terms of both the number and the value of the mergers which took place. In a sense, we can perceive the beginnings of the 1960s peak as early as 1948–50 when the

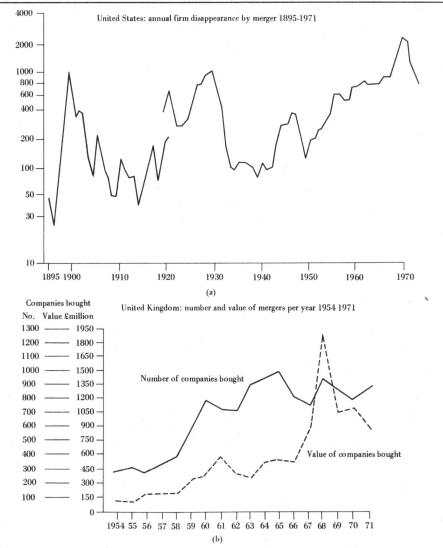

Figure 9.8
Merger activity. (a)
United States 1895–1971.
(b) United Kingdom
1954–1971. [*Source:* (a)
U.S. Federal Trade
Commission, 1969. (b)
Institute of Economic
Affairs, 1973.]

curve of Figure 9.8 turns upwards again, but the peak of intensity was not reached until the middle and late 1960s. Figure 9.8 shows that in 1966 more firms disappeared in the United States through merger than in either of the previous periods and that, in 1968 alone, well over 2,000 firms disappeared by merger. Between 1959 and 1968, a total of 11,142 manufacturing and mining firms were acquired, representing a total value of $54,550 million.

Although we have discussed mergers among manufacturing firms, the same general trends were evident in most other sectors. For example, Figure 9.9 shows how the intensity of merger activity in both wholesale and retail trade and services also reached a peak of intensity in the late 1960s. The merger activity of the late 1960s was not only greater in terms of the *number* of firms involved but also in the *value* of assets acquired. Between 1964 and 1966, there were 283 mergers in which the acquired companies had assets of more than $10

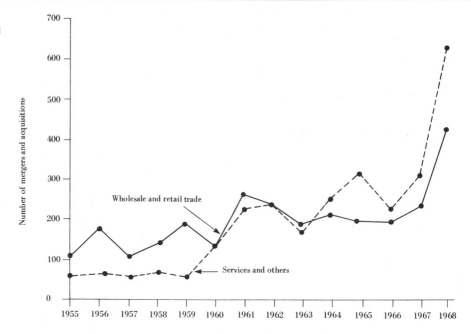

million; between 1967 and 1970 there were 530 such mergers. In the 1964-1966 period, the average value of each transaction was $38 million; in the 1967-1970 period it was $64 million.

Our earlier statement that growth by merger has become relatively more significant than growth by internal expansion is corroborated by evidence collected by the U.S. Federal Trade Commission. The Commission estimated that, in 1952, 3.6 percent of total corporate spending on new capital investment was devoted to the acquisition of other companies. In 1968, *more than half* of all corporate spending on new investment—54.6 percent—was used for acquisition. It seems likely that the entire *relative* growth of the leading 200 industrial corporations since World War II has been brought about by acquisition. Table 9.8 shows just how important acquisition was for the growth of some of the leading United States' industrial corporations. Quite apart from the number of companies and their asset value, the most interesting aspects of Table 9.8 are the final three columns. Column 3 shows the relative importance of the acquired assets to the firm's total assets in 1968. In other words, it shows how much the acquisitions contributed to the firm's size and some of the percentage figures are staggering. For example, Teledyne's acquisition of 125 companies produced 90 percent of the firm's total assets in 1968. Gulf and Western and Signal were not far behind with 83 and 84 percent respectively. Figures such as these are not surprisingly reflected in the rapid ascent of the firms involved up the "league table" of the largest companies. Comparison of columns 4 and 5 show how spectacular such movements could be. In 1960, Gulf and Western, Tenneco and Teledyne were not sufficiently large to rank in the leading 500 corporations in the United States; by 1968 their respective ranks were 17, 16 and 74.

Acquiring corporation	(1) Number of companies acquired 1961–1968	(2) Assets of acquired companies ($millions)	(3) Acquired assets as percentage of total assets (1968)	(4) Rank among largest industrial corporations by assets (1960)	(5) Rank among largest industrial corporations by assets (1968)
ITT	50	$3,705	59%	35	9
Gulf & Western	67	$2,882	83%	—	17
Ling-Temco-Vought	23	$1,901	72%	335	22
Tenneco	31	$1,196	31%	—	16
Teledyne	125	$1,026	90%	—	74
McDonnell-Douglas	8	$864	79%	242	62
Signal	10	$770	84%	126	66
U.S. Plywood-Champion Papers	27	$649	71%	176	74
Litton Industries	79	$609	47%	275	55
FMC	13	$497	75%	121	89
Textron	50	$453	73%	132	98

Table 9.8
Acquisitions by a sample of leading U.S. corporations, 1961–1968.

Source: U.S. Federal Trade Commission, 1969.

Reference back to Figure 9.7 reminds us that whether an enterprise expands internally or externally, the precise form of such expansion may follow one or more of three directions:

1. The enterprise may expand *horizontally*, that is by extending its production and sales of its existing product into new markets or by capturing a larger share of its existing market.
2. The enterprise may expand *vertically*, that is by involving itself further in the production sequence in two possible directions. First, a firm—say, a brewing company, may decide to operate at an earlier stage in the production sequence, that is to follow a strategy of *backward* integration by malting its own barley or, even further back, by actually growing the barley. Alternatively (or in addition) the brewing company may extend *forwards* to control the distribution and retail outlets for its products.
3. The enterprise may *diversify* into products which may be closely related to its existing activities or into products which are completely unrelated. This latter practice has become increasingly common and produced a new "breed" of enterprise: the *conglomerate*.

Each of these strategies may contribute in different ways to the twin goals of survival and growth identified in the previous section of this chapter. Horizontal expansion may ensure a greater level of demand for the firm's product by reducing the influence of competitors. Vertical expansion reduces the uncertainty inherent in inputs and outputs while diversification "spreads the risk," reducing a firm's dependence on one or a few products. It is assumed that a carefully designed diversification strategy will help to reduce a firm's vulnerability to cyclical or secular changes in demand.* If we look again at the merger

Cyclical variations in demand are those which have a recurring pattern over time. Some may be short-term, for example, seasonal variations in demand for iced drinks or for snow-   Note

Figure 9.10
Acquisitions by Textron,
1943–1968. [*Source:*
U.S. Federal Trade
Commission, 1969.]

Horizontal and Vertical

TEXTILES
(All resold by 1964)

SUNCOOK MILLS, Suncook, N.H., 1943
Cotton, rayon and other synthetic griege
goods, cotton fabrics

LONSDALE CO., Providence, R.I., 1945
Cotton fabric, chambrays, lawns and broad-
cloth, shirtings, bleaching

MANVILLE JENCKES CORP.,
Woonsocket, R.I., 1945
Cotton and rayon fabric, taffeta, drapery
fabrics, rayon

GOSSETT MILLS, 1946
Cotton and rayon fabric, cotton broad-
woven fabric

NASHUA MANUFACTURING CO.,
Nashua, N.Y. 1946
Cotton and rayon fabric, blankets,
pajamas, sheets, pillow cases, bedspreads

THE ESMOND MILLS, INC., Esmond, R.I.
1948
Subs: Clarence Whitman & Sons, Inc.
        The Esmond Mills, Limited
        Esmond Mills, Ontario, Limited
        Esmond Virginia, Inc.
        The Wilkes-Barr Mfg. Co.
Infant blankets

R. W. BATES PIECE DYE WORKS, INC
Groverville, N.Y. 1951
Cotton broad woven fabrics

VASS COTTON MILL CO., Vass, N.C. 1951
Cotton Fabrics

AMERICAN WOOLEN CO.
New York, N.Y. 1955
Woolen and worsted fabrics, blankets and
upholstery fabrics, industrial brushes, wool
yarn

ROBBINS MILLS, INC., New York, N.Y.
(incorporated New Jersey) 1955
Rayon and acetate fabrics, gray goods,
nylon

INDUSTRIAL BATTING

F. BURKHART MANUFACTURING CO.
St. Louis, Mo., 1953
Industrial batting

CAROLINA BAGGING CO.
Henderson, N.C. 1956
Industrial batting, padding, upholstery
filling, polyurethane foam

Oakland Plant of
NATIONAL AUTOMOTIVE FIBRES, INC.
Oakland, Calif., 1959
Cotton pad and batts for automobile seating

AIRCRAFT AND PARTS

M. B. MANUFACTURING CO.
New Haven, Conn., 1954
Engine mounts and vibration elimination
equipment

ACCESSORY PRODUCTS CORP.
Whittier, Calif., 1957
Servo actuators, flight control systems,
inertial guidance and navigation equipment

BELL AIRCRAFT CORP, Wheatfield,
N.Y. 1960
Defense business, including Bell Aerospace Corp. and 3 divisions. Helicopters,
rocket engines, research and development
on propulsion systems, space vehicle
equipment, etc.

ELECTRONIC EQUIPMENT

DALMO VICTOR CO.
San Carlos, Calif., 1954
Airborne radar antennas and related
equipment

RYAN INDUSTRIES, INC.
Detroit, Mich., 1955
Electromechanical products, photographic
equipment, jigs, dies and fixtures

CALIFORNIA TECHNICAL INDUSTRIES
Belmont, Calif., 1957
Electronics

GLOBE ELECTRONICS
Council Bluffs, Iowa, 1959
Radio equipment

SCHAFER CUSTOM ENGINEERING
Burbank, Calif., 1959
Automation equipment for radio and TV
broadcast equipment

ALLEGHANY INSTRUMENTS CO., INC.
Cumberland, Md., 1960
Gas regulators, thrust and pressure measuring devices, electronic and electromechanical vibration systems

ELETRONIC RESEARCH CO.
Kansas City, Mo., 1960
Electronic components, radio frequency
crystals, related power supplies, airborne
radar antennas

Nuclear energy operations of
ALCO PRODUCTS New York, N.Y. 1962

COLLEGE HILL INDUSTRIES
Warwick, R.I., 1964
Inertia compensated tape recorders for
space vehicles, specialized pressure and
inertia switches and pressure-sensing
capsules; research in other commercial
and defense electronic products

ELECTROCRAFT, INC. Chicago, Ill., 1959
Plugs and jacks

ROBOTOMICS ENTERPRISES, INC
Phoenix, Arizona, 1963
Decades and displays for electronic
counters

OPTICAL INSTRUMENTS

SHURON OPTICAL CO Geneva, N.Y., 1958
Optical lab equipment, including interfer-
ence filters, spectacle frames, cases and
lenses.

SPECTROLAB, INC.,
Hollywood, Calif., 1960
Optical lab equipment including inter-
ference filters

MODERN OPTICS; INC
Houston, Tex. 1961
Lenses, optical

CONTINENTAL OPTICAL CO
Indianapolis, Ind. 1963
Spectacle frames, cases and lenses

INDUSTRIAL FASTENERS

CAMCAR SCREW & MANUFACTURING
CORP., Rockford, Ill., 1955
Industrial fasteners, rivets, bolts

TOWNSEND CO., New Brighton, Pa., 1959
Industrial fasteners, rivets, bolts, cold-
heading machinery, wire-drawing equipment, rivet setting machines and electrical contacts.

BOOTS AIRCRAFT NUT CORP.
Norfolk, Conn., 1960
Lock nuts, engine nuts

AMERICAN SCREW CO.
Willimantic, Conn., 1962
Industrial fasteners, rivets, bolts

TUBULAR RIVET & STUD CO.
Woollaston, Mass., 1961
Rivets

FABRICATED PRODUCTS CO.
West Newton, Pa., 1960
Speciality building seals, washers, closures
and fasteners

BOSTITCH, INC.
East Greenwich, R.I., 1956
Industrial staplers and stitchers

HARMIL MANUFACTURING, INC.
Downey, Calif., 1966
Sealing washers

IRON AND STEEL CASTINGS

CAMPBELL WYANT & CANNON
FOUNDRY CO. Muskegon, Mich., 1956
Gray iron and steel castings for automotive, railroad, agricultural, implement
refrigeration, marine and other industries.

PITTSBURGH STEEL FOUNDRY CORP.
Glassport, Pa., 1959
Steel and alloy Castings

CHAIN SAWS

HOMELITE CORP., Port Chester, N.Y. 1955
Chain saws and pumps, electric power
plants, centrifugal pumps, gas engines

MEASURING INSTRUMENTS

SPRAGUE METER CO. INC
Bridgeport, Conn., 1961
Gas meters, gas regulators, thrust and
pressure measuring devices; electronic
and electromechanical vibration systems

RESEARCH

NUCLEAR METALS, INC
Cambridge, Mass. 1959
Nuclear and metallurgical research

FITTINGS AND PRESSURE VALVES

M .B. SKINNER CO.
South Bend, Ind., 1961
Service fittings for utilities, pressure valves

LEDEEN, INC. Los Angeles, Calif., 1964
Hydraulic and pneumatic control equipment.

CONGLOMERATE

DIE CASTINGS

PEAT MANUFACTURING CORP
Norfolk, Calif., 1956
Nonferrous die castings

METAL STAMPINGS

THE RANDALL CO., Cincinnati, Ohio 1959
Wagner Mfg. Co., Sydney, Ohio, 1959
(Subsidiary)
Appliance stampings and aluminum kitchen utensils

ZENITE METALS CORP.
Blythville, Ark., 1963
Trim for auto and appliance industry

METAL PIPE AND TUBING

CROWELL TUBE CO., INC.
Lexington, Mass. 1960
Small-diameter metal tubing

ERI TOOLWORKS AND LAKEVIEW
FORGE CO., Erie, Pa., 1965
Pipe, wrenches, vices and bomb lugs

BATHROOM FIXTURES

HALL-MACK CO., Los Angeles, Calif. 1956
Bathroom fixtures and accessories

**METAL WORKING
MACHINERY**

PRECISION METHODS AND MACHINES
Waterbury, Conn., 1958
Rolling mill machinery and equipment

BRIDGEPORT MACHINES, INC.
Bridgeport, Conn., 1968
Small milling machines

MACHINE TOOLS

WATERBURY FARREL FOUNDRY &
MACHINE CO., Waterbury, Conn. 1958
Cold-heading machinery; wire-drawing
equipment; rivet setting machines

JONES & LAMSON MACHINE CO.
Springfield, Vt., 1963
Machine tools

THOMPSON GRINDER CO.
Springfield, Ohio, 1967
Precision grinders

FOUNDRY SUPPLIES

FANNER MANUFACTURING CO.
Cleveland, Ohio, 1958
Foundry supplies, Industrial hardware for
iron and steel foundries, machine tools

AMSLER MORTON CORP
Pittsburgh, Pa., 1959
Industrial hardware for iron and steel
foundries; metal processing, industrial
furnaces

**MOTOR VEHICLE PARTS
AND ACCESSORIES**

VAN NORMAN INDUSTRIES
Springfield, Mass., 1958
Automotive replacement antennae

MILFORD MACHINE CO.
Leesburg, Ind., 1960
Crank shafts and connecting rods

**ELECTRICAL TRANSMISSION
EQUIPMENT**

Underfloor division of
WALKER BROTHERS, 1964
Underfloor line for electrical distribution
system

AMERICAN CROSSARM & CONDUIT CO.
Niles, Ill., 1967
Crossarms, braces, insulator pins

BROADCASTING EQUIPMENT

American Microphone Division of
ELGIN NATIONAL WATCH CO.
Elgin, Ill., 1958
Broadcasting equipment

PAINTS

VITA VAR CORP., Newark, N.J. 1962
Industrial paints and protective coatings

FLOOD AND CONKLIN
MANUFACTURING
CO., Newark, N.J. 1964
Paints and industrial coatings

Patterson-Sargent and Allied Divisions of
H. K. PORTER CO., No. Brunswick, N.J.
1965
Paints

BEARINGS

FAFNIR BEARING CO.
New Britain, Conn., 1968
Precision ball and roller bearings

PARKERSBURG-AETNA CORP.
Parkersburg, W. Va., 1963
Ball and roller bearings, oil field production equipment, pre-engineered metal
buildings

PLYWOOD

COQUILLE PLYWOOD CO.
Coquille, Ore., 1955
Plywood

MYRTLE POINT VENEER CO.
Norway, Ore., 1956
Plywood

BANDON VENEER & PLYWOOD
ASSOCIATION, Bandon, Ore., 1956
Plywood

PLASTIC PRODUCTS

KORDITE CORP., Macedon, N.Y., 1955
Plastic products, specialty food and
industrial bags

FEDERAL LEATHER COMPANIES
Belleville, N.J., 1956
Proxylin-coated fabric and vinyl coated
fabric

OLD KING COLE, INC
Louisville, Ohio, 1965
Vacuum and rotary forming of plastic

ABRASIVE PRODUCTS

CLEVELAND METAL ABRASIVE CO.
Cleveland, Ohio, 1965
Iron and steel shot and grit

A. P. De SANNO & SON, INC.
Phoenixville, Pa., 1967
Grinding wheels and abrasive products

**BOAT BUILDING AND
MARINE HARDWARE**

FAEGEOL MARINE ENGINE CO.
San Diego, Calif., 1958
Rights to manufacture marine engines
and turbines

DORSETT PLASTIC CORP.
(Dorset Marine), Santa Clara, Calif., 1960
Inboard and outboard runabout cruisers

SOUTH COAST MARINE CO.
Newport Beach, Calif., 1965
Marine hardware

PASSENGER LINER

S. S. La GUARDIA renamed
S.S. LEILANI, 1956
Tourist passenger line

FURNITURE

Ames Maid Division of
O. AMES CO., Parkersburg, W. Va., 1963
Kitchen and juvenile furniture

Pennant division of
NOVO INDUSTRIAL CORP.
New York, N.Y. 1964
Kitchen and bar stools, juvenile furniture

DURHAM MANUFACTURING CO.
Muncie, Ind., 1964
Folding metal furniture

UNDERWATER EXPLORATION

GERALDINES, LTD., Annapolis, Md., 1962
Products and services for commercial and
underwater exploration

AGROCHEMICALS

SPENCER KELLOG & SONS, INC.
Buffalo, N.Y., 1961
Soybean oil, soybean oil meal, lechitin,
linseed oil, castor oil, linseed oil meal,
livestock feed

S. R. MILLS FEED CO.
Freehold, N.J., 1966
Poultry and livestock feeds

POULTRY FARMING

BYARD V. CARMEAN INC.
Laurel, Del., 1963
Poultry Farm

CAROLINE POULTRY FARMS, INC.
Federalsburg, Md., 1963
Grower and processor of poultry

PHARMACEUTICALS

ZOTOX PHARMACAL CO.
Stanford, Conn., 1961
Pharmaceutical preparations

TILDEN CO., New Lebanon, N.Y., 1961
Pharmaceutical preparations

SHOES

ALBERT H. WEINBRENNER CO.
Milwaukee, Wis., 1960
Men's, boys' and childrens' shoes

STORM DOORS

BENANDA ALUMINUM PRODUCTS CO.
Girard, Ohio, 1956
Storm doors and windows, awnings,
siding material for building

GOLF CARTS

E-Z-GO CAR CORP., Augusta, Ga., 1960
Electric golf carts

WATCH BRACELETS

SPEIDEL CORP., Providence, R.I. 1964
Watch bracelets, chains, identification
bracelets

WRITING INSTRUMENTS

W. A. SHEAFFER PEN CO.
Ft. Madison, Iowa, 1965
Writing instruments, electronic hearing
aids

ZIPPERS

TALON, INC., Meadville, Pa., 1968
Slide fasteners (zippers)

SILVERWARE

GORHAM CORP., Providence, R.I. 1967
Fine silverware, school supplies and
stationery

DISTRIBUTORS

HENRY W. SAARI, INC.
Seatle, Wash., 1967
Distributor, Bostitch products

EDWARD SICKLES & CO.
Philadelphia, Pa., 1967
Distributor, Speidel products

OTHER

NEWMARKET MANUFACTURING CO.
Lowell, Mass, 1954

Walsco-Schott division of
TELAUTOGRAPH CORP.
Los Angeles, Calif., 1956

COMPONENT PARTS CO.
Whittier, Calif. 1959

FUEL ENGINEERING CORP.
Torrance, Calif. 1962

mobiles; others may be longer in periodicity and less predictable, for example, variations in the *business cycle* (periods of prosperity and periods of recession). *Secular* changes in demand are patterns which, for a particular good, do not recur (or, at least, not for a very long period of time). An example would be the demand for penny-farthing bicycles or crystal radio receivers. In some cases, however, what appears to be a secular decline in demand for a good may be completely reversed by circumstances. Thus, the secular decline in demand for bicycles has been reversed by the energy crisis and by the increasing desire to keep fit.

activity of the present century we can discern a temporal pattern in the emphasis by firms engaged in merger activities on each of these three types of strategy. The first of the merger peaks (that of the 1890s and early 1900s) was characterized by mergers which were predominantly *horizontal*, the aim being to reduce competition by swallowing up competing firms. The 1920s mergers, though they continued this trend, were characterized more especially by *vertical* mergers, while the distinguishing feature of the 1960s mergers was their *diversified*—and especially, *conglomerate*—nature. (The FTC estimated that more than four-fifths of all mergers in the United States in 1968 were conglomerate in type.)

Though not necessarily applicable to all firms, it does seem that this pattern forms a kind of three-stage evolutionary sequence which is intuitively convincing (see Bannock, 1971).

1. Early growth emphasized the removal of competition by absorption, leading to oligopolistic industry structures.
2. The next logical step for the large oligopolistic firm was to protect both its sources of supply and its markets by vertical integration.
3. The third step, having ensured protection of supplies and outlets and a high level of market concentration, is to expand and diversify into new markets.

The extent of such diversification can be seen by referring back to Figure 9.1 and by looking at the acquisition behavior of one of the major conglomerates, Textron, as shown in Figure 9.10, which reveals the enormous diversity of activities acquired by Textron between 1943 and 1968, activities ranging from aircraft to zip-fasteners, from pressure valves to kitchen furniture, from die castings to children's shoes, from poultry farming to nuclear research. Similarly, Gulf and Western operates investment and finance companies, sugar, tobacco, and metal manufacturing companies and motion pictures. Litton Industries moved from electronic work in defence industries into calculator and typewriter manufacture, machine tools, frozen food and shipbuilding. The list is endless, the variety enormous, and most of it has come about by acquisition and merger. It is not surprising that such corporations have been the object of much concern and criticism in recent years.

As business enterprises have evolved and implemented the kinds of strategies we have been discussing they have also had to initiate and modify their *organizational structures* in order to carry out such strategies. Again, following Chandler and his associates, it is possible to discern certain patterns in such developments, patterns which have a very important geographical expression. Figure 9.11 shows a three-stage sequence in the development of organizational structures which is broadly parallel to the evolution in strategy outlined above.

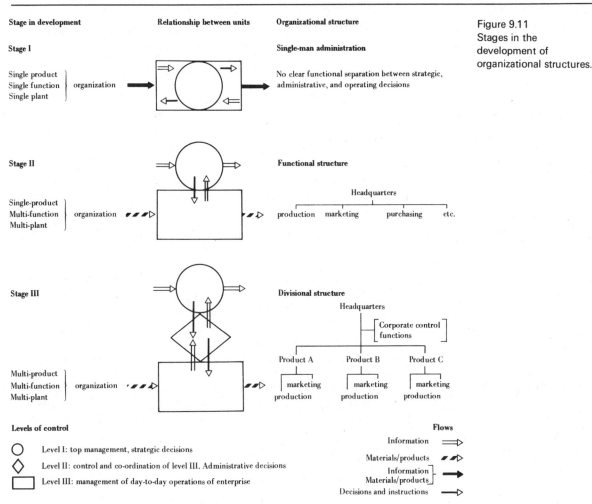

Stage in development — Relationship between units — Organizational structure

Stage I

Single product ⎫
Single function ⎬ organization
Single plant ⎭

Single-man administration

No clear functional separation between strategic, administrative, and operating decisions

Stage II

Single-product ⎫
Multi-function ⎬ organization
Multi-plant ⎭

Functional structure

Headquarters

production   marketing   purchasing   etc.

Stage III

Multi-product ⎫
Multi-function ⎬ organization
Multi-plant ⎭

Divisional structure

Headquarters

Corporate control functions

Product A   Product B   Product C

marketing   marketing   marketing
production   production   production

Levels of control

○ Level I: top management, strategic decisions
◇ Level II: control and co-ordination of level III. Administrative decisions
▭ Level III: management of day-to-day operations of enterprise

Flows

Information ⇒
Materials/products ⇒
Information ⎫
Materials/products ⎬ →
Decisions and instructions ⇒

Figure 9.11
Stages in the development of organizational structures.

The critical feature of such organizational development is the increasing separation between different *levels of control*. Stage I represents the kind of simple enterprise discussed in Chapter Eight, where there is no clear separation between strategic, administrative, and operational decisions.* Such an organization is adequate for a modest scale of business operations but as enterprises expand both in sheer size of output and, more importantly, in the *geographical* spread of their operations, the need arises for an "organizational division of labor" in which specialist departments are created to undertake specific functions. Such functional specialization, together with the operation of several dispersed plants rather than only one, demands a far greater degree of central control. Thus developed the separate *headquarters unit* whose basic function is to plan the

---

*These three categories represent the major decisions which an organization has to make. We have already defined *strategic* decisions (see p. 359) as decisions concerned with the long-term goals and objectives. *Administrative* decisions are concerned with the coordination of the firm's activities, while *operational* decisions are those which relate to the day-to-day production processes.

Note

overall policy of the enterprise as a whole and to coordinate the activities of all the other organizational units. Chandler and Redlich (1961, p. 6) are quite categorical in attributing primary importance to the role of geography in this organizational development. "*Geographical dispersion,*" they argue, "*was the first step in making modern industrial enterprise,* because it made necessary the distinction between headquarters and field."

This stage II structure is appropriate for a strategy which concentrates upon a single line of products or a group of closely related products (for example, in a vertically integrated framework). But is is too inflexible and rigid for a strategy which emphasizes increasing diversification. Hence a new kind of organizational structure has emerged—the divisional structure (Stage III in Figure 9.11). Here instead of having departments organized on functional lines, each major product is centered in a *division* which, in a sense, is a microcosm of the single-product firm. In addition, however, another level of control becomes identifiable—that concerned with administering the divisional structure.

The increasingly common structure of multi-product, multi-plant enterprises, therefore, is rather like a "three-tiered cake"—

> In the bottom layer we have the basic work processes—in the case of a manufacturing organization, the processes that procure raw materials, manufacture the physical product, warehouse it, and ship it. In the middle layer, we have the programed decision-making processes, the processes that govern the day-to-day operation of the manufacturing and distribution system. In the top layer, we have the nonprogramed decision-making processes, the processes that are required to design and redesign the entire system, to provide it with its basic goals and objectives, and to monitor its performance.
> *Simon (1960), p. 40*

We noted earlier Chandler and Redlich's emphasis on the importance of geography in the evolution of the organizational structure of business enterprise. In other words, geographical space is a fundamental *input* to the business enterprise. But there is also a very clear *geographical output* of the organizational transition we have been looking at. Each of the three levels of control and activity have distinguishable spatial patterns of arrangement and it is to these that we now turn.

Geographical organization of multi-plant enterprises

> Every business is a package of functions, and within limits these functions can be separated and located at different places.
> *R. M. Haig (1926), p. 416.*

Since Robert Haig wrote these words some half a century ago, technological developments in production technology in general and in transportation and communications in particular, have greatly increased the potential ability of business enterprises to arrange their administrative and operating units in ways which best fit their overall corporate requirements. Haig's "limits" have been greatly extended. In particular—largely because of innovations in the transmission, receipt and storage of messages—contact between administrative and operating units no longer depends necessarily on their being located at the same place. Each can be located according to its own specific needs. Recent work by geographers, especially Tornquist and Thorngren in Sweden and Goddard in Britain, has done much to increase our understanding of the locational requirements and tendencies of the *information processing units* of large organizations (Levels I and II of Figure 9.11).

Level I functions, the head office and overall control functions of the enterprise, are concerned, as we have seen, with the general long-term planning of the enterprise's activities rather than with its day-to-day operations. In other words, Level I functions deal for the most part with *nonprogramed* situations, including negotiating and bargaining with top executives in other enterprises, meeting with government and other public officials, and so on. Tornquist argues that these important contacts

> cannot be maintained with adequate efficiency by letters and telecommunications but demand *direct personal contacts* between personnel and thus passenger transportation. That these contacts demand the personal attendance of often highly expert personnel is probably bound up with the fact that contacts in many cases involve considerable elements of what we might call problem-solving, planning, keeping an eye on the course of events, pulse-feeling and reconnaissance. The contacts often take the form of talks and discussions in which personal effort is of great importance.
> *Tornquist (1968), p. 101*

These face-to-face contacts are maintained and developed most easily if such contact-intensive activities *agglomerate* in information-rich locations. Hence the top control functions of modern business enterprises show a very strong tendency to concentrate in a few major metropolitan complexes: often, though not always (New York is the case in point), these are national capitals.

The extent of the spatial concentration of such corporate headquarters is really very considerable as Figures 9.12 and 9.13 demonstrate for the United States and Britain. Figure 9.12 maps the headquarters' locations of the leading 500 industrial corporations in the United States in 1973. Although 107 cities are represented, 71 of these (66 percent) have the headquarters of only *one* of the leading corporations and a further 11 have only two headquarters. Thus 25 cities (23 percent of the total) contain 407 of the 500 headquarters offices (81 percent). But even this does not fully indicate the degree of head office concentration. Sixty-three percent of the headquarters are in just nine cities and just one—New York City—has 30 percent of the total. In 1973, therefore, almost one out of every three of the nation's leading industrial corporations was headquartered in New York City.

Concentration of the headquarters of leading corporations is even more pronounced in Britain than in the United States. Figure 9.13 reveals the totally dominant role of London as a headquarters' center. In 1971, one out of every

Figure 9.12
Headquarters of the
leading 500 United States
industrial corporations,
1973. [*Source:* compiled
from data in *Fortune,* May
1974.]

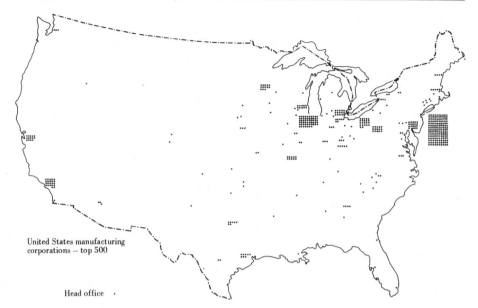

United States manufacturing
corporations — top 500

Head office   ·

two of the leading 1,000 British industrial corporations and two out of every
three of the leading 500 companies had their headquarters in London. In other
words, the concentration of leading British company headquarters in London
is more than twice as great as that of United States companies in New York.
The second-ranking metropolitan center, Birmingham, had 7 percent of the
headquarters of the leading 1,000 companies and only 5 percent of the top
500 headquarters. In comparison, Chicago, the second-ranking headquarters
center in the United States, had 11 percent of the top 500 headquarters. Table
9.9 reveals that the major concentration of headquarters of leading corporations
in Canada is evenly distributed between Montreal (38.1 percent) and Toronto
(36.7 percent). Vancouver, the next-ranking city, had only 6.3 percent of the
total. These figures are for 1965 and there is reason to believe that Toronto
has become rather more important as a headquarters center in the last ten
years.*

Level II activities, the more routine administrative functions, also tend to concentrate in information-rich locations. However because many of their contact
activities can be more readily carried out indirectly via telephone, telex and
written communications, their need to locate in the highest level metropolitan
centers is less pronounced than that of Level I activities. Nevertheless they
do, as Stephen Hymer pointed out, depend heavily upon white-collar workers,
communications systems and information, needs which can only be met in urban
centers of some size. Thus there is a very clear association between upper levels
in the organizational hierarchy and upper levels in the urban hierarchy. But

Note

*Similar levels of concentration of headquarters locations seem to exist in most industrialized
countries. Pred (1974) has gathered together a variety of statistical information on such patterns together with a lot of detail on U.S. metropolitan complexes. His attempts to relate
such concentration to the process of city-system development are discussed in Chapter 10.

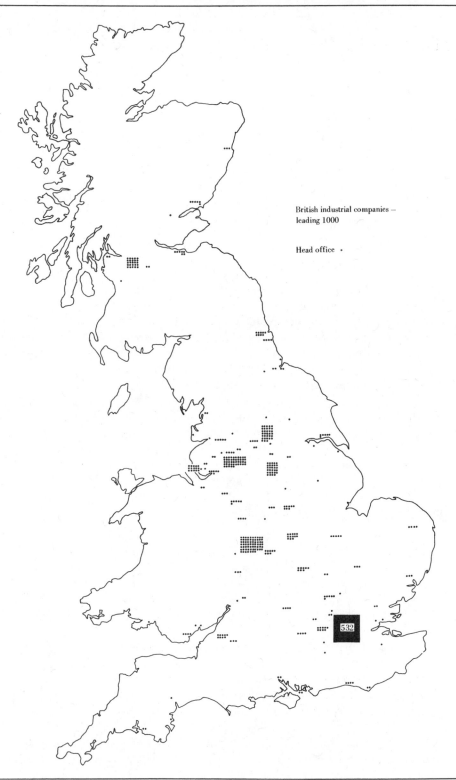

Figure 9.13
Headquarters of the
leading 1,000 British
industrial companies,
1971. [*Source:* compiled
from data in *Times 1,000,*
1972.]

British industrial companies —
leading 1000

Head office ·

Table 9.9
Assets of leading
Canadian corporations
controlled by selected
metropolitan centers,
1965.

	Corporations $000,000	% of Canadian total
Montreal	10,327	38.1
Toronto	9,901	36.7
Vancouver	1,729	6.3
Calgary	1,351	5.0
Winnipeg	536	2.0
London	138	0.5
Hamilton	1,037	3.9
Quebec City	331	1.2
Halifax	220	0.8

Source: D. Kerr (1968) Metropolitan Dominance in Canada, Table 16.6, in J. Warkentin (ed.), *Canada: A Geographical Interpretation*. Toronto: Methuen & Co.

what about Level III activities, those which produce the actual material goods of the business enterprise?

Production units of the large business enterprise show a good deal more variability in their locational requirements than do their administrative and control units simply because of the greater variability in the nature of their operations and the consequent diversity in their inputs and outputs. Despite the developments in production technology which have drastically reduced the quantities of materials required for many types of production, the fact remains that some processing units are still strongly oriented towards localized raw material sites. In the case of the multi-plant firm, of course, such a locational pull relates only to the particular processing unit itself and not to the enterprise as a whole. However, it is true to say that the general decline in such material orientation together with the decrease in the *relative* importance of transportation costs which we noted in Chapter Five has increased the potential locational flexibility of business firms. Decreases in the geographical variability of labor "costs" (in the fullest sense) *within* countries (Chapter Six) have also contributed to a widening of a firm's *spatial margins*.

Such developments have led some writers to argue that the kind of location theory we have been discussing is no longer relevant. However, just as we saw in Chapter Three that it is possible to identify some zonation of agricultural production at a continental scale (see Figures 3.22 and 3.23) it is also possible to see some evidence of the application of least-cost location theory at a similarly enlarged geographical scale. This can only occur within the context of the very large multi-plant enterprise operating at a global scale. Whereas the small single-plant firm shows little sign of abandoning existing agglomerations of economic activity (though they may move from the center of such agglomerations to their periphery) the multi-plant, and especially multi-national, firm shows far less locational conservatism. In recent years in particular, multi-national corporations with production units specializing in products with low unit weight and high labor intensity have located these units in areas of very low labor costs, especially the Third World countries of Southeast Asia, Mexico, and parts of Latin America.

Certain types of labor-oriented production are particularly susceptible to such locational tendencies. The industry which has received most attention is electronics manufacture, particularly domestic equipment such as radio, television, tape recorders and their component parts, and individual electronic components. But there are many others—cameras and photographic equipment, office machinery, garments, children's toys, to name but a few—whose production tends to be similarly located. Multi-national firms producing such goods have sought out areas of low labor costs. Just how large the difference in labor costs can be between production in the United States and in certain other countries can be seen in Figure 9.14. For example, in the case of consumer electronics production average hourly earnings for the same job were *eighteen times* higher in the United States than in Taiwan and *twelve times* higher in the United States than in Hong Kong. Garments could be manufactured in Costa Rica at one-seventh of the cost of producing them in the United States. It is hardly surprising, in the face of such large labor cost differentials, that many multi-nationals have been, and are, locating some of their production units in such countries. In terms of our discussion of Chapter Six, these labor locations fall within the *critical isodapane* for the production unit. This implies that the additional transportation costs incurred in shipping materials and other inputs to the production site and moving the finished product to the market (which is frequently another unit in the same enterprise) are more than offset by lower costs of production.

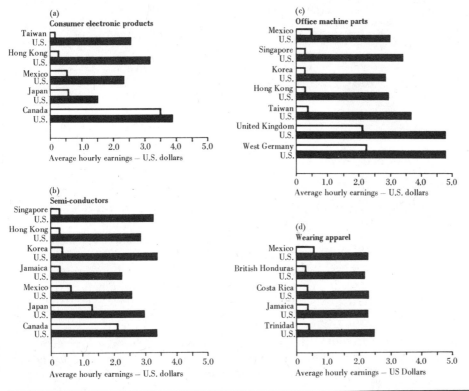

Figure 9.14 Comparison of average hourly earnings of workers processing or assembling U.S. materials in foreign establishments with estimated earnings for comparable job classifications in the United States, 1969. [*Source:* compiled from data in U.S. Tariff Commission, 1970.]

Thus, both technological and organizational developments have combined together to produce not only a multi-layered organizational structure in the multi-plant enterprise in which three primary control levels can be identified but also a very clear geographical structure of such enterprises. The individual units of an enterprise can be arranged, at least theoretically, in a variety of different ways. Figure 9.15 illustrates just three of these possibilities. In Figure 9.15(a) there is a two-fold geographical structure with the head office situated in one location and both the administrative and operating units located together at other sites (note that the diagrams do not have a scale: the degree of dispersion between units may be a few miles or thousands of miles, within a country or in different countries). In Figure 9.15(b) both control levels are located together while the operating units are dispersed. Finally, in Figure 9.15(c) there is complete separation of each level; the kind of structure which may occur particularly in multi-national corporations with the headquarters unit located in the major city of the home country, divisional or regional headquarters in key foreign metropolitan centers, and operating units in least-cost locations for their particular activities.

Figure 9.15
Alternative spatial arrangements of units of multi-plant enterprises. [*Source:* after Tornquist (1968).]

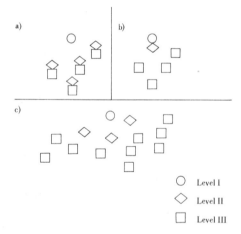

Locational decision-making in multi-plant enterprises

Even for the small single-plant firm examined in Chapter Eight the location decision is not without its complexities. But for the large multi-plant enterprise the degree of complexity is very much greater. Multi-plant firm decisions are more complex simply because such firms are themselves far more intricate structures. Not only do they experience internal pressures resulting from possible conflicts of ideas and objectives among high level decision-makers but they also have a very extensive range of "contact points" with their external environment.

But "location" decisions themselves, as we have said before, are not simply restricted to questions of locating a *new* plant (whether that is a relocated facility or a branch). As Danielsson has pointed out,

locational decisions are... involved every time a change in the extent of type of operations in one or more localities is being considered although there is not necessarily any question of building a new plant or transferring an old one... Any choice between such alternatives must take into account the consequences for a larger unit than the individual plant.
Danielsson (1964), p. 52

We should add that change in a firm's spatial organization also occurs for other reasons, particularly as a by-product of merger and acquisition. As we observed earlier, this has been a particularly important strategy in corporate growth. A very large proportion of the plants belonging to such firms as Textron and Litton, for example (Figures 9.3 and 9.4) are entirely the result of those corporations' very strong merger activity. Thus, in examining the locational behavior of multi-plant enterprises we must set such behavior within the overall framework of the enterprise's strategies and of its prevailing organizational and geographical structure. Figure 8.16, the model of locational decisions for the single-plant firm is broadly relevant even for the more complex case of the multi-plant enterprise though some modifications are obviously necessary. Readers will find it useful to refer back to this model during the ensuing discussion.

Recall the three-step view of problem-solving outlined in Chapter Eight (p. 321). In the case of the single-plant firm, identifying the stimulus for a location decision was not too difficult. However, for the multi-plant firm such stimuli may operate on one of two levels. On the one hand, the stimulus may relate to the company as a whole and concern its overall strategy and locational structure. On the other hand, the stimulus may relate to just one of the firm's plants. A further difference between large and small enterprises is that the larger ones, with their more sophisticated and specialized internal structures, have both a geographically broader outlook and a generally longer-term perspective. The more widely dispersed a firm's operations, the more extensive is its task environment and, hence, its awareness of both opportunities and problems. In a temporal context, the large firm tends to be far more *planning-oriented* than the small firm which tends to exist on a more immediate time-scale. Part of the specialized control structure of large firms is concerned with monitoring the firm's performance and with seeking out future courses of action. In fact, most large business organizations possess a highly developed and sophisticated *adaptive structure*. Individual departments, as part of their day-to-day operations, have the responsibility of collecting information concerning their own specific functions. But over and above this, most large organizations employ staff specialists whose primary function is to obtain and evaluate information regarding the firm's operation vis-à-vis, for example, the strategies of competitors, market changes, financial and technological developments, and so on. In some cases, actively searching the environment for new business opportunities may be an established part of the firm's operations. As in other respects, therefore, internal scale economies are significant in the acquisition and processing of information and, although, like all organizations, its view of the world is selective and limited, the large organization undoubtedly possesses a more extensive spatial and temporal awareness.

The planning process in large firms takes many different forms whose detail need not concern us here. It is common, however, for firms to operate, say, a "rolling five-year" plan in which forecasts for the next five years are updated annually in the light of changing conditions. Such plans generally involve forecasting sales, investment needs, market trends, and so on. The existence of such "future-scanning" procedures, however rudimentary they may be, suggests that we need to distinguish between two kinds of stimulus or stress: immediate and anticipated. The behavior of most small firms is a response to an immediate stimulus, a threat to their existence of the kind discussed in Chapter Eight (see Figure 8.17). While this may be true in specific cases for large enterprises, the fact remains that much of their behavior is initiated by the identification of problems or opportunities which seem likely to occur in the future (that is, within the time-scale of the firm's planning horizon).

Most common among such stimuli are, for example, a perceived lack of capacity to meet planned growth; competitive threat; technological change likely to render a process or product obsolescent; operating costs above those consistent with the firm's objectives; decreases in sales volume. None of these (except perhaps shortage of capacity) is an obviously and explicitly locational problem. Yet each poses two fundamental questions—*how* and *where?*—which are pregnant with locational implications. It is not possible in a book of this kind to examine possible responses to each of these stimuli. Rather than nod superficially at each, therefore, we prefer to develop one case study in some detail in order to give a clearer impression of the way in which a very large multi-plant enterprise solved a major locational problem.

*A case study of locational behavior by a multi-plant enterprise**

This case study, which concerns one of the divisions of General Foods, is based upon a detailed investigation by Whitman and Schmidt (1966). General Foods has been one of the top 50 industrial corporations in the United States for many years. In 1961, at the time of this case study, it ranked 36 in terms of sales. The company had grown to a very large extent by merger and acquisition since 1925 (the name General Foods was introduced in 1929) and produced a very wide range of food products (some 200), most of which were "household names." By the early 1960s, General Foods consisted of over 60 plants, warehouses and offices in the United States, together with 17 overseas subsidiaries. Total employment was in the region of 30,000. In common with the trend in organizational development which we discussed on p. 367, the company operated a divisional structure, the eight divisions being indicated in Figure 9.16.

Note

*Very few studies deal in any depth with the locational behavior of large business enterprises. The earliest work by a geographer is that by McNee (1958) and he has subsequently made further very valuable contributions (McNee 1960, 1963, 1974). Fleming and Krumme (1968), Krumme (1969, 1970), Hayter (1976) and Rees (1974) have also described locational adjustment processes within large enterprises. Several other works on locational decision-making also include some detail of specific cases, for example, Townroe (1971), Söderman (1975), Watts (1970, 1971). Watts (1974) has also written in general terms about the kind of spatial rationalization process discussed here.

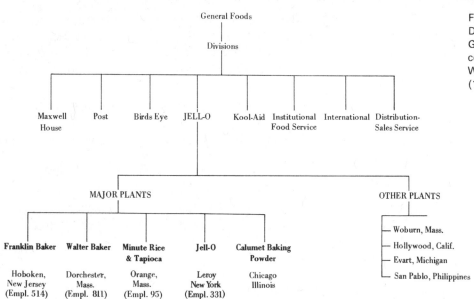

Figure 9.16
Divisional organization of
General Foods. [*Source:*
compiled from material in
Whitman and Schmidt
(1966).]

One of the most important divisions was Jell-O based upon one of the two original companies which had merged in 1925 to form the nucleus of what later became General Foods. The bulk of the Jell-O division's production of a variety of foods was concentrated in five major plants in the east and midwest (Figure 9.17), although some production was carried on elsewhere. However, it is the five main plants which are the focus of interest here. Table 9.10 outlines the process of spatial reorganization carried out by Jell-O over a four-year period. The problem which the company identified (the initial stimulus) related to the obsolescence of the five main plants, each of which was old and technologically unsuitable under 1960s conditions. None had been selected by General Foods but had been the existing plants of firms which had been acquired during the 1920s. Some kind of modernization was clearly needed but what form should

Stimulus

Figure 9.17
Geographical distribution
of major Jell-O Division
plants, 1960. [*Source:*
compiled from material in
Whitman and Schmidt
(1966).]

**Alternatives
identified**

it take? Two possibilities were identified: one, the most preferred initially, was to retain and improve the five existing plants. The other was to seek one or more new locations and consolidate production there, although the uncertainties and possible duplication of overhead costs involved in such a strategy made it an unattractive proposition at first sight.

Search

The company's search process which, as Table 9.10 indicates, was both complex and lengthy, can be divided fairly clearly into three distinct phases. Phase I was initiated by the establishment of a task force charged with making an exploratory investigation guided by a steering committee. The task force soon realized that improvement to existing location was *not* the best strategy; it was far better to seek new locations.

**Preliminary
geographical
filtering**

"The first step was to determine the optimum general geographic location in the United States for facilities to replace the five major Jell-O Division plants. Eliminating the Far West..., three geographical areas were considered—the South, East and MidWest. The initial effort proved that a separate Southern plant location was not economically advantageous at the present time because it merely replaced one existing facility, and direct and transportation savings were not sufficient to justify the investment. It became apparent that the most significant savings were obtainable through overhead reductions by consolidation of existing Jell-O plants into fewer plants. The overhead savings that have been identified represent approximately 80 percent of the total savings of this study. Direct and transportation savings represent the remainder."
Quoted in Whitman & Schmidt (1966), p. 16

**Alternative
consolidation
plans**

Thus, even at this stage and without reference to the number, let alone the specific locations, of the new plants being determined, the task force had made a commitment to a specific locational strategy. Clearly, such a consolidation strategy could take a number of different spatial forms. Table 9.11 summarizes the six alternative plans put forward for consideration by the task force. Three of the plans were based on three plants and three on two plants with varying mixtures of new, expanded or retained facilities. Comparison between the six alternatives on the basis of costs, savings, returns and "payback time" showed that the most suitable strategy was to pursue plan 6 which involved replacing all four eastern plants with *one* new plant and retaining the Calumet plant in Chicago in its existing state.

At this point, the task force's work was finished. However, problems of adopting its recommended strategy were several. One problem related to the very long-standing identification between each of the plants and the community in which it was located. Another was the potential rigidity of "putting all of Jell-O's manufacturing eggs in one basket. The proposed consolidated plant would handle approximately two-thirds of the entire production of the division... A work stoppage... would obviously be much more serious than such an occurrence at one of the old plants." Nevertheless it was felt that the economic advantages of consolidation outweighed such problems as these. (It is perhaps worth pointing out that not all business executives would necessarily take the same view.

Many would probably prefer to spread the risk and operate several separate, even if smaller, plants).

Identification of problem (early 1960): Need for "revamped and revitalized" production facilities to (a) maintain competitive position and (b) provide for new processes and products.

Alternative locational strategies identified:
(1) Expand and improve *existing* plants. This was, initially, the preferred strategy "except where other overriding advantages prevail."
(2) Seek new site(s) and consolidate production there.

Search:—carried out in three phases:

Phase I (early 1960– July 1961)	(i) Establishment of task force and steering committee. (ii) Early rejection of alternative (1); focus on consolidation. (iii) Preliminary analysis of divisional costs, esp. transportation, product allocation, construction, overhead, shutdown/startup costs. Based on three geographical areas: South, East, Midwest. South rejected. (iv) Six alternative consolidation plans formulated (see Table 9.11). (v) Task force studies select alternative 6: *one* new Eastern plant replacing all four old eastern plants plus retention of Chicago plant. *Alternative 6 recommended*

Phase II (July 1961– Sept. 1962)	(vi) Establishment of facilities improvement group. (vii) Detailed cost investigations. Confirmed likelihood of large potential savings and profit benefits. (viii) Plan submitted to Board. Sanctioned search for site. (ix) Preliminary location survey of 21 locations in 8 eastern states had "pointed strongly to a city in the Philadelphia–Wilmington–Baltimore area." (x) Appointment of plant location consultants. *Jell-O defined basic locational requirements*: (a) Plant to be within range of primary market served by four old plants, preferably within 250 miles of New York City. (b) Near an adequate ocean port(s) because of overseas origin of large quantities of raw materials. (c) Near a sugar refinery because sugar consumption more than half a million pounds per day. (d) In a community receptive to that type of industry. (xi) Consultants also recommended Philadelphia–Wilmington–Baltimore area. (xii) Specific recommendation: *Dover, Delaware*. (xiii) Jell-O employ another consulting firm to assess community of Dover as suitable location in terms of: (a) Attitudes and feelings of residents toward location of a General Foods plant in the city (b) Willingness to work in the plant (c) Work characteristics of the "employable people" (d) Status of race relations (G.F. was long-established equal opportunity employer) (e) Union attitudes (f) Availability of skilled craft labor.

Choice: Company decides to move to Dover
(September 1962)
January 1964: first production lines placed in operation
May 1965: plant officially dedicated

Source: compiled from material in Whitman and Schmidt (1966).

Table 9.10
Stages in the spatial rationalization of the Jell-O division of General Foods, 1960–1964.

Table 9.11
Alternative plant
consolidation plans for
the Jell-O division of
General Foods.

Existing plant locations, 1960:

Hoboken, N.J., Dorchester, Mass., Orange, Mass., LeRoy, N.Y., Chicago, Ill.

Plan 1.	**2 plants:**	One new plant in East
		One new plant in MidWest
Plan 2.	**2 plants:**	One new plant in East
		Expansion of Chicago plant
Plan 3.	**3 plants:**	One new plant in East
		Retention of Dorchester plant
		One new plant in Midwest
Plan 4.	**3 plants:**	One new plant in East
		Retention of Dorchester plant
		Expansion of Chicago plant
Plan 5.	**3 plants:**	One new plant in East
		Retention of Dorchester plant
		Retention of Chicago plant
Plan 6.	**2 plants:**	One new plant in East
		Retention of Chicago plant

Source: compiled from material in Whitman and Schmidt (1966).

The next stage in the search process (Phase II) was to establish a facilities improvement group to carry out detailed cost investigations. One interesting point was that the group was specifically instructed to do "*only* that work necessary to justify or reject a recommendation for building a new eastern plant consolidating the Hoboken, Dorchester, LeRoy and Orange operations." In other words, no further alternatives were to be sought. In fact the group supported the task force recommendation. It had also made a preliminary location survey and regarded the Philadelphia–Wilmington–Baltimore area as most suitable. However, such a finding was not acted upon without further analysis. In Phase III specialist location consultants were employed to carry out a detailed location survey in the East subject to the constraints listed in Table 9.10 (see section x (a-d)). As it happened, the consultants also favored the Philadelphia–Wilmington–Baltimore area and ultimately recommended the city of Dover in the State of Delaware, a community of 7,250 population.

Site selection: use of locational consultants

Use of community consultants

But the process did not end there; General Foods wanted to know more about Dover as a *community* (quite apart from the economic advantages of its location) and especially about its attitudes to a new plant, its community and race relations, and its labor force. Accordingly, another firm of consultants was engaged to "backstop" the location consultants' report with a detailed community survey. Their investigations were satisfactory, so in September 1962 the General Foods board decided to locate their new plant in Dover. Two years later the plant began limited production and was fully operational by mid-1965, some five years after the investigations began. As a result, the Jell-O Division's spatial structure was transformed from the five-plant structure shown in Figure 9.17 to the two-plant structure shown in Figure 9.18.

Final choice

General comments on locational behavior by multi-plant enterprises

Not all locational decision processes in multi-plant enterprises may be as sophis-

Figure 9.18
Location of Jell-O
Division plants after
rationalization, 1965.
[*Source:* compiled from
material in Whitman and
Schmidt (1966).]

o plant closed down
● plant retained
■ new consolidated plant

ticated and thorough as that described in this case study. The fact that the study was published at all suggests that it was regarded as a "model" example. Nevertheless, it does support our view that the locational behavior of multi-plant enterprises is complex and, in most cases, far more thorough than that of most small firms, not least because of differences in resources (both money and specialized manpower). *The important point is that location decisions are not isolated events. They arise as part of the firm's strategies* which, as we saw earlier in this chapter, can be divided broadly into horizontal, vertical or diversifying strategies. Each of these, in turn, may be pursued through internal expansion or external combination (merger/acquisition). Very often, preference for one strategy rather than another is well established and tends to be followed consistently by a particular enterprise thus lending a degree of predictability to its behavior. The General Foods case was specifically one of locational adjustment or rationalization of existing facilities and is, therefore, only one of many possible kinds of locational behavior. As Table 9.12 suggests a multi-plant enterprise can implement its strategies locationally in a variety of different ways. The table shows 27 possibilities (the General Foods case would be category 6) and this is by no means an exhaustive list.

Scale and type of operations	Locational arrangement of operations		
	Increase number of plants	No change in number	Decrease number of plants
I Increase volume of output	1	2	3
II No change in volume of output	4	5	6
III Decrease volume of output	7	8	9
IV Increase volume + new product	10	11	12
V No change in volume + new product	13	14	15
VI Decrease volume + new product	16	17	18
VII Increase volume + new process	19	20	21
VIII No change in volume + new process	22	23	24
IX Decrease volume + new process	25	26	27

Table 9.12
Categories of locational
behavior in multi-plant
enterprises.

Quite clearly, the existing spatial structure of a multi-plant enterprise—the number and location of its plants and the connections between them—exerts a very powerful influence on its subsequent behavior. In making a strategic decision the enterprise is greatly influenced by such structure. This influence is expressed in a number of ways. First, the geographical distribution of enterprise units (offices, warehouses, production plants) is the skeleton on which the firm's task environment is built. Thus both the quantity and quality of information which the firm possesses about its external environment is at least partly a reflection of the firm's geographical structure. The more extensive that structure (the more plants the firm has and the more widely they are dispersed) the more extensive is its view of the world. A second point relates to the enterprise's experience in making location decisions. We emphasized in Chapter Eight the importance of *frequency of occurrence* of problem situations because this determines the depth of experience on which to make similar decisions. The large firms we have discussed in the present chapter have large numbers of plants, yet this does not necessarily imply that they have a commensurate amount of experience in locational decision-making. On the contrary, many have rather little since most of their plants have been acquired through the process of merger and not chosen by the enterprise itself. The difference between such an enterprise and the single-plant firm, therefore, is not so much one of relevant locational experience as of possessing the resources to employ specialists to find appropriate locations. Very few small firms employ location consultants.

A third way in which the existing spatial structure of a firm is important is in its *inertial effect*. However chosen originally (even by some other firm subsequently absorbed), existing plant locations represent large fixed capital investments which are not lightly abandoned. Such inertia may well be reinforced by the long-standing relationship with the area or community in which the plant is located. Thus a multi-plant firm is just as likely to prefer to retain its existing locations and improve them (as was General Foods' original preference) as a single-plant firm. It is not surprising, therefore, that a United Nations' survey of 1967 found that between 60 and 80 percent of the new manufacturing capacity created each year is in the form of expansion to existing plants. Fourthly, when locational change is undertaken by a multi-plant enterprise its direction may well be heavily constrained by its prevailing geographical structure (again the General Foods case is instructive—see section x(a) of Table 9.10). The search process itself also seems to have certain predictable features. Again, the existing structure very likely biases the areas considered. Most locational search processes seem to fall into two distinct stages: a coarse screening at the broad geographical scale of a region or a particular city* followed by

Note

*This view is supported by a number of studies of plant location decisions. A study of a sample of single and multi-plant firms in the United States ranging in size from fewer than 500 workers to more than 20,000 workers revealed that 25 percent of plant location projects were concerned from the beginning with a single city or surrounding area and a further 25 percent were conducted within a single state (Thompson, 1961). A report by the Ontario Economic Council (1967) concerning plant location selection in Ontario reveals a similar "short-circuit" approach to locational choice. Forty-three percent of the sample firms

focused their locational search only on Toronto and sought sites within a 100–200 mile radius of that city.

Note continued

---

detailed search for a specific site *within* a pre-selected area. However, the large firm seems more likely to compare systematically a number of possible alternatives than the small firm, though much depends on how rapidly a decision has to be made. Nevertheless, the way in which General Foods compared alternative locational plans seems to fit the idea of "storing" alternatives shown in Figure 8.16.

We have traveled a long way from our early simplified model. Yet, although we have introduced a great deal of complexity by relaxing the assumptions on which the model was initially based, this does not mean that we have destroyed completely the basic theoretical principles derived from the work of such location theorists as Weber, Lösch, Isard and others. In the case of the spatial organization of manufacturing, despite the complexities of behavior and organization introduced in this and the preceding chapter, we can still observe the operation of some of these principles, albeit in more complex and larger-scale circumstances. For example, agglomeration, one of Weber's three fundamental locational forces, is especially significant for small firms (which show a very strong affinity for existing manufacturing concentrations) and for the higher-level control functions of large multi-plant enterprises. Least-cost orientation, for example, to low labor cost sites at a world scale seems to be significant in helping to explain the locational tendencies of some of the production units of multi-national enterprises. Finally, in the context of the location decision process itself, it seems possible to see the two-stage geographical search procedure as a combination of Löschian and Weberian approaches as John Rees (1974) has suggested. Thus at the broader scale, the pattern of demand for the enterprise's existing or planned output seems to be important in determining the general geographical area. This can be viewed in the kind of "market area" framework originally proposed by Lösch and developed in this book in Chapters Two and Seven. At the finer scale within the broad region chosen, Weberian least-cost considerations seem to come more into play.

Further reading

Bannock, G. (1971), *The Juggernauts: The Age of the Big Corporation*, London: Weidenfeld and Nicolson, New York: Bobbs-Merrill.

Blair, J. M. (1972), *Economic Concentration: Structure, Behavior, and Public Policy*, New York: Harcourt, Brace, Jovanovich, Chapters 1–12.

Chandler, A. D. Jr., and F. Redlich (1961), Recent Developments in American Business Administration and their Conceptualization, *Business History Review* **35**, 1–27.

Galbraith, J. K. (1974), *Economics and the Public Purpose*, Boston: Houghton Mifflin, London: Andre Deutsch.

Hamilton, F. E. I. (ed.) (1974), *Spatial Perspectives on Industrial Organization and Decision-Making*, London: John Wiley; Chapter 1 (Hamilton); Chapter 2 (McNee); Chapter 7 (Rees).

Pred, A. R. (1974), Major Job-providing Organizations and Systems of Cities, *Association of American Geographers, Commission on College Geography, Resource Paper* **27**, Chapters 1–3.

Watts, H. D. (1974), Spatial Rationalization in Multi-plant Enterprises, *Geoforum* **17**, 69–76.

CHAPTER 10

THE TIME DIMENSION: CUMULATIVE DEVELOPMENT IN SPACE

Prologue

In developing our argument throughout this book, we have quite deliberately dealt with one locational variable at a time. Although we have acknowledged the importance of temporal change in each of the individual variables our approach has been that of "comparative statics." But none of the variables conditioning the location of economic activity is constant. Over time the needs of human society change. To meet these changes new technologies develop, new production systems evolve, and the economic landscape experiences change and development. Thus the economic landscape facing the decision-maker—whether he be farmer or industrialist, single-plant entrepreneur or multinational executive—is not a static but a kaleidoscopic structure made up of elements which have evolved over a long period of time. Once set in motion, the system is never free of its antecedent states. Decisions, therefore, are set firmly within a time-stream; they have both pasts and futures.

We have now reached the stage when we must alter our approach. Instead of introducing yet another factor in the way we have done so far we need to consider *all* those factors we have discussed but in a *dynamic* or *temporal framework*. How does an economic landscape evolve? How does economic development proceed in space? These are not easy questions to answer. Our approach to them is based upon the notion that growth or development, of whatever kind, consists of two basic components (Boulding 1953):

1. The formation of the *nucleus* or initial structure.
2. The subsequent growth and development of that structure—what Maruyama (1963) calls *morphogenesis* (creation of form).

As we shall see, it is a good deal easier to gain an understanding of the second than the first of these two components.

Initial triggers to development

> Within broad limits the power of attraction today of a center has its origin mainly in the historical accident that something once started there and not in a number of other places where it could equally well or better have started and that the start met with success.
> *Myrdal (1957), p. 26*

Most writers on economic development in space would agree with Myrdal about the importance of what we shall call the *initial trigger* to an understanding of the way in which places develop over time. *How strong a trigger, what kind*, and *where it occurred* obviously have an important influence on subsequent events and on the particular arrangement of the "economic furniture" of the landscape. For the embryo central place of the simplified model of Chapter Two it was perhaps the advent of the first subsistence farmer who sufficiently understood the science of economics to make sausages or to set up a bakery, serving his neighbors more cheaply than they could supply sausages or bread to themselves. *Where* was perhaps a random event in this case, but once established, the location of the first sausage-maker would, as we have seen, influence the subsequent possible locations of other sausage-makers in relation to it. In terms of *what sort* of trigger, perhaps the significant feature here is that it was a "central" function using more labor and capital than land. *How strong*; perhaps the answer here was "not very," if one measured strength in terms of the effects of the event on the existing social and economic structure of the landscape.

Contrast this hypothetical situation, however, with the following real life example:

> The Californian gold fever is reaching its crisis. We are told that the new region that has just become a part of our possessions, is El Dorado after all. Thither is now setting a tide that will not cease its flow until either untold wealth is amassed or extended beggary is secured. By a sudden and accidental discovery the ground is represented as one vast gold mine. Gold is picked up in pure lumps, twenty-four carats fine. Soldiers are deserting their ranks, sailors their ships and everybody their employment, to speed to the region of the gold mines. In a moment, as it were, a desert country, that never deserved much notice from the world, has become the center of universal attraction.
>
> "*The Gold Fever*", Hartford Daily Courant, *December 6, 1848*

In terms of the "economic furniture" created by this trigger, the fine detail has been so effectively recreated by the movie industry that no point is served by describing it here. Just two facts will suffice. Sacramento, a collection of tents and shanties in 1849, had acquired by 1857 a population of 60,000 and become the state capital. San Francisco, with a history of previous minor triggers to growth, had a population of 1,000 in 1848 which reached 35,000 in 1850 and its "furniture" was described then as "a strange medley of buildings from the rudest hovel and canvas tent to the elegant mansion and the most substantial warehouses" (quoted in Brown, 1948, p. 504).

It is the sheer *strength* of the initial trigger in this case which is impressive. The vast mobilization of resources to tap the goldfields was of an unprecedented scale. As to the *kind* of stimulus, the gold rush embodies the hope of fast profits but the fear of overnight collapse. This gives it a particularly "speculative" flavor. Unlike the solid cabin of the homesteader—built to last—for the mining town it is the tent and shanty, mobile and ephemeral. For many boom towns this was all there was and the "spark" which mining brought to development failed to "catch on."

What both the embryo hypothetical central place and mid-century California have in common is that they both offered at a point in time some particular *advantage* in supplying a good for which a demand existed. For the "sausage-producing central place" it was a *comparatively more efficient* producer of sausages (given economies of scale). For gold-rush California it had an *absolute advantage* in providing (almost "free of charge" according to contemporary newspaper reports) a highly valued good.

Compared to other locations, then, which are probably good for other things, the two activities in question—gold mining and sausage-making—drew to them

the factors needed to produce their respective goods. Labor, capital and technical know-how, together with those skilled in making use of them, moved in
to the developing site. Linkages were established between them and the clusters
that became mining towns or central places were formed. In the simplified
model, our economic man in the guise of the entrepreneur sausage-maker saw
an immediate pay-off and was sure of this correct decision. For the goldminers,
storekeepers, hoteliers, victuallers of the gold-rush era, theirs was the judgment
of ordinary mortals that profits were to be made. For some it was so, for others
it was not, but the very fact that so many believed in the existence of "rich
pickings" pushed what are now the key cities of California into existence.

Looking back over our review of location theory, we can make the general
judgment, then, that it was the hope (or, with economic man, the certainty)
of reasonable profits which prompted decisions to locate. It prompted the assembly of capital (monetary and physical), labor and know-how at particular places.
These choices were, as we discovered, more or less constrained by the particular
spatial attributes of the inputs necessary for the production process and the
disposition of the market which was to be served. But there were no certainties
in the judgments made, as a later chapter showed. Capitalist entrepreneurs used
their best judgment of the situation and acted upon it. It would also be wrong
to emphasize the purely *material aspects* of location factors in a real world.
One only has to reflect on the origins of Salt Lake City, Utah, to realize that
more than the hope of profit may launch a small mining town into a place
of rapid growth. The advent of the Mormon Church and its particular attributes
both locationally and in terms of the social and economic way of life brought
with it are in no sense less powerful in triggering growth than the gold fever
which launched Sacramento into existence. The social and cultural forces which
trigger growth have received less than adequate attention in a text devoted
to *economic* geography, but in attempting to be more realistic about triggers
to growth we should try to bear them in mind.

Exactly *where* such triggers to growth appear is something we can attempt
to explain only with the benefit of hindsight, except where deliberate decisions
to create planned "new towns" or cities are involved. Even when we can see
them retrospectively, however, the precise origins of initial triggers to development in space are extremely difficult to disentangle. As geographers we have
often glibly spoken of cities like London growing up at the "lowest effective
bridging point" of the Thames, or Sydney as having grown up "by virtue of
its excellent natural harbor." But we sometimes tend to forget that there are
many bridging points and harbors in the world that did *not* give birth to great
cities and that the initial triggers to the growth of both London and Sydney,
or any other place for that matter, were set in the economic, social and political
events of a particular time. Their particular *physical attributes* can be seen as
necessary but *not sufficient* for the development process. Different men seeing
the physical attributes of the world in the light of different strategies might
well have come up with different locational choices. It may seem trivial to
make such a point, but in the act of generalization about complex events we
sometimes forget that triggers as we have called them belong in most cases

to another point in time: a time with different economic and social circumstances and alternative notions of locational utility. Nevertheless, once laid down, the initial network of central places, supply areas and interaction pathways in space *exerts a powerful cumulative impact on subsequent growth and development within the space economy.*

Cumulative development in space

In trying to disentangle the complexities of development in space we are, for our present purposes, more likely to succeed if we focus on the *process* of development itself rather than upon the nature and location of initial triggers. Writing of city development, Maruyama claims that

> the secret of the growth of the city is in the process of deviation-amplifying mutual positive feedback networks rather than in the initial condition or in the initial kick. This process, rather than the initial condition, has generated the complexly structured city. It is in this sense that the deviation-amplifying mutual causal process is called "morphogenesis."
> *Maruyama (1963), p. 166*

We should not be put off by the nature of Maruyama's terminology. The essence of his argument is similar to that of the development economists Myrdal (1957) and Hirschman (1958): all agree that, *once triggered by some initial motivating force, economic development tends to be a cumulative process.*

The multiplier mechanism and cumulative development

The concept of the *multiplier*—which by its very nature embodies the idea of amplification—is fundamental to an understanding of the cumulative process of development. To make explanation as simple as possible let us begin by assuming that the initial trigger for development at a particular location in a previously little-developed area is generated from *outside* the area. Such an assumption obviously fits the gold rush example mentioned above. In such cases, it is the *external demand* for a particular good which is the primary determinant of economic growth and development, at least in the early stages.

Such an approach to development can be termed *export base theory*, a theory which has a long (and somewhat controversial) history in the literature of economic development. Export base theory is founded on the observation, made mainly by economic historians with an interest in the development of the new world, that economic growth tended to come with the *export of staple products* to metropolitan markets. The work of the Canadian economic historian H. A. Innis on the mining, lumber and fur industries led him to develop what has become known as the *staple theory* of economic development.* In essence,

---

Staple theory of economic development. Staple theory appears to be especially applicable to the development of "new" countries which have a favorable man/land ratio (i.e. no population pressure on scarce resources). Thus it helps to explain the early economic development of countries such as Canada. Harold Innis, in fact, built his entire theory of Canadian development—economic, political, and social—upon the leading role of export of staple commodities

Note

(Innis and Lower, 1933). He showed how the Canadian economy evolved through a series of dominant natural resource staples, each of which in turn "left its stamp" on Canadian economic, political, and social life. The driving force was the demand generated by the metropolitan centers of the European colonial powers. The earliest of Canada's export staples was *fish*, particularly off the Grand Banks of Newfoundland and areas adjacent to the St. Lawrence. In the interior *furs* (especially beaver) followed by *lumber* were prominent. In British Columbia, *gold* followed the fur trade, but eventually lumber and fish became more significant. In time the lumber industry was supplemented by *pulp and paper* production, while agricultural products, particularly *wheat*, and *minerals* became more prominent in the twentieth century. But staple production alone does not produce self-sustaining economic growth. It may set the pace for economic growth but, ultimately, "economic development will be a process of diversification around an export base. The central concept of a staple theory, therefore, is the spread effects of the export sector, that is, the impact of export activity on domestic economy and society." (Watkins, 1963, p. 141).

this focused on the role of those products with a large natural resource content as triggers to the initial and continued growth of regional economies. Export base theory differs from this only in the respect that it concerns itself with the export of all goods and services as opposed to those of primarily natural origin. In more formal terms it hypothesizes that any region, however it may be defined, be it town, city, state, or nation, has two mutually exclusive sectors to its economy:

1. **Export base sector** (E_{ex}). This includes all those activities for which the effective demand is *external* to the region itself. That is, their level is set by forces *outside* the region. This section consists of the region's export activities.

2. **Residentiary sector** (E_{res}). This includes all those activities for which the effective demand is internal to the region itself, those production systems supplying the day-to-day needs of the resident population, for example, retail trade, local services and so on.

In shorthand terms, therefore, the total economy of a region, E_t, is

$$E_t = E_{ex} + E_{res}$$

It is the export base sector that, as in the narrower case of staple theory, is considered to play the primary part in the promotion of economic development. According to North (1955) it plays a vital role in determining levels of absolute and per capita incomes in a region, determines much of the fate of the residentiary industries, and is the carrier transmitting the effects of external income shifts to the home region.*

Export base theory is based upon the idea that at least in the *short-term*, the level of residentiary activity depends entirely upon the level of export base activity. In other words,

$$E_{res} = f(E_{ex})$$

*The export base literature is voluminous. Many of the significant contributions have been gathered into a single volume, edited by Pfouts (1960). A particularly sound discussion is provided by Tiebout (1962), while Richardson (1973) reviews export base theory in the general context of regional growth theory.

It is also assumed that the relationship between the two over time remains the same (expressed by the constant, k):

$$E_{res} = k(E_{ex})$$

On the assumption that the relative proportions of export base and residentiary activity remain the same, then it is possible to calculate the impact of a change in the export base sector on the residentiary sector and, therefore, on the regional economy as a whole. Suppose, for example, that our hypothetical region has a total labor force to begin with of 1,000. The export base sector accounts for 400 of these and the residentiary sector for 600. Thus the existing ratio between residentiary and export base activity measured in employment terms is 1:1.5 (in the statement above $k = 1.5$). In other words, for every two jobs in the export base sector there are three jobs in the residentiary sector.

On the basis of a constant relationship, we can calculate the total impact of an increase in export base activity such as for example, the opening of a new manufacturing plant employing, say, a labor force of 2,000. The residentiary sector will gain

$$E_{res} = 1.5\ (2,000)$$
$$= 3,000 \text{ new jobs}$$

Therefore, where the export base ratio is 1:1.5 an increase of 2,000 in export sector employment will yield an increase of 5,000 in total regional employment. Thus, assuming that the ratio remains constant over time it may be interpreted as a simple type of economic multiplier known as the *export base multiplier*. Written in a form more clearly identified with multiplier notation it may be expressed as:

$$E_t = \frac{1}{(1-a)}(E_{ex})$$

where E_t and E_{ex} are total and export base employment (or income) as before, and a is the parameter which determines the constant relationship between export base and residential activity. (In our example, where 60 percent of total employment is in the residentiary sector, a would have a value of 0.6.) The term $1/(1-a)$ is the multiplier which, in this case, has a value of 2.5.

Direct and indirect multiplier effects: the income multiplier

The simple example above shows only the *direct* impact on *employment* of an increase in export activities. The point about the multiplier, however, is that the direct effects are followed by a series of *indirect* effects in a chain-like sequence as expansion induced in one sector has repercussions on other sectors, though the effect gets less and less as "distance" from the original stimulus increases (just as the ripples created by throwing a stone into a pond decline in intensity outwards). Although we have visualized the relationship in terms of an *employment* multiplier, the true basis for the changes which take place "down the line" of the multiplier is *income*. This is derived from the increased demand for goods and services which in turn pulls in the full range of production factors. Labor is only one of these factors but it is often the only one which can be given any real numerical substance.

One of the most useful explanations of the income multiplier in a slightly expanded export base framework was provided by Tiebout (1962). Tiebout was concerned with it as a tool for predicting short-term economic changes while we are more interested in the multiplier as a conceptual device. However, his explanation of the way the multiplier works is so clear that we cannot do better than to base the following section on his work. Tiebout makes a basic distinction between short-term and long-term perspectives. In the short-term, let us assume that an area's economy consists of three sectors: exports, local investment, and local consumption (in other words, we sub-divide the residentiary sector into two categories). The population of the area derives income from each of these. In the short-term, income from both export and local investment sectors depends directly upon external forces while income from the local consumption sector is determined by local spending from income generated in the other two sectors. Income from local consumption is based upon two steps.

1. Residents spend *some* of their income on local goods and services. This creates what we can call *local sales dollars*. Many variable factors influence how much income is spent on local goods and services: one of the most important is, of course, the level of income. Let's suppose that, on average, local residents tend to spend 50 percent of their income on local goods and services. In technical terms, we can say that the *propensity to consume locally* is 0.5. (The other half of the residents' income may go into savings, taxes, or be spent outside the area.) If we imagine that local income from export activity increases by $1 then we might suppose that 50 cents of this would remain as local income through spending in the local consumption sector. But this is not so, because we have to take into account the second step:

2. Only part of the local sales dollar remains within the local area to become local income. In other words, some of the 50 cents of the extra dollar is used by local suppliers to pay for inputs which originate outside—imported goods, wages to non-residents, for example. But part of the 50 cents will certainly remain as local income; local wages, profits, payments to local businesses and so on. Again, assume that we can measure the average proportion which remains locally and that it is 40 percent. Using the same terminology as before we can say that the *income propensity of the local sales dollar* is 0.4.

Combining these two steps, we can say that for every dollar of local income, 50 cents will be spent locally and 40 percent of this 50 cents—that is, 20 cents—will remain as local income. But this is only the *direct* effect. Part of the additional 20 cents will be spent locally (half or 10 cents) and 0.4 of this will remain as local income—4 cents. Again, half of this is spent locally and 0.4 of this remains as local income. Thus as the multiplier process proceeds, each step contributes less and less. We can use the kind of multiplier formula introduced earlier to express this chain reaction:

$$\begin{array}{l} \text{Total income} \\ \text{increase} \end{array} = \begin{array}{l} \text{Increase in (export plus} \\ \text{local investment) income} \end{array} \times \dfrac{1}{\begin{array}{l} 1 - \text{(propensity to consume} \\ \text{locally} \times \text{income created per} \\ \text{\$ of local consumption sales)} \end{array}}$$

Inserting the values from our discussion we can calculate the total effect of increasing income by \$1:

$$\text{Total income increase} = \$1.00 \times \frac{1}{1 - (0.5 \times 0.4)} = \$1.00 \times \frac{1}{1 - 0.2} = \$1.25$$

Thus the multiplier effect of increasing income by \$1.00 is to increase total income to \$1.25 through spending in the local consumption sector.

As we observed earlier, this is a short-run view. But what if we take, say, a ten or twenty year view? In such a longer-term analysis we would expect that *local investment* income will be less dependent on external forces and influenced more by local income. For example, increases in income from export and local consumption sectors will stimulate the need for housing, plant and equipment and so on. So in addition to the propensity to consume locally we must consider the *propensity to invest in local capital goods*. Again for simplicity assume that we can calculate such a propensity and that it is 0.2 (that is, 20 cents of every dollar of local income is spent on local investment) and that the income created per dollar of local investment sales is 0.5 (that is, half of the expenditure on local investment remains in the local area).

Our multiplier formula can be adjusted to take account of these changes. In its revised form, local investment combines with local consumption. If, again, export income increases by \$1 then we can trace the total multiplier effect of this increase:

$$\begin{array}{l} \text{Total income} \\ \text{increase} \end{array} = \begin{array}{l} \text{Increase in} \\ \text{export income} \end{array} \times \dfrac{1}{\begin{array}{l} 1 - [\text{(propensity to consume locally} \times \text{income} \\ \text{created per \$ of local consumption sales)} \\ + \text{(propensity to invest locally} \times \text{income} \\ \text{created per \$ of local investment sales)}] \end{array}}$$

Inserting our hypothetical values:

$$\begin{array}{l} \text{Total income} \\ \text{increase} \end{array} = \$1.00 \times \frac{1}{1 - [(0.5 \times 0.4) + (0.2 \times 0.5)]} = \$1.00 \times \frac{1}{0.7} = \$1.43$$

Thus when both the local consumption and local investment sectors contribute to local income the multiplier value is increased. Using rather larger values, an increase in export-generated income of \$100,000 would create an additional \$43,000 through spending on local consumption and local investment.

It should now be clear that if exports are the primary determinant of local growth, those regions or cities with a *strong export orientation* and *high multipliers* will be much more sensitive to the impact of any initial kick, whether positive or negative, than those with low multiplier relations. The multiplier is thus a measure of the deviation-amplifying potential of the economic system. The actual degree of deviation depends upon the intensity and direction of the initial kick; whichever way the "kick" is dirccted the process of change tends to be cumulative. It is worth noting in passing that the multiplier relation may apply in the reverse sense. For instance, in the employment example quoted above, should redundancies or factory closures take place, for every two jobs lost in the export base sector three would be lost in the residentiary sector.

An employment multiplier of 2.5 is, as the reader will have appreciated, a pretty high one. Very few regions today would expect to generate three jobs in the residentiary sector for every two in the export sector. In fact, the strength of the multiplier depends upon something we discussed in detail in Chapter Seven—the nature of the *linkages* in the regional economy.* For some regions the new income from the expanding export base would *leak away* almost instantly as its recipients send it back home to the family, buy goods made outside the area or invest more safely elsewhere. This is, perhaps, the classic profile of the little-developed region in the present day where it is all too easy to mail money home, import fancy goods or invest with a telephone call to a big-city stockbroker. In less accessible places or at a time, say, in the pre-railway era when most places were less accessible to each other, factors of production, goods and services would have to be provided locally and so much more of the newly-won income would remain within the region to be recycled locally generating more wealth and greater multiplier effects.

Although export base theory has provided valuable insights into the operation of the growth process and has been very widely used it has been subjected to considerable criticism. Among the many technical problems is that of identifying precisely which activities form the export base since many enterprises serve

---

Note

Multipliers and linkages in different economic systems. Baldwin (1956) investigated this aspect of the export base multiplier concept through a comparison of the development effects experienced by plantation and nonplantation agriculture in two hypothetical regions. In the context of his model he hypothesized that the plantation area would develop more slowly than that growing other crops due to the low level of internal multipliers. Poorly distributed and low domestic incomes and a tendency for workers to produce most of their consumer needs themselves reduce the flow of "plantation-earned" incomes to local businesses to very low levels. Forward and backward linkages are restricted by shortages of investment funds and technical and social problems that present barriers to local expansion of economic activity. All these factors prevent the economy from breaking out of its export-dominated nature and much of the *income generated by the plantation sector is "leaked" through import purchases*. As a result, translating the situation into terms related to the development of spatial structures, morphogenetic processes are weak, few new production systems emerge and the plantation space economy experiences little change and development over time.

In the nonplantation case, by contrast, Baldwin hypothesizes faster development due to the more efficient functioning of the linkage mechanism operating from a base of higher initial incomes. Under these conditions we might foresee the operation of powerful morphogenetic forces and for the associated space economy rapid and far-reaching changes in its structural form and functional operation.

both local and export markets.* A further difficulty concerns the problem of regional delimitation, especially as with increasing size the export base:residentiary ratio changes because larger regions tend to be more self-sufficient.

For these and other reasons, including the recognition that activities other than exports exert a multiplier effect, more recent work on multiplier theory has shifted toward the notion that *regardless of its export or residentiary classification all new investment in the production system will have some multiplier effects on a regional or urban economy.* This is important nowadays because of the observed shift in emphasis from manufacturing and secondary activities in general to the tertiary and quaternary sectors. There is a strong positive association between the level of real income per head and the proportion of the population employed in tertiary or service activities. (The inverse relationship holds for primary activities.) From this empirical observation the *development stages* or *sector* theory states that a growth in real income per head within a region will be associated with a shift of structural emphasis in its economic make-up from primary to secondary to tertiary and quaternary economic activities. The

*The minimum requirements method for defining the economic base. One approach aimed at identifying export and residentiary activities is that devised by Ullman and Dacey (1962). They argued that all cities have certain *minimum requirements;* in employment terms, a certain percentage of the labor force in each industry would be engaged in producing for local needs while the remaining workers in that industry would be producing for export. The minimum requirement employment, therefore, is analogous to our residentiary sector. To identify this value Ullman and Dacey selected a group of United States cities of different sizes and calculated the percentage of the labor force in each of fourteen categories. The figure for the city with the *minimum* percentage in each category was then selected. Table 10.1 gives these minimum values for each of the fourteen functions for different city size groups. The sum of these minima (e.g. 56.7 percent for cities larger than 1 million population) represents the residentiary employment.

Note

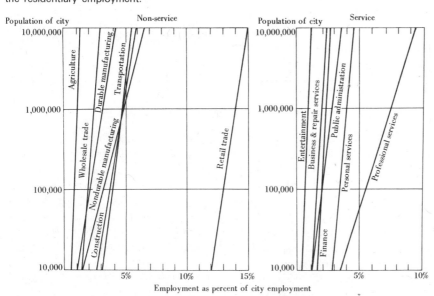

Figure 10.1
Minimum requirements for 14 industrial types, based on regression lines.
[*Source:* E. L. Ullman and M. F. Dacey (1960), paper in K. Norberg (ed.) *Proceedings of IGU Symposium in Urban Geography,* Lund Studies in Geography, Series B. 24, Figure 2.]

Note continued

Note that the size of the residentiary sector varies directly with city size. If the minimum values for each activity are plotted on semi-logarithmic paper (as in Figure 10.1) they show a linear relationship with city size, so that the minimum requirement or residentiary employment for cities of varying sizes can be read directly off the graph. For example, a city of 100,000 population would expect 3 percent of its employment in what Ullman and Dacey term "durable manufacturing" to be serving local needs.

Table 10.1
Minimum percentages employed in cities of varying size classes, 14 industry classification, 1950.

Population

Industry Type	Metropolitan Areas			Cities		
	Over 1,000,000*	300,000– 800,000	100,000– 150,000	25,000– 40,000	10,000– 12,500	2,500– 3,000
Agriculture	0.6	1.0	1.1	0.2	0.4	0.3
Mining	0.1	0.0	0.0	0.0	0.0	0.0
Construction	4.6	4.1	3.8	3.2	2.5	1.8
Manufacturing: Durable	2.3	3.1	2.0	0.8	1.2	2.8
Manufacturing: Nondurable	4.9	3.7	4.2	1.9	1.0	
Transport, Communications	6.6	4.5	3.2	3.5	3.4	2.4
Wholesale Trade	2.1	2.3	1.4	1.5	1.1	8.6
Retail Trade	14.8	13.3	12.1	13.4	11.9	
Finance, Insurance	3.1	1.9	1.8	1.8	1.6	0.8
Business, Repair Services	2.0	1.8	1.6	1.6	1.2	0.9
Personal Services	4.6	3.5	3.3	3.3	2.8	2.6
Entertainment	0.8	0.6	0.6	0.6	0.3	0.3
Professional Services	6.9	6.8	5.8	5.8	4.1	3.0
Public Administration	3.3	2.0	2.2	2.2	1.7	0.5
Total	56.7*	48.6	43.1	39.8	33.2	24.0

*Based on 14 cities; all other size classes contain 38 cities.
Source: Ullman and Dacey (1962), Table 1.

direction of the shift toward, in general, those sectors whose products enjoy a higher income elasticity of demand (that is, expand more as incomes rise) provides yet another stimulus to further investment and demand and is, in effect, a further cumulative stimulus for growth and development.

The detail of the multiplier process: input-output analysis

Tracing the actual impact of new or expanded activities through the complexities of a local economic system requires some knowledge of the inter-relationships between each sector in the economy. The technique of *input-output* analysis* allows us to do just that: it provides a detailed description of the inter-relationship between all sectors of the economy (though in practice the level of detail is restricted by difficulties of obtaining the right kind of data). As its name implies, input-output analysis shows the ways in which the inputs of one sector

Note

*This is a relatively complex technique whose technical details do not concern us here. A sound and very readable introduction is provided by Miernyk (1965). Critical evaluation will be found in Isard (1960), Chapter Eight.

are the outputs of another sector and vice versa. Table 10.2 is a hypothetical input-output table for a six-sector economy (A to F) plus the household sector (H). We can regard the household sector as the origin of labor inputs into the other sectors. Note that the order in which the sectors appear is the same in the rows as in the columns. Each entry in the table is an *input coefficient* that shows the amount of inputs from each industry needed to produce $1's worth of the output of any given industry. Thus for industry B to produce an output worth $1 it needs to purchase 26 cents of inputs from industry A, 7 cents of inputs from other firms in industry B, 4 cents of inputs from C, 2 cents from D, 11 cents from F and 32 cents from H (these represent wages paid to labor). If we assume, for simplicity, that these coefficients remain the same over time then we can easily calculate the effects of an increase (or decrease) in the output of one industry on all other sectors.

Table 10.2
A hypothetical input coefficient table (direct purchases per dollar of output).

Industries producing	Industries purchasing (in cents)						
	A	B	C	D	E	F	H[a]
A	16	26	3	5	13	13	19
B	8	7	18	3	8	18	24
C	11	4	21	3	13	7	7
D	17	2	5	21	16	9	6
E	6	0	3	36	8	4	12
F	3	11	18	15	5	13	11
H	25	32	18	13	18	20	1

[a]H represents the household sector (i.e., labor inputs).

Source: W. H. Miernyk (1965), *The Elements of Input-Output Analysis*, Table 3.4, p. 44. Reprinted by permission of Random House, Inc., New York.

The *direct* impact of an increase of $1's worth of output by sector B can be seen by reading down the B column. B is clearly a labor-intensive industry because the largest impact would be on the household sector which is the one supplying labor. Sector A is most closely linked to B so that the effect on A would be considerable; at the other extreme, the direct impact on Sector E of expansion by B would be nil. But this does not mean that E is not affected at all. As we have seen, expansion is induced in sector A, but sector A uses 6 cents worth of inputs from sector E to produce $1 of output, so E would benefit *indirectly* from expansion in sector B even though there is no direct input link from E to B. In theory, therefore, the more detailed the input-output tables the more closely we can trace the total multiplier effect (direct and indirect) of an increase in activity in one sector.

Thus the impact of increased investment not only affects the general economy of the area in question but also has a varying impact on *the individual sectors of the economy*. The export base and related approaches are concerned essentially with the aggregate effects of an increase in investment, income, or employment, while newer approaches such as input-output analysis tend to examine the *detailed effect of multiplier relations on individual sectors*.

Perhaps the reader would care to draw up for himself a notional input-output table for a growing mining town such as the one we discussed earlier. Begin with a list of sectors likely to be found. Clearly the basic ones would be mining and households, but what about livery stables, stagecoach services and so forth? Develop the table with notional weights of inputs for each sector. It should then be easy to predict the multiplier relations between sectors and how these would respond to changes or the arrival of new activities. Essentially the input-output table would form a "linkage map" of the connections between economic sectors and linkages would tend to fall into the main categories discussed in Chapter Seven (pp. 288–289).

What the reader will also discover from his input-output exercise is that he has, in effect, provided a *description of a system* of the kind we first discussed in Chapter One. Elements (sectors) are connected together by linkages along which there are flows of goods, services, and information. Changes in any one element "reverberate" through the system causing a "cascade" of changes in others. The system exists in a state of "tension" with its external environment. Periods of stability reflect the steady-state situation, periods of change the shift of the system's state to some new position. In effect, with a practice input-output table of the kind suggested the interested reader can derive and demonstrate to himself many of the key features of economic systems as we have described them throughout the book.

Taking the particular case of the *entry of a new industrial activity* into a hypothetical region, Figure 10.2 shows how it generates a set of new *local demands*. These may be derived from the requirements for local products by the factory itself, or they may be generated by the additional purchasing power associated with the arrival and settlement of the additional labor force. In this way the successful growth area draws in a whole spectrum of new businesses as the morphogenetic cycle begins at the level of the *settlement* itself. There is an early boom in the construction industries followed by new developments in the service, trade, and transportation sectors. Industries supplying needed inputs to the initial developers may then follow (*backward linkages*) and these too create more local demand by their own needs for inputs and by the increments to the area's income generated by the possibility of utilizing the outputs of the new or expanded activity (*forward linkages*). The entire process is cumulative, each new development itself generating additional multiplier effects to draw in new enterprises. This trend is reinforced as the growth of the area (in terms of population, income, and range of economic activities) increases. In effect new industrial and commercial *thresholds* are achieved, permitting the influx of larger-scale activities, *each generating its own set of multipliers*. As Figure 10.2 shows, the expansion of non-industrial activities generated by the initial multiplier itself creates a secondary multiplier, which adds to overall growth and contributes toward the attainment of even higher thresholds.

As we have seen, however, not all of the incomes earned locally are spent locally as new incomes are leaked away. In addition, as we have shown (p. 394), different production systems generate different linkages within a region. The precise nature of the local multiplier effect will, therefore, depend upon the

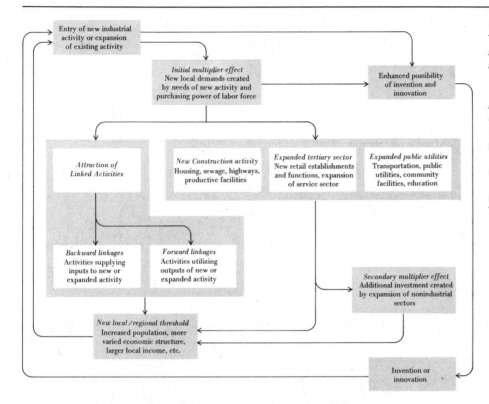

Figure 10.2
The multiplier mechanism and the process of circular and cumulative growth. [*Source:* based on A. Pred (1966), *The Spatial Dynamics of U.S. Urban-Industrial Growth*, Figure 2.1. Reprinted by permission of the M.I.T. Press, Cambridge, Massachusetts. Copyright © 1966 by the Massachusetts Institute of Technology.]

particular characteristics of the new industry's production function and upon the proportion of the total induced income spent locally compared to that leaked through the purchase of goods produced elsewhere and imported.

Empirical studies of the multiplier mechanism

The complex manner in which the multiplier operates makes its empirical study rather difficult. Few studies, in fact, attempt to trace the individual links in the chain. One which does in a rather simple way is the study by Barfod (1938) of the multiplier effects generated by the arrival of a new oil factory in the town of Aarhus, Denmark. Barfod carefully documented the income flows in the town which occurred as a result of the new installation. Figure 10.3 shows just part of this process. Suppose that the new factory, Aarhus Oliefabrik, makes a payment of 100 Kr. to a local supplier A for supplying the factory with some of its input needs. What effect does this payment have on local net income and how is it spread through the local economy? Figure 10.3 shows that 25 Kr. goes to another local supplier, B, who provides A with materials. Of this 25 Kr., 15 Kr. are spent outside the city by B; the remaining 10 Kr. are divided equally between B's net profit and the wages for B's workers. A further 20 Kr. are spent by A on "trade expenses" of which 10 Kr. go outside the city to pay interest charges on capital borrowed. The largest proportion of the original 100 Kr. (40 Kr.) goes to pay the wages for A's workers. Some of this is spent outside so that 30 Kr. remains as local wage income. The *net* gain in local

Figure 10.3
Hypothetical income
flows within the Aarhus
economy. [*Source:* B.
Barfod (1938), *Local
Economic Effects of a
Large Scale Industrial
Undertaking,*
Copenhagen:
Munksgaard. Reproduced
by permission of Aarhus
Oliefabrik A/S.]

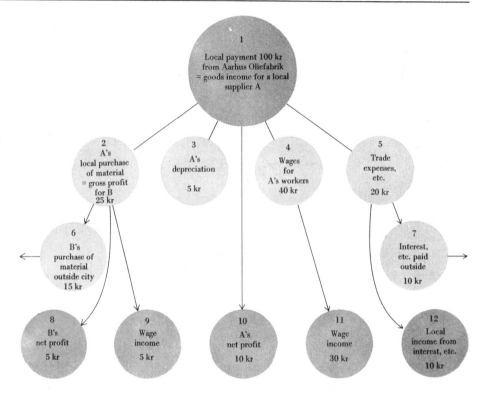

Local net income = 60 kr

income from the original 100 Kr. payment to A is 60 Kr. We can envisage
the *overall* impact of the new factory as being made up of a whole series of
such transactions, with varying amounts being retained within the city and
the rest consisting of leakages outside. Overall, Barfod calculated that the total
increment to local income derived from payments made by the new factory
was some 27 percent greater than the initial amount.

A more detailed attempt to measure the multiplier effect of increased economic
activity at a particular location makes use of input-output relationships. A
pioneering study of this kind is that by Isard and Kuenne (1953) in which
they set out to calculate the impact on employment in the Greater New York–
Philadelphia region of a proposed large-scale increase in steel production in
the region. Table 10.3 summarizes their results and is included here because
it illustrates a number of interesting features relevant to our discussion. Column
1 gives estimates of the inputs required from each of the 45 sectors by the
new steel and steel-fabricating activities. Obviously inputs from the iron and
steel industry itself are particularly important and the new installation requires
$121,170,500 of iron and steel inputs (13.4 percent of all inputs)—but many
other sectors are also significantly affected. However, not all the input requirements will be produced locally as Column 2 shows. Most services (rows 34–44)
will be supplied locally as the high percentage values in Column 2 reveal, but
the extent to which other inputs are supplied locally depends on the area's

Table 10.3
Direct and indirect
repercussions of the
installation of new steel
capacity, Greater New
York–Philadelphia region.

	requirements of initial steel and steel fabricating activities (in $ thousand) (1)	percentage of input requirements to be produced in area (2)	First-round expansions in area (in $ thousand) (3)	Second-round expansions in area (in $ thousand) (4)	Third-round expansions in area (in $ thousand) (5)	Sum of round expansions in area (in $ thousand) (6)	Total new employees corresponding to round expansions (7)	total new employees in initial steel and steel fabricating activities (8)	Overall total of new employees (9)
1. Agriculture and fisheries	50.0	0	0.0	0.	0.	0.	0		0
2. Food and kindred products	294.6	60	176.8	17,660.	8,249.	42,492.	1,833		1,833
3. Tobacco manufacturers	0.0	0	0.0	0.	0.	0.	0		0
4. Textile mill products	3,864.7	10	386.5	406.	39.	1,280.	142		142
5. Apparel	1,285.6	75	964.2	10,124.	3,461.	21,155.	2,302		2,302
6. Lumber and wood products	5,610.7	5	280.5	93.	36.	450.	64		64
7. Furniture and fixtures	1,753.4	33	578.6	802.	198.	2,000.	234		234
8. Paper and allied products	4,818.7	40	1,927.5	1,674.	1,297.	6,574.	426		426
9. Printing and publishing	425.5	90	383.0	5,929.	3,014.	14,617.	1,667		1,667
10. Chemicals	10,626.4	45	4,781.9	3,599.	1,630.	12,077.	601		601
11. Products of petroleum and coal	10,936.6	25	2,734.2	2,547.	1,118.	7,634.	228		228
12. Rubber products	8,381.5	15	1,257.2	355.	102.	1,879.	169		169
13. Leather and leather products	647.7	20	129.5	679.	194.	1,371.	150		150
14. Stone, clay, and glass products	9,031.7	15	1,354.8	441.	139.	2,083.	268		268
15. Iron and steel	121,170.5	50	60,585.3	13,566.	2,965.	78,335.	6,093	11,666	17,759
16. Nonferrous metals	33,997.4	20	6,799.5	1,667.	381.	9,063.	505		505
17. Plumbing and heating supplies	3,192.4	25	798.1	248.	50.	1,189.	118	3,640	3,758
18. Fabricated structural metal products	3,480.7	40	1,392.3	312.	33.	1,809.	151	1,420	1,571
19. Other fabricated metal products	31,770.9	40	12,708.4	2,146.	561.	16,121.	1,537	10,060	11,597
20. Agricultural, mining, and construction machinery	3,651.3	5	182.6	46.	11.	251.	22	707	729
21. Metal-working machinery	7,389.1	25	1,847.3	270.	43.	2,210.	289	2,705	2,994
22. Other machinery (except electric)	28,463.6	40	11,385.4	2,675.	551.	15,384.	1,486	28,607	30,093
23. Motors and generators	11,265.9	20	2,253.2	226.	42.	2,560.	301	⎫	
24. Radios	4,562.2	30	1,368.7	428.	101.	2,026.	192	10,392	12,312
25. Other electrical machinery	21,773.9	50	10,887.0	2,011.	432.	13,903.	1,427	⎭	
26. Motor vehicles	50,530.8	10	5,053.1	742.	260.	6,421.	389	8,770	9,159
27. Other transportation equipment	2,605.5	20	521.1	276.	69.	958.	117	4,605	4,722
28. Professional and scientific equipment	3,221.4	50	1,610.7	801.	287.	3,123.	416		416
29. Miscellaneous manufacturing	5,116.8	60	3,070.1	2,888.	982.	8,418.	845	6,108	6,953
30. Coal, gas, and electric power	7,767.0	50	3,883.5	1,843.	2,693.	11,079.	1,100		1,100
31. Railroad transportation	13,575.8	75	10,181.9	6,010.	2,390.	21,532.	3,308		3,308
32. Ocean transportation	457.3	75	343.0	331.	170.	1,021.	110		110
33. Other transportation	4,179.4	95	3,970.4	8,422.	2,836.	19,694.	2,394		2,394
34. Trade	13,969.8	95	13,271.3	36,585.	11,855.	83,642.	13,874		13,874
35. Communications	1,790.7	90	1,611.6	2,409.	1,283.	7,305.	1,191		1,191
36. Finance and insurance	3,086.2	90	2,777.6	9,472.	5,062.	25,252.	2,329		2,329
37. Rental	3,018.8	95	2,867.9	26,222.	9,603.	55,680.	909		909
38. Business services	5,338.5	95	5,071.6	2,385.	2,406.	13,384.	1,305		1,305
39. Personal and repair services	396.9	95	377.1	14,399.	5,688.	24,212.	4,443		4,443
40. Medical, educational and nonprofit org's	000.0	90	0.0	9,811.	2,160.	17,271.	4,370		4,370
41. Amusements	000.0	90	0.0	3,677.	1,066.	6,591.	1,100		1,100
42. Scrap and miscellaneous industries	8,388.2	50	4,194.1	2,054.	727.	7,411.	771		771
43. Undistributed	103,638.6	50	51,819.3	5,875.	6,019.	69,236.	7,208		7,208
44. Eating and drinking places	000.0	50	0.0	16,916.	3,903.	29,551.	3,705		3,705
45. Households	348,281.0	82	285,590.4	63,002.	80,894.	509,578.			
Total	**903,807.7**		**521,377.2**	**282,024.**	**164,400.**	**1,177,822.**	**70,089**	**88,680**	**158,769**

Source: W. Isard and R. Kuenne (1953), The Impact of Steel on the Greater New York–Philadelphia Region, Review of Economics and Statistics 35, Table 5, p. 297. Reproduced with permission of the author and editor.

existing economic structure. Column 3 shows how much each local sector must expand to keep the new steel production in operation. But this expansion itself generates further input requirements and a second round of expansion is generated (Column 4).

Column 6 shows the cumulative result of six rounds of expansion. Thus the overall impact of installing new steel capacity was calculated as $1,177,822,000. In employment terms the impact is as shown in Columns 7, 8 and 9. The total impact is an increase of 158,769 employees. Of these, 88,680 are the direct result of the steel expansion itself but a further 70,089 jobs are created by the induced expansion of the other sectors. Figure 10.4 places this new steel installation in the context of our cumulative growth model of Figure 10.2. Each box in the diagram is drawn at a scale proportional to the increased employment in each sector which results from the new steel installation.

Figure 10.4
The multiplier effects of the location of an integrated steel plant in the New York-Philadelphia area.
[*Source:* F. E. I. Hamilton (1967), Models of Industrial Location in R. J. Chorley and P. Haggett (eds.) *Models in Geography,* Figure 10.15, London: Methuen & Co.]

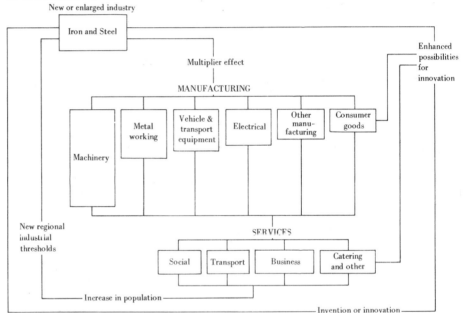

No time period is laid down for the achievement of these changes.
The increases in employment (shown proportionately by the size of each box) in each activity were calculated for six rounds of chain expansions.

At a very much smaller scale Yeates and Lloyd (1970) made a study of the multiplier effects created in the southern Georgian Bay area of Ontario by a government industrial assistance program. In the period up to 1968, government sponsorship brought over $80 million to the region in the form of industrial investment. New industries were established, chiefly in the automobile and electronic equipment field, and existing industries were subsidized to expand. As a *direct* result of the program during its first two years more than 2000 new jobs were created, many of them in particularly well-paid occupations. Over $8 million was added to the regional payroll and a further $500,000 went into the tax base.

Although initially most of the new industries retained their primary contacts with businesses outside Georgian Bay, local industrial linkages began to appear even during the first twelve months of the scheme. For example, a new firm making seat belts quickly took advantage of the facilities offered by a local metal stamping business. Other early links connected a hardware manufacturer with a new telecommunications equipment firm and a furniture maker with local suppliers of veneer and plywood. On the services side a local plant maintenance and heating engineer was quick to benefit from the opportunity to do business with the new firms. These embryonic input-output connections between businesses in the assisted area were envisaged as being only the start of a linkage process which the study predicted would eventually create an integrated industrial base for the region. In the long-run it was anticipated that over 5000 new jobs, $20 millions increase in payroll and $1 million input to the local tax base would result from the direct and indirect multiplier impact of the assistance scheme.

Given the projection of new jobs and the associated growth of population, the study went further. It pursued the multiplier concept into the likely effect which the scheme would have on the functional structure of central places. To do this it applied an element of central place theory which we have already touched on in Chapter Three (p. 73). Recall that the theory predicted, given certain assumptions, that a generalized relationship would exist between the population of each settlement and the number of central place functions it would contain. Taking this one step further, regression equations (see note on p. 74) were established for the study area which "predicted" the average number of functions of each particular type (pharmacies, food stores etc.) which would exist in each settlement *given its population*. These were expressed in the form of a *nomogram* (Figure 10.5) which is basically a kind of graph. Population, the predictor variable, appears on the extreme left and the predicted levels for each of the service functions are represented by the vertical scales running from left to right. Notice how the threshold population required for each functional type rises with the order of the good or service.

In the specific case where the effects of a *population increase* are to be estimated, reading across from left to right gives the predicted number of establishments of each functional type at each size level. For example, while a town of 500 people would have perhaps 30 business establishments in 21 types of activity, one with 5000 would be expected to have 210 establishments and 41 different functions. The particular functional types likely to appear and the number of establishments in each one can be determined by reading horizontally across all the vertical scales. Thus, where a town is expected to grow in population a generalized picture of the expected changes in its functional structure can be gained by looking at the nomogram profile for the existing situation and for the projected situation in the future.

In this way the Georgian Bay study showed how the multiplier effects from increased industrial investment could be passed not only through the manufacturing but also the retail and service sectors of particular settlements. The central place structure and *geographical* form of each settlement therefore, responds to income, employment and population changes as expanding demand promotes new threshold conditions and draws in new businesses.

Figure 10.5
A nomogram showing the relationship between population size and various tertiary activities, Georgian Bay region, southern Ontario.
[*Source:* M. H. Yeates and P. E. Lloyd (1970), *Impact of Industrial Incentives: Southern Georgian Bay Region, Ontario,* Ottawa, Queen's Printer, Figure 6.2. Reproduced by permission of the Minister of Supply and Services Canada.]

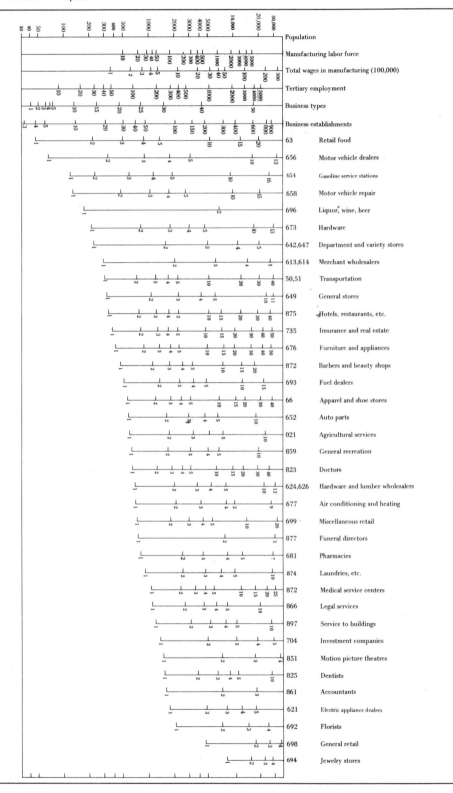

Much of the success of such schemes as that in Georgian Bay depends upon the ability of development agencies to attract industries with good growth prospects, potentially high wages and a propensity to develop local linkages to an area. The key requirement is for industries likely to exert a "propulsive effect" on the multiplier process.

Propulsive industry—key triggers to cumulative growth

It should now be clear that some economic activities exert a more powerful effect on development in an economic system than others. But we need to be careful in distinguishing between the impact of new or expanded activity on *the economy* and its impact on *the area* in which the expanded activity is located. The two should not be confused, though they often are. If we examine the development of an economy we can observe that *certain sectors* are especially important (though their precise identity is likely to change over time). The French economist Francois Perroux identified these sectors as *poles* of growth.*

Writing of economic growth in general, Perroux claimed:

> growth does not appear everywhere at the same time; it becomes manifest at points or poles of growth, with variable intensity; it spreads through different channels with variable terminal effects on the whole economy. *Perroux (1955), p. 93*

In Perroux's terms, then, "poles" are industries or firms, not geographical locations. We can perhaps best envisage them as sectors in an input-output matrix of the kind discussed above. Polarization in this sense depends on the development of a *propulsive* industry or firm which seems to have certain important characteristics. First, the industry or firm should be relatively large if it is to generate sufficient direct and indirect effects, though size alone is not sufficient. Second, it should be relatively fast-growing. Third, it should have a high intensity of input-output relationships (or linkages) with other industries or firms in order for the effect of its growth to be transmitted. Fourth, it should be innovative.

Industries or firms with these characteristics are likely to be the leaders, the "poles" around which the economy clusters. But it does not necessarily follow that *geographical* clustering will occur. One example can illustrate this: the natural gas installation at Lacq in southwestern France. It was widely believed in the early 1960s that the discovery of large natural gas supplies at Lacq would act as an important geographical pole around which other economic activities would cluster. In fact this has not occurred on any significant scale.

*The term *growth pole* has become both widely used and abused. Though completely non-geographical in Perroux's original conception it became transformed into a geographical concept particularly by regional planners. It is better to use the term *growth center* for geographical applications, reserving the term *growth pole* to its original meaning. For a comprehensive discussion of growth poles, see Darwent (1969), Hansen (1967), Lasuen (1969), Hermansen (1972).

Note

The Lacq resource has acted as a growth pole for the French economy as a whole but not for the local area itself.

Thus, for a new manufacturing development the *locational impact* of the linkage factor will depend among other things on the spatial mobility of inputs and outputs to local businesses and the overall importance of agglomeration economies. Where both are relatively high as, for example, in iron and steel manufacture during the nineteenth century, the localizing pull will be strong (See Chapter Four). A whole complex of technically linked suppliers and further processing plants will be drawn to a single location. By contrast, however, for modern fabricating industries, like automobile manufacture, the high mobility of inputs and outputs encourages greater spatial dispersion. Even here though the importance of other non-material localization economies would tend to draw investment to established growth centers. In the case of expanded economic activity in the southern Georgian Bay area of Ontario, for example, the new developments tended in particular to favor existing higher order central places. This accentuated the already existing differences between them and centers of lower order. Thus again in geographical terms the final demand impact of the new developments exerted a deviation-amplifying force on existing spatial structures, *intensifying previous levels of differentiation.*

Overall generalization is difficult on the precise spatial impact of the multiplier process, more especially since it forms only a part of the complex cumulative growth mechanism. However, *there do appear to be significant spatial polarizing influences present in the working of the multiplier,* influences which are reinforced by other considerations, in particular the operation of scale factors, the geographical clustering of innovations, and the nature of decision-making processes. Let us look briefly at each of these in turn.

Scale factors and cumulative growth

Most writers looking at the way in which growth and development tends to become concentrated in the same companies, industries, regions or nations, sooner or later turn to *economies of scale* as a basic determinant. The old adage expressed variously as "much makes more" or "them as has gits" seems to imply that the bigger and more powerful the object of the comment the more likely it is that it will grow bigger and still more powerful. In short, they are commenting on the *cumulative* properties of growth.

In previous chapters we have tried to show how locations of particular initial advantage have drawn to themselves men, money and machines. These in their turn have attracted more investment through the demands which they have exerted and which others have come in to satisfy. Each successive phase of development in a growing region has itself created an expanding source of demand both for capital and consumer goods. Bearing this in mind, let us now apply what we learned in Chapter Seven about internal and external economies of scale to see how these demand increases influence regional growth. What we shall discover is another force for deviation-amplifying or cumulative growth.

Take a typical firm in an undeveloped but developing region. Factor inputs have been assembled by it to reap the profits anticipated by its controlling organization. Assuming a U-shaped scale-cost curve at the plant (see Figure 7.8b), it is reasonable to assume that at this early stage of development scale economies will be forthcoming as output builds up. As this happens unit costs will fall sharply as the fixed costs of the initial start-up are spread over more units of output. With any luck this will enable the firm to set lower delivered prices to its customers. These may stimulate still more demand and raise output levels further to approach the minimum efficient scale for the particular plant under current technology. For a booming export sector plant with perhaps a temporary monopoly of the market (perhaps it controls some new breakthrough in technology) the rise in output may be sharp enough to take it rapidly through the threshold levels needed to support more advanced and even more cost-efficient machinery. At the level of the single producing unit, then, there will be *internal scale economies* as output rises. But, as we saw in Chapter Seven in the context of external economies of scale other industries will benefit from the internal economies of the growing plant. Depending upon the type and strength of its linkages with other plants and businesses in the region the growth impulses derived from one plant will be passed on to others.

If the plant in question is one of the region's export leaders, attracting large income from demand outside the region but still dependent on strong local linkages, then it would exert a propulsive force on the regional economy. Let us follow the situation through. Suppose, for example, a mining concern sub-contracts work to local trucking undertakings to carry materials from the mine to the processing plant. Other sub-contractors might provide maintenance services, security patrols, workers' canteen facilities, accountancy services and so on. In addition, power, gas and water might be drawn from local utility companies and a contribution to local taxes would pay for public services of various kinds.

Suppose that output rises rapidly in the mine in response to external demand which responds well to the firm's competitive prices. What happens to the subcontractors and linked services? Demands upon *them* clearly increase. Perhaps for the trucking company it presents the opportunity to buy for the first time a giant mineral transporter with ten times the capacity of its existing equipment. Ten potentially costly trucks can be "written off" and the wages of nine drivers saved—the trucking company moves to a new, vastly more efficient scale consistent with the new level of output demanded from it. For the security sub-contractor the physical expansion of the workings permits them to buy an all-purpose jeep covering a wider area more efficiently. Here, too, one or two workers may be dispensed with as the more mechanized operation comes into being. The point need not be labored further. The increased demand by the propulsive sector industry raises the level of output in the first round for its linked suppliers giving them effective *external economies of scale* and making them more cost-efficient. They, too, pass on further scale economies by exerting extra demand in the second round to still another group of enterprises. The impulse from the growth sector then works its way through that part of the regional economy to which it has income links, offering others the opportunity to benefit from external economies of scale. Benefits are passed on to utility companies—perhaps it is worth building a new, more efficient, gas plant or power station. The demand for public-sector services like schools for the children of the expanding work force at the mine, highways, sanitation works, is similarly increased, and the region's tax base (ideally) increases with it. Thus, through the general impact of external economies of scale, *the rising income derived from more efficient production in one sector is passed through the economy.* It passes through by means of the multiplier effect as gains in one sector rebound on others. What the scale mechanism does then is to "give an extra twist" to the income benefits of the multiplier.

As Weber pointed out, scale economies also offer a stimulus towards spatial agglomeration when it comes to deciding a location for new investment. More than this, however, each new investment in an area of agglomeration tends to enhance cost efficiency (generates economies of scale *internal* to the region) and, through the multipler-accelerator-scale mechanism, strengthens its pull on future investment decisions. This continues until some point of diseconomy is reached and deglomerative forces set in.

At least in the early stages of growth then, there are substantial cumulative, self-multiplying forces at work in the impact of scale economies on economic development in space. The early progression tends to be *exponential in form* with the rate of growth a positive function of the size already attained. But at a later stage growth rates fall as scale diseconomies begin to appear. In this context we can again return to the concept of *threshold* which we introduced early in Chapter Two. Recall that the term was defined as the minimum demand necessary for a firm to function. In terms of the economic development of an area, as its "size" increases it provides increasingly higher thresholds for businesses to operate. More specifically, however, some writers argue that we can envisage a certain threshold—a critical minimum size—which is necessary for economic growth to become self-sustaining. In the case of urban areas, for example, Wilbur Thompson describes such a threshold as one

> short of which growth is not inevitable and even the very existence of the place is not assured, but beyond which absolute contraction is highly unlikely, even though the growth rate may slacken, at times even to zero. In sum, at a certain range of scale...some growth mechanism, similar to a ratchet, comes into being, locking in past growth and preventing contraction.
> *Thompson (1965), p. 22*

Thompson goes on to identify a number of possible reasons for the survival of the very large urban center. Large centers tend to be more economically diversified than small centers, thus cushioning themselves against decline associated with obsolescent activities. Large centers tend to be politically more powerful—they represent more votes—and as such they may be able to acquire government aid in times of adversity. (Thompson was, of course, writing long before the New York financial crisis of the mid-1970s.) Whether this is true or not, the massive fixed capital of large cities makes total contraction unlikely. As Thompson observed, "no nation is so affluent that it can afford to throw away a major city." The very large urban center also is self-justifying as a product market, with its concentration of both economic activities and consumer population.

Although there is a good deal of apparent logic in the argument for the existence of regional thresholds there has been singularly little success in attempts to define them more closely. Nevertheless, it is clear that scale, once achieved, is a powerful influence on subsequent growth. But such influence is *more than simply economic*; *it also has behavioral connotations*, particularly in terms of the concentration of innovative activity and the nature of decision-making processes.

Innovation and cumulative growth

Since the writings of Marx it has been acknowledged in growth economics that technological change has a powerful part to play in the process of economic development. It is the volatile factor which permits a constant re-evaluation of the production possibilities of various factor combinations, off-setting the appearance of diminishing returns. In short, technological improvements allow for increasing productivity and are a key part of the mechanism for increasing returns to scale.

As we have seen earlier (Chapter Six) invention and innovation constitute the ingredients of technological progress. Invention may be autonomous or induced—in the first case largely a random process, in the second the result of deliberate expenditure of resources and effort. Innovation represents the adoption of inventions and their application to the actual production process and is heavily dependent upon the availability of investment funds and the right entrepreneurial climate.

Both induced invention and innovation are frequently closely associated with the existence of successful, expanding economic systems possessing the appropriate resources and entrepreneurial attitudes. Even autonomous invention has a greater probability of occurrence under conditions favoring high levels of human interaction and in situations where inventiveness is socially acceptable— that is in *growth situations*.

Thus one may envisage the situation of a growing, successful economic system, say an industrial city, drawing to it the ideas of spatially dispersed inventors searching for sponsorship, pulling in the skills of migrants, investing its own funds in the search for invention and using its accumulating capital and labor to convert this flood of new technology into effective use. Pred described this situation as it applied to urban-industrial centers in the United States toward the end of the nineteenth century and concluded that:

> new or enlarged urban industries and their multiplier effects created the employment opportunities that successively attracted "active" and "passive" migrants to the infant metropolises, and eventually led to additional

> manufacturing growth by directly or indirectly enhancing the possibility
> of invention and innovation.
> *Pred (1966), p. 39*

This effect is shown in Figure 10.2 where the multiplier effects are further streng-
thened by the innovative process. Here then is another of the powerful forces
for cumulative growth, and for the spatial concentration of growth at focal
points in the network of human interaction.

Wilbur Thompson in fact suggests that increasingly the major advantage of
the large metropolitan center is not so much its *economic* base in the traditional
sense of the term but rather its *innovative strength* as reflected in its university
and research institutions and other bodies whose concern is creativity and
change. He emphasizes particularly the key role of *entrepreneurial skill* in
regional growth. In his words,

> the large urban area would seem to have a great advantage in the critical
> functions of invention, innovation, promotion, and rationalization of the
> new. The stabilization and even institutionalization of entrepreneurship
> may be the principal strength of the large urban area.... A population
> of 50,000 that gives birth to, say, only one commercial or industrial genius
> every decade might get caught between geniuses at a time of great econo-
> mic trial such as the loss of a large employer, but in a population cluster
> of 5 million, with an average flow of ten per year, a serious and prolonged
> crisis in local economic leadership seems highly improbable.
> *Thompson (1968), p. 53*

Once again, therefore, there appears to be a positive relationship between the
rate of growth experienced and the scale of development already attained. Success tends to breed success in this respect and, as Schumpeter (1939) pointed
out, an important ingredient in this relationship is the particular set of behavior
attributes of the society operating the economic system. The spirit of adventure,
commercial optimism and what Hansen called "'frontier-mindedness" all contribute to stimulate invention and, more importantly, encourage risk-taking in
innovation. Where such optimism meets with success a powerful behavioral
mechanism for self-cycling growth is brought into being.

The tendency for entrepreneurial skill to be concentrated in large agglomerations is reinforced by the kinds of structural changes in business enterprise
which we discussed in Chapter Nine. *The higher control functions of modern
business enterprise—the Level I activities of Figure 9.11—have become increasingly concentrated in the larger metropolitan centers.* These provide the kinds
of information-rich environment which are perceived to be necessary for the
control and contact activities of high-level business executives. Thus the agglomeration of business headquarters in certain key centers gives a further twist
to the cumulative spiral in that such decision-making and information-process-
ing units create demands for related service activities. Because they employ
predominantly highly-paid personnel the final-demand linkage tends to be very
strong (though as we shall see in a later section, pp. 422–425, much depends

on the overall organization of a firm's activities in relation to urban centers of varying size).

Decision-making and cumulative growth

Further development of growth centers tends to be aided by the nature of decision-making itself, particularly the imperfections of information on which decisions are made. As we saw in Chapters Eight and Nine, the decision-maker does not have all the answers, he does not know all the alternatives, and he cannot attach payoffs to those alternatives which he can identify. The information on which he evaluates even those alternatives which he does perceive is presented to him in a biased form and his own ordering of that information is far from objective.

Let us examine decision-making under such conditions, remembering that economic development is, in its most disaggregated form, simply a function of individual investment decisions. Where such development is concentrated in time, in space, or within a given economic system this derives from the "clustering" of such decisions. Take the case of the industrial or commercial entrepreneur with funds available to him for investment. Following the logic reviewed in Chapter Eight he assembles information about investment alternatives. The nature of this information will depend to an appreciable degree on his own task environment and the network of interpersonal and media contacts within which he operates.

It is perhaps worth noting at the outset that the fact that he has accumulated funds for investment gives a high probability that he is *already* associated with some expanding economic system and that his task environment is biased towards it. There is similarly a high probability that his first impulse in investment is to repeat his previous behavior if this proved successful, returning his funds to the system from which they were derived. Strong conservative forces thus exist in most investment behavior. We saw in Chapter Eight that most new business firms tend to remain in the area in which their founders were already located. It is likely, therefore, that large agglomerations will spawn many more new firms than small agglomerations and that they will tend to remain there, at least in the early stages of their existence. This, to use a phrase employed earlier, is "seed-bed" growth. Many new firms have a very short life but if our discussion in Chapter Seven of external economies of agglomeration is valid, then such firms may have a greater chance of survival in large centers than in small, isolated locations. We also noted in Chapter Nine that strong inertial forces also exist in the locational behavior of large, multi-plant enterprises in that they do not readily abandon their existing plants.

If, however, for some reason the decision-maker cannot minimize his uncertainty about the results of his investment by repeating his own previous behavior the search for a satisfactory solution begins. From among the information available to him he selects a set of feasible alternatives. For the most part these will derive from his own "view" of his environment formed through his personal actions and through his interactions with other people. However, he will also respond to information provided through the communications media.

If success in investment is what he seeks then information about success, the profitable experience of others, will have a strong appeal. In attempting to resolve the uncertainty problem, where it is impossible to depend on previous personal experience a common alternative strategy is to imitate the apparently successful behavior of others. It is in this way that human behavior provides a powerful stimulus for the recycling of economic development—*investment decisions tend to favor those systems in which previous investment has apparently met with favorable returns.* If the capital itself was generated in such a system then the probability is that it will be ploughed back. Where capital has been formed elsewhere and is mobile it will tend to flow to those systems which, on the basis of available information, are perceived to be successful. We have already established that such growth-oriented systems are powerful sources of demand for investment funds as a result of their propensity to create expanding opportunities for innovation.

In more specifically spatial terms human behavior also tends to favor a cluster of new investment decisions. We have already suggested that invention and innovation occur with greater probability at the pivotal points in the interaction network, at the higher order urban centers. In addition the spatial dissemination of information is also focused upon such centers both as places of lowest mean contact distance between individuals and also as the points of origin for the dissemination of information through the public and private communications media. Thus there is an inherent behavioral bias toward the large city which occupies a prominent place on an individual's mental map and carries the attribute of a "prestige" location for the establishment of a business enterprise.

However, the decision-makers' perception of the "large" city is selective and it is here perhaps, as was pointed out earlier, that the effective *threshold* concept has its impact. A city must reach a certain size before it becomes a universal element on the mental map of a given society and is thus a starter in the contest for site selection by other than local enterprises. To classify as a prestige location it must rank still higher on the merit list of such starters.

Once established as a "large" city (in the perceptual sense) this piece of information alone is often sufficient to maintain some impact on the locational decision. Even though the initial forces which powered its growth may have evaporated and diseconomies set in, having penetrated the large city threshold is perhaps sufficient to provide the ratchet effect which Thompson (1965) identified in city growth. For the first-rank prestige city like London, Paris or New York the metropolitan tag alone may be sufficient to promote self-generating growth even if all the other advantages which they possess prove illusory in reality. Of course illusion and reality may also operate in the reverse direction. Some large cities *suffer from notoriety* as opposed to thriving on fame. A city may be big with all the advantages that size and scale bestow but it may be perceived as bad and ugly. Certainly many cities which carry the imprint of early industrialization are unattractive to investors as are those with high crime rates. Image and reputation frequently over-ride the dictates of location theory.

Transmission of growth impulses: center periphery relationships

At various points throughout this book we have emphasized the existence of a strong *localizing* or *polarizing* principle in the spatial organization of economic activity. The essence of our discussion in this chapter so far has been that, whatever the basis of the initial trigger to development at a particular location in space, the *process* of development tends to be *cumulative*. Such cumulative development is based on mutually-reinforcing multiplier and linkage effects, internal and external economics of scale, the clustering of innovative activity, and the concentration of big business, entrepreneurial talent and economic power in the widest sense.

But although development in space is cumulative *we cannot assume that the continued growth of any particular agglomeration is inevitable*. Some agglomerations do indeed continue to grow without much apparent slackening, but many get so far and no further while others experience rapid growth followed by equally rapid decline. The key to such differential growth rates is found not only in the internal operation of multiplier and linkage effects of the kind discussed above but also in the *external* relationships of agglomerations. Of course, the existence of external links has been implicit throughout our discussion; indeed we argued that the initiation and early stages of growth at a specific location would be very largely externally induced. Even where an agglomeration has made the necessary transition from total external dependence to a more self-sustaining economic structure, the fact remains that it is a system both open to external influences and one which also influences other systems outside itself.

Our concern now is to look more closely at these external relationships. In general we can depict the spatial structure of an economic system as consisting of two major components: the *core* or *center* and the *periphery* or *hinterland*. This is a very useful concept, not least because it is applicable at a variety of spatial and organization scales. In fact, we have already used the center-periphery idea to distinguish relationships between types of business enterprise in Chapter Nine. In a *spatial* context we can apply it to relationships at the level of an individual urban center and its surrounding hinterland, an entire urban system within a nation and its rural supply areas, and on an international scale to relationships between the wealthy urban-industrial nations and the poorer developing countries.

Whatever the level of resolution—and for the most part we are concerned here with the first two—the distinguishing feature of center-periphery structures is that the center tends to *dominate* the periphery in most economic, political, and social respects. In other words, the relationship is essentially a *colonial* relationship. According to John Friedmann, one of the leading proponents of the center-periphery hypothesis,

> core regions are defined as territorially organized sub-systems of society which have a high capacity for generating and absorbing innovative change; peripheral regions are sub-systems whose development path is determined chiefly by core region institutions with respect to which they

> stand in a relation of substantial dependency. Core and periphery together
> constitute a complete spatial system.
> *Friedmann (1973), p. 67*

In taking a dynamic view of the spatial organization of economic activities
which emphasizes its center-periphery structure we need to recognize the existence of two sets of interdependencies: those *within the core* (inter-urban interdependencies) and those *between the core and the periphery* (urban-rural and inter-
urban). We can further divide these interdependencies into those which have
a *polarizing* effect (Myrdal refers to these as *backwash* effects) and those which
have a *spread* effect. The relative strength of these two forces determines whether
the gap between center and periphery is likely to narrow, widen, or remain
much the same—an issue of great social and political, as well as economic,
importance in the present day.

Classical equilibrium theory sees the *spread effects* of development as the
mechanism by which the growth process is transmitted widely throughout the
economic system, evening out distributional imbalances. Hicks (1959) for
example distinguishes three ways in which this process of evening out supposedly takes place. First, the demand generated outside the center for goods
and services will enable peripheral areas to grow richer. This may occur simply
by the outflow of money in payment for materials, goods, or services supplied
by the periphery to the center. Second, the movement of labor to the center
in response to new employment opportunities will in the long-run create a
shortage of labor in the periphery and result in a rise of wages and incomes
there. Third, the need for inputs from the periphery will promote a compensatory movement of the capital accumulated in the center, seeking out more profitable investment opportunities. In other words, new production systems may
be established in the periphery—possibly to process natural resources—which
will themselves act as initial triggers to development and set in motion cumulative growth processes at the production location. In effect, the equilibrium view
is based upon the idea that both capital and labor will tend to flow freely
from areas of low return (interest, wages) to areas of high return and that,
in doing so, the resulting shortages of supply of capital and labor in the periphery will raise their price and lead to an eventual equalization between center
and periphery. (We saw earlier in Chapter Six, however, that infinite factor
mobility is a feature of economists' models but not necessarily of real life.)

However, Myrdal (1957) and Hirschman (1958) strongly dispute the effectiveness
of such spread effects particularly at the international but also at the sub-
national level. Myrdal does not deny that spread effects exist but argues that
the market mechanism does not inevitably produce them in such a way as
to promote an evening-out of growth imbalances. *Within* developed economies
which are highly integrated economic systems there is little doubt that spread
effects do exist but their spatial impact is by no means evenly spread throughout
the system.

As we shall see later, spread effects are for the most part limited to the *immediate
vicinity of growth centers* and to other centers in the urban hierarchy, favoring

especially the higher order centers. For the peripheral areas outside their influence and often for lower order centers the characteristic effect is that of
backwash, whereby the growth of the center produces not a parallel growth
but a counterpoised decline. This is caused by the continued inflow of factor
and product supplies in response to the *growing demands of the growth center.*

Polarizing or backwash effects

We noted above three major ways in which classical equilibrium theory sees
growth being transmitted to the periphery. We can take each of these and
argue that each frequently operates in exactly the opposite way—as a backwash
effect instead of a spread effect—and thus increases, rather than decreases, the
center-periphery disparity.

1. *Purchase of goods by the center from the periphery.* There is no doubt that
this occurs. Most of the primary resources of agriculture, minerals, and other
raw materials for industry which are consumed by center businesses and population do of course originate in the periphery. Consequently, there *is* a flow
of money from center to periphery in payment for such goods. Many peripheral
areas also tend to have considerable tourist potential and this, though seasonal,
also promotes an income flow from the center to the periphery. The problem
is that, with the exception of tourism, the demand for many of the periphery's
primary goods tends to be highly inelastic. In other words, it does not change
in proportion with the changing income of the center: *as income levels rise
in the center its demands for primary resources do not grow at the same rate.*
(The post-1973 oil crisis is one of the few cases where the terms of trade have
shifted in favor of periphery producers, though this may, of course, mark a
major turning point.) Not only are primary goods, in general, relatively low
earners but also, as we have shown, the income earned by the periphery tends
to be leaked away by being spent on goods which *the periphery itself cannot
provide.* Such urban centers as exist in the periphery tend to be lower order
centers which we know have a restricted variety of goods to offer. The production of high-order consumer goods—cars, refrigerators, television sets, for example—tend to be largely in the control of businesses in the core centers. Thus
much of the income generated by the center tends to *return to the center* in
payment for goods and services. The scale economies existing in the center
and the accumulated competitive benefits of its early start inhibit the production
of such goods and services in the periphery.

2. *Migration of labor from periphery to center.* Proponents of equilibrium argue
that as labor flows from the low-wage periphery to high-wage urban centers
certain equalizing forces come into play. First, within the periphery there is
assumed to be a situation of diminishing returns to land in agricultural production. (Some degree of rural overpopulation is usually postulated.) Under these
conditions a loss of population has economic benefit. It takes the periphery
from a less efficient to a more efficient combination of land and labor in its
factor mix. Second, the falling supply of labor in the periphery relative to
demand will produce a rise in wages. This increase in wage levels will enable

the periphery to "close-up" on the center where the opposite supply-demand situation for labor will prevail.

There can be no doubt that massive migrations have taken place from rural to urban areas, particularly since the Industrial Revolution. "How're ya gonna keep 'em down on the farm, after they've seen Paree" could well have been the theme song for very many rural communities. Our concern here is not with the mechanism of migration itself but with its effects. There is no clear evidence that the income levels of the periphery *have* converged with those of the center as a result of such migration. (A glance back at Figure 6.7 will confirm this.) On the other hand, there is no unequivocal evidence that it is the *selectivity* of migration which makes this equalizing process fail. Many writers, including Myrdal, have argued that it is the young, the educated, the skilled, the adventurous who tend to form an excessive proportion of migrants. As Parr writes:

> one adverse feature of outmigration is its selective character. Generally the migrants represent the best workers (who may not even be unemployed), the younger elements (good trainee material) and would-be local administrators and entrepreneurs: in other words, the area is sapped of its vital and most needed elements. Also the age distribution of the population may well become skewed in favor of the older groups.
> *Parr (1966), pp. 152–3*

Though the selectivity argument may be less clear than such statements suggest (Okun and Richardson, 1961, for example, argue that it oversimplifies the migration mechanism), any loss of active population by migration will result in some loss of local income. The local tax base may fall, local spending may be lower and, consequently, local thresholds may decline thus either inhibiting the entry of new businesses or leading to the failure of those already there.

3. *Flows of capital between center and periphery.* Classical theory pointed to the role of capital flows as an equilibrating factor inducing investment and income formation in the periphery. Capital was seen to flow out in search of the high interest rates and greater marginal productivity in resource-rich but capital-poor regions. However, in reality the greater part of the returns to investment, the profits from new production systems, and the multiplier effect from production linkages *accrues in the growth center* to the finance houses and corporations sponsoring and providing equipment for new development. Indeed there is evidence of a net capital transfer from lagging to growing regions. This phenomenon is discussed by Williamson (1965), Robock (1963), Hay and Smith (1966).*

True, local suppliers may receive a boost from new projects in the periphery and local incomes and purchasing power may rise. However, in general a good deal of the final demand impact of new development is lost from the local

Note   *The analysis of inter-regional capital flows is a complex subject. Our brief discussion cannot even begin to do it justice. The interested reader is advised to consult Richardson (1969, pp. 304-310) for a more rounded view.

multiplier mechanism and finds its way back to the growth center in exchange for those consumer goods which the new levels of income bring within the range of the population. As Myrdal observes:

> trade operates with the same fundamental bias (as capital movement) in favor of the richer and progressive regions against the other regions.
> *Myrdal (1957), p. 28*

This bias is reinforced by the tendency to which Hirschman pointed for entrepreneurs to over-estimate the attractiveness of investment opportunities in the center and to under-estimate opportunities in the periphery. This is a point touched on earlier in our discussion of decision-making and the biased information on which many investment decisions are based. As Friedmann comments,

> regional economic growth is, above all, a competitive game.... It is... with respect to the quality of a region's infrastructure and the more generalized regional *image* that productive investment decisions are generally made.
> *Friedmann (1966), p. 24*

The image of the center tends to be clearer and more attractive as an investment area than that of much of the periphery.

Thus, where compensatory factors (such as government measures) are not in operation migration losses and net capital transfers promote trigger effects through falling local demand which generate cumulative multiplier effects in the reverse direction to those which we have previously discussed. Such a mechanism may be triggered not only by the effects of migration and capital outflow but by increasing unemployment or any force which reduces aggregate regional demand in a long-run sense. This, in essence, is the motivating force for *cumulative negative development* which Myrdal envisaged in his notion of backwash.

Spread effects

(i) *The attenuating effect of distance.* A recurring theme throughout this book and in most modern work in human geography is the attenuating effect of distance on the intensity of human activity: what Warntz called the *tyranny of distance.* Insofar as the spread effect is simply a blanket term for a number of phenomena which have a spatial expression, then we should not be surprised to find that the spread of growth impulses tends to fall off very rapidly with distance from their source. In other words, the spread effects exerted by the development of a growth node are *most effective in areas close to the node itself.*

We have already referred to some of these short-distance spread effects at various points in this book. The desire to minimize transportation costs has led to the exploitation of the nearest resources first, whether these are industrial raw materials or agricultural products. We saw in Chapter Five how the increased demand generated by the expanding urban-industrial core of northwestern Europe in the nineteenth century led to a progressive outward shift of agricultural supply zones (see Figure 5.31). Similarly, industries such as iron and steel manufacture in Britain and North America began by using local ores (usually associated with coal measures) and gradually substituted long distance sources of iron ore. As Norcliffe points out, therefore:

> the tendency is to exhaust raw material supplies in the heartland first; this exhaustion process concentrates material-oriented activity in the periphery.
> *Norcliffe* (1975), *p. 38*

A further impetus towards spread at the *edges* of growth centers is the need for increasing inputs of land. As an immobile factor land draws uses to itself. Space for residential development, for "distance-sensitive" agricultural practices like intensive horticulture and for recreational needs, are primary requirements. For the most part the land required to produce them is appropriated by the physical expansion of the growth node. This results in a movement outwards of the bid-rent and land-use surfaces as the factor is drawn into use. At the margins of urban areas rural land is converted to urban uses. As we pointed out in Chapter Three, one likely repercussion of actual or anticipated urban expansion is the inversion of the agricultural land-use pattern in the innermost zones. Thus Sinclair's adaptation of Von Thünen is based upon the short-distance spread effects of expanding urban areas.

A similar distance-decay influence characterizes the more general spatial changes which have been occurring *within* urban and metropolitan centers. The large-scale exodus of both people and manufacturing activities from the center of urban areas has been predominantly directed towards the edges of such centers rather than toward new centers in the periphery itself though there are certain exceptions, one of which is the demand for recreation and amenity.* Where

---

Note

Amenities as a factor in regional growth. The major exceptions are those in which "amenity" is an important attractive force. Obviously this is a very broad term but such variables as climate, landscape and scenic attributes and a perhaps indefinable "quality of life" have become increasingly important in circumstances where affluence and mobility have reached a high level. Edward Ullman drew attention to this more than twenty years ago in his paper "Amenities as a factor in regional growth." While being careful to avoid the pitfalls of environmental determinism, Ullman argues for the growing importance of amenities, especially climate, in certain kinds of location decision-making:

> for the first time in the world's history pleasant living conditions—amenities—instead of more narrowly defined economic advantages are becoming the sparks that generate significant population increase, particularly in the United States. In spite of the handicaps of remote location and economic isolation, the fastest-growing states are California, Arizona and Florida. The new "frontier" of America is thus a frontier of comfort in contrast with the traditional frontier of hardship.
> *Ullman (1954), p. 119*

But it would be a mistake to see such factors as operating in isolation; they can only exert a locational influence where other constraining factors such as access to materials, transport costs and so on have become relatively less important. In any case the initial trigger may well have been quite unrelated to amenity—we have already mentioned the gold-induced settlement boom of nineteenth-century California. But as with all initial triggers subsequent growth is based upon the continued ability of a location to attract other activities. If growth

Note continued

proceeds sufficiently far through increasing thresholds then other self-sustaining forces operate (for example, the resultant consumer market itself becomes an attractive force). Where growth takes place in "attractive" locations then this simply adds a further twist to the cumulative spiral. Thus there may well be a transfer of activities to peripheral towns which offer the amenities and life-styles attractive to particular groups of people.

this is not the case it is frequently a response to the efforts of government to control the evolution of the urban system rather than a reflection of the normal working of market forces. The issue of suburbanization is too wide to be taken up in detail here although two key features can be identified. First, spatial changes in the growth and location of manufacturing industry have led to major shifts at the intra-urban scale. In the period since the Second World War in particular, industry has shown a marked tendency to move out to the suburbs. The blight, congestion, and latterly security problems of operating in the traditional inner urban areas have combined with the effects of planning policy to "push" industry outwards. The "pull" of the suburban industrial park with all its amenities has drawn new and expanding manufacturing plants in all but those activities still tied to the inner city (as we saw in Chapter Seven).

The second feature of the suburbanization of people and activities is reflected in the extension of commuting fields, indicating the enormous attractive power of the center on daily journey to work patterns. Figure 10.6 shows the extent of areas within commuting range of United States cities in 1960. In the northeast and along the west coast in particular these commuting fields overlap in complex ways. The unshaded areas represent the peripheral areas which lie outside the

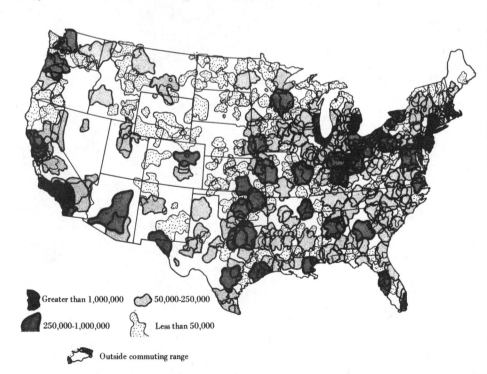

Figure 10.6
Areas within commuting range of cities of various sizes. [*Source:* B. J. L. Berry (1968), Metropolitan Area Definition: A Re-evaluation of Concept and Statistical Practice, Washington D.C.: Bureau of the Census, Working Paper No. 28.]

Greater than 1,000,000   50,000-250,000

250,000-1,000,000   Less than 50,000

Outside commuting range

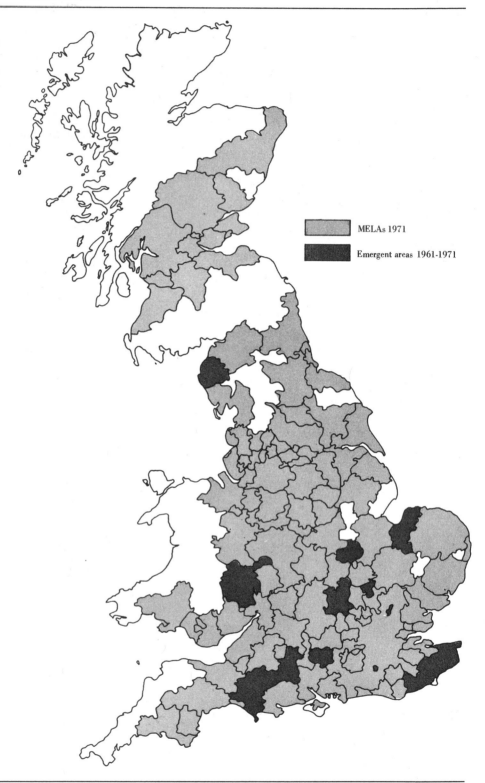

Figure 10.7
Great Britain, metropolitan
economic labor areas.
[*Source:* R. Drewett, J. B.
Goddard and N. Spence
(1976), *British Cities,
Urban Population and
Employment Trends,
1951–1971,* London:
D.O.E. Research Report,
10.]

MELAs 1971

Emergent areas 1961-1971

commuting range of the cities. Figure 10.7 is the equivalent map for Britain in 1971. Given the much smaller spatial extent of the country it is not surprising that most parts of the country are within Metropolitan Economic Labor Areas (MELAs) which are the daily commuting zones for British urban centers.

In both cases the spread is relatively limited spatially; there is a strong distance-decay component whereby the economic momentum of the center loses its impact with increasing distance. For other input needs as well as land the sensitivity of factor movements in one direction and investment flows in the other to distance, ensures that the *nearer opportunities are the first absorbed*. The development of production linkages inside and outside the center tends to conserve space for reasons which our study of location theory has made clear. Thus in a sense Hicks' view of the equalizing properties inherent in the spread effect mechanism was based, like much classical trade theory, on unrealistic assumptions of a spaceless world.

(*ii*) *The role of the urban hierarchy.* The second way in which growth impulses are transmitted in a spatial system with a center-periphery structure is from town to town through the *urban hierarchy*. Again, we have already discussed the basis of inter-urban interaction at several points in earlier chapters. The basis of such interaction is the degree of *complementarity* between places as modified by the existence of intervening opportunity and distance (transferability). We observed as early as Chapter Two that the direction of flow (whether of tangible objects such as materials and goods, or less tangible phenomena like information and innovation) depends very much on the kind of urban hierarchy considered.

In the particular case of the diffusion of innovations, Pred observes that:

> regardless of where a growth-inducing innovation originates or initially enters a system of cities, it is very likely to quickly appear in some or all of the system's largest units. That is, even if an innovation did not originate or first enter a system of cities at one of a few nationally dominant metropolitan areas, those places would tend to be early to adopt because of their high contact probabilities with a number of other places.... It is also clear that, within this probabilistic contact-field framework, large cities would benefit additionally from indirect contacts. More precisely, because of their high frequency of direct contacts with one another, large cities have the potential to quickly snap up innovations originating or entering at smaller centers with which they have no direct contact, but which lie within each other's regional sphere of influence. *Pred (1973), p. 36*

Insofar as the less rigid hierarchical structure devised by Lösch seems more realistic than that of Christaller then we would not expect the transmission of growth impulses necessarily to follow *a rigid progression from high to low-order centers* (that is passed down from big cities to towns and villages). On the contrary, the observed tendency is for both information and innovation activity to be *concentrated and recycled* in larger, higher order urban centers and for interaction to be greatest between large centers. Once again this means that the *large, already existing centers have a pronounced growth advantage which they tend to conserve among themselves.* In essence, therefore, the economic system is structured on the urban hierarchy and on the links and flows within the hierarchy. The hierarchy articulates economic activity at any given point in time and also channels growth over time, though in more complex and conservative ways than a direct high-order to low-order progression would suggest.

(iii) The role of the multi-locational business organization. The operation of spread effects and, indeed, the entire spatial center-periphery structure of economic activities is made even more complex by the increasingly dominant economic role of the very large multi-product, multi-plant business enterprise, with its highly specialized organizational and geographical structure which we discussed in Chapter Nine. Recall that we distinguished between three types or level of function: levels I and II which are administrative in type and level III which relate to operational (manufacturing or processing) activities. The precise way in which such units are organized in space, and the links that are established between them, are of very great importance in "steering" growth impulses through the space economy. Norcliffe (1975) subdivides the equivalent of our level III into those activities which mainly *process* raw materials, those which *fabricate* such processed materials into finished or intermediate products, and those which *integrate* fabricated inputs without further processing. In dynamic terms the locational shifts in each of these functions show distinct patterns. As we saw in Chapter Nine, the administrative and control functions have a marked tendency to concentrate in large agglomerations because of their information-rich and contact-intensive qualities.

Fabricating activities are tending to be moved out of the inner parts of large centers either to the edges (as discussed earlier) or to medium and small-sized centers within the core or even in the periphery. The kinds of activity involved in such a "filtering-down" process are almost invariably those of a routine and standardized nature using semi-skilled, often female, labor. Integrative activities, which require access to suppliers, and specialized functions such as research and development tend to remain closely associated with the core. Figure 10.8 depicts a suggested relationship between such plant functions and city size. *The larger the city, the greater the frequency of administrative (level I and II) activities.* Small towns, on the other hand, tend to lack these functions and to have a dominance of processing and fabricating plants.*

Note

*Figure 10.8 also suggests a direct relationship between size of plant and city size. The diagram shows two threshold levels: one (BB) below which both medium and large plants are absent, the other (AA) represents the minimum threshold for the largest plants. Thus plants of all sizes may be present in the largest towns whereas only small plants are likely to be present in small towns (except where a plant located in a small town has remained there for a long period of time and grown into a large plant *in situ*.) Norcliffe explains this size variation in terms of threshold. He argues that large plants have different requirements from small plants and that this helps to determine the possible location of new plants:

a minimum threshold size of town exists for plants of any given size, and towns below the threshold size are not likely to be selected as locations, so that large plants tend

to be confined to large towns. This does not imply that the plants located in large towns are exclusively large ones: small plants may be located in towns both large and small because their minimum threshold is commensurately small.
Norcliffe (1975), p. 42

Note continued

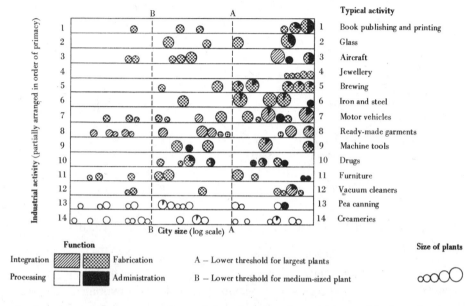

Typical activity

1 Book publishing and printing
2 Glass
3 Aircraft
4 Jewellery
5 Brewing
6 Iron and steel
7 Motor vehicles
8 Ready-made garments
9 Machine tools
10 Drugs
11 Furniture
12 Vacuum cleaners
13 Pea canning
14 Creameries

Figure 10.8
A summary of the proposed relationship between city size and activity of a plant. [*Source:* G. Norcliffe (1975), A Theory of Manufacturing Places in L. Collins and D. Walker (eds.), *Locational Dynamics of Manufacturing Activity*, Figure 1.1, Reproduced by permission of John Wiley & Sons, New York.]

Function

Integration | Fabrication
Processing | Administration

A — Lower threshold for largest plants
B — Lower threshold for medium-sized plant

Size of plants

Such geographical segregation of functional units within multi-plant business enterprises has some far-reaching spatial implications. In terms of a single multi-plant firm, decisions affecting its individual units sited in different locations (to expand or contract, to close or to modify and so on) are taken at its *headquarters location*. This has very important repercussions for the operation of multiplier effects and for differential growth both within the core and between the core and the periphery. In this respect, Pred (1973, 1974a,b) identifies three ways in which the decisions made by the multi-plant enterprise are significant.

In the first place, a change in the *scale* of activity of a multi-plant enterprise creates rather more complex *multiplier* effects than those discussed in the earlier part of this chapter. For example, suppose that a multi-plant enterprise headquartered in a major metropolitan center takes a decision to expand the output of one of its products. Wherever in the organization such expansion takes place it will have a differential effect both on other linked units within the same organization (*intra*-organizational effects) and on units of other enterprises with which it has functional relationships (*inter*-organizational effects). We already know that such linkages may be either forward or backward depending on their input-output character. Thus, insofar as one unit's expansion creates the need for additional or new inputs, for example, then multiplier effects will occur in those other units which are affected, either directly or indirectly. But these multiplier effects not only have an organizational dimension, they also have a *geographical* dimension. The multiplier effect of the expanded unit may be both *local* (other enterprise units in the same locality) and *non-local* (enterprise units located in other places). Figure 10.9 summarizes this interlocking set of multiplier relationships. Note that the process can be negative as well as positive: a decision to close down a unit or to transfer part of its operation will have multiplier effects in the opposite direction.

Figure 10.9
Categories of direct
multiplier effects.
[*Source:* Reproduced by
permission from the
Association of American
Geographers' Commission
on College Geography
Resource Paper Series,
27, *Major Job-Providing
Organizations and
Systems of Cities,* 1974,
A. R. Pred, Figure 5.]

		Local	Non-local
Intra-organizational	Backward linkage		
	Forward linkage		
Inter-organizational	Backward linkage		
	Forward linkage		

The second way in which multi-plant enterprises influence spatial change relates to their role as transmitters, processors, and receivers of specialized information, particularly that involved in "growth-inducing" innovations. Pred identifies three types of growth-inducing innovations which have effects within the urban system:

1. Innovations which provide new *products* or services for intermediate or final demand markets.
2. Innovations which involve the use of new production *processes*.
3. Innovations which relate to changes in the *organization* itself, for example, new organizational structures, new planning and decision-making procedures.

These three are, of course, not mutually exclusive categories; adopting one often involves adopting either one or both of the others. Any one of these innovations may lead to increased employment at the location involved and, through the intra and inter-organizational multiplier, possibly at other locations. More generally, much of the flow of information in modern society is *within* multi-unit organizations so that their locational characteristics have an important influence on information flows and, therefore, on the kinds of decisions made. There is a tendency for many innovations to be introduced first at or very close to the enterprise's headquarters' location and only later diffused to the chosen subordinate units at other locations.

The third influence of multi-plant enterprises on center-periphery development relates to what Pred calls the *accumulation of operational decisions.* Quite apart from the decision to do something "new"—the growth-inducing innovations discussed above—there are many operational decisions, some of them highly routine which, as they are implemented by multi-plant enterprises, again have spatial growth repercussions. Each decision individually may not have a very pronounced spatial impact; *taken as a "cluster" of decisions made by organizations whose control units are themselves geographically clustered,* the accumulated effect of such operational decisions can be very considerable. This is particularly true if we remind ourselves of some of the characteristics of decision-making behavior discussed in Chapter Nine. One important point made there was that the existing spatial structure of a firm—the geographical arrangement of its component parts—exerts an extremely powerful influence on decision-making.

Not only is there a strong inertial effect whereby existing units tend to be favored over new ones, but also the prevailing structure filters and channels the information on which enterprise decisions are made.

Thus the various kinds of operational decision which concern us here, *purchase-source* decisions, *market-outlet* decisions and *private investment* decisions, are made largely within the constraints of the organization's existing structure. How this organizational structure is arranged within the urban system or between center and periphery greatly determines differential growth at different locations. Just one example can serve to illustrate this. In Chapter Seven we discussed linkages between firms, noting that location in an urban agglomeration enabled firms to utilize specialized services—processing, financial, legal, advertising, transportation, and so on—which would not generally be available in isolated locations or small urban centers. In this sense, external economies of scale are in operation. But a very pronounced tendency is for the large multi-plant firm to provide such services from *within* its own organization. One effect of this, in Britton's words, is that:

> short circuits will be created within the urban system. Some firms contain plants which interact at a low level with service firms in their particular regions while substantial volumes of business may be created in the urban center where the company head office is located.
> *Britton (1974), p. 367*

In his study of manufacturing linkages in various metropolitan and urban centers in southern Ontario, Britton was able to demonstrate that "high-order office services" (legal; banking, where loans for capital equipment or expansion were involved; auditing and other financial services) showed a strong tendency to be "internalized." In other words, *many multi-plant organizations derived these services from other units within the same organization* rather than from independent firms in the same locality. Thus an increase in the demand for such services may well be satisfied in an entirely different urban center, generally the head-quarters' location itself. In this way, growth impulses in the form of expenditure on business services find their way to other locations rather than stimulating activity in the location where the demand is actually created.

The essence of our argument relating the behavior of large multi-plant enterprises to developments within the urban system and between center and periphery is that it results in the emergence of *centers of control* with very high concentrations of decision-making and innovative activity. Decisions made in these centers "steer" growth impulses and thus have tremendous repercussions throughout the economic system. In general the accumulated effect of these decisions is to reinforce still further the strength of existing concentrations and to perpetuate the distinction between center and periphery.

Cumulative growth and time-space convergence: a summary model

Our attention so far has been focused on the mechanics of the growth process. By way of a summary let us return more explicitly to a primary concern with space and spatial models. We can effectively do this by taking the model of transportation change introduced in Chapter Five (Figure 5.27) and integrating it with the cumulative growth model just outlined. Figure 10.10 shows how the two sub-models might be linked together (the expanded version of Janelle's model is used in this case). The emphasis in the composite model is on *the interdependence between growth at particular points in space and the evolving transport links between these growth points.*

Two processes are in operation, both of which are cumulative and circular in their own right but which are also *mutually reinforcing*: changes in the one influencing, and being influenced by, changes in the other. Let us set out the stages involved remembering that the process is circular and any starting point is bound to be arbitrary.

1. Expansion of activity leads to a demand for better communication or accessibility—to suppliers of materials, to customers, to other functionally linked activities.
2. This leads by way of technological change and its diffusion to the adoption of transport innovations and in turn to improved communication between places. Time-space or cost-space convergence is made possible.
3. The combination of stages one and two enhances the potential for specialization in the developing economic system as the effective market is expanded. Greater spatial concentration and centralization of control is facilitated.
4. The accumulated result of the changes so far permits still greater demand for accessibility which, when satisfied, produces still higher levels of interaction. The attractiveness of the pivotal centers is further enhanced and new investment flows in. In-migration is stimulated and new thresholds of consumer demand are attained. A new cycle of mutually reinforcing changes is begun.

Figure 10.10
Cumulative development and time-space convergence. [*Source:* based on A. Pred (1966), *The Spatial Dynamics of U.S. Urban-Industrial Growth,* Figure 2.1. Reprinted by permission of the M.I.T. Press, Cambridge, Massachusetts. Copyright © 1966 by the Massachusetts Institute of Technology; and D. G. Janelle (1969), Spatial Reorganization: A Model and a Concept. Reproduced by permission from the *Annals of the Association of American Geographers,* Volume 59, 1969.]

Recycling growth of this kind, however, produces its problems and, in particular, resource limitations appear. In the long-run the need for additional space becomes one such major problem. Space has to be adapted to accommodate new or growing activities. As we suggested earlier this will tend to occur on the edges of the growth center. Figure 10.10 (steps 9 and 10) reflects this and also the possibility of expansion vertically through skyscraper construction.

The key point in this general spatial reorganization process is that:

> the process of spatial reorganization in the form of centralization and specialization will accelerate most rapidly at those places which stand to benefit most from increasing accessibility. In other words, transport innovations are most likely between those places which will benefit most from a lessening in the expenditure of time (cost or effort) to attain needed and desirable goods and services.
> *Janelle (1969), p.357*

Once again it can be shown that *places which gain some initial advantage are likely to retain such an advantage*, benefiting from the cumulative processes of growth and transportation change. Places which are already large and economically powerful will be the most likely beneficiaries of innovations which will

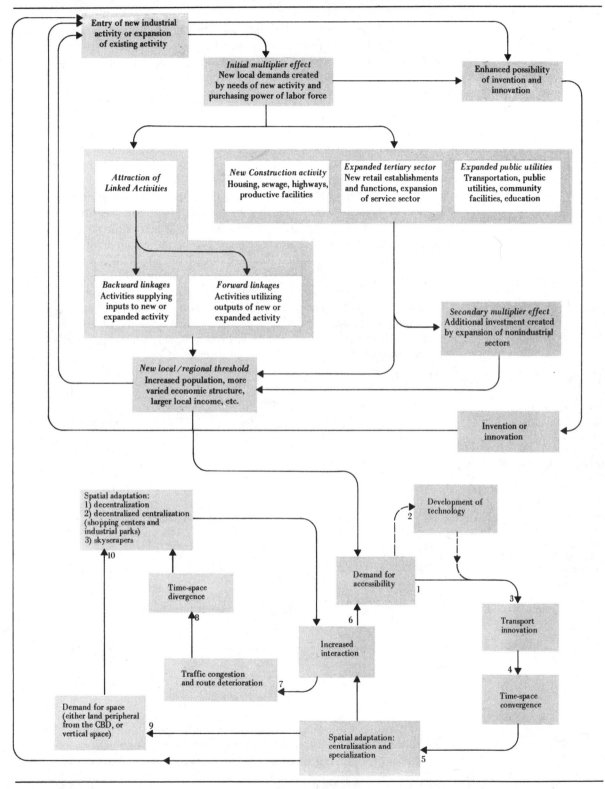

still further enhance their accessibility to other important places. In this way, the already high levels of interaction between high-order, key centers are likely to be increased even further while smaller, less significant, places may well be by-passed by the development of high-order transport linkages (such as the motorway system in Britain and the interstate highway system in the United States).

Again in the interests of integration we can usefully see Taaffe, Morrill and Gould's model of transportation development as a broad summary of this two-fold process of urban growth and change in accessibility. Figure 10.11 shows that as the network evolves certain routes develop to a greater extent than others in association with the increased importance of particular urban centers. The "ideal-typical sequence" begins (Stage 1) as a pattern of scattered, poorly connected small ports along the coastline. In Stage 2, two major routes penetrate inland, perhaps in order to tap a valuable mineral resource or to facilitate the movement of desired agricultural produce from an area in the interior to the coastal market. The result of the increased interaction is to increase the size of the two terminal ports and (Stage 3) to initiate new urban growth at strategic points on the routes. Stage 4 shows how, as a consequence of lateral route development, the competitive position of the two major centers and of those at the interior terminal points is further enhanced. Subsequently (Stage 5) almost complete interconnection may be achieved but because certain centers are already more powerful than others the further development of high priority linkages (Stage 6) is likely.

Figure 10.11
An "ideal-typical sequence" of the development of a transportation network. [*Source:* E. J. Taaffe, R. L. Morrill, and P. R. Gould (1963), Transport Expansion in Underdeveloped Countries, *Geographical Review,* 53, copyrighted by the American Geographical Society of New York.]

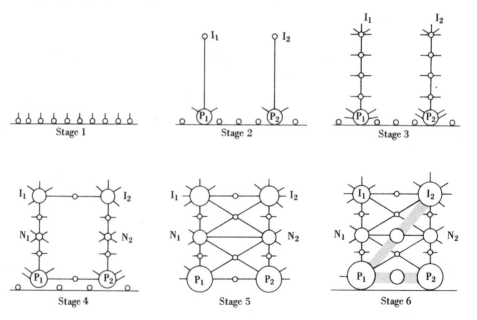

The overall result of these spatial changes is a constantly evolving and changing space economy in which *forces of polarization tend to outweigh the forces of spread.* But as Friedmann has shown, the *degree* of imbalance between center and periphery is very much related to a country's level of economic, social and political development. He identifies four major stages in the sequence of spatial organization (Figure 10.12), stages which have certain broad parallels with the transportation model of Figure 10.11. The diagram is self-explanatory though we should observe that the final stage (4) implies a deliberate planning policy aimed at totally integrating the urban-economic system. Whether or not such a fully integrated system, with "minimum essential regional imbalances" has been achieved even in the highly urbanized countries is an issue we cannot pursue here.

Figure 10.12   A sequence of stages in spatial organization. [*Source:* J. Friedmann (1966), *Regional Development Policy: A Case Study of Venezuela,* Figure 2.1. Reprinted by permission of the M.I.T. Press, Cambridge, Massachusetts. Copyright © 1966 by the Massachusetts Institute of Technology.]

1   *Independent local centers, no hierarchy.* Typical preindustrial structure; each city lies at the center of a small regional enclave; growth possibilities are soon exhausted; the economy tends to stagnate.

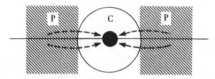

2   *A single strong center.* Structure is typical for the period of incipient industrialization; a periphery (P) emerges; local economies are undermined in consequence of a mass movement of would-be entrepreneurs, intellectuals, and labor to the center (C); the national economy is virtually reduced to a single metropolitan region, with only limited growth possibilities; continued stagnation of the periphery may lead to social and political unrest.

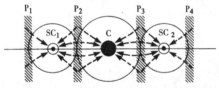

3   *A single national center, strong peripheral subcenters.* The first stage toward a solution during the period of industrial maturation; strategic subcenters (SC_n) are developed, thereby reducing the periphery on a national scale to smaller, more manageable inter-metropolitan peripheries (P_n); hypertrophy of national center is avoided while important resources from the periphery are brought into the productive cycle of the national economy; growth potential for the nation is enhanced, but problems of poverty and cultural backwardness persist in intermetropolitan peripheries.

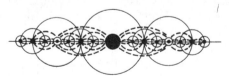

4   *A functionally interdependent system of cities.* Organized complexity is the final solution to be aimed for during the period of industrial maturation, but it will subsequently give place to other configurations; major goals of spatial organization are fulfilled: national integration, efficiency in location, maximum growth potential, minimum essential interregional balances.

Evolution of the North American urban-economic system

In case the reader should find the highly simplified patterns produced by the models far-removed from reality we will conclude by showing briefly how the spatial economic development of the United States and Canada broadly exemplifies the process we have explored in general terms. Obviously, we cannot do justice to such a vast topic here. Our aim is simply to suggest that in the *particular* circumstances where geographical space is fundamentally important (because of the vast scale of the countries) and where development occurred very rapidly from very small beginnings, the kind of development process we have been discussing is a reasonably accurate model of what has actually happened. The model is specifically "new world" in its assumptions (it might equally well be applied to conditions in Australasia, colonial Africa or South America). For the European "heartland" it is less appropriate except perhaps at lower levels of resolution in a *regional*, rather than a continental context.

The recurring theme throughout is that development occurred within an evolving heartland-hinterland (center-periphery) framework. Initially, (by this we mean the eighteenth century) both the United States and Canada were themselves peripheral or hinterland areas oriented towards the European heartland, to Britain and France in particular. Much of their early development, therefore, was based upon their ability to supply materials and resources to satisfy the colonial demands of the heartland economy. Early dependence on primary staples was thus common to both colonial America and Canada. The fact that Canada retained its hinterland status much longer than the United States, because of its persistence as a British colony, goes a long way toward explaining both the later development of a self-sustaining economy and Canada's present situation in relation to the United States.

As it happens the spatial evolution of the United States urban-economic system is very much better documented than that of Canada. Borchert (1967) and Lukermann (1966) have made particularly detailed studies and much of what follows is based upon their work. Borchert summarizes the major features in the following manner:

> Most American metropolitan areas, throughout much of their history, have functioned chiefly as collectors, processors and distributors of raw materials and goods. Consequently, it might be expected that their growth rates would have been particularly sensitive to changes in (1) the size and resource base of the hinterland and (2) the technology of transport and industrial energy for the processing of primary resources. These two sets of variables are interrelated. The technology partly defines the resource base, and the transportation technology, in particular, strongly affects the size, and therefore the resources, of a city's hinterland. There is, of course, no implication that the technological changes have been independent variables or basic causes of growth. The presumptions are, rather, that within the given framework of values and institutions they were stimulated by the economic growth and geographical expansion of the nation and that

they in turn not only further stimulated growth but also helped to differentiate it geographically.
Borchert (1967), pp. 302–303

Borchert identifies three major pairs of innovations which he sees to have had particularly important effects on the spatial organization of the economy:

1. *Steamboat and "Iron Horse"*—beginning with the application of steam engines to both water and land transportation. The result during the nineteenth century was the development of major transportation corridors along the Great Lakes and the major rivers. Subsequent development of railroads led to the integration of water and rail transport networks. Ports with favorable locations with respect to both harbor facilities and natural resources grew at the expense of other small ports. Application of steam power to manufacturing industry had a particularly localizing effect for reasons discussed in Chapter Four: high weight-loss and low burning efficiency. Waterpower sites were important: Borchert points out that in 1870, waterwheels were still providing approximately 50 percent of the inanimate energy for manufacturing and half of all the inanimate native power for industry was concentrated in the five states of Massachusetts, Connecticut, New York, Pennsylvania and Ohio.

2. *Steel rails and electric power*—particularly in the 1870s large quantities of low-priced steel became available. "A number of related events, each with geographical ramifications of great importance, occurred in dramatic sequence in the decade of the 1870's." In terms of transportation, the adoption of steel rails, standard gauges, refrigerator cars made possible a greater degree of regional specialization. Coal could be moved over much greater distances at lower cost; new fields, for example, the huge deposits of the central Appalachians, were exploited and coal could be moved to the growing ports. After the 1880s, electric power became widely available. Large market concentrations favored the development of major urban agglomerations while many waterway towns lost their growth momentum.

3. *Internal combustion engine and shift to services.* The internal combustion engine not only revolutionized movement in and between urban areas, it also revolutionized agriculture through the development of mechanized farming. Since 1920, too, major structural changes have occurred in employment with the steady decline of employment in agriculture and the more recent expansion of "service" employment. Cities are no longer primarily processors of resources and assemblers of components:

with a fast-growing majority of new jobs since 1920 in the least mechanized and least automated part of our economy—the personal and professional services—*the most likely locations for new employment growth have been the places where there were already large concentrations of people to be served. Hence—in the auto-air age, even more than in the preceding epoch—growth breeds growth.* (present authors' italics)
Borchert (1967), pp. 306–307

Using these innovation clusters as a basis, Borchert identifies four significant epochs in the evolution of the urban-economic landscape of the United States.

1. *The Sail-Wagon Epoch, 1790–1830*. Figure 10.13 shows the urban pattern of 1790. At that time, despite the nation's newly won political independence, the early cities—which essentially meant those on the northeastern seaboard—were still, in effect, an integral part of the European urban-economic system. They faced outward across the Atlantic rather than inland so that, for the most part, their hinterlands were small. In 1790, all the major urban centers were ports, located either on the bays or estuaries of the Atlantic coast or on the navigable stretches of the major east-flowing rivers. From the outset, there was no clearly defined, single, dominant or primate city, the larger coastal cities such as New York, Boston, and Philadelphia were of broadly similar size.

Figure 10.13
Distribution of major cities in the United States, 1790. [*Source:* J. R. Borchert (1967), American Metropolitan Evolution, Figure 6. Reprinted, with permission, from the *Geographical Review,* Vol. 57, 3, 1967.]

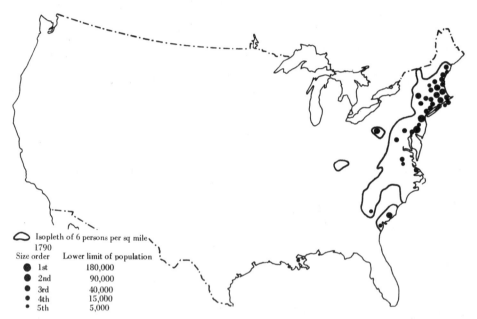

Isopleth of 6 persons per sq mile
1790

Size order	Lower limit of population
1st	180,000
2nd	90,000
3rd	40,000
4th	15,000
5th	5,000

Between 1790 and 1830 there was no spectacular change in the spatial structure of the urban system. Places with relatively faster growth rates were, in general, located in areas of frontier expansion and especially related to the exploitation of natural resources. Particularly rapid growth was largely confined to strategic locations on the major inland waterways, again emphasizing the key role of the communications media. The Atlantic urban centers maintained their importance for the most part because, as Borchert shows, there was little, if any, major change in the technology of inland transportation up to 1830. Overland movement was both difficult and costly. The "center" was effectively confined to the northeastern coast with New York emerging as the major center.

2. *Iron-Horse Epoch, 1830–1870*. The impact of the railroad brought fundamental changes; the Appalachians were effectively breached. Convergence of rail and waterway networks enhanced the significance of key port locations as the

agricultural resources of the interior were tapped; "boom" centers grew rapidly on the coalfields; cities like Pittsburg climbed the urban hierarchy; New York's growth as the major port and commercial center was rapid; having been similar in size to Philadelphia in 1830, it was double the size of Philadelphia by 1870. The Iron-Horse epoch provided the early outlines of the U.S. economic heartland which was to dominate economic life for decades. Figures 10.14 and 10.15 show how far both the major frontier of settlement and the urban centers of differing order had developed between 1830 and 1870.

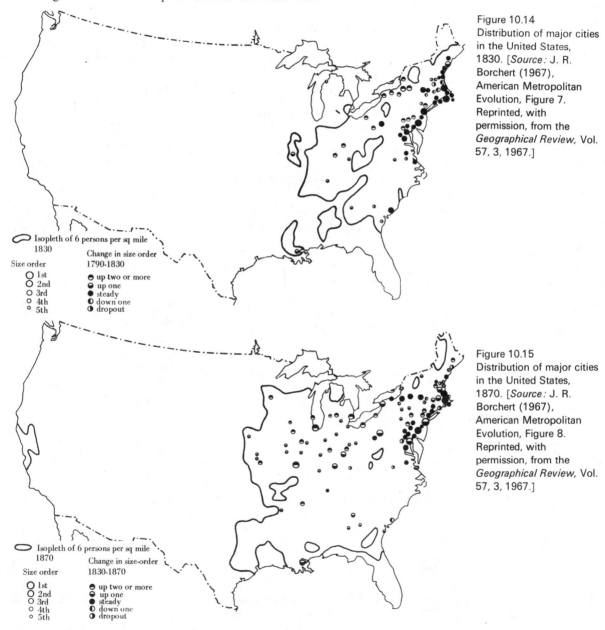

Figure 10.14
Distribution of major cities in the United States, 1830. [*Source:* J. R. Borchert (1967), American Metropolitan Evolution, Figure 7. Reprinted, with permission, from the *Geographical Review,* Vol. 57, 3, 1967.]

Figure 10.15
Distribution of major cities in the United States, 1870. [*Source:* J. R. Borchert (1967), American Metropolitan Evolution, Figure 8. Reprinted, with permission, from the *Geographical Review,* Vol. 57, 3, 1967.]

3. *Steel-Rail Epoch, 1870–1920.* The cumulative growth of manufacturing was particularly marked in this epoch as coal, the modern iron and steel industry and related activities developed in the heartland. Recall from Chapter Nine that this was the age of the first really large mergers between the industrial companies of the United States. The development of new urban centers occurred mainly in the newly exploited resource areas of the west. Conversely a number of centers experienced decline as they were unable to sustain growth compared with the heartland cities. Two groups of centers were most affected. One group consisted mainly of old waterpower sites in New England and New York state. The other was some of the river towns along the Ohio, Missouri, Mississippi river system. The five largest metropolitan areas increased their size at a faster rate than ever before as cumulative growth processes reinforced initial advantage.

4. *Auto-Air Amenity Epoch, 1920-present.* By 1920 the modern structure of the U.S. economy was established (Figure 10.16). The heartland-dominated structure which had evolved in the previous century set the pace for the subsequent changes which have occurred. Technological changes in communication in particular have enabled the influence of the growth impulses to spread, though as we observed earlier, much of the spread has been on the periphery of existing centers, within the heartland itself or in the "amenity" areas of the southwest. As Figure 10.6 showed, the daily commuting zones of the present metropolitan centers interpenetrate and coalesce, especially in the northeast—again emphasizing the historic leading role of the initial heartland.

Figure 10.16
Distribution of major cities in the United States, 1920. [*Source:* J. R. Borchert (1967), American Metropolitan Evolution, Figure 9. Reprinted, with permission, from the *Geographical Review,* Vol. 57, 3, 1967.]

Yet the center-periphery structure remains despite the massive urban growth of recent decades. As Friedmann and Miller point out:

it has become increasingly possible to interpret the spatial structure of the United States in ways that will emphasize a pattern consisting of *one*, metropolitan areas, and *two*, the inter-metropolitan periphery. Except for thinly populated parts of the American interior, the inter-metropolitan periphery includes all areas that intervene among metropolitan regions that are, as it were, the reverse image of the trend towards large-scale concentrated settlement that has persisted in this country for over half a century. Like a devil's mirror, much of it has developed a socio-economic profile that perversely reflects the very opposite of metropolitan virility. Economically, the inter-metropolitan periphery includes most of the areas that have been declared eligible for federal area development assistance.... Situated almost entirely outside the normal reach of the larger cities, these areas are shown to be clearly peripheral. They have a disproportionately large share of low-growth and declining industries and a correspondingly antiquated economic structure. Nevertheless, one-fifth of the American people are living in these regions of economic distress. Demographically, the inter-metropolitan periphery has been subject to a long-term, continuous decline... This trend reflects the movement of people to cities, especially to the large metropolitan concentrations.... The emergence in large sections of the country of the inter-metropolitan periphery as a major problem area has been the direct result of the concentration of people and activities around closely contiguous metropolitan cores.
Friedmann and Miller (1965), p. 313

The pen picture we have been developing in what must of necessity be a "sketchy" review of the spatial growth process in the United States would be incomplete if we left the reader with the impression that only the periphery has its problems. The other side of the periphery "coin" is the center, which in the North American case has become identified with the concept of *megalopolis*. Jean Gottman has given the term its widest currency. His archetypal megalopolis was the 400 mile stretch between Boston and Washington along the northeastern seaboard of the United States. In 1960 this accounted for 34.2 million of the country's residents—some 18 percent of the total. Another megalopolis may be recognized in the area of the Great Lakes. This is less homogeneous than the first and can be subdivided into three distinct groups of metropolitan areas. The first centers on Chicago, the second on Detroit and the third on Cleveland–Pittsburgh. Doxiadis suggested that this cluster transcended national boundaries through an incipient expansion into Canada along the Windsor-Hamilton-Toronto-Montreal-Ottawa axis. He went on to foresee the two major clusters—Great Lakes and northeastern—merging together by way of the "Mohawk Bridge" (Doxiadis, 1969). Although the fulfillment of his projection lies somewhere in the future, present trends point toward urbanized living on a gigantic scale.

Megalopolis America, for all the virility of its growth, has become the scene of massive problems in the wake of its very success. Congestion, pollution, crime, urban poverty, racial conflict and the growing powerlessness of the metropolitan authorities to provide financial support for the services they have to provide are one legacy of the "success" of the center as compared with the periphery. The "flight to the suburbs" has become a popular description of the spread effect generated by the *social* rather than purely economic pressures of urban living in the last quarter of the twentieth century. We can do the topic scant justice here but it is as well to remind ourselves that the "colonial" domination which the center exerts over the periphery is a matter for economic accounting. It does reflect a necessary difference in the real income of the residents of the two elements when all is taken into account.

A similar kind of heartland-hinterland structure has evolved in Canada but because of the smaller population size (one-tenth of the United States), vast unpopulated areas in the north, a longer colonial history, and the operation of both English and French cultural traditions, the precise form of the center-periphery structure is different. However the same basic forces have molded the Canadian structure. Early (and in this case, long-lived) reliance on providing staple products for the colonial heartland was a major formative influence on Canadian development (see p. 389). Early Canadian towns were essentially collection and distribution points for staple products, their locations reflecting accessibility in relation to the staple and the prevailing transportation system. Both because of developments in the United States (many early Canadian settlers were in fact loyalists who left the American colonies when the United States became independent) and the "grain" of early transportation routes (the St. Lawrence and the Great Lakes), Canadian settlement became closely tied to a relatively narrow strip along the U.S.-Canadian border. It is surely no accident that southern Ontario—the area closest to the United States manufacturing heartland—developed into the leading economic concentration in Canada, with its focus upon Toronto and the northern and western shores of Lake Ontario. The concentration of French colonial interests in the east and the development of major manufacturing activity focused on Montreal forms the other major pivot of the Canadian heartland.

Although some cities away from this core have grown very rapidly, often as resource-based centers (Winnipeg, Edmonton, Calgary, for example, and on the Pacific Coast where Vancouver has emerged as the third-ranking Canadian city) the cumulative development of the heartland has continued to dominate. The bulk of Canadian economic activity and population is in fact concentrated in the relatively narrow strip stretching from Windsor to Quebec City with major metropolitan concentrations focused on the Toronto-Hamilton region and Montreal. In fact some 75 percent of the Canadian population live in urban areas within 100 miles of the U.S. border and 25 percent in the two metropolitan areas of Toronto and Montreal.

Maxwell (1965) was able to demonstrate that a significant functional difference exists between urban centers located in the heartland (which he defines as the densely populated St. Lawrence lowlands and southern Ontario) and the periphery. Figure 10.17 shows just how far manufacturing activity is concentrated in the heartland. As Maxwell notes:

> although manufacturing is almost ubiquitous as a dominant function, it achieves an especially important position in the functional profiles of heart-

land cities. Even within the heartland there is a high concentration of manufacturing dominance.... Manufacturing generally plays a much less significant role as a dominant function in the profiles of periphery cities than in those of the heartland cities. All but two of the forty-five heartland cities have manufacturing as their dominant function. In contrast, just over one-third of the periphery cities are similarly characterized; the balance have transportation, retail trade, or some other function as the dominant activity.

Maxwell (1965), pp. 89,91

Figure 10.17
Canada's heartland and hinterland. [*Source:* J. Maxwell (1965), The Functional Structure of Canadian Cities, Figure 3. Reprinted, with permission, from the *Geographical Bulletin,* 7, 1965.]

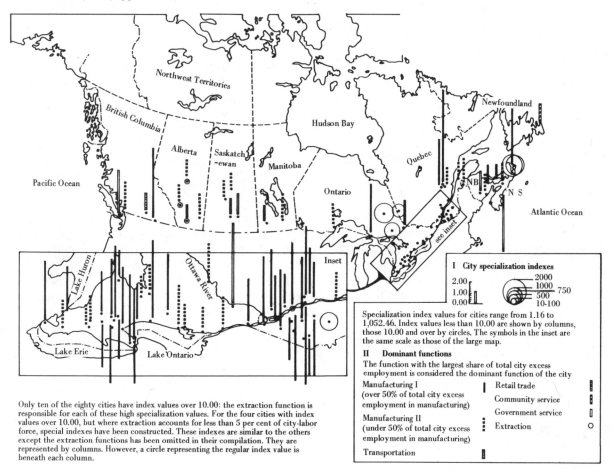

Only ten of the eighty cities have index values over 10.00: the extraction function is responsible for each of these high specialization values. For the four cities with index values over 10.00, but where extraction accounts for less than 5 per cent of city-labor force, special indexes have been constructed. These indexes are similar to the others except the extraction functions has been omitted in their compilation. They are represented by columns. However, a circle representing the regular index value is beneath each column.

The center-periphery structure is especially distinct in Canada. But it is possible to go one stage further and see the Canadian economy as a whole as being functionally a component of a North American-scale center-periphery structure. Indeed, many Canadians are fearful of the degree of U.S. dominance of Canadian economic life, whether expressed in terms of the very high degree of U.S. ownership of Canadian economic activity—Canada has been termed "the largest branch-plant economy in the world"—or in more general social, political and cultural terms. Quite apart from the deep issues involved here, it is undoubtedly true that the Canadian and United States heartlands are so closely juxtaposed and interrelated that they are functionally very closely related.

Such case studies exemplify the point that in general we can identify in the space economy powerful forces which serve to amplify by means of "mutual-causal" processes the impulses set up by initial triggers to geographical differentiation. In spatial terms, given that there are no serious blockages in factor inputs or in the willingness of society to consume the products of its leading economic subsystems, the end product of the cumulative process in a free market system tends to be the creation of localized growth centers. A characteristic feature of such centers is that beyond a certain stage of development—the threshold— they appear to exert a considerable influence on the subsequent development of the space economy while acquiring themselves a strong self-perpetuating momentum through derived advantages of their early growth. Away from the localized growth centers the intensity and rate of development has a marked tendency to decline with distance, though their expansionary momentum results in spread effects which raise levels of development in their immediate proximity. As a result of time-lags in development the periphery often remains in nearly permanent subordination to the center, cumulative growth in the one being associated with cumulative decline in the other.

Throughout our discussion of the time dimension and its impact on economic development in space we have demonstrated that market forces, technology and, in particular, the single-minded pursuit of self-interest have conspired in the western world to create huge centers of power, control and economic wealth. Space and the constraints which it imposes has had its particular impact in molding the geographical forms that the growth process has produced. We have made no value judgments on the nature of the process and economic furniture which it has produced. But western society as a whole *has* made its own value judgments about the human habitat which cumulative growth has generated. Human behavior reflects those judgments and since economic development is, at base, a reflection of that behavior we devote a final chapter in the form of an epilogue to it.

Further reading

Borchert, J. R. (1967) American Metropolitan Evolution, *Geographical Review*, **57**, 301–332.

Friedmann, J. (1966) *Regional Development Policy: A Case Study of Venezuela*, Cambridge, Mass: M.I.T. Press, Chapters 1 and 2.

Isard, W., and R. E. Kuenne (1953), The Impact of Steel on the Greater New York–Philadelphia Industrial Region, *Review of Economics and Statistics*, **35**, 289–301.

Maruyama, M. (1963), The Second Cybernetics: Deviation Amplifying Mutual Causal Processes, *American Scientist* **51**, 164–179.

Miernyk, W. H. (1965), *The Elements of Input-Output Analysis*, New York: Random House.

Myrdal, G. (1957), *Rich Lands and Poor*, New York: Harper & Row.

Norcliffe, G. (1975), A theory of manufacturing places, in L. Collins & D. F. Walker (eds.), *Locational Dynamics of Manufacturing Activity*, New York: John Wiley, pp. 19–57.

Pred, A. R. (1966), *The Spatial Dynamics of U.S. Urban-Industrial Growth, 1800–1914*, Cambridge, Mass.: M.I.T. Press, Chapters 2 and 3.

Pred, A. R. (1973), The growth and development of systems of cities in advanced economies, in A. R. Pred and G. E. Tornquist, Systems of Cities and Information Flows, *Lund Studies in Geography, Series B*, **38**, pp. 9–82.

Pred, A. R. (1974), Industry, information and city-system interdependencies, in F. E. I. Hamilton (ed.), *Spatial Perspectives on Industrial Organization and Decision-Making*, New York: John Wiley, pp. 105–139.

Thompson, W. R. (1965), *A Preface to Urban Economics*, Baltimore: Johns Hopkins Press, Chapter 1.

Thompson, W. R. (1968), Internal and External Factors in the Development of Urban Economies, in H. S. Perloff and L. Wingo, Jr. (eds.), *Issues in Urban Economics*, Baltimore: Johns Hopkins Press, pp. 43–62.

Tiebout, C. M. (1962), *The Community Economic Base Study*, New York: Committee for Economic Development.

CHAPTER II

"GROWTH CREATES FORM BUT FORM LIMITS GROWTH": AN EPILOGUE

The concise but highly significant statement in the chapter heading is derived from Kenneth Boulding, one of the most stimulating writers of the last quarter century in the social sciences. We propose to use it here as a "text" for our epilogue.

Growth has been set out in this and the previous chapter to be a result of deviation-amplifying forces at work in the economic system. We have largely rejected the pious hopes of classical equilibrium theory that the forces of the market will make everything turn out right in the end. Indeed we go along with Hirschman who complained that:

> Tradition seems to require that economists argue forever about the question whether market forces acting alone are likely to restore equilibrium. Now this is certainly an interesting question. But as social scientists we surely must address ourselves to the broader question: is the disequilibrium situation likely to be corrected at all, by market or non-market forces or by both acting jointly?
> *Hirschman (1958), p. 63*

In a particularly spatial context, we have accepted the view set forward by Ullman (1958), that "concentration within countries is the rule..." and that of Friedmann regarding the inter-metropolitan periphery as an area predisposed to decline. Thus, the *form* which has become the economico-geographic product of the growth process has been patterned on the center-periphery principle.

None of these features—the particular characteristics of the growth process or the specific spatial form—is particularly new or modern in its appearance. Indeed, as Lampard (1955) pointed out, the process which we can describe more simply as *urbanization* has been going on for about 7000 years. From the time of the earliest urban societies "centers" have grown up and taken on a dominant role in controlling the re-investment of whatever surplus income (capital) a society generated.

What makes the modern period so remarkable, however, is the *sheer scale on which this process now takes place*. At the highest level of aggregation, the controlling power of the "world metropolis" (North America and Western Europe) in both realizing and distributing the global surplus income remains intact. Though severely shaken by the post-1973 oil crises and the bout of severe inflation which followed, "recovery", we are promised, "is on the way." Warntz's maps of world income potential (Figure 11.1a) compared with population potential (Figure 11.1b) provide the sharpest visual summary of center-periphery relationships at the global level.

Below the global level of spatial aggregation we have already pointed to the arrival of megalopolis within North America. Following Hall (1973) we could add to it three other such concentrations:

1. *Japanese Megalopolis*: Centered on Tokyo, Yokohama, Nagoya, Osaka-Kobe. Population in 1960: 40.5 millions.
2. *Northwest European Megalopolis*: Includes Amsterdam, Rotterdam, Essen,

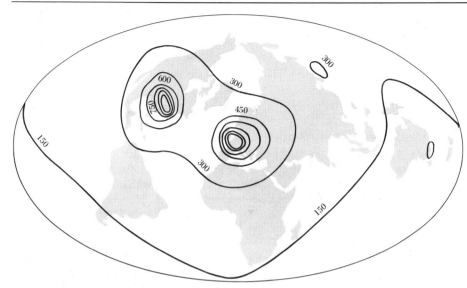

In millions, equivalent U S dollars per mile (based upon persons weighted by their incomes)

(a)

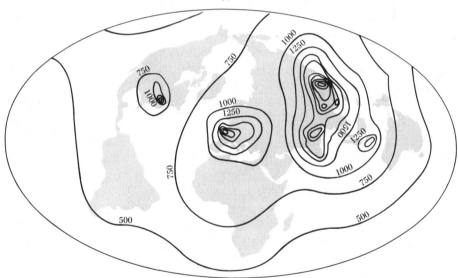

In thousands, persons per mile (all persons considered to have equal, ie, unit weight)

(b)

Figure 11.1
(a) World income potentials circa 1960.
(b) World population potential circa 1960.
[*Source:* W. Warntz (1956), *Macrogeography and Income Fronts,* Figures 19 and 24, Regional Science Research Institute, University of Pennsylvania.]

Dortmund, Duisberg, Dusseldorf, Frankfurt, Mainz, Mannheim, Stuttgart. Population in 1960: 29.2 millions.

3. *Megalopolis England*: Stretches from south coast northwards to Lancashire and Yorkshire. Includes most of the major cities e.g. London, Birmingham, Manchester, Liverpool, Leeds. Population in 1961: 32.2 millions.

At the next lowest level—the city level—literally millions of words have been written describing the process of clustering in urban agglomerations and we shall do no more than comment on it here.

Despite the early origins of the city as a social and spatial form, rapid and universal urbanization is a twentieth century phenomenon. As late as 1900 only Great Britain could be classified as predominantly urbanized. Today this label describes all industrialized nations. In 1800 probably less than 2 percent of the world's population lived in the 20 or so cities of larger than 100,000 population. In 1870 there were only seven cities with populations greater than 1 million (they contained roughly 1 percent of the world's population). By 1964 there were more than 150 "million metropolises" accommodating more than 11 percent of a very much larger world population. In the industrialized nations the degree of urbanization has been, of course, very much greater. In the early 1920s roughly 50 percent of the United States population lived in urban areas. By 1970 73.5 percent of the population was urbanized. The comparable figures for Canada were 47 percent and 76.1 percent (1971).

Not only has population become increasingly concentrated in urban agglomerations but also the spatial impact of these agglomerations has been on an unprecedented scale. As we saw in Chapter 10, the majority of people in the more populated areas of the United States are, in fact, within the commuting areas of Standard Metropolitan Statistical Areas (SMSAs). These people generate massive daily flows into and out of the metropolitan centers even though, by the 1960 census definition, they live outside the SMSA boundary. The distribution of SMSAs, in effect, provides a much more realistic picture of the general spatial clustering of the United States population and the nation's economic activities (see Figure 10.6). Over time, as would be anticipated, the SMSA's relative share of national growth has been increasing.

What we currently experience as the urban miracle, the urban crisis, or the urban tragedy (depending on viewpoint) is the product of economic and social events effective only during the past 150 years. The fact that center-periphery forms have been with us for at least 7,000 years pales into insignificance beside this fact. Using a parallel to Kingsley Davis's analogy of population growth will give some idea of the suddenness of its arrival. If the whole of man's history on earth up to now is taken as representing a single year, then urbanization and the rapid growth of population associated with it begins to occur only after one minute to midnight on New Year's Eve: its final "flowering" into conurbation and megalopolis follows only seconds before "year's end".

More economic furniture has sprung up in this short period of the earth's history than ever before as cities have been thrust into existence in response to the ever-increasing demands of exponential economic growth. Indeed, the very speed at which urban-industrial growth and its associated problems seem to have overtaken us has latterly awakened a growing anxiety about the availability of both the physical and social necessities required to support it into the future. Findings such as those in the Club of Rome group's *Limits to Growth* go wider to predict *global* shortages in the resources needed to maintain the future demands of mankind. But in a predominantly urban and urbanizing society the side effects of man's profligate use of resources and in particular the physical degradation of his environment have become especially obvious.

This has made the 1970s in particular a potential turning-point for the acquiescence of many advanced societies in the face of cumulative development.

Throughout the book, although it has not been our primary purpose to explore the origins of economic growth, we have touched upon many of the key elements which contributed to the exponential growth process. Underlying much of it was the critical interaction between technological innovation and the production possibilities open to society. From this came those increases in real productivity that created increased wealth and which in turn permitted increasing returns to scale up to the level permitted by the increased size of the market.

In a particularly spatial context we were able to show how the re-evaluation of space, made possible by the application of production innovations like the steam engine to transport, both freed resources and made new ones more accessible. The amount of total energy from all sources available for human use that was tied up in just moving people, objects and information around was enormous in the period before 1750. After the so-called transport revolution new modes of transport and the removal of much of the tyranny of distance both opened up new areas to exploitation and offered the opportunities to indulge in this exploitation to those centers with experience in the investment of surplus—the urban cores.

Perhaps then the reduction of the tyranny of distance brought with it the tyranny of urbanism—the ever-increasing subservience of the periphery to the *centers of control* at the apex of the urban hierarchy. As our conceptual model of cumulative growth showed, the process of transport innovation, the increased size of the potential market, and the economies of scale which it brought interacted in a recycling process to promote sustained growth. In the recycling process, control of the new surpluses created remained strongly urban-centered so that being at the top of the hierarchy acquired both a spatial and an organizational connotation.

The dominance of the urban centers of control—their ability by either formal or informal means to control what functions other elements in the system performed—rested in part on their *specialization*. Lampard expresses the essence of the idea in the following way:

> specialization will thrive best where it is most developed. Specialization tends to breed specialization. It develops furthest where it is most prized; where socio-economic institutions are best adapted to its forms ... If specialization makes for higher productivity over time, it also tends to concentrate production activities over space. It is a dynamic process which transforms the spatial order of production and distribution ... (thus) ... *the growth of the modern city and the march of the industrial revolution are joint products of a single cultural strand—specialization.*
> *Lampard (1955), pp. 89,90,91*

Here, then, lie the keys to the process of cumulative economic growth and spatial morphogenesis which have characterized the last century and a half. But there is another feature which, though it has been implied all along in what we have said, has never been treated explicitly as a variable in its own right. In part, this is because the conceptual framework necessary for the effective development of the discussion demands different "building blocks" from those at our disposal in a text on economic geography.

Parallel with the revolutions in material and transport technology came a *revolution in social technology* (the way society organizes itself to get things done). It, too, was based upon the principles of specialization (division of labor we have seen as an economic force) and a hierarchical system of control favoring the holders of capital and institutions at the apex of the social hierarchy. And yet the necessary social order was not, as the Introduction in Chapter One pointed out, a subject of command or *overt* control at all in its heyday. Control was vested in the "invisible hand of the market." Perhaps, then, it is best described as a social system based on *covert* control (an argument we shall seek to avoid at this stage). However control was exercised, the net effect was to promote (at least notionally) *free enterprise*—to remove institutional and social shackles from the factors of production in the interests of economic growth. The enclosure movement "freed" land from collective ownership; the joint stock company "freed" holders of capital from the most extreme risks associated with investment; labor was "free" to seek its fair return (but not until latterly to organize and constrain its availability).

The goals underlying the new ethic, however they motivated the men who pursued them, tended to stress production and the increase in overall wealth. Remember Adam Smith's famous work, *The Wealth of Nations*, set the tone. The paradigm—as it is now fashionable to call it—or the overall "model" by which society worked was one of *free enterprise capitalism*. This was largely the paradigm on which location theory was built; the best judgments of economic men free to seek an appropriate return on their resources. It has, therefore, been implicit from the very outset in almost all of our conceptualization.

In part, one can find in this one reason why our simplified model fits reality reasonably well. If the entrepreneurs who contributed to the creation of today's economic furniture during the past one hundred and fifty years believed that they were economic men in a world of free enterprise and, more importantly, *acted as though they were*, then we should not be surprised at a certain correspondence between theory and reality. Thus under the heading of keys to cumulative growth we must insert the impact of social and, in particular, institutional changes. As the railways freed society from spatial bounds and the steam engine freed it from energy shortages, so free enterprise capitalism "freed" it from institutional forces standing to disrupt its productive efforts.

It is when we turn our attention to the contemporary problems created by the center-periphery structure that the *social setting* for its growth becomes critical to our understanding. One of the features to which we pointed earlier in the case of both center and periphery was what we can call for brevity's sake the *emergence of stress*. In the periphery it was the twin scourges of unemployment and low living standards. In the center it was the more complex problems generated by what Hauser (1969) termed the "population implosion," together with growing environmental difficulties. High densities of population in the city tend to exaggerate almost every stress symptom of society. There are more people to suffer from acts of pollution and anti-social or criminal acts of all kinds. Again the literature is voluminous on the crisis in urban society and we shall not extend it here. In both cases, then, stress symptoms have been "signaled" in an age of mass communications by the *social* and *political* connotations of the cumulative growth mechanism.

The problems of the periphery were signaled first. The widespread strikes and hunger marches of the inter-war depression years in Britain, culminating in the Jarrow march of the unemployed to London, provoked government intervention in the working of cumulative growth in space. Legislation was enacted for *social reasons* which attempted to promote the equalizing processes which classical theory had postulated for the periphery but which still had not materialized. In addition, and as part of the same process of re-appraisal, other features of free enterprise capitalism as a paradigm were questioned. The emergence of the *welfare* state brought forward a wholly new set of goals and priorities which, in the case of the United Kingdom in particular, have fundamentally altered the economic geography of the nation since the last war.

In their turn, most other governments in western industrial nations have been forced to *intervene* in the workings of the cumulative growth process. For France, the imposition of deliberate growth restrictions on the center—Paris —was combined with policies to promote growth in the periphery. For the United States and Canada reaction came later but both became involved from the early 1960s onwards in selective area development schemes to "prop up" the periphery against the forces of polarization and backwash.

In the case of the center, it was again the United Kingdom—the pioneer of the industrial revolution—which pioneered the search for solutions of those problems which were generated by the aftermath of industrial success. Town planning emerged in 1947 out of a general dissatisfaction with the current state of urbanism in the industrial cities. Again almost without exception the rest of the western industrial nations were to follow. The imposition of control on the spatial operation of the cumulative growth process became a declared objective of each government's policy. Few, however, sought seriously to question the underlying basis for the kind of spatial morphogenesis we have been describing. For many, the problems were seen to be both spatially generated and spatially cured, usually by resort to little more than cosmetic surgery.

Thus, for better or worse, most modern industrial states operate under a more interventionist paradigm (at least with regard to the creation of spatial form) than that which underpins "classical" location theory. For many of them, *social welfare* criteria are beginning to emerge to complement the *production efficiency* criteria of the "high capitalism" phase of economic development. The capitalist-free enterprise system provided a most efficient force for the creation of a surplus and for its efficient (in production terms) recycling. It largely failed, however, to look to questions of the allocation of the created wealth and perhaps to social goals of higher order. As a result, the paradigm is being reworked in practice and there are now many hues of *mixed* economy operating, at least in Western Europe (though the degree of government involvement in the North American economies is greater than many people imagine). Under these circumstances the new minimizing and maximizing assumptions applied to economic and spatial forms may well be different. We have developed the "tools" by which to examine productive efficiency: we are, as yet, some way from developing similar tools for the determination of *welfare* efficiency. Smith (1974) sets out the new problem as "who gets what *where*, and how" while Chisholm (1971) provides some guidelines in search of a new basis for location theory.

We began by considering Boulding's statement that "growth creates form, but form limits growth." We showed throughout the book the building blocks and later the way they were put together so that "growth could create form." The building blocks were those derived for the most part from classical microeconomics, and the tools by which they were put together were those appropriate to the workings of the capitalist-free enterprise paradigm. The question of whether "form limits growth" *in economic terms* must be answered "not proven" —at least not within the range of the methods of economic analysis. Where form *can* be seen to limit growth is in the context of the *social or general welfare connotations of the growth process*. These have found their expression not in graphs, tables and national income accounts but in demonstrations (in the widest sense), political activity and the shifting of consensus opinion. As we pointed out earlier, the tools for the analysis of these events are those of sociology, social psychology and politics, as well as economics and geography. To investigate their spatial impact more effectively we need to go back to the beginning and attempt to see the same processes of growth and change from a new perspective.

BIBLIOGRAPHY

A

Aaronovitch, S. and M. C. Sawyer (1974), The Concentration of British Manufacturing, *Lloyds Bank Review*, October 1974, 114, 14–23.

Abler, R., J. S. Adams and P. R. Gould (1971), *Spatial Organization: The Geographer's View of the World*, Englewood Cliffs, N.J.: Prentice-Hall.

Ackerman, E. A. (1958), Geography as a Fundamental Research Discipline, *University of Chicago, Department of Geography Research Paper*, 53.

Ackerman, E. A. (1963), Where is a Research Frontier? *Annals of the Association of American Geographers* **53**, 429–440.

Alchian, A. (1950), Uncertainty, Evolution and Economic Theory, *Journal of Political Economy* **58**, 211–221.

Alexander, J. W. (1963), *Economic Geography*, Englewood Cliffs, N.J.: Prentice-Hall.

Alexander, J. W., S. E. Brown and R. E. Dahlberg (1958), Freight Rates: Selected Aspects of Uniform and Nodal Regions, *Economic Geography* **34**, 1–18.

Alonso, W. (1960), A Theory of the Urban Land Market, *Papers and Proceedings, Regional Science Association* **6**, 149–157.

Alonso, W. (1964), *Location and Land Use: Toward a General Theory of Land Rent*, Cambridge, Mass.: Harvard University Press.

Alonso, W. (1967), A Reformulation of Classical Location Theory and Its Relation to Rent Theory, *Papers and Proceedings, Regional Science Association* **19**, 23–44.

Appleton, J. H. (1963), The Efficacy of the Great Australian Divide as a Barrier to Railway Communications, *Transactions of the Institute of British Geographers* **33**, 101–122.

Armstrong, A. and A. Silberston (1965), Size of Plant, Size of Enterprise and Concentration in British Manufacturing Industry, 1935–1958, *Journal of the Royal Statistical Society*, **A, 128**, 395–420.

Arndt, H. W. (1955), External Economies in Economic Growth, *Economic Record* **31**, 192–214.

Artle, R. (1959), *Studies in the Structure of the Stockholm Economy*, Stockholm: Business Research Institute.

Averitt, R. T. (1968), *The Dual Economy: The Dynamics of American Industry Structure*, New York: Norton.

B

Bain, J. S. (1954), Economies of Scale, Concentration and the Condition of Entry in 20 Manufacturing Industries, *American Economic Review* **44**, 15–39.

Bain, J. S. (1968), *Industrial Organization*, 2nd ed. New York: Wiley.

Baker, O. E. (1921), Increasing Importance of the Physical Conditions in Determining the Utilization of Land for Agriculture and Forest Production in the U.S., *Annals of the Association of American Geographers* **11**, 17–46.

Baldwin, R. E. (1956), Patterns of Development in Newly Settled Regions, *Manchester School of Economic and Social Studies* **24**, 161–179.

Ball, C. and M. Teitz (1958), Expressways and Industrial Location, *Traffic Quarterly* **12**, 589–601.

Ballabon, M. B. (1957), Putting the "Economic" into Economic Geography, *Economic Geography* **33**, 217–223.

Bannock, G. (1971), *The Juggernauts: The Age of the Big Corporation*, Harmondsworth: Penguin Books; Indianapolis: Bobbs-Merrill.

Barfod, B. (1938), *Local Economic Effects of a Large Scale Industrial Undertaking*, Copenhagen: Munksgaard.

Barloon, M. J. (1965), Interrelationship of the Changing Structure of American Transportation and Changes in Industrial Location, *Land Economics* **41**, 169–182.

Barnum, H. G. (1966), Market Centers and Hinterlands in Baden-Würtemberg, *University of Chicago, Department of Geography Research Paper*, 103.

Bater, J. H. and D. F. Walker (1974), Aspects of Industrial Linkage: The Example of the Hamilton Metalworking Complex, Ontario, *Révue Géographique Montreal* **28**, 233–243.

Beacham, A. and W. T. Osborn (1970), The Movement of Manufacturing Industry, *Regional Studies* **4**, 41–47.

Beavon, K. S. O. and A. S. Mabin (1975), The Lösch System of Market Areas: Derivation and Extension, *Geographical Analysis* **7**, 131–151.

Beckmann, M. (1955a), Some Reflections on Lösch's Theory of Location, *Papers and Proceedings, Regional Science Association* **1**, N2–N8.

Beckmann, M. J. (1955b), The Economics of Location, *Kyklos* **8**, 416–421.

Beckmann, M. J. (1958), City Hierarchies and the Distribution of City Size, *Economic Development and Cultural Change* **6**, 243–248.

Beckmann, M. J. and J. C. McPherson (1970), City Size Distribution in a Central Place Hierarchy: An Alternative Approach, *Journal of Regional Science* **10**, 25–33.

Beesley, M. (1955), Birth and Death of Industrial Establishments: Experience in the West Midlands Conurbation, *Journal of Industrial Economics* **4**, 45–61.

Berry, B. J. L. (1961), City Size Distributions and Economic Development, *Economic Development and Cultural Change* **9,** 573–588.

Berry, B. J. L. (1963), Commercial Structure and Commercial Blight, *University of Chicago, Department of Geography Research Paper,* 85.

Berry, B. J. L. (1964a), Approaches to Regional Analysis: A Synthesis, *Annals of the Association of American Geographers* **54,** 2–12.

Berry, B. J. L. (1964b), Cities as Systems within Systems of Cities, *Papers and Proceedings, Regional Science Association* **13,** 147–163.

Berry, B. J. L. (1967), *Geography of Market Centers and Retail Distribution,* Englewood Cliffs, N.J.: Prentice-Hall.

Berry, B. J. L. (1968), *Metropolitan Area Definition: A Re-evaluation of Concept and Statistical Practice,* Washington, DC: Bureau of the Census Working Paper, no. 28.

Berry, B. J. L. (1972), Hierarchical Diffusion: The Basis of Developmental Filtering and Spread in a System of Growth Centers, in N. M. Hansen (ed.), *Growth Centers in Regional Economic Development,* New York: Free Press, 108–138.

Berry, B. J. L. and H. G. Barnum (1962), Aggregate Relations and Elemental Components of Central Place Systems, *Journal of Regional Science* **4,** 35–68.

Berry, B. J. L., H. G. Barnum and R. J. Tennant (1962), Retail Location and Consumer Behavior, *Papers and Proceedings, Regional Science Association* **9,** 65–106.

Berry, B. J. L. and W. L. Garrison (1958a), Functional Bases of the Central Place Hierarchy, *Economic Geography* **34,** 145–154.

Berry, B. J. L. and W. L. Garrison (1958b), A Note on Central Place Theory and the Range of a Good, *Economic Geography* **34,** 304–311.

Berry, B. J. L. and W. L. Garrison (1958c), Recent Developments of Central Place Theory, *Papers and Proceedings, Regional Science Association* **4,** 107–120.

Berry, B. J. L. and W. L. Garrison (1958d), Alternate Explanations of Urban Rank Size Relationships, *Annals of the Association of American Geographers* **48,** 83–91.

Berry, B. J. L. and D. F. Marble (eds.) (1967), *Spatial Analysis: A Reader in Statistical Geography,* Englewood Cliffs, N.J.: Prentice-Hall.

Berry B. J. L. and E. Neils (1969), Location, Size and Shape of Cities as Influenced by Environmental Factors, in H. S. Perloff (ed.), *The Quality of the Urban Environment,* Baltimore: Resources for the Future, 257–302.

Berry, B. J. L. and A. Pred (1965), *Central Place Studies: A Bibliography of Theory and Applications,* Philadelphia: Regional Science Research Institute.

Berry, B. J. L., J. W. Simmons and R. J. Tennent (1963), Urban Population Densities: Structure and Change, *Geographical Review* **53,** 389–405.

Bertalanffy, L. von (1951), An Outline of General System Theory, *British Journal of the Philosophy of Science* **1,** 134–165.

Bertalanffy, L. von (1968), *General System Theory,* New York: Braziller.

Blaikie, P. M. (1971), Spatial Organization of Agriculture in Some North Indian Villages, Part I, *Transactions, Institute of British Geographers* **52,** 1–40; Part II, *Transactions, Institute of British Geographers* **53,** 15–30.

Blair, J. M. (1972), *Economic Concentration: Structure, Behavior and Public Policy,* New York: Harcourt Brace Jovanovich.

Board of Trade (1968), *The Movement of Manufacturing Industry in the United Kingdom,* London: H.M.S.O.

Bogue, D. J. (1949), *The Structure of the Metropolitan Community,* Ann Arbor: University of Michigan Press.

Borchert, J. R. (1967), American Metropolitan Evolution, *Geographical Review* **57,** 301–332.

Borts, G. H. (1960), The Equalization of Returns and Regional Economic Growth, *American Economic Review* **50,** 319–347.

Borts, G. H. and J. L. Stein (1964), *Economic Growth in a Free Market,* New York: Columbia University Press.

Boulding, K. E. (1953), Toward a General Theory of Growth, *Canadian Journal of Economics and Political Science* **19,** 326–340.

Boulding, K. E. (1956), General Systems Theory—The Skeleton of Science, *Management Science* **2,** 197–208.

Boventer, E. von (1963), Towards a United Theory of Spatial Economic Structure, *Papers and Proceedings, Regional Science Association* **10,** 163–187.

Bowen, H. R. (1955), *The Business Enterprise as a Subject for Research,* New York: Social Science Research Council Pamphlet, 11.

Britton, D. K. and K. Ingersent (1964), Trends in Concentration in British Agriculture, *Journal of Agricultural Economics* **21,** 26–52.

Britton, J. N. H. (1969), A Geographical Approach to the Examination of Industrial Linkages, *Canadian Geographer* **13,** 185–198.

Britton, J. N. H. (1974), Environmental Adaptation of Industrial Plants: Service Linkages, Locational Environment and Organization, in F. E. I. Hamilton (ed.), *Spatial Perspectives on Industrial Organization and Decision Making,* London: Wiley, 363–390.

Bromley, R. J. (1971), Markets in the Developing Countries: A Review, *Geography* **56,** 124–132.

Brown, L. A. (1968a), Diffusion Dynamics: A Review and Revision of the Quantitative Theory of the Spatial Diffusion of Innovation, *Lund Studies in Geography, Series B*, 29.

Brown, L. A. (1968b), *Diffusion Processes and Location: A Conceptual Framework and Bibliography*, Philadelphia: Regional Science Research Institute.

Brown, L. A. and K. R. Cox (1971), Empirical Regularities in the Diffusion of Innovation, *Annals of the Association of American Geographers* **61**, 551–559.

Brown, R. (1948), *Historical Geography of the United States*, New York: Harcourt Brace Jovanovich.

Brush, J. E. (1953), The Hierarchy of Central Places in Southwestern Wisconsin, *Geographical Review* **43**, 380–402.

Brush, J. E. and H. E. Bracey (1955), Rural Service Centers in Southwestern Wisconsin and Southwestern England, *Geographical Review* **45**, 559–569.

Buckley, W. (ed.) (1968), *Modern Systems Research for the Behavioral Scientist*, Chicago: Aldine.

Bunge, W. (1966), Theoretical Geography, *Lund Studies in Geography, Series C*, 1, 2nd ed.

Burton, I. (1963), The Quantitative Revolution and Theoretical Geography, *Canadian Geographer* **7**, 151–162.

C

Cameron, G. C. and B. D. Clark (1966), *Industrial Movement and the Regional Problem*, Glasgow: Oliver & Boyd.

Carrothers, G. A. P. (1956), An Historical Review of the Gravity and Potential Concepts of Human Interaction, *Journal of the American Institute of Planners* **22**, 94–102.

Carruthers, W. I. (1957), The Classification of Service Centers in England and Wales—An Analysis of Public Road Transport Services, *Geographical Journal* **122**, 371–385.

Carruthers, W. I. (1967), Major Shopping Centers in England and Wales 1961, *Regional Studies* **1**, 65–81.

Carter, H. (1976), *The Study of Urban Geography*, 2nd ed., London: Edward Arnold; New York: Crane, Russak.

Casetti, E. (1966), Optimal Location of Steel Mills Serving the Quebec and Southern Ontario Steel Market, *Canadian Geographer* **10**, 27–39.

Chandler, A. D. Jr. (1962), *Strategy and Structure: Chapters in the History of the Industrial Enterprise*, Cambridge, Mass.: MIT Press.

Chandler, A. D. Jr. (ed.) (1965), *The Railroads: The Nation's First Big Business*, New York: Harcourt Brace Jovanovich.

Chandler, A. D. Jr. and F. Redlich (1961), Recent

Developments in American Business Administration and their Conceptualization, *Business History Review* **35**, 1–27.

Chinitz, B. (1960), *Freight and the Metropolis*, Cambridge, Mass.: Harvard University Press.

Chinitz, B. (1961), Contrasts in Agglomeration: New York and Pittsburgh, *American Economic Review, Proceedings* **51**, 279–289.

Chinitz, B. and R. Vernon (1960), Changing Forces in Industrial Location, *Harvard Business Review* **38**, 126–136.

Chisholm, M. (1962), *Rural Settlement and Land Use*, London: Hutchinson.

Chisholm, M. (1963), Tendencies in Agricultural Specialization and Regional Concentration of Industry, *Papers and Proceedings, Regional Science Association* **10**, 157–162.

Chisholm, M. (1966), *Geography and Economics*, London: Bell; New York: Praeger.

Chisholm, M. (1967), General Systems Theory and Geography, *Transactions of the Institute of British Geographers* **42**, 45–52.

Chisholm, M. (1971), In Search of a Basis for Location Theory: Micro-economics or Welfare Economics, in C. Board, R. J. Chorley, P. Haggett, D. R. Stoddart (eds.), *Progress in Geography*, Vol. 3, London: Edward Arnold, 111–133.

Chorley, R. J. (1962), Geomorphology and General Systems Theory, *U.S. Geological Survey, Professional Paper*, 500B.

Chorley, R. J. (1964), Geography and Analogue Theory, *Annals of the Association of American Geographers* **55**, 351–359.

Chorley, R. J. and P. Haggett (1967), *Models in Geography*, London: Methuen; New York: Barnes & Noble.

Christaller, W. (1966), *Central Places in Southern Germany* (C. W. Baskin, trans.), Englewood Cliffs, N.J.: Prentice-Hall.

Clark, C. (1940), *The Conditions of Economic Progress*, London: Macmillan.

Clark, C. (1951), Urban Population Densities, *Journal of the Royal Statistical Society*, Series A, **114**, 490–496.

Clark, P. J. and F. C. Evans (1954), Distance to Nearest Neighbor as a Measure of Spatial Relationships in Population, *Ecology* **35**, 445–453.

Cliff, A. D. (1968), The Neighbourhood Effect in the Diffusion of Innovations, *Transactions of the Institute of British Geographers* **44**, 75–84.

Cliffe, R. A. (1961), A Reconnaissance of National Transportation, in National Academy of Science, *Transportation Design Considerations*, Washington, DC.

Cootner, P. H. (1963), The Role of the Railroads in United States Economic Growth, *Journal of Economic History* **23,** 477–521.

Craig, P. G. (1957), Location Factors in the Development of Steel Centers, *Papers and Proceedings, Regional Science Association* **3,** 249–265.

Crowe, P. R. (1938), On Progress in Geography, *Scottish Geographical Magazine* **54,** 1–19.

Currie, A. W. (1965), Freight Rates and Regionalism, in J. J. Deutsch *et al.* (eds.), *The Canadian Economy: Selected Readings*, Toronto: Macmillan.

Curry, L. (1964), The Random Spatial Economy: An Explanation in Settlement Theory, *Annals of the Association of American Geographers* **54,** 138–146.

Curry, L. (1966), Chance and Landscape, in J. W. House (ed.), *Northern Geographical Essays*, Newcastle: Oriel Press, 40–55.

Curry, L. (1967), Quantitative Geography, *Canadian Geographer* **11,** 265–279.

Cyert, R. M. and J. G. March (1963), *A Behavioral Theory of the Firm*, Englewood Cliffs, N.J.: Prentice-Hall.

D

Dacey, M. F. (1962), Analysis of Central Place Patterns by Nearest Neighbor Analysis, *Lund Studies in Geography, Series B*, 24.

Daggett, S. (1955), *Principles of Inland Transportation*, New York: Harper & Row.

Daggett, S. (1968), The System of Alfred Weber, in R. H. T. Smith, E. J. Taafe and L. J. King (eds.), *Readings in Economic Geography*, Skokie, Ill.: Rand McNally, 58–64.

Daly, M. T. (1972), *Techniques and Concepts in Geography*, Melbourne: Nelson, Chapter 4.

Danielsson, A. (1964), The Locational Decision from the Point of View of the Individual Company, *Ekonomisk Tidskrift* **66,** 47–87.

Darwent, D. F. (1969), Growth Poles and Growth Centers in Regional Planning—A Review, *Environment and Planning* **1,** 5–31.

Davies, W. K. D. (1967), Centrality and the Central Place Hierarchy, *Urban Studies* **4,** 61–79.

Davis, L. (1966), The Capital Markets and Industrial Concentration, *Economic History Review* **19,** 255–272.

Dicken, P. (1971), Some Aspects of the Decision-Making Behavior of Business Organizations, *Economic Geography* **47,** 426–437.

Dodd, S. C. (1950), The Interactance Hypothesis, *American Sociological Review* **15,** 245–256.

Dodd, S. C. (1953), Testing Message Diffusion in Controlled Experiments: Charting the Distance and Time Factors—The Interactance Hypothesis, *American Sociological Review* **18,** 410–416.

Dodd, S. C. (1955), Diffusion is Predictable: Testing Probability Models for Laws of Interaction, *American Sociological Review* **20,** 292–401.

Doxiadis, C. (1969), The Prospect of an International Megalopolis, in M. Wade (ed.), *The International Megalopolis*, Windsor, Ont.: University of Windsor Press, 3–32.

Downs, R. M. and D. Stea (eds.) (1973), *Image and Environment: Cognitive Mapping and Spatial Behavior*, Chicago: Aldine.

Drewett, R., J. Goddard and N. Spence (1976), *British Cities: Urban Population and Employment Trends, 1951–1971*, London: Department of the Environment.

Duncan, O. D. *et al.* (1960), *Metropolis and Region*, Baltimore: Johns Hopkins Press.

Dunn, E. S. (1954), *The Location of Agricultural Production*, Gainesville: University of Florida Press.

Dunn, E. S. (1956), The Market Potential Concept and the Analysis of Location, *Papers and Proceedings, Regional Science Association* **2,** 183–194.

Dunning, J. (ed.) (1971), *The Multinational Enterprise*, London: George Allen & Unwin.

Durand, L. (1964), The Major Milksheds of the Northeastern Quarter of the United States, *Economic Geography* **40,** 9–33.

E

Edwards, R. S. and H. Townsend (1958), *Business Enterprise*, London: Macmillan.

Eighmy, T. H. (1972), Rural Periodic Markets and the Extension of an Urban System: a Western Nigeria Example, *Economic Geography* **48,** 299–315.

Eliot Hurst, M. E. (1972) *A Geography of Economic Behavior*, North Scituate, Mass.: Duxbury Press.

Ellis, G. H. (1949), Why New Manufacturing Establishments Located in New England, Aug. 1945–June 1948, *Federal Reserve Bank of Boston, Monthly Review* **31,** 1–12.

Emery, F. E. and O. A. Oeser (1958), *Information, Decision and Action: A Study of the Psychological Determinants of Changes in Farming Techniques*, Melbourne: Melbourne University Press.

Estall, R. C. (1972) *A Modern Geography of the United States*, London: Pelican.

Estall, R. C. and R. O. Buchanan (1973), *Industrial Activity and Economic Geography*, 3rd ed., London: Hutchinson; New York: Humanities Press.

F

Fay, C. R. (1950), *Great Britain: From Adam Smith to the Present Day*, 5th ed., London: Longmans Green & Co.; New York: Humanities Press.

Ferguson, C. E. (1960), Relationship of Business Size to Stability. An Empirical Approach, *Journal of Industrial Economics* **9**, 43–62.

Fetter, F. A. (1924), The Economic Law of Market Areas, *Quarterly Journal of Economics* **38**, 520–523.

Firey, W. (1960), *Man, Mind and Land: A Theory of Resource Use*, New York: Free Press.

Fleming, D. K. and G. Krumme (1968), The Royal–Hoesch Union: Case Analysis of Adjustment Patterns in the European Steel Industry, *Tijdschrift voor Economische en Sociale Geografie* **59**, 177–199.

Florence P. Sargant (1933), *The Logic of Industrial Organization*, London: Routledge & Kegan Paul.

Florence P. Sargant (1948), *Investment Location and Size of Plant*, London: National Institute of Economic and Social Research.

Florence P. Sargant (1962), *Postwar Investment, Location, and Size of Plant*, London: National Institute of Economic and Social Research.

Foley, D. L. (1956), Factors in the Location of Administrative Offices, with Particular Reference to the San Francisco Bay Area, *Papers and Proceedings, Regional Science Association* **2**, 318–326.

Forrester, J. W. (1968), *Principles of Systems*, Cambridge, Mass.: Wright-Allen Press.

Found, W. C. (1971), *A Theoretical Approach to Rural Land Use Patterns*, London: Edward Arnold; New York: St Martin's Press.

Friedmann, J. (1966), *Regional Development Policy: A Case Study of Venezuela*, Cambridge, Mass.: M.I.T. Press.

Friedmann, J. (1972), A General Theory of Polarized Development, in N. M. Hansen (ed.), *Growth Centers in Regional Economic Development*, New York: Free Press, 82–107.

Friedmann, J. (1973), *Urbanization, Planning and National Development*, Beverly Hills, Calif.: Sage.

Friedmann, J. and W. Alonso (1964), *Regional Development and Planning: A Reader*, Cambridge, Mass.: M.I.T. Press.

Friedmann, J. and J. Miller (1965), The Urban Field, *Journal of the American Institute of Planners* **31**, 312–320.

Fuchs, V. R. (1959), Changes in the Location of U.S. Manufacturing since 1929, *Journal of Regional Science* **1**, 1–18.

Fuchs, V. R. (1962), *Changes in the Location of Manufacturing in the United States since 1929*, New Haven, Conn.: Yale University Press.

Fuchs, V. R. (1967), *Differentials in Hourly Earnings by Region and City Size, 1959*, New York: Columbia University Press.

Fulton, M. and L. C. Hoch (1959), Transportation Factors Affecting Location Decisions, *Economic Geography* **35**, 51–59.

G

Galbraith, J. K. (1966), *The New Industrial State*, Boston: Houghton Mifflin; London: Hamish Hamilton.

Galbraith, J. K. (1974), *Economics and the Public Purpose*, Boston: Houghton Mifflin; London: Andre Deutsch.

Garner, B. J. (1966), The Internal Structure of Retail Nucleations, *Northwestern University, Department of Geography, Research Paper*, 12.

Garner, B. J. (1967), Models of Urban Geography and Settlement Location, in R. J. Chorley and P. Haggett (eds.), *Models in Geography*, London: Methuen; New York: Barnes & Noble, 303–360.

Garrison, W. L. (1959–1960), Spatial Structure of the Economy, *Annals of the Association of American Geographers* **49**, 232–239; **49**, 471–482; **50**, 357–373.

Garrison, W. L. (1960), Connectivity of the Inter-State Highway System, *Papers and Proceedings, Regional Science Association* **6**, 121–137.

Garrison, W. L. and D. F. Marble (1957), The Spatial Structure of Agricultural Activities, *Annals of the Association of American Geographers* **47**, 137–144.

Gasson, R. (1966), The Changing Location of Intensive Crops in England and Wales, *Geography* **51**, 16–28.

Getis, A. (1963), The Determination of the Location of Retail Activities with the use of a Map Transformation, *Economic Geography* **39**, 14–22.

Gibrat, R. (1927), *Les Inégalités Économiques*, Paris: Sirey.

Gilmour, J. M. (1974), External Economies of Scale, Inter-Industrial Linkages and Decision Making in Manufacturing, in F. E. I. Hamilton (ed.), *Spatial Perspectives on Industrial Organization and Decision Making*, London: Wiley, 363–393.

Gitlow, A. L. (1954), Wages and the Allocation of Employment, *Southern Economic Journal* **21**, 62–83.

Goddard, J. B. (1975a) *Office Location in Urban and Regional Development*, London: Oxford University Press.

Goddard, J. B. (1975b), Organizational Information Flows and the Urban System, *Economie Appliquée* **38**, 125–164.

Golledge, R. G. (1967), Conceptualizing the Market Decision Process, *Journal of Regional Science* **7**, 2S, 239–258.

Golledge, R. G. and D. Amedeo (1968), On Laws in Geography, *Annals of the Association of American Geographers* **58**, 760–774.

Golledge, R. G. and L. A. Brown (1967), Search, Learning and the Market Decision Process, *Geografiska Annaler* **49B**, 116–124.

Golledge, R. G., G. Rushton and W. A. V. Clark (1966), Some Spatial Characteristics of Iowa's Dispersed Farm Population and Their Implications for the Grouping of Central Place Functions, *Economic Geography* **42**, 261–272.

Gottmann, J. (1961), *Megalopolis*, Cambridge, Mass.: M.I.T. Press.

Gould, P. R. (1963), Man against his Environment: A Game Theoretic Framework, *Annals of the Association of American Geographers* **53**, 290–297.

Gould, P. R. (1966), On Mental Maps, *Michigan Inter-University Community of Mathematical Geographers, Discussion Paper 9.*

Gould, P. R. (1969), Spatial Diffusion, *Association of American Geographers, Commission on College Geography Resource Paper 4.*

Gould, P. R. and R. R. White (1968), The Mental Maps of British School Leavers, *Regional Studies* **2**, 2, 161–182.

Gould, P. R. and R. R. White (1974), *Mental Maps*, Harmondsworth: Penguin.

Greenhut, M. L. (1956), *Plant Location in Theory and Practise*, Chapel Hill: University of North Carolina Press.

Greenhut, M. L. (1959), An Empirical Model and a Survey: New Plant Location in Florida, *Review of Economics and Statistics* **61**, 433–48.

Greenhut, M. L. (1960), Size of Markets v. Transport Costs in Industrial Location Surveys and Theory, *Journal of Industrial Economics* **8**, 172–184.

Greenhut, M. L. (1964), When is the Demand Factor of Location Important? *Land Economics* **40**, 175–184.

Griliches, Z. (1957), Hybrid Corn: An Exploration in the Economics of Technological Change, *Econometrica* **25**, 501–522.

Grotewold, A. (1959), Von Thünen in Retrospect, *Economic Geography* **35**, 346–355.

Groves, P. A. (1971), Towards a Typology of Intrametropolitan Manufacturing, *University of Hull, Department of Geography, Occasional Papers*, 16.

H

H.M.S.O. (1973), *Regional Development Incentives, Report, Session 1973–74*, House of Commons Expenditure Committee (Trade and Industry Sub-Committee), No. 665107, London.

Hägerstrand, T. (1952), The Propagation of Innovation Waves, *Lund Studies in Geography, Series B*, 4.

Hägerstrand, T. (1957), Migration and Area: Survey of a Sample of Swedish Migration Fields, in D. Hannerberg, T. Hägerstrand, and B. Odeving (eds.), Migration in Sweden: A Symposium, *Lund Studies in Geography, Series B*, 13, 27–158.

Hägerstrand, T. (1960), Aspects of the Spatial Structure of Social Communication and the Diffusion of Information, *Papers and Proceedings, Regional Science Association* **16**, 27–42.

Hägerstrand, T. (1967a), *Innovation Diffusion as a Spatial Process* (trans. and postscript by A. Pred), Chicago: University of Chicago Press.

Hägerstrand, T. (1967b), On Monte Carlo Simulation of Diffusion, in W. L. Garrison and D. F. Marble (eds.), Quantitative Geography Part I, Economic and Cultural Topics, *Northwestern University Studies in Geography*, 13, 1–32.

Haggett, P. (1965), *Locational Analysis in Human Geography*, London: Edward Arnold; New York: St Martin's Press.

Haggett, P. (1966), Changing Concepts in Economic Geography, in R. J. Chorley and P. Haggett (eds.), *Frontiers in Geographical Teaching*, London: Methuen; New York, Barnes & Noble, 101–117.

Haggett, P. (1975), *Geography: A Modern Synthesis*, 2nd ed., New York, Harper & Row.

Haggett, P. and R. J. Chorley (1967), Models, Paradigms, and the New Geography, in R. J. Chorley and P. Haggett (eds.), *Models in Geography*, London: Methuen; New York, Barnes & Noble, 19–41.

Haggett, P. and R. J. Chorley (1969), *Network Analysis in Geography*, London: Edward Arnold; New York: St Martin's Press.

Haig, R. M. (1926), Toward an Understanding of the Metropolis, *Quarterly Journal of Economics* **40**, 421–433.

Hale, C. W. (1967), The Mechanism of the Spread Effect in Regional Development, *Land Economics* **43**, 434–445.

Hall, A. D. and R. E. Fagen (1956), Definition of System, *General Systems* **1**, 18–28.

Hall, M. (ed.) (1959), *Made in New York: Case Studies in Metropolitan Manufacturing*, Cambridge, Mass.: Harvard University Press.

Hall, P. (1962), *The Industries of London*, London: Hutchinson.

Hall, P. (1966a), *The World Cities*, London: Weidenfeld & Nicholson; New York: McGraw-Hill.

Hall, P. (ed.) (1966b), *Von Thünen's Isolated State*, London: Pergamon.

Hall, P. (1966c), Britain's Uneven Shrinkage, *New Society*, April 1966, 18–19.

Hall, P., H. Gracey, R. Drewett and R. Thomas (1973), *The Containment of Urban England, Volume I: Urban and Metropolitan Growth Processes*, London: George Allen & Unwin.

Hamilton, F. E. I. (1967), Models of Industrial Location, in R. J. Chorley and P. Haggett (eds.), *Models in Geography*, London: Methuen; New York: Barnes & Noble, 361–424.

Hamilton, F. E. I. (1974), A View of Spatial Behavior, Industrial Organizations and Decision-making, in F. E. I. Hamilton (ed.), *Spatial Perspectives on Industrial Organization and Decision-Making*, London: John Wiley, 3–43.

Hannerberg, D., T. Hägerstrand and B. Odeving (eds.) (1957), Migration in Sweden: A Symposium, *Lund Studies in Geography, Series B*, 13.

Hansen, N. M. (1967a), Human Resources and Regional Development: Some Lessons from French Experience, *Southern Economic Journal* **34**, 123–132.

Hansen, N. M. (1967b), Toward a New Approach in Regional Economic Policy, *Land Economics* **43**, 377–383.

Hansen, N. M. (1968), Regional Development and the Rural Poor, *Journal of Human Resources* **4**, 205–214.

Harris, C. D. (1943), Functional Classification of Cities in the United States, *Geographical Review* **33**, 86–99.

Harris, C. D. (1954), The Market as a Factor in the Localization of Industry, in the U.S., *Annals of the Association of American Geographers* **44**, 315–348.

Harris, C. D. and E. L. Ullman (1945), The Nature of Cities, *Annals of the American Academy of Political and Social Science* **242**, 7–17.

Hartshorne, R. (1939), *The Nature of Geography*, Washington, DC: Association of American Geographers.

Hartshorne, R. (1959), *Perspective on the Nature of Geography*, Skokie, Ill.: Rand McNally.

Harvey, D. W. (1963), Locational Change in the Kentish Hop Industry and the Analysis of Land Use Patterns, *Transactions of the Institute of British Geographers* **33**, 123–144.

Harvey, D. W. (1966), Theoretical Concepts and the Analysis of Agricultural Land Use Patterns in Geography, *Annals of the Association of American Geographers* **56**, 361–374.

Harvey, D. W. (1967), Models of the Evolution of Spatial Patterns in Human Geography, in R. J. Chorley and P. Haggett (eds.), *Models in Geography*, London: Methuen; New York: Barnes & Noble, 549–608.

Harvey, D. W. (1969a), Conceptual and Measurement Problems in the Cognitive–Behavioral Approach to Location Theory, in K. R. Cox and R. G. Golledge (eds.), Behavioral Problems in Geography: A Symposium, *North Western University Studies in Geography*, 17, 35–67.

Harvey, D. W. (1969b), *Explanation in Geography*, London: Edward Arnold; New York: St Martin's Press.

Hay, A. M. (1971), Notes on the Economic Basis for Periodic Marketing in Developing Countries, *Geographical Analysis* **3**, 393–401.

Hay, A. M. (1973), *Transport for the Space Economy: A Geographical Study*, London: Macmillan; Seattle: University of Washington Press.

Hay, A. and R. H. T. Smith (1966), Preliminary Estimates of Nigeria's Interregional Trade and Associated Money Flows, *Nigerian Journal of Economic and Social Studies* **8**, 9–35.

Hayter, R. (1976), Corporate Strategies and Industrial Change in the Canadian Forest Product Industries, *Geographical Review* **66**, 209–228.

Heilbroner, R. L. (1972), *The Economic Problem*, 3rd ed., Englewood Cliffs, N.J.: Prentice-Hall.

Helvig, M. (1964), Chicago's External Truck Movements, *University of Chicago, Department of Geography Research Paper*, 90.

Hermansen, T. (1972), Development Poles and Related Theories, in N. M. Hansen (ed.), *Growth Centers in Regional Economic Development*, New York: Free Press, 160–203.

Hicks, J. R. (1959), *Essays in World Economics*, Oxford: Oxford University Press.

Hidore, J. J. (1963), The Relations Between Cash Grain Farming and Land Forms, *Economic Geography* **39**, 84–89.

Hill, P. and R. H. T. Smith (1972), The Spatial and Temporal Synchronization of Periodic Markets: Evidence from Four Emirates in Northern Nigeria, *Economic Geography* **48**, 345–355.

Hirsch, W. Z. (1959), Interindustry Relations of a Metropolitan Area, *Review of Economics and Statistics* **41**, 360–369.

Hirsch, W. Z. (1961), Regional Fiscal Development and Local Industrial Development, *Papers and Proceedings, Regional Science Association* **7**, 119–130.

Hirsch, W. Z. (ed.) (1966), *Regional Accounts for Policy Decisions*, Baltimore: Johns Hopkins Press.

Hirschman, A. O. (1958), *The Strategy of Economic Development*, New Haven, Conn.: Yale University Press.

Hodge, G. (1966), Urban Systems and Regional Policy, *Canadian Public Administration* **9**, 181–193.

Hodge, G. (1968), Urban Structure and Regional Development, *Papers and Proceedings, Regional Science Association* **21,** 101–124.

Hoover, E. M. (1937), *Location Theory and the Shoe and Leather Industries*, Cambridge, Mass.: Harvard University Press.

Hoover, E. M. (1948), *The Location of Economic Activity*, New York: McGraw-Hill.

Hoover, E. M. (1964), Spatial Economics: The Partial Equilibrium Approach, *University of Pittsburgh Center for Regional Economic Studies, Occasional Paper*, 2.

Hoover, E. M. and R. Vernon (1959), *Anatomy of a Metropolis*, Cambridge, Mass.: Harvard University Press.

Horvath, R. J. (1969), Von Thünen's Isolated State and the Area Around Addis Ababa, Ethiopia, *Annals of the Association of American Geographers* **59,** 308–323.

Hotelling, H. (1929), Stability in Competition, *Economic Journal* **39,** 41–57.

Huff, D. L. (1960), A Topographical Model of Consumer Space Preferences, *Papers and Proceedings, Regional Science Association* **6,** 159–173.

Hunker, H. L. (1958), Industrial Evolution of Colombus, Ohio, *Bureau of Business Research Monograph No. 93,* Ohio State University.

Hurd, R. M. (1924), *Principles of City Land Values*, New York: The Record and Guide.

Huxley, J. S. (1932), *Problems of Relative Growth*, London: Methuen.

Hymer, S. (1972), The Multinational Corporation and the Law of Uneven Development, in J. N. Bhagwati (ed.), *Economics and World Order*, London: Macmillan, 113–140.

I

Innis, H. A. and A. R. M. Lower (1936), *Settlement and the Forest and Mining Frontier*, Toronto: Macmillan.

Institute of Economic Affairs (1973), *Mergers, Takeovers and the Structure of Industry*, London: Institute of Economic Affairs.

Isard, W. (1948), Some Locational Factors in the Iron and Steel Industry since the Early 19th Century, *Journal of Political Economy* **56,** 203–217.

Isard, W. (1956), *Location and Space Economy*, Cambridge, Mass.: M.I.T. Press.

Isard, W. (1960), *Methods of Regional Analysis*, Cambridge, Mass.: M.I.T. Press.

Isard, W. (1967), Game Theory, Location Theory and Industrial Agglomeration, *Papers and Proceedings, Regional Science Association* **18,** 1–11.

Isard, W. and J. H. Cumberland (1950), New England as a Possible Location for an Integrated Iron and Steel Works, *Economic Geography* **26,** 245–259.

Isard, W. and R. E. Kuenne (1953), The Impact of Steel on the Greater New York–Philadelphia Industrial Region, *Review of Economics and Statistics* **35,** 289–301.

Isard, W. and T. A. Reiner (1962), Aspects of Decision Making Theory and Regional Science, *Papers and Proceedings, Regional Science Association* **9,** 25–34.

Isard, W. and T. H. Tung (1964), Some Concepts for the Analysis of Spatial Organization, *Papers and Proceedings, Regional Science Association* **11,** 17–40; **12,** 1–25.

J

Janelle, D. G. (1968), Central Place Development in a Time–Space Framework, *Professional Geographer* **20,** 5–10.

Janelle, D. G. (1969), Spatial Reorganization: A Model and a Concept, *Annals of the Association of American Geographers* **59,** 348–364.

Jerome, H. (1934), *Mechanization in Industry*, National Bureau of Economic and Social Research.

Johnson, P. S. (1975), *The Economics of Invention and Innovation*, London: Martin Robertson.

Johnston, R. J. (1966), Central Places and the Settlement Pattern, *Annals of the Association of American Geographers* **56,** 541–549.

Jonasson, O. (1925), The Agricultural Regions of Europe, *Economic Geography* **1,** 277–314.

K

Kansky, K. J. (1963), Structure of Transportation Networks, *University of Chicago, Department of Geography Research Paper*, 84.

Kaplan, A. D. H. (1948), *Small Business: Its Place and Problems*, New York: McGraw-Hill.

Karaska, G. J. (1966), Interindustry Relations in the Philadelphia Economy, *East Lakes Geographer* **2,** 80–96.

Karaska, G. J. and D. F. Bramhall (1969), *Locational Analysis for Manufacturing: A Selection of Readings*, Cambridge, Mass.: M.I.T. Press.

Katona, G. and J. Morgan (1952), The Quantitative Study of Factors Determining Business Decisions, *Quarterly Journal of Economics* **66,** 67–90.

Katz, D. and R. L. Kahn (1966), *The Social Psychology of Organizations*, New York: Wiley.

Katzman, M. T. (1974), The Von Thünen Paradigm, the Industrial–Urban Hypothesis, and the Spatial Structure of Agriculture, *American Journal of Agricultural Economics* **56,** 683–697.

Keeble, D. E. (1968), Industrial Decentralization and the Metropolis: The N.W. London Case, *Transactions of the Institute of British Geographers* **44,** 1–54.

Keeble, D. E. (1969), Local Industrial Linkage and Manufacturing Growth in Outer London, *Town Planning Review* **40,** 163–188.

Keeble, D. E. (1972), Industrial Movement and Regional Development in the United Kingdom, *Town Planning Review* **43,** 3–25.

Kemeny, J. G. and G. L. Thompson (1957), Attitudes and Game Outcomes, in M. Dresher, A. W. Tucker and P. Wolfe (eds.), *Contributions to the Theory of Games, Vol. 3, Annals of Mathematical Studies* **39.**

Kennelly, R. A. (1954), The Location of the Mexican Steel Industry, in R. H. T. Smith, E. J. Taaffe and L. J. King (eds.), *Readings in Economic Geography*, Skokie, Ill.: Rand McNally, 126–157.

Kerr, D. P. (1968), Metropolitan Dominance in Canada, in J. Warkentin (ed.), *Canada: A Geographical Interpretation*, Toronto: Methuen, 531–555.

Keynes, J. M. (1936), *The General Theory*, London: Macmillan; New York: Harcourt Brace Jovanovich.

King, L. J. (1961), A Multivariate Analysis of the Spacing of Urban Settlements in the United States, *Annals of the Association of American Geographers* **51,** 222–233.

King, L. J. (1962), A Quantitative Expression of the Pattern of Urban Settlements in Selected Areas of the U.S., *Tijdschrift Voor Economische En Sociale Geografie* **53,** 1–7.

King, L. J. (1966), Approaches to Locational Analysis: An Overview, *East Lakes Geographer* **2,** 1–16.

King, L. J. (1969), *Statistical Analysis in Geography*, Englewood Cliffs, N.J.: Prentice-Hall.

Kirk, W. (1963), Problems of Geography, *Geography* **48,** 357–371.

Knos, D. S. (1962), *Distribution of Land Values in Topeka, Kansas*, Lawrence: University of Kansas Press.

Kolars, J. F. and J. D. Nystuen (1974), *Geography: The Study of Location, Culture and Environment*, New York: McGraw-Hill.

Krumme, G. (1969a), Notes on Locational Adjustment Patterns in Industrial Geography, *Geografiska Annaler* **51B,** 15–20.

Krumme, G. (1969b), Toward a Geography of Enterprise, *Economic Geography* **43,** 30–40.

Krumme, G. (1970), The Inter-Regional Corporation and the Region, *Tijdschrift Voor Economische en Sociale Geografie* **61,** 318–333.

L

Lampard, E. (1955), The History of Cities in the Economically Advanced Areas, *Economic Development and Cultural Change* **3,** 81–136.

Lasuen, J. R. (1969), On Growth Poles, *Urban Studies* **6,** 137–161.

Leibenstein, H. (1954), *Economic Backwardness and Economic Growth*, New York: Wiley.

Lewis, P. W. (1969), A Numerical Approach to the Location of Industry, *University of Hull, Department of Geography, Occasional Papers* 13.

Lewis, W. A. (1955), *The Theory of Economic Growth*, London: Allen & Unwin; New York: Harper & Row.

Lewthwaite, G. R. (1964), Wisconsin Cheese and Farm Type: A Locational Hypothesis, *Economic Geography* **40,** 95–112.

Lichtenberg, R. M. (1960), *One Tenth of a Nation*, Cambridge, Mass.: Harvard University Press.

Lindberg, O. (1953), An Economic–Geographic Study of the Swedish Paper Industry, *Geografiska Annaler* **35,** 28–40.

Lionberger, H. F. (1960), *Adoption of New Ideas and Practices*, Ames: Iowa State University Press.

Lipsey, R. G. (1975), *An Introduction to Positive Economics*, 4th ed., London: Weidenfeld & Nicolson (British Commonwealth only).

Lipsey, R. G. and P. O. Steiner (1975), *Economics*, 4th ed., New York: Harper & Row (U.S. only).

Locklin, D. P. (1960), *The Economics of Transportation*, Homewood, Ill.: Irwin.

Logan, M. I. (1966), Locational Behavior of Manufacturing Firms in Urban Areas, *Annals of the Association of American Geographers* **56,** 451–466.

Lösch, A. (1954), *The Economics of Location*, New Haven, Conn.: Yale University Press.

Lukermann, F. (1966), Empirical Expressions of Nodality and Hierarchy in a Circulation Manifold, *East Lakes Geographer* **2,** 17–44.

Luttrell, W. F. (1962), *Factory Location and Industrial Movement*, London: National Institute of Economic and Social Research.

Lynch, K. (1960), *The Image of the City*, Cambridge, Mass.: M.I.T. Press.

M

McCarty, H. H. and J. B. Lindberg (1966), *A Preface to Economic Geography*, Englewood Cliffs, N.J.: Prentice-Hall.

McDaniel, R. and M. E. Eliot Hurst (1968), A Systems Analytic Approach to Economic Geography, *Association of American Geographers, Commission on College Geography, Publication 8.*

Machlup, F. (1949), *The Basing Point System*, Homewood, Ill.: Irwin.

Mackay, J. R. (1958), The Interactance Hypothesis and Boundaries in Canada, *Canadian Geographer* **11,** 1–8.

McKim, W. (1972), The Periodic Market System in Northeastern Ghana, *Economic Geography* **48,** 333–344.

McNee, R. B. (1958), Functional Geography of the Firm, with an Illustrated Case Study from the Petroleum Industry, *Economic Geography* **34,** 321–327.

McNee, R. B. (1959), The Changing Relationships of Economics and Economic Geography, *Economic Geography* **35,** 189–198.

McNee, R. B. (1960), Towards a More Humanistic Economic Geography: The Geography of Enterprise, *Tijdschrift voor Economische en Sociale Geografie* **51,** 201–205.

McNee, R. B. (1963), The Spatial Evolution of the Sun Oil Company, *Annals of the Association of American Geographers* **53,** 609.

McNee, R. B. (1974), A Systems Approach of Understanding the Geographic Behavior of Organizations, especially Large Corporations, in F. E. I. Hamilton (ed.), *Spatial Perspectives on Industrial Organization and Decision-Making*, London: Wiley, 47–75.

Madden, C. H. (1956), Some Indicators of Stability in the Growth of Cities in the United States, *Economic Development and Cultural Change* **4,** 236–252.

Mansfield, E. (1968a), *The Economics of Technological Change*, New York: Norton.

Mansfield, E. (1968b), *Industrial Research and Technological Innovation*, New York: Norton.

Marble, D. F. and J. D. Nystuen (1963), An Approach to the Direct Measurement of Community Mean Information Fields, *Papers and Proceedings, Regional Science Association* **11,** 99–109.

March, J. G. and H. A. Simon (1958), *Organizations*, New York: Wiley.

Marcus, M. (1965), Agglomeration Economies: A Suggested Approach, *Land Economics* **41,** 279–284.

Marshall, A. (1920), *Principles of Economics*, 8th ed., London: Macmillan.

Marshall, J. U. (1969), The Location of Service Towns, *University of Toronto, Department of Geography, Research Paper,* 3.

Martin, J. E. (1966), *Greater London: An Industrial Geography*, London: Bell; Chicago: University of Chicago Press.

Maruyama, M. (1963), The Second Cybernetics: Deviation Amplifying Mutual Causal Processes, *American Scientist* **51,** 164–179.

Mattingly, P. F. (1972), Intensity of Agricultural Land Use Near Cities: A Case Study, *Professional Geographer* **24,** 1, 7–10.

Maxwell, J. W. (1965), The Functional Structure of Canadian Cities, *Geographical Bulletin* **7,** 79–104.

Meier, R. L. (1962), *A Communications Theory of Urban Growth*, Cambridge, Mass.: M.I.T. Press.

Meinig, D. W. (1962), A Comparative Historical Geography of Two Railnets: Columbia Basin and South Australia, *Annals of the Association of American Geographers* **52,** 394–413.

Melamid, A. (1962), Geography of the World Petroleum Price Structure, *Economic Geography* **38,** 283–298.

Miernyk, W. H. (1965), *The Elements of Input–Output Analysis*, New York: Random House.

Miller, J. G. (1955), Toward a General Theory for the Behavioral Sciences, *American Psychologist* **10,** 513–531.

Mills, E. S. and M. R. Lav (1964), A Model of Market Areas with Free Entry, *Journal of Political Economy* **72,** 278–288.

Moroney, J. R. (1972), *The Structure of Production in American Manufacturing*, Chapel Hill: University of North Carolina Press.

Moroney, J. R. and J. M. Walker (1966), A Regional Test of the Heckscher-Ohlin Hypothesis, *Journal of Political Economy* **74,** 573–586.

Morrill, R. L. (1963a), The Distribution of Migration Distances, *Papers and Proceedings, Regional Science Association* **11,** 75–84.

Morrill, R. L. (1963b), The Development and Spatial Distribution of Towns in Sweden, *Annals of the Association of American Geographers* **53,** 1–14.

Morrill, R. L. (1965), Migration and the Spread and Growth of Urban Settlement, *Lund Studies in Geography, Series B* 26.

Morrill, R. L. (1968), Waves of Spatial Diffusion, *Journal of Regional Science* **8,** 1–18.

Morrill, R. L. and F. R. Pitts (1967), Marriage, Migration and Mean Information Field, *Annals of the Association of American Geographers* **57,** 401–422.

Moser, C. A. and W. Scott (1961), *British Towns: A Statistical Study of Their Social and Economic Differences*, London: Oliver & Boyd.

Moses, L. N. (1958), Location and the Theory of Production, *Quarterly Journal of Economics* **72,** 259–272.

Mueller, E. and J. N. Morgan (1962), Location Decisions of Manufacturers, *American Economic Review, Papers and Proceedings* **502,** 204–217.

Mueller, E., A. Wilken and M. Wood (1961), *Location Decisions and Industry Mobility in Michigan, 1961,* Ann Arbor: Institute for Social Research, University of Michigan.

Muller, P. O. (1973), Trend Surfaces of American Agricultural Patterns: A Macro-Thünian Analysis, *Economic Geography* **49,** 228–242.

Mumford, L. (1934), *Technics and Civilization,* New York: Harcourt Brace Jovanovich.

Murdie, R. A. (1965), Cultural Differences in Consumer Travel, *Economic Geography* **41,** 211–233.

Myrdal, G. (1957), *Rich Lands and Poor,* New York: Harper & Row.

N

National Bureau of Economic Research (1962), *The Rate and Direction of Inventive Activity: Economic and Social Factors,* Princeton, N.J.: Princeton University Press.

Nelson, H. J. (1955), A Service Classification of American Cities, *Economic Geography* **31,** 189–210.

Nelson, R. L. (1963), *Concentration in the Manufacturing Industries of the United States; A Mid-Century Report,* New Haven, Conn.: Yale University Press.

Neuhoff, M. C. (1953), *Techniques of Plant Location,* Washington, D.C.: U.S.G.P.O.

Newby, P. (1971), Attitudes to a Business Environment: the Case of the Assisted Areas of the South West, in K. J. Gregory and W. L. D. Ravenhill (eds.), *Exeter Essays in Geography in Honour of Arthur Davies,* Exeter: University of Exeter, 185–199.

Nichols, V. (1969), Growth Poles: An Evaluation of Their Propulsive Effect, *Environment and Planning* **1,** 193–208.

Niedercorn, J. H. and E. F. R. Hearle (1964), Recent Land Use Trends in 48 Large American Cities, *Land Economics* **40,** 105–110.

Norcliffe, G. (1975), A Theory of Manufacturing Places, in L. Collins and D. F. Walker (eds.), *Locational Dynamics of Manufacturing Activity,* London: Wiley, 19–57.

Nordbeck, S. (1971), Urban Allometric Growth, *Geografiska Annaler* **53B,** 54–67.

North, D. C. (1955), Location Theory and Regional Economic Growth, *Journal of Political Economy* **63,** 243–258.

North, D. C. (1956), The Spatial and Interregional Framework of the U.S. Economy, *Papers and Proceedings, Regional Science Association* **2,** 201–209.

North, D. (1974), The Process of Locational Change in Different Manufacturing Organizations, in F. E. I. Hamilton (ed.), *Spatial Perspectives on Industrial Organization and Decision-Making,* London: Wiley, 213–244.

O

Okun, B. and R. W. Richardson (1961), Regional Income Inequality and Internal Population Migration, *Economic Development and Cultural Change* **9,** 128–143.

Olsson, G. (1965a), Distance and Human Interaction: A Migration Study, *Geografiska Annaler* **47B,** 3–43.

Olsson, G. (1965b), *Distance and Human Interaction: A Review and Bibliography,* Philadelphia: Regional Science Research Institute.

Olsson, G. (1967), Central Place Systems, Spatial Interaction and Stochastic Processes, *Papers and Proceedings, Regional Science Association* **18,** 13–46.

Olsson, G. and A. Persson (1964), The Spacing of Central Places in Sweden, *Papers and Proceedings, Regional Science Association* **12,** 87–93.

Ontario Economic Council (1967), *Why, Where and How and Would They Do It Again?* Toronto.

P

Parker, J. E. S. (1974), *The Economics of Innovation: The National and Multinational Enterprise in Technological Change,* London: Longmans.

Parr, J. (1966), Out Migration and the Depressed Area Problem, *Land Economics* **42,** 149–159.

Parr, J. (1969), City Hierarchies and the Distribution of City Size: A Reconsideration of Beckmann's Contribution, *Journal of Regional Science* **9,** 239–253.

Pedersen, P. O. (1970), Innovation Diffusion Within and Between National Urban Systems, *Geographical Analysis* **2,** 203–254.

Peet, J. R. (1969), The Spatial Expansion of Commercial Agriculture in the Nineteenth Century, *Economic Geography* **45,** 283–301.

Penrose, E. (1959), *The Theory of the Growth of the Firm,* Oxford: Basil Blackwell.

Perloff, H. S., E. S. Dunn, E. E. Lampard and R. F. Muth (1960), *Regions, Resources, and Economic Growth,* Baltimore: Johns Hopkins Press.

Perloff, H. S. and L. Wingo, Jr. (eds.) (1968), *Issues in Urban Economics,* Baltimore: Johns Hopkins Press.

Perroux, F. (1950), Economic Space: Theory and Application, *Quarterly Journal of Economics* **64,** 89–104.

Perroux, F. (1955), Note sur la notion de 'pôle de croissance', *Économie Appliquée* **8**. Translated version in D. L. McKee, R. D. Dean and W. H. Leahy (1970), *Regional Economics*, New York: Free Press, 93–103.

Pfouts, R. W. (1960), *The Techniques of Urban Economic Analysis*, New York: Chandler Davis.

Phillips, A. (1956), Concentration, Scale and Technological Change in Selected Manufacturing Industries, 1899–1939, *Journal of Industrial Economics* **4**, 179–193.

Pratten, C. and R. M. Dean (1965), *The Economics of Large-Scale Production in British Industry*, Cambridge: Cambridge University Press.

Pratten, C. F. (1971), *Economies of Scale in Manufacturing Industry*, Cambridge: Cambridge University Press.

Pred, A. R. (1964), The Intra-Metropolitan Location of Manufacturing, *Annals of the Association of American Geographers* **54**, 165–180.

Pred, A. R. (1965a), Industrialization, Initial Advantage and American Metropolitan Growth, *Geographical Review* **55**, 158–185.

Pred, A. R. (1965b), The Concentration of High-Value-Added Manufacturing, *Economic Geography* **41**, 108–132.

Pred, A. R. (1966), *The Spatial Dynamics of U.S. Urban–Industrial Growth, 1800–1914*, Cambridge, Mass.: M.I.T. Press.

Pred, A. R. (1967a), Behavior and Location, Part 1, *Lund Studies in Geography*, Series B 27.

Pred, A. R. (1967b), Behavior and Location, Part 2, *Lund Studies in Geography*, Series B 29.

Pred, A. R. (1971), Large-city Interdependence and the Pre-electronic Diffusion of Innovations in the U.S., *Geographical Analysis* **3**, 165–181.

Pred, A. R. (1973), The Growth and Development of Systems of Cities in Advanced Economies, in A. R. Pred and G. E. Tornquist, Systems of Cities and Information Flows, *Lund Studies in Geography*, Series B 38, 9–82.

Pred, A. R. (1974a), Industry, Information and City-System Interdependencies, in F. E. I. Hamilton (ed.), *Spatial Perspectives on Industrial Organization and Decision-Making*, London: Wiley, 105–139.

Pred, A. R. (1974b), Major Job-providing Organizations and Systems of Cities, *Association of American Geographers, Commission on College Geography Resource Paper* 27.

R

Rawstron, E. M. (1958), Three Principles of Industrial Location, *Transactions of the Institute of British Geographers* **25**, 135–142.

Ray, D. M. (1967), Cultural Differences in Consumer Travel Behavior in Eastern Ontario, *Canadian Geographer* **11**, 143–156.

Ray, D. M., P. Y. Villeneuve and R. A. Roberge (1974), Functional Prerequisites, Spatial Diffusion, and Allometric Growth, *Economic Geography* **50**, 341–351.

Rees, J. (1972), The Industrial Corporation and Location Decision Analysis, *Area* **4**, 199–205.

Rees, J. (1974), Decision-making, the Growth of the Firm and the Business Environment, in F. E. I. Hamilton (ed.), *Spatial Perspectives on Industrial Organization and Decision-Making*, London: Wiley, 189–211.

Reynolds, D. R. and M. L. McNulty (1968), On the Analysis of Political Boundaries, a Perceptual Approach, *East Lakes Geographer* **4**, 21–38.

Richardson, H. W. (1969), *Regional Economics*, London: Weidenfeld & Nicholson; New York: Praeger.

Richardson, H. W. (1973), *Regional Growth Theory*, London: Macmillan; New York: Halsted Press.

Richter, C. E. (1969), The Impact of Industrial Linkages on Geographic Association, *Journal of Regional Science* **9**, 19–28.

Robinson, E. A. G. (1958), *The Structure of Competitive Industry*, Cambridge: Cambridge University Press.

Rodgers, A. L. (1952), Industrial Inertia: A Major Factor in the Location of the Steel Industry in the U.S., *Geographical Review* **42**, 56–66.

Rodgers, H. B. (1962), The Changing Geography of the Lancashire Cotton Industry, *Economic Geography* **38**, 299–314.

Rushton, G. (1969), Analysis of Spatial Behavior by Revealed Space Preference, *Annals of the Association of American Geographers* **59**, 391–400.

S

Sampson, R. J. and M. T. Farris (1966), *Domestic Transportation: Practise, Theory and Policy*, Boston: Houghton Mifflin.

Schlebecker, J. T. (1960), The World Metropolis and the History of American Agriculture, *Journal of Economic History* **20**, 187–208.

Schumpeter, J. A. (1939), *Business Cycles: A Theoretical Historical and Statistical Analysis of the Capitalist Process*, New York: McGraw-Hill.

Scitovsky, T. (1954), Two Concepts of External Economies, *Journal of Political Economy* **LXII**, 2, 143–151.

Scott, E. P. (1970), The Spatial Structure of Rural Northern Nigeria: Farmers, Periodic Markets, and Villages, *Economic Geography* **48**, 316–332.

Segal, M. (1960), *Wages in the Metropolis*, Cambridge, Mass.: Harvard University Press.

Seidman, J. (1942), *The Needle Trades*, New York: Oxford University Press.

Seyfried, W. R. (1963), The Centrality of Urban Land Values, *Land Economics* **39**, 275–285.

Shubik, M. (ed.) (1964), *Game Theory and Related Approaches to Social Behavior*, New York: Wiley.

Siebert, H. (1969), *Regional Economic Growth: Theory and Policy*, Scranton, Pa.: International Textbook.

Simon, H. A. (1952), A Behavioral Model of Rational Choice, *Quarterly Journal of Economics* **69**, 99–118.

Simon, H. A. (1959), Theories of Decision Making in Economics and Behavioral Sciences, *American Economic Review* **49**, 253–283.

Simon, H. A. (1960), *The New Science of Management Decision*, New York: Harper & Row.

Sinclair, R. (1967), Von Thünen and Urban Sprawl, *Annals of the Association of American Geographers* **57**, 72–87.

Skinner, G. W. (1964), Marketing and Social Structure in Rural China, *Journal of Asian Studies* **24**, 3–43.

Smailes, P. (1969), Some Aspects of the South Australian Urban System, *Australian Geographer* **11**, 29–51.

Smith, D. L. (1966), Market Gardening on Adelaide's Urban Fringe, *Economic Geography* **42**, 19–36.

Smith, D. M. (1966), A Theoretical Framework for Geographical Studies of Industrial Location, *Economic Geography* **42**, 95–113.

Smith, D. M. (1971), *Industrial Location*, New York: Wiley.

Smith, D. M. (1974), Who Gets What *Where*, and How: A Welfare Focus for Human Geography, *Geography* **59**, 289–297.

Smith, P. J. (1962), Calgary: A Study in Urban Pattern, *Economic Geography* **38**, 315–329.

Smith, R. D. P. (1968), The Changing Urban Hierarchy, *Regional Studies* **2**, 1–19.

Smith, R. H. T. (1964), Toward a Measure of Complementarity, *Economic Geography* **40**, 1–8.

Smith, R. H. T. (1965a), Method and Purpose in Functional Town Classification, *Annals of the Association of American Geographers* **55**, 539–548.

Smith, R. H. T. (1965b), The Functions of Australian Towns, *Tijdschrift Voor Economische En Sociale Geografie* **53**, 81–92.

Smith, R. H. T., E. J. Taaffe and L. J. King (eds.), *Readings in Economic Geography*, Skokie, Ill.: Rand McNally.

Smith, W. (1955), The Location of Industry, *Transactions of the Institute of British Geographers* **21**, 1–18.

Söderman, S. (1975), *Industrial Location Planning*, Stockholm: Almquist & Wiksell Intl. (Halsted Press).

Spiegelman, R. G. (1966), Analysis of Urban Agglomeration, *U.S. Department of Agriculture, Economic Report 96*.

Stafford, H. A. Jr. (1963), The Functional Basis of Small Towns, *Economic Geography* **39**, 165–175.

Starbuck, W. H. (1965), Organizational Growth and Development, in J. G. March (ed.), *Handbook of Organizations*, Skokie, Ill.: Rand McNally, 451–522.

Steed, G. P. F. (1971a), Changing Processes of Corporate Environment Relations, *Area* **3**, 207–211.

Steed, G. P. F. (1971b), Forms of Corporate Environmental Adaptation, *Tijdschrift Voor Economische En Sociale Geografie* **62**, 90–94.

Steed, G. P. F. (1971c), Locational Implications of Corporate Organization of Industry, *Canadian Geographer* **15**, 54–57.

Steed, G. P. F. (1971d), Plant Adaptation, Firm Environments and Location Analysis, *Professional Geographer* **23**, 324–328.

Stevens, B. H. (1961), An Application of Game Theory to a Problem in Location Strategy, *Papers and Proceedings, Regional Science Association* **7**, 143–157.

Stevens, B. H. (1968), Location Theory and Programming Models: The Von Thünen Case, *Papers and Proceedings, Regional Science Association* **11**, 19–34.

Stewart, C. T. (1958), The Size and Spacing of Cities, *Geographical Review* **48**, 222–245.

Stewart, J. Q. (1942), A Measure of the Influence of Population at a Distance, *Sociometry* **5**, 63–71.

Stewart, J. Q. (1947), Empirical Mathematical Rules Governing the Distribution and Equilibrium of Population, *Geographical Review* **37**, 461–485.

Stewart, J. Q. (1948), Demographic Gravitation—Evidence and Applications, *Sociometry* **11**, 31–58.

Stewart, J. Q. and W. Warntz (1958a), Physics of Population Distribution, *Journal of Regional Science* **1**, 99–123.

Stewart, J. Q. and W. Warntz (1958b), Macrogeography and Social Science, *Geographical Review* **48**, 167–184.

Stine, J. H. (1962), Temporal Aspects of Tertiary Production Elements in Korea, in F. R. Pitts (ed.), *Urban Systems and Economic Development*, Eugene: University of Oregon Press.

Stocking, G. W. (1954), *Basing Point Pricing and Regional Development*, Chapel Hill: University of North Carolina Press.

Stolper, W. (1955), Spatial Order and the Economic Growth of Cities, *Economic Development and Cultural Change* **3,** 137–146.

Stouffer, S. A. (1940), Intervening Opportunities: A Theory Relating Mobility and Distance, *American Sociological Review* **5,** 845–867.

T

Taaffe, E. J. (ed.) (1970), *Geography*, Englewood Cliffs, N.J.: Prentice-Hall.

Taaffe, E. J. and H. Gauthier (1973), *Geography of Transportation*, Englewood Cliffs, N.J.: Prentice-Hall.

Taaffe, E. J., R. L. Morrill and P. R. Gould (1963), Transport Expansion in Under-Developed Countries, *Geographical Review* **53,** 503–529.

Tarrant, J. (1973), Comments on the Lösch Central Place System, *Geographical Analysis* **5,** 113–121.

Tattersall, J. N. (1962), Exports and Economic Growth: The Pacific Northwest, 1880–1960, *Papers and Proceedings, Regional Science Association* **9,** 215–234.

Taylor, M. J. (1969), Industrial Linkage, Seed-Bed Growth and the Location of Firms, *University College London, Department of Geography, Occasional Paper* 3.

Teitz, M. B. (1968), Towards a Theory of Public Facility Location, *Papers and Proceedings, Regional Science Association* **21,** 35–51.

Thoman, R. S. and P. Corbin (1974), *The Geography of Economic Activity*, 2nd ed., New York: McGraw-Hill.

Thomas, E. N. (1961), Towards an Expanded Central Place Model, *Geographical Review* **51,** 400–411.

Thomas, E. N. (1962), The Stability of Distance— Population Size Relationships for Iowa Towns from 1900–1950, *Lund Studies in Geography, Series B* 24.

Thomas, R. W. (1975), Some Functional Characteristics of British City Central Areas: An Application of Allometric Principles, *Regional Studies* **9,** 369–378.

Thompson, J. H. (1961), *Methods of Plant Site Selection Available to Small Manufacturing Firms*, Morgantown: West Virginia University Press.

Thompson, W. R. (1965), *A Preface to Urban Economics*, Baltimore: Johns Hopkins Press.

Thompson, W. R. (1968), Internal and External Factors in the Development of Urban Economies, in H. S. Perloff and L. Wingo, Jr. (eds.), *Issues in Urban Economics*, Baltimore: Johns Hopkins Press, 43–62.

Thorngren, B. (1970), How Do Contact Systems Affect Regional Development? *Environment and Planning* **2,** 409–427.

Tiebout, C. M. (1956), Exports and Regional Economic Growth, *Journal of Political Economy* **64,** 160–169.

Tiebout, C. M. (1957), Location Theory, Empirical Evidence and Economic Evolution, *Papers and Proceedings, Regional Science Association* **3,** 74–86.

Tiebout, C. M. (1962), *The Community Economic Base Study*, New York: Committee for Economic Development.

Tobler, W. R. (1963), Geographic Area and Map Projections, *Geographical Review* **53,** 59–78.

Tornquist, G. (1968), Flows of Information and the Location of Economic Activites, *Lund Studies in Geography, Series B* 30.

Tornquist, G. (1970), Contact Systems and Regional Development, *Lund Studies in Geography, Series B* 35.

Townroe, P. M. (1969), Locational Choice and the Individual Firm, *Regional Studies* **3,** 15–24.

Townroe, P. M. (1971), Industrial Location Decisions, *Centre for Urban and Regional Studies, Birmingham, Occasional Paper* 15.

Townroe, P. M. (1972), Some Behavioral Considerations in the Industrial Location Decision, *Regional Studies* **6,** 261–272.

U

Ullman, E. L. (1940–1941), A Theory of Location for Cities, *American Journal of Sociology* **46,** 853–864.

Ullman, E. L. (1954), Amenities as a Factor in Regional Growth, *Geographical Review* **44,** 119–132.

Ullman, E. L. (1956), The Role of Transportation and the Bases for Interaction, in W. L. Thomas (ed.), *Man's Role in Changing the Face of the Earth*, Chicago: University of Chicago Press, 862–880.

Ullman, E. L. (1957), *American Commodity Flow*, Seattle: University of Washington Press.

Ullman, E. L. (1958), Regional Development and the Geography of Concentration, *Papers and Proceedings, Regional Science Association* **4,** 179–198.

Ullman, E. L. (1962), The Nature of Cities Reconsidered, *Papers and Proceedings, Regional Science Association* **9,** 7–24.

Ullman, E. L. and M. F. Dacey (1962), The Minimum Requirements Approach to the Urban Economic Base, *Lund Studies in Geography, Series B*, 24, 121–143.

U.S. Federal Trade Commission (1969), *Economic Report on Corporate Mergers*, Washington D.C.

U.S. National Science Foundation (1963), *Research and Development in Industry*, Washington D.C.

V

Vajda, S. (1960), *Introduction to Linear Programming and*

the Theory of Games, London: Methuen; New York: Barnes & Noble.

Valavanis, S. (1955), Lösch on Location: A Review Article, *American Economic Review* **45**, 637–644.

Van Valkenberg, S. and C. C. Held (1952), *Europe*, New York: Wiley.

Vining, R. (1955), A Description of Certain Spatial Aspects of an Economic System, *Economic Development and Cultural Change* **3**, 147–195.

Vyver, F. T. de (1951), Labor Factors in the Industrial Development of the South, *Southern Economic Journal* **18**, 189–205.

W

Warntz, W. (1959), *Toward A Geography of Price*, Philadelphia: University of Pennsylvania Press.

Warntz, W. (1961), Transatlantic Flights and Pressure Patterns, *Geographical Review* **51**, 187–212.

Warntz, W. (1965), *Macrogeography and Income Fronts*, Philadelphia: Regional Science Research Institute.

Warntz, W. (1967), Global Science and the Tyranny of Space, *Papers and Proceedings, Regional Science Association* **19**, 7–19.

Warren, K. (1973), *American Steel Industry, 1850–1970: A Geographical Interpretation*, Oxford: Clarendon Press.

Watkins, M. H. (1963), A Staple Theory of Economic Growth, *Canadian Journal of Economics and Political Science* **XXIX**, part 2, 141–158.

Watts, H. D. (1970), The Location of Aluminium Reduction Plants in the U.K., *Tijdschrift Voor Economische En Sociale Geografie* **61**, 148–159.

Watts, H. D. (1971), The Location of the Beet Sugar Industry in England and Wales, 1912–1936, *Transactions of the Institute of British Geographers* **53**, 95–116.

Watts, H. D. (1974), Spatial Rationalization in Multi-Plant Enterprises, *Geoforum* **17**, 69–76.

Weber, A. (1909), *Theory of the Location of Industries*, Chicago: University of Chicago Press.

Werner, C. (1968), The Law of Refraction in Transportation Geography: Its Multivariate Extensions, *Canadian Geographer* **12**, 28–40.

Whitman, E. S. and W. J. Schmidt (1966), *Plant Relocation*, New York: American Management Association.

Williams, J. D. (1966), *The Compleat Strategyst*, New York: McGraw-Hill.

Williamson, J. G. (1965), Regional Inequality and the Process of National Development: A Description of the Patterns, *Economic Development and Cultural Change* **13**, Part 2.

Winsborough, H. H. (1959), Variations in Industrial Composition with City Size, *Papers and Proceedings, Regional Science Association* **5**, 121–131.

Wise, M. J. (1949), On the Evolution of the Jewellery and Gun Quarters in Birmingham, *Transactions of the Institute of British Geographers* **15**, 57–72.

Woldenberg, M. J. (1968), Energy Flow and Spatial Order: Mixed Hierarchies of Central Places, *Geographical Review* **58**, 552–574.

Woldenberg, M. J. and B. J. L. Berry (1968), Rivers and Central Places: Analogous Systems? *Journal of Regional Science* **7**, 129–139.

Wolfe, R. I. (1962), Transportation and Politics: The Example of Canada, *Annals of the Association of American Geographers* **52**, 176–190.

Wolpert, J. (1964), The Decision Process in Spatial Context, *Annals of the Association of American Geographers* **54**, 537–558.

Wolpert, J. (1965), Behavioral Aspects of the Decision to Migrate, *Papers and Proceedings, Regional Science Association* **15**, 159–172.

Wolpert, J. (1966), Migration as an Adjustment to Environmental Stress, *Journal of Social Issues* **22**, 92–102.

Wonnacott, R. J. (1964), Wage Levels and Employment Structure in United States Regions, *Journal of Political Economy* **72**, 414–419.

Wood, P. A. (1969), Industrial Location and Linkage, *Area* **2**, 32–39.

Y

Yeates, M. H. (1965), Some Factors Affecting the Spatial Distribution of Chicago Land Values, *Economic Geography* **41**, 55–70.

Yeates, M. H. (1974), *An Introduction to Quantitative Analysis in Human Geography*, New York: McGraw-Hill.

Yeates, M. H. and B. J. Garner (1976), *The North American City*, 2nd ed., New York: Harper & Row.

Yeates, M. H. and P. E. Lloyd (1970), *Impact of Industrial Incentives: Southern Georgian Bay Region, Ontario*, Ottawa: Queen's Printer.

Z

Zimmerman, E. W. (1951), *World Resources and Industry*, New York: Harper & Row.

Zipf, G. K. (1946), The P_1P_2/D Hypothesis and Intercity Movement of Persons, *American Sociological Review* **11**, 677–686.

Zipf, G. K. (1949), *Human Behavior and the Principle of Least Effort*, Reading, Mass.: Addison-Wesley.

Index